Practical C++ STL Programming

Real-World Applications with C++20 and C++23

Daniel Kusswurm

Apress®

Practical C++ STL Programming: Real-World Applications with C++20 and C++23

Daniel Kusswurm
Geneva, IL, USA

ISBN-13 (pbk): 979-8-8688-0773-2
ISBN-13 (electronic): 979-8-8688-0774-9
https://doi.org/10.1007/979-8-8688-0774-9

Copyright © 2024 by Daniel Kusswurm

This work is subject to copyright. All rights are reserved by the Publisher, whether the whole or part of the material is concerned, specifically the rights of translation, reprinting, reuse of illustrations, recitation, broadcasting, reproduction on microfilms or in any other physical way, and transmission or information storage and retrieval, electronic adaptation, computer software, or by similar or dissimilar methodology now known or hereafter developed.

Trademarked names, logos, and images may appear in this book. Rather than use a trademark symbol with every occurrence of a trademarked name, logo, or image we use the names, logos, and images only in an editorial fashion and to the benefit of the trademark owner, with no intention of infringement of the trademark.

The use in this publication of trade names, trademarks, service marks, and similar terms, even if they are not identified as such, is not to be taken as an expression of opinion as to whether or not they are subject to proprietary rights.

While the advice and information in this book are believed to be true and accurate at the date of publication, neither the authors nor the editors nor the publisher can accept any legal responsibility for any errors or omissions that may be made. The publisher makes no warranty, express or implied, with respect to the material contained herein.

Managing Director, Apress Media LLC: Welmoed Spahr
Acquisitions Editor: Melissa Duffy
Development Editor: James Markham
Editorial Assistant: Gryffin Winkler

Cover designed by eStudioCalamar

Cover image designed by Héctor J. Rivas on Unsplash

Distributed to the book trade worldwide by Springer Science+Business Media New York, 1 New York Plaza, Suite 4600, New York, NY 10004-1562, USA. Phone 1-800-SPRINGER, fax (201) 348-4505, e-mail orders-ny@springer-sbm.com, or visit www.springeronline.com. Apress Media, LLC is a California LLC and the sole member (owner) is Springer Science + Business Media Finance Inc (SSBM Finance Inc). SSBM Finance Inc is a Delaware corporation.

For information on translations, please e-mail booktranslations@springernature.com; for reprint, paperback, or audio rights, please e-mail bookpermissions@springernature.com.

Apress titles may be purchased in bulk for academic, corporate, or promotional use. eBook versions and licenses are also available for most titles. For more information, reference our Print and eBook Bulk Sales web page at http://www.apress.com/bulk-sales.

Any source code or other supplementary material referenced by the author in this book is available to readers on GitHub. For more detailed information, please visit https://www.apress.com/gp/services/source-code.

If disposing of this product, please recycle the paper

Table of Contents

About the Author xi

About the Technical Reviewer xiii

Acknowledgments xv

Introduction xvii

Prologue xxi

Chapter 1: C++ Review 1

    Templates 1

        Source Code Overview 11

    Containers and Iterators 12

    Strings 17

    User-Defined Classes 23

    User-Defined Template Classes 34

    Lambda Expressions 41

    Three-Way Comparison Operator 48

    Exceptions 58

    Summary 61

Chapter 2: Formatted I/O 63

    Formatted Output Using std::printf( ) 63

    Formatted Output Using Streams 68

    Formatted Output Using std::format( ) 80

    Formatted Output Using std::print( ) 93

    Formatted File I/O Using Streams 97

    Summary 103

TABLE OF CONTENTS

Chapter 3: Sequence Containers – Part 1 105

Overview of Sequence Containers 105

Using std::array 106

Using std::vector 116

More Algorithms Using std::array and std::vector 128

Summary 134

Chapter 4: Sequence Containers – Part 2 137

Using std::deque 137

Using std::list 148

Using std::forward_list 158

Understanding Iterators 165

Summary 171

Chapter 5: General Utilities Library 173

Heterogeneous Containers 173

    Using std::pair 174

    Using std::tuple 180

Utility Classes 190

    Using std::variant 190

    Using std::optional 200

    Using std::any 219

    Using std::expected 223

Summary 231

Chapter 6: Smart Pointers 233

Smart Pointer Primer 233

Using std::unique_ptr 235

Using std::shared_ptr 248

Using std::weak_ptr 254

Summary 258

Chapter 7: Associative Containers 259
Using std::set 259
Using std::multiset 271
Using std::map 276
Using std::multimap 292
Summary 300

Chapter 8: Unordered Associative Containers 301
Unordered Associative Container Primer 301
    Hash Functions and Concepts 302
Using std::unordered_set 303
Using std::unordered_multiset 326
Using std::unordered_map 333
Using std::unordered_multimap 345
Summary 352

Chapter 9: Container Adaptors 355
Container Adaptor Primer 355
Using std::stack 357
Using std::queue 370
Using std::priority_queue 375
Flat Container Adaptors 387
Summary 388

Chapter 10: Algorithms – Part 1 391
Algorithm Primer 391
Counting Algorithms 393
Minimum and Maximum Algorithms 408
Copy Algorithms 414
Move Algorithms 420
Reversal Algorithms 425
Replacement Algorithms 428

TABLE OF CONTENTS

    Removal Algorithms 436

    Fill Algorithms 443

    Summary 447

Chapter 11: Algorithms – Part 2 449

    For_Each Algorithms 449

    Transformation Algorithms 454

    Generation Algorithms 459

    Find Algorithms 464

    Contains Algorithms 483

    More Find Algorithms 491

    Search Algorithms 494

    Accumulate and Fold Algorithms 503

    Summary 511

Chapter 12: Algorithms – Part 3 513

    Sorting Algorithms 513

    Binary Search Algorithms 523

    Partition Algorithms 531

    Heap Algorithms 535

    Summary 542

Chapter 13: Algorithms – Part 4 545

    Merge Algorithms 545

    Shuffle and Sample Algorithms 553

    Rotate and Shift Algorithms 557

    Set Algorithms 564

    Permutation Algorithms 568

    Summary 572

Chapter 14: Ranges – Part 1 575
Range Views and Adaptors Primer 575
Range Views and Adaptors 577
Range Adaptors and Pipelines 584
Range Projections 590
More Range Adaptors 598
Range Views and Adaptors Minutiae 604
Summary 609

Chapter 15: Ranges – Part 2 611
Tuple Views 611
More Tuple Views 616
Join, Split, and Cartesian Product Views 626
Slide, Stride, and Chunk Views 633
Range Factories 642
Summary 647

Chapter 16: Time Library 649
Ratios 649
Durations 656
Clocks and Timepoints 665
More Clocks and Timepoints 675
Software Benchmarking 680
Summary 687

Chapter 17: File Systems 689
File System Path Classes 689
File System Directory Iterator Classes 699
File System Helper Functions 709
File System Copy Functions 718
Summary 725

TABLE OF CONTENTS

Chapter 18: Numerical Processing – Part 1 .... **727**
Mathematical Constants 727
Complex Numbers 734
Random Number Generation 743
Using Generators and Distributions 747
Dice Games 755
Vector of Random Numbers 764
Summary 767

Chapter 19: Numerical Processing – Part 2 .... **769**
Class std::valarray 769
Arithmetic Functions 770
Statistical Calculations 777
Class std::slice 785
Basic Operations 785
Covariance Matrix 794
Inner Products and Reductions 799
Summary 808

Chapter 20: Concurrency – Part 1 .... **811**
Concurrency Primer 811
Execution Policies 813
Mutexes 821
Threads 825
Atomic Operations 833
Multithreaded Algorithms 841
Summary 851

Chapter 21: Concurrency – Part 2 .... **853**
    Semaphores 853
    Latches 861
    Condition Variables 866
    Futures 873
    Summary 886

Appendix A: Source Code and Development Tools **887**

Appendix B: References and Resources **895**

Index **899**

About the Author

Daniel Kusswurm has 40+ years of professional experience as a software developer, computer scientist, and author. During his career, he has developed innovative software for medical devices, scientific instruments, and image processing applications. On many of these projects, he successfully utilized ISO C++ and the standard template libraries to create quality software and solve unique programming challenges. His educational background includes a BS in electrical engineering technology from Northern Illinois University along with an MS and PhD in computer science from DePaul University.

Kusswurm is the author of multiple computer programming books, including *Modern X86 Assembly Language Programming* (Third Edition), *Modern Arm Assembly Language Programming*, and *Modern Parallel Programming with C++ and Assembly Language*, all published by Apress.

About the Technical Reviewer

Sri Manikanta Palakollu is a seasoned software developer with four years of experience. He has acquired deep expertise across a wide range of technologies, including Java, AEM, Python, C++, C, JavaScript, TypeScript, MERN, databases, AI, and System Design.

In addition to his technical prowess, Sri Manikanta is a prolific writer. He has authored numerous articles on diverse domains such as AI, ML, programming, data science, and cybersecurity. These articles have been published on prominent platforms like Medium, HackerNoon, and Analytics Vidhya.

Furthermore, Sri Manikanta has provided technical guidance for many books from well-known publishers such as Packt and Apress. He has also authored the book *Practical System Programming with C*.

Beyond his writing achievements, Sri Manikanta has showcased his talent and innovation by securing a national-level hackathon and participating in several open source projects. He is also a dedicated mentor, having coached more than 5,000 students in various coding hackathons hosted by different organizations and institutions across the nation and overseas.

Acknowledgments

It is impossible to write and publish a book without the dedication, expertise, and creativity of a professional behind-the-scenes team. This book is no exception. I would like to thank the talented editorial team at Apress, including Melissa Duffy, Sowmya Thodur, James Markham, and Gryffin Winkler. I would also like to thank the entire production staff at Apress for their enthusiasm and hard work.

Sri Manikanta Palakollu merits a sincere thank-you for his technical review and constructive feedback. Ed Kusswurm is gratefully acknowledged for his methodical scrutiny of each chapter and sensible suggestions. I accept full responsibility for any remaining imperfections.

Thanks to my professional colleagues for their support. Finally, I would like to recognize parental nodes Armin (RIP) and Mary along with sibling nodes Mary, Tom, Ed, and John for their encouragement during the writing of this book.

Introduction

Perhaps the most remarkable aspect of modern C++ programming is not the expressive syntax and semantics of the language itself, but the Standard Template Libraries (STL). The STL is a vast collection of versatile template classes and algorithms. When used properly, STL facilitates and streamlines the development of high-performance quality software. However, learning how to effectively exploit STL's programming constructs is often overwhelming for many C++ programmers, both beginners and veterans.

Practical C++ STL Programming is an instructional text that teaches you how to successfully apply STL's classes, algorithms, and other programming constructs. It covers a wide range of STL topics, including many new elements from the C++20 and C++23 standards. Before continuing, it warrants mentioning that it's utterly impractical for one book to completely explain every STL component. This book emphasizes *practical* C++ STL programming. By that I mean it teaches you how to properly apply what I believe are STL's most essential and worthwhile classes and algorithms. The specific topics covered in this book along with its numerous source code examples are designed to accelerate comprehension of STL in general and motivate further study.

The target audience for *Practical C++ STL Programming* is professional C++ programmers, students, or anyone who has an interest in learning more about the STL. To reap maximum benefits from this book, you should have a rudimentary understanding of C++11 or later, including namespaces, classes (constructors, destructors, operators, inheritance, etc.), function overloading, lambda expressions, exceptions, and templates. Previous experience with at least one of the C++ compilers mentioned in the "Source Code" section will also be helpful.

Content Overview

The primary objective of this book is to teach you C++ STL programming and how to best utilize its components. Here's a brief overview of what you can expect to learn.

C++ Review - Chapter 1 reviews essential C++ programming topics, including classes, iterators, strings, templates, and lambda expressions. It also explains C++20's new three-way comparison operator.

INTRODUCTION

Formatted I/O – Chapter 2 discusses formatted I/O using streams. It also details how to properly use the new string formatting capabilities of C++20/23, including `std::format()` and `std::println()`.

Sequence Containers – Chapter 3 examines sequence containers `std::array` and `std::vector`. The former is a modern substitute for a C-style array, while the latter is undoubtedly the most important STL container. Chapter 4 covers additional sequence containers including `std::deque`, `std::list`, and `std::forward_list`. This chapter also explains iterators in greater detail and the new iterator concepts of C++20.

General Utilities Library – Chapter 5 reviews principal classes from STL's general utilities library, including `std::pair` and `std::tuple`. It also explains how to best employ other utility classes, including `std::variant`, `std::optional`, `std::any`, and `std::expected`.

Smart Pointers – Modern C++ discourages the use of raw pointers. Instead, programmers are encouraged to use smart pointers in their programs as explained in Chapter 6.

Associative Containers – Chapter 7 considers associative containers, including `std::set`, `std::multiset`, `std::map`, and `std::multimap`.

Unordered Associative Containers – Chapter 8 explains how to use unordered associative containers `std::unordered_set`, `std::unordered_multiset`, `std::unordered_map`, and `std::unordered_multimap`. This chapter also includes a primer on hash functions and their connection with unordered associative containers.

Container Adaptors – Many programs require simple stacks and queues to carry out specific processing. Chapter 9 surveys container adaptor classes `std::stack`, `std::queue`, and `std::priority_queue`.

Algorithms – Chapters 10–13 expound usages of numerous STL algorithms. The discussions and source code examples in these chapters cover both the long-established algorithms of C++11 along with the new range variants of C++20/23.

Ranges – Chapters 14 and 15 explicate C++20 ranges and views, which can be used to simplify the coding of algorithms that perform pipeline processing. These chapters also explain range adaptors, projections, and range factories.

Time Library – The STL's time library encompasses classes that streamline date/time calculations. Chapter 16 covers prominent classes and algorithms from this library, including clock classes, timepoints, durations, and date/time formatting.

INTRODUCTION

File Systems – Chapter 17 describes important file system classes, including `std::filesystem::path`, `std::filesystem::recursive_directory_iterator`, and `std::filesystem::directory_entry`. It also explains how to use STL's directory and file create, copy, and remove algorithms.

Numerical Processing – Chapters 18 and 19 spotlight STL numerical processing features, including complex numbers and random number generators/distributions. These chapters also explain how to use classes `std::valarray` and `std::slice`, which can be exploited to implement algorithms that perform calculations using numerical arrays or matrices.

Concurrency – Chapters 20 and 21 examine essential features from STL's concurrency support library. These chapters describe the classes and algorithms that facilitate the development of multithreaded applications. Topics covered include STL algorithm execution policies, thread classes, atomic operations, mutexes and semaphores, condition variables, and promise/future classes.

Source Code

The source code published in this book is available on GitHub at https://github.com/Apress/Practical-CPP-STL-Programming. Appendix A contains additional information regarding the source code, including download and setup instructions.

Caution The sole purpose of the source code is to elucidate programming topics that are directly related to the content of this book. Minimal attention is given to essential software engineering concerns such as robust error handling, security risks, numerical stability, rounding errors, or ill-conditioned functions. You are responsible for addressing these concerns should you decide to use any of the source code in your own programs.

The source code for *Practical C++ STL Programming* was developed using Windows 11 and Visual Studio 2022. The source code examples were also tested on computers running Ubuntu (GCC and Clang) and macOS (GCC) as described in Appendix A.

INTRODUCTION

Additional Resources

Appendix B lists several useful C++ and STL resources that will appeal to both novice and experienced programmers. Two of these resources warrant special mention. The first one is the draft (or final) ISO C++23 specification document. The primary audience for this document is programmers who create C++ compilers and companion development tools. For developers who merely use C++, the ISO C++23 specification document is likely an arduous read whose content is often abstruse. However, for those individuals who aspire to be a world-class C++ programmer, becoming familiar with the ISO C++ specification document is a worthwhile endeavor given that it's the ultimate arbitrator of required C++ behavior and, perhaps more importantly, undefined or unspecified behavior.

The second noteworthy resource is the website cppreference.com (`https://en.cppreference.com/w/`). This site contains indispensable (and appreciated) content regarding STL's classes and algorithms, including comprehensive descriptions, template parameters, class data members, and member/non-member functions. It also details specific language and library features for ISO standards C++11 to C++23.

Prologue

Practical C++ STL Defined

The C++ Standard Template Library (STL) is a multifarious collection of classes, algorithms, and utility functions that enable software developers to create high-performance quality code without having to reinvent the wheel. It is virtually impossible for a software developer to write C++ code of any consequence without explicitly or implicitly using STL resources since it forms the foundation of modern C++ programming. Consider that even a novice C++ programmer typically exercises elementary STL features when coding their first "hello, world" program (e.g., `std::cout << "hello, world\n";` or `std::println("hello, world");`).

It is interesting to note that despite its widespread use, the ISO C++23 standards document does not expressly mention the acronym STL. It uses the phrase "C++ standard library." However, internet searches for STL are common, and many experienced C++ programmers use STL colloquially. This book also uses the acronym STL.

Learning how to effectively exploit STL's capabilities is often a daunting task for both C++ novices and experts. The STL itself is an enormous assortment of mostly C++ template code that lacks a precise definition and starting point. It is also important to keep in mind that it's utterly impossible for one book to completely explain every STL component and usage alternative. This book emphasizes practical C++ STL programming. By that I mean it teaches you how to utilize its most important classes, algorithms, and utility functions. Admittedly, what constitutes STL's most important capabilities is decidedly subjective. However, the specific STL topics and source code examples that I have chosen are designed to accelerate comprehension of STL in general and motivate further study.

In the sections that follow, I've partitioned STL's capabilities into the following general categories:

- Containers, iterators, and algorithms
- Strings and formatted I/O

PROLOGUE

- General-purpose utilities
- Numerical programming
- Concurrency

I should note that these categories are somewhat arbitrary and do not necessarily match any categories or groupings published in the ISO C++23 standards document. They are merely used as an instrument to introduce some of the STL topics that you'll learn about in this book.

Containers, Iterators, and Algorithms

Perhaps the most important constituent of the STL is its collection of containers, iterators, and algorithms. An STL container is a data construct that holds objects (or elements). Examples of STL container objects include the following:

- Sequence containers
- Associative containers
- Unordered associative containers
- Container adaptors

The sequence container group includes arrays (`std::array`), vectors (`std::vector`), double-ended queues (`std::deque`), and lists (`std::list`, `std::forward_list`). The ordering of elements in a sequence container is the responsibility of the programmer.

Examples of associative containers include sets (`std::set`, `std::multiset`) and maps (`std::map`, `std::multimap`). Associative containers differ from sequence containers in that the objects they hold are organized using a key value and relational operator.

An unordered associative container resembles an associative container sans the underlying ordering scheme. Examples of unordered containers include unordered sets (`std::unordered_set`, `std::unordered_multiset`) and unordered maps (`std::unordered_map`, `std::unordered_multimap`).

A container adaptor class utilizes the capabilities of another STL class (usually a sequence container) to implement a universal programming construct. Container adaptor classes include stacks (`std::stack`) and queues (`std::queue`, `std::priority_queue`).

Modern C++ programs make extensive use of iterators to access or manipulate the elements of a container. Conceptually, an iterator is a generalization of a pointer. The primary difference between an iterator and a pointer is that the former facilitates element access in a uniform manner that's independent of a container's underlying data structure. STL defines a variety of iterator types whose specific capabilities vary depending on the container.

The largest component of STL is undoubtedly its extensive collection of predefined algorithms. Examples of STL algorithms include container counting (`std::count()`, `std::count_if()`), sorting (`std::sort()`), searching (`std::binary_search()`, `std::contains()`, `std::find()`), modifications (`std::merge()`, `std::reverse()`, `std::replace()`), and transformations (`std::for_each()`, `std::transform()`). The default behavior of most STL algorithms can be overridden using a programmer-defined lambda expression. A sizeable portion of this book is dedicated to explaining STL algorithms, both the time-tested forms of C++11/14/17 and the new range variants of C++20/23.

Strings and Formatted I/O

Unlike many other programming languages, a text string is not an intrinsic data type in C++. Instead, C++ programs (implicitly) use the STL template class `std::basic_string` to create and manipulate string objects. One of the parameters for template `std::basic_string` is a character type. Supported character types include `char`, `wchar_t`, `char8_t`, `char16_t`, and `char32_t`. The primary difference between types `char` and `char8_t` (C++20) is that the latter is guaranteed to be unsigned, while the sign of type `char` is implementation defined. To simplify string declarations, STL defines several aliases, including `std::string`, `std::wstring`, `std::u8string`, `std::u16string`, and `std::u32string`, for the previously mentioned character types.

A C++ program can also employ template class `std::basic_string_view`, which references a constant contiguous sequence of characters. Template class `std::basic_string_view` supports the same character types as template class `std::basic_string`. C++ programs normally work with instances of `std::basic_string_view` using the aliases `std::string_view`, `std::wstring_view`, `std::u8string_view`, `std::u16string_view`, and `std::u32string_view`.

C++ defines a comprehensive template class hierarchy that performs formatted input and output. This class hierarchy supports read and write operations using either file or string streams. Stream classes for formatted file I/O include `std::ifstream`, `std::oftsream`, and `std::fstream`; for string streams, the corresponding classes are `std::istringstream`, `std::ostringstream`, and `std::stringstream`.

Prior to C++20, most programs performed formatted I/O operations using overloads of `operator<<` and `operator>>` along with a somewhat confusing set of stream state flags and manipulators. The C++20 specification defines a new formatting library. The functions of this new library (e.g., `std::format()`, `std::format_to()`, `std::vformat()`, `std::vformat_to()`, etc.) utilize format specification strings that mimic the ones used in Python. A user-defined class can also create custom functions and specifiers for formatted output. C++23 adds `std::println()` and other functions for direct formatted output to `std::cout` or other output stream object.

General-Purpose Utilities

The C++ specification defines numerous general-purpose utility classes and functions, many of which are used by other STL classes. A C++ program can use `std::pair` or `std::tuple` to group a collection of heterogeneous elements. The former maintains two elements, while the latter supports an arbitrary number of elements. A C++ function can also use `std::pair` and `std::tuple` to return multiple values to its caller.

An instance of the STL class `std::variant` holds multiple values of different types, but only one at a time. This class is often used as a type-safe replacement for a C-style union. Class `std::optional` holds an optional value, which may or may not be present. For example, a function can return an "empty" `std::optional` value if it detects an error condition or an actual value of another type if it succeeds. Class `std::any` is a type-safe container for a single value, while class `std::expected` combines two values – an expected type and an error type – into a single entity.

Modern C++ programming discourages explicit use of operators `new` and `delete` to dynamically allocate and free memory during program execution. Instead, programs are strongly encouraged to use a smart pointer class such as `std::unique_ptr` or `std::shared_ptr`. Class `std::unique_ptr` is an object that manages another object via a pointer and maintains sole ownership of that object. Instances of `std::shared_ptr` are similar to `std::unique_ptr` but can share ownership of the managed object. Smart pointers perform automatic object deletion, which significantly reduces the risk of a memory leak compared to the manual use of `new` and `delete`.

STL includes a chrono library (namespace `std::chrono`) for time and date manipulation. Included in this library are a variety of clock objects – `std::chrono::system_clock` (wall time), `std::chrono::steady_clock` (elapsed time), `std::chrono::high_resolution_clock` (precision elapsed time) – that provide time values in the form of a `std::chrono::timepoint` object. Starting with C++20, a program can use the new calendar classes to perform year-month-day calculations and time zone conversions.

The file system library (`std::filesystem`) defines useful templates that a program can use to carry out typical file system operations, including file and directory creations, copies, searches, status queries, etc. Classes contained in this library include `std::filesystem:path`, `std::filesystem::directory_entry`, and `std::filesystem::directory_iterator`. This library also incorporates convenient helper functions that facilitate less common but still important file system operations, including symbolic link manipulation and file system queries.

Numerical Programming

The STL includes a variety of template classes that simplify numerical programming. For example, a program no longer needs to define universal math constants such as π and e. It can use the constant expression templates defined in namespace `std::numbers` (e.g., `std::numbers::pi_v` and `std::numbers::e_v`). STL also incorporates class `std::complex` for performing arithmetic using complex numbers. A program can use `std::valarray` to create arrays of numerical values. Class `std::valarray` also provides overloads of common math functions (e.g., `std::log()`, `std::sin()`, `std::sqrt()`, etc.). Class `std::slice` facilitates using class `std::valarray` to perform matrix operations.

Another useful STL numerical programming capability is the classes that support the generation of (pseudo-) random numbers. A program typically uses a random number engine in conjunction with a random number distribution to generate sequences of random numbers. Examples of random number engines include `std::linear_congruential_engine` and `std::mersene_twister_engine`. Since the underlying mathematics of random number generation is complex, STL provides several preconfigured random number engines, including `std::minstd_rand` and `std::mt19937`. Random number distributions include uniform (`std::uniform_int_distribution`, `std::uniform_real_distribution`), Poisson (`std::poisson_distribution`, `std::exponential_distribution`), and normal (`std::normal_` distribution and std::lognormal_distribution). Uniform distributions are often used in game applications to simulate the rolling of dice, dealing of playing cards, etc. The other distribution types are handy for creating synthetic data sets to test numerical algorithms.

Concurrency

The final STL grouping of this section is concurrency. Many of the STL container algorithms that you'll study in later chapters support an execution policy argument. This argument designates the method of parallelization that an algorithm is allowed to utilize. Execution policies provide a straightforward technique, provided certain constraints are observed, for an algorithm to better exploit the parallel processing capabilities of a modern processor.

A program can use the thread support classes (std::thread, std::this_thread, std::jthread, std::stop_token, std::stop_source) to manage thread execution. For resource synchronization, STL includes mutexes (std::mutex, std::timed_mutex, etc.), mutex management (std::lock_guard, std::unique_lock, etc.), semaphores (std::counting_semaphore, std::binary_semaphore), and condition variables (std::condition_variable, std::condition_variable_any, etc.).

It is often necessary for a parallel algorithm to ensure that access to a critical variable is performed atomically (i.e., the operation is performed such that it won't be interrupted by another atomic operation on the same variable). The STL includes numerous atomic template classes and functions (e.g., std::atomic, std::atomic_load, std::atomic_store, etc.) that streamline these types of operations.

An application can utilize STL's futures classes (std::promise, std::future, std::async, etc.) to perform asynchronous thread execution. This group also includes several ancillary classes (e.g., std::future_category, std::future_error, and std::future_errc) that facilitate the processing of a return value or exception from an asynchronous thread.

Summary

As mentioned earlier, the STL is the foundation of modern C++ programming. It is virtually impossible to write any meaningful C++ program without employing some of its components. In the chapters that follow, you'll learn how to successfully exploit the STL classes and algorithms introduced in this prologue.

CHAPTER 1

C++ Review

As mentioned in the Introduction, the content of this book assumes that you're somewhat familiar with the basics of C++ syntax and elementary programming features, including classes, inheritance, overloading, and templates. This chapter reviews important C++ programming concepts that you must understand to fully exploit the capabilities of STL. It also explains several new features from C++20/23. Topics covered include

- Templates
- Containers and iterators
- Strings
- User-defined classes
- User-defined template classes
- Lambda expressions
- Three-way comparison operator
- Exceptions

If your comprehension of a specific topic is sufficient, feel free to either skim or skip that section. If, however, your understanding of a subject is lacking, Appendix B contains a list of C++ references that you can consult for more information.

Templates

A C++ template is a parameterized data type. Programmers use templates to define functions, classes, and algorithms in a manner that's type independent. For example, suppose you want to code a new sorting algorithm and you want to use the algorithm with a variety of data types, such as integers, floating-point values, strings, and

CHAPTER 1 C++ REVIEW

user-defined data types. In many other programming languages, you would need to code a "different" algorithm for each desired type even though each implementation performs the same fundamental operations (e.g., compares, assignments, swaps, etc.). The use of C++ templates facilitates the coding of a single algorithm so long as the data types in use support the required operations.

Let's look at a few template examples. Listing 1-1-1 shows the header file for source code example Ch01_01. Each source code example presented in this book incorporates an example-specific header file. For source code example Ch01_01, header file Ch01_01.h contains a single function declaration.

Listing 1-1-1. Example Ch01_01 – Ch01_01.h

```
//-------------------------------------------------------------------
// Ch01_01.h
//-------------------------------------------------------------------

#ifndef CH01_01_H_
#define CH01_01_H_
#include "Common.h"

extern void Ch01_01_ex();

#endif
```

The other item of note in Listing 1-1-1 is the statement #include "Common.h". This file contains template code that facilitates the use of C++23 functions std::print() and std::println() with a compiler that supports the C++20 formatting functions (e.g., std::format(), std::vformat(), etc.). You can find Common.h in a subdirectory named Common along with other shared files. For the current example, it is not necessary to understand the template code contained in Common.h.

Listing 1-1-2 shows the source code for file Ch01_01.cpp. Like the previously described header file, each source code example presented in this book incorporates a similar file. The primary purpose of file Ch01_01.cpp is to provide a top-level exception handler.

Listing 1-1-2. Example Ch01_01 - Ch01_01.cpp

```
//------------------------------------------------------------------------
// Ch01_01.cpp
//------------------------------------------------------------------------

#include <stdexcept>
#include "Ch01_01.h"

int main(int, char** argv)
{
    int rc {};

    try
    {
        std::println("\n----- Results for example Ch01_01 -----");
        Ch01_01_ex();
    }

    catch (const std::exception& ex)
    {
        rc = 1;
        std::println("Exception occurred in program {:s}", argv[0]);
        std::println("{:s}", ex.what());
    }

    return rc;
}
```

The pertinent STL code for example Ch01_01 is in file Ch01_01_ex.cpp as shown in Listing 1-1-3.

Listing 1-1-3. Example Ch01_01 - Ch01_01_ex.cpp

```cpp
//-------------------------------------------------------------------
// Ch01_01_ex.cpp
//-------------------------------------------------------------------

#include <string>
#include "Ch01_01.h"
#include "Point2D.h"

// function template - adds values
template <typename T> T add_values(T a, T b, T c)
{
    return a + b + c;
}

void Ch01_01_ex1()
{
    // uniform initialization
    int a {10};
    int b {20};
    int c {30};
//  int x = 2.1;        // compiler warning (maybe), x = 2
//  int y {2.1};        // compiler error

    // using template function add_values()
    int sum1 = add_values(a, b, c);
    std::println("a: {}  b: {}  c: {}  sum1: {}", a, b, c, sum1);

    // using template function add_values()
    double d {100.0};
    double e {200.0};
    double f {300.0};
    double sum2 = add_values(d, e, f);
    std::println("d: {}  e: {}  f: {}  sum2: {}", d, e, f, sum2);

    // add_values() works for any class that defines operator+
    std::string s1 {"one "};
    std::string s2 {"two "};
```

```cpp
    std::string s3 {"three"};
    std::string s4 = add_values(s1, s2, s3);
    std::print("s1: \"{}\"  s2: \"{}\"  s3: \"{}\"", s1, s2, s3);
    std::println(" - s4: \"{}\"", s4);
}

// abbreviated function template - calculates mean
double calc_mean(auto a, auto b, auto c)
{
    return (a + b + c) / 3.0;
}

void Ch01_01_ex2()
{
    // using calc_mean() - same data types
    int a {12};
    int b {28};
    int c {36};
    double mean1 = calc_mean(a, b, c);
    std::println("a: {}  b: {}  c: {}  mean1: {}", a, b, c, mean1);

    // using calc_mean() - different data types
    float x {201.1f};
    long long y {108};
    unsigned short z {307};
    double mean2 = calc_mean(x, y, z);
    std::println("x: {}  y: {}  z: {}  mean3: {}", x, y, z, mean2);

    // calc_mean() - operator+ must be defined for all argument types
//  auto mean3 = calc_mean(a, b, "thirty");    // compiler error
}

void Ch01_01_ex3()
{
    // using template function add_values() with type Point2D<int>
    Point2D<int> p1 {10, 20};
    Point2D<int> p2 {30, 40};
    Point2D<int> p3 {50, 60};
```

CHAPTER 1 C++ REVIEW

```cpp
    Point2D<int> p4 = add_values(p1, p2, p3);
    std::println("p1: {}  p2: {}  p3: {}  p4: {}", p1, p2, p3, p4);

    // using Point2D equality operators
    std::println("p1 == p2: {}", p1 == p2);
    std::println("p1 != p2: {}", p1 != p2);

    // using Point2D accessors & mutators
    int x = p1.X() * 10;
    int y = p1.Y() * 20;
    std::println("x: {}, y: {}", x, y);
    p1.X() -= 1;
    p1.Y() -= 2;
    std::println("p1: {}", p1);

    // using Point2D::distance()
    std::println("p1.distance(p2): {}", p1.distance());

    // using template function add_values() with type Point2D<double>
    Point2D<double> p5 {100.0, 200.0};
    Point2D<double> p6 {300.0, 400.0};
    Point2D<double> p7 {500.0, 600.0};
    Point2D<double> p8 = add_values(p5, p6, p7);
    std::println("p5: {}  p6: {}  p7: {}  p8: {}", p5, p6, p7, p8);
}
void Ch01_01_ex()
{
    std::println("\n---- Ch01_01_ex1() -----");
    Ch01_01_ex1();

    std::println("\n---- Ch01_01_ex2() -----");
    Ch01_01_ex2();

    std::println("\n---- Ch01_01_ex3() -----");
    Ch01_01_ex3();
}
```

File `Ch01_01_ex.cpp` opens with several `#include` statements. The first statement, `#include <string>`, facilitates the use of class `std::string`. Recall that class `std::string` is an alias for STL class `std::basic_string<char>`. The next statement, `#include "Ch01_01.h"`, incorporates the previously described example-specific header file. The final header file, `"Point2D.h"`, contains the definition of a template class named `Point2D`. More on this shortly.

Following the `#include` statements is the definition of a template function named `add_values()`. This function returns the sum of its three argument values. The statement `template <typename T> T add_values(T a, T b, T c)`[1] defines `add_values()` as a template function, and T is the data type for argument values a, b, and c. The sole statement of `add_values()`, `return a + b + c`, returns the sum of a, b, and c to the caller. The most important detail to understand about template function `add_values()` is that it can be used with any data type that supports `operator+` as you will soon see.

Next in Listing 1-1-3 is a function named `Ch01_01_ex1()`. This function begins with the definition of three integer variables named a, b, and c. Note that `Ch01_01_ex1()` uses uniform initializers instead of assignments to initialize these variables. Recall that C++ uniform initializers are type-safe; the compiler will flag a narrowing conversion as an error instead of a warning. The next executable statement, `int sum1 = add_values (a, b, c)`, calculates a + b + c using the previously defined template function. The ensuing statement, `std::println("a: {}, b: {}, c: {}, sum1: {}", a, b, c, sum1)`, prints the results. You'll learn how to use `std::println()` in Chapter 2. For the examples presented in this chapter, the most important thing to note is that each occurrence of `{}` in the supplied text string signifies that the corresponding data value should be displayed using the type's default format.

The next code block in function `Ch01_01_ex1()` utilizes template function `add_values()` to compute the sum of three doubles. As previously mentioned, many other programming languages would require distinct functions to carry out the same summing operation: one for integers and one for floating-point values. The final code block uses `add_values()` to "sum" three objects of type `std::string`. This works since `std::string::operator+` is defined and it performs string concatenation.

---

[1] The keyword `class` can also be used here instead of `typename`.

Immediately following function ChO1_01_ex1() in Listing 1-1-3 is another template function definition named calc_mean(). Note that the definition of this function differs from calc_sum() in that it employs an alternative syntax that uses the keyword auto. This style is called an abbreviated function template. During compilation, the C++ compiler will automatically deduce the data types for argument values a, b, and c.

Function ChO1_01_ex2() demonstrates the use of calc_mean(). The first code block exercises calc_mean() using three values of type int. The second code block in ChO1_01_ex2() uses calc_mean() with three different types. This form of usage is acceptable since operator+ is defined for each of the types and appropriate conversions are available. The final usage example of calc_mean() is invalid and commented out since operator+ is not defined for a numerical and std::string types.

Listing 1-1-4 shows the code for a template class named Point2D. Near the top of this listing is the definition of a template constraint named PointCoord2D. This constraint restricts PointCoord2D's T parameter to integral and floating-point types. PointCoord2D uses predefined concepts std::integral and std::floating_point, which are defined in <concepts>. You can also create your own custom concepts to limit the types that can be used with a user-defined template class. Using constraints enables the compiler to flag invalid template parameters much sooner; it also facilitates more meaningful error messages. Template concepts and constraints became available with C++20.

Listing 1-1-4. Example Ch01_01 - Point2D.h

```
//-------------------------------------------------------------------------
// Point2D.h
//-------------------------------------------------------------------------

#ifndef POINT2D_H_
#define POINT2D_H_
#include <cmath>
#include <concepts>
#include <format>
#include <ostream>
#include <string>

// Point2D coordinate constraint
template <typename T> concept
PointCoord2D = std::integral<T> || std::floating_point<T>;
```

```cpp
template <PointCoord2D T> class Point2D
{
    friend struct std::formatter<Point2D<T>>;

public:
    Point2D() = default;
    Point2D(T x, T y) : m_X {x}, m_Y {y} {};

    // accessors
    T X() const { return m_X; }
    T Y() const { return m_Y; }
    T& X() { return m_X; }
    T& Y() { return m_Y; }

    // operators
    friend bool operator==(const Point2D<T>& p1, const Point2D<T>& p2)
        { return p1.m_X == p2.m_X && p1.m_Y == p2.m_Y; }

    friend bool operator!=(const Point2D<T>& p1, const Point2D<T>& p2)
        { return !(p1 == p2); }

    friend Point2D operator+(const Point2D& p1, const Point2D& p2)
        { return Point2D(p1.m_X + p2.m_X, p1.m_Y + p2.m_Y); }

    friend std::ostream& operator<< (std::ostream& os, const Point2D& p)
    {
        os << p.to_str();
        return os;
    }

    // member functions
    double distance() const
        { return std::hypot(m_X, m_Y); }    // distance from (0, 0)
private:
    std::string to_str() const
    {
        std::string s;
        std::format_to(std::back_inserter(s), "({}, {})", m_X, m_Y);
```

```
        return s;
    }

    T m_X {};
    T m_Y {};
};

// class Point2D formatter
template <typename T> struct std::formatter<Point2D<T>> :
    std::formatter<std::string>
{
    constexpr auto parse(std::format_parse_context& fpc)
        { return fpc.begin(); }

    auto format(const Point2D<T>& point, std::format_context& fc) const
        { return std::format_to(fc.out(), "{}", point.to_str()); }
};

#endif
```

Class Point2D utilizes PointCoord2D as a constraint on template parameter T. With this constraint in place, any declarations of Point2D objects that violate the constraint such as Point2D<std::string> are immediately flagged as an error by the compiler. The first statement of class Point2D's definition, friend struct std::formatter<Point2D<T>>, is provided for the Point2D formatting functions that appear near the end of file Point2D.h. These functions handle the requisite operations when Point2D objects are formatted using std::format() or std::println(). You'll learn more about this in Chapter 2. The remaining code in Point2D defines the requisite constructors, accessors for the attributes m_X and m_Y, a few operators, and a member function named distance() that calculates the Euclidean distance between points (0, 0) and (m_X, m_Y).

Function Ch01_01_ex3(), shown in Listing 1-1-3. illustrates the use of class Point2D. In the first code block, note that add_values() is used to sum points p1, p2, and p3. The use of add_values() is valid here since class Point2D defines operator+. The remaining code blocks in function Ch01_01_ex3() demonstrate usage of Point2D's operators, accessors, mutators, and distance functions. It also shows an example of Point2D using type double. Here are the results for source code example Ch01_01:

```
----- Results for example Ch01_01 -----

---- Ch01_01_ex1() -----
a: 10   b: 20   c: 30   sum1: 60
d: 100  e: 200  f: 300  sum2: 600
s1: "one " s2: "two " s3: "three" - s4: "one two three"

---- Ch01_01_ex2() -----
a: 12   b: 28   c: 36   mean1: 25.3333333333333332
x: 201.1  y: 108  z: 307  mean3: 205.36665852864584

---- Ch01_01_ex3() -----
p1: (10, 20)  p2: (30, 40)  p3: (50, 60)  p4: (90, 120)
p1 == p2: false
p1 != p2: true
x: 100, y: 400
p1: (9, 18)
p1.distance(p2): 20.12461179749811
p5: (100, 200)  p6: (300, 400)  p7: (500, 600)  p8: (900, 1200)
```

Source Code Overview

Before continuing to the next example, a few words about the source code are warranted. Most of source code examples published in this book follow the same design pattern that was used in example Ch01_01. Each source code example utilizes an example-specific header file named ChXX_YY.h, a top-level file named ChXX_YY.cpp that contains main() and a default exception handler, and a file named ChXX_YY_ex.cpp. This last file is the most important since it contains the code that demonstrates STL usage and programming techniques. Going forward, I won't show the listings for files ChXX_YY.h and ChXX_YY.cpp unless they contain code that's necessary to understand the example. If you haven't already done so, now is probably a good time to download the source code. Appendix A contains download instructions along with important C++ compiler details.

If you've been following the evolution of C++, you may be wondering why I used header files in source example Ch01_01 instead of C++ modules (e.g., import std;). There are several reasons for this. First, I started writing the source code using compilers that didn't fully support modules. One of my goals for this book was to develop code that could be successfully compiled using multiple mainstream C++ compilers, including Visual Studio (MSVC), GCC, and Clang. Doing this is often more challenging than one might expect. As I write this, these compilers vary in their support for modules as specified by the ISO C++23 standard.

Another reason is that many companion C++ development tools also do not fully support modules. Modules are a welcome and significant addition to C++, but one can still successfully learn and effectively exploit the C++ STL without using modules. As many others have noted, the transition from header files to modules will be both gradual and methodical.

Containers and Iterators

It is impossible for a programmer to effectively utilize the resources of STL without an understanding of containers and iterators. The next source code example, named Ch01_02, introduces these topics. Listing 1-2 shows the principal source code for example Ch01_02.

Listing 1-2. Example Ch01_02 - Ch01_02_ex.cpp

```
//-------------------------------------------------------------
// Ch01_02_ex.cpp
//-------------------------------------------------------------

#include <typeinfo>
#include <vector>
#include "Ch01_02.h"

void Ch01_02_ex1()
{
    std::vector<int> x_vals {10, 20, 30, 40, 50, 60, 70, 80, 90, 100};

    // access element using operator[]
    for (std::size_t i = 0; i < x_vals.size(); ++i)
        std::print("{} ", x_vals[i]);
    std::println("");
```

```cpp
    // access elements using at()
    for (std::size_t i = 0; i < x_vals.size(); ++i)
        std::print("{} ", x_vals.at(i));
    std::println("");
//  x_vals[42] = -1         // error, no exception, trouble
//  x_vals.at(42) = -1;     // error, throws exception
}

void Ch01_02_ex2()
{
    std::vector<long long> y_vals {10, 20, 30, 40, 50,
        60, 70, 80, 90, 100};

    // print elements of y_vals using iterators
    for (auto iter = y_vals.begin(); iter != y_vals.end(); ++iter)
        std::print("{} ", *iter);
    std::println("");

    // print iterator type
    std::println("\nvector<long long> iterator type:\n{}\n",
        typeid(y_vals.begin()).name());

    // print elements of y_vals in reverse order
    for (auto iter = y_vals.rbegin(); iter != y_vals.rend(); ++iter)
        std::print("{} ", *iter);
    std::println("\n");

    // using std::begin() and std::end()
    for (auto iter = std::begin(y_vals); iter != std::end(y_vals); ++iter)
    {
        *iter *= 5;
        std::print("{} ", *iter);
    }
    std::println("");
}
```

CHAPTER 1 C++ REVIEW

```cpp
void Ch01_02_ex3()
{
    std::vector<std::string> s_vals
        {"adenine", "cytosine", "guanine", "thymine", "uracil"};

    // display s_vals - in order, const iterator
    for (auto iter = s_vals.cbegin(); iter != s_vals.cend(); ++iter)
        std::print("{} ", *iter);
    std::println("");

    // display s_vals, reverse order, const iterator
    for (auto iter = s_vals.crbegin(); iter != s_vals.crend(); ++iter)
        std::print("{} ", *iter);
    std::println("");
}

void Ch01_02_ex()
{
    std::println("\n---- Ch01_02_ex1() -----");
    Ch01_02_ex1();

    std::println("\n---- Ch01_02_ex2() -----");
    Ch01_02_ex2();

    std::println("\n---- Ch01_02_ex3() -----");
    Ch01_02_ex3();
}
```

The first function of Listing 1-2, Ch01_02_ex1(), commences with the definition of a std::vector<int> named x_vals. Class std:vector is a sequence container object that supports random access of its elements using either iterators or indices. It is often used when implementing algorithms that require array-like functionality but whose size (or number of elements) is not known until runtime. In the current function, the declaration of x_vals includes an initializer list. During program execution, this initialize list is passed to the constructor of x_vals, which uses it to initialize a vector of ten elements.

The next code block in Ch01_02_ex1() prints the elements of x_vals using a conventional for loop and std::vector::operator[]. Note that the syntax used here is the same as one would use to access the elements of the C-style array. In this for loop, std::vector::size() returns the number of elements currently stored in x_vals. The ensuing code block uses the std::vector::at() function to access the elements of x_vals. The difference between operator[] and at() is that the latter throws an exception if the supplied index is invalid.

Function Ch01_02_ex2() demonstrates how to access the elements of std::vector<long long> y_vals using iterators. The first for loop uses std::vector::begin() and std::vector::end() to obtain start and end iterators for y_vals. Figure 1-1 illustrates the meaning of these iterators in greater detail. Note in this figure that the value returned by end() actually points to the "element" that follows the last element of y_vals. It is also important to note that auto was used as the type for iterator iter. This instructs the compiler to automatically deduce the correct type for iter. More about this shortly. The std::print() statement that's within the body of the for loop dereferences iter using the same syntax as one would use for a native pointer.

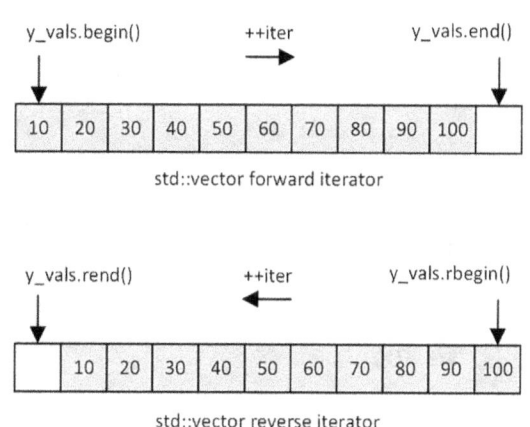

Figure 1-1. *Class* std::vector *forward and reverse iterators*

You may have noticed that the for loop in Ch01_02_ex2() uses prefix operator++ instead of postfix. The reason for this is that the prefix form is usually faster for iterator incrementing.

The next code block uses typeid(y_vals.begin()).name() to display the data type for y_val's iterators. If you scan ahead to the results section for this example, you'll immediately appreciate why the keyword auto was used to declare iter within the for loop. It warrants mentioning here that starting with C++20, a program is ill-formed[2] if it uses operator typeid without including <typeinfo>.

---

[2] A program that is constructed in violation of C++'s syntactical and semantic rules.

CHAPTER 1   C++ REVIEW

The second for loop in Ch01_02_ex2() also uses iterators to reference the elements of y_vals, but the for loop uses rbegin() and rend() to reference the elements of y_vals in reverse order as shown in Figure 1-1. In the third for loop, Ch01_02_ex2() employs global iterator functions std::begin() and std::end() for iterator initialization and loop termination testing. The global iterator functions are often used in generic programming when the specific container type is unknown. They also facilitate the use of iterators with C-style arrays. Within the third for loop, note that the syntax used to multiply each element of y_vals by five is the same syntax that one would use with a native pointer.

Function Ch01_02_ex3() demonstrates using iterators with an instance of std::vector<std::string>. Note in this example the use of functions cbegin(), cend(), crbegin(), and crend(), which return const iterators. Like a const pointer, the compiler will flag any attempt to modify a container element using a const iterator. Here are the results for example Ch01_02:

```
----- Results for example Ch01_02 -----

---- Ch01_02_ex1() -----
10 20 30 40 50 60 70 80 90 100
10 20 30 40 50 60 70 80 90 100

---- Ch01_02_ex2() -----
10 20 30 40 50 60 70 80 90 100

vector<long long> iterator type:
class std::_Vector_iterator<class std::_Vector_val<struct std::_Simple_types<__int64>>>

100 90 80 70 60 50 40 30 20 10

50 100 150 200 250 300 350 400 450 500

---- Ch01_02_ex3() -----
adenine cytosine guanine thymine uracil
uracil thymine guanine cytosine adenine
```

The string returned by typeid(y_vals.begin()).name() varies depending on the C++ compiler. The results section for example Ch01_02 shows the output from a 64-bit executable compiled using MSVC.

Strings

C++ defines strings that one can use like an intrinsic data type even though they're implemented using templates. As mentioned earlier, the base template class for C++ strings is std::basic_string. However, most programs don't use this class directly; they use one of the following alias classes: std::string, std::wstring, std::u8string, std::u16string, or std::u32string. These classes utilize char, wchar_t, char8_t, char16_t, and char32_t, respectively, for the string's character type. In this book, the source code examples mostly use std::string. Any comments or explanations that you read about std::string also apply to the other string types unless otherwise mentioned.

Listing 1-3 shows the source code for example Ch01_03. The first function in this listing, Ch01_03_ex1(), demonstrates string concatenation using std::string::operator+. You can also use std::string::operator+= to append one string to another. Class std::string includes numerous overloads that facilitate operations using a single character or C-style string. This facilitates the coding of concatenating expressions that encompass a mixture of object types such as std::string, char, and const char*. Function Ch01_03_ex1() also illustrates the use of std::string's relational operators.

Listing 1-3. Example Ch01_03 – Ch01_03_ex.cpp

```cpp
//-------------------------------------------------------------
// Ch01_03_ex.cpp
//-------------------------------------------------------------

#include <string>
#include <string_view>
#include <version>
#include "Ch01_03.h"

void Ch01_03_ex1(const std::string& s1, const std::string& s2,
    char c, const char* s)
{
    std::println("s1: '{}'", s1);
    std::println("s2: '{}'", s2);
    std::println("c:  '{}'", c);
    std::println("s:  '{}'", s);
```

CHAPTER 1   C++ REVIEW

```cpp
    // string concatenation
    std::string s3 = s1 + ' ' + s2;
    std::string s4 = s3 + c + s;
    std::println("\ns3: '{}'", s3);
    std::println("s4: '{}'", s4);

    // using std::string relational operators
    std::println("\ns1 <  s2: {}", s1 < s2);
    std::println("s1 <= s2: {}", s1 <= s2);
    std::println("s1 == s2: {}", s1 == s2);
    std::println("s1 != s2: {}", s1 != s2);
    std::println("s1 >  s2: {}", s1 > s2);
    std::println("s1 >= s2: {}", s1 >= s2);
}

void Ch01_03_ex2(const std::string& s1, const std::string s_find)
{
    std::println("s1: '{}'", s1);
    std::println("substring: {}", s_find);

    // find substring
    std::size_t pos = s1.find(s_find);

    if (pos == std::string::npos)
        std::println("not found");
    else
        std::println("found at position {}", pos);
}

void Ch01_03_ex3(const std::string& s1, const std::string& s_old,
    const std::string& s_new)
{
    std::println("\ns1: '{}'", s1);
    std::string s2 {s1};

    // using find and replace
    auto n_find = s2.find(s_old);

    if (n_find != std::string::npos)
```

```cpp
    {
        std::string s3 {s2};
        s3.replace(n_find, s_old.size(), s_new);
        std::println("s3: '{}'", s3);
    }
    else
        std::println("substring '{}' not found", s_old);
}

void Ch01_03_ex4(const std::string& s1, const std::string& s_find,
    const std::string& s_insert)
{
    std::println("\ns1: '{}'", s1);
    std::string s2 {s1};

    // using find, insert
    auto n_find = s2.find(s_find);

    if (n_find != std::string::npos)
    {
        s2.insert(n_find + s_find.size(), s_insert);
        std::println("s2: '{}'", s2);
    }
    else
        std::println("substring '{}' not found", s_find);
}

void Ch01_03_ex5(const std::string& s1, const std::string_view& s_test)
{
    // using starts_with, ends_with
    bool b_sw = s1.starts_with(s_test);
    bool b_ew = s1.ends_with(s_test);

    std::println("\n'{}' starts with string '{}' - {}", s1, s_test, b_sw);
    std::println("'{}' ends with string '{}' - {}", s1, s_test, b_ew);

    // using contains
#ifdef __cpp_lib_string_contains
```

CHAPTER 1   C++ REVIEW

```cpp
    bool b_c = s1.contains(s_test);
    std::println("'{}' contains string '{}' - {}", s1, s_test, b_c);
#else
    std::println("Ch01_03_ex5() uses string::contains() - requires C++23");
#endif
}

void Ch01_03_ex()
{
    std::println("\n----- Ch01_03_ex1() -----");
    const std::string s1 {"Hello"};
    const std::string s2 {"World"};
    const char c {'='};
    const char* s = "Hallo Welt";
    Ch01_03_ex1(s1, s2, c, s);

    std::println("\n----- Ch01_03_ex2() -----");
    const std::string s3 {"one two three four five "
                          "six seven eight nine ten"};
    Ch01_03_ex2(s3, "eight");
    Ch01_03_ex2(s3, "eleven");

    std::println("\n---- Ch01_03_ex3() -----");
    const std::string s4 {"red green blue cyan magenta "
                          "yellow orange brown purple gray"};
    Ch01_03_ex3(s4, "blue", "BLUE");
    Ch01_03_ex3(s4, "cyan", "TAN");
    Ch01_03_ex3(s4, "magenta", "**MAGENTA**");
    Ch01_03_ex3(s4, "indigo", "INDIGO");

    std::println("\n---- Ch01_03_ex4() -----");
    Ch01_03_ex4(s3, "four", " (4)");
    Ch01_03_ex4(s3, "ten", " (10)");
    Ch01_03_ex4(s3, "eleven", " (11)");

    std::println("\n---- Ch01_03_ex5() -----");
    const std::string s5 {"apple banana orange raspberry pear"};
    const std::string_view sv1 {"apple"};
```

```
    const std::string_view sv2 {"pear"};
    const std::string_view sv3 {"raspberry"};
    Ch01_03_ex5(s5, sv1);
    Ch01_03_ex5(s5, sv2);
    Ch01_03_ex5(s5, sv3);
}
```

Function Ch01_03_ex2() uses std::string::find() to search for the first occurrence of a substring within another string. If the specified substring is found, find() returns the index (position) of the substring's first character; otherwise, it returns std::string::npos. Function Ch01_03_ex3() also exercises find() to locate a substring. If a substring match is found, it uses std::string::replace() to overwrite the found substring with a new string. Modifying member function std::string::insert() inserts a new string within another string as shown in Ch01_03_ex4().

The final exposition function of Listing 1-3, Ch01_03_ex5(), demonstrates how to use a few std::string member functions new to C++20/23. Before examining these functions, note that function Ch01_03_ex5() includes an argument of type std::string_view. A std::string_view object possesses a constant pointer and a length as shown in Figure 1-2. It is often used instead of std::string when working with constant strings since it avoids std::string's higher constructor costs. The drawback of using std::string_view is that it supports a smaller set of operations than std::string.

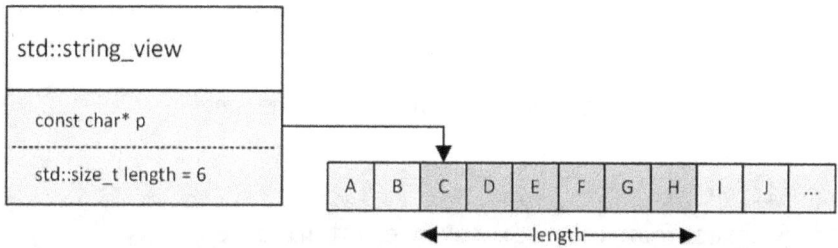

Figure 1-2. *Class* std::string_view

The first code block in Ch01_03_ex5() uses std::string::starts_with() and std::string::ends_with() to determine if string s1 starts with or ends with a substring that matches s_test. Note that these C++20 member functions return a value of type bool. The next code block exercises std::string::contains() (C++23) whose bool return value signifies the existence of substring s_test anywhere within string s1. This code block also demonstrates a technique that you can use to determine if the

CHAPTER 1   C++ REVIEW

C++ implementation supports a specific feature. In the current example, preprocessor symbol __cpp_lib_string_contains is defined if the C++ implementation supports std::string::contains(). The C++20 header file <version> defines over 200 feature detection macros that you can use to perform compile-time detection of specific features. Here are the results for example Ch01_03:

```
----- Results for example Ch01_03 -----
----- Ch01_03_ex1() -----
s1: 'Hello'
s2: 'World'
c:  '='
s:  'Hallo Welt'

s3: 'Hello World'
s4: 'Hello World=Hallo Welt'

s1 <  s2: true
s1 <= s2: true
s1 == s2: false
s1 != s2: true
s1 >  s2: false
s1 >= s2: false
----- Ch01_03_ex2() -----
s1: 'one two three four five six seven eight nine ten
substring: eight
found at position 34
s1: 'one two three four five six seven eight nine ten
substring: eleven
not found
---- Ch01_03_ex3() -----

s1: 'red green blue cyan magenta yellow orange brown purple gray'
s3: 'red green BLUE cyan magenta yellow orange brown purple gray

s1: 'red green blue cyan magenta yellow orange brown purple gray'
s3: 'red green blue TAN magenta yellow orange brown purple gray
```

```
s1: 'red green blue cyan magenta yellow orange brown purple gray'
s3: 'red green blue cyan **MAGENTA** yellow orange brown purple gray

s1: 'red green blue cyan magenta yellow orange brown purple gray'
substring 'indigo' not found

---- Ch01_03_ex4() -----

s1: 'one two three four five six seven eight nine ten'
s2: 'one two three four (4) five six seven eight nine ten

s1: 'one two three four five six seven eight nine ten'
s2: 'one two three four five six seven eight nine ten (10)

s1: 'one two three four five six seven eight nine ten'
substring 'eleven' not found

---- Ch01_03_ex5() -----

'apple banana orange raspberry pear' starts with string 'apple' - true
'apple banana orange raspberry pear' ends with string 'apple' - false
'apple banana orange raspberry pear' contains string 'apple' - true

'apple banana orange raspberry pear' starts with string 'pear' - false
'apple banana orange raspberry pear' ends with string 'pear' - true
'apple banana orange raspberry pear' contains string 'pear' - true

'apple banana orange raspberry pear' starts with string 'raspberry' - false
'apple banana orange raspberry pear' ends with string 'raspberry' - false
'apple banana orange raspberry pear' contains string 'raspberry' - true
```

Class `std::string` supports numerous other operations besides the ones demonstrated in this example. Appendix B contains a list of references that you can consult for additional information regarding `std::string` and `std::string_view`.

User-Defined Classes

Having the means to define custom data types is an essential feature of most programming languages. In C++ this is frequently accomplished using the `class` construct. Listing 1-4-1 shows the definition of a class named Image, which exemplifies

CHAPTER 1 C++ REVIEW

the typical design pattern of a user-defined class. The source code example of this section, Ch01_04, utilizes class Image to highlight important issues you need to be aware of when creating a user-defined class. Before continuing, it should be noted that class Image is incomplete, but adequate for the instructive purposes of this section.

Listing 1-4-1. Example Ch01_04 - Image.h

```
//---------------------------------------------------------------------------
// Image.h
//---------------------------------------------------------------------------
#ifndef IMAGE_H_
#define IMAGE_H_
#include <cstdint>
#include <format>
#include <ostream>
#include <string>
#include <vector>
#include "Common.h"

class Image
{
    using pixel_t = uint8_t;                            // alias for image
                                                        //   pixel type

    friend struct std::formatter<Image>;
public:
    Image() = default;                                  // default constructor

    Image(std::size_t height, std::size_t width);       // parameterized
                                                        //   constructor

    Image(const Image& im);                             // copy constructor
    Image(Image&& im) noexcept;                         // move constructor

    virtual ~Image();                                   // destructor

    Image& operator=(const Image& im);                  // copy assignment
    Image& operator=(Image&& im) noexcept;              // move assignment
```

```cpp
    // accessors
    std::size_t height() const {return m_Height;}
    std::size_t width() const {return m_Width;}
    std::size_t num_pixels() const {return m_Height * m_Width;}

    // relational operators
    friend bool operator==(const Image& im1, const Image& im2);
    friend bool operator!=(const Image& im1, const Image& im2);

    // other operators
    friend std::ostream& operator<<(std::ostream& os, const Image& im);
private:
    // private member functions
    void reset();
    std::string to_str() const;

    // attributes
    std::size_t m_Height {};
    std::size_t m_Width {};
    std::vector<pixel_t> m_PixelBuff {};
};

// class Image formatter
template <> struct std::formatter<Image> : std::formatter<std::string>
{
    constexpr auto parse(std::format_parse_context& fpc)
        { return fpc.begin(); }

    auto format(const Image& im, std::format_context& fc) const
        { return std::format_to(fc.out(), "{:s}", im.to_str()); }
};

#endif
```

The declaration of non-template class Image begins with the definition of an alias named pixel_t that defines the integer type. An alias is used here since it simplifies experimentation using different numerical types – simply change uint8_t to another numerical type and recompile. The public section of Image opens with the statement

`Image() = default` that instructs the compiler to generate a default constructor. A compiler-generated default constructor will initialize all class attributes that include an in-class member initializer. The private attributes for `Image` (located near the bottom of Listing 1-4-1) are `m_Height`, `m_Width`, and `m_PixelBuff`. Note that all three attributes are declared using initializer `{}`. This means that the compiler-generated default constructor for `Image` will set both `m_Height` and `m_Width` to zero, and `std::vector<pixel_t> m_PixelBuff` will be initialized with zero elements.

The next set of statements declares the standard set of constructors, including a parameterized constructor, copy constructor, and move constructor. Class `Image` defines its destructor as a `virtual` to facilitate its use as a base class. The copy and move assignment operators are declared next.

The remaining public declarations of class `Image` are simple accessors, relational operators, and an overload for `operator<<`. The private section of class `Image` opens with the declarations of several member functions. This is followed by a section that contains the previously described attributes.

Listing 1-4-2 shows the function definitions for class `Image`. Near the top of this listing is the parameterized constructor that expects two argument values of type `std::size_t`: height and width. Following initialization of `m_Height` and `m_Width`, the constructor exercises `m_PixelBuff.resize(m_Height * m_Width)` to properly size the pixel buffer. Function `std::vector::resize()` also initializes each pixel element in `m_PixelBuff` to zero. When the size of a `std::vector` is increased, `resize()` appends default-constructed elements to the end of the vector. For `m_PixelBuff`, the default-constructed elements are `pixel_t {}` or zero.

Listing 1-4-2. Example Ch01_04 - Image.cpp

```
//-------------------------------------------------------------------------
// Image.cpp
//-------------------------------------------------------------------------

#include <cstdint>
#include <format>
#include <ostream>
#include <string>
#include <vector>
#include "Image.h"
```

```cpp
#define IMAGE_DTOR_PRINTLN        // comment out to disable dtor
std::println

// parameterized constructor
Image::Image(std::size_t height, std::size_t width) : m_Height {height},
    m_Width {width}
{
    m_PixelBuff.resize(m_Height * m_Width);
}

// copy constructor
Image::Image(const Image& im) : m_Height {im.m_Height}, m_Width
{im.m_Width},
    m_PixelBuff {im.m_PixelBuff}
{
}

// move constructor
Image::Image(Image&& im) noexcept : m_Height {im.m_Height}, m_Width
{im.m_Width},
    m_PixelBuff {std::move(im.m_PixelBuff)}
{
    im.reset();
}

Image::~Image()
{
#ifdef IMAGE_DTOR_PRINTLN
    // std::println used for demonstration purposes
    std::println("Image::~Image() {}", *this);
#endif
}

// copy assignment
Image& Image::operator=(const Image& im)
{
    m_Height = im.m_Height;
    m_Width = im.m_Width;
```

CHAPTER 1   C++ REVIEW

```cpp
    m_PixelBuff = im.m_PixelBuff;
    return *this;
}

// move assignment
Image& Image::operator=(Image&& im) noexcept
{
    m_Height = im.m_Height;
    m_Width = im.m_Width;
    m_PixelBuff = std::move(im.m_PixelBuff);
    im.reset();
    return *this;
}

// relational operators
bool operator==(const Image& im1, const Image& im2)
{
    if (im1.m_Height != im2.m_Height || im1.m_Width != im2.m_Width)
        return false;

    return im1.m_PixelBuff == im2.m_PixelBuff;
}

bool operator!=(const Image& im1, const Image& im2)
{
    return !operator==(im1, im2);
}

// other operators
std::ostream& operator<<(std::ostream& os, const Image& im)
{
    os << im.to_str();
    return os;
}
```

```cpp
void Image::reset()
{
    m_Height = 0;
    m_Width = 0;
}

std::string Image::to_str() const
{
    std::string s {};
    std::format_to(std::back_inserter(s), "[{:5d} ", m_Height);
    std::format_to(std::back_inserter(s), "{:5d} ", m_Width);
    std::format_to(std::back_inserter(s), "{:8d} ", m_Height * m_Width);

    constexpr int pb_w {(sizeof(void*) <= 4) ? 8 : 16};
    std::uintptr_t pb = reinterpret_cast<std::uintptr_t>
    (m_PixelBuff.data());
    std::format_to(std::back_inserter(s), "0x{:0>{}X}]", pb, pb_w);
    return s;
}
```

A brief digression. You may be wondering why class Image utilizes std::vector for its pixel buffer instead of allocating the buffer using operator new (e.g., m_PixelBuffer = new pixel_t[m_Height * m_Width]). The use of the former simplifies the coding of Image's copy and move constructors along with the corresponding assignment operators. These functions can utilize functions provided by std::vector to perform pixel buffer copies and size adjustments when necessary. More importantly, the use of class std::vector ensures that the allocated pixel buffer is automatically deleted when ~Image() is called. This significantly reduces the risk of a memory leak. Modern C++ discourages direct use of operators new and delete for dynamic memory allocations since such use is error prone. Using an STL container object is usually a much better option. For design cases where explicit use of new and delete is necessary, you can use a smart pointer such as std::unique_ptr<>. Using std::unique_ptr<pixel_t> for the pixel buffer in class Image would eliminate the previously described automatic zeroing of elements, which adversely affects performance. The downside is code that's a bit more complex. You'll learn more about smart pointers in Chapter 6.

The next item in Listing 1-4-2 is Image's copy constructor, which uses the attributes and data from source image im to construct a new image. Note that the initializer m_PixelBuff {im.m_PixelBuff} utilizes std::vector's copy constructor to copy initialize m_PixelBuff.

Class Image's move constructor handles the transfer of ownership from one Image object to another. The constructor's Image&& im argument references a temporary (rvalue) object that is the source for the move. Note the use of m_PixelBuff {std::move(im.m_PixelBuffer)}, which moves the im's pixel buffer. The move constructor also calls reset() to reset the source image to its default state. Following execution of Image's move constructor, object im can be safely destroyed when its destructor is called (a move constructor should always leave the source object in state that's suitable for use by a destructor).

Assignments are handled by Image's copy assignment (Image& Image::operator=(const Image& im)) and move assignment (Image& Image::operator=(Image&& im)) operators. The operations performed by both assignment operators mimic the corresponding constructors. Class Image also defines relational operators operator== and operator!=. The statement im1.m_PixelBuff == im2.m_PixelBuff performs an element-by-element comparison of the pixel values in the two vectors using std::vector::operator==.

The final item of note in class Image is the private member function to_str(). This function is called to format a string for display purposes (e.g., when one uses std::cout << im or std::println("im: {}", im)).

Listing 1-4-3 shows the source code for file Ch01_04_ex.cpp, which contains two functions that exercise class Image. The first function, Ch01_04_ex1(), commences with the declaration Images im0, im1, and im2. The ensuing std::println() statements display each image's attributes on std::cout. If you scan ahead to the results section, note that the formatted output also includes the address of the pixel buffer.

CHAPTER 1　C++ REVIEW

Listing 1-4-3. Example Ch01_04 - Ch01_04_ex.cpp

```cpp
//---------------------------------------------------------------------
// Ch01_04_ex.cpp
//---------------------------------------------------------------------

#include <utility>
#include "Ch01_04.h"
#include "Image.h"

void Ch01_04_ex1()
{
    // create image objects
    Image im0 {};
    std::println("im0: {} - after ctor", im0);
    Image im1 {100, 200};
    std::println("im1: {} - after ctor", im1);
    Image im2 {300, 400};
    std::println("im2: {} - after ctor", im2);

    // using std::move
    Image im3 = std::move(im1);
    std::println("im3: {} - after move ctor", im3);

#pragma warning(disable:26800)   // disable MSVC warning (use of
                                 //                  moved object)
    std::println("im1: {} - after move (bad!)", im1);
#pragma warning(default:26800)
}

void Ch01_04_ex2()
{
    // create image objects
    Image im0 {1000, 2000};
    std::println("im0: {} - after ctor", im0);
    Image im1 {im0};
    std::println("im1: {} - after ctor", im1);
```

31

CHAPTER 1   C++ REVIEW

```
    Image im2 {3000, 4000};
    std::println("im2: {} - after ctor", im2);

    // using relational operators
    std::println("im1 == im2 (expect false): {}", im1 == im2);
    std::println("im1 != im2 (expect true):  {}", im1 != im2);

    // using operator=
    Image im3 {5000, 6000};
    std::println("im3: {} - after ctor", im3);

    im1 = im3;
    std::println("im1: {} - after assignment", im1);
    std::println("im1 == im3 (expect true):  {}", im1 == im3);
    std::println("im1 != im3 (expect false): {}", im1 != im3);
}

void Ch01_04_ex()
{
    std::println("\n---- Ch01_04_ex1() -----");
    Ch01_04_ex1();

    std::println("\n---- Ch01_04_ex2() -----");
    Ch01_04_ex2();
}
```

The next code block in Ch01_04_ex1() demonstrates an explicit Image move operation using std::move(). Note in the results section that the attributes of im1 following the move are all set to zero including m_PixelBuffer's data pointer. It warrants mentioning here that using an object after it has been moved is a potentially dangerous operation since the moved object is often in an unknown state (for class Image, the state of a moved Image is the same as that of a default initialized Image). This is the reason for the #pragma statements that surround the final call to std::println() – the Visual C+ compiler (MSVC) displays a warning message if a moved object is used. The second function in Listing 1-4-3, Ch01_04_ex2(), exercises additional operators of class Image.

The purpose of this example was to review the basics of a user-defined class and classes in general. When creating a user-defined class, you need to decide if the compiler-supplied default constructors and assignment operators are acceptable or if custom versions need to be coded. For class Image, the defaults could have been used, but explicit versions were coded for demonstration purposes. Here are the results for example Ch01_04:

```
---- Ch01_04_ex1() -----
im0: [    0     0          0 0x0000000000000000] - after ctor
im1: [  100   200      20000 0x000001FC05559FE0] - after ctor
im2: [  300   400     120000 0x000001FC0555EE40] - after ctor
im3: [  100   200      20000 0x000001FC05559FE0] - after move ctor
im1: [    0     0          0 0x0000000000000000] - after move (bad!)
Image::~Image() [  100   200     20000 0x000001FC05559FE0]
Image::~Image() [  300   400    120000 0x000001FC0555EE40]
Image::~Image() [    0     0         0 0x0000000000000000]
Image::~Image() [    0     0         0 0x0000000000000000]

---- Ch01_04_ex2() -----
im0: [ 1000  2000  2000000 0x000001FC057C1060] - after ctor
im1: [ 1000  2000  2000000 0x000001FC059BE060] - after ctor
im2: [ 3000  4000 12000000 0x000001FC05BB6060] - after ctor
im1 == im2 (expect false): false
im1 != im2 (expect true):  true
im3: [ 5000  6000 30000000 0x000001FC06737060] - after ctor
im1: [ 5000  6000 30000000 0x000001FC083E4060] - after assignment
im1 == im3 (expect true):  true
im1 != im3 (expect false): false
Image::~Image() [ 5000  6000 30000000 0x000001FC06737060]
Image::~Image() [ 3000  4000 12000000 0x000001FC05BB6060]
Image::~Image() [ 5000  6000 30000000 0x000001FC083E4060]
Image::~Image() [ 1000  2000  2000000 0x000001FC057C1060]
```

CHAPTER 1   C++ REVIEW

User-Defined Template Classes

User-defined classes can also be implemented using C++ templates. Recall from earlier discussions that a template is a parameterized data type. During template instantiation, the compiler substitutes the specified template parameters to generate parameter-specific code. For example, when using std::basic_string<class CharT>[3] (std::string), the compiler substitutes type char for template parameter CharT and generates code (constructors, operations, member functions, etc.) for a string based on type char. If the same program utilizes std::basic_string<class CharT> with a wchar_t (std::wstring), the compiler generates a second set of constructors, operators, etc. In other words, each distinct template instantiation results in a distinct set of code.

Listing 1-5-1 shows another Image class that's implemented using templates.

Listing 1-5-1. Example Ch01_05 - ImageT.cpp

```
//----------------------------------------------------------------
// ImageT.h
//----------------------------------------------------------------

#ifndef IMAGE_T_H_
#define IMAGE_T_H_
#include <concepts>
#include <cstdint>
#include <format>
#include <ostream>
#include <string>
#include <vector>
#include "Common.h"

#define IMAGE_T_DTOR_PRINTLN    // comment out to disable dtor std::println
```

---

[3] Class std::basic_string<> includes other template parameters besides CharT, but these are not shown.

```cpp
template <typename T> requires std::unsigned_integral<T>
class Image
{
    friend struct std::formatter<Image<T>>;
public:
    // default constructor
    Image() = default;

    // parameterized constructor
    Image(std::size_t height, std::size_t width) : m_Height {height},
        m_Width {width}
    {
        m_PixelBuff.resize(m_Height * m_Width);
    }

    // copy constructor
    Image(const Image& im) : m_Height {im.m_Height}, m_Width {im.m_Width},
        m_PixelBuff {im.m_PixelBuff}
    {
    }

    // move constructor
    Image(Image&& im) noexcept : m_Height {im.m_Height},
    m_Width {im.m_Width},
        m_PixelBuff {std::move(im.m_PixelBuff)}
    {
        im.reset();
    }

    // destructor
    virtual ~Image()
    {
#ifdef IMAGE_T_DTOR_PRINTLN
        // std::println used for demonstration purposes
        std::println("Image::~Image() {}", *this);
#endif
    }
```

```cpp
    // copy assignment
    Image& operator=(const Image& im)
    {
        m_Height = im.m_Height;
        m_Width = im.m_Width;
        m_PixelBuff = im.m_PixelBuff;
        return *this;
    }

    // move assignment
    Image& operator=(Image&& im) noexcept
    {
        m_Height = im.m_Height;
        m_Width = im.m_Width;
        m_PixelBuff = std::move(im.m_PixelBuff);
        im.reset();
        return *this;
    }

    // accessors
    std::size_t height() const {return m_Height;}
    std::size_t width() const {return m_Width;}
    std::size_t num_pixels() const {return m_Height * m_Width;}

    // relational operators
    friend bool operator==(const Image& im1, const Image& im2)
    {
        if (im1.m_Height != im2.m_Height || im1.m_Width != im2.m_Width)
            return false;

        return im1.m_PixelBuff == im2.m_PixelBuff;
    }

    friend bool operator!=(const Image& im1, const Image& im2)
    {
        return !operator==(im1, im2);
    }
```

```
        // other operators
        friend std::ostream& operator<<(std::ostream& os, const Image& im)
        {
            os << im.to_str();
            return os;
        }
private:
        void reset()
        {
            m_Height = 0;
            m_Width = 0;
        }

        std::string to_str() const
        {
            std::string s {};
            std::format_to(std::back_inserter(s), "[{:5d} ", m_Height);
            std::format_to(std::back_inserter(s), "{:5d} ", m_Width);
            std::format_to(std::back_inserter(s), "{:8d} ", m_Height *
            m_Width);

            constexpr int pb_w {(sizeof(void*) <= 4) ? 8 : 16};
            std::uintptr_t pb = reinterpret_cast<std::uintptr_t>
            (m_PixelBuff.data());
            std::format_to(std::back_inserter(s), "0x{:0>{}X}]", pb, pb_w);
            return s;
        }

        // attributes
        std::size_t m_Height {};
        std::size_t m_Width {};
        std::vector<T> m_PixelBuff {};
};
// class Image<T> formatter
template <typename T> struct std::formatter<Image<T>> :
std::formatter<std::string>
```

```
{
    constexpr auto parse(std::format_parse_context& fpc)
        { return fpc.begin(); }

    auto format(const Image<T>& im, std::format_context& fc) const
        { return std::format_to(fc.out(), "{}", im.to_str()); }
};

#endif
```

The design pattern for class `Image<>` mirrors its non-template counterpart from the previous example. The definition of this class begins with the statement `template <typename T> requires std::unsigned_integral<T> class Image`. The keyword `template` signifies the start of a template definition. Keyword `typename` denotes a template parameter. In this example, `Image<>` requires a single parameter named T that signifies the pixel data type. The `requires` clause that follows constrains parameter T to an unsigned integral type. If one wanted `Image<>` to also support floating-point values for pixel type parameter T, a `requires` clause of `std::unsigned integral<T> || std::floating_point<T>` would suffice.

The most obvious difference between classes `Image<>` and `Image` is that the former requires its constructors, operators, etc., to be defined within the class. The actual code for each constructor and operator is essentially the same; the size attributes are also identical. Note that `Image<>` uses type `std::vector<T>` for `m_PixelBuffer` instead of `std::vector<pixel_t>`.

Listing 1-5-2 shows the source code for example Ch01_05. This example includes several functions that demonstrate the use of class `Image<>`. The first two example functions, `Ch01_05_ex1()` and `Ch01_05_ex2()`, illustrate the use of `Image<uint8_t>` (`uint8_t` is an unsigned 8-bit integer that's defined in `<cstdint>`). The third demonstration function, `Ch01_05_ex3()`, spotlights the use of `Image<uint16_t>` and `Image<uint32_t>`. The lines commented out near the end of `Ch01_05_ex3()` demonstrate errors flagged by the compiler due to `Image<>`'s type constraint. The results for example Ch01_05 are not shown since they're basically the same as the results for example Ch01_04.

Listing 1-5-2. Example Ch01_05 - Ch01_05_ex.cpp

```cpp
//-----------------------------------------------------------------------
// Ch01_05_ex.cpp
//-----------------------------------------------------------------------

#include <cstdint>
#include <utility>
#include "Ch01_05.h"
#include "ImageT.h"

void Ch01_05_ex1()
{
    // create image objects
    Image<uint8_t> im0 {};
    std::println("im0: {} - after ctor", im0);
    Image<uint8_t> im1 {100, 200};
    std::println("im1: {} - after ctor", im1);
    Image<uint8_t> im2 {300, 400};
    std::println("im2: {} - after ctor", im2);

    // using std::move
    Image<uint8_t> im3 = std::move(im1);
    std::println("im3: {} - after move ctor", im3);
#pragma warning(disable:26800)   // disable MSVC warning (use of
                                 //                moved object)
    std::println("im1: {} - after move (bad!)", im1);
#pragma warning(default:26800)
}

void Ch01_05_ex2()
{
    // create image objects
    Image<uint8_t> im0 {1000, 2000};
    std::println("im0: {} - after ctor", im0);
    Image<uint8_t> im1 {im0};
    std::println("im1: {} - after ctor", im1);
```

CHAPTER 1   C++ REVIEW

```
    Image<uint8_t> im2 {3000, 4000};
    std::println("im2: {} - after ctor", im2);

    // using relational operators
    std::println("im1 == im2 (expect false): {}", im1 == im2);
    std::println("im1 != im2 (expect true):  {}", im1 != im2);

    // using operator=
    Image<uint8_t> im3 {5000, 6000};
    std::println("im3: {} - after ctor", im3);

    im1 = im3;
    std::println("im1: {} - after assignment", im1);
    std::println("im1 == im3 (expect true):  {}", im1 == im3);
    std::println("im1 != im3 (expect false): {}", im1 != im3);
}

void Ch01_05_ex3()
{
    // create image objects (uint16_t)
    Image<uint16_t> im0 {1000, 2000};
    std::println("im0: {} - after ctor", im0);

    Image<uint16_t> im1 {3840, 2160};
    std::println("im1: {} - after ctor", im1);

    // using operator=
    im0 = im1;
    std::println("im0: {} - after assignment", im0);
    std::println("im0 == im1 (expect true):  {}", im0 == im1);
    std::println("im0 != im1 (expect false): {}", im0 != im1);

    // create image objects (uint32_t)
    Image<uint32_t> im2 {3840, 2160};
    std::println("im2: {} - after ctor", im2);
    Image<uint32_t> im3 {1920, 1080};
    std::println("im3: {} - after ctor", im3);
```

```
    // using operator=
    Image<uint32_t> im4 {im3};
    std::println("im4: {} - after ctor", im4);
    std::println("im4 == im2 (expect false): {}", im4 == im2);
    std::println("im4 == im3 (expect true):  {}", im4 == im3);

//  Image<int16_t> im5;         // compiler error - constraints not satisfied
//  Image<std::string> im5;     // compiler error - constraints not satisfied
}
void Ch01_05_ex()
{
    std::println("\n---- Ch01_05_ex1() -----");
    Ch01_05_ex1();

    std::println("\n---- Ch01_05_ex2() -----");
    Ch01_05_ex2();

    std::println("\n---- Ch01_05_ex3() -----");
    Ch01_05_ex3();
}
```

Lambda Expressions

Lambda expressions facilitate the definition of unnamed (anonymous) functions and named function objects, which can be stored for later use or passed as data to another function. Many C++ STL algorithms utilize lambda expressions to either modify or augment their behaviors. For example, operator< is the default binary compare operator for std::sort(). This STL algorithm sorts the elements of a container in ascending order. A program can also pass a lambda expression to std::sort() to alter its default use of operator< (e.g., operator> or a custom binary operator).

Figure 1-3 illustrates the principal elements[4] of a lambda expression. The lambda expression's capture list specifies which variables from the expression's enclosing scope are usable within the body. The parameter list specifies types and names for the argument values just like a regular function. The specifier section accepts optional

---

[4] Some lesser-used optional elements are not shown to improve readability.

CHAPTER 1   C++ REVIEW

keywords that affect constness or mutability. The lambda expression's optional trailing return type follows; this defaults to auto if it's not explicitly specified. Finally, the body section contains the actual code. Figure 1-3 also shows a lambda expression with an explicit template parameter list (C++20). This type of lambda expression accepts a template parameter list and an optional requires clause, just like a regular template.

Lambda expression

[capture-list] (parameter-list) specifiers -> return-type { body }

Lambda expression with explicit template parameters

[capture-list] <template-parameters> requires (parameter-list) specifiers -> return-type { body }

specifiers: consteval, constexpr, mutable, static

Figure 1-3. *Elements of a lambda expression*

Listing 1-6 shows the C++ code for example Ch01_06. This example illustrates how to define and use typical lambda expressions.

Listing 1-6. Example Ch01_06 - Ch01_06_ex.cpp

```
//------------------------------------------------------------------------
// Ch01_06_ex.cpp
//------------------------------------------------------------------------

#include <cmath>
#include <functional>
#include <vector>
#include "Ch01_06.h"

namespace
{
    std::vector<int> s_ValuesInt
    {
         1,  4,  7,  9, 12, 13, 15, 22, 27, 33, 38, 44,
        51, 58, 63, 68, 71, 77, 82, 87, 93, 95, 98, 99
    };

    std::vector<double> s_ValuesDouble
```

```cpp
    {
        10.0, 20.0, 30.0, 40.0, 50.0, 60.0, 70.0, 80.0
    };
}
void Ch01_06_ex1()
{
    std::vector<int> vec1 {s_ValuesInt};

    // lambda expression
    auto is_even = [](int x) { return (x % 2) == 0; };

    // using is_even
    int sum_even {};
    for (int x : vec1)
    {
        if (is_even(x))
            sum_even += x;
    }

    std::println("sum_even: {}", sum_even);
}
int sum_if(const std::vector<int>& vec, const std::function<bool(int)>& predicate)
{
    int sum {};
    for (int x : vec)
    {
        if (predicate(x))
            sum += x;
    }

    return sum;
}
```

CHAPTER 1   C++ REVIEW

```cpp
void Ch01_06_ex2()
{
    std::vector<int> vec1 {s_ValuesInt};

    // passing a lambda expression to another function
    auto is_even = [](int x) { return (x % 2) == 0; };
    int sum_even = sum_if(vec1, is_even);

    auto is_odd = [](int x) { return (x % 2) != 0; };
    int sum_odd = sum_if(vec1, is_odd);

    std::println("sum_even: {}, sum_odd: {}", sum_even, sum_odd);
}

void Ch01_06_ex3()
{
    double cap_val {2.0};
    std::vector<double> vec1 {s_ValuesDouble};

    // using a captured (by value) variable
    auto calc1 = [cap_val] (double x) { return std::sqrt(x) + cap_val; };

    for (double x : vec1)
    {
        double y = calc1(x);
        std::println("x: {:.2f}, y: {:.4f}", x, y);
    }
}

void Ch01_06_ex4()
{
    double cap_val {1.0};
    std::vector<double> vec1 {s_ValuesDouble};

    // using a captured (by reference) variable
    auto calc1 = [&cap_val] (double x) -> double
        { double y = std::sqrt(x + cap_val); cap_val *= 2.0; return y; };

    std::println("cap_val (before range for loop): {:.2f}", cap_val);
```

44

```cpp
    for (double x : vec1)
    {
        double y = calc1(x);
        std::println("x: {:.2f}, y: {:.4f}", x, y);
    }

    std::println("cap_val (after range for loop): {:.2f}", cap_val);
}

void Ch01_06_ex5()
{
    std::vector<double> vec1 {s_ValuesDouble};

    // using a local captured variable (requires mutable)
    auto calc1 = [local_val = 1.0] (double x) mutable -> double
        { double y = std::sqrt(x + local_val); local_val *= 2.0;
        return y; };

    for (double x : vec1)
    {
        double y = calc1(x);
        std::println("x: {:.2f}, y: {:.4f}", x, y);
    }
}

void Ch01_06_ex()
{
    std::println("\n---- Ch01_06_ex1() -----");
    Ch01_06_ex1();

    std::println("\n---- Ch01_06_ex2() -----");
    Ch01_06_ex2();

    std::println("\n---- Ch01_06_ex3() -----");
    Ch01_06_ex3();

    std::println("\n---- Ch01_06_ex4() -----");
    Ch01_06_ex4();
```

CHAPTER 1　C++ REVIEW

```
    std::println("\n---- Ch01_06_ex5() -----");
    Ch01_06_ex5();
}
```

Listing 1-6 opens with an anonymous namespace that defines two `std::vectors` for later use. Using an anonymous namespace here limits the scope of the enclosed vectors to the current file. Function `Ch01_06_ex1()` opens with the declaration of `std::vector<int>` vec1. Note that this declaration uses s_ValuesInt to initialize the elements of vec1. The statement `auto is_even = [](int x) { return (x % 2) == 0; }` defines a lambda expression named is_even. This expression tests x and returns true if it's an even number; otherwise, false is returned. Keyword auto is generally for a lambda expression's type since actual lambda type names are lengthy. The ensuing range for loop sums the even elements of vec1 using is_even as a test predicate.

The next item in Listing 1-6 is the definition of a function named `sum_if()`. This function utilizes function object predicate to selectively sum elements of vec. Note that function object predicate requires a single value of type int (i.e., it's a unary predicate) and returns a bool. Function `Ch01_06_ex2()` exercises `sum_if()` using two different lambda expressions, is_even and is_odd, to calculate sum_even and sum_odd. The design pattern demonstrated here is representative of the many STL algorithms that accept lambda expressions as arguments.

Function `Ch01_06_ex3()` defines a lambda expression that utilizes a capture variable. The lambda expression calc1 uses variable capval to perform an arbitrary calculation. During execution, capval is passed by value to calc1, which means that the compiler needs to create a copy of capval. Since capval is an integer, the copy overhead is essentially nothing. However, for types where the copy costs are higher, it's usually better for a lambda expression to capture a variable by reference. In function `Ch01_06_ex4()`, note that the definition of calc1 contains &capval in its capture list, which captures the variable by reference. Also, note the use of an explicit lambda expression trailing return type. An explicit return type is not necessary for this example but included for demonstration purposes.

The reason calc1 captures capval by reference in `Ch01_06_ex4()` is that it wants to modify the value. Following the calculation of y = std::sqrt(x + capval), the lambda expression executes capval *= 2.0, which modifies capval (another arbitrary calculation). If you scan ahead to the results section, you'll notice that the value of cap_val is different before and after the range for loop.

The final function in Listing 1-6, Ch01_06_ex5(), demonstrates the capture of a lambda expression local variable. In this example, local_var is initialized to one in the capture list, and its scope is localized to the lambda expression. When a lambda expression captures a local variable, it must also use the mutable specifier. Here are the results for example Ch01_06:

```
----- Results for example Ch01_06 -----

---- Ch01_06_ex1() -----
sum_even: 426

---- Ch01_06_ex2() -----
sum_even: 426, sum_odd: 741

---- Ch01_06_ex3() -----
x: 10.00, y: 5.1623
x: 20.00, y: 6.4721
x: 30.00, y: 7.4772
x: 40.00, y: 8.3246
x: 50.00, y: 9.0711
x: 60.00, y: 9.7460
x: 70.00, y: 10.3666
x: 80.00, y: 10.9443

---- Ch01_06_ex4() -----
cap_val (before range for loop): 1.00
x: 10.00, y: 3.3166
x: 20.00, y: 4.6904
x: 30.00, y: 5.8310
x: 40.00, y: 6.9282
x: 50.00, y: 8.1240
x: 60.00, y: 9.5917
x: 70.00, y: 11.5758
x: 80.00, y: 14.4222
cap_val (after range for loop): 256.00
```

CHAPTER 1   C++ REVIEW

```
---- Ch01_06_ex5() -----
x: 10.00, y: 3.3166
x: 20.00, y: 4.6904
x: 30.00, y: 5.8310
x: 40.00, y: 6.9282
x: 50.00, y: 8.1240
x: 60.00, y: 9.5917
x: 70.00, y: 11.5758
x: 80.00, y: 14.4222
```

Lambda expressions are permitted to use [=] and [&] as capture lists. The former captures by value all variables in the enclosing scope that it uses. Keep in mind that capturing variables by values involves copy operations, which might be time-consuming. Using a capture list of [&] captures all used variables from the enclosing scope by reference. You can also use a combination of capture by value and reference (e.g., [=, &x], [&, x]). The best design pattern for capture lists is to explicitly list the variables to capture, either by value or reference. This makes the intent clear. You'll see more examples of lambda expressions in later chapters.

Three-Way Comparison Operator

C++20 introduced a new three-way comparison operator <=>, which is often called a "spaceship" operator since it evidently resembles the character-based spaceships of yesteryear's ASCII terminal games. This operator returns a class result that can be compared to zero to determine if a < b, a == b, or a > b is true. The three-way comparison operator reduces the amount of coding needed for a class to implement the six standard relational operators.

Listing 1-7-1 shows the source code for example Ch01_07. The first function in this listing, Ch01_07_ex1(), demonstrates how to explicitly use operator<=> to compare two integer values. Near the top of Listing 1-7-1 is an #include <compare> statement. This file should be included with any code that utilizes operator<=>. Inside the for loop, the expression a_vals[i] <=> b_vals[i] returns an ordering class whose value can be compared *only to zero*. This is different than the standard relational operators, which return a value of type bool. Note that the std::println() statements don't print cmp_ab, but print cmp_ab > 0, cmp_ab == 0, and cmp_ab > 0 (all values of type bool). Function Ch01_07_ex2() highlights the use of operator<=> with floating-point values.

Listing 1-7-1. Example Ch01_07 – Ch01_07_ex.cpp

```
//-------------------------------------------------------------------------
// Ch01_07_ex.cpp
//-------------------------------------------------------------------------
#include <compare>
#include <vector>
#include "Ch01_07.h"
#include "Line.h"

void Ch01_07_ex1()
{
    std::vector<int> a_vals {5, -8,  37};
    std::vector<int> b_vals {7, -15, 37};

    for (std::size_t i = 0; i < a_vals.size(); ++i)
    {
        auto cmp_ab = a_vals[i] <=> b_vals[i];

        std::println("\ntest case #{:d}:   a = {:d}, b = {:d}",
            i, a_vals[i], b_vals[i]);

        std::println("cmp_ab <   0 | {:s}", cmp_ab <  0);
        std::println("cmp_ab ==  0 | {:s}", cmp_ab == 0);
        std::println("cmp_ab >   0 | {:s}", cmp_ab >  0);
    }
}

void Ch01_07_ex2()
{
    std::vector<double> a_vals {5.0, -8.0,  37.0};
    std::vector<double> b_vals {7.0, -15.0, 37.0};
```

```cpp
    for (std::size_t i = 0; i < a_vals.size(); ++i)
    {
        auto cmp_ab = a_vals[i] <=> b_vals[i];

        std::println("\ntest case #{:d}:  a = {:.1f}, b = {:.1f}",
            i, a_vals[i], b_vals[i]);

        std::println("cmp_ab <   0 | {:s}", cmp_ab <  0);
        std::println("cmp_ab ==  0 | {:s}", cmp_ab == 0);
        std::println("cmp_ab >   0 | {:s}", cmp_ab >  0);
    }
}

void Ch01_07_ex3()
{
    std::vector<Line<int>> lines1
    {
        Line<int> {0, 0, 3, 4}, Line<int> {90, 100, 125, 130},
        Line<int> {8, 41, 17, 44}
    };

    std::vector<Line<int>> lines2
    {
        Line<int> {0, 0, 6, 8}, Line<int> {100, 100, 110, 115},
        Line<int> {8, 41, 17, 44}
    };

    for (std::size_t i = 0; i < lines1.size(); ++i)
    {
        auto& line1 = lines1[i];
        auto& line2 = lines2[i];

        std::println("\nline1: {}\nline2: {}", line1, line2);
        std::println("line1 == line2): {:s}", line1 == line2);
        std::println("line1 != line2): {:s}", line1 != line2);
        std::println("line1 <  line2): {:s}", line1 <  line2);
        std::println("line1 <= line2): {:s}", line1 <= line2);
```

```cpp
        std::println("line1 >  line2): {:s}", line1 >  line2);
        std::println("line1 >= line2): {:s}", line1 >= line2);
    }
}
void Ch01_07_ex()
{
    std::println("\n---- Ch01_07_ex1() -----");
    Ch01_07_ex1();

    std::println("\n---- Ch01_07_ex2() -----");
    Ch01_07_ex2();

    std::println("\n---- Ch01_07_ex3() -----");
    Ch01_07_ex3();
}
```

The ordering class that's returned by operator<=> varies depending on the types being compared. Table 1-1 lists the various ordering classes.

Table 1-1. *Ordering Class Return Values for Three-Way Compare Operator*

Compare Class	Return Type	Condition
strong_ordering	strong_ordering::equal	a == b (same as equivalent)
	strong_ordering::equivalent	a == b (same as equal)
	strong_ordering::less	a < b
	strong_ordering::greater	a > b
partial_ordering	partial_ordering::equivalent	a == b (may not be equal)
	partial_ordering::less	a < b
	partial_ordering::greater	a > b
	partial_ordering::unordered	not comparable

(*continued*)

Table 1-1. (*continued*)

Compare Class	Return Type	Condition
weak_ordering	weak_ordering::equivalent	a == b (may not be equal)
	weak_ordering::less	a < b
	weak_ordering::greater	a > b

When comparing two integer types (char, int, long, etc.) or pointers, operator<=> returns a std::strong_ordering result. This means that exactly one of the conditions shown in Table 1-1 is true. Note that result types std::strong_ordering::equal and strong_ordering::equivalent are the same.

For floating-point types, operator<=> returns one of the std::partial_ordering results. A std::partial_ordering differs from a std::strong_ordering in two ways. First, values a and b can be equivalent but not equal. For example, -0.0 and +0.0 are equivalent but not equal.[5] The other difference is the unordered result. This result signifies that neither a nor b are comparable. The floating-point NaN (Not a Number) is an example of a value that's not comparable.

Type std::weak_ordering is the least stringent of the three ordering types and employed exclusively in user-defined classes; a user-defined class can also return a result of std::strong_ordering or std::partial_ordering. The archetypal example of a weakly ordered result is the case-insensitive compare of two text strings.

The final function of Listing 1-7-1, named Ch01_07_ex3(), contains code that exercises the six standard relational operators of template class Line. Listing 1-7-2 shows the code for Line. This class realizes the six standard binary relational operators by defining binary versions of operator<=> and operator==.

---

[5] The IEEE 754 standard for floating-point arithmetic defines two distinct values for zero: -0.0 and +0.0.

CHAPTER 1 C++ REVIEW

Listing 1-7-2. Example Ch01_07 - Line.h

```cpp
//-------------------------------------------------------------------
// Line.h
//-------------------------------------------------------------------

#ifndef LINE_H_
#define LINE_H_
#include <cmath>
#include <compare>
#include <concepts>
#include <format>
#include <limits>
#include <ostream>
#include <string>

// Line coordinate constraint
template <typename T> concept
LineCoord = std::integral<T> || std::floating_point<T>;

// simple line class
template <LineCoord T> class Line
{
    friend struct std::formatter<Line<T>>;

public:
    Line() = default;
    Line(T x0, T y0, T x1, T y1) :
        m_X0{x0}, m_Y0{y0}, m_X1{x1}, m_Y1{y1} {};

    // accessors
    T X0() const { return m_X0; }
    T Y0() const { return m_Y0; }
    T X1() const { return m_X1; }
    T Y1() const { return m_Y1; }
```

```cpp
    T& X0() { return m_X0; }
    T& Y0() { return m_Y0; }
    T& X1() { return m_X1; }
    T& Y1() { return m_Y1; }

    friend std::ostream& operator<<(std::ostream& os, const Line<T>& line)
    {
        os << line.to_str();
        return os;
    }

    double length() const
    {
        double dx = static_cast<double>(m_X1) - m_X0;
        double dy = static_cast<double>(m_Y1) - m_Y0;
        return std::hypot(dx, dy);
    }

    double slope(double epsilon = 1.0e-15) const
    {
        double dx = static_cast<double>(m_X1) - m_X0;
        double dy = static_cast<double>(m_Y1) - m_Y0;

        return std::fabs(dx) > epsilon ?
            dy / dx : std::numeric_limits<double>::quiet_NaN();
    }

private:
    std::string to_str() const
    {
        std::string s{};
        std::format_to(std::back_inserter(s), "[({}, {}, ", m_X0, m_Y0);
        std::format_to(std::back_inserter(s), "{}, {}) | ", m_X1, m_Y1);
        std::format_to(std::back_inserter(s), "({:.4f}, ", length());
        std::format_to(std::back_inserter(s), "{:.4f})]", slope());

        return s;
    }
```

```cpp
    // attributes
    T m_X0 {};
    T m_Y0 {};
    T m_X1 {};
    T m_Y1 {};
};

// non-member relational operators
template <LineCoord T>
auto operator<=>(const Line<T>& line1, const Line<T>& line2)
{
    return line1.length() <=> line2.length();
}

template <LineCoord T>
bool operator==(const Line<T>& line1, const Line<T>& line2)
{
    return line1.length() == line2.length();
}

// class Line formatter
template <typename T> struct std::formatter<Line<T>> :
std::formatter<std::string>
{
    constexpr auto parse(std::format_parse_context& fpc)
        { return fpc.begin(); }

    auto format(Line<T> line, std::format_context& fc) const
        { return std::format_to(fc.out(), "{}", line.to_str()); }
};

#endif
```

Before examining the code for operator<=> and operator==, a few general comments about class Line are required. In Listing 1-7-2, note that class Line includes attributes m_X0, m_Y0, m_X1, and m_Y1. These attributes define the start (m_X0, m_Y0) and end (m_X1, m_Y1) points of a line on a 2D plane. Class Line defines a member function named length(), which calculates the line's length using its coordinate points. There's also a member function named slope().

CHAPTER 1   C++ REVIEW

Near the bottom of Listing 1-7-2 is the definition of operator<=> for Line. This function utilizes the three-way comparison operator to compare the lengths of line1 and line2. The return type for operator<=>(const Line<T>& line1, const Line<T>& line2) is one of the std::partial_ordering values shown in Table 1-1 since length() returns a double. Function operator==(const Line<T>& line1, const Line<T>& line2) compares the lengths of line1 and line2 for equivalence and returns a bool. Note that if a user-defined class defines operator<=>, it must also define operator==. Having an explicit operator== also provides optimization opportunities for classes with multiple members since operator== usually returns an equal/equivalent result faster than operator<=>. By providing definitions for operator<=> and operator==, the compiler can generate code that implements the six standard binary relational operators for class Line. Here are the results for example Ch01_07:

```
----- Results for example Ch01_07 -----

---- Ch01_07_ex1() -----
test case #0:  a = 5, b = 7
cmp_ab <    0 | true
cmp_ab ==   0 | false
cmp_ab >    0 | false

test case #1:  a = -8, b = -15
cmp_ab <    0 | false
cmp_ab ==   0 | false
cmp_ab >    0 | true

test case #2:  a = 37, b = 37
cmp_ab <    0 | false
cmp_ab ==   0 | true
cmp_ab >    0 | false

---- Ch01_07_ex2() -----
test case #0:  a = 5.0, b = 7.0
cmp_ab <    0 | true
cmp_ab ==   0 | false
cmp_ab >    0 | false
```

```
test case #1:  a = -8.0, b = -15.0
cmp_ab <   0 | false
cmp_ab ==  0 | false
cmp_ab >   0 | true

test case #2:  a = 37.0, b = 37.0
cmp_ab <   0 | false
cmp_ab ==  0 | true
cmp_ab >   0 | false

---- Ch01_07_ex3() -----

line1: [(0, 0, 3, 4) | (5.0000, 1.3333)]
line2: [(0, 0, 6, 8) | (10.0000, 1.3333)]
line1 == line2): false
line1 != line2): true
line1 <  line2): true
line1 <= line2): true
line1 >  line2): false
line1 >= line2): false

line1: [(90, 100, 125, 130) | (46.0977, 0.8571)]
line2: [(100, 100, 110, 115) | (18.0278, 1.5000)]
line1 == line2): false
line1 != line2): true
line1 <  line2): false
line1 <= line2): false
line1 >  line2): true
line1 >= line2): true

line1: [(8, 41, 17, 44) | (9.4868, 0.3333)]
line2: [(8, 41, 17, 44) | (9.4868, 0.3333)]
line1 == line2): true
line1 != line2): false
line1 <  line2): false
line1 <= line2): true
line1 >  line2): false
line1 >= line2): true
```

CHAPTER 1   C++ REVIEW

Exceptions

In C++, exceptions provide a means of transferring program control from one execution point in a thread to a previously passed execution point. Exceptions and return codes are often used to report and recover from error conditions.

Listing 1-8 shows the code for a simple program that utilizes exceptions to process invalid user input. In this listing, note the `try` and `catch` blocks. A `try` block encompasses the normal code that requires execution. In the current example, the `try` block reads a string from the keyboard, converts the string to floating-point using `std::stod()`, and calculates a square root. Prior to calculating the square root, the code tests `x < 0.0`; if true, an exception of type `std::domain_error` is thrown. Class `std::domain_error` is one of STL's predefined standard exception classes. When throwing an exception, a program can utilize an STL-defined exception class or derive a custom exception class from an existing one.

Listing 1-8. Example Ch01_08 - Ch01_08_ex.cpp

```
//-------------------------------------------------------------------
// Ch01_08_ex.cpp
//-------------------------------------------------------------------

#include <cmath>
#include <iostream>
#include <string>
#include <stdexcept>
#include "Ch01_08.h"

void Ch01_08_ex1()
{
    const char* de_text =
        "std::sqrt() domain error, try again";

    while (true)
    {
        std::print("\nEnter a positive number, ctrl-z to exit: ");
```

```cpp
try
{
    std::string x_str {};
    std::getline(std::cin, x_str);

    if (!std::cin.good())
    {
        if (!std::cin.eof())
            std::println("std::cin error");
        return;
    }

    double x = std::stod(x_str);

    if (x < 0.0)
        throw std::domain_error(de_text);

    double x_sqrt = std::sqrt(x);
    std::println("x: {:f} x_sqrt: {:.4f}", x, x_sqrt);
}
// catch std::domain_error from above
catch (const std::domain_error& ex)
{
    std::println("{}", ex.what());
}

// catch std::invalid_argument or std::out_of_range
// (thrown by std::stod())
catch (const std::invalid_argument& ex)
{
    std::println("{}", ex.what());
}
catch (const std::out_of_range& ex)
{
    std::println("{}", ex.what());
}
```

CHAPTER 1   C++ REVIEW

```
        // catch all other exceptions
        catch (...)
        {
            std::println("unknown exception has occurred");
        }
    }
}
void Ch01_08_ex()
{
    std::println("\n----- Ch01_08_ex1() -----");
    Ch01_08_ex1();
}
```

After exception std::domain_error is thrown, program control is transferred to the catch (const std::domain_error& ex) block. Function ex.what() returns a C-style pointer to the text message that was passed via std::domain_error's constructor when the exception was thrown. The next two catch blocks in Ch01_08_ex1() process exceptions thrown by std::stod(). Note that each catch block catches the thrown exception by reference. The final catch (...) block provides a default for handling any other exceptions. Here are the results for example Ch01_08:

```
----- Ch01_08_ex1() -----

Enter a positive number, ctrl-z to exit: 100
x: 100.000000 x_sqrt: 10.0000

Enter a positive number, ctrl-z to exit: 200
x: 200.000000 x_sqrt: 14.1421

Enter a positive number, ctrl-z to exit: -300
std::sqrt() domain error, try again

Enter a positive number, ctrl-z to exit: hello
invalid stod argument

Enter a positive number, ctrl-z to exit: 400
x: 400.000000 x_sqrt: 20.0000
Enter a positive number, ctrl-z to exit:
```

When creating a user-defined class, it is sometimes unclear whether it should employ return codes or exceptions. One common guideline is to employ return codes to recover from errors that are likely to occur and use exceptions for rare or unrecoverable errors. The principal advantage of using exceptions over return codes is that the former guarantees any applicable destructors get executed while program control is transferred to the appropriate `catch` block. With return codes, a program usually needs to add extra code to ensure applicable destructor execution – a task that is often error prone and a producer of obfuscated code. It is important to note that a user-defined class should never throw an exception in a destructor. It is also imperative for any C++ program to develop a strategy for handling exceptions since they're used by many standard library classes and functions. Appendix B contains additional resources that you can consult for more information regarding the particulars of C++ exceptions.

Summary

Here are the key learning points:

- The STL is the foundation of modern C++ programming. It is virtually impossible to write any meaningful C++ program without employing some of its components.

- A template is a parameterized data type that facilitates the development of generic functions, algorithms, and classes. The C++ compiler instantiates code for each distinct template type.

- When developing a user-defined class, ensure that the following essential operations are defined – either explicitly coded or implicitly defined using the compiler-supplied default – or deleted:

  - Default constructor
  - Parameterized constructor(s)
  - Copy and move constructors
  - Copy and move assignments
  - Destructor

- Lambda expressions are used to create anonymous functions. They can also be used to override the default behavior of many STL algorithms.

- A class can use the three-way comparison operator to generate a complete set of relational operators.

- A class can employ exceptions to report an error or atypical condition that requires special handling by its user. The primary advantage of exceptions vs. return codes is that the former ensures any applicable destructors are automatically called. Many STL classes and algorithms use exceptions to report errors.

CHAPTER 2

Formatted I/O

This chapter explains how to perform formatted I/O operations using a variety of techniques, including

- Formatted output using `std::printf()`
- Formatted output using streams
- Formatted output using `std::format()`
- Formatted output using `std::print()`
- Formatted file I/O using streams

You are encouraged to peruse the sections that explain how to use `std::format()` and `std::print()` since they cover important details regarding these C++20/23 functions. For all other topics, you can either skim or skip the sections that you already understand.

Formatted Output Using std::printf()

C++ provides a variety of functions, classes, and operators for formatted I/O. Listing 2-1 shows the source code for example Ch02_01, which illustrates the use of function `std::printf()`. Despite its C pedigree, many C++ programs still utilize `std::printf()` (or one of its sibling functions) to generate simple formatted output. Having a basic understanding of how `std::printf()` works is often essential when maintaining a legacy code base.

Listing 2-1. Example Ch02_01 – Ch02_01_ex.cpp

```
//-------------------------------------------------------------
// Ch02_01_ex.cpp
//-------------------------------------------------------------
```

CHAPTER 2   FORMATTED I/O

```cpp
#include <cstdio>
#include <iostream>
#include <iomanip>
#include <format>
#include <numbers>
#include <string>
#include "Ch02_01.h"

void Ch02_01_ex1(int a, unsigned long long b, double c, const std::string& d)
{
    std::printf("Values using printf()\n");
    std::printf("a: %d\n", a);
    std::printf("b: 0x%016llX\n", b);
    std::printf("c: %-10.8lf\n", c);
    std::printf("d: %40s\n", d.c_str());
}

void Ch02_01_ex2(int a, unsigned long long b, double c, const std::string& d)
{
    std::cout << "Values using ostream operator<<\n";
    std::cout << "a: " << a << '\n';
    std::cout << std::setfill('0')
              << "b: 0x" << std::hex << std::setw(16) << b << '\n';
    std::cout << std::setfill(' ')
              << "c: " << std::fixed << std::setprecision(8)
              << std::left << std::setw(10) << c << '\n';
    std::cout << "d: " << std::right << std::setw(40) << d << '\n';
}

void Ch02_01_ex3(int a, unsigned long long b, double c, const std::string& d)
{
    std::cout << "Values using std::format()\n";
    std::cout << std::format("a: {}\n", a);
    std::cout << std::format("b: 0x{:016X}\n", b);
```

```cpp
    std::cout << std::format("c: {:<10.8f}\n", c);
    std::cout << std::format("d: {:>40s}\n", d);
}

void Ch02_01_ex4(int a, unsigned long long b, double c, const
std::string& d)
{
    std::println("Values using std::println()");
    std::println("a: {}", a);
    std::println("b: 0x{:016X}", b);
    std::println("c: {:<10.8f}", c);
    std::println("d: {:>40s}", d);
}

void Ch02_01_ex()
{
    constexpr int a {100};
    constexpr unsigned long long b {0x4444'3333'2222'1111};
    constexpr double c {std::numbers::pi};
    std::string d {"Four score and seven years ago, ..."};

    std::println("\n----- Ch02_01_ex1() -----");
    Ch02_01_ex1(a, b, c, d);

    std::println("\n----- Ch02_01_ex2() -----");
    Ch02_01_ex2(a, b, c, d);

    std::println("\n----- Ch02_01_ex3() -----");
    Ch02_01_ex3(a, b, c, d);

    std::println("\n----- Ch02_01_ex4() -----");
    Ch02_01_ex4(a, b, c, d);
}
```

Listing 2-1 opens with a function named Ch02_01_ex1() that demonstrates the use of std::printf(). This variadic function writes text to the predefined output stream stdout. The first argument of std::printf() is a C-style null-terminated format string that can include optional conversion specifiers. These specifiers direct the formatting of the argument values that trail the format string.

CHAPTER 2 FORMATTED I/O

Within the format string, the % symbol denotes the start of a conversion specifier. For example, the first call to std::printf() in Ch02_01_ex1() uses the conversion specifier %d to format argument value int a as a signed decimal integer. The next std::printf() call employs conversion specifier %016llX to format unsigned long long b as a hexadecimal integer using a minimum field width of 16 characters with leading zeros. A typical format specifier employs the following pattern:

%[modifier][width][.precision][length]spec-char

Valid symbols for the modifier field include - (left justify), + (always print sign), # (use alternate form), or 0 (use zero instead of spaces for left padding). The width field specifies the minimum size of the field in characters. The precision field denotes the number of digits to print after the decimal point (floating-point values), minimum number of digits to print (integers), or maximum number of characters to print when using %s. The length field is a modifier for the spec-char. Common length modifiers include h (short int), l (long int), and ll (long long int). Table 2-1 shows supported values for the specification character spec-char.

Table 2-1. *Specification Characters for* std::printf()

Character	Output Type
d, i	Signed decimal integer
u	Unsigned decimal integer
o	Unsigned octal integer
x, X	Unsigned hexadecimal integer, lowercase (%x), uppercase (%X)
f, F	Floating-point, decimal, lowercase (%f), uppercase (%F)
e, E	Floating-point, scientific notation, lowercase (%e), uppercase (%E)
g, G	Floating-point, shorter of %f (%F) or %e (%E)
a, A	Floating-point hexadecimal notation, lowercase (%a), uppercase (%A)
c	Character
s	C-style null-terminated character string
%	Percent symbol

CHAPTER 2   FORMATTED I/O

Before continuing, I should note that std::printf() supports additional forms besides those discussed in this section. You're likely to encounter uses of std::printf() or one of its sibling functions (std::fprintf(), std::sprintf(), etc.) in legacy code. However, modern C++ discourages the use of these functions for several reasons. First, they are only useful for formatting fundamental types, such as char, int, float, etc. Second, std::printf() doesn't support overloading or any other mechanism for formatting a user-defined class. Third, and perhaps most important, they are not type-safe. Using std::printf() on a memory-constrained system (e.g., Raspberry Pi Pico) might be justifiable. For nearly all other use cases, you are better off using a different method for formatted output.

The remaining functions in Listing 2-1 are modern alternatives that generate the same formatted output as Ch02_01_ex1(). These are shown for comparison purposes. Modern alternatives include formatted output using output streams and overloads of operator<<, std::format() (C++20), and std::println() (C++23). You'll learn more about these later in this chapter. Here are the results for example Ch02_01:

```
----- Results for example Ch02_01 -----

----- Ch02_01_ex1() -----
Values using std::printf()
a: 100
b: 0x4444333322221111
c: 3.14159265
d:      Four score and seven years ago, ...

----- Ch02_01_ex2() -----
Values using ostream operator<<
a: 100
b: 0x4444333322221111
c: 3.14159265
d:      Four score and seven years ago, ...

----- Ch02_01_ex3() -----
Values using std::format()
a: 100
b: 0x4444333322221111
c: 3.14159265
```

67

d: Four score and seven years ago, ...

----- Ch02_01_ex4() -----
Values using std::println()
a: 100
b: 0x4444333322221111
c: 3.14159265
d: Four score and seven years ago, ...

Formatted Output Using Streams

In C++, a stream is an object that performs data reads (input stream) or data writes (output stream). Input and output streams are often linked to an underlying file or string. Like template class `std::basic_string<>` that you learned about in Chapter 1, stream template classes are parameterized using a character type such as `char` or `wchar_t`.

Figure 2-1 shows the template class hierarchy for I/O streams. From a programming perspective, the most important classes are those situated toward the bottom of the figure. The lighter-colored rectangles denote file stream objects, while the darker-colored ones signify string streams. For each leaf class, STL defines an alias using types `char` and `wchar_t`. For example, `std::ifstream` and `std::wifstream` are aliases for `std::basic_ifstream<char>` and `std::basic_ifstream<wchar_t>`, respectively. These are file input streams. Similarly, output streams `std::ostringstream` and `std::wostringstream` are aliases for `std::basic_ostringstream<char>` and `std::basic_ostringstream<wchar_t>`.

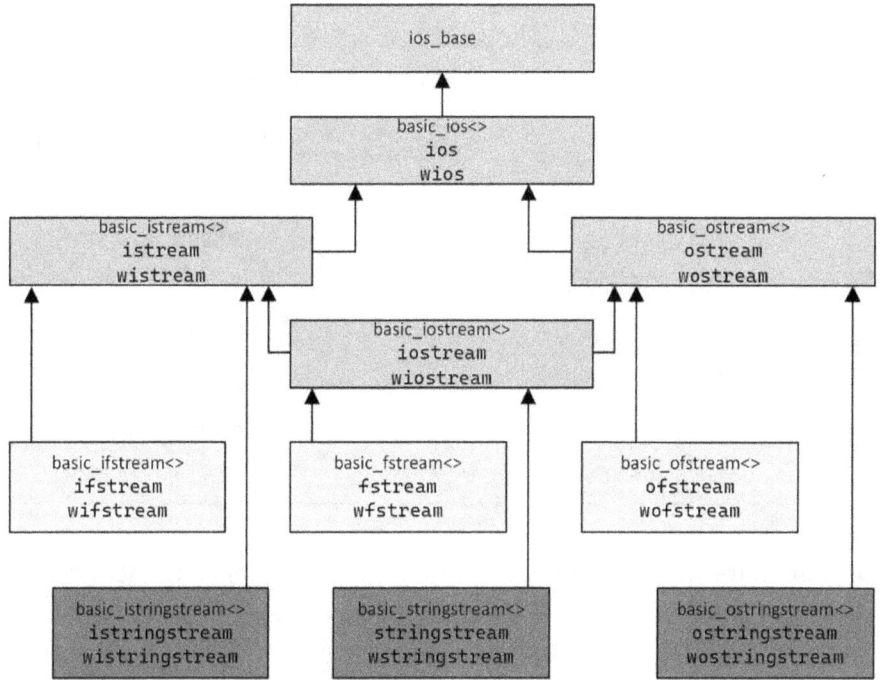

Figure 2-1. *Class hierarchy for input and output streams*

Table 2-2 shows the global stream objects for standard I/O operations. Standard I/O is normally performed using a terminal or a GUI application that emulates a terminal. This means that unless redirection is in effect, a program can acquire keyboard input by reading `std::cin` and write text to `std::cout`, `std::cerr`, or `std::clog`. The corresponding wide versions can also be used. The I/O streams shown in Table 2-2 are typically used in command-line programs and may not be available in GUI applications. GUI applications normally use platform-specific APIs for keyboard input and display output.

Table 2-2. *Global I/O Streams*

I/O Stream	Class	C Stream	Description
std::cerr std::wcerr	std::ostream std::wostream	stderr	Standard error stream
std::cin std::wcin	std::istream std::wistream	stdin	Standard input stream
std::clog std:wlog	std::ostream std::wostream	stderr	Standard log stream
std::cout std::wcout	std::ostream std::wostream	stdout	Standard output stream

The primary difference between std::cerr and std::clog (and the corresponding wide stream objects) is that output to the former is not buffered (default operation) while output to the latter is. A C++ program can read data from an input stream std::ifstream or std::istringstream using an overload of operator>> or one of the member functions provided by std::istream. Similarly, a program can write data to an output stream std::ofstream or std::ostringstream using an overload of operator<< or one of the member functions provided by std::ostream. The same operators and inheritance relationships also apply to the corresponding wchar_t overloads.

The base I/O stream class std::ios_base maintains a series of format and state flags that a program can use to specify formatting options or detect error conditions. A program can employ manipulators or member functions to modify the formatting flags maintained by std::ios_base.

At first glance, the C++ I/O stream libraries may seem a little bewildering. The best way to learn C++ I/O streams is by example, and you'll examine several examples in this and subsequent chapters. These examples demonstrate basic I/O stream operations that you need to understand to effectively exploit STL classes and algorithms. It should be noted that the examples and associated discussions do not explicate the entire C++ I/O stream library. Appendix B contains a list of references that you can consult for additional information regarding advanced I/O stream use.

Source code example Ch02_02 demonstrates formatted writes using output streams. Listing 2-2-1 shows the first function for this example.

CHAPTER 2   FORMATTED I/O

Listing 2-2-1. Example Ch02_02 – Ch02_02_ex1()

```
//-------------------------------------------------------------------------
// Ch02_02_ex.cpp
//-------------------------------------------------------------------------

#include <bitset>
#include <fstream>
#include <iostream>
#include <iomanip>
#include <numbers>
#include <ostream>
#include <string>
#include "Ch02_02.h"
#include "Line.h"
#include "MF.h"

void Ch02_02_ex1()
{
    constexpr int a {100};
    constexpr long long b {-300};

    // bool output
    std::cout << "a == 100: ";
    std::cout << (a == 100);
    std::cout << '\n';
    std::cout << "a == 100: " << std::boolalpha << (a == 100) << '\n';

    // decimal output
    std::cout << "a: " << a << '\n';
    std::cout << "b: " << b << '\n';

    // hex output
    std::cout << std::hex << std::showbase;
    std::cout << "a: " << a << '\n';
    std::cout << "b: " << b << '\n';

    // hex output using uppercase and fill character
    constexpr int w = (sizeof(void*) <= 4) ? 8 : 16;
```

71

CHAPTER 2 FORMATTED I/O

```cpp
    std::uintptr_t a_addr = reinterpret_cast<uintptr_t>(&a);
    std::cout << std::noshowbase << std::uppercase << std::setfill('0');
    std::cout << "\na_addr: 0X" << std::setw(w) << a_addr << '\n';

    // hex output using lower case and same fill char
    std::cout << std::nouppercase;
    std::cout << "a_addr: 0x" << std::setw(w) << a_addr << '\n';

    // binary output
    std::bitset<sizeof(uintptr_t) * 8> a_addr_bin(a_addr);
    std::cout << "a_addr: 0b" << a_addr_bin << '\n';

    // reset std::cout to decimal
    std::cout << std::dec;
}
```

The first executable statement of Ch02_02_ex1(), std::cout << "a == 100: ", uses operator<< to write a C-style text string to std::cout. More specifically, this expression calls std::ostream& operator<<(std::ostream&, const char*) to write a null-terminated string to global std::ostream object std::cout. Header file <ostream> defines operator<< overloads for all fundamental C++ types (e.g., char, int, long, float, etc.). A user-defined class can also define its own overloads for operator<< as you'll soon see. The next statement, std::cout << (a == 100), writes the result of a Boolean expression to std::cout. This is followed by std::cout << '\n';, which writes a newline character to std::cout.

The subsequent expression chains together multiple uses of operator<<. This is possible since each use of std::cout << value returns a reference to std::cout. This chaining capability is supported by all std::ostream objects and not just std::cout. Also, note the use of the manipulator std::boolalpha in the chain.

Manipulators are distinct objects that can be employed to specify formatting options when reading from an input or writing to an output stream. For example, the manipulator std::boolalpha instructs an output stream to format bools as a string ("false" or "true") instead of a number (0 or 1). Manipulators are also utilized to perform control operations such as flushing an output stream's buffer. Table 2-3 lists some frequently used manipulators; these are defined in header file <iomanip>.

The next code block in function Ch02_02_ex1() writes values a and b to std::cout. This is followed by a code block that also writes values a and b to std::cout but uses manipulators to format the output. Manipulator std::hex instructs std::cout to format

CHAPTER 2　FORMATTED I/O

integers as hexadecimal values, and manipulator `std::showbase` enables insertion of prefix "0x" or "0X" when formatting a hexadecimal value (it also inserts a "0" prefix when using `std::oct`). Table 2-3 lists common I/O stream manipulators.

Table 2-3. *Common I/O Stream Manipulators*

Manipulator	Description
boolalpha, noboolalpha	Selects text or numbers for bool values
dec, hex, oct	Selects numeric base for integer input and output
endl	Writes newline char, flushes output stream buffer
ends	Writes null character, no flush of stream
fixed, scientific, hexfloat, defaultfloat	Selects floating-point notation
flush	Flushes output stream buffer
left, right	Selects left/right justification using current fill character
showbase, noshowbase	Enable/disable base prefix (e.g., 0x) for numeric values
showpos, noshowpos	Enable/disable plus sign for positive numerical values
showpoint, noshowpoint	Enable/disable explicit decimal point for floating-point values
skipws, noskipws	Enable/disable skips of leading whitespace during input
uppercase, nouppercase	Enable/disable uppercase letters for numeric values
unitbuf, nouintbuf	Enable/disable output buffer flush after each write
ws	Ignores leading whitespace from input stream
resetioflags()	Clears specified I/O format flags
setbase()	Sets numeric base (8, 10, or 16) for integer input or output
setfill()	Sets fill character (default fill character is space)
setioflags()	Sets specified I/O format flags
setprecision()	Sets precision for floating-point values
setw()	Sets field width for next input or output operation

Scanning ahead a few lines, other manipulators are exercised, including `std::noshowbase`, `std::uppercase`, and `std::setfill('0')`. The manipulator `std::setw(w)` sets the field width for the output stream. The field width value w affects only the next data value written to the output stream. This means manipulator `std::setw()` must be used for each data value that requires an explicit field width.

The I/O stream library does not include a manipulator for binary output. However, you can exploit class `std::bitset<>` to produce binary output as demonstrated in `Ch02_02_ex1()`. Class `std::bitset<>` is a template class that represents a fixed-size sequence of bits. The expression `std::bitset<sizeof(uintptr_t) * 8> a_addr_bin(a_addr)` creates a bit set of length `sizeof(uintptr_t) * 8` using the bits of `uintptr_t a_addr`. The next statement writes the bit values stored in `a_addr_bin` to `std::cout`.

The final statement of `Ch02_02_ex1()`, `std::cout << std::dec`, resets the formatting of integers for global stream `std::cout` back to decimal. When using I/O streams, it is important to keep in mind that a stream remembers any changes to its formatting attributes following the use of a manipulator. For the current example, failure to use manipulator `std::dec` prior to exiting `Ch02_02_ex1()` means that subsequent writes of integer values to `std::cout` will continue to use hexadecimal formatting. Programs that utilize manipulators with streams, especially global stream objects, usually need to define rules for modifying or preserving a stream's formatting attributes across function boundaries.

Listing 2-2-2 shows the code for `Ch02_02_ex2()`. This function highlights several formatting options for floating-point values. Note that this function requires an argument value of type `std::ostream&`. In the current example, `Ch02_02_ex2()` is called using `std::cout` as the argument, but it could also be called using a file output stream argument as you'll soon see.

Listing 2-2-2. Example Ch02_02 – Ch02_02_ex2()

```
void Ch02_02_ex2(std::ostream& os)
{
    using namespace std::numbers;

    // save current flags and precision
    auto old_flags = os.flags();
    auto old_precision = os.precision(4);
    os << "old_precision: " << old_precision << '\n';
```

CHAPTER 2 FORMATTED I/O

```cpp
    // floating-point output using fixed
    os << std::fixed;
    os << "\ne:  " << e << '\n';
    os << "pi: " << pi << '\n';

    // floating-point output using setprecision()
    os << std::setprecision(10);
    os << "e:  " << e << '\n';
    os << "pi: " << pi << '\n';

    // floating-point output using scientific notation
    double a = e / 10000.0;
    double b = pi * 10000.0;
    os << std::scientific << std::setprecision(6);
    os << "\na: " << a << '\n';
    os << "b: " << b << '\n';

    // floating-point output using showpos
    a = -a;
    os << std::fixed << std::showpos;
    os << "\na: " << a << '\n';
    os << "b: " << b << '\n';

    // restore original flags and precision
    os.flags(old_flags);
    os.precision(old_precision);
}
```

Function Ch02_02_ex2() opens with a using namespace std::numbers (C++20) statement that facilitates direct use of the numerical constants pi and e, which are defined in <numbers>. The first code block in Ch02_02_ex2() uses os.flags() and os.precision(4) to save the current format flags and precision setting for stream os. The latter call also sets the new precision value to four. One advantage of using a member function (inherited from std::ios_base) to modify the precision (or any other values shown in Table 2-3) is that the function returns the old setting. If necessary, this value can be used to restore the caller's setting.

CHAPTER 2   FORMATTED I/O

The next code block in ChO2_02_ex2() utilizes manipulator std::fixed to specify decimal notation for floating-point values (the default notation uses decimal or scientific depending on fit). It then writes pi and e to os using four digits of precision. The ensuing code block performs the same operation but utilizes manipulator std::setprecision(10) to change the stream's precision setting prior to the writes.

The final code blocks of ChO2_02_ex2() highlight the use of manipulators std::scientific (format floating-point value using scientific notation) and std::showpos (insert leading + character for positive numbers). The last two statements of ChO2_02_ex2() restore the caller's original flag and precision settings for stream os.

Function ChO2_02_ex3(), shown in Listing 2-2-3, utilizes manipulator std::setfill('_') to change the fill character (the default fill character for std::ostream objects is a space). It also utilizes manipulators std::left and std::right to perform left and right justifications of text strings. The final two statements of ChO2_02_ex3() apply manipulator std::quoted(). This manipulator inserts quotes around the specified string. The default quote character is ", but this can be changed to another character as demonstrated.

Listing 2-2-3. Example Ch02_02 – Ch02_02_ex3()

```
void ChO2_02_ex3(std::ostream& os)
{
    constexpr int w {40};
    std::string s1 {"0123456789"};
    std::string s2 {"abcdefghijklmnopqrstuvwxyz"};

    // string output using left, right, and setw
    os << std::setfill('_');
    os << "s1: " << std::left << std::setw(w) << s1 << '\n';
    os << "s2: " << std::left << std::setw(w) << s2 << '\n';
    os << "s1: " << std::right << std::setw(w) << s1 << '\n';
    os << "s2: " << std::right << std::setw(w) << s2 << '\n';

    // string output using quoted
    os << std::setfill(' ');
    os << "\ns1 quoted: " << std::quoted(s1) << '\n';
    os << "s2 quoted: " << std::quoted(s2, '|') << '\n';
}
```

Listing 2-2-4 shows the code for Ch02_02_ex4(). This function highlights the basic use of output file class std::ofstream. The opening statement of this function employs MF::mk_test_filename() to construct a filename string. This function prepends a directory name and filename prefix string to the specified base name. The directory name and filename prefix strings are defined in Common/MF.h; you can change these to whatever suits your needs. Namespace MF[1] also contains additional miscellaneous functions that are exploited in multiple source code examples. The filename string fn is used to initialize and open std::ofstream ofs.

Listing 2-2-4. Example Ch02_02 - Ch02_02_ex4()

```
void Ch02_02_ex4()
{
    // open test file
    std::string fn = MF::mk_test_filename("ch02_02_ex4.txt");
    std::ofstream ofs {fn};

    // open success?
    if (!ofs.good())
    {
        std::println("open failed using file {}", fn);
        return;
    }

    // write to std::ofstream
    Ch02_02_ex2(ofs);
    ofs.close();
    std::println("results saved to file {}", fn);
}
void Ch02_02_ex()
{
    std::println("\n----- Ch02_02_ex1() -----");
    Ch02_02_ex1();

    std::println("\n----- Ch02_02_ex2() -----");
```

---

[1] The source code in this book utilizes capital letters for its namespaces to avoid confusion with any C++ defined namespaces.

```
    Ch02_02_ex2(std::cout);

    std::println("\n----- Ch02_02_ex3() -----");
    Ch02_02_ex3(std::cout);

    std::println("\n----- Ch02_02_ex4() -----");
    Ch02_02_ex4();
}
```

The next code block uses ofs.good() to determine if file fn was successfully opened by the constructor. If true, function Ch02_02_ex4() calls Ch02_02_ex2() using ofs as the argument, which means Ch02_02_ex2() writes its results to file fn instead of std::cout. The ofs.close() that follows is technically not necessary since the destructor of ofs will automatically close an open file stream. However, it is considered good programming practice to explicitly close a file following the completion of all I/O operations to avoid needless consumption of a system resource.

Table 2-4 lists other the std::basic_ios<> functions that a program can use to determine the state of a file stream following its constructor or any I/O operation. Class std::basic_ios<> is a base class of the file stream classes as shown in Figure 2-1.

Table 2-4. State Functions and State Bits for std::basic_ios<> and std::ios_base

State Function std::basic_ios<>	State Bit std::ios_base	Description
good()		True if eofbit, failbit, and badbit are all false
eof()	eofbit	True if end-of-file detected, otherwise false
fail()	failbit	True if stream error has occurred, otherwise false
bad()	badbit	True if non-recoverable error has occurred, otherwise false
rdstate()		Returns std::ios_base::iostate<> mask of all state bits
setstate()		Sets state bits using std::ios_base::iostate<> mask
clear()		Clears all state bits; sets state bits to new values
operator!()		Returns true if badbit or failbit is true

CHAPTER 2 FORMATTED I/O

You'll see other examples of I/O streams later in this and subsequent chapters. Here are the results for source code example Ch02_02:

```
----- Results for example Ch02_02 -----

----- Ch02_02_ex1() -----
a == 100: 1
a == 100: true
a: 100
b: -300
a: 0x64
b: 0xfffffffffffffed4

a_addr: 0X000000DB15EFFB10
a_addr: 0x000000db15effb10
a_addr: 0b0000000000000000000000001101101100010101111011111111101100010000

----- Ch02_02_ex2() -----
old_precision: 6

e:  2.7183
pi: 3.1416
e:  2.7182818285
pi: 3.1415926536

a: 2.718282e-04
b: 3.141593e+04

a: -0.000272
b: +31415.926536

----- Ch02_02_ex3() -----
s1: 0123456789_____
s2: abcdefghijklmnopqrstuvwxyz_____
s1: _____0123456789
s2: _____abcdefghijklmnopqrstuvwxyz
```

CHAPTER 2   FORMATTED I/O

```
s1 quoted: "0123456789"
s2 quoted: |abcdefghijklmnopqrstuvwxyz|

----- Ch02_02_ex4() -----
results saved to file ./~~ch02_02_ex4.txt
```

The examples of this section used stream objects parameterized with type char (e.g., std::cout, std::ofstream, etc.), but you can also use the wchar_t counterparts std::wcout and std::wofstream to perform formatted stream output.

Formatted Output Using std::format()

Compared to the legacy C functions for formatted I/O, the C++ I/O stream functions discussed in the previous section are a worthwhile upgrade. However, there is a conspicuous lack of succinctness when a function is required to employ multiple manipulators to perform what should be a simple formatting operation. Moreover, keeping track of stream state changes across function boundaries can be challenging. The formatting libraries of C++20 remedy this situation by employing format specifiers that mimic the ones used in Python.

The C++20 formatting library <format> includes numerous practical functions for generating formatted output. The quintessential member of this library is std::format(), which is a variadic template function that formats a pack of argument values according to a first-argument format string. For example, consider the following code:

```cpp
#include <cmath>
#include <format>
#include <iostream>
#include <string>
#include "Ch02_03.h"

void format_ex1()
{
    int a {100};
    unsigned int b {200};
    unsigned long long c {0x123456789ABC};
    float d = std::sqrt(300.0f);
```

```
    double e = std::log(400.0);
    double f = e * -0.5;
    std::string g {"abcdefghij"};

    std::string s1 = std::format("a={:d}, b={:6d}, c={:#016X}", a, b ,c);
    std::string s2 = std::format("f={2:.4f}, e={1:<12.8f}, d={0:.2f}",
    d, e, f);
    std::string s3 = std::format("{0:~<20s}, {0:#^20s}, {0:=>20s}", g);

    std::cout << s1 << '\n';
    std::cout << s2 << '\n';
    std::cout << s3 << '\n';
}
```

Execution of function format_ex1() yields the following result:

```
a=100, b=   200, c=0X00123456789ABC
f=-2.9957, e=5.99146455  , d=17.32
abcdefghij~~~~~~~~~~, #####abcdefghij#####, ==========abcdefghij
```

For now, don't worry about the contents of the format specification string and just observe that std::format() returns a value of type std::string. An overload that returns a value of type std::wstring is also available. Also, note the use of {}, which denotes a format specifier. The syntax of a format specifier is

{arg-id:fill-and-align sign # 0 width precision L type}

Table 2-5 describes the meaning of each format specifier field. All fields between the curly braces are optional. Using a format specifier of {} instructs std::format() to format a value using a default specifier that varies depending on the type.

Table 2-5. Format Specifier Fields

Field	Description
arg-id	Index of argument
fill-and-align	Fill character (any character other than { or }, followed by one of < (left alignment), ^ (center alignment), or > (right alignment)
sign	One of + (always show sign), - (default, show sign for negative values only), space (add leading space for non-negative values, otherwise use -)
#	Integers – add leading 0b, 0B, 0, 0x, 0X for binary, octal, hexadecimal values) Floating-point – always show decimal point for floating-point values
0	Pad value with leading zeros (ignored if align is used)
width	Integer value that specifies minimum field width (default is 0)
.precision	Floating-point – precision String – longest prefix of formatted argument to be included in a nested replacement field
L	Perform locale conversions for arithmetic types (e.g., digit separators)
type	b or B – binary, base prefix is 0b or 0B c – character d – decimal o – octal, base prefix is 0 for nonzero value x, X – hexadecimal, base prefix is 0x or 0X a, A – floating-point hexadecimal e, E – floating-point scientific (default precision is 6) f, F – floating-point fixed (default precision is 6) g, G – Floating-point general (default precision is 6) none – use default for type p, P – pointer type

A nested replacement field is a second set of {} that's enclosed within the first set of {}. Nested replacement fields can be used to specify runtime values for width and precision.

Like most C++ programming features, the best way to learn about std::format() and format specifiers is to study a few examples. Source code example Ch02_03 demonstrates typical usages of std::format() along with various format specifiers. Listing 2-3-1 shows the code for function Ch02_03_ex1().

Listing 2-3-1. Example Ch02_03 – Ch02_03_ex1()

```cpp
//-------------------------------------------------------------------------
// Ch02_03_ex.cpp
//-------------------------------------------------------------------------

#include <format>
#include <fstream>
#include <iostream>
#include <numbers>
#include "Ch02_03.h"
#include "Line.h"
#include "MF.h"

void Ch02_03_ex1()
{
    constexpr int a {100};
    constexpr int b {-200};
    constexpr long long c {300};
    constexpr long long d {-400};

    // bool format
    std::cout << std::format("a == 100: {:d}\n", a == 100);
    std::cout << std::format("b == 400: {:d}\n", b == 400);
    std::cout << std::format("a == 100: {}\n", a == 100);
    std::cout << std::format("b == 400: {:s}\n", b == 400);

    // decimal format
    std::cout << std::format("\na: {}\n", a);
    std::cout << std::format("b: {:d}\n", b);

    // decimal format fill char, alignment, and width
    std::cout << std::format("\na: {:_>10d}\n", a);
    std::cout << std::format("a: {:_<10d}\n", a);
    std::cout << std::format("a: {:_^10d}\n", a);
```

CHAPTER 2 FORMATTED I/O

```cpp
    // hex format
    std::cout << std::format("\na: {:x}\n", a);
    std::cout << std::format("b: {:x}\n", b);         // includes leading
                                                      //   minus sign

    std::cout << std::format("a: {:#010x}\n", static_cast<unsigned int>(a));
    std::cout << std::format("b: {:#010x}\n", static_cast<unsigned int>(b));
    std::cout << std::format("c: {:#018X}\n", static_cast<unsigned long long>(c));
    std::cout << std::format("d: {:#018X}\n", static_cast<unsigned long long>(d));

    // binary format
    std::cout << std::format("\na: {:#034b}\n", static_cast<unsigned int>(a));
    std::cout << std::format("b: {:#034b}\n", static_cast<unsigned int>(b));
    std::cout << std::format("c: {:#066b}\n", static_cast<unsigned int>(c));
    std::cout << std::format("b: {:#066b}\n", static_cast<unsigned long long>(d));

    // decimal format using arg ids
    std::cout << std::format("\na: {0:d} c: {2:d} b: {1:d} c: {2:d} a: {0:d}\n",
        a, b, c);
    std::cout << std::format("a: {0:_>10d} a: {0:_<10d} a: {0:_^10d}\n", a);
}
```

The first code block in Ch02_03_ex1() demonstrates bool formatting. For bools, using a specifier of {:d} instructs std::format() to output a numerical value (0 = false, 1 = true). Using a format specifier of {} or {:s} yields a textual output ("false" or "true"). Note that output from std::format() is directed to std::cout using operator<<.

The next code block in Ch02_03_ex1() spotlights the formatting of decimal integers. The first two statements utilize format specifiers {} and {:d} to default format a decimal integer. The ensuing code block utilizes a fill character, an alignment character, and a width specifier of ten. If you scan ahead to the results section for example Ch02_03, you can see how the alignment character affects the output. It merits mentioning here that the format specifiers utilized by std::format() do not require any size modifiers like those used for std::printf(). A format specifier of {:d} can be used for any fundamental integer type, signed or unsigned.

To output an integer using hexadecimal notation, a function can use specifier {:x} as illustrated in the next code block. When using {:x} with a signed integer type, the output will include a leading minus sign if the value is less than zero. This is why the next four instances of std::format() apply static_cast<> conversions. Note that format specifier {:#010x} incorporates a # symbol, which instructs std::format() to output leading text "0x" (or "0X" for type X). The ensuing 0 is the fill character, and 10 specifies the minimum field width. The outputting of an integer value using binary digits is basically the same as hexadecimal except for the use of b (or B) instead of x (or X) as demonstrated.

The final code block of Ch02_03_ex1() illustrates the use of argument ids to select specific values from the argument pack. Argument id 0 corresponds to the first argument after the format string, 1 to the second argument, etc. Note that the argument ids in the format string need not be consecutively specified and that each argument id can be used multiple times. When using argument ids, they must be used with all format specifiers or none of them.

Listing 2-3-2 shows the source code for function Ch02_03_ex2(), which exercises std::format() using floating-point specifiers. Note that this function includes an argument of type std::ostream& for the output.

Listing 2-3-2. Example Ch02_03 – Ch02_03_ex2()

```
void Ch02_03_ex2(std::ostream& os)
{
    using namespace std::numbers;

    // floating-point format
    os << std::format("\ne: {}, pi: {}\n", e, pi);
    os << std::format("e: {:f}, pi: {:f}\n", e, pi);       // precision = 6

    // floating-point format using width & precision
    // (+ shows sign char for positive values)
    os << std::format("\ne: {:10.6f}, pi: {:10.6f}\n", e, pi);
    os << std::format("e: {:14.10f}, pi: {:14.10f}\n", e, pi);
    os << std::format("e: {:+10.6f}, pi: {:+10.6f}\n", e, pi);

    // floating-point format using fill char and alignment
```

```
    os << std::format("\ne: {:_<12.6f}, pi: {:_<12.6f}\n", e, pi);
    os << std::format("e: {:_>12.6f}, pi: {:_>12.6f}\n", e, pi);
    os << std::format("e: {:_^12.6f}, pi: {:_^12.6f}\n", e, pi);

    // floating-point format using nested replacement
    os << std::format("\ne:  {:{}.{}f}\n", e, 6, 3);
    os << std::format("pi: {:{}.{}f}\n", pi, 16, 8);

    // floating-point format using scientific notation
    double a = e * 10000.0;
    double b = pi / 100000.0;
    os << std::format("\na: {:8.4e}, b: {:8.4e}\n", a, b);
    os << std::format("a: {:16.8e}, b: {:16.8e}\n", a, b);
}
```

The first code block in ChO2_03_ex2() utilizes format specifiers {} and {:f}. The difference between these two is that the latter one defaults to six digits of precision. The next code block exercises format specifiers that include explicit values for width and precision. Note the use of the + sign that instructs std::format() to add a leading plus sign for a positive value. Fill characters and alignments are demonstrated in the next set of calls to std:format(). This is followed by code block that employs a nested replacement specifier, which is useful for runtime calculations of width and precision (the current example just uses integer literals). The final code block in function ChO2_03_ex2() utilizes format specifiers for scientific notation.

Listing 2-3-3 shows the code for function ChO2_03_ex3(). This function exemplifies the use of format specifiers for values of type std::string.

Listing 2-3-3. Example Ch02_03 – Ch02_03_ex3()

```
void Ch02_03_ex3(std::ostream& os)
{
    std::string s1 {"0123456789"};
    std::string s2 {"abcdefghijklmnopqrstuvwxyz"};
    std::string sr {"red"};
    std::string sg {"green"};
    std::string sb {"blue"};

    // string format (default)
```

```
    os << std::format("\ns1: {}\n", s1);
    os << std::format("s2: {}\n", s2);

    // string format using fill char and alignment
    os << std::format("\ns1: {:~<40s}\n", s1);
    os << std::format("s1: {:~>40s}\n", s1);
    os << std::format("s1: {:~^40s}\n", s1);

    // string format using arg ids
    os << std::format("\n{0:s} {0:s} {1:s} {1:s} {2:s} {2:s}\n",
        sr, sg, sb);
    os << std::format("{0:_>10s} {0:_<10s} {0:_^10s}\n", sg);
}
```

One extremely important protection feature of std::format() is the checking, both compile time and runtime, that's performed on the format specification string. For example, a C++ compiler is *required* to flag an error if a function attempts to use a floating-point format specifier such as {:f} to format an integer value. The first two uses of std::format() in function Ch02_03_ex4(), shown in Listing 2-3-4, provide an example. Remove the comments from either of these lines, and the source code will fail to compile.

Listing 2-3-4. Example Ch02_03 – Ch02_03_ex4()

```
void Ch02_03_ex4(std::ostream& os)
{
    int x {10};
    float y{22.5f};
    std::string fmt1 {"{:d}, {:f}"};
    std::string fmt2 {"{:f}, {:d}"};
//  os << std::format("x: {:f}\n", x);          // bad - compiler error
//  os << std::format("y: {:d}\n", y);          // bad - compiler error
    try
    {
        auto args {std::make_format_args(x, y)};
```

```
            std::string s1 {std::vformat(fmt1, args)};   // ok
            os << s1 << '\n';

            std::string s2 {std::vformat(fmt2, args)};   // throws std::format_
                                                                         error
            os << s1 << '\n';
        }
        catch (const std::format_error& fe)
        {
            os << "\ncaught std::format_error exception" << '\n';
            os << "fe.what() text: " << fe.what() << '\n';
        }
    }
```

Another item of significance regarding std::format()'s format specification string is that it must be a compile-time constant, which means std::format() can't be used in situations where runtime creation of a format specifier is necessary. However, the formatting library contains a function named std::vformat() that supports a non-const format specification string. Like its counterpart std::format(), std::vformat() also performs runtime checks on the supplied format specification string.

The try block of Ch02_03_ex4() exemplifies the runtime error checking of a format specification string. The first statement inside the try block utilizes std::make_format_args(x, y) to create an object of argument values that can be passed to std::vformat(). The next statement employs std::vformat() to format args (i.e., x and y) using format specification string fmt1. The formatted string s1 is then written to std::ostream os. The next two statements carry out the same operations. However, note that the format specifiers in fmt2 are incorrect; {:f} is used for int x and {:d} is used for float y. Upon detection of this formatting gaffe, std::vformat() throws an exception of std::format_error.

Listing 2-3-5 shows the code for Ch02_03_ex5(), which demonstrates the use of std::format() with template class Line<>.

CHAPTER 2　FORMATTED I/O

Listing 2-3-5. Example Ch02_03 - Ch02_03_ex5()

```
void Ch02_03_ex5(std::ostream& os)
{
    Line<short> line1 {0, 0, 3, 4};
    Line<int> line2 {1, 12, 12, -1};
    Line<float> line3 {10.0f, 15.0f, 10.0f, 22.0f};
    Line<double> line4 {-8.0, 8.0, 8.0, -8.0};

    // Line format
    os << std::format("line1: {}\n", line1);
    os << std::format("line2: {}\n", line2);
    os << std::format("line3: {}\n", line3);
    os << std::format("line4: {}\n", line4);
}

void Ch02_03_ex()
{
    std::println("\n----- format_ex1 -----");
    format_ex1();

    std::println("\n----- Ch02_03_ex1() -----");
    Ch02_03_ex1();

    std::println("\n----- Ch02_03_ex2() -----");
    Ch02_03_ex2(std::cout);

    std::println("\n----- Ch02_03_ex3() -----");
    Ch02_03_ex3(std::cout);

    std::println("\n----- Ch02_03_ex4() -----");
    Ch02_03_ex4(std::cout);

    std::println("\n----- Ch02_03_ex5() -----");
    Ch02_03_ex5(std::cout);
}
```

CHAPTER 2 FORMATTED I/O

Using `std::format()` with a user-defined class is not much different than using it with a fundamental type. However, before this is possible, the user-defined class must define a structure and a couple of member functions to handle the necessary formatting operations. Listing 2-3-6 shows a portion of the code for class Line<> (see Listing 1-7-2 for the complete code).

Listing 2-3-6. Example Ch02_03 – Line.h (partial)

```
private:
    std::string to_str() const
    {
        std::string s{};
        std::format_to(std::back_inserter(s), "[({}, {}, ", m_X0, m_Y0);
        std::format_to(std::back_inserter(s), "{}, {}) | ", m_X1, m_Y1);
        std::format_to(std::back_inserter(s), "({:.4f}, ", length());
        std::format_to(std::back_inserter(s), "{:.4f})]", slope());

        return s;
    }

    // attributes
    T m_X0 {};
    T m_Y0 {};
    T m_X1 {};
    T m_Y1 {};
};

// class Line formatter
template <typename T> struct std::formatter<Line<T>> :
std::formatter<std::string>
{
    constexpr auto parse(std::format_parse_context& fpc)
        { return fpc.begin(); }

    auto format(Line<T> line, std::format_context& fc) const
        { return std::format_to(fc.out(), "{}", line.to_str()); }
};
```

Class Line<> defines a private member function named to_str(). This function builds a text string using the line's attributes. Function to_str() is called by the functions that std::format() calls to format a Line<>. It's also called by operator<< (std::stream& const Line<T>& line). Within to_str(), note the use of std::format_to(). This function performs formatting just like std::format() but writes the resultant string to the output iterator that's specified by the first argument. Function std::back_inserter() is a template function that returns an iterator of type std::back_insert_iterator, and std::format_to() uses this iterator to append a new string to target string s. You'll learn more about std::back_inserter() in Chapter 3. For the current example, it's only necessary to understand that std::back_inserter(s) appends a new string to the end of string s.

Function std::format_to() utilizes the same format specifiers as std::format(). The string built by to_str() includes coordinate attributes m_X0, m_Y0, m_X1, and m_Y1, along with the line's length and slope.

Toward the bottom of Listing 2-3-6 is the definition of a template structure named std::formatter<Line<>>. Note that this structure contains two member functions. Both parse() and format() are called whenever std::format() (or a related format library function) is used to format an instance of Line<>. The purpose of parse() is to process a custom format specifier for Line<>. Class Line<> doesn't define a custom format specifier, so parse() returns fpc.begin(). Function format() handles the actual formatting. This function writes the std::string built by to_str() to the output iterator returned by fc.out(). The organization of std::formatter<Line<T>> is typical for a user-defined class that's used with std::format() to perform simple formatting. Later in this book, you'll learn how to create a custom format specifier for a user-defined class. You'll also learn how to use the chrono format specifiers for dates and times. Here are the results for example Ch02_03:

```
----- Results for example Ch02_03 -----

----- Ch02_03_ex1() -----
a == 100: 1
b == 400: 0
a == 100: true
b == 400: false

a: 100
b: -200
```

CHAPTER 2   FORMATTED I/O

a: _____100
a: 100_____
a: ___100____

a: 64
b: -c8
a: 0x00000064
b: 0xffffff38
c: 0X000000000000012C
d: 0XFFFFFFFFFFFFFE70

a: 0b0000000000000000000000000001100100
b: 0b11111111111111111111111100111000
c: 0b0000000000000000000000000000000000000000000000000000000100101100
b: 0b1111111111111111111111111111111111111111111111111111111001110000

a: 100 c: 300 b: -200 c: 300 a: 100
a: _____100 a: 100_____ a: ___100____

----- Ch02_03_ex2() -----

e: 2.718281828459045, pi: 3.141592653589793
e: 2.718282, pi: 3.141593

e: 2.718282, pi: 3.141593
e: 2.7182818285, pi: 3.1415926536
e: +2.718282, pi: +3.141593

e: 2.718282____, pi: 3.141593____
e: ____2.718282, pi: ____3.141593
e: __2.718282__, pi: __3.141593__

e: 2.718
pi: 3.14159265

a: 2.7183e+04, b: 3.1416e-05
a: 2.71828183e+04, b: 3.14159265e-05

----- Ch02_03_ex3() -----

92

s1: 0123456789
s2: abcdefghijklmnopqrstuvwxyz

s1: 0123456789~~~~~~~~~~~~~~~~~~~~~~
s1: ~~~~~~~~~~~~~~~~~~~~~~~~0123456789
s1: ~~~~~~~~~~~~~0123456789~~~~~~~~~~~

red red green green blue blue
____green green____ __green__

----- Ch02_03_ex4() -----
10, 22.500000

caught std::format_error exception
fe.what() text: Invalid presentation type for integer

----- Ch02_03_ex5() -----
line1: [(0, 0, 3, 4) | (5.0000, 1.3333)]
line2: [(1, 12, 12, -1) | (17.0294, -1.1818)]
line3: [(10, 15, 10, 22) | (7.0000, nan)]
line4: [(-8, 8, 8, -8) | (22.6274, -1.0000)]

Formatted Output Using std::print()

C++23 adds new print functions for formatted output, including std::print() and std::println(). The difference between these functions is that the latter automatically appends a newline character to the output. Both std::print() and std::println() functions utilize the same format specifiers that you learned about in the previous section. They also write their results to output stream std::cout. Overloads are defined in <print> that facilitate the use of std::print() and std::println() using any object of type std::ostream or std::wostream.

Listing 2-4 shows the source code for example Ch02_04, which demonstrates the use of std::println(). In this listing, function Ch02_04_ex1() utilizes std::print() to print formatted integers on std::cout. The format specifiers exercised here are identical to the ones used in Ch02_03_ex1(). This is also true in Ch02_04_ex2(), which prints formatted floating-point values. Note that the std::println() calls in Ch02_04_ex2() utilize an argument of type std::ostream&.

CHAPTER 2   FORMATTED I/O

Listing 2-4. Example Ch02_04 – Ch02_04_ex.cpp

```
//-------------------------------------------------------------------------
// Ch02_04_ex.cpp
//-------------------------------------------------------------------------

#include <iostream>
#include <numbers>
#include "Ch02_04.h"
#include "Line.h"
#include "MF.h"

void Ch02_04_ex1()
{
    constexpr int a {1000};
    constexpr int b {-2000};
    constexpr long long c {3000};

    // bool print
    std::println("b == 400: {:d}", b == 400);
    std::println("b == 400: {:s}", b == 400);

    // decimal print
    std::println("a: {}", a);
    std::println("b: {:d}", b);

    // decimal print using fill char, alignment and width specifier
    std::println("a: {:_>10d}", a);
    std::println("a: {:_<10d}", a);
    std::println("a: {:_^10d}", a);

    // hex print
    std::println("a: {:x}", a);
    std::println("c: {:X}", c);

    // binary print
    std::println("a: {:#034b}", a);
    std::println("c: {:#066b}", c);

    // decimal print using arg ids
```

```cpp
    std::println("a: {0:d} c: {2:d} b: {1:d} c: {2:d} a: {0:d}", a, b, c);
}
void Ch02_04_ex2(std::ostream& os)
{
    using namespace std::numbers;

    // floating-point print
    std::println(os, "e: {:f}, pi: {:f}", e, pi);

    // floating-point print using width & precision
    std::println(os, "e: {:10.6f}, pi: {:10.6f}", e, pi);
    std::println(os, "e: {:14.10f}, pi: {:14.10f}", e, pi);

    // floating-point print using scientific notation
    double a = e * 10000.0;
    double b = pi / 100000.0;
    std::println(os, "a: {:8.4e}, b: {:8.4e}", a, b);
    std::println(os, "a: {:16.8e}, b: {:16.8e}", a, b);
}
void Ch02_04_ex3(std::ostream& os)
{
    std::string s1 {"0123456789"};
    std::string sr {"red"};
    std::string sg {"green"};
    std::string sb {"blue"};

    // string print using alignment and fill char
    std::println(os, "s1: {:~<40s}", s1);
    std::println(os, "s1: {:~>40s}", s1);
    std::println(os, "s1: {:~^40s}", s1);

    // string print using arg ids
    std::println(os, "{2:s} {1:s} {0:s} {0:s} {1:s} {2:s}", sr, sg, sb);
}
void Ch02_04_ex()
{
```

CHAPTER 2 FORMATTED I/O

```
    std::println("\n----- Ch02_04_ex1() -----");
    Ch02_04_ex1();

    std::println("\n----- Ch02_04_ex2() -----");
    Ch02_04_ex2(std::cout);

    std::println("\n----- Ch02_04_ex3() -----");
    Ch02_04_ex3(std::cout);
}
```

The remaining functions of Listing 2-4 underscore additional uses of std::println(). Here are the results for example Ch02_04:

```
----- Results for example Ch02_04 -----

----- Ch02_04_ex1() -----
b == 400: 0
b == 400: false
a: 1000
b: -2000
a:       1000
a: 1000_____
a:    1000
a: 3e8
c: BB8
a: 0b00000000000000000000001111101000
c: 0b00000000000000000000000000000000000000000000000000101110111000
a: 1000 c: 3000 b: -2000 c: 3000 a: 1000

----- Ch02_04_ex2() -----
e: 2.718282, pi: 3.141593
e:    2.718282, pi:    3.141593
e:    2.7182818285, pi:    3.1415926536
a: 2.7183e+04, b: 3.1416e-05
a:    2.71828183e+04, b:    3.14159265e-05
```

```
----- Ch02_04_ex3() -----
s1: 0123456789~~~~~~~~~~~~~~~~~~~~~~~~~~~
s1: ~~~~~~~~~~~~~~~~~~~~~~~~~~~0123456789
s1: ~~~~~~~~~~~~~~0123456789~~~~~~~~~~~~~~
blue green red red green blue
```

Formatted File I/O Using Streams

The final example of this chapter, named Ch02_05, illustrates additional operations using file streams `std::ofstream` and `std::ifstream`. Listing 2-5 shows the source code for this example.

Listing 2-5. Example Ch02_05 - Ch02_05_ex.cpp

```
//-------------------------------------------------------------------------
// Ch02_05_ex.cpp
//-------------------------------------------------------------------------

#include <fstream>
#include <stdexcept>
#include <string>
#include "Ch02_05.h"
#include "MF.h"

namespace
{
    const char* s_Strings[]
    {
        "zero", "one", "two", "three", "four", "five", "six", "seven", "eight",
        "nine", "ten", "eleven", "twelve", "thirteen", "fourteen", "fifteen",
        "sixteen", "seventeen", "eighteen", "nineteen"
    };
}

void Ch02_05_ex1(const std::string& filename)
{
    std::ofstream ofs {filename};
```

CHAPTER 2   FORMATTED I/O

```cpp
    if (!ofs.good())
    {
        std::println("file open error: {:s}", filename);
        return;
    }

    std::println("writing data to file: {:s}", filename);

    // using iterators to access elements of C-style array
    for (auto iter = std::begin(s_Strings); iter != std::end(s_Strings); ++iter)
    {
        std::println(ofs, "{:s}", *iter);

        if (!ofs.good())
        {
            std::println("file write error: {:s}\n", filename);
            return;
        }
    }

    ofs.close();
}
void Ch02_05_ex2(const std::string& filename)
{
    std::ifstream ifs {filename};

    if (!ifs.good())
    {
        std::println("file open error: {:s}", filename);
        return;
    }

    std::println("reading data from file: {:s}", filename);

    size_t i {};
    std::string str {};

    while (1)
```

```cpp
    {
        // get next string value from ifs
        ifs >> str;

        if (ifs.eof())
            break;

        if (ifs.fail())
        {
            std::println("file read error: {:s}", filename);
            break;
        }

        // verify string value
        std::print("test string: {:15s} | compare: ", str);

        if (str == s_Strings[i++])
            std::println("OK");
        else
        {
            std::println("failed!");
            break;
        }
    }

    ifs.close();
}

void Ch02_05_ex3(const std::string& filename)
{
    std::ifstream ifs {filename};

    if (!ifs.good())
    {
        std::println("file open error: {:s}", filename);
        return;
    }

    std::println("reading data from file: {:s}", filename);
```

```cpp
        size_t num_lines {};
        std::string line {};

        while (1)
        {
            // read next line from ifs
            std::getline(ifs, line);

            if (ifs.eof())
                break;

            if (ifs.fail())
            {
                std::println("file read error: {:s}", filename);
                break;
            }

            std::println("line {:4d}: {:s}", ++num_lines, line);
        }

        std::println("\nnum_lines: {:d}\n", num_lines);
        ifs.close();
    }

    void Ch02_05_ex()
    {
        std::string fn1 = MF::mk_test_filename("ch02_05.txt");

        std::println("\n----- Ch02_05_ex1() -----");
        Ch02_05_ex1(fn1);

        std::println("\n----- Ch02_05_ex2() -----");
        Ch02_05_ex2(fn1);

        std::println("\n----- Ch02_05_ex3() -----");
        Ch02_05_ex3(fn1);
    }
```

In Listing 2-5, function Ch02_05_ex1() writes text strings to a file. There are two important programming techniques to recognize in this function. First, the elements of C-style array s_Strings are accessed using an iterator. This is accomplished using global functions std::begin() and std::end(). Using iterators to access the elements of a C-style array is advantageous here since it sidesteps any applications of operator sizeof() to determine the number of text strings in s_Strings. The other item is the statement std::println(ofs, "{:s}", *iter), which writes the specified string to output stream ofs. The same operation also could have been performed using std::ofs << *iter << '\n'. However, it should be readily apparent from the examples in this chapter that using std::println() with or without an explicit output stream yields easier-to-read code (compared to the use of operator<< and manipulators), especially when writing multiple values.

Function Ch02_05_ex2() employs operator>> to read data from an input file stream. Within the while loop, note the use of the statement ifs >> str, which reads the next string value from input file stream ifs. The next statement, ifs.eof(), tests ifs's eofbit for an end-of-file condition; if true, the while loop is terminated. This is followed by an ifs.fail(), which checks input stream ifs for an error condition.

The final function in Listing 2-5, Ch02_05_ex3(), also reads data from an input file stream but utilizes std::getline() to read an entire line from file stream ifs. When working with text files where each line contains multiple values (e.g., a comma-separated value file), using std::getline() is often more convenient than multiple uses of operator>>. The acquired std::string can be passed as an argument to another function for additional parsing. Here are the results for example Ch02_05:

```
----- Results for example Ch02_05 -----

----- Ch02_05_ex1() -----
writing data to file: ./~~ch02_05.txt

----- Ch02_05_ex2() -----
reading data from file: ./~~ch02_05.txt
test string: zero           | compare: OK
test string: one            | compare: OK
test string: two            | compare: OK
test string: three          | compare: OK
test string: four           | compare: OK
test string: five           | compare: OK
test string: six            | compare: OK
```

```
test string: seven        | compare: OK
test string: eight        | compare: OK
test string: nine         | compare: OK
test string: ten          | compare: OK
test string: eleven       | compare: OK
test string: twelve       | compare: OK
test string: thirteen     | compare: OK
test string: fourteen     | compare: OK
test string: fifteen      | compare: OK
test string: sixteen      | compare: OK
test string: seventeen    | compare: OK
test string: eighteen     | compare: OK
test string: nineteen     | compare: OK
----- Ch02_05_ex3() -----
reading data from file: ./~~ch02_05.txt
line     1: zero
line     2: one
line     3: two
line     4: three
line     5: four
line     6: five
line     7: six
line     8: seven
line     9: eight
line    10: nine
line    11: ten
line    12: eleven
line    13: twelve
line    14: thirteen
line    15: fourteen
line    16: fifteen
line    17: sixteen
```

```
line    18: seventeen
line    19: eighteen
line    20: nineteen
num_lines: 20
```

Summary

Here are the key learning points for this chapter:

- A C++ program can use the legacy C function `std::printf()` or one of its sibling functions to perform formatted output. However, type-safe alternatives should be used in new code.

- The C++ input/output library defines a class hierarchy (Figure 2-1) for formatted input and output. Template classes within the hierarchy are parameterized using a character type.

- A function can use manipulators to specify stream formatting options or perform control operations.

- C++20 includes a new formatting library that utilizes Python-like format specifiers. Format specifiers are defined for fundamental types and common string classes. A user-defined class can also define a custom format specifier and formatting function for use with `std::format()`, `std::format_to()`, etc.

- C++23 incorporates new print functions that utilize the same format specifiers as `std::format()`. The default output stream for `std::print()` and `std::println()` is `std::cout`, but overloads are defined that facilitate writes to any output stream.

CHAPTER 3

Sequence Containers – Part 1

This chapter introduces sequence containers, including

- An overview of sequence containers
- How to use `std::array`
- How to use `std::vector`
- Additional algorithms using `std::array` and `std::vector`

The discussions and source code examples of this chapter expound typical uses for classes `std::array` and `std::vector`. You'll study additional examples for these classes in later chapters.

Overview of Sequence Containers

A sequence container organizes a finite collection of objects (or elements), all of which must be the same type. The ordering of objects within a sequence container is linear and determined programmatically. Table 3-1 summarizes the five STL sequence container classes.

CHAPTER 3   SEQUENCE CONTAINERS – PART 1

Table 3-1. *STL Sequence Container Classes*

Sequence Container	Description	Key Feature
`std::array`	Fixed-size collection of objects	No insert or erase operations
`std::vector`	Adjustable size collection of objects	Most frequently used container; best for insertions and removals at the end of the container
`std::deque`	Double-ended queue	Similar to `std::vector` but optimized for fast insertions and removals at the beginning and end of the container
`std::list`	Abstraction of a doubly linked list	Optimized for constant time insertions and removals anywhere in the container
`std::forward_list`	Abstraction of a singly linked list	Similar to `std::list` but supports forward-only traversals

In this chapter, you'll learn how to use `std::array` and `std::vector`. Chapter 4 covers the other sequence container classes mentioned in Table 3-1.

Using std::array

STL class `std::array` is a sequence container that implements a fixed-size array. It is often used as a safer alternative to a C-style array. Instances of `std::array` are an encapsulation of a continuous block of memory and a size attribute as shown in Figure 3-1. Compared to a C-style array, `std::array` provides a couple of noteworthy advantages. First, the number of elements is incorporated within the object. Second, the public interface for `std::array` facilitates the use of many STL algorithms. Instances of `std::array` can also be utilized in a manner that resembles a C-style array. For example, elements within a `std::array` are accessible using `operator[]`.

CHAPTER 3   SEQUENCE CONTAINERS – PART 1

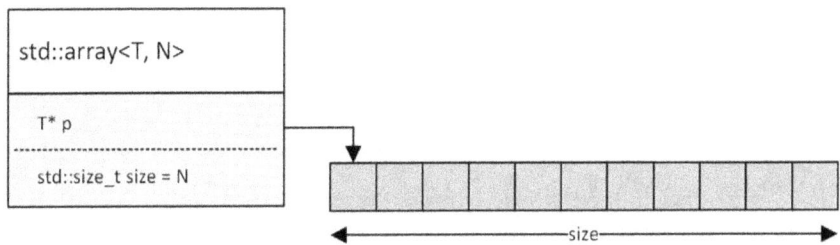

Figure 3-1. *Sequence container* `std::array`

The source code in Listing 3-1-1 illustrates basic use of class `std::array`. The first statement of function `Ch03_01_ex1()`, `std::array<int, 9> x_vals {100, 200, 300, 400, 500, 600, 700, 800, 900}`, defines a `std::array` of nine elements of type `int` whose initial values correspond to those within the initializer list. Note that the template parameter list for `std::array` requires two items: the object type and the number of array elements. The number of elements must be a compile-time constant.

Listing 3-1-1. Example Ch03_01 – Ch03_01_ex1()

```
//------------------------------------------------------------------
// Ch03_01_ex.cpp
//------------------------------------------------------------------

#include <algorithm>
#include <array>
#include <format>
#include <numbers>
#include <numeric>
#include <string>
#include "Ch03_01.h"
#include "MT.h"
#include "RN.h"

void Ch03_01_ex1()
{
    std::array<int, 9> x_vals {100, 200, 300, 400, 500, 600, 700,
        800, 900};

    // print elements of x_vals using operator[]
```

107

```cpp
        std::println("\narray x_vals: ");
        for (size_t i = 0; i < x_vals.size(); ++i)
            std::print("{:6d} ", x_vals[i]);
        std::println("");
        std::println("x_vals.size(): {:d}", x_vals.size());

        // using at()
    //  x_vals.at(42) *= 10;       // invalid index, throws exception

        // print elements of x_vals using forward iterator
        std::println("\narray x_vals: ");
        for (auto iter = x_vals.begin(); iter != x_vals.end(); ++iter)
            std::print("{:6d} ", *iter);
        std::println("");

        // print elements of x_vals using reverse iterator
        std::println("\nx_vals (reversed): ");
        for (auto iter = x_vals.rbegin(); iter != x_vals.rend(); ++iter)
            std::print("{:6d} ", *iter);
        std::println("");
    }
```

The next code block utilizes a for loop to print the elements of x_vals. Note that x_vals.size() obtains the number of elements in x_vals. Also, note that elements of x_vals are referenced using std::array::operator[] just like a C-style array. You can also use std::array::at() to reference elements. The difference between operator[] and at() is that the latter throws an exception if the supplied index is invalid (i.e., index >= size()). You can observe this by removing the comment that precedes the statement vals.at(42) *= 10 and executing the code.

The next code block in Ch03_01_ex1() employs a forward iterator to print the elements of x_vals. Recall from the discussions in Chapter 1 that an iterator is a generalization of a pointer. Iterators are frequently used to access the elements in a container. The for loop's initializer statement utilizes x_vals.begin() to obtain an iterator to the first element in x_vals. The condition section of the for loop compares iter against x_vals.end(). If iter equals x_vals.end(), the for loop terminates. Member function end() returns a value that points to the "element" that follows the array's last element as shown in Figure 3-2. The iterator value returned by end() should only be used to perform a loop termination test; it should never be dereferenced. The expression ++iter updates iter so that it points to the next element in x_vals. Prefix operator++ is generally employed when updating an iterator since it's usually faster than the postfix variant.

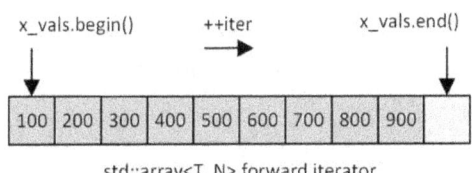

std::array<T, N> forward iterator

Figure 3-2. Using std::array forward iterator

Within the iterator for loop, note that std::print() employs the expression *iter to dereference (access) the current element of x_vals. It is important to keep in mind that while iterators are often used in a manner that mimics native pointers, they are not pointers. Iterators are types that support pointer-like operations such as *, ++, --, etc., to facilitate access to a variety of container types in a uniform manner. C++ defines several different iterator categories with distinct operational capabilities. You'll learn more about iterators and iterator categories in Chapter 4.

The final code block in Ch03_01_ex1() utilizes a reverse iterator to print the elements of x_vals in reverse order. Member functions rbegin() and rend() are the reverse iterator counterparts of begin() and end() as shown in Figure 3-3.

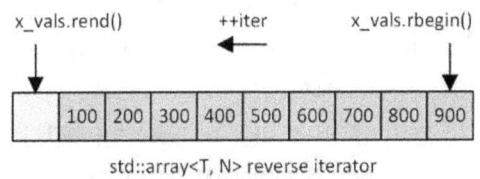

std::array<T, N> reverse iterator

Figure 3-3. Using std::array reverse iterator

Listing 3-1-2 shows the source code for function Ch03_01_ex2(), which exploits a forward iterator to modify the elements of a std::array. The initial code block of Ch03_02_ex() initializes and prints the values of std::array<long, 10> x_vals using functions begin() and end() just like function Ch03_01_ex1(). The next for loop utilizes a forward iterator to perform an arithmetic operation using each element in x_vals. Note the use of the expression *iter += 5, which adds five to the element of x_vals "pointed" to by iter.

CHAPTER 3   SEQUENCE CONTAINERS – PART 1

Listing 3-1-2. Example Ch03_01 - Ch03_01_ex2()

```
void Ch03_01_ex2()
{
    // create array x_vals and print elements
    std::array<long, 10> x_vals {10, 20, 30, 40, 50, 60, 70, 80, 90, 100};
    std::println("\nx_vals (original values): ");
    for (auto iter = x_vals.begin(); iter != x_vals.end(); ++iter)
        std::print("{:6d} ", *iter);
    std::println("");

    // add 5 to each element of x_vals[i] using forward iterators
    for (auto iter = x_vals.begin(); iter != x_vals.end(); ++iter)
        *iter += 5;

    // print modified elements
    std::println("\nx_vals (after adds): ");
    for (auto iter = x_vals.begin(); iter != x_vals.end(); ++iter)
        std::print("{:6d} ", *iter);
    std::println("");
}
```

Function Ch03_01_ex3(), shown in Listing 3-1-3, employs forward iterators to carry out an arithmetic calculation using two containers of type std::array<double, 8>. This function opens with the definition of container std::array<double, 8> radii. The ensuing statement, std::array<double, radii.size()> areas {}, defines another array of doubles whose size matches that of radii. Using radii.size() for areas size parameter is permissible here since it's a constexpr function that can be compile-time evaluated. The empty initializer list {} that's included with the declaration of areas ensures that each element of the array is initialized to zero.

Listing 3-1-3. Example Ch03_01 - Ch03_01_ex3()

```
void Ch03_01_ex3()
{
    using namespace std::numbers;

    std::array<double, 8> radii {1.0, 1.4, 2.0, 2.8, 4.0, 5.6, 8.0, 11.0};
    std::array<double, radii.size()> areas {};
```

```
    // using iterators to perform arithmetic calculation
    auto iter_a = areas.begin();
    for (auto iter_r = radii.begin(); iter_r != radii.end(); ++iter_r,
    ++iter_a)
        *iter_a = pi * *iter_r * *iter_r;

    // print results
    std::println("radius            area\n{:s}", std::string(25, '='));
    iter_a = areas.begin();
    for (auto iter_r = radii.begin(); iter_r != radii.end(); ++iter_r,
    ++iter_a)
        std::println("{:6.1f} {:15.6f}", *iter_r, *iter_a);
}
```

The next code block opens with the expression auto iter_a = areas.begin() that initializes iterator iter_a to the beginning of areas. The ensuing for loop utilizes forward iterators to calculate circle areas using the values in radii. Note that the for loop's iteration expression updates both iter_r and iter_a. The final code block of Ch03_01_ex3() prints the values of arrays radii and areas.

Listing 3-1-4 shows the code for function Ch03_01_ex4(), which exploits a predefined STL algorithm to sum the elements of an std::array. The first code block of Ch03_01_ex4() utilizes template function RN::fill_ctr() (located in Common/RN.h) to fill container arr1 with random numbers. You'll learn about STL's random number classes and functions in Chapter 18. For the current example, it's only necessary to understand that RN::fill_ctr() fills arr1 using a distribution model that uniformly selects random numbers from the interval [rng_min, rng_max]. Value rng_seed seeds the underlying random number engine.

Listing 3-1-4. Example Ch03_01 – Ch03_01_ex4()

```
void Ch03_01_ex4()
{
    constexpr size_t n {20};
    constexpr int rng_min {1};
    constexpr int rng_max {1000};
    constexpr unsigned int rng_seed {3};

    // fill arr1 with random values
```

```
    std::array<int, n> arr1;
    RN::fill_ctr(arr1, rng_min, rng_max, rng_seed);

    // print elements of arr1
    const char* fmt = "{:7d}";
    constexpr size_t epl_max {10};
    MT::print_ctr("\nelements of arr1:\n", arr1, fmt, epl_max);

    // sum elements of arr1 using iterators
    int sum1 {};
    for (auto iter = arr1.begin(); iter != arr1.end(); ++iter)
        sum1 += *iter;
    std::println("sum1: {:d}", sum1);

    // sum elements of arr1 using std::accumulate()
    int sum2 = std::accumulate(arr1.begin(), arr1.end(), 0);
    std::println("sum2: {:d}", sum2);
}
```

The next code block in Ch03_01_ex4() employs MT::print_ctr() (located in Common/MT.h) to print the elements of container arr1. Arguments required by this function include a message text string, the container, a format specifier (fmt), and the maximum number of elements per line (epl_max). Going forward, most of the source code examples will utilize MT::print_ctr() or one of the other print functions defined in namespace MT to display a container's elements instead of using an explicit for loop or similar programming construct. This will enable you to focus on the principal STL code for each example and not be distracted by repetitive boilerplate code.

Following the print operation, Ch03_01_ex4() sums the elements of arr1 using a for loop that employs iterators to reference each element in the container. Many programs perform summing operations like this, so you might be wondering if there's a predefined algorithm that you can use to sum the elements of a std::array or other container type. Yes, there is. The final code block utilizes STL algorithm std::accumulate(), which is declared in <numeric>, to sum the elements of arr1. The first two arguments of this function specify the range of elements that std::accumulate will operate over. For the current example, the range is [arr1.begin(), arr1.end()) or all of the elements in arr1. The final argument of std::accumulate() specifies the initial value for sum. STL function std::accumulate essentially performs the same summing operation as the preceding for loop. This function also accepts a fourth argument that allows a program to supply a different binary operator to replace the default operator+.

Listing 3-1-5 shows the code for Ch03_01_ex5(). This function demonstrates the use of STL algorithm std::sort(), which is declared in <algorithm>. The version of std::sort() that's utilized in Ch03_01_ex5() sorts the elements of range [colors. begin(), colors.end()) using operator< (i.e., elements are sorted in ascending order). Overloaded versions of std::sort() that accept a binary compare predicate to override the algorithm's default use of operator< are also available.

Listing 3-1-5. Example Ch03_01 - Ch03_01_ex5()

```
void Ch03_01_ex5()
{
    const char* fmt = "{:15s}";
    constexpr size_t epl_max {5};

    // create test arrays of std::string
    std::array<std::string, 15> colors1 {"Red", "Green", "Blue", "Cyan",
        "Magenta", "Yellow", "Black", "White", "Gray", "Orange", "Brown",
        "Pink", "Purple", "Amber", "Teal"};

    auto colors2 {colors1};

    // using std::sort
    std::sort(colors1.begin(), colors1.end());
    MT::print_ctr("\ncolors1 - after std::sort():\n", colors1, fmt,
        epl_max);

    // using std::ranges::sort (C++20)
    std::ranges::sort(colors2);
    MT::print_ctr("\ncolors2 - after std::ranges::sort():\n",
        colors2, fmt, epl_max);

    // using operator==
    std::println("\ncolors1 == colors2: {:s}", colors1 == colors2);
}
```

CHAPTER 3   SEQUENCE CONTAINERS – PART 1

Prior to C++20, most STL algorithm functions required the caller to supply two iterators just like `std::sort()`. This is useful when the algorithm needs to carry out a calculation using a subrange of the container's elements. For most use cases, however, you want the STL algorithm to work with the entire container. Repeatedly typing `begin()` and `end()` gets monotonous very quickly.

C++20 introduced a new set of range algorithms. The next code block in Ch03_01_ex5() demonstrates the use of `std::ranges::sort()`. Note that this function requires a single container (i.e., range) argument instead of two iterators. Also, note the different namespace, which differentiates `std::ranges::sort()` from its pre-C++20 counterpart. Like `std::sort()`, `std::ranges::sort()` defines distinct overloads that modify its default use of `operator<`.

The final code block of Ch03_ex5() demonstrates the use of `operator==` using colors1 and colors2. This performs a lexicographical compare of the elements in colors1 and colors2. More about this shortly.

Example Ch03_01 exercised `std::accumulate()`, `std::sort()`, and `std::ranges::sort()` as means of gradually introducing STL algorithms. There are over 100 STL algorithms, and you'll learn how to use many of these later in this and in subsequent chapters. Here are the results for example Ch03_01:

```
----- Results for example Ch03_01 -----

----- Ch03_01_ex1() -----

array x_vals:
    100    200    300    400    500    600    700    800    900
x_vals.size(): 9

array x_vals:
    100    200    300    400    500    600    700    800    900

x_vals (reversed):
    900    800    700    600    500    400    300    200    100

----- Ch03_01_ex2() -----

x_vals (original values):
    10    20    30    40    50    60    70    80    90    100

x_vals (after adds):
```

```
   15      25      35      45      55      65      75      85      95     105
----- Ch03_01_ex3() -----
radius              area
=========================
    1.0           3.141593
    1.4           6.157522
    2.0          12.566371
    2.8          24.630086
    4.0          50.265482
    5.6          98.520346
    8.0         201.061930
   11.0         380.132711
----- Ch03_01_ex4() -----
elements of arr1:
     551      71     709     840     291     122     511     570     893     438
     897      19     126      41     208     248      52      94     441     695
sum1: 7817
sum2: 7817
----- Ch03_01_ex5() -----
colors1 - after std::sort():
Amber           Black           Blue            Brown           Cyan
Gray            Green           Magenta         Orange          Pink
Purple          Red             Teal            White           Yellow
colors2 - after std::ranges::sort():
Amber           Black           Blue            Brown           Cyan
Gray            Green           Magenta         Orange          Pink
Purple          Red             Teal            White           Yellow
colors1 == colors2: true
```

As mentioned earlier, the primary purpose of `std::array` is to provide a safer and more convenient alternative to C-style arrays. It is important to keep in mind that the number of elements maintained by `std::array` is fixed. Unlike other sequence container objects, you can't insert or remove elements from a `std::array`; you can only replace existing elements. For local instances of `std::array`, the contiguous block of memory for the array's elements is often situated on the stack. For some C++ implementations, this can preclude using `std::array` with a large number of elements.

A function can use `operator=` to create a copy of a `std::array`. It can also utilize one of the standard relational operators to lexicographically compare two `std::array` containers. When using relational operators, the `std::array` containers must be parameterized using the same type and size. The reason for this is that parameterized template objects such as `std::array<int, 5>` and `std::array<int, 10>` are *different* types. Examples of valid and invalid `std::array` relational operator use include

```
std::array<int, 4> a {10, 20, 30, 40};
std::array<int, 4> b {-10, -20, -30, -40};
std::array<long, 4> c {100, 200, 300, 400};
std::array<long, 5> d {100, 200, 300, 400, 500};

bool b1 = a == b;       // ok
bool b2 = a >= b;       // ok
a = b;                  // ok

//  bool b3 = a == c;   // error - different types
//  bool b4 = c == d;   // error - different sizes
//  a = c;              // error - different types and sizes
```

Using std::vector

Class `std::array` is a practical but somewhat limited sequence container. The biggest drawback of `std::array` is its compile-time fixed size. Many programs require the ability to allocate and utilize array-like data structures whose size is not known until runtime. Programs also require the ability to insert and/or remove elements. STL class `std::vector` is a container that eliminates the limitations of `std::array` while providing the same array-like usage capabilities.

Figure 3-4 shows the internal organization of a `std::vector`. Like `std::array`, `std::vector` encapsulates a size attribute along with a block of elements in contiguous memory. It also incorporates a capacity attribute that helps to improve performance when adding new elements to the end of a `std::vector`. You'll learn more about this attribute later in this section.

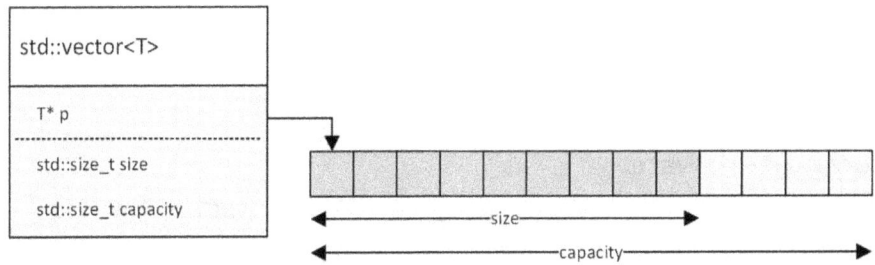

Figure 3-4. *Sequence container* `std::vector`

Listing 3-2-1 shows the first `std::vector` exposition function for example Ch03_02. Near the top of this function is the definition of `std::vector<int> vec1`, which includes an initializer list. This statement initializes a vector of five elements. Unlike the definitions of `std::array` that you saw in the previous example, class `std::vector` does not require a size parameter. The next statement, `std::vector<int> vec2(vec1.size())`, utilizes `std::vector::size()` to create a `std::vector<int>` of five elements, and each element is initialized to zero. In this statement, it's important to recognize the parentheses that surround constructor argument `vec1.size()`. The use of the statement `vec2{vec1.size()}` would instantiate a one-element vector whose value equals `vec1.size()`. The definition of `vec3` that follows demonstrates creation of a vector using an explicit fill value of seven.

Listing 3-2-1. Example Ch03_02 – Ch03_02_ex1()

```
//-------------------------------------------------------------
// Ch03_02_ex.cpp
//-------------------------------------------------------------

#include <algorithm>
#include <cmath>
#include <format>
#include <sstream>
#include <stdexcept>
#include <string>
#include <vector>
#include "Ch03_02.h"
#include "MT.h"
#include "Point2D.h"
```

CHAPTER 3   SEQUENCE CONTAINERS – PART 1

```cpp
void Ch03_02_ex1()
{
    const char* fmt = "{:6d}";

    // create test vectors
    std::vector<int> vec1 {10, 20, 30, 40, 50};    // vec1 = {10, 20,
                                                   // 30, 40, 50}
    std::vector<int> vec2(vec1.size());            // vec2 = {0, 0, 0, 0, 0}
    std::vector<int> vec3(vec1.size(), 7);         // vec3 = {7, 7, 7, 7, 7}

    MT::print_ctr("\nvec1: ", vec1, fmt);
    MT::print_ctr("vec2: ", vec2, fmt);
    MT::print_ctr("vec3: ", vec3, fmt);

    // using operator[] and .at()
    for (size_t i = 0; i < vec1.size(); ++i)
        vec2[i] = vec1.at(i) * vec3.at(i);
    MT::print_ctr("\nvec2 (after calculation): ", vec2, fmt);

    // create more test vectors
    std::vector<unsigned long long> vec4 {100, 200, 300, 400, 500, 600,
        700, 800};
    std::vector<unsigned long long> vec5(vec4.size(), 100);
    std::vector<unsigned long long> vec6 {vec4.size()};    // vec6 = {8}
    std::vector<unsigned long long> vec7 {};               // vec7 = {}

    MT::print_ctr("\nvec4:  ", vec4, fmt);
    MT::print_ctr("vec5:  ", vec5, fmt);
    MT::print_ctr("vec6: ", vec6, fmt);
    MT::print_ctr("vec7: ", vec7, fmt);

    // using iterators
    auto iter4 = vec4.begin();
    auto iter5 = vec5.begin();
    for (; iter4 != vec4.end(); ++iter4, ++iter5)
        *iter5 += *iter4 / 2;
    MT::print_ctr("\nvec5:  ", vec5, fmt);
```

```
    // using front() and back()
    std::println("\nvec4.front(): {:6d}", vec4.front());
    std::println("vec4.back():  {:6d}", vec4.back());

    // using clear()
    vec5.clear();
    MT::print_ctr("\nvec5 (after clear): ", vec5, fmt);
    std::println("vec5.size(): {:d}", vec5.size());
}
```

Following the prints of vectors vec1, vec2, and vec3 is a code block that demonstrates the use of std::vector::operator[] and std::vector member function std::vector::at() to access vector elements. The next code block declares three std::vector<unsigned long long> vectors named vec4, vec5, and vec6. Note that vec6 is defined using curly braces around vec4.size(), which signifies an initializer list. This statement constructs a single-element vector, and the value of that element is vec4.size() (eight). The next definition statement, std::vector<unsigned long long> vec7 {}, constructs a vector of unsigned long longs containing zero elements.[1] The ensuing code block utilizes iterators to calculate vec5[i] += vec4[i] / 2.

The final two code blocks of Ch03_02_01() spotlight the use of several member functions of std::vector. Functions std::vector::front() and std::vector::back() print the first and last elements of vec4. The std::vector::clear() function removes all elements from vec5.

Listing 3-2-2 shows the code for function Ch03_02_ex2(). Near the top of this function is the definition of a lambda expression that prints the size attributes for vec1. More on this shortly. The statement std::vector<double> vec1 {} creates an empty vector of doubles. In the next code block, Ch03_02_ex2() utilizes a for loop and std::vector::push_back() to add elements to the end of vec1. Each call to push_back() adds a new element to the end of vec1.

---

[1] Member function std::vector::resize() can be used to change the size of a std::vector.

Listing 3-2-2. Example Ch03_02 – Ch03_02_ex2()

```
void Ch03_02_ex2()
{
    const char* fmt = "{:9.4f}   ";
    constexpr size_t epl_max {6};
    constexpr size_t n {10};
    std::vector<double> vec1 {};          // empty vector

    // lambdas expression for printing size attributes
    auto print_size_cap = [&vec1] ()
    {
        std::println("vec1.size(): {:d}   vec1.capacity(): {:d}",
            vec1.size(), vec1.capacity());
    };

    // add elements to vec1 using push_back()
    for (size_t i = 0; i < n; ++i)
        vec1.push_back(std::sqrt(static_cast<double>(i + 1)));
    MT::print_ctr("\nvec1 - initial values:\n", vec1, fmt, epl_max);
    print_size_cap();

    // remove elements from vec1 using pop_back()
    while (vec1.size() >= n / 2)
        vec1.pop_back();
    MT::print_ctr("\nvec1 - after pop_back operations:\n", vec1, fmt,
        epl_max);
    print_size_cap();

    // add elements to middle of vec1 using insert
    std::array<double, 8> arr1 {10.0, 20.0, 30.0, 40.0, 50.0, 60.0,
        70.0, 80.0};
    vec1.insert(vec1.begin() + 2, arr1.begin(), arr1.end());
    MT::print_ctr("\nvec1 - after middle inserts:\n", vec1, fmt, epl_max);
    print_size_cap();

    // add elements to end of vec1 using insert
    std::array<double, 6> arr2 {-10.0, -20.0, -30.0, -40.0, -50.0, -60.0};
```

```
vec1.insert(vec1.end(), arr2.begin(), arr2.end());
MT::print_ctr("\nvec1 - after end inserts:\n", vec1, fmt, epl_max);
print_size_cap();

// remove elements from vec1 using member erase (erases vec1[3] and
vec1[4])
vec1.erase(vec1.begin() + 3, vec1.begin() + 5);
MT::print_ctr("\nvec1 - after erase operation:\n", vec1, fmt, epl_max);
print_size_cap();
}
```

An object of type std::vector maintains two different "size" attributes as shown in Figure 3-4. The attribute named size signifies the number of elements currently stored in a std::vector, while the capacity attribute denotes the maximum number of elements for which space is allocated. Member functions std::vector::size() and std::vector::capacity() can be used to query these attributes.

The capacity of a std::vector is often larger than its size to facilitate faster end-of-container insertions. Whenever the capacity of a vector becomes too small due to a std::vector::push_back() or other insertion operations, class std::vector will allocate a new block of memory to accommodate the new elements. This reallocation of storage space is a potentially time-consuming operation since it often requires copying (or moving) elements from the old memory buffer to the new one. A std::vector storage space reallocation also invalidates all iterators that reference elements in the container. If you scan ahead to the results section, you will notice that following the push_back() insertions, vec1's size is 10, but its capacity is 13. A function can also utilize std::vector::reserve() to explicitly change the capacity of a std::vector.

The next code block contains a for loop that removes elements from vec1 using std::vector::pop_back(). Like its push_back() counterpart, each call to pop_back() removes the last element (i.e., vec1[vec1.size() - 1]) from vec1. Note that pop_back() should not be called if the std::vector object is empty. You can utilize size() or std::vector::empty() to test for an empty container.

Class std::vector also defines member functions that can be used to insert multiple elements into a vector. The statement vec1.insert(vec1.begin() + 2, arr1.begin(), arr1.end()) inserts all elements from arr1 into vec1. The elements are copied from arr1 and inserted into vec1 before element vec1.begin() + 2 (or vec1[2]). Note that arr1 is a container of type std::array. Many other STL algorithm functions also carry out their operations using iterators from two different containers.

The next code block also utilizes insert() to insert elements from arr2 to the end of vec1. Similar to the previous insert(), the elements to be inserted are copied from a container of type std::array. The final code block of Ch03_02_ex2() employs vec1.erase(vec1.begin() + 3, vec1.begin() + 5) to erase elements [vec1.begin() + 3, vec1.begin() + 5) (i.e., vec[3] and vec[4]) from vec1. Erasing elements from a std::vector container invalidates any iterators from the insertion point to the end of the container. Performing erasures on a std:vector may also trigger the container into performing element copy or move operations, which may be time-consuming depending on the size of the vector or the element type.

Function Ch03_02_ex3(), shown in Listing 3-2-3, demonstrates additional methods of inserting elements into a std::vector. This function utilizes std::copy() to insert elements from planets_cstr1 into std:vector<std::string>> planets1. In the current example, the first two iterator arguments of std::copy() specify the range of source elements to copy. The third argument, std::back_inserter(planets1), constructs an iterator of type std::back_inserter_iterator that enables std::copy() to employ std::vector::push_back() to perform the insertions.

Listing 3-2-3. Example Ch03_02 – Ch03_02_ex3()

```
void Ch03_02_ex3()
{
    const char* fmt = "{:s} ";
    std::vector<std::string> planets1;
    const char* planets_cstr1[] {"Mercury", "Venus", "Earth", "Mars"};
    const char* planets_cstr2[] {"Jupiter", "Saturn", "Uranus", "Neptune"};

    // using std::copy
    std::copy(std::begin(planets_cstr1), std::end(planets_cstr1),
        std::back_inserter(planets1));
    MT::print_ctr("planets1: ", planets1, fmt);

    // using assignment ctor and emplace_back
    std::vector<std::string> planets2 {planets1};
    planets2.emplace_back(planets_cstr2[0]);
    planets2.emplace_back(planets_cstr2[1]);
```

```cpp
    planets2.emplace_back(planets_cstr2[2]);
    planets2.emplace_back(planets_cstr2[3]);
    MT::print_ctr("planets2: ", planets2, fmt);

    // using std::find
    auto iter_mars = std::find(planets2.begin(), planets2.end(), "Mars");
    bool found_mars = iter_mars != planets2.end();
    std::println("\nfound_mars:  {:s}", found_mars);

    // using std::ranges::find (C++20)
    auto iter_pluto = std::ranges::find(planets2, "Pluto");
    bool found_pluto = iter_pluto != planets2.end();
    std::println("found_pluto: {:s}", found_pluto);

    // using std::sort
    auto planets3 {planets2};
    std::sort(planets2.begin(), planets2.end());
    MT::print_ctr("\nplanets2 sorted: ", planets2, fmt);

    // using std::ranges::sort (C++20)
    std::ranges::sort(planets3);
    MT::print_ctr("planets3 sorted: ", planets3, fmt);

    // using operators
    std::println("planets2 == planets3 (expect true): {:s}", planets2 == planets3);
    std::swap(planets2[3], planets2[4]);
    MT::print_ctr("\nplanets2 after swap: ", planets2, fmt);
    MT::print_ctr("planets3 after swap: ", planets3, fmt);
    std::println("planets2 >  planets3 (expect true):  {:s}", planets2 > planets3);
    std::println("planets2 <  planets3 (expect false): {:s}", planets2 < planets3);
}
```

The ensuing code block in Ch03_02_ex3() opens with the statement std::vector<std::string> planets2 {planets1}, which utilizes the copy constructor of std::vector to instantiate container planets2. Following execution of this statement, std::vectors planets1 and planets2 are identical (i.e., the corresponding element positions of both vectors contain the same value). The next statement, planets2.emplace_back(planets_cstr2[0]), inserts a new element into planets2. Member function std::vector::emplace_back() differs from push_back() in that the former performs an in-place construction of its argument at the memory location provided by the container. For non-fundamental types, using emplace_back() is often faster than defining an object and using push_back() since the latter entails execution of both a constructor and a copy operation.

One ubiquitous programming operation is to search a container for the existence of a specific value. The next code block in Ch03_02_ex3() utilizes STL algorithm std::find() (<algorithm>) to search planets2. The first two iterator arguments of std::find(), planets2.begin() and planets2.end(), define a range over which it will search for the value specified by the third argument. Function std::find() returns an iterator to the first element in the target container that matches the specified search value; if no match is found, it returns end().

In the subsequent code block, Ch03_02_ex3() exercises std::ranges::find(planets2, "Pluto"), which searches planets2 for an occurrence of std::string {"Pluto"}. As mentioned earlier, many C++11 algorithms have a C++20 counterpart in namespace std::ranges that you can use. For example, the next two code blocks demonstrate the use of STL algorithms std::sort() and std::ranges::sort(). These two variants perform the same sorting operation, but the latter is easier to read and type.

The final code block in Ch03_02_ex3() demonstrates how to perform relational comparisons using std::vector objects. The first statement utilizes operator== to compare planets2 and planets3 for equality. The lexicographical compare is performed using corresponding elements from the two vectors. Unlike template class std::array<, a function can compare two std::vectors of the same type but different sizes. Note the use of std::swap(planets2[3], planets2[4]), which swaps values of the specified elements, prior to the use of relational operators operator> and operator<.

The final function of example Ch03_02 demonstrates how to remove a specific value from a std::vector. In Listing 3-2-4, function Ch03_02_ex4() opens with the creation of a std::vector<Point2D<int>> named points. Class Point2D is the same template class that you studied in Chapter 1 (see Listing 1-1-4). Following this is the definition of another std::vector<Point2d<int>> vector named points_to_erase.

Listing 3-2-4. Example Ch03_02 – Ch03_02_ex4()

```cpp
void Ch03_02_ex4()
{
    const char* fmt {"{} "};
    constexpr size_t epl_max {6};

    // create  point vectors
    std::vector<Point2D<int>> points {{3, 4}, {7, 9}, {-2, -4}, {-5, 6},
    {12,10}, {3, -4}, {10, 2}, {3, -4}, {12, 10}, {-9, -2}, {-6, 4}, {12, 10}};
    std::vector<Point2D<int>> points_to_erase
        {{3, -4}, {-7, 6}, {7, 9}, {12,10}};

    MT::print_ctr("\nvector points (initial values):\n", points, fmt,
    epl_max);
    std::println("points.size(): {:d}\n", points.size());

    // perform erasures
    for (const auto& point : points_to_erase)
    {
        // using std::erase (C++20) - erases all occurrences of point
        from points
        auto num_erased = std::erase(points, point);

        // print results
        std::print("current point {} - ", point);

        if (num_erased)
        {
            std::string s = (num_erased > 1) ? "s\n" : "\n";
            std::print("erased {:d} point{:s}", num_erased, s);
        }
        else
            std::print("not found\n");
    }
```

CHAPTER 3   SEQUENCE CONTAINERS – PART 1

```
        MT::print_ctr("\nvector points (after erasures):\n", points, fmt,
        epl_max);
        std::println("points.size(): {:d}", points.size());
}
```

Within the range for loop that's shown in Listing 3-2-4, Ch03_02_ex4() utilizes std::erase(points, point) (C++20) to erase (remove) all occurrences of point from vector points. STL function std::erase() returns the number of matching elements it erased, and this value is used to print a suitable status message. A function can also exploit std::erase_if() to perform a predicate-controlled erasure. You'll learn how to use this function in Chapter 8. Here are the results for example Ch03_02:

```
----- Results for example Ch03_02 -----

----- Ch03_02_ex1() -----

vec1:       10      20      30      40      50
vec2:       0       0       0       0       0
vec3:       7       7       7       7       7

vec2 (after calculation):       70      140     210     280     350

vec4:       100     200     300     400     500     600     700     800
vec5:       100     100     100     100     100     100     100     100
vec6:       8
vec7: <empty>

vec5:       150     200     250     300     350     400     450     500

vec4.front():       100
vec4.back():        800

vec5 (after clear): <empty>
vec5.size(): 0

----- Ch03_02_ex2() -----

vec1 - initial values:
    1.0000      1.4142      1.7321      2.0000      2.2361      2.4495
    2.6458      2.8284      3.0000      3.1623
```

```
vec1.size(): 10  vec1.capacity(): 13

vec1 - after pop_back operations:
   1.0000      1.4142      1.7321      2.0000
vec1.size(): 4  vec1.capacity(): 13

vec1 - after middle inserts:
   1.0000      1.4142     10.0000     20.0000     30.0000     40.0000
  50.0000     60.0000     70.0000     80.0000      1.7321      2.0000
vec1.size(): 12  vec1.capacity(): 13

vec1 - after end inserts:
   1.0000      1.4142     10.0000     20.0000     30.0000     40.0000
  50.0000     60.0000     70.0000     80.0000      1.7321      2.0000
 -10.0000    -20.0000    -30.0000    -40.0000    -50.0000    -60.0000
vec1.size(): 18  vec1.capacity(): 19

vec1 - after erase operation:
   1.0000      1.4142     10.0000     40.0000     50.0000     60.0000
  70.0000     80.0000      1.7321      2.0000    -10.0000    -20.0000
 -30.0000    -40.0000    -50.0000    -60.0000
vec1.size(): 16  vec1.capacity(): 19

----- Ch03_02_ex3() -----
planets1: Mercury Venus Earth Mars
planets2: Mercury Venus Earth Mars Jupiter Saturn Uranus Neptune

found_mars:  true
found_pluto: false

planets2 sorted: Earth Jupiter Mars Mercury Neptune Saturn Uranus Venus
planets3 sorted: Earth Jupiter Mars Mercury Neptune Saturn Uranus Venus
planets2 == planets3 (expect true): true

planets2 after swap: Earth Jupiter Mars Neptune Mercury Saturn Uranus Venus
planets3 after swap: Earth Jupiter Mars Mercury Neptune Saturn Uranus Venus
planets2 >  planets3 (expect true):  true
planets2 <  planets3 (expect false): false

----- Ch03_02_ex4() -----
```

```
vector points (initial values):
(3, 4) (7, 9) (-2, -4) (-5, 6) (12, 10) (3, -4)
(10, 2) (3, -4) (12, 10) (-9, -2) (-6, 4) (12, 10)
points.size(): 12

current point (3, -4) - erased 2 points
current point (-7, 6) - not found
current point (7, 9) - erased 1 point
current point (12, 10) - erased 3 points

vector points (after erasures):
(3, 4) (-2, -4) (-5, 6) (10, 2) (-9, -2) (-6, 4)
points.size(): 6
```

Class std::vector is undeniably the most useful of all STL sequence container classes. When deciding which sequence container to use for a particular algorithm, the ISO C++23 specification document states: "When choosing a container, remember vector is best; leave a comment to explain if you choose from the rest!" Regardless of whether you agree with this statement, most modern C++ programs utilize std::vector in a multiplicity of use cases, both ordinary and imaginative. This means that it's important for you to fully understand how to properly utilize this class. You'll study additional examples of std::vector usage later in this and subsequent chapters.

More Algorithms Using std::array and std::vector

Prior to C++20, programs were required to employ a different technique to remove all occurrences of an element value from a std::vector container. Listing 3-3-1 shows the source code for function Ch03_03_ex1(), which exemplifies the use of the erase-remove idiom for a std::vector. It's important for you to understand this software idiom since you're extremely likely to encounter it in pre-C++20 code.

Listing 3-3-1. Example Ch03_03 - Ch03_03_ex1()

```cpp
//----------------------------------------------------------------------
// Ch03_03_ex.cpp
//----------------------------------------------------------------------

#include <algorithm>
#include <array>
#include <string>
#include <vector>
#include "Ch03_03.h"
#include "MT.h"

void Ch03_03_ex1()
{
    const char* fmt = "{:6.1f}";
    constexpr size_t epl_max {10};
    constexpr double rem_val {-1.0};
    std::println("\nrem_val: {:.1f}", rem_val);

    // create test vectors
    std::vector<double> vec1 {10.0, 20.0, rem_val, 30.0, 40.0,
        rem_val, 50.0, rem_val, 60.0, 70.0};
    std::vector<double> vec2 {vec1};

    // using std::remove
    MT::print_ctr("\nvec1 (initial values):\n", vec1, fmt, 10);
    auto iter_rem = std::remove(vec1.begin(), vec1.end(), rem_val);
    MT::print_ctr("\nvec1 (after remove):\n", vec1, fmt, epl_max);
    std::println("vec1.size(): {:d}", vec1.size());

    // using std::vector::erase()
    auto num_erased1 = vec1.end() - iter_rem;
    vec1.erase(iter_rem, vec1.end());
    MT::print_ctr("\nvec1 (after erase):\n", vec1, fmt, epl_max);
    std::println("num_erased1: {:d}", num_erased1);
    std::println("vec1.size(): {:d}", vec1.size());

    // using std::erase (C++20)
```

```
    MT::print_ctr("\nvec2 (initial values):\n", vec2, fmt, 10);
    auto num_erased2 = std::erase(vec2, rem_val);
    MT::print_ctr("\nvec2 (after std::erase):\n", vec2, fmt, epl_max);
    std::println("num_erased2: {:d}", num_erased2);
    std::println("vec2.size(): {:d}", vec2.size());
}
```

Function Ch03_03_ex1() begins its execution with the creation of two type std::vector<double> vectors named vec1 and vec2. Note that rem_val occurs multiple times in each vector. The initial statement of the ensuing code block utilizes std::remove(vec1.begin(), vec1.end(), test_val) to "remove" all occurrences of rem_val from vec1. Figure 3-5 illustrates execution of this function in greater detail. Note that std::remove() didn't actually remove any elements from vec1; it merely overwrites any occurrence of rem_val by moving other elements toward the front of the container. Following execution of std::remove(), vec1 still contains n elements, but all element positions between iter_rem and vec1.end() contain unspecified values.[2] The ensuing vec1.erase(iter_rem, vec1.end()) statement removes all values from vec1 between [iter_rem, vec1.end()). Note that prior to execution of vec1.erase(), Ch03_03_ex1() utilized iterator arithmetic to calculate num_erased1.

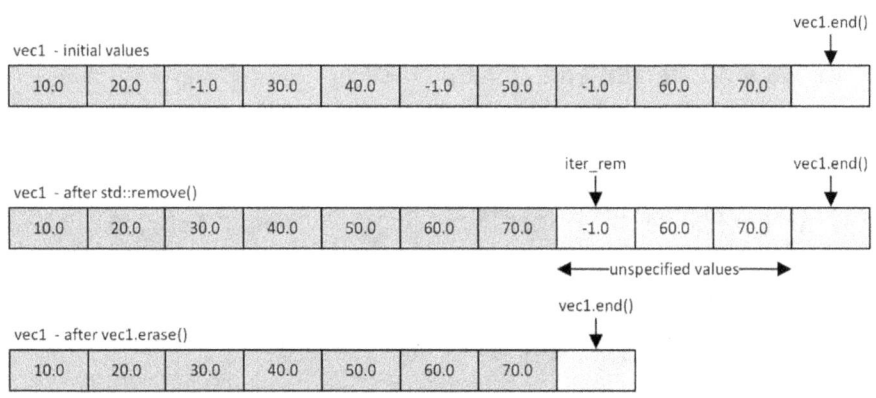

Figure 3-5. *Illustration of erase-remove idiom for container class* std::vector

---

[2] Elements at these locations can be dereferenced using an iterator (or accessed using operator[ ] or at()), but C++ does not guarantee any specific values.

The final code block utilizes std::erase() to perform the same operation and is shown for comparison purposes. Function std::erase() essentially implements the erase-remove idiom as a single algorithm.

For the final example of this chapter, let's look at a few algorithms that can be used to replace all occurrences of a value in a std::array or std::vector. Listing 3-3-2 shows the code for function Ch03_03_ex2(). Near the top of this function is a code block that initializes a std::array<std::string> of text values named arr1. Initialization of std::vector<std::string>> vec1 is next. Note that the constructor for vec1 utilizes iterators arr1.begin() and arr1.end(). Following execution of vec1's constructor, both arr1 and vec1 contain the same number of elements, and each element position contains the same string value.

Listing 3-3-2. Example Ch03_03 – Ch03_03_ex2()

```
void Ch03_03_ex2()
{
    const char* fmt = "{:15s}";
    constexpr size_t epl_max {6};

    // initialize test containers
    std::array<std::string, 12> arr1
    {
        "Hydrogen", "Helium", "Lithium", "Beryllium", "Boron", "Carbon",
        "Nitrogen", "Oxygen", "Fluorine", "Neon", "Sodium", "Magnesium",
    };
    MT::print_ctr("\narr1 (initial values):\n", arr1, fmt, epl_max);

    std::vector<std::string> vec1(arr1.begin(), arr1.end());
    MT::print_ctr("\nvec1 (initial values):\n", vec1, fmt, epl_max);

    // using std::replace and std::ranges::replace (C++20) with std::array
    std::replace(arr1.begin(), arr1.end(), "Neon", "NEON");
    std::ranges::replace(arr1, "Nitrogen", "NITROGEN");
    MT::print_ctr("\narr1 (after replace):\n", arr1, fmt, epl_max);

    // using std::replace and std::ranges::replace (C++20) with std::vector
    std::replace(vec1.begin(), vec1.end(), "Neon", "NEON");
    std::ranges::replace(vec1, "Nitrogen", "NITROGEN");
```

```
    MT::print_ctr("\nvec1 (after replace):\n", vec1, fmt, epl_max);

    // define unary predicate for later use
    auto replace_if_pred = [](std::string& s) { return s[0] == 'N'; };

    // using std::ranges::replace_if with std::array (C++20)
    std::ranges::replace_if(arr1, replace_if_pred, "########");
    MT::print_ctr("\narr1 (after replace_if):\n", arr1, fmt, epl_max);

    // using std::ranges::replace_if with std::vector (C++20)
    std::ranges::replace_if(vec1, replace_if_pred, "########");
    MT::print_ctr("\nvec1 (after replace_if):\n", vec1, fmt, epl_max);
}
```

The next code block utilizes STL algorithms `std::replace()` and `std::ranges::replace()` (C++20) to modify specific values within `arr1`. Like the sorting algorithms that you saw earlier in this chapter, `std::replace()` is a C++11 function that utilizes iterator arguments to define a range over which it will operate; the C++20 variant `std::ranges::replace()` is more convenient to employ when replacing an element value using the entire container. The ensuing code block also utilizes `std::replace()` and `std::ranges::replace()` to carry out the same operation using vec1. One important detail to note here is that except for the actual containers, both uses of `std::replace()` and `std::ranges::replace()` are identical. Many STL algorithms are designed to be used with a variety of container types.

Execution of `Ch03_03_ex2()` continues with the definition of a lambda expression named `replace_if_pred`. This expression requires a single argument of type `std::string&` and returns `true` if the first letter of string s equals `'N'`; otherwise, it returns `false`. The following code block utilizes `replace_if_pred` as an argument to `std::ranges_replace_if()`. This algorithm applies the specified predicate to each element of arr1. If the predicate returns `true`, the element is overwritten using "########". A predicate result of `false` leaves the element unaltered. The final code block in `Ch03_03_02()` also exploits `replace_if_pred` and `std::ranges::replace_if()` to perform the same replacement operation using vec1. Here are the results for example Ch03_03:

```
----- Results for example Ch03_03 -----

----- Ch03_03_ex1() -----

rem_val: -1.0

vec1 (initial values):
  10.0  20.0  -1.0  30.0  40.0  -1.0  50.0  -1.0  60.0  70.0

vec1 (after remove):
  10.0  20.0  30.0  40.0  50.0  60.0  70.0  -1.0  60.0  70.0
vec1.size(): 10

vec1 (after erase):
  10.0  20.0  30.0  40.0  50.0  60.0  70.0
num_erased1: 3
vec1.size(): 7

vec2 (initial values):
  10.0  20.0  -1.0  30.0  40.0  -1.0  50.0  -1.0  60.0  70.0

vec2 (after std::erase):
  10.0  20.0  30.0  40.0  50.0  60.0  70.0
num_erased2: 3
vec2.size(): 7

----- Ch03_03_ex2() -----

arr1 (initial values):
```

Hydrogen	Helium	Lithium	Beryllium	Boron	Carbon
Nitrogen	Oxygen	Fluorine	Neon	Sodium	Magnesium

vec1 (initial values):

Hydrogen	Helium	Lithium	Beryllium	Boron	Carbon
Nitrogen	Oxygen	Fluorine	Neon	Sodium	Magnesium

arr1 (after replace):

Hydrogen	Helium	Lithium	Beryllium	Boron	Carbon
NITROGEN	Oxygen	Fluorine	NEON	Sodium	Magnesium

vec1 (after replace):

| Hydrogen | Helium | Lithium | Beryllium | Boron | Carbon |
| NITROGEN | Oxygen | Fluorine | NEON | Sodium | Magnesium |

arr1 (after replace_if):

| Hydrogen | Helium | Lithium | Beryllium | Boron | Carbon |
| ######## | Oxygen | Fluorine | ######## | Sodium | Magnesium |

vec1 (after replace_if):

| Hydrogen | Helium | Lithium | Beryllium | Boron | Carbon |
| ######## | Oxygen | Fluorine | ######## | Sodium | Magnesium |

There are two takeaway points from the code in Ch03_03_ex2(). First, many STL algorithms accept lambda expression predicates that modify an algorithm's default behavior. Some STL algorithms like std::ranges::replace_if() require a predicate. Second, most STL algorithms can be applied to a variety of container types. For an algorithm to be usable with a specific container type, suitable iterator types must be supported by both the algorithm and container. You'll learn more about iterator types in Chapter 4.

Summary

Here are the key learning points for this chapter:

- A sequence container holds a collection of objects. Each object's position within the container is determined programmatically.

- There are five STL sequence container classes: std::array, std::vector, std::deque, std::list, and std::forward_list.

- Template class std::array is a sequence container whose size must be a compile-time constant. Objects can neither be inserted nor removed from a std::array.

- Template class std::vector is a sequence container whose size is specified at runtime. Objects can be inserted or removed anywhere from a std::vector; however, std::vector is most efficient when these operations are performed using the back end of the container.

- Both std::array and std::vector support indexed access to their elements using operator[] or member function at(). The latter throws an exception if it's used with an invalid index.

- Both std::array and std::vector support traversals using forward and reverse iterators.

- Both std::array and std::vector can be used with a variety of STL algorithms. This includes the classic algorithms of C++11 and the C++20 variants of namespace std::ranges.

CHAPTER 4

Sequence Containers – Part 2

This chapter covers additional sequence containers, including

- How to use `std::deque`
- How to use `std::list`
- How to use `std::forward_list`
- Iterators

The source code examples and accompanying explanations of this chapter focus on typical usages for sequence container classes `std::deque`, `std::list`, and `std::forward_list`. You'll also learn more about iterators and the various iterator categories.

Using std::deque

A `std::deque` (double-ended queue) is a vector-like sequence container that's optimized for insertions and removals at both ends. Programs often employ `std::deques` to implement algorithms that require last-in-first-out (LIFO) or first-in-first-out (FIFO) processing. Figure 4-1 illustrates the logical structure of a `std::deque`. Unlike a `std::vector`, the elements of a `std::deque` are not stored contiguously in a single block of memory but in multiple blocks, which facilitates faster dual-end insertions and removals. The downside of this scheme is higher memory usage and somewhat slower access for indexed references (e.g., `operator[]` and `at()`) compared to a `std::vector`.

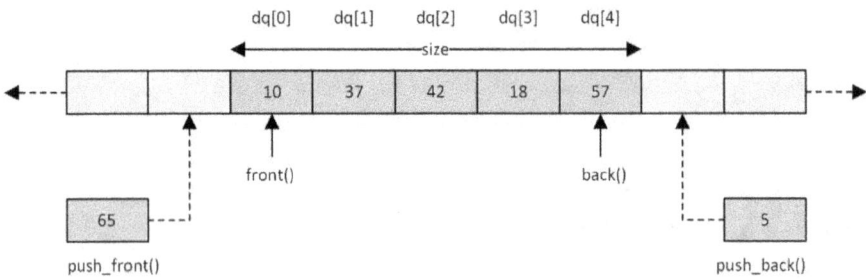

Figure 4-1. *Logical structure of a* `std::deque`

Source code example Ch04_01 illustrates how to perform ordinary operations using a `std::deque`. Listing 4-1-1 shows the code for `Ch04_01_ex1()`. In the opening code block of this function, the statement `std::deque<int> deq1 {10, 20, 30, 40, 50}` creates a `std::deque` that holds five objects of type `int` whose initial values are specified in the initializer list. The next statement, `std::deque<int> deq2 (deq1.size())`, instantiates a second `std:deque` of five `int`s, and each element is initialized to zero.

Listing 4-1-1. Example Ch04_01 - Ch04_01_ex1()

```
//------------------------------------------------------------------
// Ch04_01_ex.cpp
//------------------------------------------------------------------
#include <algorithm>
#include <array>
#include <deque>
#include <functional>
#include <string>
#include <version>
#include "Ch04_01.h"
#include "Line.h"
#include "MT.h"

void Ch04_01_ex1()
{
    const char* fmt = "{:5d} ";
```

```
    // create deques
    std::deque<int> deq1 {10, 20, 30, 40, 50};
    std::deque<int> deq2 (deq1.size());

    // access deque elements using operator[] and .at()
    for (size_t i = 0; i < deq1.size(); ++i)
        deq2[i] = deq1.at(i) * 5;

    MT::print_ctr("\ndeq1: ", deq1, fmt);
    MT::print_ctr("deq2: ", deq2, fmt);

    // create deques
    std::deque<long> deq3 {100, 200, 300, 400, 500, 600};
    std::deque<long> deq4(deq3.size(), 1000);

    // using iterators
    auto iter3 = deq3.begin();
    auto iter4 = deq4.begin();
    for (; iter3 != deq3.end(); ++iter3, ++iter4)
        *iter4 += *iter3 / 2;

    MT::print_ctr("\ndeq3: ", deq3, fmt);
    MT::print_ctr("deq4: ", deq4, fmt);
}
```

The subsequent code block spotlights the use of std::deque member functions operator[] and at(). Just like std::vector, the difference between these two is that the latter throws an exception if the supplied index is invalid. Skipping ahead a few lines, the statement std::deque<long> deq4(deq3.size(), 1000) instantiates a std::deque that holds deq3.size() elements and initializes each element to 1000. The final code block in Ch04_01_ex1() exercises iterators to carry out a simple arithmetic calculation using the elements of deq3 and deq4.

Listing 4-1-2 shows the code for Ch04_01_ex2(). This function utilizes std::deque::push_back() and std::deque::push_front() to insert elements into the back and front ends of deq1. To remove an element from the back end of a std::deque, Ch04_01_ex2() employs member function pop_back(). The corresponding std::deque front-end removal function is pop_front(). The final code block in Ch04_01_ex2() exploits deq1.insert(deq1.begin() + 2, arr1.begin(), arr1.end()) to insert new elements into deq1 immediately before deq[2]. One item that should be noted here is that except for push_front() and pop_front(), the member functions and operators utilized thus far to perform std::deque manipulations are the same as the ones you learned about in the previous chapter for std::vector.

Listing 4-1-2. Example Ch04_01 - Ch04_01_ex2()

```
void Ch04_01_ex2()
{
    std::deque<double> deq1 {};
    const char* fmt {"{:7.1f} "};

    // using deque::push_back
    deq1.push_back(50.0);
    deq1.push_back(60.0);
    deq1.push_back(70.0);
    deq1.push_back(80.0);
    MT::print_ctr("\ndeq1 (after push_back operations):\n", deq1, fmt);

    // using deque::push_front
    deq1.push_front(40.0);
    deq1.push_front(30.0);
    deq1.push_front(20.0);
    deq1.push_front(10.0);
    MT::print_ctr("\ndeq1 (after push_front operations):\n", deq1, fmt);

    // using deque::pop_back
    deq1.pop_back();
    deq1.pop_back();
    MT::print_ctr("\ndeq1 (after pop_back operations):\n", deq1, fmt);

    // using deque::pop_front
    deq1.pop_front();
    deq1.pop_front();
    MT::print_ctr("\ndeq1 (after pop_front operations):\n", deq1, fmt);
```

```cpp
    // add elements to "middle" of deq1 using insert
    std::array<double, 5> arr1 {1000.0, 2000.0, 3000.0, 4000.0, 5000.0};
    deq1.insert(deq1.begin() + 2, arr1.begin(), arr1.end());
    MT::print_ctr("\ndeq1 (after insert):\n", deq1, fmt);
}
```

The next example function, named Ch04_01_ex3(), illustrates the use of std::deque member functions emplace_front() and emplace_back() using template class Line. Listing 4-1-3 shows the source code for Ch04_01_ex3(), while the source code for class Line was previously shown in Listing 1-7-2.

Listing 4-1-3. Example Ch04_01 – Ch04_01_ex3()

```cpp
void Ch04_01_ex3()
{
    using line_t = Line<double>;

    const char* fmt = "{} ";
    constexpr size_t epl_max {2};

    // using deque::emplace_front
    std::deque<line_t> deq1 {};
    deq1.emplace_front(line_t {0.0, 0.0, 3.0, 4.0});
    deq1.emplace_front(line_t {0.0, 1.0, 3.0, 4.0});
    deq1.emplace_front(line_t {1.0, 0.0, 3.0, 4.0});
    deq1.emplace_front(line_t {1.0, 1.0, 3.0, 4.0});
    MT::print_ctr("\ndeq1 (initial values):\n", deq1, fmt, epl_max);

    // using deque::emplace_back
    std::deque<line_t> deq2 {};
    deq2.emplace_back(line_t {10.0, 10.0, 30.0, 40.0});
    deq2.emplace_back(line_t {10.0, 20.0, 30.0, 40.0});
    deq2.emplace_back(line_t {20.0, 10.0, 30.0, 40.0});
    deq2.emplace_back(line_t {20.0, 20.0, 30.0, 40.0});
    MT::print_ctr("\ndeq2: (initial values):\n", deq2, fmt, epl_max);
```

CHAPTER 4   SEQUENCE CONTAINERS – PART 2

```
    // using deque::insert_range (C++23)
    auto iter_insert = deq1.begin() + deq1.size() / 2;
#ifdef __cpp_lib_containers_ranges
    deq1.insert_range(iter_insert, deq2);
#else
    deq1.insert(iter_insert, deq2.begin(), deq2.end());
#endif
    MT::print_ctr("\ndeq1 (after insert_range):\n", deq1, fmt, epl_max);
}
```

Function Ch04_01_ex3() opens with a using line_t = Line<double> statement that defines an alias line type for this example to improve readability. Following the declaration of deq1, Ch04_01_ex3() employs four emplace_front() calls to insert four line_t objects into deq1. Member function emplace_front() differs from push_front() in that the former constructs the object at the proper position within the container. Emplace member functions are often faster than declaring an object and performing a discrete push since this requires execution of both a constructor and a copy operation. The ensuing code block illustrates the use of emplace_back(), which performs an emplace construction at the back end of deq1. Following the emplacement operations, Ch04_01_ex3() utilizes std::deque::insert_range() (C++23) to insert additional line_t objects into deq1. Note the use of the preprocessor statement #ifdef __cpp_lib_containers_ranges to verify compiler support for insert_range(). If the current C++ implementation doesn't support insert_range(), Ch04_01_ex3() uses std::deque::insert() to carry out the same operation.

In Listing 4-1-4, function Ch04_01_ex4() employs function std::deque::append_range() (C++23) to append elements from array arr1 to the end of deq1. Note that this code block also utilizes macro __cpp_lib_containers_ranges to confirm compiler support for append_range().

Listing 4-1-4. Example Ch04_01 – Ch04_01_ex4()

```
void Ch04_01_ex4()
{
    const char* fmt {"{:5s}"};

    // initialize deque of strings
    std::deque<std::string> deq1 {"Jan", "Feb", "Mar", "Apr",
    "May", "Jun"};
```

```cpp
    MT::print_ctr("\ndeq1 (initial values):\n", deq1, fmt);

    // using append_range (C++23)
    std::array<std::string, 6> arr1 {"Jul", "Aug", "Sep", "Oct",
    "Nov", "Dec"};
#ifdef __cpp_lib_containers_ranges
    deq1.append_range(arr1);
#else
    deq1.insert(deq1.end(), arr1.begin(), arr1.end());
#endif
    MT::print_ctr("\ndeq1 (after append_range):\n", deq1, fmt);

    // using std::sort
    std::sort(deq1.begin(), deq1.end());
    MT::print_ctr("\ndeq1 (after sort using operator<):\n", deq1, fmt);

    std::sort(deq1.begin(), deq1.end(), std::greater<>());
    MT::print_ctr("deq1 (after sort using operator>):\n", deq1, fmt);

    // using std::ranges::sort
    std::deque deq2 {deq1};
    std::ranges::sort(deq2);
    MT::print_ctr("\ndeq2 (after ranges::sort using operator<):\n",
    deq2, fmt);

    std::ranges::sort(deq2, std::greater<>());
    MT::print_ctr("deq2 (after ranges::sort using operator>):\n",
    deq2, fmt);

    // using relational operators
    std::println("\ndeq1 == deq2: {:s}", deq1 == deq2);
    std::swap(deq1[5], deq1[7]);
    std::println("deq1 <= deq2: {:s}", deq1 <= deq2);
    std::println("deq1 >= deq2: {:s}", deq1 >= deq2);
}
```

Following the insertions, Ch04_01_ex4() exercises std::sort() to sort the elements of deq1 in ascending order. Recall that the default relational operator utilized by std::sort() is operator<. The next call to std::sort() utilizes function object std::greater<>() as an argument to sort the elements of deq1 in descending. Function object std::greater<>() is a wrapper for a class's operator> and is often utilized to override the default behavior of std::sort() and other algorithm functions. The next code block utilizes algorithm std::ranges::sort() (C++20) to perform the same sorting operations using deq2. It's important to recognize here that except for the container type, Ch04_01_ex4()'s use of std::sort() and std::ranges::sort() are identical to the usages that you saw in example Ch03_01 for std::vector.

The final code block of Ch04_01_ex4() illustrates the use of relational operators with deques. These expressions perform lexicographical compares using corresponding element positions of deq1 and deq2.

Listing 4-1-5 shows the code for the concluding function of example Ch04_01. Following the creation of std::deques deq1 and deq2, Ch04_01_ex5() exercises std::remove() and std::deque::erase() to remove all occurrences of rem_value from deq1. This code is the std::deque counterpart of the std::vector erase-remove idiom that you learned about in Chapter 3 (see example Ch03_03 and Figure 3-5). The ensuing code block utilizes function std::erase() (C++23) to carry out the same erase operation using deq2.

Listing 4-1-5. Example Ch04_01 - Ch04_01_ex5()

```
void Ch04_01_ex5()
{
    const char* fmt = "{:6.1f}";
    constexpr size_t epl_max {10};
    constexpr double rem_val {-1.0};
    std::println("\nrem_val: {:.1f}", rem_val);

    // create test deques
    std::deque<double> deq1 {10.0, 20.0, rem_val, 30.0, 40.0,
        rem_val, 50.0, rem_val, 60.0, 70.0};
    std::deque<double> deq2 {deq1};

    MT::print_ctr("\ndeq1 (initial values):\n", deq1, fmt, 10);
    std::println("deq1.size(): {:d}", deq1.size());
```

```cpp
    // using std::remove and std::deque::erase (erase-remove idiom)
    auto iter_rem = std::remove(deq1.begin(), deq1.end(), rem_val);
    MT::print_ctr("\ndeq1 (after std::remove):\n", deq1, fmt, epl_max);
    std::println("deq1.size(): {:d}", deq1.size());

    auto num_erased1 = deq1.end() - iter_rem;
    deq1.erase(iter_rem, deq1.end());
    MT::print_ctr("\ndeq1 (after erase):\n", deq1, fmt, epl_max);
    std::println("num_erased1: {:d}", num_erased1);
    std::println("deq1.size(): {:d}", deq1.size());

    // using std::erase (C++20)
    MT::print_ctr("\ndeq2 (initial values):\n", deq2, fmt, 10);
    std::println("deq2.size(): {:d}", deq2.size());
    auto num_erased2 = std::erase(deq2, rem_val);
    MT::print_ctr("\ndeq2 (after std::erase):\n", deq2, fmt, epl_max);
    std::println("num_erased2: {:d}", num_erased2);
    std::println("deq2.size(): {:d}", deq2.size());
}
```

Here are the results for example Ch04_01:

```
----- Results for example Ch04_01 -----

----- Ch04_01_ex1() -----

deq1:      10    20    30    40    50
deq2:      50   100   150   200   250

deq3:     100   200   300   400   500   600
deq4:    1050  1100  1150  1200  1250  1300

----- Ch04_01_ex2() -----

deq1 (after push_back operations):
    50.0    60.0    70.0    80.0
deq1 (after push_front operations):
    10.0    20.0    30.0    40.0    50.0    60.0    70.0    80.0
```

deq1 (after pop_back operations):
   10.0   20.0   30.0   40.0   50.0   60.0

deq1 (after pop_front operations):
   30.0   40.0   50.0   60.0

deq1 (after insert):
   30.0   40.0   1000.0   2000.0   3000.0   4000.0   5000.0   50.0   60.0

----- Ch04_01_ex3() -----

deq1 (initial values):
[(1, 1, 3, 4) | (3.6056, 1.5000)] [(1, 0, 3, 4) | (4.4721, 2.0000)]
[(0, 1, 3, 4) | (4.2426, 1.0000)] [(0, 0, 3, 4) | (5.0000, 1.3333)]

deq2: (initial values):
[(10, 10, 30, 40) | (36.0555, 1.5000)] [(10, 20, 30, 40) | (28.2843, 1.0000)]
[(20, 10, 30, 40) | (31.6228, 3.0000)] [(20, 20, 30, 40) | (22.3607, 2.0000)]

deq1 (after insert_range):
[(1, 1, 3, 4) | (3.6056, 1.5000)] [(1, 0, 3, 4) | (4.4721, 2.0000)]
[(10, 10, 30, 40) | (36.0555, 1.5000)] [(10, 20, 30, 40) | (28.2843, 1.0000)]
[(20, 10, 30, 40) | (31.6228, 3.0000)] [(20, 20, 30, 40) | (22.3607, 2.0000)]
[(0, 1, 3, 4) | (4.2426, 1.0000)] [(0, 0, 3, 4) | (5.0000, 1.3333)]

----- Ch04_01_ex4() -----

deq1 (initial values):
Jan Feb Mar Apr May Jun

deq1 (after append_range):
Jan Feb Mar Apr May Jun Jul Aug Sep Oct Nov Dec

deq1 (after sort using operator<):
Apr Aug Dec Feb Jan Jul Jun Mar May Nov Oct Sep
deq1 (after sort using operator>):
Sep Oct Nov May Mar Jun Jul Jan Feb Dec Aug Apr

```
deq2 (after ranges::sort using operator<):
Apr  Aug  Dec  Feb  Jan  Jul  Jun  Mar  May  Nov  Oct  Sep
deq2 (after ranges::sort using operator>):
Sep  Oct  Nov  May  Mar  Jun  Jul  Jan  Feb  Dec  Aug  Apr

deq1 == deq2: true
deq1 <= deq2: true
deq1 >= deq2: false

----- Ch04_01_ex5() -----

rem_val: -1.0

deq1 (initial values):
  10.0  20.0  -1.0  30.0  40.0  -1.0  50.0  -1.0  60.0  70.0
deq1.size(): 10

deq1 (after std::remove):
  10.0  20.0  30.0  40.0  50.0  60.0  70.0  -1.0  60.0  70.0
deq1.size(): 10

deq1 (after erase):
  10.0  20.0  30.0  40.0  50.0  60.0  70.0
num_erased1: 3
deq1.size(): 7

deq2 (initial values):
  10.0  20.0  -1.0  30.0  40.0  -1.0  50.0  -1.0  60.0  70.0
deq2.size(): 10

deq2 (after std::erase):
  10.0  20.0  30.0  40.0  50.0  60.0  70.0
num_erased2: 3
deq2.size(): 7
```

CHAPTER 4 SEQUENCE CONTAINERS – PART 2

Compared to container class std::vector, std::deque provides additional capabilities that are advantageous in many applications. As mentioned earlier, std::deques are often utilized to implement algorithms that require LIFO or FIFO processing. You probably already know that stacks and queues are exemplars of LIFO and FIFO containers, respectively. Before using a std::deque as a stack or queue, you should consider using a container adaptor class such as std::stack and std::queue. You'll study container adaptor classes in Chapter 9.

Using std::list

A std::list is a sequential container that's an abstraction of a doubly linked list. Figure 4-2 illustrates the logical structure of a std::list. Like a std::deque, std::lists support fast constant-time insertions and removals using either container end. Mid-container insertions and removals are also performed in constant time since these operations are achievable using pointer manipulations instead of object copies or moves. And unlike the other sequence containers that you've learned about thus far, inserting or removing elements from a std::list doesn't invalidate any iterators, except those that reference a removed element.

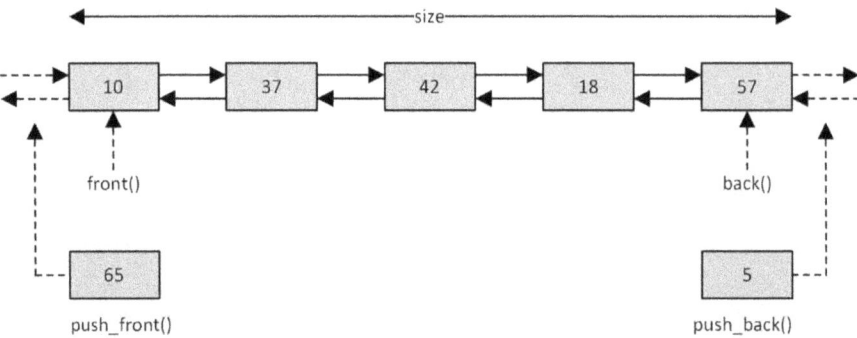

Figure 4-2. Logical structure of a std::list

A std::list container does not support random access operations, which means a program can't access its elements using operator[] or at(). A program must exploit iterators to traverse a std::list container, but this movement can be carried out in either direction. Lack of random access operations also means that some STL algorithms can't be used with std::lists; however, class std::list defines suitable alternatives for some of these algorithms.

Source code example Ch04_02 demonstrates how to carry out common operations using std::lists. Listing 4-2-1 shows the source code for function Ch04_02_ex1(). In the opening code block, note that the declaration of list1 includes an initializer list, which specifies the initial elements. The next code block utilizes push_front() and push_back() to add an element to the front and back ends of list1, respectively. A program can also employ pop_front() and pop_back() to remove elements from a std::list.

Listing 4-2-1. Example Ch04_02 – Ch04_02_ex1()

```
//-------------------------------------------------------------------
// Ch04_02_ex.cpp
//-------------------------------------------------------------------

#include <algorithm>
#include <array>
#include <iterator>
#include <list>
#include <stdexcept>
#include "Ch04_02.h"
#include "MT.h"
#include "Point2D.h"

void Ch04_02_ex1()
{
    const char* fmt = "{:<5d}";
    std::list<int> list1 {20, 30, 40, 40, 50, 60, 70, 70, 70, 80};
    MT::print_ctr("list1 (initial values):\n", list1, fmt);

    // using list::push_front and list::push_back
    list1.push_front(10);
    list1.push_back(90);
    MT::print_ctr("\nlist1 (after push_front, push_back):\n", list1, fmt);
    std::print("list1.size():   {:d}\n", list1.size());
    std::print("list1.front():  {:d}\n", list1.front());
    std::print("list1.back():   {:d}\n", list1.back());
```

```cpp
    // using std::advance
    auto iter_mid = list1.begin();
    std::advance(iter_mid, list1.size() / 2);

    // using list::insert
    std::array<int, 3> more_vals {-40, -50, -60};
    list1.insert(iter_mid, more_vals.begin(), more_vals.end());
    MT::print_ctr("\nlist1 (after insert):\n", list1, fmt);
    std::print("list1.size():  {:d}\n", list1.size());
    std::print("list1.front(): {:d}\n", list1.front());
    std::print("list1.back():  {:d}\n", list1.back());

    // using remove
    list1.remove(40);
    list1.remove(70);
    MT::print_ctr("\nlist1 (after remove):\n", list1, fmt);
    std::print("list1.size():  {:d}\n", list1.size());
    std::print("list1.front(): {:d}\n", list1.front());
    std::print("list1.back():  {:d}\n", list1.back());

    // using remove_if
    auto rem_op = [] (int x) { return x % 60 == 0; };
    list1.remove_if(rem_op);
    MT::print_ctr("\nlist1 (after remove_if):\n", list1, fmt);
    std::print("list1.size():  {:d}\n", list1.size());
    std::print("list1.front(): {:d}\n", list1.front());
    std::print("list1.back():  {:d}\n", list1.back());
}
```

The statement auto iter_mid = list1.begin() initializes an iterator to the first element in list1. The next expression, std::advance(iter_mid, list1.size() / 2), adjusts iter_mid so that it points to the middle element in list1. Function std::advance() is an iterator helper function that increments iter_mid by list.size1() / 2. The reason std::advance() is utilized here instead of calculating iter_mid + list1.size() / 2 directly is that class std::list iterators only support operator++ and operator--, both prefix and postfix. You'll learn more about the different iterator types and which operations they support later in this chapter. For the current example, using std::advance() is more convenient than having to code a for loop that performs ++iter_mid list1.size() / 2 times.[1]

The next code block employs std::list::insert() to insert the elements from std::array more_vals into list1. The elements are inserted into list1 before iter_mid. If you scan ahead to the results section for example Ch04_02, you'll notice that the elements from move_vals are inserted before value 50.

Examples Ch03_03 and Ch04_01 exploited global algorithm std::remove() to remove all occurrences of a value from a std::vector and std::deque. This same function can also be utilized to perform removals using a std::list. However, the next code block applies std::list::remove() to remove all occurrences of 40 and 70 from list1. Some STL container classes define member functions that carry out the same operation as a global algorithm. Whenever this occurs, you should favor the use of the member function instead of the global algorithm since the former is likely to be optimized for the container's internal data structures. Another advantage of using std::list::remove() here is that this function also erases elements from the list, which means a subsequent call to std::list::erase() is not necessary.

The final code block of Ch04_02_ex1() exercises std::line::remove_if() instead of std::remove_if() to remove all elements from list1 that return true for predicate rem_pred.

Listing 4-2-2 shows the source code for Ch04_02_ex2(), which demonstrates the use of std::list::splice().

Listing 4-2-2. Example Ch04_02 - Ch04_02_ex2()

```
void Ch04_02_ex2()
{
    const char* fmt = "{:s} ";

    // create lists
    std::list<std::string> list1 {"Jan", "Feb", "Mar", "Apr",
        "Sep", "Oct", "Nov", "Dec"};
    std::list<std::string> list2 {"May", "Jun", "Jul", "Aug"};
```

---

[1] Function std::advance() essentially performs this calculation.

```
    MT::print_ctr("\nlist1 (initial values): ", list1, fmt);
    MT::print_ctr("list2 (initial values): ", list2, fmt);

    // using list::splice
    auto iter_splice = list1.begin();
    std::advance(iter_splice, 4);

    list1.splice(iter_splice, list2);
    MT::print_ctr("\nlist1 (after splice): ", list1, fmt);
    MT::print_ctr("list2 (after splice): ", list2, fmt);
}
```

Following initialization of list1 and list2, Ch04_02_ex2() exercises std::advanced() to calculate an arbitrary point in list1 for the splice. The next statement, list1.splice(iter_splice, list2), inserts list2 into list1 just before iter_splice as shown in Figure 4-3. Note in this figure that following the splice operation, list2 is empty. The splicing of two std::lists is a fast operation since it doesn't require any element copy or move operations; it merely updates the internal node pointers of the two std::lists.

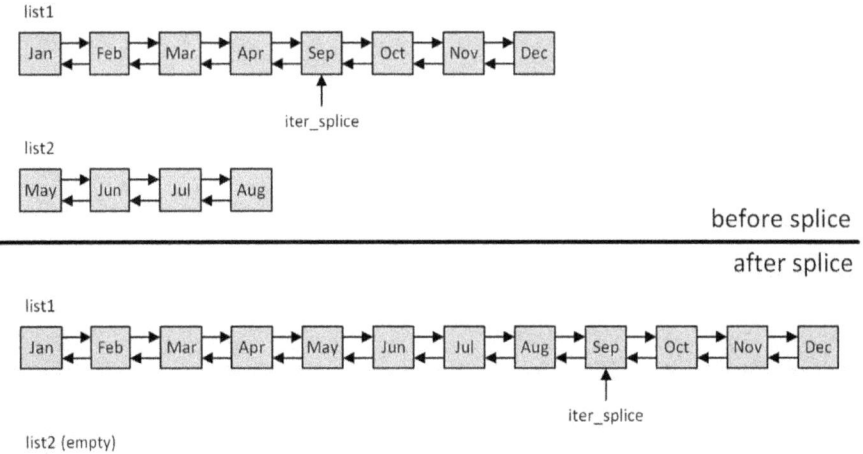

Figure 4-3. *List splicing using* std::list

In Listing 4-2-3, function Ch04_02_ex3() performs a simple calculation using containers of type line_t (alias for List<Point2D<double>>) and iterators (see Listing 1-1-4 for class Point2D). Near the top of Listing 4-2-3 are the declarations of three std::lists named list1, list2, and list3. Note that list3 contains list1.size() elements, and these are initialized using the Point2D's default constructor.

Listing 4-2-3. Example Ch04_02 – Ch04_02_ex3()

```
void Ch04_02_ex3()
{
    const char* fmt = "{} ";
    constexpr size_t epl_max {4};

    // create lists
    using list_t = std::list<Point2D<double>>;
    list_t list1 { {10.0, 10.0}, {20.0, 20.0}, {30.0, 30.0},
    {40.0, 40.0} };
    list_t list2 { {-1.0, -2.0}, {-3.0, -4.0}, {-5.0, -6.0},
    {-7.0, -8.0} };
    list_t list3 (list1.size());

    if (list1.size() != list2.size())
        throw std::runtime_error("Ch04_02_ex3() - list size error");

    MT::print_ctr("\nlist1 (initial values): ", list1, fmt, epl_max);
    MT::print_ctr("list2 (initial values): ", list2, fmt, epl_max);
    MT::print_ctr("list3 (initial values): ", list3, fmt, epl_max);

    // using iterators
    auto iter1 = list1.cbegin();
    auto iter2 = list2.cbegin();
    auto iter3 = list3.begin();
    for (; iter1 != list1.cend(); ++iter1, ++iter2)
        *iter3++ = *iter1 + *iter2;

    MT::print_ctr("\nlist3 (after for loop): ", list3, fmt, epl_max);
}
```

Prior to the for loop, Ch04_02_ex3() initializes iterators iter1, iter2, and iter3, all of which point to the first elements of their respective lists. Iterators iter1 and iter2 are initialized using cbegin(), which means they're const iterators and can only be used to read elements from list1 and list2. Besides cbegin(), most container classes define const iterator functions cend(), crbegin(), and crend(). Just like a const pointer, using a `const` iterator precludes inadvertent value modifications and may enable the compiler to generate more efficient code. The arbitrary calculation within the `for` loop adds corresponding `Point2D` elements from `list1` and `list2` and saves the sum in `list3`.

The final `std::list` example, shown in Listing 4-2-4, utilizes `emplace_back()` and `emplace_front()` to initialize two lists of type `std::list<std::string>>`. Following initialization of these lists, `Ch04_02_ex4()` utilizes `std::list::sort()` to sort the elements of `list1` and `list2`. Global function `std::sort()` cannot be used here since it requires random access iterators (i.e., an iterator that defines `operator[]`), which class `std::list` does not support. Function `std::list::sort()` performs a stable sort[2] using `operator<`. An overload of `std::list::sort()` that accepts a binary compare predicate is also available. You'll learn more about sorting algorithms in Chapter 12.

Listing 4-2-4. Example Ch04_02 - Ch04_02_ex4()

```
void Ch04_02_ex4()
{
    const char* fmt = "{:14s} ";
    constexpr size_t epl_max {5};

    // using list::emplace_back and list::emplace_front
    std::list<std::string> list1 {};
    std::list<std::string> list2 {};
    list1.emplace_back("Alanine");
    list2.emplace_back("Arginine");
    list1.emplace_front("Asparagine");
    list2.emplace_front("Aspartate");
    list1.emplace_back("Cysteine");
    list2.emplace_back("Glutamine");
    list1.emplace_front("Glutamate");
    list2.emplace_front("Glycine");
    list1.emplace_back("Histidine");
    list2.emplace_back("Isoleucine");
```

---

[2] A stable sort preserves the order of equivalent elements.

```
    list1.emplace_front("Leucine");
    list2.emplace_front("Lysine");
    list1.emplace_back("Methionine");
    list2.emplace_back("Phenylalanine");
    list1.emplace_front("Proline");
    list2.emplace_front("Serine");
    list1.emplace_back("Threonine");
    list2.emplace_back("Tryptophan");
    list1.emplace_front("Tyrosine");
    list2.emplace_front("Valine");

    MT::print_ctr("\nlist1 (initial values):\n", list1, fmt, epl_max);
    MT::print_ctr("\nlist2 (initial values):\n", list2, fmt, epl_max);

    // using list::sort
    list1.sort();
    list2.sort();
    MT::print_ctr("\nlist1 (after sort):\n", list1, fmt, epl_max);
    MT::print_ctr("\nlist2 (after sort):\n", list2, fmt, epl_max);

    // using list::merge
    list1.merge(list2);
    MT::print_ctr("\nlist1 (after merge):\n", list1, fmt, epl_max);
    MT::print_ctr("\nlist2 (after merge):\n", list2, fmt, epl_max);

    // using list::reverse
    list1.reverse();
    MT::print_ctr("\nlist1 (after reverse):\n", list1, fmt, epl_max);
}
```

Following the sorts of list1 and list2, ChO4_02_ex4() utilizes list1.merge(list2) to merge list2 into list1. Member function std::list::merge() only works with sorted lists. Like the splice operation that you saw earlier, std::list::merge() updates internal pointers of the two std::lists; it does not execute any object copy or move operations. Following execution of list1.merge(list2), list1 contains all elements from the pre-merger lists and list2 is empty. Note in the results section that the

CHAPTER 4   SEQUENCE CONTAINERS – PART 2

elements of list1 are sorted. The final code block of Ch04_02_ex2() demonstrates how to use list1.reverse(), which reverses the order of elements in list1. Here are the results for example Ch04_02:

```
----- Results for example Ch04_02 -----
----- Ch04_02_ex1() -----
list1 (initial values):
20   30   40   40   50   60   70   70   70   80

list1 (after push_front, push_back):
10   20   30   40   40   50   60   70   70   70   80   90
list1.size():   12
list1.front():  10
list1.back():   90

list1 (after insert):
10   20   30   40   40   50   -40   -50   -60   60   70   70   70   80   90
list1.size():   15
list1.front():  10
list1.back():   90

list1 (after remove):
10   20   30   50   -40   -50   -60   60   80   90
list1.size():   10
list1.front():  10
list1.back():   90

list1 (after remove_if):
10   20   30   50   -40   -50   80   90
list1.size():   8
list1.front():  10
list1.back():   90

----- Ch04_02_ex2() -----

list1 (initial values): Jan Feb Mar Apr Sep Oct Nov Dec
list2 (initial values): May Jun Jul Aug
```

```
list1 (after splice): Jan Feb Mar Apr May Jun Jul Aug Sep Oct Nov Dec
list2 (after splice): <empty>

----- Ch04_02_ex3() -----

list1 (initial values): (10, 10) (20, 20) (30, 30) (40, 40)
list2 (initial values): (-1, -2) (-3, -4) (-5, -6) (-7, -8)
list3 (initial values): (0, 0) (0, 0) (0, 0) (0, 0)

list3 (after for loop): (9, 8) (17, 16) (25, 24) (33, 32)

----- Ch04_02_ex4() -----

list1 (initial values):
Tyrosine        Proline         Leucine         Glutamate       Asparagine
Alanine         Cysteine        Histidine       Methionine      Threonine

list2 (initial values):
Valine          Serine          Lysine          Glycine         Aspartate
Arginine        Glutamine       Isoleucine      Phenylalanine   Tryptophan

list1 (after sort):
Alanine         Asparagine      Cysteine        Glutamate       Histidine
Leucine         Methionine      Proline         Threonine       Tyrosine

list2 (after sort):
Arginine        Aspartate       Glutamine       Glycine         Isoleucine
Lysine          Phenylalanine   Serine          Tryptophan      Valine

list1 (after merge):
Alanine         Arginine        Asparagine      Aspartate       Cysteine
Glutamate       Glutamine       Glycine         Histidine       Isoleucine
Leucine         Lysine          Methionine      Phenylalanine   Proline
Serine          Threonine       Tryptophan      Tyrosine        Valine

list2 (after merge):
<empty>
```

list1 (after reverse):
Valine	Tyrosine	Tryptophan	Threonine	Serine
Proline	Phenylalanine	Methionine	Lysine	Leucine
Isoleucine	Histidine	Glycine	Glutamine	Glutamate
Cysteine	Aspartate	Asparagine	Arginine	Alanine

The primary advantage of container `std::list` compared to `std::vector` and `std::deque` is that class `std::list` performs fast element insertions and removals without invalidating existing iterators, except for the removed element. Operations such as merging, sorting, and splicing are also relatively fast since these operations are carried out sans any element copies or moves. The one notable drawback of `std::list` is its lack of random access operations.

Using std::forward_list

Container class `std::forward_list` is an abstraction of a singly linked list as shown in Figure 4-4. Operationally, a `std::forward_list` resembles a `std::list` in that element insertions and removals are relatively fast since no copy or move operations are performed; only internal pointers are manipulated. However, a `std::forward_list` can only be traversed using forward iterators. Bidirectional iterators like those of `std::list` are not supported. The lack of bidirectional iterator support also means that a `std::forward_list` does not support common container member functions including `rbegin()` and `rend()`. There's also no `size()` function. More about this later. From a resource perspective, a `std::forward_list` is marginally better than a `std::list`, both in terms of memory space and execution time.

CHAPTER 4   SEQUENCE CONTAINERS – PART 2

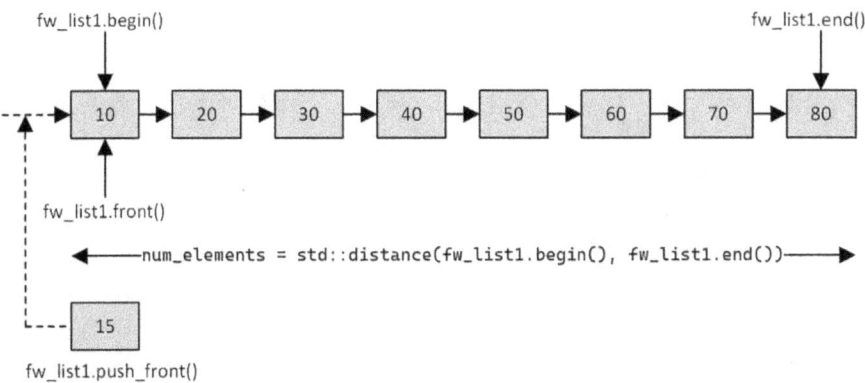

Figure 4-4. *Logical structure of a* `std::forward_list`

Listing 4-3-1 shows the source code for the first function of source code example Ch04_03. In this listing, function Ch04_03_ex1() commences its execution with the creation of a std::forward_list named fw_list1. Next is a series of push_front() calls that add a few more elements to the front end of fw_list1. You can also use pop_front() to remove an element from the front of a std::forward_list. It warrants mentioning here that std::forward_list doesn't support back-end insertions or removals, which means that push_back() and pop_back() are not defined.

Listing 4-3-1. Example Ch04_03 – Ch04_03_ex1()

```
//-------------------------------------------------------------------------
// Ch04_03_ex.cpp
//-------------------------------------------------------------------------

#include <array>
#include <forward_list>
#include <functional>
#include <iterator>
#include <string>
#include "Ch04_03.h"
#include "MT.h"

void Ch04_03_ex1()
{
    const char* fmt = "{:3d} ";
```

```cpp
    // create forward_list
    std::forward_list<int> fw_list1 {10, 20, 30, 40, 50, 60, 70, 80};
    MT::print_ctr("\nfw_list1 (initial values):\n", fw_list1, fmt);

    // using forward_list::push_front
    fw_list1.push_front(15);
    fw_list1.push_front(25);
    fw_list1.push_front(35);
    fw_list1.push_front(45);
    fw_list1.push_front(55);
    fw_list1.push_front(65);
    fw_list1.push_front(75);
    MT::print_ctr("\nfw_list1 (after push_front):\n", fw_list1, fmt);

    // calculate num_elements
    auto num_elements = std::distance(fw_list1.begin(), fw_list1.end());
    std::println("num_elements: {:d}", num_elements);

    // using forward_list::sort
    fw_list1.sort();
    MT::print_ctr("\nlist1 (after sort):\n", fw_list1, fmt);

    // using forward_list::reverse
    fw_list1.reverse();
    MT::print_ctr("\nlist1 (after reverse):\n", fw_list1, fmt);
}
```

As mentioned earlier, class std::forward_list doesn't define a size() function. The reason for this is that maintaining an element count would burden all instances of std::forward_list with additional execution overhead, including use cases where it's not needed.[3] The next code block in Ch04_03_ex1() demonstrates the use of helper function std::distance() to calculate the number of elements in a std::forward_list. In the current example, std::distance() essentially counts the number of iterator operator++ executions needed to traverse fw_list1 from begin() to end().

---

[3] The primary design objective for class std::forward_list is zero overhead, both space and time, relative to a hand-coded C-style singly linked list. Maintaining an element count would compromise this objective.

The time required to do this will, of course, vary depending on the number of elements in fw_list1. For use cases where determining (in constant time) the number of elements in a std::forward_list is critical, you should consider using a std::list instead of a std::forward_list.

The next code block in Ch04_03_ex1() demonstrates the use of std::forward_list::sort(). Like class std::list, global algorithm std::sort() cannot be used with instances of std::forward_list since this class doesn't support bidirectional iterators. The final code block of Ch04_03_ex1() utilizes std::forward_list::reverse() to reverse the elements of fw_list1.

Function Ch04_03_ex2(), shown in Listing 4-3-2, starts with the creation of two lists of type fw_list_t (alias for std::forward_list<std::string>). The code blocks that follow the creation of fw_list1 and fw_list2 demonstrate the use of std::forward_list::splice_after(). In this example, execution of splice_after(iter_splice, fw_list2) inserts fw_list2 into fw_list1 immediately after string element "tangerine". Note that std::advance() is applied to calculate the correct splice position. Following the splice_after() operation, fw_list1 contains nine std::string elements, while fw_list2 is empty.

Listing 4-3-2. Example Ch04_03 – Ch04_03_ex2()

```
void Ch04_03_ex2()
{
    const char* fmt = "{:s} ";
    constexpr size_t epl {6};
    using fw_list_t = std::forward_list<std::string>;

    // initialize lists
    fw_list_t fw_list1 {"lemon", "lime", "orange", "tangerine",
    "grapefruit"};
    MT::print_ctr("\nfw_list1 (initial values):\n", fw_list1, fmt, epl);

    fw_list_t fw_list2 {"raspberry", "strawberry", "blueberry",
    "blackberry"};
    MT::print_ctr("\nfw_list2 (initial values):\n", fw_list2, fmt, epl);

    // using forward_list::splice
    auto iter_splice = fw_list1.begin();
    std::advance(iter_splice, 3);
```

```
    fw_list1.splice_after(iter_splice, fw_list2);
    MT::print_ctr("\nfw_list1 (after splice):\n", fw_list1, fmt, epl);
    MT::print_ctr("\nfw_list2 (after splice):\n", fw_list2, fmt, epl);

    // using forward_list::remove_if
    const std::string find_ss {"berry"};
    auto rem_op = [&find_ss](std::string s)
        {return s.find(find_ss) != std::string::npos;};

    fw_list1.remove_if(rem_op);
    MT::print_ctr("\nfw_list1 (after remove_if):\n", fw_list1, fmt, epl);
}
```

In its final code block, Ch04_03_ex2() defines a unary lambda expression named rem_pred that returns true if string argument s contains substring find_ss ("berry"). This lambda expression is used as an argument to std::forward_list::remove_if() to remove all strings that contain substring find_ss from fw_list1.

Listing 4-3-3 shows the code for the concluding function of example Ch04_03. Function std::forward_list::prepend_range() (C++ 23) is a member function that appends a range of elements to the beginning of a std::forward_list. Like some of the previous examples that you've seen, Ch04_03_ex3() utilizes preprocessor macro __cpp_lib_containers_ranges to confirm compiler support for prepend_range().

Listing 4-3-3. Example Ch04_03 - Ch04_03_ex3()

```
void Ch04_03_ex3()
{
    const char* fmt = "{:4d} ";
    constexpr size_t epl_max {10};

    // create forward_list
    std::forward_list<int> fw_list1 {60, 70, 80, 90, 100};
    MT::print_ctr("\nfw_list1 (initial values):\n", fw_list1, fmt,
        epl_max);
```

```cpp
    // using forward_list::prepend_range
    const std::array<int, 5> arr1 {10, 20, 30, 40, 50};
#ifdef __cpp_lib_containers_ranges
    fw_list1.prepend_range(arr1);
#else
    fw_list1.insert_after(fw_list1.before_begin(), arr1.cbegin(),
    arr1.cend());
#endif
    MT::print_ctr("\nfw_list1 (after prepend_range):\n", fw_list1, fmt,
    epl_max);

    // using forward_list::insert_range_after
    auto iter = fw_list1.begin();
    std::advance(iter, 3);
    const std::array<int, 9> arr2 {41, 42, 43, 44, 45, 46, 47, 48, 49};
#ifdef __cpp_lib_containers_ranges
    fw_list1.insert_range_after(iter, arr2);
#else
    fw_list1.insert_after(iter, arr2.begin(), arr2.end());
#endif
    MT::print_ctr("\nfw_list1 (after insert_range_after):\n",
    fw_list1, fmt,
        epl_max);

    // using std::erase_if
    std::erase_if(fw_list1, [](int x) { return x % 3 == 0; });
    MT::print_ctr("\nfw_list1 (after erase_if):\n", fw_list1, fmt,
    epl_max);
}
```

The next code block in Listing 4-3-3 utilizes `insert_range_after()` (C++23) to insert elements from `arr2` into `fw_list1` immediately after element value 40. Once again, `std::advance()` is applied to calculate a target insert position in `fw_list1`. The final code block in `Ch04_03_ex3()` exploits `std::erase_if()` to erase all evenly divisible-by-three values from `fw_list1`. Note that the predicate expression for `erase_if()` is defined not as a named function object but inline as part of the call, which is typical for a short single-use function object. Here are the results for example Ch04_03:

```
----- Results for example Ch04_03 -----

----- Ch04_03_ex1() -----

fw_list1 (initial values):
  10  20  30  40  50  60  70  80

fw_list1 (after push_front):
  75  65  55  45  35  25  15  10  20  30  40  50  60  70  80
num_elements: 15

list1 (after sort):
  10  15  20  25  30  35  40  45  50  55  60  65  70  75  80

list1 (after reverse):
  80  75  70  65  60  55  50  45  40  35  30  25  20  15  10

----- Ch04_03_ex2() -----

fw_list1 (initial values):
lemon lime orange tangerine grapefruit

fw_list2 (initial values):
raspberry strawberry blueberry blackberry

fw_list1 (after splice):
lemon lime orange tangerine raspberry strawberry
blueberry blackberry grapefruit

fw_list2 (after splice):
<empty>
```

```
fw_list1 (after remove_if):
lemon lime orange tangerine grapefruit

----- Ch04_03_ex3() -----

fw_list1 (initial values):
   60    70    80    90   100

fw_list1 (after prepend_range):
   10    20    30    40    50    60    70    80    90   100

fw_list1 (after insert_range_after):
   10    20    30    40    41    42    43    44    45    46
   47    48    49    50    60    70    80    90   100

fw_list1 (after erase_if):
   10    20    40    41    43    44    46    47    49    50
   70    80   100
```

Understanding Iterators

Each source code example discussed in this (and the previous) chapter exercised iterators to reference a container's elements or to specify a range for an STL algorithm. For some examples, an iterator could only perform certain operations. The reason for this is that each container is designed to work with a specific iterator type, and each iterator type supports a specific set of operations.

Recall that an iterator is an abstraction of a pointer. Iterators facilitate pointer-like operations that are independent of a container's internal data structure. For example, operator++ can be utilized to advance an iterator to the next element of a container. For a std::vector container, iterator operator++ performs simple pointer arithmetic. However, for a std::list iterator, operator++ must traverse to the next node in the list. Without iterators, the C++ STL algorithm library would be significantly larger and more complicated since numerous function overloads would be required for each container type.

C++17 defines six iterator types or categories. Each iterator category supports a different set of operational capabilities as shown in Table 4-1.

CHAPTER 4   SEQUENCE CONTAINERS – PART 2

Table 4-1. *C++17 Iterator Categories*

Iterator Category	Supported Capabilities	Example Class
Output	*iter = val, ++iter, iter++, *iter++ = val	std::basic_ostream
Input	*iter = val, iter1 == iter2, iter1 != iter2, iter->member, ++iter, iter++, *iter++	std::basic_istream
Forward	Extension of input iterator that adds: val = *iter, iter1 = iter2	std::forward_list
Bidirectional	Extension of forward iterator that adds: --iter, iter--, *iter--	std::list
Random Access	Extension of bidirectional iterator that adds: iter += n, iter -= n, iter + n, n + iter, iter - n, iter1 - iter2, inter[n], iter1 < iter2, iter1 <= iter2, iter1 > iter2, iter1 >= iter2	std::deque
Contiguous	Same as random access iterator; elements are guaranteed to be stored contiguously in memory	std::basic_string, std::array, std::vector

In Table 4-1, symbol iter denotes an iterator, n signifies an integer value, member is a class attribute, and val is a data value. The important takeaway point from Table 4-1 is that starting from iterator category input, each subsequent category provides additional capabilities. Iterator category output is a distinct category unto itself.

C++20 defines iterators using a taxonomy of concepts instead of categories. Recall that a C++20 concept is a named constraint that defines valid parameter types for a template class or function. There are 13 iterator concepts. These are listed in Table 4-2.

Table 4-2. *C++20 Iterator Concepts*

Iterator Concept (namespace std::)	Capabilities
indirectly_readable	Readable using val = *iter Used for pointers, smart pointers, and iterators
indirectly_writable	Writable using *iter = val
weakly_incrementable	Incrementable using ++iter and iter++ Does not preserve equality
incrementable	Incrementable using ++iter and iter++ Preserves equality
input_or_output_iterator	Extension of weakly_incrementable that adds *iter Universal concept for all iterators
sentinel_for	Iterator used to locate a sentinel (terminating) value
sized_sentinel_for	Supports it - sent_for and sent_for - it to determine the distance between sentinel_for iterators in constant time
output_iterator	Extension of indirectly_writable that adds *iter++ = val
input_iterator	Extension of indirectly_readable that adds ++iter and iter++
forward_iterator	Extension of input_iterator, incrementable, and sentinel_for that adds copyability, equality comparison, and a multi-pass guarantee
bidirectional_iterator	Extension of forward_iterator that adds --iter and iter--
random_access_iterator	Extension of bidirectional_iterator that adds iter += n, iter -= n, iter + n, n + iter, iter - n, and iter[n]
contiguous_iterator	Extension of random_access_iterator that guarantees elements are stored contiguously in memory

CHAPTER 4   SEQUENCE CONTAINERS – PART 2

A sentinel value is a special value that signifies the end of a sequence such as the terminating null character for a C-style string. A multi-pass guarantee means that iter1 == iter2 implies ++iter1 == ++iter2. Note in Table 4-2 that the bottom six concepts are consistent with the categories presented in Table 4-1. C++20's use of iterator concepts instead of categories facilitates improved compiler error checking and specializations for template algorithms.

You've already seen several examples of iterator usage. Source code example Ch04_04 spotlights iterator categories for various containers. Listing 4-4 shows the C++ code for this example.

Listing 4-4. Example Ch04_04 – Ch04_04_ex1()

```
//-------------------------------------------------------------------
// Ch04_04_ex.cpp
//-------------------------------------------------------------------
#include <array>
#include <deque>
#include <forward_list>
#include <iterator>
#include <list>
#include <set>
#include <unordered_set>
#include <vector>
#include <typeinfo>
#include "Ch04_04.h"

template <typename T>
void print_concepts(const char* msg, T& ctr)
{
    // test for const iterator
    std::string s{};
    auto iter = ctr.begin();
    auto citer = std::make_const_iterator(iter);
    bool is_const_iter = typeid(iter) == typeid(citer);
```

```cpp
    // add surrounding {} or []
    auto mk_str = [is_const_iter](const char* s1)
    {
        // {} used for const iterator, [] for non-const
        std::string s2 {};
        s2 += (is_const_iter) ? "{" : "[";
        s2 += s1;
        s2 += (is_const_iter) ? "} " : "] ";
        return s2;
    };

    // construct string of iterator concepts for ctr
    if (std::input_iterator<decltype(iter)>)
        s += mk_str("input");
    if (std::forward_iterator<decltype(iter)>)
        s += mk_str("forward");
    if (std::bidirectional_iterator<decltype(iter)>)
        s += mk_str("bidirectional");
    if (std::random_access_iterator<decltype(iter)>)
        s += mk_str("random access");
    if (std::contiguous_iterator<decltype(iter)>)
        s += mk_str("contiguous");

    std::println("\niterator concepts for {:s}:\n{:s}", msg, s);
}
void Ch04_04_ex1()
{
    // print iterator concepts for different container types
    std::string str1 {};
    print_concepts("str1", str1);
    std::array<int, 2> arr1 {};
    print_concepts("arr1", arr1);

    std::vector<int> vec1 {};
    print_concepts("vec1", vec1);
    std::deque<int> deq1 {};
    print_concepts("deq1", deq1);
```

CHAPTER 4   SEQUENCE CONTAINERS – PART 2

```
    std::list<int> list1 {};
    print_concepts("list1", list1);
    std::forward_list<int> fw_list1 {};
    print_concepts("fw_list1", fw_list1);

    std::set<int> set1 {};
    print_concepts("set1", set1);
    std::unordered_set<int> uno_set1 {};
    print_concepts("uno_set1", uno_set1);
}
void Ch04_04_ex()
{
    std::println("\n----- Ch04_04_ex1() -----");
    Ch04_04_ex1();
}
```

Near the top of Listing 4-4, template function print_concepts() contains code that prints the iterator concepts for container argument ctr. The first code block in this function checks to see if the iterators for ctr are const. More about this shortly. Next is a lambda expression named mk_str() that adds surrounding {} (const iterator) or [ ] (non-const iterator) to argument s1. The remaining code in print_concepts() utilizes various C++20 iterator concepts to ascertain valid iterator operations for container ctr.

Function Ch04_04_ex1() applies print_concepts() using the different types of sequence containers. It also exercises print_concepts() using containers std::set and std::unordered_set, whose iterators are const. You'll learn more about these container classes in Chapters 7 and 8. Here are the results for example Ch04_04:

```
----- Results for example Ch04_04 -----

----- Ch04_04_ex1() -----

iterator concepts for str1:
[input] [forward] [bidirectional] [random access] [contiguous]

iterator concepts for arr1:
[input] [forward] [bidirectional] [random access] [contiguous]
```

```
iterator concepts for vec1:
[input] [forward] [bidirectional] [random access] [contiguous]

iterator concepts for deq1:
[input] [forward] [bidirectional] [random access]

iterator concepts for list1:
[input] [forward] [bidirectional]

iterator concepts for fw_list1:
[input] [forward]

iterator concepts for set1:
{input} {forward} {bidirectional}

iterator concepts for uno_set1:
{input} {forward} {bidirectional}
```

Earlier in this chapter, you saw typical usages of iterator helper functions std::advance() and std::distance(). A program can also utilize std::next() and std::prev() to increment or decrement an iterator by n counts (i.e., n applications of iterator operator++ or operator--). Unlike std::advance(), which returns nothing, both std::next() and std::prev() return an updated iterator. Helper function std::next() can be used with a std::input_iterator iterator argument, while std::prev() requires an iterator argument that supports std::iterator_bidirectional.

Summary

Here are the key learning points for this chapter:

- Template class std::deque is a sequence container that models a double-ended queue. This class is optimized for element insertions and removals at both ends, which makes it suitable for use cases that require a LIFO or FIFO container.

- Template class `std::list` is an abstraction of a doubly linked list. This class supports fast constant-time insertions and removals at the front end, middle, and back end without copy or move operations. Instances of `std::list` do not support random accesses using `operator[]` or `at()`.

- Template class `std::forward_list` is an abstraction of a singly-linked list that's optimized for front-end insertions and removals in constant time. This class is marginally more efficient, both time and space, than `std::list` since it supports traversals using only forward iterators. Class `std::forward_list` does not define a `size()` member function.

- A C++ iterator is an abstraction of a pointer. Iterators facilitate pointer-like operations with a container in a manner that's independent of a container's internal data structure.

- C++17 defines six iterator categories that support different operational capabilities. C++20 defines a more comprehensive taxonomy of iterator concepts that facilitate improved compiler error messages and template specializations.

CHAPTER 5

General Utilities Library

This chapter covers principal classes from the general utilities library, including

- `std::pair`
- `std::tuple`
- `std::variant`
- `std::optional`
- `std::any`
- `std::expected`

Classes `std::pair` and `std::tuple` are heterogeneous template containers that the STL itself uses. These classes are also handy in many real-world programs. The other four classes incorporate other object(s) and are occasionally used as surrogates for simple structures. Some of these classes also maintain state information regarding the object(s) they hold.

Heterogeneous Containers

In many programs, it is often necessary to bundle two or more heterogeneous objects as a single unit. For example, a function might need to return multiple values – perhaps an `int` and a `std::string` – to its caller. Another common example is the bundling of a key with one or more data values. The classic approach to these scenarios is to declare a small class or structure that maintains the bundled objects as a single unit. While this approach is fine for many use cases, it doesn't lend itself to contexts where either the types or number of objects are unknown.

In Chapter 7, you'll learn how to use STL container class `std::map`. This template class arranges data using key-value pairs. Class `std::map` utilizes template parameters to specify the object types for both the key and value. For a class like `std::map` to be useful, the key and value must support any object type including user-defined classes. To handle these types of scenarios, the STL provides two template classes named `std::pair` and `std::tuple`. Class `std::pair` bundles two objects into a single unit, while class `std::tuple` bundles an arbitrary number of objects. The STL itself makes use of these classes. For example, the aforementioned `std::map` class utilizes `std::pair` along with other STL classes that you'll learn about later in this book. The remainder of this section explains how to use `std::pair` and `std::tuple`.

Using std::pair

A `std::pair` is a template class that bundles two heterogeneous objects into a single unit. The elements of a `std::pair` can be accessed using structure-like named members or via constant indices. Class `std::pair` defines an extensive set of constructors for object creation. Non-member functions include the standard set of relational operators and a non-constructor object creator.

Listing 5-1-1 shows the source code for function `Ch05_01_ex1()`. This function expounds several methods that create objects of type `std::pair`. In the initial code block of `Ch05_01_ex1()`, the statement `std::pair<int, double> pair1 {100, 200.0}` constructs a `std::pair` object that bundles values of type `int` and `double`. The accompanying initializer list supplies the initial values for `pair1`. The next statement utilizes `std::println()` to print the data values of `pair1`. Note that this statement utilizes `pair1.first` and `pair1.second` to access the first (100) and second (200.0) elements of `pair1`. The two elements of any `std::pair` can be referenced using names `first` and `second` as demonstrated in this example.

Listing 5-1-1. Example Ch05_01 – Ch05_01_ex1()

```
//-------------------------------------------------------------------------
// Ch05_01_ex.cpp
//-------------------------------------------------------------------------

#include <algorithm>
#include <format>
#include <string>
#include <utility>
#include <vector>
#include "Ch05_01.h"
```

```
void Ch05_01_ex1()
{
    using namespace std::string_literals;

    // pair<int, double>
    std::pair<int, double> pair1 {100, 200.0};
    std::println("pair1.first: {:d}   pair1.second: {:.1f}",
        pair1.first, pair1.second);

    // pair<std::string, long long>
    std::pair<std::string, long long> pair2 {"Hello, World!", 42LL};
    std::println("pair2.first: {:s}   pair2.second: {:d}",
        pair2.first, pair2.second);

    // using std::make_pair()
    auto pair3 = std::make_pair("cm / inch", 2.54f);
    std::println("pair3.first: {:s}   pair3.second: {:.2f}",
        pair3.first, pair3.second);

    // pair<> - type deduction
    std::pair pair4 {"L / U.S. gallon"s, 3.785411784};
    std::println("pair4.first: {:s}   pair4.second: {:.9f}",
        pair4.first, pair4.second);
}
```

The next code block in Ch05_01_ex1() constructs pair2, which bundles values of type std::string and long long. In the third code block, Ch05_01_ex1() utilizes helper function std::make_pair() to create pair3, which is an object of type std::pair<const char*, float>. The final code block in Ch05_01_ex1() utilizes the expression std::pair pair4 {"L / U.S. gallon"s, 3.785411784} to construct pair4. Note in this statement that std::pair is used without explicit types; the compiler deduces the types for pair4. Also, note in this statement the use of the literal suffix s; this suffix forces deduction for pair4 as a std::pair<std::string, double>. Without the string literal suffix, the compiler will deduce pair4 as type std::pair<const char*, double>.

Listing 5-1-2 shows the code for Ch05_01_ex2(). The opening code block in this function contains definitions for pair1 to pair5, all of which are type std::pair<int, double>. Note that pair3 is copy constructed using pair1. For pair4 and pair5, the empty initializer list will default initialize elements first and second to zero.

Listing 5-1-2. Example Ch05_01 – Ch05_01_ex2()

```
void Ch05_01_ex2()
{
    // create std::pairs
    std::pair<int, double> pair1 {100, 200.0};
    std::pair<int, double> pair2 {300, 400.0};
    std::pair<int, double> pair3 {pair1};
    std::pair<int, double> pair4 {};
    std::pair<int, double> pair5 {};

    // using first and second
    pair4.first = pair1.first;
    pair4.second = 350.0;

    // using std::get<>
    std::get<0>(pair5) = pair1.first;    // pair5.first = pair1.first
    std::get<1>(pair5) = -150.0;         // pair5.second = -150.0

    // display values
    std::println("pair1.first: {:d}   pair1.second: {:.1f}",
        pair1.first, pair1.second);
    std::println("pair2.first: {:d}   pair2.second: {:.1f}",
        pair2.first, pair2.second);
    std::println("pair3.first: {:d}   pair3.second: {:.1f}",
        pair3.first, pair3.second);
    std::println("pair4.first: {:d}   pair4.second: {:.1f}",
        pair4.first, pair4.second);
    std::println("pair5.first: {:d}   pair5.second: {:.1f}",
        pair5.first, pair5.second);

    // relational operators
    std::println("\npair1 == pair2: {:s}", pair1 == pair2);
    std::println("pair1 == pair3: {:s}", pair1 == pair3);
    std::println("pair1 >  pair4: {:s}", pair1 >  pair4);
    std::println("pair1 <  pair4: {:s}", pair1 <  pair4);
}
```

The code block that follows the creation of pair1 to pair5 demonstrates the use of assignment statements to modify the elements of pair4. Note that the syntax utilized here is the same as that used to reference the members of a structure. The next code block utilizes std::get<0> and std::get<1> to assign values to pair5.first and pair5.second. Global function std::get<I>(std::pair) returns a reference to the *i-th* element of a std::pair. Since a std::pair contains only two elements, indices 0 and 1 correspond to std::pair elements first and second, respectively. The index value I that's specified within the <> must be a compile-time constant that equals 0 or 1.

Following the series of std::println() statements, the final code block in Ch05_01_ex2() illustrates relational operator usage between two std::pairs. Execution of a relational operator using std::pairs initially compares the two first elements of each std::pair. If the two firsts are equivalent, the two seconds are then compared to determine the result. When comparing two objects of type std::pair, the element types for the firsts and seconds must be the same, or a suitable conversion must be available. For example, comparing two objects of type std::pair<int, float> and std::pair<int, double> is acceptable since appropriate type conversions are available. However, comparing a std::pair<int, float> against a std::pair<int, std::string> will fail to compile.

The final std::pair example, shown in Listing 5-1-3, opens with the initialization of std::vector vec1. Note that this vector holds objects of type std::pair<std::string, double> (alias pair_t). The next code block adds more objects of type pair_t to the back end of vec1 using emplace_back(). Following the emplacement operations is the definition of a lambda expression named print_vec() that's used to print the elements of vec1.

Listing 5-1-3. Example Ch05_01 – Ch05_01_ex3()

```
void Ch05_01_ex3()
{
    // create vector of pair_t elements
    using pair_t = std::pair<std::string, double>;

    std::vector<pair_t> vec1 { {"Beryllium", 9.0122}, {"Helium", 4.0026},
        {"Neon", 20.180}, {"Nitrogen", 14.007}, {"Oxygen", 15.999} };

    // using emplace_back to add more elements
    vec1.emplace_back(std::make_pair("Lithium", 6.94));
```

```
    vec1.emplace_back(std::make_pair("Fluorine", 18.998));
    vec1.emplace_back(std::make_pair("Boron", 10.81));
    vec1.emplace_back(std::make_pair("Hydrogen", 1.0080));
    vec1.emplace_back(std::make_pair("Carbon", 12.011));

    // print lambda for std::vector<pair_t>
    auto print_vec = [](const char* msg, const std::vector<pair_t>& vec)
    {
        std::print("{:s}", msg);

        for (const auto& v : vec)
            std::println("{:<12s} {:12.4f}", v.first, v.second);
    };

    print_vec("\nvec1 (initial values):\n", vec1);

    // using std::ranges::sort (operator<)
    std::ranges::sort(vec1);
    print_vec("\nvec1 (after first sort):\n", vec1);

    // using std::ranges::sort (custom predicate)
    auto cmp_op = [](const pair_t& pair1, const pair_t& pair2)
        { return pair1.second < pair2.second; };

    std::ranges::sort(vec1, cmp_op);
    print_vec("\nvec1 (after second sort):\n", vec1);
}
```

Following the first print_vec() call, Ch05_01_ex3() exploits std::ranges::sort() to sort the elements of vec1. Recall from the discussions in Chapter 3 that the default relational operator for std::ranges::sort() is operator<. For the current example, this means comparing two values of type pair_t using operator< on pair1.first and (if necessary) pair1.second. The ensuing code block Ch05_01_ex3() also utilizes std::ranges::sort(), but defines a custom compare predicate that compares pair1.second against pair2.second. This modifies the sorting algorithm so that it sorts vec1 in ascending order using atomic mass instead of the element name. Here are the results for example Ch05_01:

----- Results for example Ch05_01 -----

----- Ch05_01_ex1() -----
pair1.first: 100   pair1.second: 200.0
pair2.first: Hello, World!   pair2.second: 42
pair3.first: cm / inch   pair3.second: 2.54
pair4.first: L / U.S. gallon   pair4.second: 3.785411784

----- Ch05_01_ex2() -----
pair1.first: 100   pair1.second: 200.0
pair2.first: 300   pair2.second: 400.0
pair3.first: 100   pair3.second: 200.0
pair4.first: 100   pair4.second: 350.0
pair5.first: 100   pair5.second: -150.0

pair1 == pair2: false
pair1 == pair3: true
pair1 > pair4: false
pair1 < pair4: true

----- Ch05_01_ex3() -----
vec1 (initial values):
Beryllium   9.0122
Helium   4.0026
Neon   20.1800
Nitrogen   14.0070
Oxygen   15.9990
Lithium   6.9400
Fluorine   18.9980
Boron   10.8100
Hydrogen   1.0080
Carbon   12.0110

vec1 (after first sort):
Beryllium   9.0122
Boron   10.8100
Carbon   12.0110

Fluorine	18.9980
Helium	4.0026
Hydrogen	1.0080
Lithium	6.9400
Neon	20.1800
Nitrogen	14.0070
Oxygen	15.9990

vec1 (after second sort):

Hydrogen	1.0080
Helium	4.0026
Lithium	6.9400
Beryllium	9.0122
Boron	10.8100
Carbon	12.0110
Nitrogen	14.0070
Oxygen	15.9990
Fluorine	18.9980
Neon	20.1800

Using std::tuple

A std::tuple is a template class that bundles a heterogeneous collection of *N* objects into a single object. Class std::tuple is a generalization of class std::pair that you learned about in the previous section. Like class std::pair, you can reference the elements of a std::tuple using std::get<I>(std::tuple) and a compile-time constant index. Unlike class std::pair, std::tuple does not define named members (i.e., first and second).

Listing 5-2-1 shows the source code for function Ch05_02_01(), which highlights various std::tuple instantiation techniques. The first code block in Ch05_02_ex1() defines a four-element tuple named tup1 whose type is std::tuple<int, double, std::string_view, char>. The connected initializer list supplies the initial values for each element of tup1. The subsequent series of std::println() statements utilize std::get<I>() to obtain references to the elements of tup1.

Listing 5-2-1. Example Ch05_02 – Ch05_02_ex1()

```
//--------------------------------------------------------------------------
// Ch05_02_ex.cpp
//--------------------------------------------------------------------------

#include <numbers>
#include <string>
#include <string_view>
#include <typeinfo>
#include <utility>
#include "Ch05_02.h"
#include "Point2D.h"

void Ch05_02_ex1()
{
    using namespace std::string_view_literals;

    // four-element tuple - explicit types
    std::tuple<int, double, std::string_view, char> tup1
        {10, 20.123456, "Hello, World!", '#'};

    std::println("\nstd::get<0>(tup1): {:d}", std::get<0>(tup1));
    std::println("std::get<1>(tup1): {:f}", std::get<1>(tup1));
    std::println("std::get<2>(tup1): {:s}", std::get<2>(tup1));
    std::println("std::get<3>(tup1): {:c}", std::get<3>(tup1));

    // four-element tuple - std::make_tuple
    auto tup2 {std::make_tuple(100, 200.123456, "Bonjour le
    Monde!"sv, '&')};
    static_assert(typeid(tup1) == typeid(tup2));

    std::println("\nstd::get<0>(tup2): {:d}", std::get<0>(tup2));
    std::println("std::get<1>(tup2): {:f}", std::get<1>(tup2));
    std::println("std::get<2>(tup2): {:s}", std::get<2>(tup2));
    std::println("std::get<3>(tup2): {:c}", std::get<3>(tup2));

    // four-element tuple - type deduction
    std::tuple tup3 {1000, 2000.123456, "Hallo Welt!"sv, '*'};
    static_assert(typeid(tup1) == typeid(tup3));
```

CHAPTER 5 GENERAL UTILITIES LIBRARY

```
    std::println("\nstd::get<0>(tup3): {:d}", std::get<0>(tup3));
    std::println("std::get<1>(tup3): {:f}", std::get<1>(tup3));
    std::println("std::get<2>(tup3): {:s}", std::get<2>(tup3));
    std::println("std::get<3>(tup3): {:c}", std::get<3>(tup3));

    // using std::tuple_size
    std::println("\ntup3_size {:d}", std::tuple_size<decltype(tup3)>::value);

    // using std::tuple_element
    std::println("\ntup3 types:");
    std::println("{:s}", typeid(std::tuple_element
    <0, decltype(tup3)>::type).name());
    std::println("{:s}", typeid(std::tuple_element
    <1, decltype(tup3)>::type).name());
    std::println("{:s}", typeid(std::tuple_element
    <2, decltype(tup3)>::type).name());
    std::println("{:s}", typeid(std::tuple_element
    <3, decltype(tup3)>::type).name());
}
```

The next code block in Ch05_02_ex2() instantiates tup2 using std::make_tuple(). Note that the third argument of std::make_tuple(), "Bonjour le Monde!"sv, includes std::string_view literal suffix sv. This ensures identical types for both tup1 and tup2, which is confirmed by the subsequent static_assert(typeid(tup1) == typeid(tup2)) statement. The ensuing code block exploits type deduction to instantiate tup3. Like tup2, the type of tup3 matches that of tup1.

The final two code blocks in Ch05_02_ex1() demonstrate the use of std::tuple_size<> and std::tuple_element<>. Both of these are std::tuple helper classes. The former obtains the number of elements in the specified tuple. The expression std::tuple_size<decltype(tup3)> is a class, and ::value is a constant member of this class that denotes the number of tuple elements. The C++ keyword decltype retrieves the type for tup3. Similarly, std::tuple_element<0, decltype(tup3)> is a class, and constant member ::type yields the type for element 0 of tup3.

CHAPTER 5   GENERAL UTILITIES LIBRARY

Demo function Ch05_02_ex2(), shown in Listing 5-2-2, illustrates a few common operations using std::tuples and std::tuple elements. This function opens with the definition tup_t as an alias for std::tuple<std::string, int, double>. Following the declarations of tuples tup0 to tup3 is the definition of lambda expression print_tup(), which prints the elements of a tup_t.

Listing 5-2-2. Example Ch05_02 – Ch05_02_ex2()

```
void Ch05_02_ex2()
{
    using tup_t = std::tuple<std::string, int, double>;

    // create test tuples
    tup_t tup0 {"aaaa", 1, 100.0};
    tup_t tup1 {"bbbb", 2, 200.0};
    tup_t tup2 {"cccc", 3, 300.0};
    tup_t tup3 {"dddd", 4, 400.0};

    // print test tuples
    auto print_tup = [](const char* msg, const tup_t& tup)
    {
        std::println("{:s}: [{:s} | {:d} | {:.2f}]", msg,
            std::get<0>(tup), std::get<1>(tup), std::get<2>(tup));
    };

    print_tup("\ntup0 (initial value)", tup0);
    print_tup("tup1 (initial value)", tup1);
    print_tup("tup2 (initial value)", tup2);
    print_tup("tup3 (initial value)", tup3);

    // modification of elements
    tup_t tup4 {tup0};
    print_tup("\ntup4 (initial value)", tup4);
    std::get<0>(tup4) = "AAAA";
    std::get<1>(tup4) *= -1;
    std::get<2>(tup4) /= std::get<2>(tup3);
    print_tup("tup4 (after modifications)", tup4);
```

```
    // relational operators
    auto tup5 {tup0};
    print_tup("\ntup5 (initial value)", tup5);
    std::println("tup0 == tup5: {:s}", tup0 == tup5);

    std::get<2>(tup5) *= 1.5;
    print_tup("\ntup5 (after modification)", tup5);
    std::println("tup0 <  tup5: {:s}", tup0 <  tup5);

    std::get<1>(tup5) -= 7;
    print_tup("\ntup5 (after modification)", tup5);
    std::println("tup0 <  tup5: {:s}", tup0 <  tup5);
}
```

Subsequent to the tuple prints, Ch05_02_ex2() utilizes std::get<I>() to perform simple calculations using the elements of tup4. The final code block in Ch05_02_ex2() demonstrates the use of std::tuple relational operators. These operators perform lexicographical compares of corresponding elements in the two std::tuples. The compare operations terminate following the determination of a definitive result. This means for the first tup0 < tup5 operation, all three tuple elements are checked; for the second tup0 < tup5 operation, a definitive result is obtained without comparing the two doubles.

Listing 5-2-3 shows the source code for template function print_tuple() and example function Ch05_02_ex3(). The purpose of Ch05_02_ex3() is to explicate the workings of print_tuple(), which prints the elements of a std::tuple.

Listing 5-2-3. Example Ch05_02 - Ch05_02_ex3()

```
template <size_t I = 0, typename... TUP_Ts>
constexpr void print_tuple(const char* msg, const std::tuple<TUP_Ts...>& tup)
{
    if constexpr(I == 0)
        std::print("{:s}", msg);

    if constexpr(I < sizeof...(TUP_Ts))
    {
```

```cpp
        std::print(" | {}", std::get<I>(tup));
        print_tuple<I + 1>(msg, tup);
    }
    else
        std::println(" |");
}
void Ch05_02_ex3()
{
    using namespace std::numbers;
    using namespace std::string_literals;
    using namespace std::string_view_literals;
    using point2d_t = Point2D<unsigned int>;

    // using print_tuple
    auto tup1 = std::make_tuple("Black"s, 1, pi);
    print_tuple("tup1:", tup1);

    auto tup2 = std::make_tuple(pi * 2, "Blue"s, -1, "NFC North"sv);
    print_tuple("tup2:", tup2);

    auto tup3 = std::make_tuple("Chicago Bears"sv, "Detroit Lions"sv,
        "Green Bay Packers"sv, "Minnesota Vikings"sv);
    print_tuple("tup3:", tup3);

    auto tup4 = std::make_tuple(point2d_t {10, 20}, "upper left"s,
        point2d_t {100, 125}, "lower right"s, ln2_v<float>);
    print_tuple("tup4:", tup4);
}
```

In Listing 5-2-3, note that template function print_tuple() specifies two parameters. Parameter size_t I corresponds to the element index that's required for std::get<I>(). Observe that the default value for I is zero. The other template parameter, typename... TUP_Ts, is a template parameter pack.[1] A template parameter pack is a template parameter that accepts zero or more template arguments.

---

[1] The notation ... signifies a template parameter pack.

For template function print_tuple(), TUP_Ts embodies the element types for argument const std::tuple<TUP_Ts...>& tup). The syntax that's used here facilitates using print_tuple() to print the elements of any valid std::tuple.

The best way to understand how print_tuple() works is to dive into an example. Following its using statements, function Ch05_02_ex3() exploits std::make_tuple("Black"s, 1, pi) to construct tup1, whose type corresponds to std::tuple<std::string, int, double>. Function Ch05_02_ex3() then employs print_tuple("tup1:", tup1) to print the elements of tup1. Note here that template argument I is not specified, which means that it defaults to zero. Also, note that parameter pack TUP_Ts for tup1 corresponds to std::string, int, and double.

The first expression of print_tuple() compares I == 0. If true, the ensuing std::print("{:s}", msg) prints msg, which occurs upon first entry to print_tuple(). The next expression in print_tuple(), if constexpr(I < sizeof...(TUP_Ts)),[2] compares I against the number of template arguments in TUP_Ts. If constexpr (I < sizeof... (TUP_Ts)) is false, all tuple elements have been printed and print_tuple() calls std::println(" |") to conclude the std::tuple print action.

If constexpr (I < sizeof... (TUP_Ts)) is true, print_tuple() exercises std::get<I>(tuple) to retrieve and print the *i-th* element of tup. Note that std::println() utilizes format specifier {}. Recall that {} is the default format specifier for a given type (assuming it's been defined). Using type-specific format specifiers (e.g., {:d}, {:s}, etc.) here is not feasible since print_tuple() is expected to work with any std::tuple.

Following the std::println() call, print_tuple() utilizes print_tuple<I + 1>(msg, tup) to recursively print the next element of tup. It is important to recognize here that template function print_tuple() is *compile-time* recursive.[3] During template instantiation, every use of print_tuple<I+1>(msg, tup) compels the compiler to generate code for another instance of print_tuple().[4] The remaining code in Ch05_02_ex3() demonstrates additional usages of print_tuple() using assorted test tuples.

---

[2] The sizeof... operator counts the number of arguments in a template parameter pack.
[3] This is why print_tuple() uses if constexpr().
[4] During its optimization phase, the C++ compiler may combine the different instantiations of print_tuple() into a single runtime function. This optimization is performed for each distinct template parameter pack.

Listing 5-2-4 shows the source code for Ch05_02_ex4(), which exploits std::tie() to unpack the elements of a std::tuple. The first use of std::tie() unpacks all elements of tup1 and assigns these values to local variables. More specifically, std::tie() returns a std::tuple of references to the specified variables. Execution of the assignment operator std::tuple<Types...>operator= then copies each element of tup1 to its corresponding std::tie() variable. The second occurrence of std::tie() demonstrates the use of std::ignore, which represents an unspecified type that essentially skips the corresponding element when unpacking tup1.

Listing 5-2-4. Example Ch05_02 – Ch05_02_ex4()

```
void Ch05_02_ex4()
{
    using namespace std::string_literals;

    // using std::tie to unpack tuple
    int x1 {};
    std::string s1 {}, s2 {}, s3 {};

    auto tup1 = std::make_tuple(1, "one"s, "eins"s, "uno"s);
    std::tie(x1, s1, s2, s3) = tup1;
    std::println("x1: {:d}   s1: {:s}   s2: {:s}   s3: {:s}", x1, s1, s2, s3);

    // using std::tie and std::ignore to unpack tuple
    s2 = "****";
    std::tie(x1, s1, std::ignore, s3) = tup1;
    std::println("x1: {:d}   s1: {:s}   s2: {:s}   s3: {:s}", x1, s1, s2, s3);

    // using structured binding to unpack tuple
    auto tup2 {std::make_tuple(2, "two"s, "zwei"s, "dos"s)};
    auto [x2, s4, s5, s6] = tup2;
    std::println("x2: {:d}   s4: {:s}   s5: {:s}   s6: {:s}", x2, s4, s5, s6);

    // using std::tuple_cat (example 1)
    auto tup3 {std::make_tuple(3, "three"s, "drei"s, "tres"s)};
    auto tup4 {std::make_tuple(4, "four"s, "veir"s, "cuatro"s)};
    auto tup5 = std::tuple_cat(tup3, tup4);
```

```
        print_tuple("\ntup5: ", tup5);
        std::println("tup5 size: {:d}", std::tuple_size
        <decltype(tup5)>::value);

        // using std::tuple_cat (example 2)
        auto tup6 = std::tuple_cat(tup3, std::make_tuple(10.5, 20.8), tup4);

        print_tuple("\ntup6: ", tup6);
        std::println("tup6 size: {:d}", std::tuple_size
        <decltype(tup6)>::value);
}
```

The next code block utilizes structured binding to unpack the elements of tup2. Note that when using structured binding, the auto keyword must be employed since this construct exploits automatic type deduction. Besides std::tuple, structured binding can be applied to unpack the elements of a std::pair, struct, std::array, or C-style array. It also can be exploited to return multiple values from a function. You'll see additional examples of structured binding in Chapter 7.

The final two code blocks of Ch05_02_ex4() employ std::tuple_cat() to perform std::tuple concatenation. In the first code block, the expression tup5 = std::tuple_cat(tup3, tup4) concatenates tup3 and tup4 into a newly constructed std::tuple named tup5. The concatenation operation is performed left to right using the source std::tuples' types and values. A function can also utilize std::tuple_cat() to concatenate more than two std::tuples as demonstrated in the second std::tuple usage example. Here are the results for example Ch05_02:

```
----- Results for example Ch05_02 -----

----- Ch05_02_ex1() -----

std::get<0>(tup1): 10
std::get<1>(tup1): 20.123456
std::get<2>(tup1): Hello, World!
std::get<3>(tup1): #

std::get<0>(tup2): 100
std::get<1>(tup2): 200.123456
std::get<2>(tup2): Bonjour le Monde!
std::get<3>(tup2): &
```

```
std::get<0>(tup3): 1000
std::get<1>(tup3): 2000.123456
std::get<2>(tup3): Hallo Welt!
std::get<3>(tup3): *

tup3_size 4

tup3 types:
int
double
class std::basic_string_view<char,struct std::char_traits<char> >
char

----- Ch05_02_ex2() -----

tup0 (initial value): [aaaa | 1 | 100.00]
tup1 (initial value): [bbbb | 2 | 200.00]
tup2 (initial value): [cccc | 3 | 300.00]
tup3 (initial value): [dddd | 4 | 400.00]

tup4 (initial value): [aaaa | 1 | 100.00]
tup4 (after modifications): [AAAA | -1 | 0.25]

tup5 (initial value): [aaaa | 1 | 100.00]
tup0 == tup5: true

tup5 (after modification): [aaaa | 1 | 150.00]
tup0 <  tup5: true

tup5 (after modification): [aaaa | -6 | 150.00]
tup0 <  tup5: false

----- Ch05_02_ex3() -----
tup1: | Black | 1 | 3.141592653589793 |
tup2: | 6.283185307179586 | Blue | -1 | NFC North |
tup3: | Chicago Bears | Detroit Lions | Green Bay Packers | Minnesota Vikings |
tup4: | (10, 20) | upper left | (100, 125) | lower right | 0.6931472 |
```

```
----- Ch05_02_ex4() -----
x1: 1   s1: one   s2: eins   s3: uno
x1: 1   s1: one   s2: ****   s3: uno
x2: 2   s4: two   s5: zwei   s6: dos

tup5:  | 3 | three | drei | tres | 4 | four | veir | cuatro |
tup5 size: 8

tup6:  | 3 | three | drei | tres | 10.5 | 20.8 | 4 | four | veir | cuatro |
tup6 size: 10
```

Utility Classes

The section explains how to use STL utility classes std::variant, std::optional, std::any, and std::expected. These classes generally hold zero or more objects along with state information. They are typically used to simplify data exchange between functions.

Using std::variant

A std::variant is a C++ template class that holds a single value from a specified set of alternative types. The purpose of this template class is to provide a type-safe replacement for a C-style union. Before continuing, it warrants mentioning that despite its intended usage, std::variants and unions are different constructs, and the former doesn't fully replicate the capabilities of the latter. In most use cases, however, a std::variant is a superior alternative to union. And you can still exploit a union in those situations where its unique capabilities are necessary, such as low-level byte manipulations of fundamental types.

Source code example Ch05_03 spotlights elementary operations using std::variants. Listing 5-3-1 shows the source code for Ch05_03_ex1().

CHAPTER 5 GENERAL UTILITIES LIBRARY

Listing 5-3-1. Example Ch05_03 – Ch05_03_ex1()

```cpp
//--------------------------------------------------------------------------
// Ch05_03_ex.cpp
//--------------------------------------------------------------------------

#include <numbers>
#include <utility>
#include <variant>
#include "Ch05_03.h"
#include "Rect.h"

void Ch05_03_ex1()
{
    std::variant<double, int> var1 {};

    // using var1 with double
    var1 = std::numbers::pi;
    std::println("\nstd::get<0>(var1):      {}", std::get<0>(var1));
    std::println("std::get<double>(var1): {}", std::get<double>(var1));

    // using var1 with int
    var1 = 100;
    std::println("\nstd::get<1>(var1):      {}", std::get<1>(var1));
    std::println("std::get<int>(var1):    {}", std::get<int>(var1));

    // bad variant access generates exception
    try
    {
        auto bad_access = std::get<double>(var1);
        std::println("\nbad_access: {}", bad_access);
    }
    catch (const std::bad_variant_access& ex)
    {
        std::println("\ncaught exception:       {}", ex.what());
    }
```

191

```cpp
    // using std::get_if (example 1)
    std::print("\nget_if<double>(var1):   ");
    if (const double* p_double = std::get_if<double>(&var1))
        std::println("*p_double = {}", *p_double);
    else
        std::println("failed as expected\n");

    // using std::get_if (example 2)
    std::print("get_if<int>(var1):      ");
    if (const int* p_int = std::get_if<1>(&var1))
        std::println("*p_int = {}", *p_int);
    else
        std::println("unexpected error");
}
```

Function Ch05_03_ex1() opens with the statement std::variant<double, int> var1 {}. This defines var1 as a std::variant capable of holding two alternative values, either a double or int. The first expression of the ensuing code block utilizes the expression var1 = std::numbers::pi to store pi in var1. The next two std::println() statements demonstrate two different methods for accessing the current value in a std::variant. The first method utilizes std::get<0>(var1). When using std::get<>() to access the value in a std::variant, index 0 corresponds to the first alternative, index 1 the second alternative, and so on. For var1, this means that indices 0 and 1 can be used to access the double and int, respectively. The second std::println() statement utilizes std::get<double>(var1) to retrieve the double value that's currently stored in var1. The succeeding code block in Ch05_03_ex1() demonstrates using var1 with an int. Note that the two std::get<> statements utilize template arguments 1 and int, respectively.

Helper function std::get<>() will throw a std::bad_variant_access exception if it's used to access a std::variant alternative that doesn't hold the current value. The try-catch construct of Ch05_03_ex1() demonstrates this. The first statement of the try block, std::get<double>(var1), is invalid since var1 currently holds an int. Execution of this statement generates an exception that's caught in the subsequent catch block.

CHAPTER 5 GENERAL UTILITIES LIBRARY

Values of std::variant can also be accessed using std::get_if<>(). The template argument for std::get_if<>() can be a constant index or type just like std::get<>(). The primary difference between these two non-member functions is that std::get_if<>() returns a nullptr on an invalid access instead of throwing an exception. The final two code blocks in Ch05_03_ex1() demonstrate proper usage of std::get_if().

Listing 5-3-2-1 shows the source code for class Rect, which is used later in this and other examples. Class Rect maintains attributes for a rectangle. It also defines relevant relational operators and formatting functions. Note that operator<=> and operator== carry out their operations using area().

Listing 5-3-2-1. Example Ch05_03 – Class Rect

```cpp
//------------------------------------------------------------------
// Rect.h
//------------------------------------------------------------------
#ifndef RECT_H_
#define RECT_H_
#include <format>
#include <ostream>
#include <string>

class Rect
{
    friend struct std::formatter<Rect>;
public:
    // constructors
    Rect() = default;

    Rect(unsigned int x, unsigned int y, unsigned int w, unsigned int h) :
        m_X(x), m_Y(y), m_W(w), m_H(h) {}

    ~Rect();

    // accessors
    unsigned int X() const { return m_X; }
    unsigned int Y() const { return m_Y; }
    unsigned int W() const { return m_W; }
    unsigned int H() const { return m_H; }
```

193

```cpp
    unsigned int& X() { return m_X; }
    unsigned int& Y() { return m_Y; }
    unsigned int& W() { return m_W; }
    unsigned int& H() { return m_H; }

    void set(unsigned int x, unsigned int y, unsigned int w,
    unsigned int h)
        { m_X = x; m_Y = y; m_W = w; m_H = h; }

    // public member functions
    unsigned int area() const { return m_W * m_H; }

    // operators (see Rect.cpp)
    friend std::ostream& operator<<(std::ostream& os, const Rect& rect);
private:
    std::string to_str() const;

    // private attributes
    unsigned int m_X {};
    unsigned int m_Y {};
    unsigned int m_W {};
    unsigned int m_H {};
};
// relational operators
inline auto operator<=>(const Rect& rect1, const Rect& rect2)
    { return rect1.area() <=> rect2.area(); }

inline bool operator==(const Rect& rect1, const Rect& rect2)
    { return rect1.area() == rect2.area(); }

// class Rect formatter
template <> struct std::formatter<Rect> : std::formatter<std::string>
{
    constexpr auto parse(std::format_parse_context& fpc)
        { return fpc.begin(); }
```

```cpp
    auto format(const Rect& rect, std::format_context& fc) const
        { return std::format_to(fc.out(), "{}", rect.to_str()); }
};

#endif
```

```cpp
//---------------------------------------------------------------------------
// Rect.cpp
//---------------------------------------------------------------------------

#include <format>
#include <ostream>
#include <string>
#include "Rect.h"
#include "Common.h"

Rect::~Rect()
{
//   std::println("Rect::~Rect()");     // for demo purposes only
}

std::ostream& operator<<(std::ostream& os, const Rect& rect)
{
    os << rect.to_str();
    return os;
}

std::string Rect::to_str() const
{
    std::string s{};
    std::format_to(std::back_inserter(s), "[({:d}, {:d}, {:d}, {:d}) ",
        m_X, m_Y, m_W, m_H);
    std::format_to(std::back_inserter(s), "{:d}]", area());
    return s;
}
```

Listing 5-3-2-2 shows the source code for function Ch05_02_ex2(). Function Ch05_02_ex2() demonstrates the use of a std::variant that holds an object of type Rect or std::string. The first code block in this function uses var1.emplace<0>(Rect(10, 20, 30, 40)) to store a Rect in var1. The std::variant::emplace<>() functions perform in-place object construction just like the other emplace() functions that you've already seen. The ensuing call to std::holds_alternative<Rect>(var1) returns true if var1 currently holds a value of type Rect; otherwise, it returns false. Also, note in this code block the use of var1.index(), which returns the index of the currently held object.

Listing 5-3-2-2. Example Ch05_03 – Ch05_03_ex2()

```
void Ch05_03_ex2()
{
    std::variant<Rect, std::string> var1 {};

    // using emplace and holds_alternative (example 1)
    var1.emplace<0>(Rect(10, 20, 30, 40));
    if (std::holds_alternative<Rect>(var1))
        std::println("\nvar1 (Rect):    {}", std::get<Rect>(var1));
    std::println("var1.index(): {:d}", var1.index());

    // using emplace and holds_alternative (example 2)
    var1.emplace<1>("one, two, three, four");
    if (std::holds_alternative<std::string>(var1))
        std::println("\nvar1 (std::string): {}",
            std::get<std::string>(var1));
    std::println("var1.index(): {:d}", var1.index());
}
```

The second code block in Ch05_03_ex2() employs var1.emplace<1>("one, two, three, four") to store a std::string into var1. It warrants mentioning here that unlike a union, class std::variant ensures that any applicable destructors are executed whenever a new object is stored. To observe this, remove the comment from the std::println() statement in Rect's destructor and run the code.

Listing 5-3-3 shows the source code for the Ch05_03_ex3(). This example spotlights the use of relational operators and std::variants.

Listing 5-3-3. Example Ch05_03 - Ch05_03_ex3()

```
void Ch05_03_ex3()
{
    using namespace std::string_literals;
    using var_t = std::variant<std::string, int>;

    var_t var1 {"red"s};
    var_t var2 {"red"s};
    var_t var3 {"green"s};
    var_t var4 {10};

    // relational operators (same index, same value)
    std::println("\nvar1 == var2: {:s}", var1 == var2);
    std::println("var1 != var2: {:s}", var1 != var2);
    std::println("var1 <  var2: {:s}", var1 <  var2);
    std::println("var1 <= var2: {:s}", var1 <= var2);
    std::println("var1 >  var2: {:s}", var1 >  var2);
    std::println("var1 >= var2: {:s}", var1 >= var2);

    // relational operators (same index, different value)
    std::println("\nvar1 == var3: {:s}", var1 == var3);
    std::println("var1 != var3: {:s}", var1 != var3);
    std::println("var1 <  var3: {:s}", var1 <  var3);
    std::println("var1 <= var3: {:s}", var1 <= var3);
    std::println("var1 >  var3: {:s}", var1 >  var3);
    std::println("var1 >= var3: {:s}", var1 >= var3);

    // relational operators (different index, different value)
    std::println("\nvar1 == var4: {:s}", var1 == var4);
    std::println("var1 != var4: {:s}", var1 != var4);
    std::println("var1 <  var4: {:s}", var1 <  var4);
    std::println("var1 <= var4: {:s}", var1 <= var4);
    std::println("var1 >  var4: {:s}", var1 >  var4);
    std::println("var1 >= var4: {:s}", var1 >= var4);
}
```

CHAPTER 5 GENERAL UTILITIES LIBRARY

Table 5-1 summarizes the specific actions and results for each relational operator. In this table, v and w are objects of type std::variant and i = v.index(). Function std::variant::valueless_by_exception() returns false if and only if the variant contains a value. A variant can become valueless_by_exception() if an exception is thrown during value initialization or a type change. Reading from top to bottom, the condition column of Table 5-1 shows the distinct comparisons (in order of execution) for each relational operator. This column is somewhat unwieldy since the relational operators consider indices and valueless_by_exception(). What's important to recognize here is that if the indices are identical and the std::variants are not valueless_by_exception(), the relational operators carry out standard comparisons.

Table 5-1. Relational Operators for std::variant

Operator	Condition	Return Value
v == w	v.index() != w.index()	false
	v.valueless_by_exception()	true
	otherwise	get<i>(v) == get<i>(w)
v != w	v.index() != w.index()	true
	v.valueless_by_exception()	false
	otherwise	get<i>(v) != get<i>(w)
v < w	w.valueless_by_exception()	false
	v.valueless_by_exception()	true
	v.index() < w.index()	true
	v.index() > w.index()	false
	otherwise	get<i>(v) < get<i>(w)
v > w	v.valueless_by_exception()	false
	w.valueless_by_exception()	true
	v.index() > w.index()	true
	v.index() < w.index()	false
	otherwise	get<i>(v) > get<i>(w)

(*continued*)

Table 5-1. (*continued*)

Operator	Condition	Return Value
v <= w	v.valueless_by_exception()	true
	w.valueless_by_exception()	false
	v.index() < w.index()	true
	v.index() > w.index()	false
	otherwise	get<i>(v) <= get<i>(w)
v >= w	w.valueless_by_exception()	true
	v.valueless_by_exception()	false
	v.index() > w.index()	true
	v.index() < w.index()	false
	otherwise	get<i>(v) >= get<i>(w)
v <=> w	v.valueless_by_exception() && w.valueless_by_exception()	strong_ordering::equal
	v.valueless_by_exception()	strong_ordering::less
	w.valueless_by_exception()	strong_ordering::greater
	c = v.index() <=> w.index();	c
	c != 0	get<i>(v) <=> get<i>(w)
	otherwise	

Here are the results for example Ch05_03:

```
----- Results for example Ch05_03 -----

----- Ch05_03_ex1() -----

std::get<0>(var1):      3.141592653589793
std::get<double>(var1): 3.141592653589793

std::get<1>(var1):      100
std::get<int>(var1):    100

caught exception:       bad variant access

get_if<double>(var1):   failed as expected
```

CHAPTER 5 GENERAL UTILITIES LIBRARY

```
get_if<int>(var1):      *p_int = 100

----- Ch05_03_ex2() -----

var1 (Rect):    [(10, 20, 30, 40) 1200]
var1.index(): 0

var1 (std::string): one, two, three, four
var1.index(): 1

----- Ch05_03_ex3() -----

var1 == var2: true
var1 != var2: false
var1 <  var2: false
var1 <= var2: true
var1 >  var2: false
var1 >= var2: true

var1 == var3: false
var1 != var3: true
var1 <  var3: false
var1 <= var3: false
var1 >  var3: true
var1 >= var3: true

var1 == var4: false
var1 != var4: true
var1 <  var4: true
var1 <= var4: true
var1 >  var4: false
var1 >= var4: false
```

Using std::optional

A std::optional object is a template class that encompasses and manages another object, which may or may not be present. Objects of std::optional are sometimes exploited to return a value from a function that might fail. The state of a std::optional object is binary; it either contains an object or it contains nothing. If a `std::optional` object contains another object, that object's destructor is executed during execution of the holding `std::optional`'s destructor.

Source code example Ch05_04 spotlights a few conventional usages of `std::optional` objects. Listing 5-4-1-1 shows the source code for class Nut. Example Ch05_04 utilizes this class to illustrate the use of `std::optional` objects. It's also used in later chapters.

Listing 5-4-1-1. Example Ch05_04 – Class Nut

```
//-----------------------------------------------------------------
// Nut.h
//-----------------------------------------------------------------
#ifndef NUT_H_
#define NUT_H_
#include <format>
#include <ostream>
#include <string>
#include <vector>

class Nut
{
    friend struct std::formatter<Nut>;
public:
    // order of elements in enum Type must match elements in s_Nuts (see
    Nut.cpp)
    enum class Type : unsigned int
        {Almond, Cashew, Chestnut, Hazelnut, Pecan, Pistachio, Walnut};

    // constructors
    Nut() = default;

    Nut(const std::string& name, unsigned int energy_kj, float
    carbohydrates,
        float fat, float protein) : m_Name {name}, m_EnergyKj {energy_kj},
        m_Carbohydrates {carbohydrates}, m_Fat {fat}, m_Protein {protein}
```

```cpp
    {
        m_EnergyKcal = static_cast<unsigned int>(m_EnergyKj * 0.239f
        + 0.5f);
    }

    // accessors
    std::string Name() const { return m_Name; }
    unsigned int EnergyKj() const { return m_EnergyKj; }
    unsigned int EnergyKcal() const { return m_EnergyKcal; }
    float Carbohydrates() const { return m_Carbohydrates; }
    float Fat() const { return m_Fat; }
    float Protein() const { return m_Protein; }

    // operators
    friend auto operator<=>(const Nut& nut1, const Nut& nut2)
        { return nut1.m_Name <=> nut2.m_Name; }

    friend bool operator==(const Nut& nut1, const Nut& nut2)
        { return nut1.m_Name == nut2.m_Name; }

    friend std::ostream& operator<<(std::ostream& os, const Nut& nut)
        { os << nut.to_str(); return os; }

    // miscellaneous (see Nut.cpp)
    static Nut get_nut(Nut::Type type);
    static std::string get_type_string(Nut::Type type);
    static std::vector<Nut> get_vector();
    static std::string title_str();

private:
    // private member functions (see Nut.cpp)
    std::string to_str() const;

    // private attributes
    std::string m_Name {};              // nut name
    unsigned int m_EnergyKj {};         // energy (kilojoules) per 100g
    unsigned int m_EnergyKcal {};       // energy (kilocalories) per 100g
    float m_Carbohydrates {};           // carbohydrates (g) per 100g
```

CHAPTER 5   GENERAL UTILITIES LIBRARY

```
    float m_Fat {};                 // fat (g) per 100g
    float m_Protein {};             // protein (g) per 100g
};

// class Nut formatter
template <> struct std::formatter<Nut> : std::formatter<std::string>
{
    constexpr auto parse(std::format_parse_context& pc)
        { return pc.begin(); }

    auto format(const Nut& nut, std::format_context& fc) const
        { return std::format_to(fc.out(), "{}", nut.to_str()); }
};

#endif


//---------------------------------------------------------------------
// Nut.cpp
//---------------------------------------------------------------------

#include <array>
#include <format>
#include <stdexcept>
#include <string>
#include <vector>
#include "Nut.h"

namespace
{
    const std::array<Nut, 7> s_Nuts
    {
        // order of objects below must match enum Nut::Type (see Nut.h)
        Nut {"Almond",    2423, 21.6f,  49.9f,  21.2f},
        Nut {"Cashew",     553, 30.19f, 43.85f, 18.22f},
        Nut {"Chestnut",   820, 28.0f,   1.3f,   1.6f},
        Nut {"Hazelnut",  2629, 16.7f,  60.75f, 15.95f},
        Nut {"Pecan",     2889, 13.86f, 71.97f,  9.17f},
        Nut {"Pistachio", 2351, 27.51f, 45.39f, 20.27f},
```

CHAPTER 5   GENERAL UTILITIES LIBRARY

```cpp
        Nut {"Walnut", 2738, 13.71f, 65.21f, 15.23f},
    };
}

Nut Nut::get_nut(Nut::Type type)
{
    auto t = static_cast<unsigned int>(type);

    if (t >= s_Nuts.size())
        throw std::runtime_error("Nut::get_nut() - invalid type");

    return s_Nuts[t];
}

std::string Nut::get_type_string(Nut::Type type)
{
    auto t = static_cast<unsigned int>(type);

    if (t >= s_Nuts.size())
        throw std::runtime_error("Nut::get_type_string() - invalid type");

    return s_Nuts[t].m_Name;
}

std::vector<Nut> Nut::get_vector()
{
    std::vector<Nut> nuts(s_Nuts.begin(), s_Nuts.end());
    return nuts;
}

std::string Nut::to_str() const
{
    std::string s {};
    std::format_to(std::back_inserter(s), "[{:<13s}", m_Name);
    std::format_to(std::back_inserter(s), "{:>11d}", m_EnergyKj);
    std::format_to(std::back_inserter(s), "{:>11d}", m_EnergyKcal);
    std::format_to(std::back_inserter(s), "{:>11.2f}", m_Carbohydrates);
    std::format_to(std::back_inserter(s), "{:>11.2f}", m_Fat);
    std::format_to(std::back_inserter(s), "{:>11.2f}]", m_Protein);
```

```cpp
    return s;
}
std::string Nut::title_str()
{
    std::string s {};
    std::format_to(std::back_inserter(s), "\n{:<13s}", "Name");
    std::format_to(std::back_inserter(s), "{:>11s}", "EnKj");
    std::format_to(std::back_inserter(s), "{:>12s}", "EnKcal");
    std::format_to(std::back_inserter(s), "{:>11s}", "Carbs");
    std::format_to(std::back_inserter(s), "{:>11s}", "Fat");
    std::format_to(std::back_inserter(s), "{:>12s}\n", "Protein");

    s += std::string(72, '=');
    s += '\n';
    return s;
}
```

The first part of Listing 5-4-1-1 shows the header file for class Nut. Near the top of the class definition is an enum named Type, which defines symbolic names for the predefined Nut objects in Nut.cpp. The parameterized constructor for class Nut requires a name std::string along with various nutritional values. Next is a series of accessor functions. This is followed by the definitions for operator<=> and operator==.[5] Note that these operators perform comparisons using attribute m_Name. The miscellaneous section contains declarations for static functions that the example programs use to obtain Nut objects or other related data. File Nut.cpp begins an anonymous namespace that contains a std::array of predefined Nut objects. The remaining code in Nut.cpp includes definitions for the previously mentioned static functions along with some formatting functions.

Function Ch05_04_ex1() demonstrates how to determine if a std::optional object contains a value. Listing 5-4-1-2 shows the code for Ch05_04_ex1().

---

[5] Recall that the C++ compiler can automatically generate code for the six standard relational operators from these two operators.

CHAPTER 5   GENERAL UTILITIES LIBRARY

Listing 5-4-1-2. Example Ch05_04 – Ch05_04_ex1()

```cpp
//--------------------------------------------------------------------
// Ch05_04_ex.cpp
//--------------------------------------------------------------------

#include <array>
#include <cmath>
#include <optional>
#include <string>
#include "Ch05_04.h"
#include "Nut.h"

void Ch05_04_ex1()
{
    // std::optional objects
    std::optional<Nut> nut1 {Nut::get_nut(Nut::Type::Almond)};
    std::optional<Nut> nut2 {Nut::get_nut(Nut::Type::Pecan)};
    std::optional<Nut> nut3 {};

    std::print("{:s}", Nut::title_str());

    // using has_value()
    if (nut1.has_value())
        std::println("{}", nut1.value());
    else
        std::println("no value");

    // using operator bool()
    if (nut2)
        std::println("{}", *nut2);
    else
        std::println("no value");

    if (nut3)
        std::println("{}", *nut3);
    else
        std::println("no value");
}
```

In Listing 5-4-1-2, function `Ch05_04_ex1()` opens with the definition of several `std::optional<Nut>` objects. The first two objects, `nut1` and `nut2`, contain `Nut` objects that encompass nutritional data for almonds and pecans. Object `nut3` is a `std::optional<Nut>` object without a contained `Nut`. While not used in this example, a function could exercise `std::optional::operator=` to assign a value to `nut3`.

The second code block in `Ch05_04_ex1()` uses `nut1.has_value()` to test `nut1` for a contained value. Member function `has_value()` returns a `bool` signifying the presence (`true`) or absence (`false`) of a contained value. If `nut1` contains a value, the subsequent `std::println()` call exercises `nut1.value()` to obtain a reference to the current `Nut` value for printing. One important item to note here is that `std::optional::value()` throws a `std::bad_optional_access` exception if it's used with an object that doesn't contain a value.

The next code block demonstrates an alternative method of checking a `std::optional` object for a contained value. The statement `if (nut2)` exploits `std::optional::bool()`, which performs the same operation as `has_value()`. Note the use of (dereference) `operator*()` in the ensuing `std::println()` statement to access the contained value in `nut2`. The final code block demonstrates the use of a `std::optional<Nut>` object without a contained value.

Listing 5-4-2 shows the code for function `Ch05_04_ex2()`, which illustrates `std::optional` relational operator usage. Following the initializations of `nut1` to `nut5`, `Ch05_04_ex2()` performs comparisons using objects `nut1` to `nut3`, all of which have contained values. For these comparisons, the relational operators defined by class `Nut` get employed. The next code block compares `nut1` and `nut4`. Note that `nut4` lacks a contained value.

Listing 5-4-2. Example Ch05_04 – Ch05_04_ex2()

```
void Ch05_04_ex2()
{
    // create std::optional<Nut> test objects
    std::optional<Nut> nut1 {Nut::get_nut(Nut::Type::Pecan)};
    std::optional<Nut> nut2 {nut1};
    std::optional<Nut> nut3 {Nut::get_nut(Nut::Type::Walnut)};
    std::optional<Nut> nut4 {};
    Nut nut5 {Nut::get_nut(Nut::Type::Almond)};      // value object
```

```cpp
std::println("nut1 name: {}", nut1.has_value() ? nut1->Name() :
"no value");
std::println("nut2 name: {}", nut2.has_value() ? nut2->Name() :
"no value");
std::println("nut3 name: {}", nut3.has_value() ? nut3->Name() :
"no value");
std::println("nut4 name: {}", nut4.has_value() ? nut4->Name() :
"no value");
std::println("nut5 name: {}", nut5.Name());

// Relational operators - example 1
std::println("\ncomparisons using two std::optional<Nut>");
std::println("nut1 == nut2: {:s}", nut1 == nut2);
std::println("nut1 <  nut2: {:s}", nut1 <  nut2);
std::println("nut1 >  nut2: {:s}", nut1 >  nut2);

std::println("\nnut1 == nut3: {:s}", nut1 == nut3);
std::println("nut1 <  nut3: {:s}", nut1 <  nut3);
std::println("nut1 >  nut3: {:s}", nut1 >  nut3);

// Relational operators - example 2
std::println("\ncomparisons using std::optional<Nut> and no value");
std::println("nut1 == nut4: {:s}", nut1 == nut4);
std::println("nut1 <  nut4: {:s}", nut1 <  nut4);
std::println("nut1 >  nut4: {:s}", nut1 >  nut4);

// Relational operators - example 3
std::println("\ncomparisons using std::optional<Nut> and
std::nullopt");
std::println("nut1 == std::nullopt: {:s}", nut1 == std::nullopt);
std::println("nut1 <  std::nullopt: {:s}", nut1 <  std::nullopt);
std::println("nut1 >  std::nullopt: {:s}", nut1 >  std::nullopt);

std::println("\nnut4 == std::nullopt: {:s}", nut4 == std::nullopt);
std::println("nut4 <  std::nullopt: {:s}", nut4 >  std::nullopt);
std::println("nut4 >  std::nullopt: {:s}", nut4 <  std::nullopt);
```

```
    // Relational operators - example 4
    std::println("\ncomparisons using using std::optional<Nut> and Nut");
    std::println("nut1 == nut5: {:s}", nut1 == nut5);
    std::println("nut1 <  nut5: {:s}", nut1 <  nut5);
    std::println("nut1 >  nut5: {:s}", nut1 >  nut5);
}
```

Table 5-2 summarizes `std::optional` relational operator usages. In this table, symbols x and y denote objects of type `std::optional<T>`, and v denotes an object of type T. Table 5-2 contains three relational operator groupings: x op y, x op `std::nullopt`, and x op v (or v op x) where op denotes a relational operator. The important item to recognize in Table 5-2 is that when comparing two `std::optional<T>` objects, a normal comparison is performed if both `x.has_value()` and `y.has_value()` are true. When comparing a `std::optional<T>` against an object of type T, a normal comparison is performed if `x.has_value()` is true.

Table 5-2. Relational Operators for std::optional

Operator	Condition	Return Value
x == y	x.has_value() != y.has_value()	false
	x.has_value() == false	true
	otherwise	*x == *y
x != y	x.has_value() != y.has_value()	true
	x.has_value() == false	false
	otherwise	*x != *y
x < y	!y	false
	!x	true
	otherwise	*x < *y

(continued)

Table 5-2. (*continued*)

Operator	Condition	Return Value
x > y	!x	false
	!y	true
	otherwise	*x > *y
x <= y	!x	true
	!y	false
	otherwise	*x <= *y
x >= y	!y	true
	!x	false
	otherwise	*x >= *y
x <=> y	x && y	*x <=> *y
	otherwise	x.has_value() <=> y.has_value()
x == std::nullopt		!x
x <=> std::nullopt		x.has_value() <=> false
x == v		x.has_value() ? *x == v : false
v == x		x.has_value() ? v == *x : false
x != v		x.has_value() ? *x != v : true
v != x		x.has_value() ? v != *x : true
x < v		x.has_value() ? *x < v : true
v < x		x.has_value() ? v < *x : false
x > v		x.has_value() ? *x > v : false
v > x		x.has_value() ? v > *x : true
x <= v		x.has_value() ? *x <= v : true
v <= x		x.has_value() ? v <= *x : false

(*continued*)

CHAPTER 5 GENERAL UTILITIES LIBRARY

Table 5-2. (*continued*)

Operator	Condition	Return Value
x >= v		x.has_value() ? *x >= v : false
v >= x		x.has_value() ? v >= *x : true
x <=> v		x.has_value() ? *x <=> v : strong_ordering::less

One real-world downside of std::optional usage is the repeated checking (using has_value() or operator bool()) that a program typically performs to confirm that a std::optional object contains a value. To mitigate this problem, C++23 adds several monadic operations to class std::optional<>. A monadic operation is a member function that conditionally executes a supplied function based on the state of a std::optional object. Monadic operations reduce the number of if-else code blocks necessary to execute a series of operations using a std::optional object.

Listing 5-4-3 shows the source code example function Ch05_04_ex3(). This function demonstrates basic usage of std::optional<> monadic operations and_then(), transform(), and or_else().

Listing 5-4-3. Example Ch05_04 – Ch05_04_ex3()

```
void Ch05_04_ex3()
{
#if __cpp_lib_optional >= 202110L

    std::array<std::optional<double>, 2> arr1
        { std::optional<double> {}, std::optional<double> {2.0} };

    for (const std::optional<double>& opt : arr1)
    {
        // print opt.value()
        std::print("\nopt.value(): ");
        if (opt)
            std::println("{:f}", opt.value());
        else
```

211

```cpp
        std::println("no value");

    // using std::optional<T>::and_then
    auto func_and_then = [](double x) -> std::optional<double>
        { return std::sqrt(x); };

    std::optional<double> result_and_then = opt.and_then
    (func_and_then);

    std::print("result_and_then.value(): ");
    if (result_and_then)
        std::println("{:f}", result_and_then.value());
    else
        std::println("no value");

    // using std::optional<T>::transform
    auto func_transform = [](double x) -> int
        { return static_cast<int>(x * x * x); };

    std::optional<int> result_transform = opt.transform
    (func_transform);

    std::print("result_transform.value(): ");
    if (result_transform)
        std::println("{:d}", result_transform.value());
    else
        std::println("no value");

    // using std::optional<T>::or_else
    auto func_or_else = []() -> std::optional<double>
        { return 20.0; };

    std::optional<double> result_or_else = opt.or_else(func_or_else);

    std::print("result_or_else.value(): ");
    if (result_or_else)
        std::println("{:f}", result_or_else.value());
    else
        std::println("no value");
}
```

```
#else
    std::println("Example Ch05_04_ex3() "
        "requires std::optional monadic operations (C++23)");
#endif
}
```

Near the top of Ch05_04_ex3() is the definition of std::array<std::optional<double>, 2> arr1. Note that the first std::optional<double> object is empty, while the second object contains a value of 2.0. The first code block within the for loop prints the contained value of opt (if present). Next is the definition of lambda expression func_and_then. Note that this expression requires an argument of type double. Also, note that func_and_then() calculates the square root of x and returns this value in an object of type std::optional<double>. The next statement, result_and_then = opt.and_then(func_and_then), calls func_and_then(). If opt contains a value (opt1.has_value() is true), function func_and_then() gets executed, which calculates the square root of opt.value(). The result of this calculation is returned in an object of type std::optional<double>. If opt1 doesn't contain a value (i.e., opt1.has_value() is false), and_then() returns an empty object of type std::optional<double>.

The next for loop code block in Ch05_04_ex3() demonstrates the use of monadic member function transform(), which performs a transformation using the value of a std::optional object. Lambda expression func_transform() defines the transformation to perform. Note that this expression requires an argument of type double (the same type as the std::optional object) but returns a value of type int. Similar to and_then(), opt.transform(func_transform) executes func_transform(opt.value()) provided opt.has_value() is true. What's important to recognize here is that opt.transform(func_transform) takes the int value calculated by func_transform() and automatically converts this value to an object of type std::optional<int>. Note that result_transform is declared as a std::optional<int>.[6]

The final for loop code block spotlights the use of monadic member function or_else(). This function executes lambda expression func_or_else() if opt.has_value() is false; otherwise, it returns opt. Note that func_or_else() returns an object of type std::optional<double>. Monadic member function or_else() is often utilized

---

[6] Explicit types are used here instead of keyword auto to accentuate the actual types.

CHAPTER 5 GENERAL UTILITIES LIBRARY

to provide a default value for a std::optional<> object that lacks a value. Before proceeding, you may want to take a quick look at the results section for this example to confirm your understanding of the code in Ch05_04_ex3().

Listing 5-4-4 shows the source code for the next std::optional example. This listing begins with the definition of a helper function named get_test_nut(), which returns a std::optional<Nut>. Note that std::nullopt is returned for types Nut::Type::Pecan and Nut::Type::Pistachio to simulate an error condition. The next helper function, protein_per_gram(), calculates the amount of protein (grams) in a one gram serving. Note that the return type for this function is std::optional<float>. The final helper function, protein_per_ounce(), calculates grams of protein per one ounce serving.

Listing 5-4-4. Example Ch05_04 - Ch05_04_ex4()

```
// helper functions
std::optional<Nut> get_test_nut(Nut::Type type)
{
    // return nullopt to simulate error
    if (type == Nut::Type::Pecan || type == Nut::Type::Pistachio)
        return std::nullopt;

    // return valid Nut
    return Nut::get_nut(type);
}

std::optional<float> protein_per_gram(const Nut& nut)
{
    // calculate grams of protein in 1 gram serving
    return nut.Protein() / 100.0f;
}

float protein_per_ounce(float ppg)
{
    // calculate grams of protein in 1 ounce serving
    return ppg * 28.3495f;
}

void Ch05_04_ex4()
{
```

```cpp
#if __cpp_lib_optional >= 202110L

    Nut::Type nut_types[] { Nut::Type::Almond, Nut::Type::Cashew,
        Nut::Type::Pecan, Nut::Type::Walnut };

    for (Nut::Type nut_type : nut_types)
    {
        std::print("nut type: {:10s}", Nut::get_type_string(nut_type));

        // lambda expression for std::optional::or_else
        auto func_or_else = [nut_type]()
            { return std::optional<Nut> { Nut::get_nut(nut_type) }; };

        std::optional<Nut> nut1 = get_test_nut(nut_type);
        std::optional<Nut> nut2 = nut1.or_else(func_or_else);

        if (nut2)
        {
            // display protein per ounce (ppo)
            std::optional<float> ppg = nut2.and_then(protein_per_gram);
            std::optional<float> ppo = ppg.transform(protein_per_ounce);

            if (ppo)
                std::println("protein: {:.4f} g per ounce", ppo.value());
            else
                std::println("ppo has no value");
        }
        else
            std::println("nut2 has no value");
    }
#else
    std::println("Example Ch05_04_ex4() "
                 "requires std::optional monadic operations (C++23)");
#endif
}
```

CHAPTER 5   GENERAL UTILITIES LIBRARY

Function Ch05_04_ex4() spotlights a series of monadic operations using instances of std::optional<Nut>. Within the for loop, nut1 is initialized using helper function get_test_nut(). Recall that get_test_nut() may return a std::nullopt to simulate an error condition. The next statement, nut2 = nut1.or_else(func_or_else), calls func_or_else() to initialize nut2 if nut1.has_value() equals false; otherwise, or_else() returns nut1. In the next code block, Ch05_04_ex4() utilizes ppg = nut2.and_then(protein_per_gram) and ppo = ppg.transform(protein_per_ounce) to calculate the amount of protein in a one ounce serving.

Listing 5-4-5 shows the code for Ch05_04_ex5(), which exemplifies a chained series of monadic operations. The calculation carried out in this function is the same as the one in Ch05_04_ex4(), but the code that's utilized within the for loop is shorter and – more importantly – underscores the ultimate intent of the calculation.

Listing 5-4-5. Example Ch05_04 – Ch05_04_ex5()

```
void Ch05_04_ex5()
{
#if __cpp_lib_optional >= 202110L

    Nut::Type nut_types[] { Nut::Type::Almond, Nut::Type::Cashew,
        Nut::Type::Pecan, Nut::Type::Walnut };

    for (Nut::Type nut_type : nut_types)
    {
        std::print("nut type: {:10s}", Nut::get_type_string(nut_type));

        // lambda expression for std::optional::or_else
        auto func_or_else = [nut_type]()
            { return std::optional<Nut> { Nut::get_nut(nut_type) }; };

        // display protein per ounce (ppo)
        auto ppo = get_test_nut(nut_type)
                    .or_else(func_or_else)
                    .and_then(protein_per_gram)
                    .transform(protein_per_ounce);

        if (ppo)
            std::println("protein: {:.4f} g per ounce", ppo.value());
        else
```

```
            std::println("ppo has no value");
    }
#else
    std::println("Example Ch05_04_ex5() "
        "requires std::optional monadic operations (C++23)");
#endif
}
```

Here are the results for example Ch05_04:

```
----- Results for example Ch05_04 -----

----- Ch05_04_ex1() -----

Name              EnKj        EnKcal      Carbs       Fat         Protein
==========================================================================
[Almond           2423         579        21.60       49.90        21.20]
[Pecan            2889         690        13.86       71.97         9.17]
no value

----- Ch05_04_ex2() -----
nut1 name: Pecan
nut2 name: Pecan
nut3 name: Walnut
nut4 name: no value
nut5 name: Almond

comparisons using two std::optional<Nut>
nut1 == nut2: true
nut1 <  nut2: false
nut1 >  nut2: false

nut1 == nut3: false
nut1 <  nut3: true
nut1 >  nut3: false

comparisons using std::optional<Nut> and no value
nut1 == nut4: false
nut1 <  nut4: false
```

CHAPTER 5   GENERAL UTILITIES LIBRARY

```
nut1 >   nut4: true

comparisons using std::optional<Nut> and std::nullopt
nut1 == std::nullopt: false
nut1 <  std::nullopt: false
nut1 >  std::nullopt: true

nut4 == std::nullopt: true
nut4 <  std::nullopt: false
nut4 >  std::nullopt: false

comparisons using using std::optional<Nut> and Nut
nut1 == nut5: false
nut1 <  nut5: false
nut1 >  nut5: true

----- Ch05_04_ex3() -----

opt.value(): no value
result_and_then.value(): no value
result_transform.value(): no value
result_or_else.value(): 20.000000

opt.value(): 2.000000
result_and_then.value(): 1.414214
result_transform.value(): 8
result_or_else.value(): 2.000000

----- Ch05_04_ex4() -----
nut type: Almond    protein: 6.0101 g per ounce
nut type: Cashew    protein: 5.1653 g per ounce
nut type: Pecan     protein: 2.5996 g per ounce
nut type: Walnut    protein: 4.3176 g per ounce

----- Ch05_04_ex4() -----
nut type: Almond    protein: 6.0101 g per ounce
nut type: Cashew    protein: 5.1653 g per ounce
nut type: Pecan     protein: 2.5996 g per ounce
nut type: Walnut    protein: 4.3176 g per ounce
```

Using std::any

Class std::any is a simple *non-template* container that can hold a single value of any type, which must be copy constructable (i.e., the type defines a copy constructor). The state of a std::any object corresponds to whether it contains a value. A std::any object without a value is considered empty. Objects of type std::any are often utilized to safely convey a single value whose type may vary.

Source code example Ch05_05 highlights the use of std::any. Function Ch05_05_ex1(), shown in Listing 5-5-1, begins its execution with the statement std::any val1 {100}. Following execution of this statement, val1 contains an int and its value is 100. In the ensuing std::println() statement, the expression val1.type().name() returns a string for the type of value contained in val1. The next std::println() statement utilizes std::any_cast<int>(val1) to obtain the value of the int that's stored in val1.

Listing 5-5-1. Example Ch05_05 – Ch05_05_ex1()

```
//-------------------------------------------------------------------
// Ch05_05_ex.cpp
//-------------------------------------------------------------------

#include <any>
#include <numbers>
#include <typeinfo>
#include "Ch05_05.h"
#include "Rect.h"

void Ch05_05_ex1()
{
    using namespace std::string_literals;

    // using std::any - initial value is int
    std::any val1 {100};
    std::println("\nval1 type:  {:s}", val1.type().name());
    std::println("val1 value: {:d}", std::any_cast<int>(val1));

    // change val1 to std::string (literal suffix required)
    val1 = "one, two, three"s;
    std::println("\nval1 type:  {:s}", val1.type().name());
```

```
    std::println("val1 value: {:s}", std::any_cast<std::string>(val1));

    // using std::any - initial value is double
    std::any val2 {std::numbers::pi};
    std::println("\nval1 type:  {:s}", val2.type().name());
    std::println("val2 value: {:.4f}", std::any_cast<double>(val2));

    // throws std::bad_any_cast exception
//  auto val3 = std::any_cast<std::string>(val2);
}
```

In the next code block, the expression val1 = "one, two, three"s changes both the type and value of the object maintained in val1. Note that this expression employs literal suffix s. This is required to ensure that val1 contains an object of type std::string. Without the literal suffix, val1 would hold an object of type const char*. The following code block creates std::any object val2, which contains a double that equals the constant π. The final statement of Ch05_05_ex1() is commented out since it generates an exception. When using std::any_cast<T>(const std::any& any_obj), the value that's contained in any_obj must be one of type T. If it isn't, std::any_cast throws a std::bad_any_cast exception.

Listing 5-5-2 shows the source code for the next std::any example. Function Ch05_05_ex2() opens with the definition of an empty std::any object named val1. The val1.emplace<Rect>(0, 0, 3, 4) statement that follows emplaces an object of type Rect (see Listing 5-3-2-1) into val1. In the ensuing if statement, val1.has_value() returns true if val1 contains a value; otherwise, it returns false. The next code block utilizes val1.emplace<std::string>("eins zwei drei") to store an object of type std::string in val. When changing the value of a std::any object, any applicable destructors are automatically executed. Function Ch05_05_ex2()'s final code block utilizes val1.reset(), which resets val1 to the empty state.

Listing 5-5-2. Example Ch05_05 – Ch05_05_ex2()

```
void Ch05_05_ex2()
{
    std::any val1 {};

    // using emplace - change to Rect
    val1.emplace<Rect>(0, 0, 3, 4);
```

```
    if (val1.has_value())
    {
        if (val1.type() == typeid(Rect))
            std::println("val1: {}", any_cast<Rect>(val1));
    }

    // using emplace - change to std::string
    val1.emplace<std::string>("eins zwei drei");

    if (val1.has_value())
    {
        if (val1.type() == typeid(std::string))
            std::println("val1: {}", any_cast<std::string>(val1));
    }

    // manual reset
    val1.reset();

    if (val1.has_value())
        std::println("val1.reset() failed!");
    else
        std::println("val1.reset() successful");
}
```

The final std::any example of Ch05_05, shown in Listing 5-5-3, begins with the definition of a function named process_message(). Note that this function requires an argument of type const std::any&. Within process_message() is a series of val.type() checks that test val for specific type. If a type match is found, the ensuing std::println() statement prints the contained value. If val is empty, val.type() returns typeid(void). The next function in Listing 5-5-3, Ch05_05_ex3(), exercises process_message() using a variety of std::any objects. Note that the last call to process_message() utilizes an empty std::any object.

Listing 5-5-3. Example Ch05_05 – Ch05_05_ex3()

```
void process_message(const std::any& val)
{
    if (val.type() == typeid(int))
        std::println("val: {:d}", any_cast<int>(val));
```

```cpp
    if (val.type() == typeid(long))
        std::println("val: {:d}", any_cast<long>(val));

    else if (val.type() == typeid(double))
        std::println("val: {:f}", any_cast<double>(val));

    else if (val.type() == typeid(std::string))
        std::println("val: {:s}", any_cast<std::string>(val));

    else if (val.type() == typeid(Rect))
        std::println("val: {}", any_cast<Rect>(val));

    else
        std::println("unexpected type: {:s}", val.type().name());
}
void Ch05_05_ex3()
{
    process_message(std::make_any<int>(100));
    process_message(std::make_any<long>(200L));
    process_message(std::make_any<long long>(300LL));
    process_message(std::make_any<double>(std::numbers::pi));
    process_message(std::make_any<std::string>("lemon lime orange"));
    process_message(std::make_any<Rect>(Rect {0, 0, 30, 40}));
    process_message(std::any {});
}
```

Example function Ch05_05_ex3() and process_message() utilized std::any objects that contained simple types, but it's easy to envision a real-world message processing algorithm that processes different message types embedded within a std::any object. The results for Ch05_05 follow this paragraph. Note that the text output shown for "val1 type" is compiler dependent.

```
----- Results for example Ch05_05 -----
----- Ch05_05_ex1() -----
val1 type:   int
val1 value: 100
```

```
val1 type:   class std::basic_string<char,struct std::char_
traits<char>,class std::allocator<char> >
val1 value: one, two, three

val1 type:   double
val2 value: 3.1416

----- Ch05_05_ex2() -----
val1: [(0, 0, 3, 4) 12]
val1: eins zwei drei
val1.reset() successful

----- Ch05_05_ex3() -----
val: 100
unexpected type: int
val: 200
unexpected type: __int64
val: 3.141593
val: lemon lime orange
val: [(0, 0, 30, 40) 1200]
unexpected type: void
```

Using std::expected

A std::expected<T, E> (C++23) object is a template class that *always* contains a value of type T or type E where T is the type of an expected value and E is the type of an unexpected value. Class std::expected objects are handy for function return values since they can encompass either a success (expected) or an error (unexpected) result.

Listing 5-6-1 shows the source code for example Ch05_06_ex1(). The first item to note in this listing is the preprocessor statement #if __cpp_lib_expected >= 202211L, which confirms compiler support for class std::expected. Next is the definition of enum class ErrorCode. This enum defines a few symbolic names for errors that example Ch05_06 generates. The function that follows, std::string to_string(ErrorCode ec), returns an ErrorCode's string representation for display purposes.

CHAPTER 5   GENERAL UTILITIES LIBRARY

Listing 5-6-1. Example Ch05_06 – Ch05_06_ex1()

```
//-----------------------------------------------------------------
// Ch05_06_ex.cpp
//-----------------------------------------------------------------

#include <cerrno>
#include <cfenv>
#include <cmath>
#include <concepts>
#include <filesystem>
#include <format>
#include <fstream>
#include <string>
#include <vector>
#include <version>
#include "Ch05_06.h"
#include "MF.h"

#if __cpp_lib_expected >= 202211L
#include <expected>

enum class ErrorCode
    {OpenError, WriteError, CloseError, DomainError, RangeError};

std::string to_string(ErrorCode ec)
{
    static std::string ec_strings[]
        {"OpenError", "WriteError", "CloseError", "DomainError",
        "RangeError"};

    switch (ec)
    {
        case ErrorCode::OpenError:
        case ErrorCode::WriteError:
        case ErrorCode::CloseError:
        case ErrorCode::DomainError:
        case ErrorCode::RangeError:
```

```cpp
                return ec_strings[static_cast<int>(ec)];
            default:
                return "unknown error code";
        }
    }
}

std::expected<std::string, ErrorCode> file_op(const std::string& base_fn)
{
    // add name of results dir to base_fn
    std::string fn = MF::mk_test_filename(base_fn);

    // create test file (fails on invalid base_fn)
    std::ofstream ofs {fn, std::ios_base::out | std::ios_base::trunc};

    if (!ofs.good())
        return std::unexpected(ErrorCode::OpenError);

    // test file writes
    for (char c {'A'}; c <= 'Z'; ++c)
    {
        ofs << std::string(72, c) << '\n';

        if (!ofs.good())
            return std::unexpected(ErrorCode::WriteError);
    }

    // explicit close
    ofs.close();
    if (ofs.fail())
        return std::unexpected(ErrorCode::CloseError);

    // return final filename to caller
    return fn;
}

void Ch05_06_ex1()
{
    // test base name strings (good and bad)
    const std::string base_names[] =
```

```cpp
        {"test1.txt", "test2\\.txt", "test3.txt", "test4/.txt"};

    // Perform test file operations
    for (const std::string& bn : base_names)
    {
        // build base name string
        std::string bn2 {"Ch05_06_ex1_"};
        bn2 += bn;
        std::println("\nbase name: {:s}", bn2);

        // perform file operation
        std::expected<std::string, ErrorCode> result = file_op(bn2);

        if (result.has_value())
        {
            // successful file operation, delete temp file
            std::println("file_op() successful");
            std::println("removing test file {:s}", result.value());
            std::filesystem::remove(result.value());
        }
        else
        {
            // file operation error
            ErrorCode error_code = result.error();
            std::println("file_op() failed ({:s})", to_string(error_code));
        }
    }
}
```

The next item in Listing 5-6-1 is the definition of test function file_op(), which writes character data to a test file. Note that the return value for file_op() is std::expected<std::string, ErrorCode>. The first code block in file_op() utilizes MF::mk_test_file() to prepend a directory name and prefix to base_fn.[7] The ensuing code block opens file fn for output. If the open fails, file_op() executes return std::unexpected(ErrorCode::OpenError). This returns an object of

---

[7] See MF.h for more information.

CHAPTER 5   GENERAL UTILITIES LIBRARY

std::expected<std::string, ErrorCode> that contains an unexpected value. The next code block in file_op() writes test data to the specified file. This is followed by an explicit call to close(). Note that a result of std::unexpected is generated if either of these operations fail. The final return fn statement returns the generated filename to the caller. Note that fn is an object of type std::string, which matches the expected type of return value std::expected<std::string, ErrorCode>.

The opening code block of Ch05_06_ex1() defines a C-style array of std::strings that represent base names for test files. Note that array base_names[] includes both valid and invalid names. Within the for loop, the previously described file_op() is called and its return value is saved in result. The next statement, result.has_value(), tests result to see if it contains an *expected* value. If true, the ensuing std::println() statements print appropriate status messages. Note in the second std::println() statement the use of result.value(); this returns a reference to the expected std::string value that result contains. If result.has_value() is false, the expression error_code = result.error() obtains the unexpected value from result. This value is converted to a std::string using to_string() and printed.

Listing 5-6-2 shows the source code for example function Ch05_06_ex2(). This example utilizes std::expected to report the results of a numerical calculation. Listing 5-6-2 opens with the definition of template function calc_result(). Note that this function requires an argument of type std::vector<T> and returns a std::expected<std::vector<T>, ErrorCode>. Function calc_result() computes result[i] = sqrt(log10(vec[i])). This calculation is arbitrary and inconsequential. What is important are the domain and range error checks performed within the for loop. If a domain or range error is detected, calc_result() returns std::unexpected(ErrorCode::DomainError) or std::unexpected(ErrorCode::RangeError), respectively; otherwise, std::vector<T> result is returned.

Listing 5-6-2. Example Ch05_06 – Ch05_06_ex2()

```
template <typename T> requires std::floating_point<T>
std::expected<std::vector<T>, ErrorCode> calc_result(const
std::vector<T>& vec)
{
    errno = 0;
    std::vector<T> result(vec.size());
```

```cpp
        // perform test calculation (flag domain & range errors)
        for (size_t i = 0; i < result.size(); ++i)
        {
            T temp1 = log10(vec[i]);
            if (errno == EDOM)
                return std::unexpected(ErrorCode::DomainError);
            if (errno == ERANGE)
                return std::unexpected(ErrorCode::RangeError);

            T temp2 = sqrt(temp1);
            if (errno == EDOM)
                return std::unexpected(ErrorCode::DomainError);

            result[i] = temp2;
        }

        return result;
    }
    void Ch05_06_ex2()
    {
        int test_id {};

        // test vectors
        std::vector<std::vector<double>> vecs
        {
            {10.0, 20.0, 30.0, 40.0, 50.0},
            {10.0, 20.0, 0.0, 40.0, 50.0},                  // RE - log10(0.0)
            {100.0, 200.0, 300.0, 400.0, 500.0},
            {100.0, 200.0, -300.0, 400.0, 500.0},           // DE - log10(-300.0)
            {1000.0, 2000.0, 3000.0, 4000.0, 5000.0},
            {10.0, 20.0, 0.5, 40.0, 50.0}                   // DE - sqrt(log10(0.5))
        };

        auto print_vec = [](const std::vector<double>& vec)
        {
            for (double x : vec)
```

```cpp
            std::print("{:9.4f} ", x);
        std::println("");
    };

    for (const std::vector<double>& vec : vecs)
    {
        std::print("\ntest #{:d} vec:    ", test_id);
        print_vec(vec);

        std::print("test #{:d} result: ", test_id++);

        std::expected<std::vector<double>, ErrorCode> result = calc_
        result(vec);

        if (result)
        {
            std::vector<double> result_vec = result.value();
            print_vec(result_vec);
        }
        else
        {
            ErrorCode ec = result.error();
            std::print("{:s}\n", to_string(ec));
        }
    }
}

#endif    // __cpp_lib_expected
```

Function Ch05_06_ex2(), also shown in Listing 5-6-2, contains code that exercises calc_result(). Near the top of Ch05_06_ex2() are a series of test vectors that contain purposeful values to generate domain and range errors. The for loop within Ch05_06_ex2() contains straightforward code. Function calc_result() is called for each test std::vector<double> vec in vecs. The return code from this function is tested using std::expected::operator::bool(). If true, the results of the calculation are printed using print_vec(); otherwise, result.error() is utilized to obtain the unexpected error code, and this value is then converted to a std::string prior to being printed. Here are the results for example Ch05_06:

CHAPTER 5   GENERAL UTILITIES LIBRARY

----- Results for example Ch05_06 -----

----- Ch05_06_ex1() -----

base name: Ch05_06_ex1_test1.txt
file_op() successful
removing test file ./~~Ch05_06_ex1_test1.txt

base name: Ch05_06_ex1_test2\.txt
file_op() failed (OpenError)

base name: Ch05_06_ex1_test3.txt
file_op() successful
removing test file ./~~Ch05_06_ex1_test3.txt

base name: Ch05_06_ex1_test4/.txt
file_op() failed (OpenError)

----- Ch05_06_ex2() -----

```
test #0 vec:        10.0000    20.0000    30.0000    40.0000    50.0000
test #0 result:      1.0000     1.1406     1.2154     1.2657     1.3034

test #1 vec:        10.0000    20.0000     0.0000    40.0000    50.0000
test #1 result: RangeError

test #2 vec:       100.0000   200.0000   300.0000   400.0000   500.0000
test #2 result:      1.4142     1.5169     1.5739     1.6131     1.6429

test #3 vec:       100.0000   200.0000  -300.0000   400.0000   500.0000
test #3 result: DomainError

test #4 vec:      1000.0000  2000.0000  3000.0000  4000.0000  5000.0000
test #4 result:      1.7321     1.8169     1.8647     1.8979     1.9233

test #5 vec:        10.0000    20.0000     0.5000    40.0000    50.0000
test #5 result: DomainError
```

Class `std::expected<T, E>` also supports several monadic operations, including `and_then()`, `transform()`, `or_else()`, and `transform_error()`. The first three monadic operations are analogs of the ones that you learned about earlier in this chapter for `std::optional`. The fourth one, `transform_error()`, facilitates transform operations using the value returned by `std::expected<E, T>::error()` instead of `std::expected<E, T>::value()`. Appendix B contains a list of resources that you can consult for more information regarding these operations.

Summary

Here are the key learning points for this chapter:

- A `std::pair` is a template class that bundles two heterogeneous objects into a single unit. The elements of a `std::pair` can be referenced using structure-like named members or via compile-time constant indices.

- A `std::tuple` is a template class that bundles *N* heterogeneous objects into a single unit. The elements of a `std::tuple` are referenced using compile-time constant indices.

- A `std::variant` is a type-safe alternative for a `union`. An instance of `std::variant` can hold one of several alternative types, which are specified using template parameters.

- A `std::optional` is a template class that holds an optional value of a single type. This class is sometimes utilized for return values since the presence or absence of a contained object can signify success or failure. Class `std::optional` supports monadic operations (C++23) that can be chained together to minimize boilerplate code that performs value checks.

- A `std::any` object can (optionally) hold a single value of any copy-constructable object.

- A `std::expected` (C++23) object always holds either an expected (normal) value or an unexpected (error) value. Class `std::expected` also supports monadic operations that can be chained together to minimize boilerplate value checking code.

CHAPTER 6

Smart Pointers

This chapter explains smart pointers and how to use them. Topics discussed include

- Smart pointer primer
- How to use `std::unique_ptr`
- How to use `std::shared_ptr`
- How to use `std::weak_ptr`

Smart Pointer Primer

A raw or native C++ pointer is simply the address of an object in memory. Consider the following frivolous example:

```
void test_ptr1()
{
    // pointer to a fundamental type
    int i {10};
    int* ip = &i;

    *ip += 20;
    i -= 5;
    std::println("i: {:d}", i);
}
```

CHAPTER 6   SMART POINTERS

The code in test_ptr1() uses address-of operator & to initialize pointer int* ip. The next two expressions, *ip += 20 and i -= 5, carry out their operations using the same value in memory. Here's another example that's a bit more interesting:

```
struct X
{
    int ValA {20};
    double ValB {30.0};
};

void test_ptr2()
{
    // pointer to a struct
    X* xp = new X {};

    xp->ValA *= 10;
    xp->ValB /= 5.0;
    std::println("xp->ValA: {:d}  xp->ValB: {:f}", xp->ValA, xp->ValB);
    delete xp;
}
```

Function test_ptr2() exploits operator new to dynamically allocate an instance X on the free store.[1] It then utilizes the pointer returned by new to perform calculations with structure members ValX and ValB. Following the calculations, test_ptr2() uses delete xp to release the previously allocated storage.

The final raw pointer example, test_ptr3(), allocates a C-style array and passes a pointer to the allocated array along with the number of elements to a function object that performs a calculation:

```
void test_ptr3()
{
    // pointer to C-style array
    constexpr int n {5};
    int* p = new int[n];

    auto f = [](int* p, int n)
```

---

[1] A reserved section of memory that's used for dynamic allocations.

```
    {
        for (int i = 0; i < n; ++i)
        {
            p[i] = 3 * i * i + 2 * i + 4;
            std::println("p[{:d}]: {:d}", i, p[i]);
        }
    };

    f(p, n);
    delete[] p;
}
```

The code pattern of the for loop in test_ptr3() is extremely common in legacy C++ code, especially pre-C++11 code. The "problem" with using pointers as shown in test_ptr2() and test_ptr3() is that you must remember to utilize delete or delete[] to release the storage space allocated by new. More importantly, the code in these functions doesn't account for the fact that std::println() might throw an exception. To address this situation, you can add try-catch blocks, but this often introduces unwelcome code obfuscations, especially when multiple levels of if-elses or function calls are involved.

To address situations like this, modern C++ strongly discourages the use of raw pointers. Instead, programs are encouraged to utilize smart pointers. A smart pointer is an abstraction of a raw pointer that's used just like the latter. The primary advantage of a smart pointer over a raw pointer is that a smart pointer guarantees execution of all applicable destructors if an exception is thrown. The remainder of this chapter explicates the use of C++ smart pointers std::unique_ptr, std::shared_ptr, and std::weak_ptr.

Using std::unique_ptr

A std::unique_ptr is a smart pointer that maintains exclusive ownership of an object. Compared to a raw pointer, a std::unique_ptr is expedient in that it automatically calls the destructor of the maintained object during execution of its own destructor. This reduces the risk of a memory or other resource leak.

Listing 6-1-1-1 shows the source code for class Book, which is used later in this section. Class Book is a straightforward class that holds book-related information including author, title, year published, and number of copies. The class itself defines accessor functions to facilitate retrieval of these attributes, two member functions buy()

CHAPTER 6 SMART POINTERS

and sell() that adjust the number of copies, and formatting functions. It also defines suitable constructors and a destructor. Source code examples Ch06_01 and Ch06_02 utilize class Book to demonstrate std::unique_ptr usage.

Listing 6-1-1-1. Example Ch06_01 – Class Book

```
//-----------------------------------------------------------------
// Book.h
//-----------------------------------------------------------------
#include <format>
#include <ostream>
#include <string>

class Book
{
    friend struct std::formatter<Book>;
public:
    Book();
    Book(const char* author, const char* title, int year_pub, int num_copies);
    ~Book();

    std::string Author() const { return m_Author; };
    std::string Title() const { return m_Title; };
    int YearPub() const { return m_YearPub; };
    int NumCopies() const { return m_NumCopies; };

    void set(const char* author, const char* title, int year_pub, int num_copies)
    {
        m_Author = author;
        m_Title = title;
        m_YearPub = year_pub;
        m_NumCopies = num_copies;
    }
```

```cpp
    int sell(int num_copies);
    void buy(int num_copies);
private:
    std::string to_str() const;

    std::string m_Author {};
    std::string m_Title {};
    int m_YearPub {};
    int m_NumCopies {};
};
// class Book formatter
template <> struct std::formatter<Book> : std::formatter<std::string>
{
    constexpr auto parse(std::format_parse_context& fpc)
        { return fpc.begin(); }

    auto format(const Book& book, std::format_context& fc) const
        {   return std::format_to(fc.out(), "{}", book.to_str()); }
};
//-------------------------------------------------------------------------
// Book.cpp
//-------------------------------------------------------------------------
#include <format>
#include <stdexcept>
#include <string>
#include "Book.h"
#include "Common.h"

// note: std::println() calls in ctors and dtor are for demo purposes only
Book::Book()
{
//  std::println("class Book - default ctor");
}
```

```cpp
Book::Book(const char* author, const char* title, int year_pub, int num_
copies) :
    m_Author {author}, m_Title {title},
    m_YearPub {year_pub}, m_NumCopies {num_copies}
{
//  std::println("class Book - ctor for '{:s}'", m_Title);
}

Book::~Book()
{
//  std::println("class Book - dtor for '{:s}'", m_Title);
}

int Book::sell(int num_copies)
{
    if (num_copies < 0)
        throw std::runtime_error("Book::sell() - invalid value: 'num_
        copies'");

    if (m_NumCopies >= num_copies)
    {
        m_NumCopies -= num_copies;
        return num_copies;
    }
    else
    {
        int nc_ret = m_NumCopies;
        m_NumCopies = 0;
        return nc_ret;
    }
}

void Book::buy(int num_copies)
{
    if (num_copies < 0)
        throw std::runtime_error("Book::buy() - invalid value: 'num_
        copies'");
```

```
        m_NumCopies += num_copies;
}
std::string Book::to_str() const
{
    std::string s {};

    std::format_to(std::back_inserter(s), {"[{:s}, '{:s}', {:d}, {:d}]"},
        m_Author, m_Title, m_YearPub, m_NumCopies);

    return s;
}
```

Listing 6-1-1-2 shows the source code for test function `Ch06_01_ex1()`. In the opening code block of this function, two instances of class `Book` are dynamically allocated using operator `new`. Execution of these statements calls the parameterized constructor that's defined for class `Book`. The next few code blocks carry out `std::println()` and `sell()` operations using the allocated `Book` objects. The final code block utilizes operator `delete` to release `book1` and `book2`. This action also executes the destructor for both `Book` objects.

Listing 6-1-1-2. Example Ch06_01 – Ch06_01_ex1()

```
//-------------------------------------------------------------------
// Ch06_01_ex.cpp
//-------------------------------------------------------------------

#include <cstdint>
#include <memory>
#include <stdexcept>
#include "Ch06_01.h"
#include "Book.h"
#include "RN.h"

void Ch06_01_ex1()
{
    Book* book1 = new Book("Isaac Newton", "Principia", 1687, 5);
    Book* book2 = new Book("Charles Darwin", "On the Origin of Species",
        1859, 4);
```

CHAPTER 6 SMART POINTERS

```
    // perform operations - exception unsafe
    std::println("\nInitial values:");
    std::println("book1: {}", *book1);
    std::println("book2: {}", *book2);

    book1->sell(2);
    book2->sell(3);

    std::println("\nAfter sell operations:");
    std::println("book1: {}", *book1);
    std::println("book2: {}", *book2);

    delete book1;
    delete book2;
}
```

Function Ch06_01_ex1() is correct in that it properly uses new and delete to allocate and release storage for objects book1 and book2. However, a memory leak will occur if either sell() or std::println() throws an exception. To address this flaw, Ch06_01_ex2() adds a try-catch construct to catch any exceptions thrown by sell() or std::println(). Listing 6-1-2 shows the source code for this example.

Listing 6-1-2. Example Ch06_01 – Ch06_01_ex2()

```
void Ch06_01_ex2()
{
    Book* book1 = new Book("Marie Curie", "The Discovery of Radium",
    1921, 2);
    Book* book2 = new Book("Albert Einstein", "The Meaning of Relativity",
    1923, 3);

    std::println("\nInitial values:");
    std::println("book1: {}", *book1);
    std::println("book2: {}", *book2);

    try
    {
        book1->sell(1);
        book2->sell(5);
```

```
        std::println("\nAfter sell operations:");
        std::println("book1: {}", *book1);
        std::println("book2: {}", *book2);
    }
    catch (const std::exception& ex)
    {
        std::println("caught exception Ch06_01_ex2(): {:s}", ex.what());
    }
    delete book1;
    delete book2;
}
```

The catch block in Ch06_01_ex2() only contains a call to std::println(). In a production environment, the code in this block would probably be more elaborate. The most important detail to recognize here is that following the catch block are two uses of delete, which delete book1 and book2 during normal processing or if an exception occurs.

In most C++ programs, adding code to handle potential exceptions is a requirement. However, inserting extra try-catch blocks merely to preclude a memory or other resource leak often results in code bloat and undesirable intricacies. Source code example Ch06_01_ex3(), shown in Listing 6-1-3, demonstrates how to use a std::unique_ptr, which is a simpler alternative.

Listing 6-1-3. Example Ch06_01 – Ch06_01_ex3()

```
void Ch06_01_ex3()
{
    std::unique_ptr<Book> book1 = std::make_unique<Book>("Richard Feynman",
        "Quantum Electrodynamics", 1962, 12);
    std::unique_ptr<Book> book2 = std::make_unique<Book>("Stephen Hawking",
        "A Brief History of Time", 1988, 19);

    std::println("\nInitial values:");
    std::println("book1: {}", *book1);
    std::println("book2: {}", *book2);
```

CHAPTER 6 SMART POINTERS

```
    book1->sell(9);
    book2->sell(4);

    std::println("\nAfter sell operations:");
    std::println("book1: {}", *book1);
    std::println("book2: {}", *book2);
}
```

The first statement of Ch06_01_ex3() utilizes std::make_unique<Book>() to create a smart pointer that encompasses an object of type Book. More specifically, function std::make_unique<Book>() calls operator new to allocate and construct an object of type Book; it then inserts a pointer to the newly allocated Book object in an instance of std::unique_ptr<Book> named book1. The next statement in Ch06_01_ex3() creates another std::unique_ptr<Book> instance named book2.

The remaining code in Ch06_01_ex3() exercises std::println() and sell() like the previous two functions. Note that std::unique_ptr<Book> objects book1 and book2 utilize operator-> and operator*() just like a raw pointer. Also, note that there's no extra boilerplate code to ensure deletion of the Book objects maintained by book1 and book2. These objects are automatically deleted during execution of the corresponding std::unique_ptr<Book> destructors, which occurs even if an exception is thrown. If warranted by the specific use case, you could add a try-catch block to Ch06_01_ex3() to handle any exceptions thrown by std::println() or sell(). The crucial takeaway point from this example is that extra boilerplate code is not needed to prevent a memory leak that results from failing to delete one or both of the allocated Book objects.

Near the top of example Ch06_01_ex4(), shown in Listing 6-1-4, is the definition of a lambda expression named buy_copies(). Note that this function object requires an argument of type std::unique_ptr<Book>&. A reference is used here since passing a std::unique_ptr object by value requires creating a new copy of the smart pointer, which is forbidden. Recall that a std::unique_ptr object maintains exclusive ownership of its encompassed object; allowing copy operations would violate this requisite. If you're unsure about using a reference here, change the argument of buy_copies() from a reference to a value and recompile the code. The remaining code in Ch06_01_ex4() illustrates the use of buy_copies(). Note that while Ch06_01_ex4() employs a lambda expression, you can also define a regular function that takes an argument of type std::unique_ptr&.

CHAPTER 6 SMART POINTERS

Listing 6-1-4. Example Ch06_01 – Ch06_01_ex4()

```
void Ch06_01_ex4()
{
    // std::unique_ptr<Book> passed by reference
    auto buy_copies = [](const std::unique_ptr<Book>& book)
    {
        // RN::get_value<int> returns a random integer value (see RN.h)
        int num_copies = RN::get_value<int>() % 20 + 1;
        book->buy(num_copies);
        return num_copies;
    };

    // pass std::unique_ptr<Book>& to another function
    std::unique_ptr<Book> book = std::make_unique<Book>("Isaac Newton",
        "Principia", 1687, 5);
    std::println("\nbook: {}", *book);
    int num_copies = buy_copies(book);
    std::println("num_copies: {:d}", num_copies);
    std::println("book: {}", *book);
}
```

Function Ch06_01_ex5(), shown in Listing 6-1-5, spotlights the use of a std::unique_ptr that encompasses a C-style array of Book objects. Like the previous example, function Ch06_01_ex5() commences with the definition of a lambda expression named buy_copies(). Note that for this example, buy_copies() requires an argument of type Book&.

Listing 6-1-5. Example Ch06_01 – Ch06_01_ex5()

```
void Ch06_01_ex5()
{
    auto buy_copies = [](Book& book)
    {
        int num_copies = RN::get_value<int>() % 20 + 1;
        book.buy(num_copies);
        return num_copies;
    };
```

CHAPTER 6   SMART POINTERS

```
    constexpr size_t num_books {2};
    std::unique_ptr<Book[]> books = std::make_unique<Book[]>(num_books);

    // manipulate element book[0]
    books[0].set("Isaac Newton", "Principia", 1687, 5);
    std::println("\nbooks[0]: {}", books[0]);
    int num_copies0 = buy_copies(books[0]);
    std::println("num_copies0: {:d}", num_copies0);
    std::println("books[0]: {}", books[0]);

    // manipulate element book[1]
    books[1].set("Charles Darwin", "On the Origin of Species", 1859, 4);
    std::println("\nbooks[1]: {}", books[1]);
    int num_copies1 = buy_copies(books[1]);
    std::println("num_copies1: {:d}", num_copies1);
    std::println("books[1]: {}", books[1]);
}
```

Following the definition of the lambda expression is the statement

`std::unique_ptr<Book[]> books = std::make_unique<Book[]>(num_books);`

Class `std::unique_ptr` defines a partial specialization for C-style arrays. Note that the object type for `books` is `Book[]`. Following execution of `std::make_unique()`, object `books` maintains exclusive ownership of a C-style `Book[2]` array. The first statement of the next code block, `books[0].set("Isaac Newton", "Principia", 1687, 5)`, initializes `books[0]`. In this expression, `std::unique_ptr<>::operator[]`[2] returns a reference to the first `Book` object in `books`. Following initialization is a call to `buy_copies(books[0])`. The final code block in `Ch06_01_ex5()` carries out the same operation using `books[2]`.

Listing 6-1-6 shows the source code for demo function `Ch06_01_ex6()`. This function illustrates the use of `std::move()` to transfer the ownership of a `Book` object from one `std::unique<Book>` to another. Following the `std::move()` operation, the state of `book1` is undefined. It warrants mentioning here that due to the exclusive ownership requisites of a `std::unique_ptr`, `operator=` and the copy constructor are explicitly defined as `delete`.

---

[2] For a non-array `std::unique_ptr<>`, `operator[]` is undefined.

CHAPTER 6 SMART POINTERS

Listing 6-1-6. Example Ch06_01 - Ch06_01_ex6()

```
void Ch06_01_ex6()
{
    std::unique_ptr<Book> book1 = std::make_unique<Book>("Isaac Newton",
        "Principia", 1687, 5);
    std::println("book1: {}", *book1);

    // using std::move to transfer ownership
    std::unique_ptr<Book> book2 = std::move(book1);
    std::println("book2: {}", *book2);

//  std::unique_ptr<Book> book3 = book2;    // error - use of deleted
                                            //         copy ctor
//  book3 = book2;                          // error - use of deleted
                                            //         operator=
}
```

One common use case for `std::unique_ptr` objects is the allocation of a large temporary buffer. For example, loading an entire file into a memory buffer and processing the data from that buffer is often faster than processing smaller chunks of data using multiple reads. The final example function of this section demonstrates the use of `std::make_unique_for_overwrite()`. Listing 6-1-7 shows the source code for this example.

Listing 6-1-7. Example Ch06_01 - Ch06_01_ex7()

```
void Ch06_01_ex7()
{
    constexpr size_t n {10'000'000};

    // buff1 is value-initialized - all elements set to zero
    auto buff1 = std::make_unique<int[]>(n);

    // buff2 is uninitialized
    auto buff2 = std::make_unique_for_overwrite<int[]>(n);

    // fill buffers with random values
    RN::fill_buffer(buff1.get(), n);
    RN::fill_buffer(buff2.get(), n);
```

```
    // perform simulated calculation
    int sum1 {}, sum2 {};

    for (size_t i = 0; i < n; ++i)
    {
        sum1 += buff1[i];
        sum2 += buff2[i];
    }

    std::println("sum1: {:d}   sum2: {:d}", sum1, sum2);
}
```

The code in function Ch06_01_ex7() shows two methods for allocating a temporary buffer. The first method utilizes std::make_unique(); the second exploits std::make_unique_for_overwrite(). The primary difference between these two techniques is that the former initializes each int element in buff1 to zero, while the latter doesn't. Using an uninitialized buffer is faster, especially for large buffers, when the buffer is going to be overwritten soon after instantiation as demonstrated by the subsequent calls to RN::fill_buffer(). Note that buff1.get() and buff2.get() obtain the int* pointers managed by buff1 and buff2, respectively. Here are the results for example Ch06_01:

```
----- Results for example Ch06_01 -----

----- Ch06_01_ex1() -----

Initial values:
book1: [Isaac Newton, 'Principia', 1687, 5]
book2: [Charles Darwin, 'On the Origin of Species', 1859, 4]

After sell operations:
book1: [Isaac Newton, 'Principia', 1687, 3]
book2: [Charles Darwin, 'On the Origin of Species', 1859, 1]

----- Ch06_01_ex2() -----

Initial values:
book1: [Marie Curie, 'The Discovery of Radium', 1921, 2]
book2: [Albert Einstein, 'The Meaning of Relativity', 1923, 3]
```

CHAPTER 6 SMART POINTERS

After sell operations:
book1: [Marie Curie, 'The Discovery of Radium', 1921, 1]
book2: [Albert Einstein, 'The Meaning of Relativity', 1923, 0]

----- Ch06_01_ex3() -----

Initial values:
book1: [Richard Feynman, 'Quantum Electrodynamics', 1962, 12]
book2: [Stephen Hawking, 'A Brief History of Time', 1988, 19]

After sell operations:
book1: [Richard Feynman, 'Quantum Electrodynamics', 1962, 3]
book2: [Stephen Hawking, 'A Brief History of Time', 1988, 15]

----- Ch06_01_ex4() -----

book: [Isaac Newton, 'Principia', 1687, 5]
num_copies: 18
book: [Isaac Newton, 'Principia', 1687, 23]

----- Ch06_01_ex5() -----

books[0]: [Isaac Newton, 'Principia', 1687, 5]
num_copies0: 5
books[0]: [Isaac Newton, 'Principia', 1687, 10]

books[1]: [Charles Darwin, 'On the Origin of Species', 1859, 4]
num_copies1: 13
books[1]: [Charles Darwin, 'On the Origin of Species', 1859, 17]

----- Ch06_01_ex6() -----
book1: [Isaac Newton, 'Principia', 1687, 5]
book2: [Isaac Newton, 'Principia', 1687, 5]

----- Ch06_01_ex7() -----
sum1: 709820587   sum2: 709820587

Recall from the discussions in Chapter 1 that classes Image and ImageT (see Listings 1-4-1 and 1-5-1) employed container class std::vector for the pixel buffers. For these classes, using std::make_unique_for_overwrite() would be a better option since calling std::vector::resize() to adjust the buffer size can initiate a buffer zeroing operation that adversely affects performance.

Using std::shared_ptr

A std::shared_ptr is another smart pointer class. Unlike a std::unique_ptr, a std::shared_ptr shares ownership of an object. An object that's shared between one or more std::shared_ptrs is automatically destroyed during destruction of the last owning std::shared_ptr. This reduces the risk of a memory or other resource leak. Shared pointers can also be exploited to streamline access to a shared object that's used in multiple threads.

Figure 6-1 shows the logical relationships of several std::shared_ptr<T> objects in use. In this diagram, note that std::shared_ptr objects sp1, sp2, and sp3 contain a pointer of type T, and each type T pointer points to the same instance of object T. Also, note that each std::share_ptr object contains a pointer to a common ControlBlock[3] object. This object encompasses counters that track the number of std::shared_ptr and std::weak_ptr instances that share ownership of object T. Class std::weak_ptr<T> is discussed later in this chapter.

---

[3] Object ControlBlock is utilized here for exposition purposes. The actual data structures are defined by the C++ implementation.

CHAPTER 6　SMART POINTERS

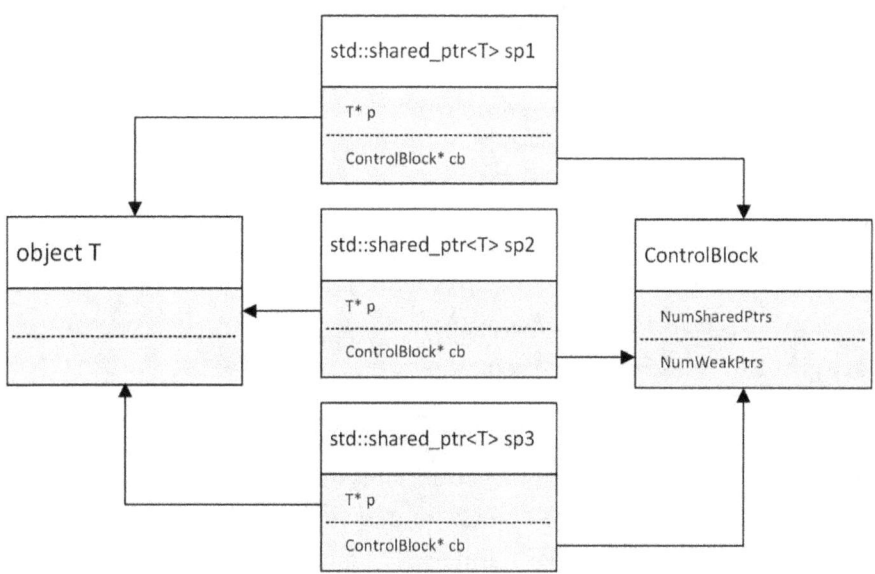

Figure 6-1. Logical relationships of multiple std::shared_ptr<T> objects

Using a std::shared_ptr is similar to using a std::unique_ptr. Listing 6-2-1 shows the source code for example Ch06_02_ex1(). This example highlights the basic use of a std::share_ptr.

Listing 6-2-1. Example Ch06_02 – Ch06_02_ex1()

```
//------------------------------------------------------------------------
// Ch06_02_ex.cpp
//------------------------------------------------------------------------

#include <memory>
#include "Ch06_02.h"
#include "Book.h"
#include "RN.h"

void Ch06_02_ex1()
{
    std::shared_ptr<Book> book1 = std::make_shared<Book>("Richard Feynman",
        "Quantum Electrodynamics", 1962, 12);
    std::shared_ptr<Book> book2 = std::make_shared<Book>("Stephen Hawking",
        "A Brief History of Time", 1988, 19);
```

249

CHAPTER 6   SMART POINTERS

```
    std::println("\nInitial values:");
    std::println("book1: {}", *book1);
    std::println("book2: {}", *book2);

    book1->sell(9);
    book2->sell(4);

    std::println("\nAfter sell operations:");
    std::println("book1: {}", *book1);
    std::println("book2: {}", *book2);
}
```

The opening code block in Ch06_02_ex1() employs std::make_shared() to create two std::shared_ptr<Book> objects named book1 and book2. The ensuing std::println() statements use book1 and book2 just like raw pointers to print the Book objects. Similarly, operator-> is exercised to call member function sell().

The next std::shared_ptr example, shown in Listing 6-2-2, begins with the definition of a lambda expression named buy_copies(). Note that argument std::shared_ptr<Book> book is passed by value instead of reference. Unlike a std::unique_ptr, passing a std::shared_ptr by value is permissible since operator= is defined.

Listing 6-2-2. Example Ch06_02 – Ch06_02_ex2()

```
void Ch06_02_ex2()
{
    // shared_ptr<Book> passed by value
    auto buy_copies = [](std::shared_ptr<Book> book)
    {
        // RN::get_value<int> returns a random integer value (see RN.h)
        int num_copies = RN::get_value<int>() % 40 + 1;
        book->buy(num_copies);
        return num_copies;
    };

    auto book1 = std::make_shared<Book>("Marie Curie",
        "The Discovery of Radium", 1921, 5);
    std::println("\nInitial value:");
    std::println("book1 (use_count: {}): {}", book1.use_count(), *book1);
```

```
    // using copy constructor
    auto book2 = book1;
    std::println("\nAfter book2 assignment:");
    std::println("book1 (use_count: {}): {}", book1.use_count(), *book1);
    std::println("book2 (use_count: {}): {}", book2.use_count(), *book2);

    // using buy_copies()
    int num_copies = buy_copies(book1);
    std::println("\nafter buy_copies() (num_copies = {:d})", num_copies);
    std::println("book1 (use_count: {}): {}", book1.use_count(), *book1);
    std::println("book2 (use_count: {}): {}", book2.use_count(), *book2);

    // using assignment operator
    std::shared_ptr<Book> book3 {};
    book3 = book2;
    num_copies = buy_copies(book3);
    std::println("\nafter buy_copies() (num_copies = {:d})", num_copies);
    std::println("book1 (use_count: {}): {}", book1.use_count(), *book1);
    std::println("book2 (use_count: {}): {}", book2.use_count(), *book2);
    std::println("book3 (use_count: {}): {}", book3.use_count(), *book3);
}
```

Following the definition of buy_copies() is a code block that creates std::shared_ptr<Book> book1. The std::println() statement in the same code block calls book1.use_count(), which returns the number std::shared_ptr instances that currently share ownership of the managed Book object. When using use_count() to track std::share_ptr usages, keep in mind that it can return zero (e.g., following a call std::shared_ptr::reset()).

In the ensuing code block, the statement auto book2 = book1 creates a second std::shared_ptr<Book> object. Following execution of this statement, book1 and book2 share ownership of the same Book object. If you scan ahead to the results section for Ch06_02_ex2(), you'll notice that use_count() returned a value of two instead of one and that identical data is printed for both book1 and book2.

The next code block utilizes num_copies = buy_copies(book1) to perform a simulated transaction that updates m_NumCopies for the Book object maintained by book1. In the results section, note that following execution of buy_copies(), m_NumCopies is the same for both book1 and book2. The final code block demonstrates the use of std::shared_ptr::operator= to initialize book3. Following the assignment, use_count() returns a value of three as shown in the results section.

Listing 6-2-3 shows the source code for example Ch06_02_ex3(). This example demonstrates the creation of additional std::shared_ptr<Book> objects in a new scope. Within the if code block, the value returned by book1.use_count() is four. Following the if code block, book1.use_count() returns a value of one since std::shared_ptr<Book> objects book2, book3, and book4 no longer exist. It warrants mentioning here that the creation and deletion of additional std::shared<Book> objects within the if block does not entail any additional class Book constructor or destructor calls. To observe this, remove the comments from the std::println() statements in Book's constructors and destructor, compile, and run the code.

Listing 6-2-3. Example Ch06_02 – Ch06_02_ex3()

```
void Ch06_02_ex3()
{
    auto book1 = std::make_shared<Book>("Marie Curie",
        "The Discovery of Radium", 1921, 5);

    std::println("\nOuter scope");
    std::println("book1 (use_count: {}): {}", book1.use_count(), *book1);

    if (book1->YearPub() == 1921)
    {
        // make copies in new scope
        auto book2 = book1;
        auto book3 = book1;
        auto book4 = book1;

        std::println("\nInner scope");
        std::println("book1 (use_count: {}): {}", book1.use_count(),
            *book1);
    }

    std::println("\nOuter scope");
    std::println("book1 (use_count: {}): {}", book1.use_count(), *book1);
}
```

Here are the results for example Ch06_02:

```
----- Results for example Ch06_02 -----

---- Ch06_02_ex1() ----

Initial values:
book1: [Richard Feynman, 'Quantum Electrodynamics', 1962, 12]
book2: [Stephen Hawking, 'A Brief History of Time', 1988, 19]

After sell operations:
book1: [Richard Feynman, 'Quantum Electrodynamics', 1962, 3]
book2: [Stephen Hawking, 'A Brief History of Time', 1988, 15]

---- Ch06_02_ex2() ----

Initial value:
book1 (use_count: 1): [Marie Curie, 'The Discovery of Radium', 1921, 5]

After book2 asignment:
book1 (use_count: 2): [Marie Curie, 'The Discovery of Radium', 1921, 5]
book2 (use_count: 2): [Marie Curie, 'The Discovery of Radium', 1921, 5]

after buy_copies() (num_copies = 23)
book1 (use_count: 2): [Marie Curie, 'The Discovery of Radium', 1921, 28]
book2 (use_count: 2): [Marie Curie, 'The Discovery of Radium', 1921, 28]

after buy_copies() (num_copies = 33)
book1 (use_count: 3): [Marie Curie, 'The Discovery of Radium', 1921, 61]
book2 (use_count: 3): [Marie Curie, 'The Discovery of Radium', 1921, 61]
book3 (use_count: 3): [Marie Curie, 'The Discovery of Radium', 1921, 61]

---- Ch06_02_ex3() ----

Outer scope
book1 (use_count: 1): [Marie Curie, 'The Discovery of Radium', 1921, 5]

Inner scope
book1 (use_count: 4): [Marie Curie, 'The Discovery of Radium', 1921, 5]

Outer scope
book1 (use_count: 1): [Marie Curie, 'The Discovery of Radium', 1921, 5]
```

CHAPTER 6 SMART POINTERS

Using std::weak_ptr

Smart pointer class `std::weak_ptr` facilitates object sharing without object ownership. Instances of `std::weak_ptr` are often used to handle cyclic references involving objects that hold `std::shared_ptr` objects.

Listing 6-3-1 shows the source code for example Ch06_03_ex1(). This example demonstrates the use of a `std::weak_ptr`. Function Ch06_03_ex1() opens with the creation of a `std::shared_ptr<Book>` instance named book1. Immediately after the two `std::println()` calls is the statement `std::weak_ptr book1_wp(book1)`. Following execution of this expression, book1_wp references the same Book object as book1, but it *does not* own the underlying object; it's still owned by book1.

Listing 6-3-1. Example Ch06_03 – Ch06_03_ex1()

```
//-------------------------------------------------------------------
// Ch06_03_ex.cpp
//-------------------------------------------------------------------

#include <memory>
#include "Ch06_03.h"
#include "Book.h"

void Ch06_03_ex1()
{
    // create std::shared_ptr
    std::shared_ptr<Book> book1 = std::make_shared<Book>("Albert Einstein",
        "The Meaning of Relativity", 1923, 3);

    std::println("\nInitial values:");
    std::println("book1 (use_count: {}): {}", book1.use_count(), *book1);

    // create std::weak_ptr
    std::weak_ptr book1_wp(book1);

    // using lock() - converts std::weak_ptr to std::shared_ptr
    std::shared_ptr<Book> book1_wp_locked = book1_wp.lock();

    if (!book1_wp_locked)
    {
```

```
        // lock() fails if std::weak_ptr object is empty
        std::println("lock failed!");
        return;
    }

    std::println("\nAfter lock()");
    std::println("book1_wp_locked (use_count: {}):\n  {}",
        book1_wp_locked.use_count(), *book1_wp_locked);

    std::println("book1 (use_count: {}): {}", book1.use_count(), *book1);

    // using reset()
    std::println("\nAfter reset()");
    std::println("book1 (use_count: {}): {}", book1.use_count(), *book1);
}
```

Unlike std::share_ptr, a function can't utilize operator-> or operator*() to dereference the underlying object of a std::weak_ptr. To do this, the std::weak_ptr must be converted to a std::shared_ptr using the member function lock(). In function Ch06_03_ex1(), the statement std::shared_ptr<Book> book1_wp_locked = book1_wp.lock() performs this operation. Note that std::weak_ptr::lock() returns an empty std::shared_ptr object if the std::weak_ptr object is empty. Following the conversion, book1_wp_locked can be used just like a regular std::shared_ptr. Near the end of Ch06_03_ex1() is the statement book1_wp_locked.reset(). Execution of this statement removes book1_wp_locked's access to the Book object that book1 maintains. Note in the results section that following execution of reset(), book1.use_count() equals one instead of two when book1_wp_locked was active.

The purpose of Ch06_03_ex1() was to illustrate basic std::weak_ptr object usage. As utilized in this function, class std::weak_ptr doesn't provide any practical advantages compared to std::shared_ptr. However, one archetypal use case for a std::weak_ptr is to avoid cyclic references between objects that maintain std::shared_ptrs. Listing 6-3-2 shows a source code example that demonstrates this capability. This listing opens with the definition of two simple structures named S1 and S2. Note that structure S1 defines attribute std::shared_ptr<S2> S2_sp, while structure S2 defines attributes std::shared_ptr<S1> S1_sp and std::weak_ptr<S1> S1_wp.

Listing 6-3-2. Example Ch06_03 - Ch06_03_ex2()

```
struct S2;

struct S1
{
    S1()  {std::println("S1 ctor");}
    ~S1() {std::println("S1 dtor");}

    std::shared_ptr<S2> S2_sp {};
};

struct S2
{
    S2()  {std::println("S2 ctor");}
    ~S2() {std::println("S2 dtor");}

    std::shared_ptr<S1> S1_sp {};
    std::weak_ptr<S1> S1_wp {};
};

void Ch06_03_ex2()
{
    // cyclic shared_ptrs - destructors not executed
    std::shared_ptr<S1> s1_sp {std::make_shared<S1>()};
    std::shared_ptr<S2> s2_sp {std::make_shared<S2>()};

    s1_sp->S2_sp = s2_sp;
    s2_sp->S1_sp = s1_sp;
}
```

Function Ch06_03_ex2(), also shown in Listing 6-3-2, opens with the creation of a std::shared_ptr<S1> object named s1_sp, which owns an object of type S1. The next statement, std::shared_ptr<S2> s2_sp {std::make_shared<S2>()}, instantiates s2_sp that owns an object of type S2. Following creation of the std::shared_ptrs, Ch06_03_ex2() utilizes s1_sp->S2_sp = s2_sp to save a copy of s2_sp in the S1 object that's owned by s1_sp. The next statement, s2_sp->S1_sp = s1_sp, saves a copy of s1_sp in the S2 object that's owned by s2_sp. If you scan ahead to the results section, you'll notice

CHAPTER 6 SMART POINTERS

that the constructors for S1 and S2 get executed but the corresponding destructors don't. The reason for this is that use_count() equals one for both S1::S2_sp and S2::S1_sp; a std::share_ptr deletes its maintained object only if use_count() equals zero.

Listing 6-3-3 shows the source code for example Ch06_03_ex3(). This example is identical to the previous example except for the last statement, s2_sp->S1_wp = s1_sp. Execution of this expression saves a copy of s1_sp in s2_sp->S1_wp whose type is std::weak_ptr<S1>. Note in the results section that the destructors for shared objects S1 and S2 are now properly executed.

Listing 6-3-3. Example Ch06_03 – Ch06_03_ex3()

```
void Ch06_03_ex3()
{
    // cyclic shared_ptr/weak_ptr - destructors executed
    std::shared_ptr<S1> s1_sp {std::make_shared<S1>()};
    std::shared_ptr<S2> s2_sp {std::make_shared<S2>()};

    s1_sp->S2_sp = s2_sp;
    s2_sp->S1_wp = s1_sp;
}
```

In example Ch06_03, the definition of structure S2 includes a std::shared_ptr and a std::weak_ptr to enable the use of struct S2 in both Ch06_03_ex2() and Ch06_03_ex3(). In production code, only the std::weak_ptr would be necessary. Here are the results for example Ch06_03:

```
----- Results for example Ch06_03 -----

----- Ch06_03_ex1() -----
Initial values:
book1 (use_count: 1): [Albert Einstein, 'The Meaning of Relativity',
1923, 3]

After lock()
book1_wp_locked (use_count: 2):
  [Albert Einstein, 'The Meaning of Relativity', 1923, 3]
book1 (use_count: 2): [Albert Einstein, 'The Meaning of Relativity',
1923, 3]
```

CHAPTER 6   SMART POINTERS

```
After reset()
book1 (use_count: 1): [Albert Einstein, 'The Meaning of Relativity',
1923, 3]

----- Ch06_03_ex2() -----
S1 ctor
S2 ctor

----- Ch06_03_ex2() -----
S1 ctor
S2 ctor
S1 dtor
S2 dtor
```

Summary

Here are the key learning points for this chapter:

- Modern C++ strongly discourages the use of raw pointers. For most use cases, smart pointer usage is generally a superior alternative since execution of all applicable destructors is assured.

- A `std::unique_ptr` smart pointer maintains exclusive ownership of an object. An instance of `std::unique_ptr` can't be copied; however, its managed object can be moved to a different `std::unique_ptr`.

- A `std::shared_ptr` shares object ownership with other `std::share_ptrs`. The object maintained by one or more `std::shared_ptrs` is automatically deleted during destruction of the last owning `std::shared_ptr`.

- A `std::weak_ptr` is a smart pointer that facilitates sharing of a non-owned object. They are primarily used to ensure appropriate destructors get executed when cyclic references exist between objects that hold `std::shared_ptr` objects.

CHAPTER 7

Associative Containers

This chapter discusses associative containers, including

- How to use `std::set`
- How to use `std::multiset`
- How to use `std::map`
- How to use `std::multimap`

An associative container maintains a collection of objects (or elements). Unlike a sequence container such as `std::vector` or `std::deque`, an associative container utilizes a comparison function to arrange its elements. This internal arrangement is independent of the element insertion order. The primary advantage of an associative container is that element insertions, searches, and removals have logarithmic instead of linear complexity.

Using std::set

A `std:set` is an associative container that holds a sorted collection of *unique* elements (or keys). In this regard, a `std::set` models a mathematical set. A `std::set` is commonly, but not necessarily, implemented using a red-black tree. A red-black tree is similar to a binary tree with the primary difference being the inclusion of extra control data to ensure that the tree remains (approximately) balanced. Unlike sequence containers such as `std::vector` and `std::deque`, you can't directly access the elements of a `std::set` using `operator[]` or `at()`, nor can you change the value of an element in a `std::set` via an iterator. Changing the value of an element in a `std::set` requires removing the old object and inserting a new one.

Listing 7-1-1 shows the source code for example `Ch07_01_ex1()`. This function demonstrates the use of a `std::set`. Near the top of `Ch07_01_ex1()` is the definition of `std::set<int>` set1 whose corresponding initializer list supplies the initial values.

CHAPTER 7 ASSOCIATIVE CONTAINERS

The `MT::print_ctr()` statement that follows prints the elements of `set1`. Note in the results section that the elements of `set1` are printed in ascending order. Class `std::set`'s default comparison function for sorting is `std::less<>` (i.e., `operator<`). You'll learn how to specify a different comparison function later in this chapter. The ensuing `std::println()` statement utilizes `set1.size()`, which prints the number of elements in `set1`.

Listing 7-1-1. Example Ch07_01 – Ch07_01_ex1()

```cpp
//------------------------------------------------------------------------
// Ch07_01_ex.cpp
//------------------------------------------------------------------------

#include <array>
#include <functional>
#include <numbers>
#include <set>
#include <string>
#include "Ch07_01.h"
#include "MT.h"

void Ch07_01_ex1()
{
    const char* fmt1 = "{:d}   ";
    constexpr size_t epl_max {5};

    // create set1 - ints
    std::set<int> set1 {20, 40, 100, 50, 90, 70, 10, 30};

    MT::print_ctr("\nset1 (initial values):\n", set1, fmt1, epl_max);
    std::println("set1.size(): {:d}", set1.size());

    // add more elements to set1 using insert()
    std::array<int, 3> vals1 {80, 50, 60};

    for (auto val1 : vals1)
    {
        auto p = set1.insert(val1);
```

```cpp
        std::println("set1.insert({:d}) - status: {:s}", *p.first,
            p.second);
    }

    MT::print_ctr("\nset1 (after insertions):\n", set1, fmt1, epl_max);
    std::println("set1.size(): {:d}", set1.size());

    // create set2 - strings
    const char* fmt2 = "{:s}  ";
    std::set<std::string> set2 {"New York", "Los Angeles", "Chicago",
        "Houston", "Phoenix", "Philadelphia", "San Antonio", "San Diego"};

    MT::print_ctr("\nset2 (initial values):\n", set2, fmt2, epl_max);
    std::println("set2.size(): {:d}\n", set2.size());

    // add more elements to set2 using emplace()
    std::array<std::string, 3> vals2 {"Dallas", "Phoenix", "Austin"};

    for (const auto& val2 : vals2)
    {
        auto p = set2.emplace(val2);
        std::println("set2.emplace(\"{:s}\") - status: {:s}", *p.first,
            p.second);
    }

    MT::print_ctr("\nset2 (after emplacements):\n", set2, fmt2, epl_max);
    std::println("set2.size(): {:d}", set2.size());
}
```

The next code block in Ch07_01_ex1() adds the elements of vals1 to set1 using set1.insert(). Member function std::set::insert() returns a std::pair. Element first of this std::pair contains a constant iterator to the inserted element or a constant iterator to an existing element in the set. Element second is a bool that signifies whether the new element was inserted (true) or if it already existed (false). Following these insertions, MT::print_ctr() prints the elements of set1 in ascending order.

Like other container objects, elements can be inserted into a std::set using emplacements as demonstrated in the subsequent code block with std::set<std::string> set2. Recall that an emplace() insertion is often faster than an `insert()` since the element is constructed using memory provided by the container. Doing this often precludes an extra copy or move operation. Note in the range for loop that `set2.emplace()` also returns a `std::pair` that contains an iterator and a `bool` value.

In Listing 7-1-2, function `Ch07_01_ex2()` demonstrates additional `std::set` insertions. The statement `std::set<std::string, std::greater<std::string>> set1` defines a `std::set` that holds `std::string` elements, but uses function object `std::greater<std::string>` for comparisons. The effect of using `std::greater<>` is that elements in `set2` are sorted in descending instead of ascending order.

Listing 7-1-2. Example Ch07_01 – Ch07_01_ex2()

```cpp
void Ch07_01_ex2()
{
    const char* fmt = "{:s}  ";
    constexpr size_t epl_max {5};

    // create set1 - using std::greater for sorting
    std::set<std::string, std::greater<std::string>> set1 { "California",
        "Texas", "Florida", "New York", "Pennsylvania", "Illinois", "Ohio"};

    MT::print_ctr("\nset1 (initial values):\n", set1, fmt, epl_max);

    // add more elements to set1 using insert
    std::array<std::string, 4> vals1
        {"Georgia", "Florida", "North Carolina", "Michigan"};

    set1.insert(vals1.begin(), vals1.end());
    MT::print_ctr("\nset1 (after insert):\n", set1, fmt, epl_max);

    // add more elements to set1 using insert_range (C++23)
#ifdef __cpp_lib_containers_ranges
    std::array<std::string, 3> vals2
        {"South Carolina", "Vermont", "Indiana"};

    set1.insert_range(vals2);
    MT::print_ctr("\nset1 (after insert_range):\n", set1, fmt, epl_max);
#else
    std::println("\nstd::set::insert_range() requires C++23");
#endif
```

CHAPTER 7   ASSOCIATIVE CONTAINERS

```
    // using iterators to access elements of set1
    std::println("\nset1 (using iterators)");

    for (auto iter = set1.begin(); iter != set1.end(); ++iter)
    {
//      *iter += " test";                   // error - modifications not allowed
        std::println("{:s}", *iter);
    }
}
```

In Ch07_01_ex2()'s next code block, the expression set1.insert(vals1.begin(), vals1.end()) inserts copies of all elements from vals1 into set1. The final code block of Ch07_01_ex2() exploits set1.insert_ranges(vals2)[1] (C++23) to insert copies of elements from vals2 into set1. This latter insertion method is certainly more convenient when inserting an entire range of elements into a std::set, assuming it's supported by the compiler.

The final code block in Ch07_01_ex2() shows how to use a for loop and iterators to access the elements of set1. Recall from earlier discussions that you can't change the value of an element in a std::set via an iterator. This is why the expression *iter += " test" is commented out. For a std::set, the iterators returned by begin() and end() are constant iterators. Class std::set also utilizes bidirectional iterators (see Chapter 4), which means that std::sets can't be used with STL algorithms that require random access iterators, such as std::sort() or std::ranges::sort().

Listing 7-1-3 shows the source code for example Ch07_01_ex3(). This example highlights the use of relational operators with std::sets. For two objects of type std::set<T> to be equal, they must contain the same number of elements, and the values in corresponding element positions must also be equal. If the two std::set<T> objects are different sizes, an element-by-element lexicographical compare is performed. This lexicographical compare is performed using the relational operators defined for T, which might be different than the comparison function used to order the elements of a std::set<T>.

---

[1] In this and later examples, preprocessor symbol __cpp_lib_containers_ranges is tested to confirm compiler support for insert_ranges().

CHAPTER 7   ASSOCIATIVE CONTAINERS

Listing 7-1-3. Example Ch07_01 – Ch07_01_ex3()

```
void Ch07_01_ex3()
{
    const char* fmt = "{:5d}";
    constexpr size_t epl_max {10};

    // using relational operators
    std::set<int> set1 {100, 200, 300, 400, 500, 600};
    std::set<int> set2 {100, 200, 150, 400, 500, 600};
    std::set<int> set3 {100, 200, 300, 400, 500, 600};
    std::set<int> set4 {100, 200, 300, 450, 500, 600};

    MT::print_ctr("\nset1 (initial values):\n", set1, fmt, epl_max);
    MT::print_ctr("\nset2 (initial values):\n", set2, fmt, epl_max);
    MT::print_ctr("\nset3 (initial values):\n", set3, fmt, epl_max);
    MT::print_ctr("\nset4 (initial values):\n", set4, fmt, epl_max);

    std::println("\nset1 == set2: {:s}", set1 == set2);
    std::println("set1 != set2: {:s}", set1 != set2);
    std::println("set1 <  set2: {:s}", set1 <  set2);
    std::println("set1 <= set2: {:s}", set1 <= set2);
    std::println("set1 >  set2: {:s}", set1 >  set2);
    std::println("set1 >= set2: {:s}", set1 >= set2);

    std::println("\nset1 == set3: {:s}", set1 == set3);
    std::println("set1 <  set3: {:s}", set1 <  set3);
    std::println("set1 >  set3: {:s}", set1 >  set3);

    std::println("\nset1 == set4: {:s}", set1 == set4);
    std::println("set1 <  set4: {:s}", set1 <  set4);
    std::println("set1 >  set4: {:s}", set1 >  set4);

    // using relational operators (elements in container sorted using
    operator>)
    using set_t = std::set<int, std::greater<int>>;
    set_t set5 {100, 300, 400, 200, 500};
    set_t set6 {100, 300, 400, 200, 600};
    set_t set7 {100, 300, 400, 200, 500};
```

CHAPTER 7 ASSOCIATIVE CONTAINERS

```cpp
    MT::print_ctr("\nset5 (initial values):\n", set5, fmt, epl_max);
    MT::print_ctr("\nset6 (initial values):\n", set6, fmt, epl_max);
    MT::print_ctr("\nset7 (initial values):\n", set7, fmt, epl_max);

    std::println("\nset5 == set6: {:s}", set5 == set6);
    std::println("set5 <  set6: {:s}", set5 <  set6);
    std::println("set5 >  set6: {:s}", set5 >  set6);

    std::println("\nset5 == set7: {:s}", set5 == set7);
    std::println("set5 <  set7: {:s}", set5 <  set7);
    std::println("set5 >  set7: {:s}", set5 >  set7);
}
```

Example Ch07_01_ex4(), shown in Listing 7-1-4, illustrates the use of std::set::find() and std::set::erase(). These member functions perform element searches and removals, respectively. Example function Ch07_01_ex4() also spotlights the use of std::set::contains() (C++20). More about this function shortly.

Listing 7-1-4. Example Ch07_01 – Ch07_01_ex4()

```cpp
void Ch07_01_ex4()
{
    const char* fmt = "{} ";
    constexpr size_t epl_max {5};

    // create set of strings
    std::set<std::string> set1 {"Wyoming", "Vermont", "Alaska", "North
    Dakota", "South Dakota", "Delaware", "Rhode Island", "Montana",
    "Maine"};

    MT::print_ctr("\nset1 (initial values):\n", set1, fmt, epl_max);
    std::println("");

    // search set1 using find, remove if found
    std::array<std::string, 4> find_vals
        {"New Hampshire", "Alaska", "Hawaii", "Maine"};

    for (const std::string& find_val : find_vals)
    {
        std::print("set1.find(\"{:s}\") - ", find_val);
```

265

```
        if (auto iter = set1.find(find_val); iter != set1.end())
        {
            set1.erase(iter);
            std::println("removed");
        }
        else
            std::println("not found");
    }

    MT::print_ctr("\nset1 (after erase operations):\n", set1, fmt,
    epl_max);
    std::println("");

    // search set1 for values using contains (C++20)
    std::array<std::string, 3> contains_vals
        {"Kansas", "South Dakota", "Nebraska"};

    for (const std::string& contain_val : contains_vals)
    {
        bool b = set1.contains(contain_val);
        std::println("set1.contains(\"{:s}\") - {:s}", contain_val, b);
    }
}
```

Function Ch07_01_ex4()'s critical code blocks are its two for loops. In the first for loop, set1.find(find_val) searches set1 for element find_val. If found, find() returns a constant iterator to find_val in set1; otherwise, find() returns set1.end(). To remove a value from set1, Ch07_01_ex4() first verifies that iter != set1.end() is true. It then utilizes set1.erase(iter) to remove find_val from set1. The second for loop in Ch07_04_ex1() exercises set1.contains(contain_val) to determine if set1 contains element contain_val. Member function contains() returns true if contain_vals exists; otherwise, false is returned.

The final std::set example function, Ch07_01_ex5(), utilizes set::merge() to merge two sets. In this example, which is shown in Listing 7-1-5, values from std::set<double> set2 are merged into set1. During execution of set1.merge(set2), elements from set2 are *moved* to set1 only if they do not already exist in set1. If you scan ahead to the results section, note that set2 still contains std::numbers::sqrt2 and std::numbers::pi since these values existed in set1 prior to the merger.

Listing 7-1-5. Example Ch07_01 – Ch07_01_ex5()

```
void Ch07_01_ex5()
{
    using namespace std::numbers;
    const char* fmt = "{:8.4f}";

    // create test sets
    std::set<double> set1 {pi, e, inv_pi, sqrt2};
    std::set<double> set2 {sqrt2, phi, pi, sqrt3, log2e};

    MT::print_ctr("\nset1 (initial values): ", set1, fmt);
    MT::print_ctr("set2 (initial values): ", set2, fmt);

    // merge sets
    set1.merge(set2);
    MT::print_ctr("\nset1 (after merge): ", set1, fmt);
    MT::print_ctr("set2 (after merge): ", set2, fmt);

    // clear set1
    set1.clear();
    MT::print_ctr("\nset1 (after clear): ", set1, fmt);
}
```

The final code block in Ch07_01_ex5() spotlights the use of std::set::clear(). This member function removes all elements from the specified set. Here are the results[2] for source code example Ch07_01:

```
----- Results for example Ch07_01 -----

----- Ch07_01_ex1() -----

set1 (initial values):
  10   20   30   40   50
  70   90  100
set1.size(): 8
```

---

[2] The results for this and later examples may vary slightly depending on compiler support for C++23 specific features.

CHAPTER 7   ASSOCIATIVE CONTAINERS

```
set1.insert(80) - status: true
set1.insert(50) - status: false
set1.insert(60) - status: true

set1 (after insertions):
10   20   30   40   50
60   70   80   90   100
set1.size(): 10

set2 (initial values):
Chicago   Houston   Los Angeles   New York   Philadelphia
Phoenix   San Antonio   San Diego
set2.size(): 8

set2.emplace("Dallas") - status: true
set2.emplace("Phoenix") - status: false
set2.emplace("Austin") - status: true

set2 (after emplacements):
Austin   Chicago   Dallas   Houston   Los Angeles
New York   Philadelphia   Phoenix   San Antonio   San Diego
set2.size(): 10

----- Ch07_01_ex2() -----

set1 (initial values):
Texas   Pennsylvania   Ohio   New York   Illinois
Florida   California

set1 (after insert):
Texas   Pennsylvania   Ohio   North Carolina   New York
Michigan   Illinois   Georgia   Florida   California

set1 (after insert_range):
Vermont   Texas   South Carolina   Pennsylvania   Ohio
North Carolina   New York   Michigan   Indiana   Illinois
Georgia   Florida   California
```

set1 (using iterators)
Vermont
Texas
South Carolina
Pennsylvania
Ohio
North Carolina
New York
Michigan
Indiana
Illinois
Georgia
Florida
California

----- Ch07_01_ex3() -----

set1 (initial values):
  100   200   300   400   500   600

set2 (initial values):
  100   150   200   400   500   600

set3 (initial values):
  100   200   300   400   500   600

set4 (initial values):
  100   200   300   450   500   600

set1 == set2: false
set1 != set2: true
set1 < set2: false
set1 <= set2: false
set1 > set2: true
set1 >= set2: true

set1 == set3: true
set1 < set3: false
set1 > set3: false

```
set1 == set4: false
set1 <  set4: true
set1 >  set4: false

set5 (initial values):
  500  400  300  200  100

set6 (initial values):
  600  400  300  200  100

set7 (initial values):
  500  400  300  200  100

set5 == set6: false
set5 <  set6: true
set5 >  set6: false

set5 == set7: true
set5 <  set7: false
set5 >  set7: false

----- Ch07_01_ex4() -----

set1 (initial values):
Alaska  Delaware  Maine  Montana  North Dakota
Rhode Island  South Dakota  Vermont  Wyoming

set1.find("New Hampshire") - not found
set1.find("Alaska") - removed
set1.find("Hawaii") - not found
set1.find("Maine") - removed

set1 (after erase operations):
Delaware  Montana  North Dakota  Rhode Island  South Dakota
Vermont  Wyoming

set1.contains("Kansas") - false
set1.contains("South Dakota") - true
set1.contains("Nebraska") - false
```

```
----- Ch07_01_ex5() -----

set1 (initial values):    0.3183  1.4142  2.7183  3.1416
set2 (initial values):    1.4142  1.4427  1.6180  1.7321  3.1416

set1 (after
merge):   0.3183  1.4142  1.4427  1.6180  1.7321  2.7183  3.1416
set2 (after merge):    1.4142  3.1416
set1 (after clear): <empty>
```

Using std::multiset

A std::multiset is an associative container that closely resembles a std::set. Like a std::set, std::multiset insertions, searches, and removals are executed in logarithmic time. Class std::multiset also supports most of the same member functions as std::set. The primary difference between std::multiset and std::set is that the former allows insertions of multiple elements (or keys) with the same value.

Example Ch07_02 highlights a few operations using std::multiset. In Listing 7-2-1, function Ch07_02_ex1() opens with the creation of std::multiset<int> mset1, whose initial values are provided in the accompanying initializer list. After creating mset1, Ch07_02_ex() utilizes mset1.insert() to add more elements – including elements that already exist – to mset1.

Listing 7-2-1. Example Ch07_02 – Ch07_02_ex1()

```
//-------------------------------------------------------------------
// Ch07_02_ex.cpp
//-------------------------------------------------------------------

#include <array>
#include <functional>
#include <set>
#include <string>
#include "Ch07_02.h"
#include "MT.h"
```

CHAPTER 7 ASSOCIATIVE CONTAINERS

```cpp
void Ch07_02_ex1()
{
    const char* fmt = "{:6d}";
    constexpr size_t epl_max {10};

    // create multiset of integers
    std::multiset<int> mset1 {20, 40, 100, 50, 90, 70, 10, 80, 30};
    MT::print_ctr("\nmset1 (initial values):\n", mset1, fmt, epl_max);
    std::println("mset1.size(): {:d}", mset1.size());

    // add more elements to mset1 using insert
    mset1.insert(110);
    mset1.insert(90);
    mset1.insert(80);
    mset1.insert(60);
    MT::print_ctr("\nmset1 (after insertions):\n", mset1, fmt, epl_max);
    std::println("mset1.size(): {:d}", mset1.size());

    // add more elements to mset1 using insert_range (C++23)
#ifdef __cpp_lib_containers_ranges
    std::array<int, 5> vals1 {70, 80, 40, 80, 30};

    mset1.insert_range(vals1);
    MT::print_ctr("\nmset1 (after insert_range):\n", mset1, fmt, epl_max);
    std::println("mset1.size(): {:d}", mset1.size());
#else
    std::println("\nstd::multiset::insert_range() requires C++23");
#endif

    // count occurences of count_val in mset1
    int count_val {80};
    auto n = mset1.count(count_val);
    std::println("\nmset1.count({:d}) = {:d}", count_val, n);
}
```

The next code block in Ch07_02_ex1() utilizes mset1.insert_range(vals1) (C++23) to insert values from vals1 into mset1. The final code block illustrates the use of mset1.count(count_val), which returns the number of elements in mset1 that equal count_val. It warrants mentioning here that class std::set also includes a count() member function, but this function always returns a value of one.

Listing 7-2-2 shows the source code for example Ch07_02_ex2(). This function begins its execution with the creation of a std::multiset<std::string, std::greater<std::string>> named mset1. Like a std::set, you can change the comparison function for a std::multiset; the default is std::less<T>().

Listing 7-2-2. Example Ch07_02 – Ch07_02_ex2()

```
void Ch07_02_ex2()
{
    const char* fmt = "{:12s}";
    constexpr size_t epl_max {5};

    // set of strings (sorted using operator>)
    std::multiset<std::string, std::greater<std::string>> mset1
        {"Pittsburg", "Atlanta", "Charlotte", "Denver", "Seattle", "Miami",
        "Atlanta", "Dallas", "Denver", "Boise"};

    MT::print_ctr("\nmset1 (initial values):\n", mset1, fmt, epl_max);
    std::println("mset1.size(): {:d}", mset1.size());

    // add new elements using emplace
    mset1.emplace("Portland");
    mset1.emplace("Atlanta");
    mset1.emplace("Cleveland");
    mset1.emplace("Detroit");
    MT::print_ctr("\nmset1 (after emplacements):\n", mset1, fmt, epl_max);
    std::println("mset1.size(): {:d}", mset1.size());

    // erase element using value
    mset1.erase("Atlanta");
    MT::print_ctr("\nmset1 (after first erase):\n", mset1, fmt, epl_max);
    std::println("mset1.size(): {:d}", mset1.size());
```

CHAPTER 7   ASSOCIATIVE CONTAINERS

```
    // erase all cities that begin with a 'D'
    auto iter = mset1.begin();

    while (iter != mset1.end())
    {
        // *iter is type std::string
        if ((*iter)[0] == 'D')
            iter = mset1.erase(iter);
        else
            ++iter;
    }

    MT::print_ctr("\nmset1 (after erase loop):\n", mset1, fmt, epl_max);
    std::println("mset1.size(): {:d}", mset1.size());
}
```

The next code block in Ch07_02_ex2() utilizes std::multiset::emplace() to add more elements to mset1. To remove an element from a std::multiset, you can use std::multiset::erase(). Note that execution of mset1.erase("Atlanta") removes *all* occurrences of std::string("Atlanta") from mset1.

The final code block in Ch07_02_ex2() contains a while loop that removes from mset1 all city names that begin with a 'D'. Note that iter is used just like any other iterator; it's initialized using mset1.begin(), and the loop terminates when iter != mset1.end() is false. Within the while loop, the first letter of the std::string pointed to by iter is compared against 'D'; if equal, execution of iter = mset1.erase(iter) deletes from mset1 the element pointed to by iter. What's important to recognize here is that mset1.erase(iter) returns an iterator value that points to the next element in mset1. This is why ++iter is executed only if (*iter)[0] == 'D' is false. Here are the results for source code example Ch07_02:

```
----- Results for example Ch07_02 -----

----- Ch07_02_ex1() -----

mset1 (initial values):
    10    20    30    40    50    70    80    90    100
mset1.size(): 9
```

```
mset1 (after insertions):
    10    20    30    40    50    60    70    80    80    90
    90    100   110
mset1.size(): 13

mset1 (after insert_range):
    10    20    30    30    40    40    50    60    70    70
    80    80    80    80    90    90    100   110
mset1.size(): 18

mset1.count(80) = 4

----- Ch07_02_ex2() -----

mset1 (initial values):
Seattle      Pittsburg   Miami        Denver       Denver
Dallas       Charlotte   Boise        Atlanta      Atlanta
mset1.size(): 10

mset1 (after emplacements):
Seattle      Portland    Pittsburg    Miami        Detroit
Denver       Denver      Dallas       Cleveland    Charlotte
Boise        Atlanta     Atlanta      Atlanta
mset1.size(): 14

mset1 (after first erase):
Seattle      Portland    Pittsburg    Miami        Detroit
Denver       Denver      Dallas       Cleveland    Charlotte
Boise
mset1.size(): 11

mset1 (after erase loop):
Seattle      Portland    Pittsburg    Miami        Cleveland
Charlotte    Boise
mset1.size(): 7
```

CHAPTER 7   ASSOCIATIVE CONTAINERS

Using std::map

A `std::map<Key, T>` is an associative container that manages key-value pairs. The primary difference between a `std::map<Key, T>` and a `std::set<T>` is that the former manages elements that contain *both* a unique Key and a data value of type T. Similarities between a `std::map` and `std::set` include the following:

- A `std::map` is commonly implemented using a red-black tree.
- The elements of a `std::map<Key, T>` are sorted using the unique key and `std::less<Key>`. The function object can be overridden.
- Common operations such as insertions, searches, and removals have logarithmic instead of linear performance.
- Class `std::map<Key, T>` supports bidirectional iterators.
- The key of a `std::map<Key, T>` element cannot be changed. To modify an element's key, the old key-value element must be removed and a new one inserted. The value component of a `std::map<Key, T>` element can be modified in place.

Listing 7-3-1 shows the source code for the first `std::map` example. This example commences with the declaration of `std::map<int, std::string> map1`. Note that the key for map1 is an `int`, while the value is a `std::string`. Also, note that the initializer list for map1 includes pairs of integers and text strings. Following the declaration of map1 is a call to `MT::print_map()` (see `Common/MT.h`), which prints the elements of a `std::map`. The `std::println()` statement that follows exercises `map1.size()`. This member function returns the number of elements in map1.

Listing 7-3-1. Example Ch07_03 – Ch07_03_ex1()

```
//-----------------------------------------------------------------------
// Ch07_03_ex.cpp
//-----------------------------------------------------------------------
#include <array>
#include <format>
#include <functional>
#include <map>
#include <ostream>
```

```cpp
#include <string>
#include <string_view>
#include <tuple>
#include <utility>
#include "Ch07_03.h"
#include "MT.h"
#include "RGB.h"

void Ch07_03_ex1()
{
    constexpr size_t epl_max {5};
    const char* fmt1 = "[{:3d}, ";
    const char* fmt2 = "{:<6s}] ";

    // simple map (int key, std::string data)
    std::map<int, std::string> map1
        {{0, "zero"}, {1, "one"}, {2, "two"}, {3, "three"}, {4, "four"},
         {5, "five"}, {6, "six"}, {7, "seven"}, {8, "eight"}, {9, "nine"}};

    MT::print_map("\nmap1 (initial values):\n", map1, fmt1, fmt2, epl_max);
    std::println("map1.size(): {:d}", map1.size());

    // using operator[] to modify values (keys are const)
    map1[0] = "null";
    map1[1] = "eins";
    map1[2] = "zwei";
    map1[3] = "drei";
    MT::print_map("\nmap1 (after modifications):\n", map1, fmt1, fmt2,
        epl_max);
    std::println("map1.size(): {:d}", map1.size());

    // using operator[] to add new elements
    map1[10] = "zehn";
    map1[11] = "elf";
    MT::print_map("\nmap1 (after insertions):\n", map1, fmt1, fmt2,
        epl_max);
    std::println("map1.size(): {:d}", map1.size());
```

```
    // using at() - throws std::out_of_range if key is invalid
    std::println("\nmap1.at(2):   {}", map1.at(2));
    std::println("map1.at(11): {}", map1.at(11));
//  std::println("map1.at(47): {}", map1.at(47));            // throws exception

    // erase elements
    map1.erase(5);
    map1.erase(6);
    MT::print_map("\nmap1 (after erase operations):\n", map1, fmt1, fmt2,
    epl_max);
    std::println("map1.size(): {:d}", map1.size());

    // clear map
    map1.clear();
    MT::print_map("\nmap1 (after clear):\n", map1, fmt1, fmt2, epl_max);
    std::println("map1.size(): {:d}", map1.size());
}
```

The next code block utilizes operator[] to modify the values of elements in map1. For example, the expression map1[0] = "null" changes the value for key 0 from "zero" to "null". You can also exploit operator[] to add new key-value pairs to a std::map. The expression map1[10] = "zehn" adds a new element to map1 whose key-value is 10 and "zehn". The ensuing std::println() statements utilize map1.at(2) and map1.at(11) to print the values associated with keys 2 and 11, respectively. Like other containers, std::map::at() throws an exception if the supplied key is invalid. To observe this, remove the comment from the line that contains map1.at(47) and run the code.

Ch07_03_ex1() applies map1.erase(5) and map1.erase(6) to remove elements with keys 5 and 6 from map1. The final code block in Ch07_03_ex1() illustrates the use of map1.clear(), which removes all elements from map1.

The next std::map example, shown in Listing 7-3-2, begins its execution with the instantiation of std::map<std::string_view, std::string> map1. Each key-value pair in map1 groups a unique three-character airport code and the airport's name. Following initialization of map1, Ch07_03_ex2() employs the expression map1["SYD"] = "Sydney Airport (Sydney, Australia)", which adds a new key-value pair to map1. Note that for a std::map, the key type supplied to operator[] must match the key type for the std::map or a suitable conversion must be available. For the current example, class std::string_view defines a constructor that accepts an argument of type const char*.

CHAPTER 7 ASSOCIATIVE CONTAINERS

Listing 7-3-2. Example Ch07_03 – Ch07_03_ex2()

```
void Ch07_03_ex2()
{
    constexpr size_t epl_max {1};
    const char* fmt1 = "[{:3s}, ";
    const char* fmt2 = "{:^35s}] ";

    // initialize map
    std::map<std::string_view, std::string> map1
        {{"ORD", "O'Hare International (Chicago, IL USA)"},
         {"LHR", "Heathrow Airport (London, England UK)"},
         {"ZRH", "Flughafen Zurich (Zurich, Switzerland)"},
         {"AKL", "Auckland Airport (Auckland, New Zealand)"}};

    MT::print_map("\nmap1 (initial values):\n", map1, fmt1, fmt2, epl_max);
    std::println("map1.size(): {:d}", map1.size());

    // insert element using new key
    map1["SYD"] = "Sydney Airport (Sydney, Australia)";
    MT::print_map("\nmap1 (after SYD insert):\n", map1, fmt1, fmt2,
    epl_max);
    std::println("map1.size(): {:d}", map1.size());

    // insert new element using emplace
    //
    // notes: emplace returns std::pair<iterator, bool>
    //        returned iterator points to std::pair<Key, T>
    auto [iter1, status1] = map1.emplace
        ( std::make_pair("NRT", "Narita International (Tokyo, Japan)") );

    if (status1)
    {
        std::println("\nmap1.emplace - new element added to map1");
        std::println("key = '{}' value: '{}'", iter1->first, iter1->
        second);
    }
    else
```

```cpp
    {
        std::println("\nmap1.emplace - element key already exists
        in map1");
        std::println("key = '{}' value: '{}'", iter1->first,
        iter1->second);
    }

    // insert new element using try_emplace
    auto [iter2, status2] = map1.try_emplace
        ("DXB", "Dubai International Airport (Dubai, UAE)");

    if (status2)
    {
        std::println("\nmap1.try_emplace - new element added to map1");
        std::println("key = '{}' value: '{}'", iter2->first,
        iter2->second);
    }
    else
        std::println("\nmap1.try_emplace - element key already exists
        in map1");

    MT::print_map("\nmap1 (after emplacements):\n", map1, fmt1, fmt2,
    epl_max);
    std::println("map1.size(): {:d}", map1.size());
    std::println("");

    // search map using key values and find()
    std::array<std::string_view, 4> keys {"ZRH", "LAX", "MCO", "AKL"};

    for (const std::string_view& key : keys)
    {
        std::print("key: '{:3s}' - ", key);

        if (auto iter = map1.find(key); iter != map1.end())
            std::println("found [{:3s}, {:35s}]", iter->first,
            iter->second);
        else
```

```
            std::println("not found");
    }
}
```

The subsequent code block in Ch07_03_ex2() adds another element to map1 using std::map::emplace(). The expression

```
auto [iter1, status1] = map1.emplace
        ( std::make_pair("NRT", "Narita International (Tokyo, Japan)") );
```

inserts a new element into map1 with key "NRT". Member function emplace() returns a value of type std::pair<iterator, bool>. Note that structured binding is exploited to unbundle the std::pair's elements. For the current example, the structured binding[3] construct executes iter1 = get<0>(pair_emp) and status1 = get<1>(pair_emp) where pair_emp is the std::pair<iterator, bool> returned by emplace(). If status1 is true, the emplace() operation successfully inserted the new element into map1 and iter1 points to a std::pair<std::string_view, std::string> node – or the inserted element – in map1. Note that the ensuing std::println() statements employ iter1->first and iter1->second to print the key and value of the newly inserted element. If status1 is false, the key already exists in map1 and iter1 points to that element.

The next code block in Ch07_03_ex2() demonstrates the use of try_emplace(). Note that try_emplace() requires separate key and value arguments; there are no overloads that accept a std::pair<Key, T> object. Execution-wise, the primary difference between emplace() and try_emplace() is that the latter first checks to see if the specified key already exists in the map. If it does, try_emplace() does nothing. Otherwise, it constructs the value object and inserts the key-value pair into the map. Member function emplace() constructs the value object *before* checking the std::map for an existing key. This execution ordering may be suboptimal in use cases that perform frequency insertions of existing keys.

The final code block in Ch07_03_ex2() demonstrates use of std::map::find(). This member function searches a std::map for a specified key and returns an iterator to a key-value pair if the key is found; otherwise, find() returns end().

---

[3] Structured binding can also be used to unbundle the elements of a std::tuple.

Listing 7-3-3-1 shows the source code for class RGB, which is used later in example Ch07_03_ex3(). Class RGB is a straightforward class that encompasses the red, green, and blue components of a color. Note that this class defines two parameterized constructors; the first one requires distinct uint8_t values for color components r, g, and b, while the second one accepts a single uint32_t[4] value. Also, note that for class RGB, operator<=> and operator== (arbitrarily) compare the uint32_t value of a color.

Listing 7-3-3-1. Example Ch07_03 – Class RGB

```
//-------------------------------------------------------------------
// RGB.h
//-------------------------------------------------------------------
#ifndef RGB_H_
#define RGB_H_
#include <compare>
#include <cstdint>
#include <format>
#include <ostream>
#include <string>

class RGB
{
    friend struct std::formatter<RGB>;
public:
    RGB() = default;
    RGB(uint8_t r, uint8_t g, uint8_t b) : m_R{r}, m_G{g}, m_B{b} {};

    RGB(uint32_t color)
    {
        m_B = color & 0xFF;
        m_G = (color >> 8) & 0xFF;
        m_R = (color >> 16) & 0xFF;
    }
```

---

[4] This format is often utilized to specify HTML colors as demonstrated in later chapters.

```cpp
    // accessors
    uint8_t R() const { return m_R; }
    uint8_t B() const { return m_B; }
    uint8_t G() const { return m_G; }
    uint8_t& R() { return m_R; };
    uint8_t& G() { return m_G; };
    uint8_t& B() { return m_B; };
    uint32_t ValUint() const { return (m_R << 16) | (m_G << 8) | m_B; }

    // operators
    friend auto operator<=>(const RGB& rgb1, const RGB& rgb2)
        { return rgb1.ValUint() <=> rgb2.ValUint(); }

    friend bool operator==(const RGB& rgb1, const RGB& rgb2)
        { return rgb1.ValUint() == rgb2.ValUint(); }

    friend std::ostream& operator<<(std::ostream& os, const RGB& rgb)
        {os << rgb.to_str(); return os;}
private:
    std::string to_str(bool use_hex = true) const;

    uint8_t m_R {};
    uint8_t m_G {};
    uint8_t m_B {};
    uint8_t m_A {};      // reserved for future use
};
// class RGB formatter
template <> struct std::formatter<RGB> : std::formatter<std::string>
{
    constexpr auto parse(std::format_parse_context& pc)
        { return pc.begin(); }

    auto format(const RGB& rgb, std::format_context& fc) const
        { return std::format_to(fc.out(), "{}", rgb.to_str()); }
};

#endif
```

CHAPTER 7   ASSOCIATIVE CONTAINERS

```cpp
//--------------------------------------------------------------------------
// RGB.cpp
//--------------------------------------------------------------------------

#include <format>
#include <string>
#include "RGB.h"

std::string RGB::to_str(bool use_hex) const
{
    std::string s {};

    if (use_hex)
    {
        uint32_t c = ValUint();
        std::format_to(std::back_inserter(s), "0x{:06X}", c);
    }
    else
    {
        std::format_to(std::back_inserter(s), "({:3d},{:3d},{:3d})",
            m_R, m_G, m_B);
    }

    return s;
}
```

The source code for example Ch07_03_ex3(), shown in Listing 7-3-3-2, opens with the definition of std::map aliases cmap_lt_t and cmap_gt_t. The difference between these two types is that the former utilizes std::less<std::string_view> for its comparison function while the latter employs std::greater<std::string_view>. Both cmap_lt_t and cmap_gt_t use a key of type std::string_view and a value type of RGB. Next in Listing 7-3-3-2 is the definition of template function print_colors(), which prints the colors of a cmap_lt_t or cmap_gt_t map.

Listing 7-3-3-2. Example Ch07_03 – Ch07_03_ex3()

```
using cmap_lt_t = std::map<std::string_view, RGB,
std::less<std::string_view>>;
using cmap_gt_t = std::map<std::string_view, RGB,
std::greater<std::string_view>>;

template <typename T>
void print_colors(const char* msg, const T& colors)
{
    std::print("{:s}", msg);

    for (const auto& color : colors)
        std::println("{:<10s} {}", color.first, color.second);
}

void Ch07_03_ex3()
{
    // create map of colors
    cmap_lt_t colors1
    {
        {"Red", 0xFF0000}, {"Green", 0x008000}, {"Blue", 0x0000FF},
        {"Yellow", 0xFFFF00}, {"Cyan", 0x00FFFF}, {"Magenta", 0xFF00FF}
    };

    print_colors("\nmap colors1 (initial values):\n", colors1);

    // std::map relational operators
    cmap_lt_t colors2 {colors1};
    print_colors("\nmap colors2 (initial values):\n", colors2);
    std::println("\ncolors2 == colors1: {:s}", colors2 == colors1);
    std::println("colors2 <  colors1: {:s}", colors2 <  colors1);
    std::println("colors2 >  colors1: {:s}", colors2 >  colors1);

    colors2.emplace("Lime", 0x00FF00);
    print_colors("\nmap colors2 (after emplace):\n", colors2);
    std::println("\ncolors2 == colors1: {:s}", colors2 == colors1);
    std::println("colors2 <  colors1: {:s}", colors2 <  colors1);
    std::println("colors2 >  colors1: {:s}", colors2 >  colors1);
```

```cpp
    // add more colors using insert_range (C++23)
#ifdef __cpp_lib_containers_ranges
    auto more_colors = { std::pair<std::string_view, RGB>
        {"Black", RGB {0x00000}}, {"Gray", RGB {0x808080}},
        {"LightGray", RGB {0xD3D3D3}}, {"White", RGB {0xFFFFFF}} };

    colors2.insert_range(more_colors);
    print_colors("\nmap colors2 (initial insert_range):\n", colors2);
#else
    std::println("\nstd::map::insert_range() requires C++23");
#endif

    // create new map using std::greater for key sorts
    cmap_gt_t colors3(colors2.begin(), colors2.end());
    print_colors("\nmap colors3 (initial values):\n", colors3);

    // invalid expressions - different template types
//  cmap_gt_t colors3(colors2);     // compiler error
//  bool colors3 < colors1;         // compiler error
}
```

Function Ch07_03_ex3() opens with the creation of cmap_lt_t maps colors1 and colors2. The next set of statements demonstrates the use of various relational operators using colors1 and colors2. The code block that occurs after the relational operators exercises colors2.insert_range(more_colors) (C++23). This expression inserts the std::pair<std::string_view, RGB> objects from more_colors into colors2. The final executable code block in Ch07_03_ex3() utilizes cmap_gt_t colors3(colors2.begin(), colors2.end()) to instantiate colors3. Note in the results section that colors2 contains the same elements as colors1, but the elements are sorted in descending order. It warrants mentioning here that cmap_lt_t and cmap_gt_t are distinct C++ types. This means that certain operations, such as those shown in the commented-out statements at the end of Ch07_03_ex3(), generate compiler errors. The constructor for colors3 is valid since maps cmap_lt_t colors2 and cmap_gt_t colors3 both use the same key-value types.

The final example function of Ch07_03, shown in Listing 7-3-4, commences with the creation of cmap_lt_t colors1 and cmap_gt_t colors2. Following the calls to print_colors(), Ch07_03_ex4() utilizes the expression colors1.merge(colors2) to merge elements from colors2 into colors1. Despite the different types for colors1 and colors2, this expression is valid since both cmap_lt_t and cmap_gt_t utilize std::string_view and RGB for the map key-value pair. Note in the results section that following the map merger, colors2 contains elements that existed in colors1 prior to the merge operation.

Listing 7-3-4. Example Ch07_03 – Ch07_03_ex4()

```
void Ch07_03_ex4()
{
    // create and print maps
    cmap_lt_t colors1
        {{"Red", 0xFF0000}, {"Maroon", 0x800000}, {"Green", 0x008000},
         {"Yellow", 0xFFFF00}};

    cmap_gt_t colors2
        {{"Aqua", 0x00FFFF}, {"Teal", 0x008080}, {"Yellow", 0xFFFF00},
         {"Red", 0xFF0000}, {"White", 0xFFFFFF}};

    print_colors("\nmap colors1 (initial values):\n", colors1);
    print_colors("\nmap colors2 (initial values):\n", colors2);

    // merge maps - ok since colors1 and colors2 use same <Key, T>
    colors1.merge(colors2);
    print_colors("\nmap colors1 (after merge):\n", colors1);
    print_colors("\nmap colors2 (after merge):\n", colors2);
}
```

Here are the results for source code example Ch07_03:

```
----- Results for example Ch07_03 -----

----- Ch07_03_ex1() -----

map1 (initial values):
[  0, zero  ] [  1, one   ] [  2, two   ] [  3, three ] [  4, four  ]
[  5, five  ] [  6, six   ] [  7, seven ] [  8, eight ] [  9, nine  ]
map1.size(): 10
```

CHAPTER 7   ASSOCIATIVE CONTAINERS

```
map1 (after modifications):
[  0, null   ] [  1, eins   ] [  2, zwei  ] [  3, drei  ] [  4, four  ]
[  5, five   ] [  6, six    ] [  7, seven ] [  8, eight ] [  9, nine  ]
map1.size(): 10

map1 (after insertions):
[  0, null   ] [  1, eins   ] [  2, zwei  ] [  3, drei  ] [  4, four  ]
[  5, five   ] [  6, six    ] [  7, seven ] [  8, eight ] [  9, nine  ]
[ 10, zehn   ] [ 11, elf    ]
map1.size(): 12

map1.at(2):  zwei
map1.at(11): elf

map1 (after erase operations):
[  0, null   ] [  1, eins   ] [  2, zwei  ] [  3, drei  ] [  4, four  ]
[  7, seven  ] [  8, eight  ] [  9, nine  ] [ 10, zehn  ] [ 11, elf   ]
map1.size(): 10

map1 (after clear):
<empty>
map1.size(): 0

----- Ch07_03_ex2() -----

map1 (initial values):
[AKL, Auckland Airport (Auckland, New Zealand)]
[LHR, Heathrow Airport (London, England UK)]
[ORD, O'Hare International (Chicago, IL USA)]
[ZRH, Flughafen Zurich (Zurich, Switzerland)]
map1.size(): 4

map1 (after SYD insert):
[AKL, Auckland Airport (Auckland, New Zealand)]
[LHR, Heathrow Airport (London, England UK)]
[ORD, O'Hare International (Chicago, IL USA)]
[SYD, Sydney Airport (Sydney, Australia) ]
[ZRH, Flughafen Zurich (Zurich, Switzerland)]
map1.size(): 5
```

```
map1.emplace - new element added to map1
key = 'NRT' value: 'Narita International (Tokyo, Japan)'

map1.try_emplace - new element added to map1
key = 'DXB' value: 'Dubai International Airport (Dubai, UAE)'

map1 (after emplacements):
[AKL, Auckland Airport (Auckland, New Zealand)]
[DXB, Dubai International Airport (Dubai, UAE)]
[LHR, Heathrow Airport (London, England UK)]
[NRT, Narita International (Tokyo, Japan)]
[ORD, O'Hare International (Chicago, IL USA)]
[SYD, Sydney Airport (Sydney, Australia) ]
[ZRH, Flughafen Zurich (Zurich, Switzerland)]
map1.size(): 7

key: 'ZRH' - found [ZRH, Flughafen Zurich (Zurich, Switzerland)]
key: 'LAX' - not found
key: 'MCO' - not found
key: 'AKL' - found [AKL, Auckland Airport (Auckland, New Zealand)]

----- Ch07_03_ex3() -----

map colors1 (initial values):
Blue        0x0000FF
Cyan        0x00FFFF
Green       0x008000
Magenta     0xFF00FF
Red         0xFF0000
Yellow      0xFFFF00

map colors2 (initial values):
Blue        0x0000FF
Cyan        0x00FFFF
Green       0x008000
Magenta     0xFF00FF
Red         0xFF0000
Yellow      0xFFFF00
```

CHAPTER 7 ASSOCIATIVE CONTAINERS

```
colors2 == colors1: true
colors2 <  colors1: false
colors2 >  colors1: false

map colors2 (after emplace):
Blue        0x0000FF
Cyan        0x00FFFF
Green       0x008000
Lime        0x00FF00
Magenta     0xFF00FF
Red         0xFF0000
Yellow      0xFFFF00

colors2 == colors1: false
colors2 <  colors1: true
colors2 >  colors1: false

map colors2 (initial insert_range):
Black       0x000000
Blue        0x0000FF
Cyan        0x00FFFF
Gray        0x808080
Green       0x008000
LightGray   0xD3D3D3
Lime        0x00FF00
Magenta     0xFF00FF
Red         0xFF0000
White       0xFFFFFF
Yellow      0xFFFF00

map colors3 (initial values):
Yellow      0xFFFF00
White       0xFFFFFF
Red         0xFF0000
Magenta     0xFF00FF
Lime        0x00FF00
LightGray   0xD3D3D3
```

```
Green      0x008000
Gray       0x808080
Cyan       0x00FFFF
Blue       0x0000FF
Black      0x000000

----- Ch07_03_ex4() -----

map colors1 (initial values):
Green      0x008000
Maroon     0x800000
Red        0xFF0000
Yellow     0xFFFF00

map colors2 (initial values):
Yellow     0xFFFF00
White      0xFFFFFF
Teal       0x008080
Red        0xFF0000
Aqua       0x00FFFF

map colors1 (after merge):
Aqua       0x00FFFF
Green      0x008000
Maroon     0x800000
Red        0xFF0000
Teal       0x008080
White      0xFFFFFF
Yellow     0xFFFF00

map colors2 (after merge):
Yellow     0xFFFF00
Red        0xFF0000
```

CHAPTER 7 ASSOCIATIVE CONTAINERS

Using std::multimap

If you were to guess that container class `std::multimap` is a `std::map` like container that supports multiple elements using the same key, you would be correct. Most of what you learned in the previous section regarding `std::maps` also applies to `std::multimaps`. Class `std::multimap` includes a few additional member functions that class `std::map` doesn't define, and you'll learn how to properly use these in this section.

Listing 7-4-1 shows the source code for the first `std::multimap` example. Near the top of `Ch07_04_ex1()` is a series of two-letter `std::string_view` objects that denote names of states in the United States. These variables are employed to avoid repetition and improve readability. Next is the declaration of `mulmap_t mmap1`, which contains key-value pairs of US states and cities. Type name `mulmap_t` is an alias for `std::multimap<std::string_view, std::string>`. Note that `mmap1` contains multiple cities from each state. The `std::println()` statement that follows the call to `MT::print_multimap()` exercises `mmap1.size()`, which returns the number of elements in `mmap1`.

Listing 7-4-1. Example Ch07_04 – Ch07_04_ex1()

```
//---------------------------------------------------------------
// Ch07_04_ex.cpp
//---------------------------------------------------------------

#include <array>
#include <iomanip>
#include <iostream>
#include <map>
#include <string>
#include <string_view>
#include "Ch07_04.h"
#include "MT.h"

using mulmap_t = std::multimap<std::string_view, std::string>;

void Ch07_04_ex1()
{
    constexpr size_t epl_max {2};
    const char* fmt1 = "[{:<14s} | ";
    const char* fmt2 = "{:>14s}] ";
```

```cpp
// state abbreviations
std::string_view ca {"California"};
std::string_view fl {"Florida"};
std::string_view il {"Illinois"};
std::string_view ny {"New York"};
std::string_view oh {"Ohio"};
std::string_view tx {"Texas"};
std::string_view wi {"Wisconsin"};

mulmap_t mmap1
    {{ca, "Los Angeles"}, {ca, "San Francisco"}, {ca, "Fresno"},
     {il, "Chicago"}, {il, "Peoria"}, {il, "Rockford"},
     {oh, "Cleveland"}, {oh, "Columbus"}, {oh, "Cincinnati"},
     {tx, "Houston"}, {tx, "Dallas"}, {tx, "Austin"}, {tx, "El Paso"}};
MT::print_multimap("\nmmap1 (initial values):\n", mmap1, fmt1, fmt2,
epl_max);
std::println("mmap1.size(): {:d}", mmap1.size());

// add new key/value pairs to mmap1 using insert
mmap1.insert(std::pair {fl, "Orlando"});
mmap1.insert(std::pair {fl, "Miami"});
mmap1.insert(std::pair {fl, "Jacksonville"});
mmap1.insert(std::pair {fl, "Orlando"});
MT::print_multimap("\nmmap1 (after insertions):\n", mmap1, fmt1, fmt2,
epl_max);
std::println("mmap1.size(): {:d}", mmap1.size());

// add new key/value pairs to mmap1 using emplace
mmap1.emplace(ny, "New York City");
mmap1.emplace(ny, "Buffalo");
mmap1.emplace(ny, "Albany");
mmap1.emplace(ny, "Yonkers");
mmap1.emplace(ny, "Syracuse");
MT::print_multimap("\nmmap1 (after emplacements):\n", mmap1, fmt1,
fmt2, epl_max);
std::println("mmap1.size(): {:d}", mmap1.size());
```

```
    // using count
    auto count_il = mmap1.count(il);
    auto count_tx = mmap1.count(tx);
    std::println("\nnumber of {:s} cities in mmap1: {:d}", il, count_il);
    std::println("number of {:s} cities in mmap1: {:d}", tx, count_tx);

    // using contains (C++20)
    std::println("\nmmap1 contains key {:s}: {:s}", oh,
    mmap1.contains(oh));
    std::println("mmap1 contains key {:s}: {:s}", wi, mmap1.contains(wi));
}
```

The next two code blocks in Ch07_04_ex1() add more elements to mmap1 using std::multimap::insert() and std::multimap::emplace(). It warrants merits mentioning here that std::multimap::try_emplace() is not defined since std::multimaps can hold multiple objects with the same key. Following the insertions, Ch07_04_ex1() utilizes count_il = mmap1.count(il) to count the number of cities from Illinois in mmap1. The next statement, count_tx = mmap1.count(tx), performs the same operation for cities in Texas. The final code block in Ch07_04_ex1() demonstrates the use of mmap1.contains() (C++20), which returns true if the specified key exists in mmap1.

Like std::map, container class std::multimap defines a member function named find() that searches for a specific key value. However, the use of the latter find() is somewhat different since a std::multimap may contain multiple elements with the same key. Example function Ch07_04_ex2(), shown in Listing 7-4-2, illustrates the use of std::multimap::find() along with another search function named std::multimap::equal_range().

Listing 7-4-2. Example Ch07_04 - Ch07_04_ex2()

```
void Ch07_04_ex2()
{
    constexpr size_t epl_max {3};
    const char* fmt1 = "[{:3s}, ";
    const char* fmt2 = "{:s}] ";

    // country abbreviations
    std::string_view ar {"Argentina"};
    std::string_view br {"Brazil"};
```

```cpp
    std::string_view ca {"Canada"};
    std::string_view in {"India"};
    std::string_view mx {"Mexico"};

    // create and initialize multimap
    mulmap_t mmap1
        {{br, "Sao Paulo"}, {br, "Rio de Janeiro"}, {br, "Brasilia"},
         {ca, "Montreal"}, {ca, "Toronto"}, {ca, "Edmonton"},
         {ca, "Calgary"}, {ca, "Vancouver"},
         {in, "New Delhi"}, {in, "Chennai"},
         {mx, "Mexico City"}, {mx, "Tijuana"}, {mx, "Ecatepec"}};

    MT::print_multimap("\nmmap1 (initial values):\n", mmap1, fmt1, fmt2,
        epl_max);
    std::println("mmap1.size(): {:d}", mmap1.size());

    // using multimap::find
    std::println("\nsearching mmap1 using find()");
    std::array<std::string_view, 3> find_keys {ar, ca, in};

    for (const auto& find_key : find_keys)
    {
        std::print("\nfind_key: {:s}\n", find_key);

        auto iter = mmap1.find(find_key);

        if (iter == mmap1.end())
            std::println("not found");
        else
        {
            while (iter->first == find_key)
            {
                std::println("found: {:s}, {:s}", iter->first,
                    iter->second);

                if (++iter == mmap1.end())
                    break;
            }
        }
    }
```

```
    }

    // using multimap::equal_range
    std::println("\nsearching mmap1 using equal_range()");

    for (const auto& find_key : find_keys)
    {
        std::println("\nfind_key: {:s}", find_key);

        auto iter_er = mmap1.equal_range(find_key);

        if (iter_er.first->first != find_key)
            std::println("not found");
        else
        {
            for (auto iter = iter_er.first; iter != iter_er.second; ++iter)
                std::println("found: {:s}, {:s}", iter->first,
                    iter->second);
        }
    }
}
```

Similar to the previous example, Ch07_04_ex2() defines a few std::string_view objects that contain country names. Next is the definition of mulmap_t mmap1, which maintains country-city key-value pairs. Following the definition of mmap1, function MT::print_multimap() prints the elements of mmap1.

The next code block in Ch07_04_ex2() utilizes mmap1.find(find_key) to search mmap1 for an element that matches find_key. If a key match is not found, find() returns mmap1.end(). Otherwise, it returns an iterator to the first element in mmap1 that matches find_key. The ensuing while loop uses iter to print the key and value of each element in mmap1 that matches find_key. There are two important details to recognize here. First, iterator iter points to an object of type std::pair<std::string_view, std::string>, which matches the element type of mulmap_t. Second, note that there are two termination checks in the while loop: iter->first == find_key (terminate if false) and ++iter == mmap1.end() (terminate if true).

CHAPTER 7 ASSOCIATIVE CONTAINERS

The final code block of Ch07_04_ex2() utilizes mmap1.equal_range(find_key) to search mmap1 for find_key. In the current example, equal_range() returns a std::pair of iterators that's saved in iter_er. Iterator iter_er.first points to the first element in mmap1 that's not less than find_key, while iter_er.second points to the first element in mmap1 that's greater than find_key. If iter_er.first->first != find_key is true, no key matches were found. Otherwise, the ensuing for loop prints all elements with key find_key; these exist in the range [iter_er.first, iter_er.second). Here are the results for source code example Ch07_04:

```
----- Results for example Ch07_04 -----

----- Ch07_04_ex1() -----
mmap1 (initial values):
[California    |     Los Angeles] [California    |    San Francisco]
[California    |          Fresno] [Illinois      |           Chicago]
[Illinois      |          Peoria] [Illinois      |          Rockford]
[Ohio          |       Cleveland] [Ohio          |          Columbus]
[Ohio          |      Cincinnati] [Texas         |           Houston]
[Texas         |          Dallas] [Texas         |            Austin]
[Texas         |         El Paso]
mmap1.size(): 13

mmap1 (after insertions):
[California    |     Los Angeles] [California    |    San Francisco]
[California    |          Fresno] [Florida       |           Orlando]
[Florida       |           Miami] [Florida       |      Jacksonville]
[Florida       |         Orlando] [Illinois      |           Chicago]
[Illinois      |          Peoria] [Illinois      |          Rockford]
[Ohio          |       Cleveland] [Ohio          |          Columbus]
[Ohio          |      Cincinnati] [Texas         |           Houston]
[Texas         |          Dallas] [Texas         |            Austin]
[Texas         |         El Paso]
mmap1.size(): 17
```

CHAPTER 7　ASSOCIATIVE CONTAINERS

mmap1 (after emplacements):
```
[California  |   Los Angeles] [California  |  San Francisco]
[California  |        Fresno] [Florida     |        Orlando]
[Florida     |         Miami] [Florida     |   Jacksonville]
[Florida     |       Orlando] [Illinois    |        Chicago]
[Illinois    |        Peoria] [Illinois    |       Rockford]
[New York    | New York City] [New York    |        Buffalo]
[New York    |        Albany] [New York    |        Yonkers]
[New York    |      Syracuse] [Ohio        |      Cleveland]
[Ohio        |      Columbus] [Ohio        |     Cincinnati]
[Texas       |       Houston] [Texas       |         Dallas]
[Texas       |        Austin] [Texas       |        El Paso]
```
mmap1.size(): 22

number of Illinois cities in mmap1: 3
number of Texas cities in mmap1: 4

mmap1 contains key Ohio: true
mmap1 contains key Wisconsin: false

----- Ch07_04_ex2() -----

mmap1 (initial values):
[Brazil, Sao Paulo] [Brazil, Rio de Janeiro] [Brazil, Brasilia]
[Canada, Montreal] [Canada, Toronto] [Canada, Edmonton]
[Canada, Calgary] [Canada, Vancouver] [India, New Delhi]
[India, Chennai] [Mexico, Mexico City] [Mexico, Tijuana]
[Mexico, Ecatepec]
mmap1.size(): 13

searching mmap1 using find()

find_key: Argentina
not found

find_key: Canada
found: Canada, Montreal
found: Canada, Toronto

```
found: Canada, Edmonton
found: Canada, Calgary
found: Canada, Vancouver

find_key: India
found: India, New Delhi
found: India, Chennai

searching mmap1 using equal_range()

find_key: Argentina
not found

find_key: Canada
found: Canada, Montreal
found: Canada, Toronto
found: Canada, Edmonton
found: Canada, Calgary
found: Canada, Vancouver

find_key: India
found: India, New Delhi
found: India, Chennai
```

When searching a `std::multimap`, the ordering of elements with equal keys is not guaranteed. The only assurance for these cases is that `std::multimap::find()` and `std::multimap::equal_ranges()` return the necessary iterator information that facilitates access to all key-matched elements. This element ordering ambiguity also applies to `std::multiset::find()`.

Summary

Here are the key learning points for this chapter:

- A `std::set<T>` is an associative container that holds a unique set of elements. The elements of a `std::set<T>` are usually stored in red-black tree; the ordering of elements in this tree is determined using a comparison function that defaults to `std::less<T>`. Element insertions, searches, and removals have logarithmic instead of linear complexity.

- A `std::multiset<T>` is similar to a `std::set<T>` but allows multiple elements of the same value.

- A `std::map<Key, T>` is an associative container that holds pairs of key-value elements. The key of each element in a `std::map<Key, T>` must be unique. Like a `std::set<T>`, the ordering of elements in a `std::map<Key, T>` is determined using a comparison function whose default is `std::less<Key>`. Element insertions, searches, and removals also have logarithmic instead of linear complexity.

- A `std::multimap<Key, T>` is similar to a `std::map<Key, T>` but allows multiple elements with the same key value.

CHAPTER 8

Unordered Associative Containers

This chapter covers unordered associative containers, including

- Unordered associative container primer
- How to use `std::unordered_set`
- How to use `std::unordered_multiset`
- How to use `std::unordered_map`
- How to use `std::unordered_multimap`

An unordered associative container holds a collection of objects or elements. Unlike the (ordered) associative containers that you studied in the previous chapter, unordered associative containers do not order their elements using a tree-like structure and comparison function. Instead, unordered associative containers order their elements using hash functions. For many use cases, the application of a hash function instead of a comparison function yields improved performance.

Unordered Associative Container Primer

In Chapter 7, you learned that compared to a sequence container, an associative container has logarithmic instead of linear complexity when performing common operations, such as element insertions, searches, and removals. You also learned that an associative container typically utilizes a red-black tree to organize its elements, which is the principal reason behind its logarithmic performance properties. For many applications, however, this algorithmic performance enhancement is inadequate, especially when working with containers that possess large numbers of elements.

CHAPTER 8 UNORDERED ASSOCIATIVE CONTAINERS

To address this imbalance, some applications exploit unordered associative containers. Unlike an associative container, an unordered associative container doesn't use an internal tree; it also doesn't order its elements using a key comparison function. Instead, an unordered associative container utilizes a hash function and a hash table to arrange its elements. Before examining the programming aspects of an unordered associative container, a brief overview of hash functions and other hashing concepts is necessary.

Hash Functions and Concepts

A hash function is a function that maps a key value to a fixed-size value. This fixed-size value, commonly an integer, is called a hash value. Once calculated, a hash value is employed as an index into a hash table, which contains (or points to) the key's data. For some containers, the key and data are the same object. Figure 8-1 illustrates the logical relationships between a key, hash function, hash table, and data.

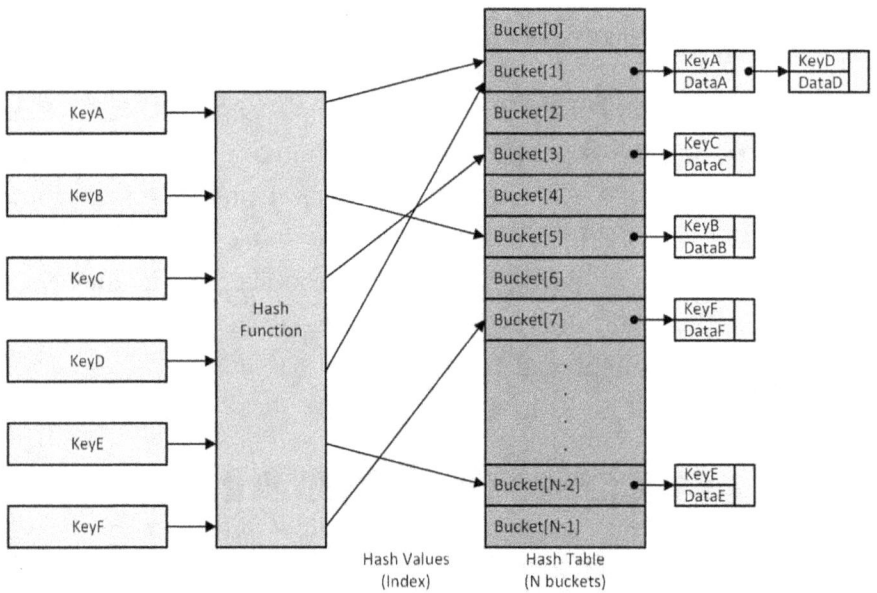

Figure 8-1. *Logical relationships between key, hash function, hash table, and data*

In Figure 8-1, note that the hash table contains *N* buckets. Each hash table bucket is often a list of key-data pairs (or just keys). Also, note in this figure that many, but not all, keys map to a unique bucket. A collision occurs when two or more keys map to the same bucket. In this situation, the bucket list is extended to accommodate the new element.

For any STL unordered associative container `ctr`, `ctr.bucket_count()` returns the number of hash table buckets. A hash table load factor is the average number of elements per bucket and can be calculated as follows: `ctr.load_factor() = ctr.size() / ctr.bucket_count()` where `ctr.size()` is the number of container elements. The maximum load factor is the largest allowable load factor. If this value is exceeded due to an element insertion, the container automatically increases the number of buckets; it then performs a rehash operation. A rehash rebuilds the entire hash table using the new bucket count. This reduces the number of elements that are maintained in each bucket, which improves search performance. The downside of a rehash is that it may be a time-consuming operation depending on the number of elements in the container.

The maximum load factor of an unordered associative container can be manually specified using `ctr.max_load_factor(float mlf)`. You can also manually change the number of hash table buckets using `ctr.rehash(std::size_t bucket_count_min)`. During execution of `ctr.rehash()`, the number of hash table buckets is adjusted to at least `bucket_count_min`. It's important to keep in mind that that the actual number of hash table buckets is always determined by the container. You'll see example usages of these hash policy functions later in this chapter.

One notable advantage of a hash algorithm is that it doesn't require execution of key comparison functions or tree node traversals to determine a key's bucket within the hash table. A key's hash table bucket can be quickly accessed using simple indexing, which makes it appropriate for use cases that perform frequent searches. Numerous tomes have been written about hash functions and algorithms. Appendix B contains a few references that you can consult for more information regarding these topics.

Using std::unordered_set

A `std::unordered_set` is an unordered associative container that incorporates a collection of unique keys. Like its ordered counterpart `std::set`, class `std::unordered_set` models a mathematical set. Its public interface for insertions, searches, and removals resembles that of a `std::set`. All STL unordered associative container classes including `std::unordered_set` define additional public member functions that facilitate customization of the container's internal hash table and hash policy.

CHAPTER 8　UNORDERED ASSOCIATIVE CONTAINERS

Source code example Ch08_01 typifies several usages of class std::unordered_set. In Listing 8-1-1-1, note that header file Ch08_01.h defines aliases uno_set_str_t = std::unordered_set<std::string> and uno_set_hc_t = std::unordered_set<HtmlColor, size_t(*)(const HtmlColor&)>. The former is a std::unordered_set that contains keys of std::string, while the latter contains keys of HtmlColor. Alias uno_set_hc_t also specifies a custom hash function. The particulars regarding class HtmlColor, shown in Listing 8-1-4-1, and uno_set_hc_t's custom hash function are explained later in this section. Listing 8-1-1-1 additionally shows the source code for Ch08_01_misc.cpp. This file defines two overloads for print_buckets(). These functions print the buckets of a uno_set_str_t or uno_set_hc_t container as expounded later in this section.

Listing 8-1-1-1.　Example Ch08_01 - Ch08_01.h and Ch08_01_misc.cpp

```
//------------------------------------------------------------
// Ch08_01.h
//------------------------------------------------------------
#ifndef CH08_01_H_
#define CH08_01_H_
#include <string>
#include <unordered_set>
#include "Common.h"
#include "HtmlColor.h"

// type aliases for unordered_set of HtmlColor values
using uno_set_str_t = std::unordered_set<std::string>;
using uno_set_hc_t = std::unordered_set<HtmlColor, size_t(*)(const HtmlColor&)>;

// Ch08_01_misc.cpp
void print_buckets(const char* msg, const uno_set_str_t& strings);
void print_buckets(const char* msg, const uno_set_hc_t& colors);

// Ch08_01_ex.cpp
extern void Ch08_01_ex();

#endif
```

```cpp
//-------------------------------------------------------------------------
// Ch08_01_misc.cpp
//-------------------------------------------------------------------------

#include "Ch08_01.h"
#include "HtmlColor.h"

template <typename T>
void print_stats(const char* msg, const T& uno_set)
{
    // print stats
    std::println("{:s}  ", msg);
    std::print("size: {:d}   ", uno_set.size());
    std::print("bucket_count: {:d}   ", uno_set.bucket_count());
    std::println("load_factor: {:..4f}\n", uno_set.load_factor());
}

void print_buckets(const char* msg, const uno_set_str_t& strings)
{
    print_stats(msg, strings);

    // print buckets of strings
    for (size_t i = 0; i < strings.bucket_count(); ++i)
    {
        if (strings.bucket_size(i) > 0)
        {
            std::print("bucket {:2d}: ", i);

            for (auto iter = strings.begin(i); iter != strings.end(i);
            ++iter)
                std::print("'{}' ", *iter);
            std::println("");
        }
    }
}
```

CHAPTER 8   UNORDERED ASSOCIATIVE CONTAINERS

```
void print_buckets(const char* msg, const uno_set_hc_t& colors)
{
    print_stats(msg, colors);

    // print buckets of colors
    for (size_t i = 0; i < colors.bucket_count(); ++i)
    {
        if (i >= HtmlColor::hash_func_bucket_count)
            break;

        if (colors.bucket_size(i) > 0)
        {
            std::print("bucket {:2d}: ", i);

            for (auto iter = colors.begin(i); iter != colors.end(i);
            ++iter)
                std::print(" {}", iter->Name());
            std::println("");
        }
    }
}
```

Listing 8-1-1-2 shows the source code for example function Ch08_01_ex1(). The open code block of this function instantiates uno_set_str_t set1 whose initializer list supplies the container's initial values. The next statement exercises print_buckets() to print the bucket contents of set1. If you scan ahead to the results section for example Ch08_01, note that set1 contains six elements and eight buckets.[1] Only three of the buckets – numbers three, five, and seven – contain elements; the remaining buckets are empty. Also shown is the current load factor for set1, which is not very meaningful right now given the small number of elements in set1.

---

[1] For each example in this chapter, the hash table parameters shown in the results section may vary depending on the C++ compiler.

Listing 8-1-1-2. Example Ch08_01 - Ch08_01_ex1()

```cpp
//--------------------------------------------------------------------------
// Ch08_01_ex.cpp
//--------------------------------------------------------------------------

#include <array>
#include <functional>
#include <string>
#include <unordered_set>
#include "Ch08_01.h"
#include "MF.h"
#include "MT.h"
#include "HtmlColor.h"

uno_set_str_t Ch08_01_ex1()
{
    // create an unordered set of strings
    uno_set_str_t set1 { "Gulf of Alaska", "Caribbean Sea", "Black Sea",
        "Red Sea", "Gulf of Thailand", "Bering Sea" };

    print_buckets("\nset1 (initial values): ", set1);

    // add more elements using insert and emplace
    set1.insert("Baltic Sea");
    set1.insert("Mediterranean Sea");
    set1.insert("Gulf of Mexico");
    set1.emplace("Ross Sea");
    set1.emplace("Yellow Sea");
    set1.emplace("Greenland Sea");

    // add more elements using insert_range (C++23) or ranges::copy (C++20)
    std::array<std::string, 6> arr1
        {"Labrador Sea", "Amundsen Gulf", "North Sea",
         "Adriatic Sea", "Scotia Sea", "Gulf of Biscay"};

#if __cpp_lib_containers_ranges >= 202202L
    set1.insert_range(arr1);
```

```
#else
    std::ranges::copy(arr1, std::inserter(set1, set1.begin()));
#endif

    print_buckets("\nset1 (after insert_range): ", set1);
    return set1;
}
```

Before continuing with Ch08_01_ex1(), let's quickly review the code for the first overload of print_buckets() in Listing 8-1-1-1. Execution of this function begins with a call to template function print_stats(). Function print_stats() prints basic statistics for std::unordered_set uno_set, including uno_set.size() (number of elements), uno_set.bucket_count() (number of hash table buckets), and uno_set.load_factor() (average number of elements per bucket). Following the call to print_stats() is a for loop that prints the elements of each bucket. Function strings.bucket_size(i) obtains the number of elements in bucket i. If strings.bucket_size(i) > 0 is true, a second for loop prints the elements of bucket i. Note that this for loop references the elements of bucket i using an iterator; functions strings.begin(i) and strings.end(i) return the requisite start and end iterators for bucket i. It warrants mentioning here that all unordered associative containers including std::unordered_set define universal iterator member functions begin(), cbegin(), end(), and cend().

Returning to the code in Listing 8-1-1-2, the code block that follows the first call to print_stats() demonstrates the use of std::unordered_set member functions insert() and emplace(). Like other containers, these functions insert a new element into a std::unordered_set. The ensuing code block utilizes set1.insert_range(arr1) (C++23) or std::ranges::copy(arr1, std::inserter(set1, set1.begin())) to insert copies of the std::string elements in arr1 into set1. STL helper function std::inserter(set1, set1.begin()) constructs an insert iterator that std::ranges::copy() utilizes to insert elements into set1.

Following the element insertions is another call to print_buckets(). Note in the results section that the number of elements in set1 is now 18. More importantly, note that the bucket count is now 64, the load factor is 0.2812, and the maximum number of elements in any bucket is two. As discussed earlier in this section, an unordered associative container will automatically increase the number of buckets and carry out a rehash operation following an insertion whenever the load factor exceeds

CHAPTER 8   UNORDERED ASSOCIATIVE CONTAINERS

std::unordered_set::max_load_factor(). The final statement of Ch08_01_ex1() returns set1 so that it can be used in example function Ch08_01_ex2(), which is shown in Listing 8-1-2.

Listing 8-1-2. Example Ch08_01 – Ch08_01_ex2()

```
void Ch08_01_ex2(uno_set_str_t set1)
{
    // create new set
    uno_set_str_t set2 {"Yellow Sea", "Red Sea", "Arabian Sea",
    "Baffin Bay",
        "North Sea", "Beaufort Sea", "Caspian Sea", "Gulf of Biscay"};

    // set1 is the same as final output from Ch08_01_ex1()
    // print_buckets("\nset1 (initial values): ", set1);

    print_buckets("\nset2 (initial values): ", set2);

    // merge sets
    set2.merge(set1);
    print_buckets("\nset1 (after merge): ", set1);
    print_buckets("\nset2 (after merge): ", set2);

    // using contains
    std::println("\nset2.contains(\"North Sea\"): {:s}", set2.
    contains("North Sea"));
    std::println("set2.contains(\"Java Sea\"): {:s}", set2.
    contains("Java Sea"));
    std::println("");

    // using extract ("Green Sea" not member of set2)
    std::array<std::string, 3> extract_seas
        {"Black Sea", "Green Sea", "Red Sea"};

    for (const std::string& extract_sea : extract_seas)
    {
        std::print("extract_sea: {:s} - ", extract_sea);

        auto node_handle = set2.extract(extract_sea);
```

CHAPTER 8   UNORDERED ASSOCIATIVE CONTAINERS

```
        if (!node_handle.empty())
        {
            std::println("found");
            node_handle.value() = MF::to_upper(node_handle.value());
            set2.insert(std::move(node_handle));
        }
        else
            std::println("not found");
    }

    print_buckets("\nset2 (after extracts): ", set2);
}
```

Function Ch08_01_ex2() opens with the creation of an unordered set named set2. Following the print_buckets() call, Ch08_01_ex2() utilizes set2.merge(set1) to merge elements from set1 into set2. Recall that a std::unordered_set doesn't allow duplicate keys. Any key that exists in both set2 and set1 will remain in set1 as shown in the results section. Following the merger, the ensuing std::println() calls demonstrates the use of contains(). This member function returns true if the specified std::string key exists in set2.

The final code block in Ch08_01_ex2() illustrates the use of std::unordered_set::extract(). This member function moves the specified key – if it exists – from a std::unordered_set into an object of std::unordered_set::node_type. Member function extract() is often utilized in tandem with insert() to modify a key value as demonstrated in the ensuing for loop. The expression node_handle = set2.extract(extract_sea) searches set2 for key extract_sea. If !node_handle.empty() is true, extract_key was found and this key moved from set2 into node_handle. Inside the subsequent if block, the expression

node_handle.value() = MF::to_upper(node_handle.value());

converts the std::string key value owned by node_handle to uppercase and re-saves this value back in node_handle. The set2.insert(std::move(node_handle)) that follows moves the modified key back into set2. It warrants mentioning here that a function can also exercise erase()/insert() to modify an existing key in a std::unordered_set; however, extract()/insert() must be used if the target container holds move-only objects.

Function Ch08_01_ex3(), shown in Listing 8-1-3, demonstrates how to use an iterator to remove keys that begin with an 'S' from a container of type uno_set_str_t. Inside this function's for loop, the expression (*iter)[0] == 'S' checks the first letter of the std::string pointed to by iter for equality to 'S'. If true, the subsequent expression iter = set1.erase(iter) removes the key pointed to by iter from set1. Execution of set1.erase(iter) also returns an iterator to the next key in set1. If (*iter)[0] == 'S' is false, the ++iter statement adjusts iter so that it points to the next key in set1.

Listing 8-1-3. Example Ch08_01 – Ch08_01_ex3()

```
void Ch08_01_ex3()
{
    uno_set_str_t set1 {"Superior", "Michigan", "Huron", "Ontario", "Erie",
        "Tahoe", "Iliamna", "Crater", "Becharof", "Clark", "Sakakawea",
        "Pyramid", "Pontchartrain", "Champlain", "Mead", "Flathead",
        "Seneca", "Yellowstone", "Cayuga", "Bear"};

    print_buckets("\nset1 (initial values): ", set1);

    // remove strings that begin with an 'S'
    for (auto iter = set1.begin(); iter != set1.end(); )
    {
        if ((*iter)[0] == 'S')
            iter = set1.erase(iter);
        else
            ++iter;
    }
    print_buckets("\nset1 (after removals): ", set1);
}
```

The final source code example of this section demonstrates how to specify a custom hash function for a std::unordered_set. Before continuing, it warrants mentioning that originating a custom hash function that's both algorithmically efficient and statistically optimal for a specific key type is a nontrivial undertaking. The STL defines hash functions for all fundamental types, and you should have a very good reason for not using one of these. For user-defined classes, consider using one of the STL's predefined hash functions along with a suitable class attribute. Chapter 11 includes an example that utilizes a predefined hash function.

Listing 8-1-4-1 shows the source code for class HtmlColor. Function Ch08_01_ex4() employs this class to explicate the creation and use of a custom hash function. Class HtmlColor is also used in later examples.

Listing 8-1-4-1. Example Ch08_01 – Class HtmlColor

```
//------------------------------------------------------------------------
// HtmlColor.h
//------------------------------------------------------------------------
#ifndef HTML_COLOR_H_
#define HTML_COLOR_H_
#include <cstdint>
#include <format>
#include <functional>
#include <ostream>
#include <string>
#include <vector>

class HtmlColor
{
    friend struct std::formatter<HtmlColor>;
    static const std::vector<HtmlColor> s_HtmlColors;   // all HTML colors
public:
    // simple structs for RGB and HSI values
    struct RGB
    {
        RGB() = default;
        RGB(uint8_t r, uint8_t g, uint8_t b) :
            R {r}, G {g}, B {b} {};
        RGB(uint32_t c)
            { B = c & 0xFF; G = (c >> 8) & 0xFF; R = (c >> 16) & 0xFF; }
        uint32_t get_uint() const
            { return static_cast<uint32_t>(B) | (G << 8) | (R << 16); }
```

```
      uint8_t R {};        // red
      uint8_t G {};        // green
      uint8_t B {};        // blue
};

struct HSI
{
   HSI() = default;

   float H {};          // hue
   float S {};          // saturation
   float I {};          // intensity
};

// hash function bucket count
static constexpr size_t hash_func_bucket_count {50};

// hash function for unordered containers
static size_t hash_func(const HtmlColor& color)
   { return color.m_ValRgb.get_uint() % hash_func_bucket_count; }

// hash function for std::searcher (uses default for std::string)
static size_t hash_func_searcher(const HtmlColor& html_color)
   { return std::hash<std::string>{} (html_color.m_Name); }

HtmlColor() = default;
HtmlColor(const HtmlColor& color) :
   m_Name {color.m_Name}, m_ValRgb {color.m_ValRgb} {};

HtmlColor(const std::string& name, uint8_t r, uint8_t g, uint8_t b) :
   m_Name {name}, m_ValRgb {RGB(r, g, b)} {};

HtmlColor(const std::string& name, uint32_t val) :
   m_Name {name}, m_ValRgb {RGB(val)} {};

HtmlColor(const std::string& name, RGB val_rgb) :
   m_Name {name}, m_ValRgb {val_rgb} {};

// accessors
std::string Name() const { return m_Name; }
```

```cpp
RGB ValRgb() const { return m_ValRgb; };
uint8_t R() const { return m_ValRgb.R; }
uint8_t G() const { return m_ValRgb.G; }
uint8_t B() const { return m_ValRgb.B; }

uint32_t ValUint() const { return m_ValRgb.get_uint(); };

HSI ValHSI() const { return get_hsi(); };
float H() const { return get_hsi().H; }
float S() const { return get_hsi().S; }
float I() const { return get_hsi().I; }

// operators
HtmlColor& operator=(const HtmlColor& c1)
    {m_Name = c1.m_Name; m_ValRgb = c1.m_ValRgb; return *this; }

friend auto operator<=>(const HtmlColor& c1, const HtmlColor& c2)
    { return c1.m_Name <=> c2.m_Name; };

friend bool operator==(const HtmlColor& c1, const HtmlColor& c2)
    { return c1.m_Name == c2.m_Name; };

friend std::ostream& operator<<(std::ostream& os, const
HtmlColor& color)
    { os << color.to_str(); return os; }

// miscellaneous HtmlColor functions (see HtmlColor.cpp)
static HtmlColor get(size_t index);
static std::string get_name(size_t index);

static std::vector<HtmlColor> get_vector();
static std::vector<HtmlColor> get_vector(const std::vector<size_t>&
indices);

static std::vector<HtmlColor> get_vector(size_t vec_size,
    bool unique_vals, unsigned int rng_seed);

static std::vector<std::string>
    get_vector_names_only(const std::vector<size_t>& indices);

static size_t num_colors() { return s_HtmlColors.size(); }
```

```cpp
private:
    HSI get_hsi() const;
    std::string to_str(bool use_hex = true) const;

    **std::string m_Name {"?"};**    // color name
    **RGB m_ValRgb {};**             // color value
};

// HtmlColor formatter
template <> struct std::formatter<HtmlColor> : std::formatter<std::string>
{
    constexpr auto parse(std::format_parse_context& pc)
        { return pc.begin(); }

    auto format(const HtmlColor& color, std::format_context& fc) const
        { return std::format_to(fc.out(), "{}", color.to_str()); }
};

#endif

//-------------------------------------------------------------------------
// HtmlColor.cpp
//-------------------------------------------------------------------------

#include <array>
#include <cmath>
#include <cstdint>
#include <random>
#include <stdexcept>
#include <string>
#include <vector>
#include "HtmlColor.h"
#include "MTH.h"

// vector s_HtmlColors contains 141 HtmlColors
const std::vector<HtmlColor> HtmlColor::s_HtmlColors
{
    HtmlColor{"AliceBlue",          0xf0f8ff},
    HtmlColor{"AntiqueWhite",       0xfaebd7},
    HtmlColor{"Aqua",               0x00ffff},
```

CHAPTER 8   UNORDERED ASSOCIATIVE CONTAINERS

```cpp
    // colors AquaMarine - White excluded from listing

    HtmlColor{"WhiteSmoke",         0xf5f5f5},
    HtmlColor{"Yellow",             0xffff00},
    HtmlColor{"YellowGreen",        0x9acd32},
};

// LUT functions
HtmlColor HtmlColor::get(size_t index)
{
    if (index >= s_HtmlColors.size())
        throw std::runtime_error("HtmlColor::get() - invalid index");

    return s_HtmlColors[index];
}

std::string HtmlColor::get_name(size_t index)
{
    if (index >= s_HtmlColors.size())
        throw std::runtime_error("HtmlColor::get_name() - invalid index");

    return s_HtmlColors[index].m_Name;
}

std::vector<HtmlColor> HtmlColor::get_vector()
{
    std::vector<HtmlColor> colors {};
    std::copy(s_HtmlColors.begin(), s_HtmlColors.end(), std::back_inserter(colors));

    return colors;
}

std::vector<HtmlColor> HtmlColor::get_vector(const std::vector<size_t>& indices)
{
    std::vector<HtmlColor> colors {};
```

```cpp
    for (auto index : indices)
        colors.push_back(get(index));

    return colors;
}

std::vector<HtmlColor> HtmlColor::get_vector(size_t vec_size,
    bool unique_vals, unsigned int rng_seed)
{
    if (unique_vals && vec_size > s_HtmlColors.size())
        throw std::runtime_error("HtmlColor::get_vector_random() - 
        bad args");

    std::mt19937 rng {rng_seed};
    std::uniform_int_distribution<size_t> dist {0, s_HtmlColors.
    size() - 1};

    std::vector<HtmlColor> colors {};

    while (colors.size() < vec_size)
    {
        const HtmlColor& color = s_HtmlColors[dist(rng)];

        if (unique_vals)
        {
            auto iter = std::find(std::begin(colors), std::end(colors),
            color);

            if (iter != std::end(colors))
                continue;
        }

        colors.push_back(color);
    }

    return colors;
}
```

CHAPTER 8   UNORDERED ASSOCIATIVE CONTAINERS

```
std::vector<std::string>
HtmlColor::get_vector_names_only(const std::vector<size_t>& indices)
{
    std::vector<std::string> color_names {};

    for (auto index : indices)
        color_names.push_back(get(index).Name());

    return color_names;
}

// Private member functions
HtmlColor::HSI HtmlColor::get_hsi() const
{
    // See Gonzalez and Woods, "Digital Image Processing (4th edition)",
    // p. 541 - 546 for more information about the RGB to HSI algorithm
    // used below.

    HSI hsi;
    constexpr float eps {0.00001f};         // prevents division by zero
    float r = m_ValRgb.R / 255.0f;
    float g = m_ValRgb.G / 255.0f;
    float b = m_ValRgb.B / 255.0f;

    // Note: theta_deg = 90.0 when r, g, b are equal
    float theta_num = 0.5f * ((r - g) + (r - b));
    float theta_den = std::sqrt((r - g) * (r - g) + (r - b) * (g - b));
    float theta_rad = std::acos(theta_num / (theta_den + eps));
    float theta_deg = MTH::rad_to_deg(theta_rad);
    hsi.H = (b > g) ? 360.0f - theta_deg : theta_deg;

    // Note: saturation is 0 when r, g, b are equal
    float min_rgb = std::min(r, std::min(g, b));
    hsi.S = 1.0f - (3.0f / (r + g + b + eps)) * min_rgb;

    hsi.I = (r + g + b) / 3.0f;
    return hsi;
}
```

```
std::string HtmlColor::to_str(bool use_hex) const
{
    std::string s {};
    std::format_to(std::back_inserter(s), "[{:20s} ", m_Name);

    if (use_hex)
    {
        uint32_t c = m_ValRgb.get_uint();
        std::format_to(std::back_inserter(s), "0x{:06X}]", c);
    }
    else
    {
        unsigned int r = m_ValRgb.R;
        unsigned int g = m_ValRgb.G;
        unsigned int b = m_ValRgb.B;
        std::format_to(std::back_inserter(s), "({:3d},{:3d},{:3d})",
            r, g, b);
    }

    return s;
}
```

The source code for class HtmlColor is admittedly lengthy but reasonably straightforward. For function Ch08_01_ex4(), you only need to understand a few features of HtmlColor. First, note that HtmlColor defines two member structures named RGB and HSI. These structures are provided to simplify color value representations using different color spaces (HSI is used in later chapters). Class HtmlColor also defines two attributes: std::string m_Name and RGB m_ValRgb. These are declared near the end of file HtmlColor.h, which is shown in Listing 8-1-4-1.

Following the structure declarations are the statements for HtmlColor's custom hash functions. These are shown using bold text. Value size_t hash_func_bucket_count specifies the number of buckets[2] (i.e., hash table indices) generated by hash function

---

[2] As mentioned earlier, the actual number of hash table buckets allocated is determined by the unordered associative container.

HtmlColor::hash_func(). Function HtmlColor::hash_func() calculates color.m_ValRgb.get_uint() % hash_func_bucket_count. HtmlColor::RGB::get_uint() converts the distinct R, G, and B color components of an RGB value to a value of type uint32_t. To summarize, HtmlColor::hash_func() returns a value between [0, hash_func_bucket_count), and this value specifies the hash table bucket that an unordered associative container will use to store an HtmlColor object whose hash value equals HtmlColor::hash_func() as you'll soon see. Hash function Html::Color::hash_func_searcher() is used in Chapter 11.

One other item to note in Listing 8-1-4-1 is the definition of std::vector<HtmlColor> HtmlColor::s_HtmlColors, which contains HtmlColor objects of all 141 possible HtmlColor values. Note that the listing only shows the first and last three colors to save some space.

Listing 8-1-4-2 shows the source code for function Ch08_01_ex4(). This function begins with the definition of a uno_set_hc_t container named colors. Alias uno_set_hc_t is a std::unordered_set of HtmlColors, and its complete definition is shown in Listing 8-1-1-1. Note that the constructor for colors specifies two parameters. The first parameter, HtmlColor::hash_func_bucket_count, denotes the minimum number of hash table buckets. The second parameter designates a custom hash function for container colors to use when adding keys (i.e., objects of type HtmlColor) to the hash table.

Listing 8-1-4-2. Example Ch08_01 – Ch08_01_ex4()

```
void Ch08_01_ex4()
{
    // instantiate uno_set_hc_t object - custom hash function
    uno_set_hc_t colors(HtmlColor::hash_func_bucket_count,
        HtmlColor::hash_func);

    // change max_load_factor to prevent a rehash
    colors.max_load_factor(100.0f);

    // add HTML colors
    size_t num_colors = HtmlColor::num_colors();

    for (size_t i = 0; i < num_colors; ++i)
        colors.emplace(HtmlColor::get(i));

    print_buckets("--- Bucket values for 'colors' ---", colors);
}
```

Following the definition of colors is the statement colors.max_load_factor(100.0f), which sets the maximum load factor for colors. A deliberately high value is used here to preclude a rehash of container colors. Next is a simple for loop that inserts HtmlColor objects into colors. Function HtmlColor::get(i) returns the *i-th* HtmlColor object from vector HtmlColor::s_HtmlColors.

The final statement of Ch08_01_ex4() prints the buckets of colors. Note in the results section that only buckets [0, hash_func_bucket_count) contain elements. Also, note the relatively high load factor, which is a consequence of the call to max_load_factor(). The number of buckets in colors was intentionally limited for exposition purposes. The earlier recommendation of using a predefined hash function along with a suitable class attribute would most certainly apply if the classes and algorithms of example Ch08_01_ex4() were to be adapted for a production environment. Here are the complete results for example Ch08_01:

```
----- Results for example Ch08_01 -----

----- Ch08_01_ex1() -----

set1 (initial values):
size: 6  bucket_count: 8  load_factor: 0.7500

bucket   3: 'Red Sea' 'Black Sea'
bucket   5: 'Bering Sea' 'Gulf of Alaska'
bucket   7: 'Gulf of Thailand' 'Caribbean Sea'

set1 (after insert_range):
size: 18  bucket_count: 64  load_factor: 0.2812

bucket   2: 'Greenland Sea' 'Yellow Sea'
bucket   3: 'Mediterranean Sea'
bucket   8: 'Amundsen Gulf'
bucket  15: 'Gulf of Thailand'
bucket  17: 'Scotia Sea'
bucket  19: 'Red Sea'
bucket  27: 'North Sea'
bucket  31: 'Adriatic Sea'
bucket  33: 'Labrador Sea'
bucket  37: 'Gulf of Alaska' 'Bering Sea'
```

CHAPTER 8 UNORDERED ASSOCIATIVE CONTAINERS

```
bucket 39: 'Gulf of Mexico' 'Caribbean Sea'
bucket 49: 'Gulf of Biscay'
bucket 51: 'Ross Sea'
bucket 59: 'Black Sea' 'Baltic Sea'

----- Ch08_01_ex2() -----

set2 (initial values):
size: 8   bucket_count: 8   load_factor: 1.0000

bucket  1: 'Gulf of Biscay'
bucket  2: 'Yellow Sea'
bucket  3: 'North Sea' 'Red Sea'
bucket  4: 'Beaufort Sea' 'Arabian Sea'
bucket  5: 'Caspian Sea'
bucket  7: 'Baffin Bay'

set1 (after merge):
size: 4   bucket_count: 64   load_factor: 0.0625

bucket  2: 'Yellow Sea'
bucket 19: 'Red Sea'
bucket 27: 'North Sea'
bucket 49: 'Gulf of Biscay'

set2 (after merge):
size: 22   bucket_count: 64   load_factor: 0.3438

bucket  2: 'Greenland Sea' 'Yellow Sea'
bucket  3: 'Mediterranean Sea'
bucket  8: 'Amundsen Gulf'
bucket 13: 'Caspian Sea'
bucket 15: 'Gulf of Thailand'
bucket 17: 'Scotia Sea'
bucket 19: 'Red Sea'
bucket 27: 'North Sea'
bucket 28: 'Arabian Sea'
bucket 31: 'Adriatic Sea'
bucket 33: 'Labrador Sea'
```

```
bucket 37: 'Gulf of Alaska' 'Bering Sea'
bucket 39: 'Gulf of Mexico' 'Caribbean Sea'
bucket 47: 'Baffin Bay'
bucket 49: 'Gulf of Biscay'
bucket 51: 'Ross Sea'
bucket 52: 'Beaufort Sea'
bucket 59: 'Black Sea' 'Baltic Sea'

set2.contains("North Sea"): true
set2.contains("Java Sea"): false

extract_sea: Black Sea - found
extract_sea: Green Sea - not found
extract_sea: Red Sea - found

set2 (after extracts):
size: 22  bucket_count: 64  load_factor: 0.3438

bucket  2: 'Greenland Sea' 'Yellow Sea'
bucket  3: 'Mediterranean Sea'
bucket  8: 'Amundsen Gulf'
bucket 13: 'Caspian Sea'
bucket 15: 'Gulf of Thailand'
bucket 17: 'Scotia Sea'
bucket 19: 'RED SEA'
bucket 27: 'North Sea'
bucket 28: 'Arabian Sea'
bucket 31: 'Adriatic Sea'
bucket 33: 'Labrador Sea'
bucket 37: 'Gulf of Alaska' 'Bering Sea'
bucket 39: 'Gulf of Mexico' 'Caribbean Sea'
bucket 47: 'Baffin Bay'
bucket 49: 'Gulf of Biscay'
bucket 51: 'Ross Sea'
bucket 52: 'Beaufort Sea'
bucket 59: 'BLACK SEA' 'Baltic Sea'
```

CHAPTER 8   UNORDERED ASSOCIATIVE CONTAINERS

----- Ch08_01_ex3() -----

set1 (initial values):
size: 20   bucket_count: 64   load_factor: 0.3125

bucket 2: 'Mead'
bucket 4: 'Seneca' 'Pontchartrain'
bucket 5: 'Huron'
bucket 12: 'Sakakawea'
bucket 20: 'Flathead'
bucket 30: 'Superior'
bucket 36: 'Champlain' 'Iliamna'
bucket 38: 'Yellowstone' 'Clark'
bucket 39: 'Pyramid'
bucket 43: 'Cayuga'
bucket 46: 'Tahoe'
bucket 51: 'Bear'
bucket 54: 'Crater'
bucket 55: 'Ontario'
bucket 56: 'Erie'
bucket 59: 'Michigan'
bucket 61: 'Becharof'

set1 (after removals):
size: 17   bucket_count: 64   load_factor: 0.2656

bucket 2: 'Mead'
bucket 4: 'Pontchartrain'
bucket 5: 'Huron'
bucket 20: 'Flathead'
bucket 36: 'Champlain' 'Iliamna'
bucket 38: 'Yellowstone' 'Clark'
bucket 39: 'Pyramid'
bucket 43: 'Cayuga'
bucket 46: 'Tahoe'
bucket 51: 'Bear'
bucket 54: 'Crater'

CHAPTER 8   UNORDERED ASSOCIATIVE CONTAINERS

```
bucket 55: 'Ontario'
bucket 56: 'Erie'
bucket 59: 'Michigan'
bucket 61: 'Becharof'

----- Ch08_01_ex4() -----
--- Bucket values for 'colors' ---
size: 141  bucket_count: 64   load_factor: 2.2031

bucket  0:   MintCream MediumTurquoise Ivory DarkGreen Crimson Black
bucket  1:   DeepSkyBlue
bucket  2:   Chartreuse BlueViolet
bucket  3:   PaleVioletRed LightSlateGray
bucket  4:   MediumSpringGreen LightBlue Gray DarkRed
bucket  5:   MediumBlue GreenYellow Blue
bucket  6:   Turquoise Silver LightGreen
bucket  7:   SpringGreen
bucket  8:   OldLace Maroon
bucket  9:   DarkKhaki
bucket 10:   Yellow PowderBlue LightGoldenrodYellow Lavender Khaki Honeydew
             Gainsboro DarkSalmon Beige
bucket 11:   SlateBlue
bucket 12:   MidnightBlue LightSalmon DarkOrchid
bucket 14:   SandyBrown AquaMarine
bucket 15:   White LightPink LavenderBlush DimGray
bucket 16:   PaleTurquoise
bucket 17:   MediumOrchid DarkGray
bucket 18:   Green
bucket 19:   RosyBrown DarkSeaGreen
bucket 20:   Orange Linen Goldenrod Gold FloralWhite DarkOrange Chocolate
bucket 21:   GhostWhite
bucket 22:   MediumAquamarine Coral
bucket 23:   PeachPuff MistyRose MediumVioletRed LightGray DarkCyan
bucket 24:   YellowGreen IndianRed
bucket 25:   Azure AntiqueWhite
bucket 26:   Olive LawnGreen
```

bucket 27:   SeaGreen PapayaWhip
bucket 28:   Navy CadetBlue
bucket 29:   Moccasin
bucket 30:   Tan SteelBlue Snow Red PaleGreen PaleGoldenrod LimeGreen Lime Indigo
bucket 31:   Wheat SkyBlue RebeccaPurple CornFlowerBlue Burlywood
bucket 32:   Salmon
bucket 33:   MediumPurple AliceBlue
bucket 34:   Orchid LightYellow LightSteelBlue Brown
bucket 35:   WhiteSmoke Pink NavajoWhite Magenta LemonChiffon Fuchsia Cyan Aqua
bucket 36:   Violet Purple LightCoral
bucket 37:   SaddleBrown Plum
bucket 38:   Thistle Seashell Cornsilk
bucket 39:   OliveDrab DarkViolet DarkGoldenrod DarkBlue
bucket 40:   MediumSlateBlue LightSeaGreen HotPink
bucket 41:   Peru
bucket 42:   ForestGreen
bucket 43:   DarkMagenta
bucket 44:   SlateGray OrangeRed Bisque
bucket 45:   Tomato RoyalBlue DarkTurquoise DarkSlateGray BlanchedAlmond
bucket 46:   Teal LightSkyBlue Firebrick
bucket 47:   Sienna MediumSeaGreen DeepPink DarkSlateBlue
bucket 49:   LightCyan DodgerBlue DarkOliveGreen

Using std::unordered_multiset

A std::unordered_multiset closely resembles a std::unordered_set. The primary difference is that a std::unordered_multiset can hold multiple instances of the same key. A std::unordered_multiset supports all of the public member functions that you learned in the previous section for std::unordered_set. It also adds a few extra functions that expedite operations with non-unique keys.

Source code example Ch08_02 spotlights a few elementary usages of class std::unordered_multiset. Listing 8-2-1-1 opens with the header file Ch08_02.h. In this file, note the definition of alias uno_mset_t = std::unordered_multiset<HtmlColor, size_t(*)(const HtmlColor&)>. This alias represents a std::unordered_multiset container that holds objects of type HtmlColor (see Listing 8-1-4-1). It also specifies custom hash functions just like you saw in example Ch08_01_ex4() (see Listing 8-1-4-2). The next file in Listing 8-2-1-1, Ch08_02_misc.cpp, contains the definition of function print_buckets(). This function prints the buckets of a uno_mset_t container and closely parallels the print_buckets() functions that you studied in the previous section (see Listing 8-1-1-1).

Listing 8-2-1-1. Example Ch08_02 – Ch08_02.h and Ch08_02_misc.cpp

```
//-------------------------------------------------------------------------
// Ch08_02.h
//-------------------------------------------------------------------------

#ifndef CH08_02_H_
#define CH08_02_H_
#include <unordered_set>
#include "Common.h"
#include "HtmlColor.h"

// type alias for example Ch08_02
using uno_mset_t = std::unordered_multiset<HtmlColor,
    size_t(*)(const HtmlColor&)>;

// Ch08_02_ex.cpp
extern void Ch08_02_ex();

// Ch08_02_misc.cpp
extern void print_buckets(const char* msg, const uno_mset_t& colors);
#endif

//-------------------------------------------------------------------------
// Ch08_02_misc.cpp
//-------------------------------------------------------------------------

#include "Ch08_02.h"
#include "HtmlColor.h"
```

```
void print_buckets(const char* msg, const uno_mset_t& colors)
{
    // print stats
    std::println("{:s}", msg);
    std::print("size: {}  ", colors.size());
    std::print("bucket_count: {}  ", colors.bucket_count());
    std::println("load_factor:  {}", colors.load_factor());

    // print buckets
    std::string sep = '\n' + std::string(11, ' ');

    for (size_t i = 0; i < colors.bucket_count(); ++i)
    {
        if (i >= HtmlColor::hash_func_bucket_count)
            break;

        if (colors.bucket_size(i) != 0)
        {
            unsigned int add_nl {};
            std::print("\nbucket {:2d}: ", i);

            // print elements in current bucket
            for (auto iter = colors.begin(i); iter != colors.end(i); ++iter)
            {
                std::print("{}  ", *iter);

                if ((++add_nl % 2) == 0 && std::next(iter) != colors.end(i))
                    std::print("{:s}", sep);
            }
        }
    }

    std::println("");
}
```

CHAPTER 8 UNORDERED ASSOCIATIVE CONTAINERS

Listing 8-2-1-2 contains the definition of function Ch08_02_ex1(). Execution of this function begins with the instantiation of a uno_mset_t named colors. Note that the definition of colors includes constructor arguments HtmlColor::hash_func_bucket_count and HtmlColor::hash_func. These arguments supply the initial bucket count along with a custom hash function for uno_mset_t container colors.

Listing 8-2-1-2. Example Ch08_02 – Ch08_02_ex1()

```
//-------------------------------------------------------------------------
// Ch08_02_ex.cpp
//-------------------------------------------------------------------------

#include <string>
#include <unordered_set>
#include "Ch08_02.h"
#include "HtmlColor.h"
#include "MF.h"

void Ch08_02_ex1()
{
    uno_mset_t colors(HtmlColor::hash_func_bucket_count,
        HtmlColor::hash_func);

    // add elements to colors using emplace
    for (size_t i = 0; i < HtmlColor::num_colors(); i += 10)
        colors.emplace(HtmlColor::get(i));

    // add elements to colors using insert
    for (size_t i = 0; i < HtmlColor::num_colors(); i += 20)
        colors.insert(HtmlColor::get(i));

    // using merge to add duplicates
    uno_mset_t more_colors(HtmlColor::hash_func_bucket_count,
        HtmlColor::hash_func);

    HtmlColor test_color1 {HtmlColor::get(HtmlColor::num_colors() / 2)};
    HtmlColor test_color2 {HtmlColor::get(HtmlColor::num_colors() / 5)};
    std::println("\ntest_color1: {}", test_color1);
    std::println("test_color2: {}", test_color2);
```

CHAPTER 8   UNORDERED ASSOCIATIVE CONTAINERS

```cpp
    more_colors.insert(test_color1);
    more_colors.insert(test_color1);
    more_colors.insert(test_color1);
    more_colors.insert(test_color2);
    more_colors.insert(test_color2);

    colors.merge(more_colors);
    print_buckets("\ncolors (initial values):", colors);

    // using extract and insert
    HtmlColor test_color3 {"FalseColor", 0x123456};
    std::vector<HtmlColor> test_colors {test_color1, test_color2,
    test_color3};

    for (auto test_color : test_colors)
    {
        auto iter = colors.find(test_color);

        for (; iter != colors.end(); iter = colors.find(test_color))
        {
            // extract node
            auto node_handle = colors.extract(test_color);

            // convert name to upper case
            HtmlColor html_color_ex = node_handle.value();
            std::string name {html_color_ex.Name()};
            MF::to_upper(name);

            // reinsert updated color
            node_handle.value() = HtmlColor {name, html_color_ex.ValRgb()};
            colors.insert(std::move(node_handle));
        }
    }

    print_buckets("\ncolors (after extract/insert operations):", colors);
}
```

CHAPTER 8 UNORDERED ASSOCIATIVE CONTAINERS

The next three code blocks in Ch08_02_ex1() spotlight various methods for adding new keys to colors. The first code block utilizes colors.emplace(HtmlColor::get(i)). Recall that function HtmlColor::get(i) returns the *i-th* color value from vector HtmlColor::s_HtmlColors (see Listing 8-1-4-1). The next code block exploits colors. insert(HtmlColor::get(i)) to add more colors. The i += 20 that the second for loop uses ensures that multiple keys get inserted into colors. The third code block exploits colors.merge(more_colors) to explicitly insert duplicate keys into colors. Execution of merge() moves all keys from more_colors into colors. Following execution of merge(), container more_colors contains zero keys.

Like a std::unordered_set, a function can't directly modify a key that's maintained in a std::unordered_multiset. To change a key, you must remove it, change its value, and reinsert it back into the container. The final code block in Ch08_02_ex1() demonstrates this technique. Within the for loop, colors.find(test_color) is exploited to determine if at least one instance of test_color exists in colors. If test_color doesn't exist, find() returns colors.end(); otherwise, find() returns an iterator to the first occurrence of test_color in colors. In the next code block, node_handle = colors.extract(test_color) extracts test_color from colors. This is followed by a code block that converts the name of html_color_ex, which is the extracted HtmlColor, to uppercase. Following the conversion, the statements node_handle.value() = HtmlColor {name, html_color_ex.ValRgb()} and colors. insert(std::move(node_handle)) reinsert the updated HtmlColor back into container colors. For the current example, the updated HtmlColor will be inserted back into the same bucket since the calculated hash function value is not dependent on the color's name. However, key ordering for this bucket may differ from the ordering that existed prior to the extract()/insert() operation. To observe this, review the results section for Ch08_02_ex1() and compare the contents of bucket number 12 before and after the extract()/insert() operation. Here are the results for example Ch08_02:

```
----- Results for example Ch08_02 -----

----- Ch08_02_ex1() -----

test_color1: [LightSalmon          0xFFA07A]
test_color2: [DarkOliveGreen       0x556B2F]

colors (initial values):
size: 28  bucket_count: 64  load_factor:  0.4375
```

CHAPTER 8 UNORDERED ASSOCIATIVE CONTAINERS

```
bucket   2: [BlueViolet          0x8A2BE2]
bucket   4: [Gray                0x808080]
bucket   8: [Maroon              0x800000]   [Maroon              0x800000]
bucket  12: [MidnightBlue        0x191970]   [LightSalmon         0xFFA07A]
            [LightSalmon         0xFFA07A]   [LightSalmon         0xFFA07A]
            [LightSalmon         0xFFA07A]   [DarkOrchid          0x9932CC]
bucket  15: [LavenderBlush       0xFFF0F5]   [LavenderBlush       0xFFF0F5]
            [DimGray             0x696969]   [DimGray             0x696969]
bucket  24: [YellowGreen         0x9ACD32]   [YellowGreen         0x9ACD32]
bucket  27: [SeaGreen            0x2E8B57]   [SeaGreen            0x2E8B57]
bucket  30: [Tan                 0xD2B48C]
bucket  33: [AliceBlue           0xF0F8FF]   [AliceBlue           0xF0F8FF]
bucket  35: [Cyan                0x00FFFF]   [Cyan                0x00FFFF]
bucket  37: [Plum                0xDDA0DD]
bucket  44: [OrangeRed           0xFF4500]   [OrangeRed           0xFF4500]
bucket  49: [DarkOliveGreen      0x556B2F]   [DarkOliveGreen      0x556B2F]

colors (after extract/insert operations):
size: 28  bucket_count: 64  load_factor: 0.4375

bucket   2: [BlueViolet          0x8A2BE2]
bucket   4: [Gray                0x808080]
bucket   8: [Maroon              0x800000]   [Maroon              0x800000]
bucket  12: [LIGHTSALMON         0xFFA07A]   [LIGHTSALMON         0xFFA07A]
            [LIGHTSALMON         0xFFA07A]   [LIGHTSALMON         0xFFA07A]
            [MidnightBlue        0x191970]   [DarkOrchid          0x9932CC]
bucket  15: [LavenderBlush       0xFFF0F5]   [LavenderBlush       0xFFF0F5]
            [DimGray             0x696969]   [DimGray             0x696969]
bucket  24: [YellowGreen         0x9ACD32]   [YellowGreen         0x9ACD32]
bucket  27: [SeaGreen            0x2E8B57]   [SeaGreen            0x2E8B57]
bucket  30: [Tan                 0xD2B48C]
bucket  33: [AliceBlue           0xF0F8FF]   [AliceBlue           0xF0F8FF]
bucket  35: [Cyan                0x00FFFF]   [Cyan                0x00FFFF]
bucket  37: [Plum                0xDDA0DD]
bucket  44: [OrangeRed           0xFF4500]   [OrangeRed           0xFF4500]
bucket  49: [DARKOLIVEGREEN      0x556B2F]   [DARKOLIVEGREEN      0x556B2F]
```

Using std::unordered_map

The next unordered associative container that you'll scrutinize is std::unordered_map. Like the (ordered) associative container std::map that you studied in Chapter 7, a std::unordered_map holds key-value (or key-data) pairs. Similarities between a std::unordered_map and a std::unordered_set include the following:

- The elements of a std::unordered_map<Key, T> are maintained using a hash function and hash table similar to the conceptual model that's shown in Figure 8-1.

- The hash function is applied to the Key; the value component T does not affect an element's position in the hash table.

- Class std::unordered_map supports forward iterators.

- The key of a std::unordered_map<Key, T> element cannot be changed. To modify an element's key, the old key-value element must be extracted and a new one inserted. The value component of a std::unordered_map<Key, T> element can be modified in place.

The public interface for std::unordered_map closely resembles the one that you learned for std::map.

Listing 8-3-1-1 shows the source code for file Ch08_03.h. The two items of interest in this file are the alias definitions for uno_map_t and uno_map_hf_t. Note that both aliases define std::unordered_map containers that use std::strings for the keys and values. The latter alias also specifies a custom hash function that requires an argument of type std::string.

Listing 8-3-1-1. Example Ch08_03 – Ch08_03.h

```
//-------------------------------------------------------------------------
// Ch08_03.h
//-------------------------------------------------------------------------

#ifndef CH08_03_H_
#define CH08_03_H_
#include <string>
#include <unordered_map>
#include "Common.h"
```

```
// type aliases for example Ch08_03
using uno_map_t = std::unordered_map<std::string, std::string>;
using uno_map_hf_t = std::unordered_map<std::string, std::string,
        size_t(*)(const std::string&)>;

// Ch08_03_ex.cpp
extern void Ch08_03_ex();

// Ch08_03_misc.cpp
uno_map_t get_airports(int id);
void get_airports(uno_map_hf_t& map, int id);
void print_buckets(const char* msg, const uno_map_hf_t& map);

#endif
```

Listing 8-3-1-2 shows the source code for Ch08_03_misc.cpp. This file contains two overloads for get_airports(), which perform std::unordered_map initializations. Note that each key-value pair consists of an airport code and airport name. Also, note that get_airports()'s integer argument selects a group of airports. The function print_buckets() prints the airport codes of a uno_map_hf_t map.

Listing 8-3-1-2. Example Ch08_03 – Ch08_03_misc.cpp

```
//-------------------------------------------------------------------
// Ch08_03_misc.cpp
//-------------------------------------------------------------------
#include <algorithm>
#include <format>
#include <iterator>
#include <string>
#include <unordered_map>
#include "Ch08_03.h"

uno_map_t get_airports(int id)
{
    uno_map_t map;

    if (id == 1)
    {
```

```cpp
        map.emplace("ABQ", "Albuquerque International");
        map.emplace("BWI", "Baltimore/Washington International");
        map.emplace("BOS", "Logan International");
        map.emplace("CLT", "Charlotte Douglas International");
        map.emplace("DEN", "Denver International");
        map.emplace("DFW", "Dallas Fort Worth International");
        map.emplace("DSM", "Des Moines International");
        map.emplace("DTS", "Detroit Metro Wayne County");
    }
    else
    {
        map.emplace("FAI", "Fairbanks International");
        map.emplace("ITO", "Hilo International");
        map.emplace("LAX", "Los Angeles International");
        map.emplace("LGA", "LaGuardia");
        map.emplace("MCO", "Orlando International");
        map.emplace("ORD", "O'Hare International");
        map.emplace("PHX", "Phoenix Sky Harbor International");
        map.emplace("SEA", "Seattle-Tacoma International");
    }

    return map;
}
void get_airports(uno_map_hf_t& map, int id)
{
    std::ranges::copy(get_airports(id), std::inserter(map, map.begin()));
}
void print_buckets(const char* msg, const uno_map_hf_t& map)
{
    // print stats
    std::println("{:s}", msg);
    std::print("size: {} ", map.size());
    std::print("bucket_count: {}  ", map.bucket_count());
    std::println("load_factor:  {}\n", map.load_factor());
```

```cpp
    // print buckets (airport code only)
    unsigned int add_nl {};
    size_t bc = map.bucket_count();

    for (size_t i = 0; i < bc; ++i)
    {
        if (map.bucket_size(i) != 0)
        {
            std::string s {};
            std::format_to(std::back_inserter(s), "bucket {:2d}: ", i);

            for (auto iter = map.begin(i); iter != map.end(i); ++iter)
                std::format_to(std::back_inserter(s), "{:4s}",
                    iter->first);

            if ((++add_nl % 2) == 0)
                std::println("{:40s}", s);
            else
                std::print("{:40s}", s);
        }
    }

    if (add_nl % 2 != 0)
        std::println("");
}
```

Example function Ch08_03_ex1(), shown near the top of Listing 8-3-1-3, utilizes get_airports() to initialize two uno_map_t containers named map1 and map2. Following the initializations, the expression map2.merge(map1) moves all elements from map1 to map2 provided the element doesn't already exist in map2. For the current example, all map1 elements are moved to map2.

Listing 8-3-1-3. Example Ch08_03 – Ch08_03_ex1()

```cpp
//-----------------------------------------------------------------
// Ch08_03_ex.cpp
//-----------------------------------------------------------------

#include <algorithm>
#include <array>
```

CHAPTER 8   UNORDERED ASSOCIATIVE CONTAINERS

```cpp
#include <cctype>
#include <iostream>
#include <iterator>
#include <string>
#include <unordered_map>
#include <utility>
#include "Ch08_03.h"
#include "MT.h"

void Ch08_03_ex1()
{
    constexpr size_t epl_max {2};
    const char* fmt1 = "[{:3s}, ";
    const char* fmt2 = "{:^35s}] ";

    // initialize unordered maps
    uno_map_t map1 = get_airports(1);
    MT::print_unordered_map("\nmap1 (initial values):\n",
        map1, fmt1, fmt2, epl_max);

    uno_map_t map2 = get_airports(2);
    MT::print_unordered_map("\nmap2 (initial values):\n",
        map2, fmt1, fmt2, epl_max);

    // merge maps
    map2.merge(map1);
    MT::print_unordered_map("\nmap1 (after merge):\n",
        map1, fmt1, fmt2, epl_max);
    MT::print_unordered_map("\nmap2 (after merge):\n",
        map2, fmt1, fmt2, epl_max);

    // insert new elements
    map2.insert(std::make_pair("COD", "Yellowstone Regional"));
    map2["MHT"] = "Manchester-Boston Regional";

    MT::print_unordered_map("\nmap2 (after insertions):\n",
        map2, fmt1, fmt2, epl_max);
```

CHAPTER 8   UNORDERED ASSOCIATIVE CONTAINERS

```cpp
    // find keys in map
    std::array<std::string, 4> keys {"LAX", "PIT", "COD", "CHS"};

    std::println("\nfind keys in map2");
    for (auto key : keys)
    {
        std::print("key: {:s} - ", key);

        if (auto iter = map2.find(key); iter != map2.end())
            std::println("{:s}", iter->second);
        else
            std::println("not found");
    }

    // erase elements from map
    auto pred = [](const auto& elem)
        { auto const& [key, value] = elem; return key[0] == 'D'; };

    auto num_erasures = std::erase_if(map2, pred);

    std::println("\nnum_erasures = {:d}", num_erasures);
    MT::print_unordered_map("\nmap2 (after erasures):\n",
        map2, fmt1, fmt2, epl_max);
}
```

The code block that follows merge() demonstrates two methods of adding new elements to a std::unordered_map(). The statement map2.insert(std::make_pair("COD", "Yellowstone Regional")) inserts a new airport key-value pair into map2. The expression map2["MHT"] = "Manchester-Boston Regional" also inserts a new element into map2. Like a std::map, class std::unordered_map overloads operator[], which facilitates its use for new element insertions or accesses of existing elements as demonstrated in this example.

The next code block in Ch08_03_ex1() consists of a range for loop that searches map2 for airport codes. Note the use of the expression iter = map2.find(key); if iter != map2.end() is true, key exists in map2 and the subsequent std::println() statement utilizes iter->second to print the airport's name.

CHAPTER 8 UNORDERED ASSOCIATIVE CONTAINERS

The final code block of Ch08_03_ex1() commences with the definition of a lambda expression named pred that returns true if the first letter of the airport code equals 'D'. The next statement, num_erasures = std::erase_if(map2, pred), exploits global algorithm std::erase_if() to erase all key-value pairs from map2 whose airport code begins with the letter 'D'. Note that erase_if() returns the number of elements that it removed from map2.

Listing 8-3-2 shows the code for the next std::unordered_map example. Function Ch08_03_ex2() opens with the definition of a lambda expression named hash_func. This crude function returns a size_t value that's derived using the first letter of an airport code.

Listing 8-3-2. Example Ch08_03 – Ch08_03_ex2()

```
void Ch08_03_ex2()
{
    // simple hash function
    auto hash_func = [](const std::string& s) -> size_t
    {
        auto c = static_cast<unsigned char>(s[0]);
        return std::isalpha(c) ? std::toupper(c) - 'A' + 1 : c % 32;
    };

    // initialize map1
    constexpr size_t num_buckets {32};
    uno_map_hf_t map1(num_buckets, hash_func);
    get_airports(map1, 1);
    print_buckets("\nmap1 (initial values)", map1);

    // initialize map2
    uno_map_hf_t map2(num_buckets, hash_func);
    get_airports(map2, 2);
    print_buckets("\nmap2 (initial values)", map2);

    // merge maps
    map2.merge(map1);
    print_buckets("\nmap2 (after merge)", map2);
```

CHAPTER 8 UNORDERED ASSOCIATIVE CONTAINERS

```
    // using relational operators (only operator== is defined)
    auto map3 {map2};
    std::println("\nmap2 == map3: {:s}", map2 == map3);
    std::println("map2 != map3: {:s}", map2 != map3);
}
```

The next code block Ch08_03_ex2() instantiates a uno_map_hf_t container named map1. In the statement uno_map_hf_t map1(num_buckets, hash_func), constructor argument num_buckets specifies the hash table's minimum bucket count, while hash_func supplants the container's default hash function. The instantiation of map2 follows map1 and utilizes the same programming construct. If you scan ahead to the results section, note that each element's bucket number corresponds to the first letter of its airport code as expected. This is also true following execution of map2.merge(map1). The final code block in Ch08_03_ex2() demonstrates the use of operator==. This is the only relational operator defined for a std::unordered_map and all other unordered associative containers (starting with C++20, operator!= is synthesized from operator==).

Example function Ch08_03_ex3(), shown in Listing 8-3-3, spotlights the use of member function std::unordered_map::insert_range() (C++23). The expression map1.insert_range(map2) inserts copies of elements from map2 into map1. When utilizing insert_range() or any other insertion function, it's important to keep in mind that an element insertion may trigger a rehash operation, which would invalidate all existing iterators.

Listing 8-3-3. Example Ch08_03 – Ch08_03_ex3()

```
void Ch08_03_ex3()
{
    constexpr size_t epl_max {2};
    const char* fmt1 = "[{:3s}, ";
    const char* fmt2 = "{:^35s}] ";

    // initialize unordered maps
    uno_map_t map1 = get_airports(1);
    uno_map_t map2 = get_airports(2);
```

```cpp
    // using insert_range, copies elements from map2 to map1
#ifdef __cpp_lib_containers_ranges
    map1.insert_range(map2);
#else
    map1.insert(map2.begin(), map2.end());
#endif
    MT::print_unordered_map("\nmap1 (after insert_range):\n",
        map1, fmt1, fmt2, epl_max);

    // modify value component of each map1 key-value pair
    const std::string str1 = "International";
    const std::string str2 = "Intl.";

    for (auto iter = map1.begin(); iter != map1.end(); ++iter)
    {
        // iter->first points to key (airport code)
        // iter->second points to value (airport name)
        auto pos = iter->second.find(str1);

        if (pos != std::string::npos)
        {
            // replace str1 with str2 using replace_with_ranges (C++23)
            auto iter_b = iter->second.begin() + pos;
            auto iter_e = iter_b + str1.size();
#ifdef __cpp_lib_containers_ranges
            iter->second.replace_with_range(iter_b, iter_e, str2);
#else
            iter->second.replace(iter_b, iter_e, str2.begin(), str2.end());
#endif
        }
    }
    MT::print_unordered_map("\nmap1 (after replace_with_ranges):\n",
        map1, fmt1, fmt2, epl_max);
}
```

CHAPTER 8   UNORDERED ASSOCIATIVE CONTAINERS

The final code block in Ch08_03_ex3() demonstrates traversing a container of type uno_map_t using iterators. A uno_map_t iterator essentially points to an object of type std::pair<std::string, std::string>. The code within the for loop replaces each occurrence of substring str1 in an airport name (iter->second) with str2. Recall that the data value of a std::unordered_map can be modified in place. Also, note the use of std::string::replace_with_range() (C++23). In the current example, execution of this function replaces characters between [iter_b, iter_e) with characters from [str2.begin(), str2.end()). Here are the results for example Ch08_03:

```
----- Results for example Ch08_03 -----

----- Ch08_03_ex1() -----

map1 (initial values):
[ABQ,       Albuquerque International   ] [BOS,        Logan International         ]
[BWI, Baltimore/Washington International ] [CLT,  Charlotte Douglas International   ]
[DEN,          Denver International      ] [DFW,  Dallas Fort Worth International   ]
[DSM,        Des Moines International    ] [DTS,     Detroit Metro Wayne County     ]

map2 (initial values):
[FAI,        Fairbanks International     ] [ITO,        Hilo International          ]
[LAX,       Los Angeles International    ] [LGA,              LaGuardia             ]
[MCO,         Orlando International      ] [ORD,        O'Hare International        ]
[PHX,  Phoenix Sky Harbor International  ] [SEA,   Seattle-Tacoma International     ]

map1 (after merge):
<empty>

map2 (after merge):
[ABQ,       Albuquerque International   ] [BOS,        Logan International         ]
[BWI, Baltimore/Washington International ] [CLT,  Charlotte Douglas International   ]
[DEN,          Denver International      ] [DFW,  Dallas Fort Worth International   ]
[DSM,        Des Moines International    ] [DTS,     Detroit Metro Wayne County     ]
[FAI,        Fairbanks International     ] [ITO,        Hilo International          ]
[LAX,       Los Angeles International    ] [LGA,              LaGuardia             ]
[MCO,         Orlando International      ] [ORD,        O'Hare International        ]
[PHX,  Phoenix Sky Harbor International  ] [SEA,   Seattle-Tacoma International     ]
```

CHAPTER 8   UNORDERED ASSOCIATIVE CONTAINERS

```
map2 (after insertions):
[ABQ,        Albuquerque International    ] [BOS,         Logan International         ]
[BWI, Baltimore/Washington International  ] [CLT, Charlotte Douglas International     ]
[COD,           Yellowstone Regional      ] [DEN,        Denver International         ]
[DFW,    Dallas Fort Worth International  ] [DSM,      Des Moines International       ]
[DTS,      Detroit Metro Wayne County     ] [FAI,      Fairbanks International        ]
[ITO,            Hilo International       ] [LAX,     Los Angeles International       ]
[LGA,                 LaGuardia           ] [MCO,        Orlando International        ]
[MHT,     Manchester-Boston Regional      ] [ORD,        O'Hare International         ]
[PHX,   Phoenix Sky Harbor International  ] [SEA,    Seattle-Tacoma International     ]

find keys in map2
key: LAX - Los Angeles International
key: PIT - not found
key: COD - Yellowstone Regional
key: CHS - not found

num_erasures = 4

map2 (after erasures):
[ABQ,        Albuquerque International    ] [BOS,         Logan International         ]
[BWI, Baltimore/Washington International  ] [CLT, Charlotte Douglas International     ]
[COD,           Yellowstone Regional      ] [FAI,      Fairbanks International        ]
[ITO,            Hilo International       ] [LAX,     Los Angeles International       ]
[LGA,                 LaGuardia           ] [MCO,        Orlando International        ]
[MHT,     Manchester-Boston Regional      ] [ORD,        O'Hare International         ]
[PHX,   Phoenix Sky Harbor International  ] [SEA,    Seattle-Tacoma International     ]

----- Ch08_03_ex2() -----

map1 (initial values)
size: 8 bucket_count: 32  load_factor:  0.25

bucket  1: ABQ                         bucket  2: BOS BWI
bucket  3: CLT                         bucket  4: DFW DEN DTS DSM

map2 (initial values)
size: 8 bucket_count: 32  load_factor:  0.25

bucket  6: FAI                         bucket  9: ITO
bucket 12: LGA LAX                     bucket 13: MCO
```

CHAPTER 8   UNORDERED ASSOCIATIVE CONTAINERS

bucket 15: ORD   bucket 16: PHX
bucket 19: SEA

map2 (after merge)
size: 16 bucket_count: 32   load_factor: 0.5

bucket 1: ABQ   bucket 2: BWI BOS
bucket 3: CLT   bucket 4: DSM DTS DEN DFW
bucket 6: FAI   bucket 9: ITO
bucket 12: LGA LAX   bucket 13: MCO
bucket 15: ORD   bucket 16: PHX
bucket 19: SEA

map2 == map3: true
map2 != map3: false

----- Ch08_03_ex3() -----

map1 (after insert_range):
[ABQ,   Albuquerque International   ] [BOS,   Logan International   ]
[BWI, Baltimore/Washington International] [CLT, Charlotte Douglas International]
[DEN,   Denver International   ] [DFW,   Dallas Fort Worth International]
[DSM,   Des Moines International   ] [DTS,   Detroit Metro Wayne County   ]
[FAI,   Fairbanks International   ] [ITO,   Hilo International   ]
[LAX,   Los Angeles International   ] [LGA,   LaGuardia   ]
[MCO,   Orlando International   ] [ORD,   O'Hare International   ]
[PHX,   Phoenix Sky Harbor International   ] [SEA,   Seattle-Tacoma International   ]

map1 (after replace_with_ranges):
[ABQ,   Albuquerque Intl.   ] [BOS,   Logan Intl.   ]
[BWI,   Baltimore/Washington Intl.   ] [CLT,   Charlotte Douglas Intl.   ]
[DEN,   Denver Intl.   ] [DFW,   Dallas Fort Worth Intl.   ]
[DSM,   Des Moines Intl.   ] [DTS,   Detroit Metro Wayne County   ]
[FAI,   Fairbanks Intl.   ] [ITO,   Hilo Intl.   ]
[LAX,   Los Angeles Intl.   ] [LGA,   LaGuardia   ]
[MCO,   Orlando Intl.   ] [ORD,   O'Hare Intl.   ]
[PHX,   Phoenix Sky Harbor Intl.   ] [SEA,   Seattle-Tacoma Intl.   ]

Using std::unordered_multimap

A `std::unordered_multimap` container replicates a `std::unordered_map` but supports multiple elements with the same key. The next example, named Ch08_04, illustrates the basics of a `std::unordered_multimap`. Listing 8-4-1-1 shows the source code for header file Ch08_04.h. This file starts with the definition of a simple structure named `Airport`, which contains a few airport-related data members. Next is the definition of alias `uno_mmap_t = std::unordered_multimap<std::string_view, Airport>`. Note that this container class type utilizes a key of type `std::string_view`. The actual key value will be a two-letter country code.

Listing 8-4-1-1. Example Ch08_04 – Ch08_04.h

```
//------------------------------------------------------------------------
// Ch08_04.h
//------------------------------------------------------------------------

#ifndef CH08_04_H_
#define CH08_04_H_
#include <string>
#include <string_view>
#include <unordered_map>
#include "Common.h"

struct Airport
{
    std::string_view IataCode {};
    double Latitude {};
    double Longitude {};
    std::string City {};
};

// unordered_multimap<country code, Airport>
using uno_mmap_t = std::unordered_multimap<std::string_view, Airport>;

// Ch08_04_ex.cpp
extern void Ch08_04_ex();
```

CHAPTER 8 UNORDERED ASSOCIATIVE CONTAINERS

```
// Ch08_04_misc.cpp
extern uno_mmap_t get_airports();
extern void print_buckets(const char* msg, const uno_mmap_t& airports);

#endif
```

Listing 8-4-1-2 shows the source code for functions get_airport() and print_buckets(). The former utilizes a series of emplace() calls to construct a uno_mmap_t of airports, while the latter prints its buckets. Please note that the geocoordinates used in get_airports() are included for exposition purposes only. They are not suitable for actual navigation.

Listing 8-4-1-2. Example Ch08_04 – Ch08_04_misc.cpp

```
//-----------------------------------------------------------------
// Ch08_04_misc.cpp
//-----------------------------------------------------------------

#include "Ch08_04.h"

uno_mmap_t get_airports()
{
    // create unordered multimap using country code as key
    uno_mmap_t airports {};

    airports.emplace("AU", Airport {"MEL", -37.6733, 144.8433,
        "Melbourne"});
    airports.emplace("AU", Airport {"SYD", -33.9461, 151.1772, "Sydney"});
    airports.emplace("CA", Airport {"YYC", 51.1225, -114.0133, "Calgary"});
    airports.emplace("CA", Airport {"YVR", 49.1947, -123.1839,
        "Vancouver"});
    airports.emplace("CA", Airport {"YYZ", 53.3100, -113.5794, "Toronto"});
    airports.emplace("CN", Airport {"PEK", 40.0725, 116.5975, "Beijing"});
    airports.emplace("CN", Airport {"PVG", 31.1433, 121.8053, "Shanghai"});
    airports.emplace("CH", Airport {"ZRH", 47.4314, 8.5492, "Zurich"});
    airports.emplace("CL", Airport {"SCL", -33.3928, -70.7911,
        "Santiago"});
    airports.emplace("DE", Airport {"BER", 52.3667, 13.5033, "Berlin"});
    airports.emplace("DE", Airport {"FRA", 50.0333, 8.5706, "Frankfurt"});
```

```cpp
    airports.emplace("DE", Airport {"MUN", 48.3539, 11.7861, "Munich"});
    airports.emplace("FR", Airport {"CDG", 49.0097, 2.5478, "Paris"});
    airports.emplace("FR", Airport {"TLS", 43.6350, 1.3678, "Toulouse"});
    airports.emplace("GB", Airport {"GLA", 55.8719, -4.4331, "Glasgow"});
    airports.emplace("GB", Airport {"LHR", 51.4775, -0.4614, "London"});
    airports.emplace("JP", Airport {"KIX", 34.4306, 135.2303, "Osaka"});
    airports.emplace("JP", Airport {"NRT", 35.7653, 140.3856, "Tokyo"});
    airports.emplace("NO", Airport {"BGO", 60.2936, 5.2181, "Bergen"});
    airports.emplace("NO", Airport {"OSL", 60.2028, 11.0839, "Oslo"});
    airports.emplace("SE", Airport {"ARN", 59.5019, 17.9186, "Stockholm"});
    airports.emplace("US", Airport {"JFK", 40.6397, -74.0789, "New York"});
    airports.emplace("US", Airport {"LAX", 33.9425, -118.4081, "Los Angeles"});
    airports.emplace("US", Airport {"ORD", 41.9786, -87.9047, "Chicago"});

    return airports;
}
void print_buckets(const char* msg, const uno_mmap_t& airports)
{
    // print stats
    std::println("{:s}", msg);
    std::print("size: {}   ", airports.size());
    std::print("bucket_count: {}   ", airports.bucket_count());
    std::println("load_factor: {}\n", airports.load_factor());

    // print buckets
    for (size_t i {0}; i < airports.bucket_count(); ++i)
    {
        if (airports.bucket_size(i) != 0)
        {
            std::println("bucket {:2d}:", i);

            for (auto iter = airports.begin(i); iter != airports.end(i); ++iter)
            {
                const Airport& ap = iter->second;
```

```
            std::println("  {:2s} | {:3s} [{:9.4f}, {:9.4f}] {:40s}",
                iter->first, ap.IataCode, ap.Latitude, ap.Longitude,
                ap.City);
        }
      }
   }
   std::println("");
}
```

Example function Ch08_04_ex1(), shown in Listing 8-4-1-3, begins its execution by calling the previously described get_airports() and print_buckets(). The declaration of array keys_codes is next. This array contains a series of two-letter country codes. Within the for loop, execution of range = airports.equal_range(key_code) returns a pair of iterators. If range.first == range.second is true; no country code match was found. Otherwise, the Airport objects between iterators [range.first, range.second) match the current key_code. Function Ch08_04_ex1() then executes a second for loop that converts the city name to uppercase. Like a std::unordered_set, the value component of a std::unordered_map element can be modified in place.

Listing 8-4-1-3. Example Ch08_04 – Ch08_04_ex1()

```
//---------------------------------------------------------------
// Ch08_04_ex.cpp
//---------------------------------------------------------------

#include <array>
#include <string_view>
#include <unordered_map>
#include "Ch08_04.h"
#include "MF.h"

void Ch08_04_ex1()
{
    // create unordered_multimap
    uno_mmap_t airports = get_airports();
    print_buckets("\nairports (initial values):", airports);
```

```cpp
// search airports for matching country codes
std::array<std::string_view, 5> key_codes {"CH", "FR", "NL",
"NO", "US"};

for (const auto& key_code : key_codes)
{
    auto range = airports.equal_range(key_code);
    std::print("\nkey_code: {:s} - match ", key_code);

    if (range.first == range.second)
        std::println("not found");
    else
    {
        std::println("found");

        // change city name to upper case
        for (auto iter = range.first; iter != range.second; ++iter)
        {
            Airport& airport = iter->second;
            airport.City = MF::to_upper(airport.City);

            std::println("  updating city name: {:s}", airport.City);

        }
    }
}

print_buckets("\nairports (after city name updates):", airports);
}
```

The results for example Ch08_04 follow this paragraph. Note in the output that bucket number 58 contains airports for two different countries and that the iterator pair returned by equal_range() spans only the elements that matched key_code "NO". Like a std::unordered_set, inserting an element into an unordered associate container will always place elements with the same key value in the same bucket, but the ordering within that bucket is not guaranteed. To observe this effect, transpose the emplace() calls for airports "BGO" and "OSL" in get_airports() and execute the code.

CHAPTER 8   UNORDERED ASSOCIATIVE CONTAINERS

----- Results for example Ch08_04 -----

----- Ch08_04_ex1() -----

airports (initial values):
size: 24   bucket_count: 64   load_factor: 0.375
bucket 9:
  CA | YYC [51.1225, -114.0133] Calgary
  CA | YVR [49.1947, -123.1839] Vancouver
  CA | YYZ [53.3100, -113.5794] Toronto
bucket 12:
  GB | GLA [55.8719,   -4.4331] Glasgow
  GB | LHR [51.4775,   -0.4614] London
bucket 17:
  FR | CDG [49.0097,   2.5478] Paris
  FR | TLS [43.6350,   1.3678] Toulouse
bucket 20:
  CN | PEK [40.0725, 116.5975] Beijing
  CN | PVG [31.1433, 121.8053] Shanghai
bucket 23:
  JP | KIX [34.4306, 135.2303] Osaka
  JP | NRT [35.7653, 140.3856] Tokyo
bucket 25:
  US | JFK [40.6397, -74.0789] New York
  US | LAX [33.9425, -118.4081] Los Angeles
  US | ORD [41.9786, -87.9047] Chicago
bucket 27:
  AU | MEL [-37.6733, 144.8433] Melbourne
  AU | SYD [-33.9461, 151.1772] Sydney
bucket 34:
  DE | BER [52.3667,   13.5033] Berlin
  DE | FRA [50.0333,   8.5706] Frankfurt
  DE | MUN [48.3539,   11.7861] Munich
bucket 37:
  SE | ARN [59.5019,   17.9186] Stockholm

```
bucket 46:
  CH | ZRH [  47.4314,    8.5492] Zurich
bucket 58:
  NO | BGO [  60.2936,    5.2181] Bergen
  NO | OSL [  60.2028,   11.0839] Oslo
  CL | SCL [ -33.3928,  -70.7911] Santiago

key_code: CH - match found
  updating city name: ZURICH

key_code: FR - match found
  updating city name: PARIS
  updating city name: TOULOUSE

key_code: NL - match not found

key_code: NO - match found
  updating city name: BERGEN
  updating city name: OSLO

key_code: US - match found
  updating city name: NEW YORK
  updating city name: LOS ANGELES
  updating city name: CHICAGO

airports (after city name updates):
size: 24  bucket_count: 64  load_factor: 0.375

bucket  9:
  CA | YYC [  51.1225, -114.0133] Calgary
  CA | YVR [  49.1947, -123.1839] Vancouver
  CA | YYZ [  53.3100, -113.5794] Toronto
bucket 12:
  GB | GLA [  55.8719,   -4.4331] Glasgow
  GB | LHR [  51.4775,   -0.4614] London
bucket 17:
  FR | CDG [  49.0097,    2.5478] PARIS
  FR | TLS [  43.6350,    1.3678] TOULOUSE
bucket 20:
```

```
  CN | PEK [  40.0725,  116.5975] Beijing
  CN | PVG [  31.1433,  121.8053] Shanghai
bucket 23:
  JP | KIX [  34.4306,  135.2303] Osaka
  JP | NRT [  35.7653,  140.3856] Tokyo
bucket 25:
  US | JFK [  40.6397,  -74.0789] NEW YORK
  US | LAX [  33.9425, -118.4081] LOS ANGELES
  US | ORD [  41.9786,  -87.9047] CHICAGO
bucket 27:
  AU | MEL [ -37.6733,  144.8433] Melbourne
  AU | SYD [ -33.9461,  151.1772] Sydney
bucket 34:
  DE | BER [  52.3667,   13.5033] Berlin
  DE | FRA [  50.0333,    8.5706] Frankfurt
  DE | MUN [  48.3539,   11.7861] Munich
bucket 37:
  SE | ARN [  59.5019,   17.9186] Stockholm
bucket 46:
  CH | ZRH [  47.4314,    8.5492] ZURICH
bucket 58:
  NO | BGO [  60.2936,    5.2181] BERGEN
  NO | OSL [  60.2028,   11.0839] OSLO
  CL | SCL [ -33.3928,  -70.7911] Santiago
```

Summary

Here are the key learning points for this chapter:

- The elements of an unordered associative container are organized using hash functions and hash tables.

- A hash function maps a key value to a fixed-size index. This index is then used to select a hash table bucket that maintains the element.

- A hash function will always map identical key values to the same bucket. The ordering of elements with a specific bucket is not guaranteed.

- Load factor is the average number of elements per hash table bucket. Maximum load factor is the maximum allowable load factor. A rehash operation, which adds more buckets to the hash table and reorders the elements, occurs if the maximum load factor is exceeded.

- Unordered associative container classes `std::unordered_set` and `std::unordered_multiset` maintain collections of keys using hash functions and hash tables. The former supports unique keys, while the latter maintains multiple keys with the same value.

- Unordered associative container classes `std::unordered_map` and `std::unordered_multimap` maintain collections of key-value pairs. The hash function is applied to the key. The value component of a key-value pair can be modified in place.

- The STL defines hash functions for fundamental types. An unordered associative container can also be configured to exploit a custom hash function when such use can be justified.

CHAPTER 9

Container Adaptors

This chapter discusses STL container adaptors, including

- Container adaptor primer
- How to use `std::stack`
- How to use `std::queue`
- How to use `std::priority_queue`
- Flat container adaptors

Container Adaptor Primer

A container adaptor is a template class that repurposes an STL sequence container class to provide specific functionality. The STL includes two varieties of container adaptors. The first variety encompasses classes `std::stack`, `std::queue`, and `std::priority_queue`. These tried-and-true container adaptors define public interfaces that are deliberately simple and intuitive. The second container adaptor variety includes `std::flat_set`, `std::flat_multiset`, `std::flat_map`, and `set::flat_multimap`. These C++23 classes utilize STL sequence containers to provide functional behavior that parallels the corresponding associative container classes (see Chapter 7) but with improved performance for certain use cases. Table 9-1 summarizes several distinguishing aspects of these container adaptors.

CHAPTER 9   CONTAINER ADAPTORS

Table 9-1. STL Container Adaptors

Container Adaptor	Default Container	Alternate Containers	Element Access, Insertions, and Removals
std::stack<T>	std::deque<T>	std::vector<T> std::list<T>	top(), push(), pop()
std::queue<T>	std::deque<T>	std::list<T>	front(), back(), push(), pop()
std::priority_queue<T>	std::vector<T>	std::deque<T>	top(), push(), pop()
std::flat_set<Key>	std::vector<Key>	std::deque<Key>	Same as std::set<Key>
std::flat_multiset<Key>	std::vector<Key>	std::deque<Key>	Same as std::multiset<Key>
std::flat_map<Key,T>	std::vector<Key> std::vector<T>	std::deque<Key> std::deque<T>	Same as std::map<Key,T>
std::flat_multimap<Key,T>	std::vector<Key> std::vector<T>	std::deque<Key> std::deque<T>	Same as std::multimap<Key,T>

While reading the rest of this chapter, keep in mind the following points:

- As mentioned earlier, all container adaptors manipulate sequence containers internally; however, they are *not* sequence containers. Think of them as wrapper classes for the underlying sequence containers that furnish specific but limited functionality.

- In Table 9-1, the column labeled "Default Container" specifies the adaptor's default underlying sequence container, while column "Alternate Containers" shows supported alternatives.

- For most use cases, the default sequence container offers the best performance. The alternate containers are normally specified only when they deliver improved element insertion or removal performance for a particular data type.

CHAPTER 9 CONTAINER ADAPTORS

- A function cannot access an adaptor's underlying sequence container(s). It must use the public interface functions.

- Iterators cannot be used to access the elements of a std::stack, std::queue, or std::priority_queue. This means that most STL algorithms will not work with these classes.

Using std::stack

A std::stack is a container adaptor that provides last-in-first-out (LIFO) functionality using push() and pop() operations. A common visual metaphor for a software stack is a pile of plates. A new plate can only be inserted (pushed) onto the pile's top, and only the topmost plate can be removed (popped). Plates within the pile are not accessible. Figure 9-1 illustrates the logical structure of a std::stack that uses a std::deque for its underlying sequence container. This figure also illustrates execution of operations push() and pop().

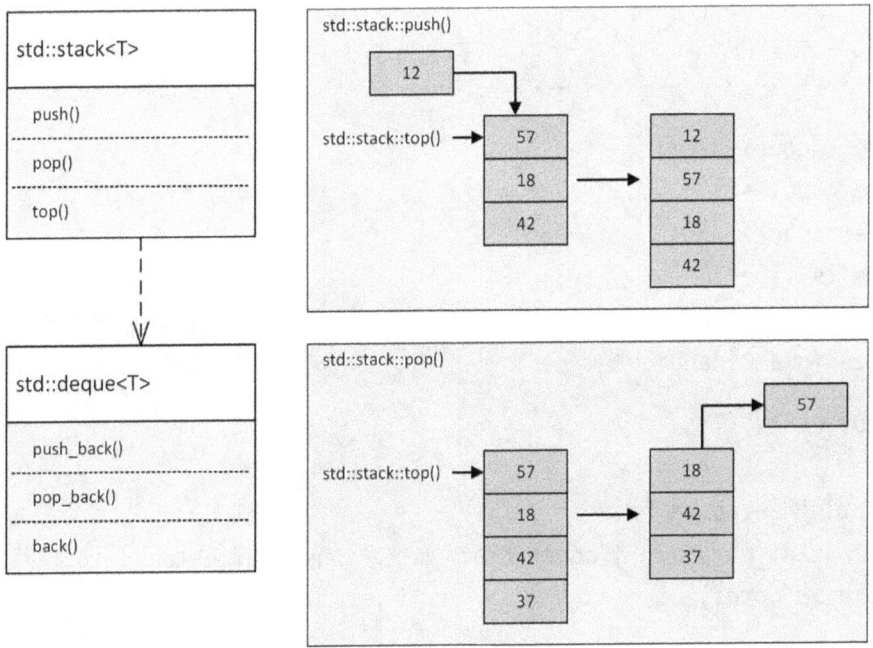

Figure 9-1. Container adaptor std::stack

CHAPTER 9   CONTAINER ADAPTORS

Recall from Table 9-1 that a `std::stack` can also utilize either a `std::vector` or `std::list` for its underlying sequence container. These containers along with `std::deque` define member functions `push_back()`, `pop_back()`, and `back()`. Container adaptor `std::stack` utilizes these functions to implement its `push()`, `pop()`, and `top()` operations, respectively.

Listing 9-1-1 shows the source code for example `Ch09_01_ex1()`. This function demonstrates how to perform elementary operations using `std::stacks`. The opening code block of `Ch09_01_ex1()` defines a lambda expression named `print_words()`, which prints the elements of a `std::stack<std::string>`. In this function, the expression `auto stk {words}` copy-constructs a new instance of argument words. The reason for creating a copy of argument words is that adaptor `std::stack` doesn't support iterators or define any public member functions that allow direct access to its elements. Currently,[1] the only straightforward means of printing a `std::stack`'s elements is to utilize sequences of `top()` and `pop()`.

Listing 9-1-1. Example Ch09_01 – Ch09_01_ex1()

```
//-------------------------------------------------------------
// Ch09_01_ex.cpp
//-------------------------------------------------------------

#include <deque>
#include <ranges>
#include <stack>
#include <string>
#include "Ch09_01.h"
#include "TowerOfHanoi.h"

void Ch09_01_ex1()
{
    // print words lambda
    auto print_words = [](const char* msg, const std::stack<std::
string>& words)
```

---

[1] The C++23 standard defines specializations of template class `std::formatter<>` for container adaptors `std::stack`, `std::queue`, and `std::priority_queue`. These specializations can be exploited to generate formatted text of a container adaptor's elements. As I write this, mainstream C++ compilers do not support the `std::formatter<>` specializations for container adaptors.

```cpp
    {
        auto stk {words};

        std::println("{:s} (size = {:d})", msg, stk.size());

        while (!stk.empty())
        {
            // using top() and pop()
            std::print("| {:s} ", stk.top());
            stk.pop();
        }

        std::println("|");
    };

    // create stack (std::stack doesn't support initializer lists)
    const auto il1 = {"brought ...", "fathers", "our", "ago",
    "years", "and"};
    std::stack<std::string> words1(il1.begin(), il1.end());
    print_words("\nwords1 (initial values)", words1);

    // using push and emplace
    words1.push("score");
    words1.emplace("four");
    print_words("\nwords1 (after push and emplace)", words1);

    // create stack (constructor initialized using std::deque)
    const std::deque<std::string> deq2
        {"apple", "banana cream", "blueberry"};

    std::stack<std::string> words2(deq2);
    print_words("\nwords2 (initial values)", words2);

    // using push_range
    std::stack<std::string> words3 {words2};
    print_words("\nwords3 (initial values)", words3);

    const auto il3 = {"cherry", "key lime", "peach", "pecan", "turtle"};
#ifdef __cpp_lib_containers_ranges
    words3.push_range(il3);
```

```
    print_words("\nwords3 (after push_range)", words3);
#else
    for (const auto& s : il3)
        words3.push(s);
    print_words("\nwords3 (after push operations)", words3);
#endif
}
```

The next code block in print_words() utilizes a while loop to print the elements of stk. Member function stk.empty() returns true if stk contains zero elements. The ensuing std::println() statement utilizes stk.top() to access and print the topmost element of stk. This is followed by a stk.pop(), which removes the topmost std::string from stk. You may be wondering why top() and pop() are defined distinctly instead of a single member function that combines both operations. Defining a top_and_pop() member function would necessitate an element copy operation even in situations where only a pop() is required. You can always define a custom top_and_pop() function, and you'll see an example of this later.

Before continuing, it warrants mentioning that using top() or pop() with an empty std::stack results in undefined behavior. A function that uses std::stack adaptors should always include appropriate checks using empty() or size(). It's also not a bad idea to throw an exception if detection of an empty stack is erroneous.

Returning to the code of Ch09_01_ex1(), the first code block following the definition of print_words() instantiates a std::stack<std::string> adaptor named words1. Note that this code block defines an explicit initializer list of text strings; iterators il1.begin() and il1.end() are passed to the constructor for words1. The reason for this is that adaptor class std::stack doesn't support object construction using an initializer list (e.g., std::stack<std::string> stk {"one", "two"} is invalid). Following the instantiation of words1, Ch09_01_ex1() utilizes print_words() to print its elements.

In the next code block, the statements words1.push("score") and words1.emplace("four") push two more elements onto words1. The code block that follows instantiates another std::stack<std::string> adaptor named words2. Note here that an object of type std::deque<std::string> is passed to the constructor of words2. This is possible since the underlying container for adaptor words2 is a std::deque<std::string>.

CHAPTER 9　CONTAINER ADAPTORS

The final code block of `Ch09_01_ex1()` demonstrates the use of `words2.push_range()` (C++ 23), which pushes the elements of `il3` onto stack `words3`. The elements of `il3` are pushed using the same order as they appear in the initializer list (i.e., `"cherry"` is pushed first followed by `"key lime"`, etc.). The actual elements pushed onto `words3` are, of course, `std::strings` that get constructed using the `const char*` members of `il3`.

The archetypal example of stack usage is the well-known Tower of Hanoi (TOH) algorithm. In this algorithm, numbered discs must be moved from a source peg to a target peg using an intermediate peg. A disc can only be moved to another peg if its value is less than the topmost disc on the target peg. A disc can also be moved to an empty peg. Figure 9-2 illustrates the TOH peg and disc arrangements in greater detail.

CHAPTER 9 CONTAINER ADAPTORS

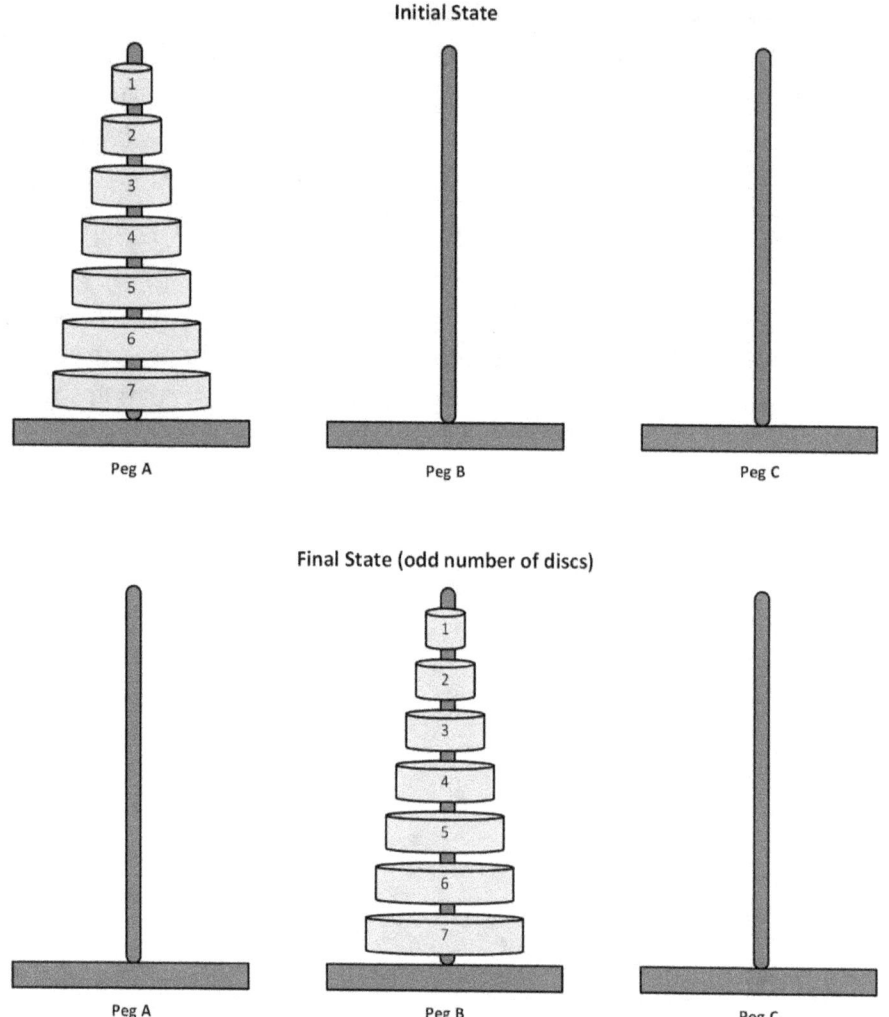

Figure 9-2. *Tower of Hanoi algorithm peg and disc arrangements*

The TOH algorithm typically starts with all of the discs on PegA as shown in Figure 9-2. If the number of discs is even, PegC is the final target; otherwise, it's PegB. The number of moves required to transfer N discs from PegA to the target peg is $2^N - 1$.

Listing 9-1-2-1 shows the source code for class TowerOfHanoi. Near the top of the class declaration is the definition of an alias named uint_t. This defines the integer type for a disc. Function TowerOfHanoi::run() is the only public member function. This function requires two arguments: the number of discs and a verbose flag that enables stack dumps and other status messages during execution. Alias peg_t is a TOH algorithm peg, which corresponds to a container adaptor of type `std::stack<uint, std::vector<uint_t>>`. Adaptor peg_t utilizes a `std::vector<uint_t>` for its underlying container since this sequence container is typically faster when used with a fundamental type such as uint_t compared to a `std::deque<uint_t>`.[2] The private member functions of class TowerOfHanoi are declared next. The attributes of class TowerOfHanoi include peg_t objects m_PegA, m_PegB, and m_PegC along with a bool named m_Verbose.

Listing 9-1-2-1. Example Ch09_02 – Class TowerOfHanoi

```
//---------------------------------------------------------------
// TowerOfHanoi.h
//---------------------------------------------------------------
#ifndef TOWER_OF_HANOI_H_
#define TOWER_OF_HANOI_H_

#include <cstdint>
#include <stack>
#include <vector>

class TowerOfHanoi
{
public:
    using uint_t = uint64_t;
    constexpr static uint_t s_NumDiscsMax {63};

    void run(uint_t num_discs, bool verbose);

private:
    using peg_t = std::stack<uint_t, std::vector<uint_t>>;

    uint_t top_and_pop(peg_t& peg);
    void move_disc(peg_t& peg_from, peg_t& peg_to, const char* msg);
```

---

[2] Recall that the elements of a `std::vector` are stored in contiguous memory, which means fast copy operations should a reallocation of `std::vector`'s internal buffer become necessary during the insertion of a new uint_t element.

```cpp
    void print_pegs();
    void print_peg(const char* msg, const peg_t& peg);

    peg_t m_PegA {};            // source peg
    peg_t m_PegB {};            // target peg (num discs is odd)
    peg_t m_PegC {};            // target peg (num discs is even)
    bool m_Verbose {};          // print status messages if true
};

#endif


//-----------------------------------------------------------------------
// TowerOfHanoi.cpp
//-----------------------------------------------------------------------

#include <stdexcept>
#include "Common.h"
#include "TowerOfHanoi.h"

TowerOfHanoi::uint_t TowerOfHanoi::top_and_pop(peg_t& peg)
{
#ifdef _DEBUG
    if (peg.empty())
        throw std::runtime_error("peg stack is empty()");
#endif

    // pop disc from peg, return value to caller
    uint_t disc = peg.top();
    peg.pop();
    return disc;
}

void TowerOfHanoi::move_disc(peg_t& peg_from, peg_t& peg_to, const char* msg)
{
    // move disc
    uint_t disc = top_and_pop(peg_from);
    peg_to.push(disc);
```

```cpp
        if (m_Verbose)
            std::println("{:s}", msg);
    }

    void TowerOfHanoi::print_pegs()
    {
        print_peg("PegA", m_PegA);
        print_peg("PegB", m_PegB);
        print_peg("PegC", m_PegC);
    }

    void TowerOfHanoi::print_peg(const char* msg, const peg_t& peg)
    {
        peg_t peg_temp {peg};
        std::print("{:s}:", msg);

        while (!peg_temp.empty())
            std::print("{:2d} ", top_and_pop(peg_temp));
        std::println("");
    }

    void TowerOfHanoi::run(uint_t num_discs, bool verbose)
    {
        if (num_discs == 0 || num_discs > s_NumDiscsMax)
            throw std::runtime_error("invalid value - 'num_discs'");

        // num_moves = pow(2, num_discs) - 1
        // target_peg = PegB/PegC for num_discs odd/even
        m_Verbose = verbose;
        uint_t num_moves = (uint_t(1) << num_discs) - 1;
        std::string target_peg = (num_discs & 1) ? "PegB" : "PegC";

        // place discs on source peg (m_PegA)
        for (uint_t i {num_discs}; i >= 1; --i)
            m_PegA.push(i);

        std::println(
            "Start (num_discs: {:d}, num_moves: {:d}, target_peg: {:s})",
            num_discs, num_moves, target_peg);
        print_pegs();
```

```cpp
    for (uint_t i {0}; i < num_moves; ++i)
    {
        if (m_Verbose)
            std::print("\nMove {:d} - ", i);
        if (i % 3 == 0)
        {
            if (!m_PegA.empty() && (m_PegB.empty() || m_PegA.top()
            < m_PegB.top()))
                move_disc(m_PegA, m_PegB, "PegA to PegB");
            else
                move_disc(m_PegB, m_PegA, "PegB to PegA");
        }
        else if (i % 3 == 1)
        {
            if (!m_PegA.empty() && (m_PegC.empty() || m_PegA.top()
            < m_PegC.top()))
                move_disc(m_PegA, m_PegC, "PegA to PegC");
            else
                move_disc(m_PegC, m_PegA, "PegC to PegA");
        }
        else
        {
            if (!m_PegB.empty() && (m_PegC.empty() || m_PegB.top()
            < m_PegC.top()))
                move_disc(m_PegB, m_PegC, "PegB to PegC");
            else
                move_disc(m_PegC, m_PegB, "PegC to PegB");
        }
        if (m_Verbose)
            print_pegs();
    }
    std::println(
        "\nStop (num_discs: {:d}, num_moves: {:d}, target_peg: {:s})",
```

        num_discs, num_moves, target_peg);
    print_pegs();
}

Also shown in Listing 9-1-2-1 are the member functions for class TowerOfHanoi, the first of which is named top_and_pop(). As implied by its name, this member function reads the topmost disc from peg_t peg. It then pops the same disc from peg and returns its value to the caller. The TowerOfHanoi algorithm performs multiple top-and-pop operations, so it makes sense to define a single function that combines both stack operations. The next member function, move_disc(), transfers a disc from peg_from to peg_to. Note that this member function exploits top_and_pop(). Adaptor member function push() is utilized to place the removed disc onto peg_to. The next two functions in TowerOfHanoi.cpp, print_pegs() and print_peg(), carry out print operations. Note that print_peg() instantiates a local copy of argument peg, and this object exploits top_and_pop() to print peg's discs.

The TOH disc move algorithm code is located in member function run(). The opening code blocks of this function carry out the requisite initializations. The first for loop in run() places the initial set of discs on m_PegA. The second for loop performs the disc moves. A legal move from peg X to peg Y requires the following conditions:

- Peg X must not be empty AND.

- Peg Y must be empty OR the topmost disc of peg X must be less than the topmost disc of peg Y.

Since there are three pegs, only three distinct move actions are possible as outlined in Table 9-2.

Table 9-2. *Tower of Hanoi Disc Moves*

Iteration	Possible Moves
i % 3 == 0	If legal, move disc from m_PegA to m_PegB; otherwise, move disc from m_PegB to m_PegA
i % 3 == 1	If legal, move disc from m_PegA to m_PegC; otherwise, move disc from m_PegC to m_PegA
i % 3 == 2	If legal, move disc from m_PegB to m_PegC; otherwise move disc from m_PegC to m_PegB

CHAPTER 9 CONTAINER ADAPTORS

Listing 9-1-2-2 shows the source code for example function Ch09_01_ex2(). This function exercises TowerOfHanoi::run() using both even and odd disc counts. To observe the actual disc moves, enable preprocessor symbol TOH_VERBOSE_TEST, recompile, and execute.

Listing 9-1-2-2. Example Ch09_01 - Ch09_01_ex2()

```
//#define TOH_VERBOSE_TEST

void Ch09_01_ex2()
{
    // verbose mode test
#ifdef TOH_VERBOSE_TEST
    TowerOfHanoi tow0 {};
    TowerOfHanoi::uint_t num_discs0 {7};

    std::println("\nbegin run0");
    tow0.run(num_discs0, true);
#endif

    // using even number of discs
    TowerOfHanoi tow1 {};
    TowerOfHanoi::uint_t num_discs1 {20};

    std::println("\nbegin run1");
    tow1.run(num_discs1, false);

    // using odd number of discs
    TowerOfHanoi tow2 {};
    TowerOfHanoi::uint_t num_discs2 {21};

    std::println("\n\nbegin run2");
    tow2.run(num_discs2, false);
}
```

CHAPTER 9 CONTAINER ADAPTORS

Container adaptor function std::queue::push() adds a new element to the back of a queue, while std::queue::pop() removes the queue's frontmost element. A function can also read the back or frontmost element of a std::queue using member functions back() and front(), respectively.

Using a std::queue is not that much different than using a std::stack. Listing 9-2-1 shows the source code for example Ch09_02_ex1(). The first code block in this function utilizes a std::deque<int> to initialize std::queue<int> queue1. Like a std::stack, adaptor std::queue does not support constructor initialization using an initializer list. The next code block demonstrates using push() and emplace() to add new elements to the back of queue1. This is followed by a series of std::println() statements that exhibit usages of member functions front(), back(), size(), and empty().

Listing 9-2-1. Example Ch09_02 – Ch09_02_ex1()

```
//-------------------------------------------------------------------
// Ch09_02_ex.cpp
//-------------------------------------------------------------------

#include <deque>
#include <queue>
#include <string>
#include "Ch09_02.h"
#include "MT.h"

void Ch09_02_ex1()
{
    const char* fmt = "{:4d}";
    constexpr size_t epl_max {15};

    // create queue (std::queue doesn't support initializer lists)
    std::deque<int> x {10, 20, 30, 40};
    std::queue<int> queue1(x);
    MT::print_queue("\nqueue1 (initial values):\n", queue1, fmt, epl_max);

    // using push() and emplace()
    queue1.push(50);
    queue1.emplace(60);
    MT::print_queue("\nqueue1 (after insertions):\n", queue1, fmt,
        epl_max);
```

```cpp
    // using front(), back(), size(), and empty()
    std::println("\nqueue1.front(): {:d}", queue1.front());
    std::println("queue1.back():  {:d}", queue1.back());
    std::println("queue1.size():  {:d}", queue1.size());
    std::println("queue1.empty(): {:s}", queue1.empty());

    // using pop()
    queue1.pop();
    queue1.pop();
    MT::print_queue("\nqueue1 (after pop operations):\n", queue1, fmt,
    epl_max);

    // using relational operators
    std::queue<int> queue2 {queue1};
    MT::print_queue("\nqueue2 (initial values):\n", queue2, fmt, epl_max);

    std::println("\nqueue1 == queue2: {:s}", queue1 == queue2);
    std::println("queue1 != queue2: {:s}", queue1 != queue2);
    std::println("queue1 <  queue2: {:s}", queue1 <  queue2);
    std::println("queue1 <= queue2: {:s}", queue1 <= queue2);
    std::println("queue1 >  queue2: {:s}", queue1 >  queue2);
    std::println("queue1 >= queue2: {:s}", queue1 >= queue2);
}
```

Following the calls to std::println() is the definition of queue2. Note that this std::queue<int> object is copy-constructed using the elements of queue1. Next is a sequence of six std::println() calls that spotlights the use of std::queue's relational operators. Like other container relational operators, these operators carry out lexicographical compares of corresponding elements in queue1 and queue2.

The next example, shown in Listing 9-2-2, highlights a few more operations using container adaptor std::queue. Near the top of Ch09_02_ex2() is the definition of alias queue_t, which corresponds to a container adaptor of type std::queue<std::string>. In the code block that follows, queue_t queue1 is initialized using iterators. The constructor overload of std::queue that accepts iterator arguments is new to C++23. The subsequent code block utilizes push_range() (C++23) to add more elements to queue2. In the current example, push_range() effectively performs multiple push operations using the strings of il2. The final code block of Ch09_02_ex2() exploits swap() to exchange the elements of queue1 and queue2.

Listing 9-2-2. Example Ch09_02 – Ch09_02_ex2()

```cpp
void Ch09_02_ex2()
{
    const char* fmt = "{:20s}";
    constexpr size_t epl_max {4};
    using queue_t = std::queue<std::string>;

    const auto il1 = {"apple", "banana cream",
        "blueberry", "cherry", "key lime", "peach", "pecan", "turtle"};

    // initialize queue1 (ctor is C++23)
#ifdef __cpp_lib_adaptor_iterator_pair_constructor
    queue_t queue1(il1.begin(), il1.end());
#else
    queue_t queue1 {};
    for (auto s : il1)
        queue1.push(s);
#endif

    MT::print_queue("\nqueue1 (initial values):\n", queue1, fmt, epl_max);

    // initialize queue2 (push_range is C++23)
    const auto il2 = {"pumpkin", "raspberry", "custard", "coconut cream",
            "lemon meringue", "strawberry"};

    queue_t queue2 {};
#ifdef __cpp_lib_containers_ranges
    queue2.push_range(il2);
    MT::print_queue("\nqueue2 (using push_range):\n", queue2, fmt,
    epl_max);
#else
    for (const auto& s : il2)
        queue2.push(s);
    MT::print_queue("\nqueue2 (using push ops):\n", queue2, fmt, epl_max);
#endif
```

CHAPTER 9 CONTAINER ADAPTORS

```
    // swap queue1 and queue2
    queue1.swap(queue2);
    MT::print_queue("\nqueue1 (after swap):\n", queue1, fmt, epl_max);
    MT::print_queue("\nqueue2 (after swap):\n", queue2, fmt, epl_max);
}
```

Here are the results for example Ch09_02:

```
----- Results for example Ch09_02 -----

----- Ch09_02_ex1() -----
queue1 (initial values):
  10  20  30  40

queue1 (after insertions):
  10  20  30  40  50  60

queue1.front(): 10
queue1.back():  60
queue1.size():  6
queue1.empty(): false

queue1 (after pop operations):
  30  40  50  60

queue2 (initial values):
  30  40  50  60

queue1 == queue2: true
queue1 != queue2: false
queue1 <  queue2: false
queue1 <= queue2: true
queue1 >  queue2: false
queue1 >= queue2: true
```

```
----- Ch09_02_ex2() -----
queue1 (initial values):
apple               banana cream        blueberry           cherry
key lime            peach               pecan               turtle

queue2 (using push_range):
pumpkin             raspberry           custard             coconut cream
lemon meringue      strawberry

queue1 (after swap):
pumpkin             raspberry           custard             coconut cream
lemon meringue      strawberry

queue2 (after swap):
apple               banana cream        blueberry           cherry
key lime            peach               pecan               turtle
```

Using std::priority_queue

A std::priority_queue is another queue-like container adaptor. The primary difference between a std::queue and a std::priority_queue is that the latter orders its elements using a compare function. The default comparison function object for a std::priority_queue is std::less<>. Note that adaptor std::priority_queue applies this function object to order its elements in *descending* order. In other words, the frontmost element is the largest.[3] To order the elements of a priority queue in *ascending* order – where the smallest element is frontmost – a std::priority_queue can be declared using function object std::greater<> as you'll soon see. Figure 9-4 depicts the logical structure of a std::priority_queue. This figure also illustrates the execution of member functions push() and pop().

---

[3] This is different than most other STL default uses of std::less<>, which arranges elements in ascending order.

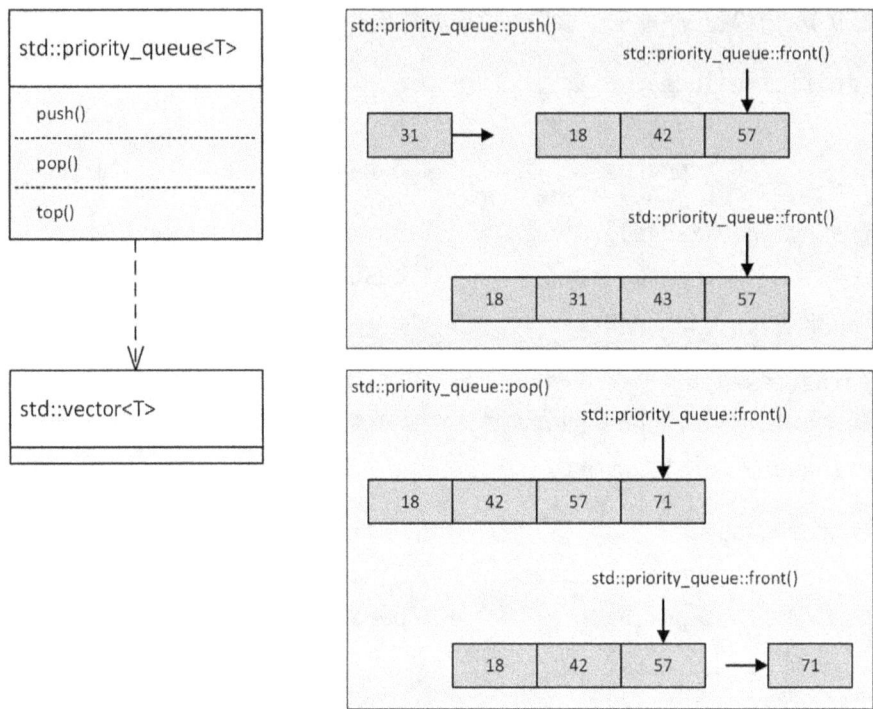

Figure 9-4. *Container adaptor* `std::priority_queue`

The default underlying sequence container of a `std::priority_queue` is a `std::vector`. You can change this to a `std::deque`. The elements of a `std::priority_queue` are arranged as a heap. A heap is a tree-like data structure that optimally orders a group of elements. Heaps are commonly exploited to implement efficient sorting algorithms and priority queues. For the current example, it's not necessary to understand the algorithmic mechanisms of a heap. You'll learn more about this data structure in Chapter 12.

Listing 9-3-1-1 shows the source code for class `RegPolygon`. The `std::priority_queue` examples that you'll examine in this section utilize this class. Class `RegPolygon` is also used in later chapters.

Listing 9-3-1-1. *Example Ch09_03 – Class RegPolygon*

```
//-------------------------------------------------------------------------
// RegPolygon.h
//-------------------------------------------------------------------------
#ifndef REG_POLYGON_H_
#define REG_POLYGON_H_
#include <format>
#include <string>
#include <vector>

class RegPolygon
{
    friend struct std::formatter<RegPolygon>;

    static constexpr int NumSidesDef = 3;
    static constexpr double Radius1Def = 1.0;
public:
    RegPolygon() { calc_values(NumSidesDef, Radius1Def); }
    RegPolygon(int num_sides, double radius1) { calc_values(num_sides,
    radius1); }

    // accessors
    int NumSides() const { return m_NumSides; }
    double Radius1() const { return m_Radius1; };
    double SideLength() const { return m_SideLength; }
    double Radius2() const { return m_Radius2; };
    double Perimeter() const { return m_Perimeter; };
    double VertexAngle() const { return m_VertexAngle; };
    double Area() const { return m_Area; };

    void set(int num_sides, double radius1) { calc_values(num_sides,
    radius1); }

    // relational operators
    friend auto operator<=>(const RegPolygon& rp1, const RegPolygon& rp2)
        { return rp1.m_Area <=> rp2.m_Area; }
```

```
    friend bool operator==(const RegPolygon& rp1, const RegPolygon& rp2)
        { return rp1.m_Area == rp2.m_Area; }

    // public member functions
    static std::vector<RegPolygon> get_random_polygons(size_t num_polygons,
        unsigned int rng_seed1, unsigned int rng_seed2);

    static std::string title_str();

private:
    void calc_values(int num_sides, double radius1);
    std::string to_str() const;

    // RegPolygon attributes
    int m_NumSides {};
    double m_Radius1 {};          // inscribed radius
    double m_SideLength {};
    double m_Radius2 {};          // circumscribed radius
    double m_Perimeter {};
    double m_VertexAngle {};      // labeled theta in figure
    double m_Area {};
};

// class RegPolygon formatter
template <> struct std::formatter<RegPolygon> : std::formatter<std::string>
{
    constexpr auto parse(std::format_parse_context& pc)
        { return pc.begin(); }

    auto format(const RegPolygon& rp, std::format_context& fc) const
        { return std::format_to(fc.out(), "{}", rp.to_str()); }
};

#endif

//-------------------------------------------------------------------------
// RegPolygon.cpp
//-------------------------------------------------------------------------
```

```cpp
#include <cmath>
#include <iomanip>
#include <numbers>
#include <ostream>
#include <random>
#include <stdexcept>
#include <sstream>
#include <vector>
#include "RegPolygon.h"
#include "MTH.h"

std::vector<RegPolygon> RegPolygon::get_random_polygons(size_t num_
polygons,
         unsigned int rng_seed1, unsigned int rng_seed2)
{
    std::mt19937 rng_num_sides {rng_seed1};
    std::uniform_int_distribution<int> dist_num_sides {3, 30};

    std::mt19937 rng_radius {rng_seed2};
    std::uniform_real_distribution<double> dist_radius {0.5, 25.0};

    std::vector<RegPolygon> polygons {};

    for (size_t i = 0; i < num_polygons; ++i)
    {
        int num_sides = dist_num_sides(rng_num_sides);
        double radius1 = dist_radius(rng_radius);

        polygons.emplace_back(num_sides, radius1);
    }

    return polygons;
}
std::string RegPolygon::title_str()
{
    static std::string s {};

    if (s.empty())
```

```
    {
        s += "Sides       ";
        s += "Radius1     ";
        s += "SideLen     ";
        s += "Radius2     ";
        s += "Perim       ";
        s += "VerAng      ";
        s += "Area\n";
        s += std::string(74, '=');
    }

    return s;
}

void RegPolygon::calc_values(int num_sides, double radius1)
{
    using namespace std::numbers;

    // validate arguments
    static std::string s1 { "RegPolygon::CalcValues(): invalid value - " };

    if (num_sides < 3)
        throw std::runtime_error(s1 + "'num_sides'");

    if (radius1 <= 0.0)
        throw std::runtime_error(s1 + "'radius1'");

    // calculate polygon parameters
    m_NumSides = num_sides;
    m_Radius1 = radius1;

    m_SideLength = 2.0 * m_Radius1 * std::tan(MTH::deg_to_rad(180.0 / m_NumSides));
    m_Perimeter = m_NumSides * m_SideLength;
    m_VertexAngle = (m_NumSides - 2) / static_cast<double>(m_NumSides)
        * 180.0;

    m_Radius2 = 0.5 * m_SideLength
                    * MTH::csc(MTH::deg_to_rad(180.0 / m_NumSides));
```

```
    m_Area = m_NumSides * m_Radius1 * m_Radius1
                        * std::tan(MTH::deg_to_rad(180.0 / m_NumSides));
}
std::string RegPolygon::to_str() const
{
    std::string s {};
    std::format_to(std::back_inserter(s), "[{:4d}, ", m_NumSides);
    std::format_to(std::back_inserter(s), "{:9.3f} | ", m_Radius1);
    std::format_to(std::back_inserter(s), "{:9.3f}, ", m_SideLength);
    std::format_to(std::back_inserter(s), "{:9.3f}, ", m_Radius2);
    std::format_to(std::back_inserter(s), "{:9.3f}, ", m_Perimeter);
    std::format_to(std::back_inserter(s), "{:9.3f}, ", m_VertexAngle);
    std::format_to(std::back_inserter(s), "{:9.3f}]", m_Area);

    return s;
}
```

The first part of Listing 9-3-1-1 shows the declaration for class RegPolygon. For the examples of this section, there are two particulars to note here. First, operator<=> and operator== carry out their comparisons using attribute m_Area. Second, the parameterized constructor for RegPolygon requires two argument values: num_sides and (inscribed radius) radius1. Member function calc_values() utilizes these values to calculate the regular polygon's circumscribed radius, side length, perimeter, vertex angle, and area. Figure 9-5 shows a six-sided (hexagon) regular polygon along with the inscribed and circumscribed circles.

CHAPTER 9   CONTAINER ADAPTORS

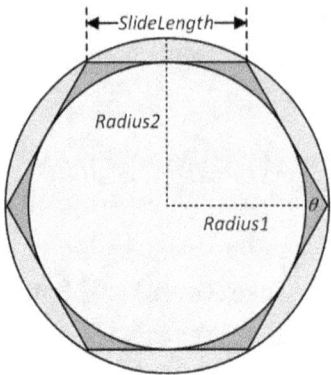

Figure 9-5. *Six-sided (hexagon) regular polygon*

File RegPolygons.cpp, also shown in Listing 9-3-1-1, contains the actual code for calc_values(). This file also includes the requisite code necessary to print the attributes of a RegPolygon object using std::println(). Member function get_random_polygons(), used in later chapters, generates a std::vector<RegPolygon> of regular polygons using random values for num_sides and radius1.

Example function Ch09_03_ex1(), shown in Listing 9-3-1-2, begins its execution with the creation of a std::priority_queue<RegPolygon> named polygons1. Note that like std::stack and std::queue, class std::priority_queue doesn't support constructor initializer lists, which is why the constructor for polygons1 uses iterator arguments. Following the creation of polygons1, MT::print_priority_queue() (see Common/MT.h) is exercised to print its elements. If you scan ahead to the results section, you'll notice that the RegPolygon objects of polygons1 are ordered by area from largest to smallest.

Listing 9-3-1-2. Example Ch09_03 – Ch09_03_ex1()

```
//------------------------------------------------------------
// Ch09_03_ex.cpp
//------------------------------------------------------------

#include <deque>
#include <functional>
#include <queue>
#include "Ch09_03.h"
#include "MT.h"
#include "RegPolygon.h"
```

CHAPTER 9 CONTAINER ADAPTORS

```cpp
void Ch09_03_ex1()
{
    const char* fmt = "{}";
    constexpr size_t epl_max {1};

    // create priority queue of RegPolygons
    // RegPolygon::operator<=> uses area
    const auto il1 =
        {RegPolygon {3, 1.0}, RegPolygon {4, 3.0}, RegPolygon {5, 2.0}};

    std::priority_queue<RegPolygon> polygons1(il1.begin(), il1.end());

    std::println("{:s}", RegPolygon::title_str());
    MT::print_priority_queue("\npolygons1 (initial values):\n",
        polygons1, fmt, epl_max);

    // add more polygons
    polygons1.push(RegPolygon {6, 4.0});
    polygons1.push(RegPolygon {4, 8.0});
    polygons1.emplace(RegPolygon {8, 5.0});
    polygons1.emplace(RegPolygon {10, 3.0});

    MT::print_priority_queue("\npolygons1 (after push/emplace operations):\n",
        polygons1, fmt, epl_max);
    std::println("\npolygons1.size(): {}", polygons1.size());
    std::println("\npolygons1.top():\n{}", polygons1.top());

    // remove elements
    polygons1.pop();
    polygons1.pop();

    MT::print_priority_queue("\npolygons1 (after pop operations):\n",
        polygons1, fmt, epl_max);
    std::println("\npolygons1.size(): {}", polygons1.size());
    std::println("\npolygons1.top():\n{}", polygons1.top());
}
```

The next code block demonstrates the use of member functions push() and emplace() to add more polygons to polygons1. During execution of each call to push() or emplace(), the new RegPolygon object is inserted into polygons1, and the internal heap is adjusted to maintain proper (largest to smallest) ordering by area as shown in the results section. The ensuing two calls to std::println() demonstrate the use of size() and top(). The former returns the number of elements in polygons1, while top() returns the frontmost (largest) element. Calling top() or pop() using an empty std::priority_queue results in undefined behavior. The final code block of Ch09_03_ex1() spotlights the use of pop(), which removes the frontmost element from polygons1.

Listing 9-3-2 shows the source code for example Ch09_03_ex2(). Prior to the start of this function are several alias definitions. Note that type pq_t is a std::priority_queue and that it holds RegPolygons. Also, note that function object std::greater<RegPolygon> is utilized to order the elements of a pq_t, which means that the frontmost element will contain the smallest by area RegPolygon object.

Listing 9-3-2. Example Ch09_03 – Ch09_03_ex2()

```cpp
// type aliases for custom priority_queue
using value_t = RegPolygon;
using container_t = std::deque<RegPolygon>;
using cmp_t = std::greater<RegPolygon>;
using pq_t = std::priority_queue<value_t, container_t, cmp_t>;

void Ch09_03_ex2()
{
    const char* fmt = "{}";
    constexpr size_t epl_max {1};

    // create priority queue of RegPolygons
    // add polygons using push_range
    pq_t polygons1 {};

    const auto il1 = {RegPolygon {3, 1.0}, RegPolygon {4, 3.0},
        RegPolygon {5, 2.0}, RegPolygon {6, 4.0}};

#ifdef __cpp_lib_containers_ranges
    polygons1.push_range(il1);
```

```cpp
#else
    for (const auto rp : il1)
        polygons1.push(rp);
#endif

    std::println("{:s}", RegPolygon::title_str());
    MT::print_priority_queue("\npolygons1 (initial values):\n",
        polygons1, fmt, epl_max);

    // add more polygons
    polygons1.emplace(RegPolygon {3, 0.5});
    polygons1.emplace(RegPolygon {10, 0.25});
    polygons1.emplace(RegPolygon {12, 0.0125});

    MT::print_priority_queue("\npolygons1 (after emplace operations):\n",
        polygons1, fmt, epl_max);

    // remove elements
    polygons1.pop();
    polygons1.pop();
    MT::print_priority_queue("\npolygons1 (after pop operations):\n",
        polygons1, fmt, epl_max);
}
```

The opening code block of Ch09_03_ex2() utilizes push_range() (C++23) to add elements to polygons1. Note in the results section that the elements of polygons1 are arranged in ascending order by area. The ensuing code block utilizes emplace() to add more RegPolygons to polygons1. The final code block of Ch09_03_ex2() exercises member function pop() twice to remove the two smallest RegPolygons from polygons1. Here are the results for example Ch09_03:

```
----- Results for example Ch09_03 -----

----- Ch09_03_ex1() -----

Sides      Radius1     SideLen    Radius2     Perim       VerAng      Area
===========================================================================

polygons1 (initial values):
[    4,      3.000 |    6.000,     4.243,    24.000,     90.000,    36.000]
```

```
[    5,    2.000 |    2.906,    2.472,   14.531,   108.000,   14.531]
[    3,    1.000 |    3.464,    2.000,   10.392,    60.000,    5.196]
```

polygons1 (after push/emplace operations):
```
[    4,    8.000 |   16.000,   11.314,   64.000,    90.000,  256.000]
[    8,    5.000 |    4.142,    5.412,   33.137,   135.000,   82.843]
[    6,    4.000 |    4.619,    4.619,   27.713,   120.000,   55.426]
[    4,    3.000 |    6.000,    4.243,   24.000,    90.000,   36.000]
[   10,    3.000 |    1.950,    3.154,   19.495,   144.000,   29.243]
[    5,    2.000 |    2.906,    2.472,   14.531,   108.000,   14.531]
[    3,    1.000 |    3.464,    2.000,   10.392,    60.000,    5.196]
```

polygons1.size(): 7

polygons1.top():
```
[    4,    8.000 |   16.000,   11.314,   64.000,    90.000,  256.000]
```

polygons1 (after pop operations):
```
[    6,    4.000 |    4.619,    4.619,   27.713,   120.000,   55.426]
[    4,    3.000 |    6.000,    4.243,   24.000,    90.000,   36.000]
[   10,    3.000 |    1.950,    3.154,   19.495,   144.000,   29.243]
[    5,    2.000 |    2.906,    2.472,   14.531,   108.000,   14.531]
[    3,    1.000 |    3.464,    2.000,   10.392,    60.000,    5.196]
```

polygons1.size(): 5

polygons1.top():
```
[    6,    4.000 |    4.619,    4.619,   27.713,   120.000,   55.426]
```

----- Ch09_03_ex2() -----

Sides	Radius1	SideLen	Radius2	Perim	VerAng	Area

===

polygons1 (initial values):
```
[    3,    1.000 |    3.464,    2.000,   10.392,    60.000,    5.196]
[    5,    2.000 |    2.906,    2.472,   14.531,   108.000,   14.531]
[    4,    3.000 |    6.000,    4.243,   24.000,    90.000,   36.000]
[    6,    4.000 |    4.619,    4.619,   27.713,   120.000,   55.426]
```

```
polygons1 (after emplace operations):
[  12,    0.013  |    0.007,    0.013,     0.080,   150.000,     0.001]
[  10,    0.250  |    0.162,    0.263,     1.625,   144.000,     0.203]
[   3,    0.500  |    1.732,    1.000,     5.196,    60.000,     1.299]
[   3,    1.000  |    3.464,    2.000,    10.392,    60.000,     5.196]
[   5,    2.000  |    2.906,    2.472,    14.531,   108.000,    14.531]
[   4,    3.000  |    6.000,    4.243,    24.000,    90.000,    36.000]
[   6,    4.000  |    4.619,    4.619,    27.713,   120.000,    55.426]

polygons1 (after pop operations):
[   3,    0.500  |    1.732,    1.000,     5.196,    60.000,     1.299]
[   3,    1.000  |    3.464,    2.000,    10.392,    60.000,     5.196]
[   5,    2.000  |    2.906,    2.472,    14.531,   108.000,    14.531]
[   4,    3.000  |    6.000,    4.243,    24.000,    90.000,    36.000]
[   6,    4.000  |    4.619,    4.619,    27.713,   120.000,    55.426]
```

Flat Container Adaptors

The ISO C++23 standard specifies four new flat container adaptors: std::flat_set, std::flat_multiset, std::flat_map, and std::flat_multimap. The public interfaces for these adaptor classes are roughly the same as the corresponding associative containers you studied in Chapter 7. Differences between a flat container adaptor and its counterpart associative container include

- The elements of a flat container adaptor are usually maintained in a std::vector or std::deque. The elements of an associative container are maintained using a red-black tree.

- Flat container adaptors have (worst case) linear complexity for element insertions and removals; associative containers have logarithmic complexity.

- Iterators for flat container adaptor iterators are random access; associative container iterators are bidirectional.

- Searching a flat container adaptor for an element is likely to be faster than the same element search using an associative container.

- A flat container adaptor consumes less memory than its counterpart associative container.

Flat container adaptors are best suited for use cases that favor frequent element searches over insertions and/or removals. The primary reason for this is that the elements of a flat container adaptor are stored in contiguous memory since the default underlying sequence container is a std::vector (for a std::deque, clusters of adjacent elements are often stored in contiguous memory). This improves processor cache utilization (fewer cache misses), which directly affects search performance. As I write this, none of the mainstream C++ compilers support flat container adaptors. Hopefully, this changes soon so that the putative search advantages of flat container adaptors can be substantiated using a multiplicity of real-world data types.

Summary

Here are the key learning points for this chapter:

- A std::stack container adaptor provides last-in-first-out functionality using std::stack::push() and std::stack::pop(). The stack's topmost element can be accessed using std::stack::top().

- A std::queue container adaptor provides first-in-first-out functionality using std::queue::push() and std::queue::pop(). You can use std::queue::front() or std::queue::back() to access the first or last elements of a std::queue.

- A std::priority_queue container adaptor is a queue-like entity that orders its elements using a compare function. The default compare function is std::less<>. A std::priority_queue uses this function to arrange its elements in descending order (i.e., the frontmost element is the largest). You can use std::greater<> to arrange the elements of a std::priority_queue in ascending order.

- The C++23 standard defines a new set of flat container adaptors: std::flat_set, std::flat_multiset, std::flat_map, and std::flat_multimap. Unlike their associative container counterparts, each flat container adaptor maintains its elements in a sequence container. Flat container adaptors are best suited for use cases that carry out frequent element searches relative to insertions and/or removals.

CHAPTER 10

Algorithms – Part 1

Thus far in this book, you've learned how to use a variety of STL container classes, including sequence containers, associative containers, and unordered associative containers. Modern C++ programming also mandates a comprehensive understanding of STL algorithms. This chapter commences your study of the STL algorithm library. In this chapter, you'll learn how to exploit a multiplicity of elementary and practical STL algorithms, including

- Counting algorithms
- Minimum and maximum algorithms
- Copy algorithms
- Move algorithms
- Reversal algorithms
- Replacement algorithms
- Removal algorithms
- Fill algorithms

The algorithms selected for coverage in this chapter will also prepare you for the more advanced algorithms that you'll study in later chapters.

Algorithm Primer

The STL algorithm library is an extensive collection of template functions that perform operations on containers or ranges. There are two distinct categories of STL algorithms. The first category includes those algorithms formalized by the C++11 standard. These algorithms typically carry out their operations over a range of elements that's specified by a pair of iterators. For example, execution of `std::sort(ctr.begin(), ctr.end())`

sorts the elements of container `ctr` between [`ctr.begin()`, `ctr.end()`) (i.e., all elements in `ctr`). The advantage of using iterator arguments is that it's straightforward to specify a subrange within a container over which an algorithm should operate. The downside is that, more often than not, a program wants an algorithm to carry out its actions using the container's complete collection of elements. Repeatedly designating `ctr.begin()` and `ctr.end()` for every algorithm entails lots of extra typing; it's also potentially error prone.

The second category of STL algorithms includes the range (or constrained) variants of C++20 and later, which are defined in namespace `std::ranges`. These algorithms support the use of container names as arguments. For instance, `std::ranges::sort(ctr)` sorts the elements of container `ctr`. In this example, argument `ctr` is the C++ shorthand for [`ctr.begin()`, `ctr.end()`). Most of the algorithms defined in `std::ranges` also support additional features including projections. These topics are covered in Chapter 14.

While reading this book's chapters that explain STL algorithms, you should keep in mind the following points:

- Some containers define member functions that carry out the same operation as a global algorithm. For example, to reverse the elements of a `std::list`, you could use member function `std::list::reverse()` or global algorithm `std::reverse()`. If possible, you should favor the use of container-specific algorithms since these functions are likely optimized for the container's internal data structures.

- Most C++ STL algorithms embrace multiple overloads. These overloads typically define parameters that modify an algorithm's default behavior. The source code examples of this book cover a wide variety of STL algorithm usages, but you should always consult a reliable C++ reference (see Appendix B) to learn more about additional overload options for each STL algorithm.

- An STL algorithm may not work with every container class. The driving factor is usually the type of iterators that the algorithm requires. For example, `std::sort()` requires random access iterators, which means that this algorithm can't be used with a `std::list` or `std::forward_list`. STL algorithms that modify a container's elements are often not usable with associative or unordered associative containers since these containers use an element's value to position it within a tree or hash table.

- Global algorithms defined in namespaces std and std::ranges cannot be used to add or remove elements from a container. You must use a container member function to carry out these actions.

- You should *never* make any assumptions regarding the performance of an STL algorithm vs. a custom-coded counterpart. *Always* perform benchmark testing to confirm any putative performance gains. You'll learn more about this in Chapter 16.

Counting Algorithms

Source code example Ch10_01 spotlights the use of several counting and counting-like algorithms. The first group includes algorithms std::count(), std::ranges::count(), std::count_if(), and std::ranges::count_if(). The former two count the number of element occurrences in a container, while the latter two count the number of elements that return true for a user-defined predicate function. The second group encompasses algorithms std::any_of(), std::all_of(), and std::none_of() along with the counterpart algorithms in namespace std::ranges. These algorithms apply a unary predicate to each element of a container and return true if the predicate returned true for some, all, or none of the container's elements.

Listing 10-1-1 shows the source code for example function Ch10_01_ex1(), which illustrates the use of std::count(). The opening code block of this function instantiates and initializes std::vector<int> vec1. In the next code block, the expression count10 = std::count(vec1.begin(), vec1.end(), 10) counts the number of elements in vec1 that equal 10. More specifically, std::count() counts the number of elements between [vec1.begin(), vec1.end()) that equal 10. Algorithm std::count() supports the use of container iterator subranges. For example, execution of std::count(vec1.begin() + 2, vec1.end(), 10) would skip the first two elements of vec1. Unsurprisingly, std::count() carries out its comparisons using operator== that's defined for the element type.

Listing 10-1-1. Example Ch10_01 - Ch10_01_ex1()

```cpp
//--------------------------------------------------------------------
// Ch10_01_ex.cpp
//--------------------------------------------------------------------

#include <algorithm>
#include <deque>
#include <set>
#include <vector>
#include <utility>
#include "Ch10_01.h"
#include "AminoAcid.h"
#include "MT.h"

namespace
{
    const std::initializer_list<int> c_Numbers { 10, 20, 30, -10, 40,
    50, 80, 10,
        50, -60, 10, 80, -90, 10, 80, 90, 60, 120, 90, 80, 60, 10,
        -20, -70 };
};

void Ch10_01_ex1()
{
    const char* fmt = "{:5d}";
    constexpr size_t epl_max {12};

    // using std::count with std::vector
    std::vector<int> vec1 {c_Numbers};
    MT::print_ctr("\nvec1:\n", vec1, fmt, epl_max);

    auto count10 = std::count(vec1.begin(), vec1.end(), 10);
    auto count75 = std::ranges::count(vec1, 75);
    std::println("\ncount10: {:d}", count10);
    std::println("count70: {:d}", count75);
```

```
    // using std::count with std::multiset
    // (elements ordered in ascending order)
    std::multiset<int> mset1 {c_Numbers};
    MT::print_ctr("\nmset1:\n", mset1, fmt, epl_max);

    auto count40 = std::count(mset1.begin(), mset1.end(), 40);
    auto count50 = std::ranges::count(mset1, 50);
    std::println("\ncount40: {:d}", count40);
    std::println("count80: {:d}", count50);
}
```

The flexibility of specifying a range using iterators for std::count() is convenient for less-frequent use cases. However, for the vast majority of use cases, you want algorithms like std::count() to carry out their operations using all container elements. The next statement in Ch10_01_ex1(), count75 = std::ranges::count(vec1, 75), counts the number of elements in vec1 that equal 75. In this expression, the use of variable name vec1 is basically an abbreviation for the range [vec1.begin(), vec1.end()). More importantly, note the use of namespace std::ranges. As mentioned earlier, this namespace defines constrained versions of most pre-C++20 algorithms.

The next code block in Listing 10-1-1 utilizes std::count() and std::ranges::count() to count matching elements in std::multiset<int> mset1. It's extremely important to recognize here that Ch10_01_ex1() utilizes algorithms std::count() and std::ranges::count() to count matching elements in a std::multiset just like it did in the previous code block to count matching elements in a std::vector. This is a fundamental advantage conveyed by the STL in that its algorithms can be applied to a variety of container types.

If you scan ahead to the results section for example Ch10_01, you'll notice that MT::print_ctr() printed different element orderings for vec1 and mset1. Recall that unlike a std::vector, a std::multiset orders its elements as explained in Chapter 7, and this ordering is reflected when MT::print_ctr() prints the specified container's elements using a range for loop (see Common/MT.h).

Source code example Ch10_01_ex2(), shown in Listing 10-1-2, demonstrates the use of std::count_if() and std::ranges::count_if(). The open code block of this function defines two unary predicates named neg_pred() and div30_pred(). The former returns true if x is negative, while the latter returns true if x is evenly divisible by 30. Next is the instantiation and initialization of std::deque<int> deq1.

CHAPTER 10   ALGORITHMS – PART 1

Listing 10-1-2. Example Ch10_01 – Ch10_01_ex2()

```
void Ch10_01_ex2()
{
    const char* fmt = "{:5d}";
    constexpr size_t epl_max {12};

    // predicates for std::count_if
    auto neg_pred = [](int x) { return x < 0; };
    auto div30_pred = [](int x) { return x % 30 == 0; };

    // using std::count_if
    std::deque<int> deq1 {c_Numbers};
    MT::print_ctr("\ndeq1:\n", deq1, fmt, epl_max);

    auto num_neg = std::count_if(deq1.begin(), deq1.end(), neg_pred);
    std::println("\nnum_neg: {:d}", num_neg);

    // using std::ranges::count_if
    auto num_div30 = std::ranges::count_if(deq1, div30_pred);
    std::println("num_div30: {:d}", num_div30);
}
```

Following the definitions of predicates neg_pred() and div30_pred(), Ch10_01_ex2() utilizes std::count_if(deq1.begin(), deq1.end(), neg_pred) to count the number of negative values in deq1. Like std::count(), algorithm std::count_if() can carry out its operations using an iterator subrange (e.g., std::count_if(deq1.begin() + 2, deq1.end() - 1, neg_pred)). The next code block exploits std::ranges::count_if(deq1, div30_pred) to count the number of elements in deq1 that are evenly divisible by 30.

The STL algorithm examples shown thus far have been applied to various containers holding elements of type int. Real-world applications normally incorporate numerous user-defined classes. The next example function, Ch10_01_ex3(), utilizes a user-defined class named AminoAcid.

Amino acids are the building blocks of proteins. Chemically, an amino acid contains an amino group (nitrogen and hydrogen), a central α-carbon atom, and a carboxyl group (carbon, oxygen, and hydrogen). Attached to the central α-carbon atom is a side chain of additional elements (hydrogen, carbon, nitrogen, oxygen, and sulfur) that differentiate

CHAPTER 10   ALGORITHMS – PART 1

one amino acid from another. Figure 10-1 depicts the general form of an amino acid. The human genome directly encodes 20 standard amino acids. Each standard amino acid is identified by a sanctioned name, a one-letter code, and a three-letter code. For example, amino acid glycine is recognizable in scientific literature by its name and the one- and three-letter codes G and Gly, respectively.

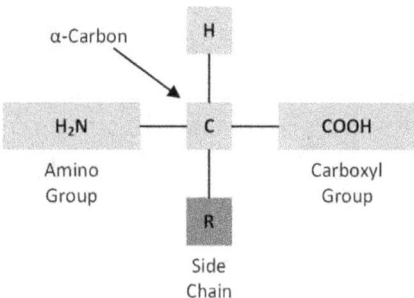

Figure 10-1. Amino acid general form

Listing 10-1-3-1 shows the source code for the definition of class AminoAcid. This class is used in Ch10_01_ex3(); it's also used in later chapters. Toward the bottom of file AminoAcid.h are the class's attributes. Note that each AminoAcid instance includes attributes m_Name, m_Code1, and m_Code3, which correspond to an amino acid's name and its two codes. Additional AminoAcid attributes include molecular mass m_MolMass and side chain (polarity) type m_SideChain. Note that enum AminoAcid::SC defines valid side chain types. Class AminoAcid's inclusion of m_MolarMass and m_SideChain were chosen as representative examples of the numerous chemical properties, both qualitative and quantitative, that characterize amino acids.

Listing 10-1-3-1. Example Ch10_01 – AminoAcid.h

```
//-------------------------------------------------------------------------
// AminoAcid.h
//-------------------------------------------------------------------------

#ifndef AMINIO_ACID_H_
#define AMINIO_ACID_H_
#include <cstddef>
#include <format>
#include <optional>
```

397

CHAPTER 10   ALGORITHMS – PART 1

```cpp
#include <string>
#include <tuple>
#include <vector>

// AA tuple <3-letter code, full name 1-letter code, molecular mass>
using AaTuple = std::tuple<std::string, std::string, char, double>;

class AminoAcid
{
    friend struct std::formatter<AminoAcid>;
    static constexpr unsigned int s_RngSeedDefault {1001};
public:
    // amino acid side chain types
    enum class SC : unsigned int
        { Unknown, Acidic, Basic, NonPolar, UnchargedPolar };

    static constexpr char BadCode1 {'?'};
    static constexpr const char* BadCode3 = "???";

    // constructors
    AminoAcid() = default;

    explicit AminoAcid(const char* name, char code1, const char* code3,
        double mol_mass, SC side_chain) : m_Name {name}, m_Code1 {code1},
        m_Code3 {code3},
        m_MolMass {mol_mass}, m_SideChain {side_chain} {};

    // accessors
    const std::string& Name() const { return m_Name; }
    char Code1() const { return m_Code1; }
    std::string Code3() const { return m_Code3; }
    double MolMass() const { return m_MolMass; }
    SC SideChain() const { return m_SideChain; }

    // operators
    friend auto operator<=>(const AminoAcid& aa1, const AminoAcid& aa2)
        { return aa1.m_Name <=> aa2.m_Name; }
    friend bool operator==(const AminoAcid& aa1, const AminoAcid& aa2)
        { return aa1.m_Name == aa2.m_Name; }
```

```cpp
    // helper functions (see AminoAcid.cpp)
    static std::optional<AminoAcid> find(char code1);
    static std::optional<AminoAcid> find(const std::string& code3);
    static bool is_valid(char code1);
    static bool is_valid(const std::string& code3);
    static char to_code1(const std::string& code3);
    static std::string to_code3(char code1);
    static std::string to_string(SC side_chain, bool short_text = true);

    // vector generators (see AminoAcid.cpp)
    static std::vector<AminoAcid> get_vector_all();
    static std::vector<char> get_vector_all_code1();
    static std::vector<std::string> get_vector_all_code3();
    static std::vector<double> get_vector_all_mol_mass();
    static std::vector<std::string> get_vector_all_name();
    static std::vector<char> get_vector_random_code1(size_t num_aa,
        unsigned int rng_seed = s_RngSeedDefault);
    static std::vector<std::string> get_vector_random_code3(size_t num_aa,
        unsigned int rng_seed = s_RngSeedDefault);
    static std::vector<AaTuple> get_vector_tuple();
private:
    std::string to_str() const;

    std::string m_Name {};              // full name
    char m_Code1 {};                    // 1-letter code
    std::string m_Code3 {};             // 3-letter code
    double m_MolMass {};                // molecular mass (g/mol)
    SC m_SideChain {SC::Unknown};       // side chain type
};

// class AminoAcid formatter
template <> struct std::formatter<AminoAcid> : std::formatter<std::string>
{
    constexpr auto parse(std::format_parse_context& fpc)
        { return fpc.begin(); }
```

```
    auto format(const AminoAcid& aa, std::format_context& fc) const
        { return std::format_to(fc.out(), "{:s}", aa.to_str()); }
};

#endif
```

Note in Listing 10-1-3-1 that class AminoAcid compares attribute m_Name during execution of operator<=> and operator==. Following the operators are the declarations for a series of helper functions and vector generator functions. More about this shortly.

Listing 10-1-3-2 shows the definition of class AminoAcid. For now, take note of these items. Near the top of file AminoAcid.cpp is an anonymous namespace that defines a std::vector<AminoAcid> of the 20 standard amino acids. About halfway down the listing are the definitions for a series of functions that begin with the prefix get_vector_. Each of these functions builds a std::vector of amino acid properties. The final function in Listing 10-1-3-2, AminoAcid::to_str(), is called by the formatter for class AminoAcid to create a std::string of an AminoAcid's attributes.

Listing 10-1-3-2. Example Ch10_01 – AminoAcid.cpp

```
//-----------------------------------------------------------------------
// AminoAcid.cpp
//-----------------------------------------------------------------------

#include <algorithm>
#include <format>
#include <optional>
#include <random>
#include "AminoAcid.h"

using SC = AminoAcid::SC;

namespace
{
    // standard amino acids
    const std::vector<AminoAcid> c_AminoAcids
    {
        AminoAcid {"Alanine",       'A', "Ala",  89.094, SC::NonPolar},
        AminoAcid {"Arginine",      'R', "Arg", 174.203, SC::Basic},
        AminoAcid {"Asparagine",    'N', "Asn", 132.119, SC::UnchargedPolar},
```

```
        AminoAcid {"AsparticAcid",    'D', "Asp", 133.104, SC::Acidic},
        AminoAcid {"Cysteine",        'C', "Cys", 121.154, SC::NonPolar},
        AminoAcid {"Glutamine",       'Q', "Gln", 146.146, SC::UnchargedPolar},
        AminoAcid {"GlutamicAcid",    'E', "Glu", 147.131, SC::Acidic},
        AminoAcid {"Glycine",         'G', "Gly",  75.067, SC::NonPolar},
        AminoAcid {"Histidine",       'H', "His", 155.156, SC::Basic},
        AminoAcid {"IsoLeucine",      'I', "Ile", 131.175, SC::NonPolar},
        AminoAcid {"Leucine",         'L', "Leu", 131.175, SC::NonPolar},
        AminoAcid {"Lysine",          'K', "Lys", 146.189, SC::Basic},
        AminoAcid {"Methionine",      'M', "Met", 149.208, SC::NonPolar},
        AminoAcid {"Phenylalanine",   'F', "Phe", 165.192, SC::NonPolar},
        AminoAcid {"Proline",         'P', "Pro", 115.132, SC::NonPolar},
        AminoAcid {"Serine",          'S', "Ser", 105.093, SC::UnchargedPolar},
        AminoAcid {"Threonine",       'T', "Thr", 119.119, SC::UnchargedPolar},
        AminoAcid {"Tryptophan",      'W', "Trp", 204.228, SC::NonPolar},
        AminoAcid {"Tyrosine",        'Y', "Tyr", 181.191, SC::UnchargedPolar},
        AminoAcid {"Valine",          'V', "Val", 117.148, SC::NonPolar},
    };
};

// helper functions
std::optional<AminoAcid> AminoAcid::find(char code1)
{
    auto pred = [code1](const AminoAcid& aa) { return aa.Code1() ==
    code1; };
    auto iter = std::ranges::find_if(c_AminoAcids, pred);
    return (iter != c_AminoAcids.end()) ? std::optional(*iter) :
    std::nullopt;
}

std::optional<AminoAcid> AminoAcid::find(const std::string& code3)
{
    auto pred = [code3](const AminoAcid& aa) { return aa.Code3() ==
    code3; };
    auto iter = std::ranges::find_if(c_AminoAcids, pred);
```

CHAPTER 10   ALGORITHMS – PART 1

```cpp
    return (iter != c_AminoAcids.end()) ? std::optional(*iter) :
    std::nullopt;
}
bool AminoAcid::is_valid(char code1)
{
    std::optional<AminoAcid> aa = AminoAcid::find(code1);
    return aa.has_value();
}
bool AminoAcid::is_valid(const std::string& code3)
{
    std::optional<AminoAcid> aa = AminoAcid::find(code3);
    return aa.has_value();
}
char AminoAcid::to_code1(const std::string& code3)
{
    std::optional<AminoAcid> aa = AminoAcid::find(code3);
    return aa.has_value() ? aa.value().Code1() : AminoAcid::BadCode1;
}
std::string AminoAcid::to_code3(char code1)
{
    std::optional<AminoAcid> aa = AminoAcid::find(code1);
    return aa.has_value() ? aa.value().Code3() : AminoAcid::BadCode3;
}
std::string AminoAcid::to_string(SC side_chain, bool short_text)
{
    switch (side_chain)
    {
        case SC::Acidic:
            return (short_text) ? "A " : "Acidic";
        case SC::Basic:
            return (short_text) ? "B " : "Basic";
        case SC::NonPolar:
            return (short_text) ? "NP" : "NonPolar";
```

```cpp
        case SC::UnchargedPolar:
            return (short_text) ? "UP" : "UnchargedPolar";
        default:
            return (short_text) ? "??" : "?????";
    }
}

// vector generators
std::vector<AminoAcid> AminoAcid::get_vector_all()
{
    return c_AminoAcids;
}

std::vector<char> AminoAcid::get_vector_all_code1()
{
    std::vector<char> amino_acids {};

    for (const AminoAcid& aa : c_AminoAcids)
        amino_acids.push_back(aa.Code1());
    return amino_acids;
}

std::vector<std::string> AminoAcid::get_vector_all_code3()
{
    std::vector<std::string> amino_acids {};

    for (const AminoAcid& aa : c_AminoAcids)
        amino_acids.push_back(aa.Code3());
    return amino_acids;
}

std::vector<double> AminoAcid::get_vector_all_mol_mass()
{
    std::vector<double> amino_acids {};

    for (const AminoAcid& aa : c_AminoAcids)
        amino_acids.push_back(aa.MolMass());
    return amino_acids;
}
```

CHAPTER 10   ALGORITHMS – PART 1

```cpp
std::vector<std::string> AminoAcid::get_vector_all_name()
{
    std::vector<std::string> amino_acids {};

    for (const AminoAcid& aa : c_AminoAcids)
        amino_acids.push_back(aa.Name());
    return amino_acids;
}

std::vector<char> AminoAcid::get_vector_random_code1(size_t num_aa,
    unsigned int rng_seed)
{
    const int dist_max = static_cast<int>(c_AminoAcids.size() - 1);
    std::mt19937 rng {rng_seed};
    std::uniform_int_distribution<int> dist {0, dist_max};

    std::vector<char> amino_acids(num_aa);

    for (size_t i = 0; i < amino_acids.size(); ++i)
        amino_acids[i] = c_AminoAcids[dist(rng)].Code1();
    return amino_acids;
}

std::vector<std::string> AminoAcid::get_vector_random_code3(size_t num_aa,
        unsigned int rng_seed)
{
    std::vector<char> amino_acids1 = get_vector_random_code1(num_aa,
    rng_seed);
    std::vector<std::string> amino_acids3{};

    for (auto aa_code1 : amino_acids1)
        amino_acids3.push_back(to_code3(aa_code1));
    return amino_acids3;
}

std::vector<AaTuple> AminoAcid::get_vector_tuple()
{
    std::vector<AaTuple> aa_vec {};
```

```
    for (const AminoAcid& aa : c_AminoAcids)
    {
        aa_vec.emplace_back(std::make_tuple(aa.m_Code3, aa.m_Name,
        aa.m_Code1,
            aa.m_MolMass));
    }

    return aa_vec;
}

// private member functions
std::string AminoAcid::to_str() const
{
    std::string s {};
    std::format_to(std::back_inserter(s), "[{:<16s}", m_Name);
    std::format_to(std::back_inserter(s), "{:c}|", m_Code1);
    std::format_to(std::back_inserter(s), "{:3s}|", m_Code3);
    std::format_to(std::back_inserter(s), "{:7.3f}|", m_MolMass);
    std::format_to(std::back_inserter(s), "{:2s}]", to_string(m_SideChain));
    return s;
}
```

Source code example Ch10_01_ex3(), shown in Listing 10-1-3-3, demonstrates the use of std::ranges::any_of(), std::ranges::all_of(), and std::ranges::none_of(). The first statement of Ch10_01_ex3() calls AminoAcid::get_vector_all().[1] The return value from this function is a std::vector<AminoAcid> that contains all 20 standard amino acids. This result is used to initialize vec1. Next is a C-style array named mm_vals that contains three molecular mass values.

Listing 10-1-3-3. *Example Ch10_01 – Ch10_01_ex3()*

```
void Ch10_01_ex3()
{
    // initialize vector of full amino acids
    std::vector<AminoAcid> vec1 {AminoAcid::get_vector_all()};
    MT::print_ctr("\nvec1:\n", vec1, "{} ", 2);
```

---

[1] You'll learn how to use the other AminoAcid::get_vector_ functions in later chapters.

```cpp
    // using std::any_of, std::all_of, std::none_of
    const double mol_mass_vals[] {75.0, 150.0, 250.0};

    for (auto mol_mass : mol_mass_vals)
    {
        auto pred_mm = [mol_mass](const AminoAcid& aa)
            { return aa.MolMass() >= mol_mass; };

        // using std::any_of, std::all_of, std::none_of
        bool b_any_of  = std::ranges::any_of(vec1, pred_mm);
        bool b_all_of  = std::ranges::all_of(vec1, pred_mm);
        bool b_none_of = std::ranges::none_of(vec1, pred_mm);

        std::println("\nMolMass >= {:.2f})", mol_mass);
        std::println("b_any_of:  {:s}", b_any_of);
        std::println("b_all_of:  {:s}", b_all_of);
        std::println("b_none_of: {:s}", b_none_of);
    }
}
```

Inside Ch10_01_ex3()'s for loop is the definition of unary lambda expression named pred_mm(). This expression returns true if aa.MolMass() is greater than captured value mol_mass. The next three statements within the for loop utilize lambda pred_mm. Execution of std::ranges::any_of(vec1, pred_mm) returns true if predicate pred_mm() is true for at least one AminoAcid object in vec1. The next statement, std::ranges::all_of(vec1, pred_mm), returns true if pred_mm() is true for all elements in vec1. Lastly, the statement std::ranges::none_of(vec1, pred_mm) returns true if pred_mm() is true for none of the elements in vec1.

The pre-C++20 counterpart functions of those demonstrated in Ch10_01_ex3() are named std::any_of(), std::all_of(), and std::none_of(). These functions carry out their respective actions using the provided iterator arguments (e.g., vec1.begin() and vec1.end()). Here are the results for example Ch10_01:

```
----- Results for example Ch10_01 -----

----- Ch10_01_ex1() -----

vec1:
```

CHAPTER 10   ALGORITHMS – PART 1

```
   10    20    30   -10    40    50    80    10    50   -60    10    80
  -90    10    80    90    60   120    90    80    60    10   -20   -70

count10:  5
count70:  0

mset1:
  -90   -70   -60   -20   -10    10    10    10    10    10    20    30
   40    50    50    60    60    80    80    80    80    90    90   120

count40:  1
count80:  2

----- Ch10_01_ex2() -----

deq1:
   10    20    30   -10    40    50    80    10    50   -60    10    80
  -90    10    80    90    60   120    90    80    60    10   -20   -70

num_neg:   5
num_div30: 8

----- Ch10_01_ex3() -----

vec1:
[Alanine          A|Ala| 89.094|NP]   [Arginine         R|Arg|174.203|B ]
[Asparagine       N|Asn|132.119|UP]   [AsparticAcid     D|Asp|133.104|A ]
[Cysteine         C|Cys|121.154|NP]   [Glutamine        Q|Gln|146.146|UP]
[GlutamicAcid     E|Glu|147.131|A ]   [Glycine          G|Gly| 75.067|NP]
[Histidine        H|His|155.156|B ]   [IsoLeucine       I|Ile|131.175|NP]
[Leucine          L|Leu|131.175|NP]   [Lysine           K|Lys|146.189|B ]
[Methionine       M|Met|149.208|NP]   [Phenylalanine    F|Phe|165.192|NP]
[Proline          P|Pro|115.132|NP]   [Serine           S|Ser|105.093|UP]
[Threonine        T|Thr|119.119|UP]   [Tryptophan       W|Trp|204.228|NP]
[Tyrosine         Y|Tyr|181.191|UP]   [Valine           V|Val|117.148|NP]

MolMass >= 75.00)
b_any_of:  true
b_all_of:  true
b_none_of: false
```

MolMass >= 150.00)
b_any_of: true
b_all_of: false
b_none_of: false

MolMass >= 250.00)
b_any_of: false
b_all_of: false
b_none_of: true

Minimum and Maximum Algorithms

Searching a container for its minimum and/or maximum element is a frequent programming task. The STL provides several straightforward algorithms that expedite the finding of a minimum and/or maximum element. Listing 10-2-1 shows the source code for example Ch10_02_ex1(). The first code block in this function utilizes RN::get_vector<double>(20) to initialize std::vector<double> vec1 with 20 random values (see Common/RN.cpp for the source code). In the next code block, execution of the statement iter_min1 = std::min_element(vec1.begin(), vec1.end()) obtains an iterator to the smallest element in vec1. Similarly, execution of iter_max1 = std::max_element(vec1.begin(), vec1.end()) returns an iterator to the largest element in vec1. The ensuing std::println() pair uses iterators iter_min1 and iter_max1 to print the actual values.

Listing 10-2-1. Example Ch10_02 – Ch10_02_ex1()

```
//---------------------------------------------------------------------
// Ch10_02_ex.cpp
//---------------------------------------------------------------------

#include <algorithm>
#include <vector>
#include "Ch10_02.h"
#include "MT.h"
#include "Nut.h"
#include "RN.h"
```

```cpp
void Ch10_02_ex1()
{
    const char* fmt = "{:7.1f} ";
    constexpr size_t epl_max {10};

    // initialize vector of doubles
    std::vector<double> vec1 = RN::get_vector<double>(20);
    MT::print_ctr("\nvec1:\n", vec1, fmt, epl_max);

    // using std::min_element and std::max_element
    auto iter_min1 = std::min_element(vec1.begin(), vec1.end());
    auto iter_max1 = std::max_element(vec1.begin(), vec1.end());
    std::println("\n*iter_min1: {:.1f}", *iter_min1);
    std::println("*iter_max1: {:.1f}", *iter_max1);

    // using std::ranges::min_element and std::ranges::max_element
    auto iter_min2 = std::ranges::min_element(vec1);
    auto iter_max2 = std::ranges::max_element(vec1);
    std::println("\n*iter_min2: {:.1f}", *iter_min2);
    std::println("*iter_max2: {:.1f}", *iter_max2);

    // using std::minmax_element, returns std::pair<iter, iter>
    auto [iter_min3, iter_max3] = std::minmax_element(vec1.begin(),
    vec1.end());
    std::println("\n*iter_min3: {:.1f}", *iter_min3);
    std::println("*iter_max3: {:.1f}", *iter_max3);

    // using std::ranges::minmax_element
    // std::ranges::minmax_element returns std::ranges::min_max_result
    auto [iter_min4, iter_max4] = std::ranges::minmax_element(vec1);
    std::println("\n*iter_min4: {:.1f}", *iter_min4);
    std::println("*iter_max4: {:.1f}", *iter_max4);
}
```

The next code block demonstrates the use of std::ranges::min_element(vec1) and std::ranges::max_element(vec1). These functions also return iterators to the minimum and maximum elements of vec1. For use cases where you need to determine both the minimum and maximum element of a container, you can exploit

CHAPTER 10   ALGORITHMS – PART 1

std::minmax_element(vec1.begin(), vec1.end()) as shown in Ch10_02_ex1(). This function returns a std::pair of iterators. Note that the code in Ch10_02_ex1() utilizes structured binding to extract the two iterators from the returned std::pair.

In the final code block of Ch10_02_ex1(), execution of the statement [iter_min4, iter_max4] = std::ranges::minmax_element(vec1) returns a structure of type std::ranges::min_max_result. Once again, structured binding is employed to extract iterators to the minimum and maximum elements. It warrants mentioning here that structure std::ranges::min_max_result contains two members named min and max. More about this shortly.

Example function Ch10_02_ex2(), shown in Listing 10-2-2, presents additional usages of std::ranges::minmax_element() using a container of type std::vector<Nut> (see Listing 5-4-1-1 for class Nut). The default comparison function used by std::ranges::minmax_element() and the other minimum/maximum finding functions of this section is std::less. For class Nut, the relational operators compare attribute Nut::m_Name.

Listing 10-2-2. Example Ch10_02 - Ch10_02_ex2()

```
void Ch10_02_ex2()
{
    const char* fmt = "{}";
    constexpr size_t epl_max {1};

    // create vector of nuts
    std::vector<Nut> nuts = Nut::get_vector();
    MT::print_ctr(Nut::title_str().c_str(), nuts, fmt, epl_max);

    // using std::ranges::minmax_element (operator<)
    // std::ranges::minmax_element returns std::ranges::min_max_result
    auto result1 = std::ranges::minmax_element(nuts);

    std::println("\nminmax_element using operator<");
    std::println("result1.min: {:s}", result1.min->Name());
    std::println("result1.max: {:s}", result1.max->Name());
```

```
    // using std::ranges::minmax_element (fat compare)
    auto cmp_fat = [](const Nut& nut1, const Nut& nut2)
        { return nut1.Fat() < nut2.Fat(); };

    auto [result2_min, result2_max] = std::ranges::minmax_element(nuts,
    cmp_fat);

    std::println("\nminmax_element using cmp_fat");
    std::println("result2_min: {:s} = {:..4f}",
        result2_min->Name(), result2_min->Fat());
    std::println("result2_max: {:s} = {:..4f}",
        result2_max->Name(), result2_max->Fat());

    // using std::ranges::minmax_element (protein compare)
    auto cmp_protein = [](const Nut& nut1, const Nut& nut2)
        { return nut1.Protein() < nut2.Protein(); };

    auto [result3_min, result3_max] = std::ranges::minmax_element(nuts,cmp_
    protein);

    std::println("\nminmax_element using cmp_protein");
    std::println("result3_min: {:s} = {:..4f}",
        result3_min->Name(), result3_min->Protein());
    std::println("result3_max: {:s} = {:..4f}",
        result3_max->Name(), result3_max->Protein());
}
```

In function Ch10_02_ex2(), execution of the statement result1 = std::ranges::minmax_element(nuts) returns a std::ranges::minmax_element. As mentioned earlier, this structure contains two members named min and max. Elements min and max can be references, copies, or iterators to elements in the target container. For the current example, result1.min and result1.max are iterators that point to the minimum and maximum elements in container nuts.

Minimum and maximum functions like std::ranges::minmax_element() define overloads that accept a user-defined binary compare function. Note in example function Ch10_02_ex2() the definition of lambda expression cmp_fat(). This expression returns nut1.Fat() < nut2.Fat(). Execution of the statement [result2_min, result2_max] = std::ranges::minmax_element(nuts, cmp_fat) obtains two iterators that point to the smallest and largest elements of nuts based on fat content.[2] In the ensuing code block, lambda expression cmp_protein() is utilized to find the smallest and largest elements of nuts based on the amount of protein.

The C++ STL also includes minimum and maximum functions that return values instead of iterators. Listing 10-2-3 shows the source code for example Ch10_02_ex3(). This function spotlights the use of std::ranges::min() and std::ranges::max(). In the current example, these functions return values of type double instead of iterators. Function Ch10_02_ex3() also demonstrates the use of std::ranges::minmax(). Following execution of result2 = std::ranges::minmax(vec1), result2.min and result2.max contain vec1's minimum and maximum values.

Listing 10-2-3. Example Ch10_02 – Ch10_02_ex3()

```
void Ch10_02_ex3()
{
    const char* fmt = "{:7.1f} ";
    constexpr size_t epl_max {10};

    // initialize vector of doubles
    std::vector<double> vec1 = RN::get_vector<double>(20);
    MT::print_ctr("\nvec1:\n", vec1, fmt, epl_max);

    // using std::ranges::min and std::ranges::max
    auto min1 = std::ranges::min(vec1);
    auto max1 = std::ranges::max(vec1);
    std::println("\nmin1: {:..1f}", min1);
    std::println("max1: {:..1f}", max1);

    // using std::ranges::minmax
    auto result2 = std::ranges::minmax(vec1);
    std::println("\nresult.min: {:..1f}", result2.min);
    std::println("result.max: {:..1f}", result2.max);
}
```

---

[2] A std::ranges projection could also be used here. You'll learn how to do this in Chapter 14.

CHAPTER 10 ALGORITHMS – PART 1

In situations where a container holds multiple instances of the same element, algorithm functions std::min_element(), std::max_element(), std::ranges::min_element(), and std::ranges::max_element() return an iterator to the first occurrence of that element in the target container. These functions also return an iterator that matches end() if the target container or range is empty. Here are the results for Ch10_02:

```
----- Results for example Ch10_02 -----

----- Ch10_02_ex1() -----

vec1:
   375.0   797.0   951.0   184.0   732.0   780.0   599.0   597.0   157.0   446.0
   156.0   100.0    59.0   460.0   867.0   334.0   602.0   143.0   709.0   651.0

*iter_min1: 59.0
*iter_max1: 951.0

*iter_min2: 59.0
*iter_max2: 951.0

*iter_min3: 59.0
*iter_max3: 951.0

*iter_min4: 59.0
*iter_max4: 951.0

----- Ch10_02_ex2() -----
Name                EnKj        EnKcal      Carbs       Fat         Protein
===========================================================================
[Almond             2423         579        21.60       49.90       21.20]
[Cashew              553         132        30.19       43.85       18.22]
[Chesnut             820         196        28.00        1.30        1.60]
[Hazelnut           2629         628        16.70       60.75       15.95]
[Pecan              2889         690        13.86       71.97        9.17]
[Pistachio          2351         562        27.51       45.39       20.27]
[Walnut             2738         654        13.71       65.21       15.23]

minmax_element using operator<
```

413

CHAPTER 10   ALGORITHMS – PART 1

```
result1.min: Almond
result1.max: Walnut

minmax_element using cmp_fat
result2_min: Chesnut = 1.3000
result2_max: Pecan = 71.9700

minmax_element using cmp_protein
result3_min: Chesnut = 1.6000
result3_max: Almond = 21.2000

----- Ch10_02_ex3() -----

vec1:
   375.0   797.0   951.0   184.0   732.0   780.0   599.0   597.0   157.0   446.0
   156.0   100.0    59.0   460.0   867.0   334.0   602.0   143.0   709.0   651.0

min1: 59.0
max1: 951.0

result.min: 59.0
result.max: 951.0
```

Copy Algorithms

Most applications need to copy elements from one container to another. The STL includes several algorithms that simplify this task. Listing 10-3-1 shows the source code for example function Ch10_03_ex1(). The opening code block of this function initializes std::array<int, 10> arr1. In the next code block, std::vector<int> vec1(arr1.size()) is constructed first. The subsequent statement, std::copy(arr1.begin(), arr1.end(), vec1.begin()), copies all elements between [arr1.begin(), arr1.end()) to vec1.begin(). Exercise care when using this form of std::copy() or std::ranges::copy(). You *must* ensure that the destination is large enough to hold all of the elements specified by the source iterators.

Listing 10-3-1. Example Ch10_03 – Ch10_03_ex1()

```cpp
//---------------------------------------------------------------------
// Ch10_03_ex.cpp
//---------------------------------------------------------------------

#include <algorithm>
#include <array>
#include <iterator>
#include <iostream>
#include <string>
#include <vector>
#include "Ch10_03.h"
#include "MT.h"
#include "Rect.h"

void Ch10_03_ex1()
{
    const char* fmt {"{:d} "};
    constexpr size_t epl_max {15};

    // create array of ints
    std::array<int, 10> arr1 {10, 20, 30, 40, 50, 60, 70, 80, 90, 100};
    MT::print_ctr("\narr1: ", arr1, fmt, epl_max);

    // using std::copy - destination iterator
    std::vector<int> vec1(arr1.size());
    std::copy(arr1.begin(), arr1.end(), vec1.begin());
    MT::print_ctr("\nvec1: ", vec1, fmt, epl_max);

    // using std:copy - std::back_inserter
    std::vector<int> vec2 {-10, 0};
    std::copy(vec1.begin(), vec1.end(), std::back_inserter(vec2));
    MT::print_ctr("\nvec2: ", vec2, fmt, epl_max);

    // using std::ranges::copy - different data types
    std::vector<double> vec3 {};
    std::ranges::copy(vec2, std::back_inserter(vec3));
    MT::print_ctr("\nvec3: ", vec3, "{:.1f} ", epl_max);
```

```cpp
    // using std::ranges::copy
    std::vector<double> vec4(vec3.size());
    std::ranges::copy(vec3, vec4.begin());
    MT::print_ctr("\nvec4: ", vec4, "{:.1f} ", epl_max);
}
```

The subsequent code block utilizes std::copy(vec1.begin(), vec1.end(), std::back_inserter(vec2)) to copy all elements in [vec1.begin(), vec1.end()) to vec2. This form of std::copy() is somewhat safer since std::back_inserter() exploits std::vector::push_back() to add new elements to vec2. The third code block in Ch10_03_ex1() utilizes std::ranges::copy(vec2, std::back_inserter(vec3)) to copy all elements from vec2 to vec3. Note here that std::vector<int> vec2 and std::vector<double> vec3 are different types. The copy works since values of type int can be safely converted to doubles.

The next example function, named Ch10_03_ex2(), highlights the use of std::copy_if(). The code for this example, shown in Listing 10-3-2, opens with an anonymous namespace that contains an initializer list of Rect objects (see Listing 5-3-2-1 for class Rect). The opening code block of Ch10_03_ex2() instantiates std::vector<Rect1> vec1 using this initializer list. Next is the definition of lambda expression copy_pred, which returns true if rect.area() is between [500,000, 4,000,000].

Listing 10-3-2. Example Ch10_03 – Ch10_03_ex2()

```cpp
namespace
{
    std::initializer_list<Rect> s_Rects
    {
        {0, 0, 640, 480},    {0, 0, 800, 600},
        {0, 0, 1024, 768},   {0, 0, 1280, 1024},
        {0, 0, 1600, 1200},  {0, 0, 1920, 1080},
        {0, 0, 3840, 2160},  {0, 0, 7680, 4320},
    };
}
```

```cpp
void Ch10_03_ex2()
{
    const char* fmt {"{} "};
    constexpr size_t epl_max {2};

    // initialize vector of Rects
    std::vector<Rect> vec1 {s_Rects};
    MT::print_ctr("\nvec1 (orginal values):\n", vec1, fmt, epl_max);

    //copy _if predicate
    auto copy_pred = [](const Rect& rect)
        { return rect.area() >= 500'000 && rect.area() <= 4'000'000; };

    // using std::copy_if
    std::vector<Rect> vec2 {};
    std::copy_if(vec1.begin(), vec1.end(), std::back_inserter(vec2),
        copy_pred);
    MT::print_ctr("\nvec2 (after copy_if):\n", vec2, fmt, epl_max);

    // using std::ranges::copy_if
    std::vector<Rect> vec3 {};
    std::ranges::copy_if(vec1, std::back_inserter(vec3), copy_pred);
    MT::print_ctr("\nvec3 (after ranges::copy_if):\n", vec3, fmt, epl_max);
}
```

Following the definition of copy_pred() is the statement std::copy_if(vec1.begin(), vec1.end(), std::back_inserter(vec2), copy_pred). During execution of this statement, copy_pred() is applied to each Rect element in vec1. If copy_pred() returns true for an element, that Rect element is copied to vec2. The next code block carries out the same operation but utilizes std::ranges::copy_if() instead of std::copy_if().

Function Ch10_03_ex3(), shown in Listing 10-3-3, demonstrates the use of std::copy_n() and std::ranges::copy_n(). Unlike the copy functions that you have seen thus far, the copy_n() variants copy exactly n elements from the specified source to the target. Note that Ch10_03_ex3() utilizes num_elem = std::distance(iter_beg, vec1.end() - 1) to calculate an arbitrary number of elements to copy.

CHAPTER 10   ALGORITHMS – PART 1

Listing 10-3-3. Example Ch10_03 - Ch10_03_ex3()

```
void Ch10_03_ex3()
{
    const char* fmt {"{} "};
    constexpr size_t epl_max {2};

    std::vector<Rect> vec1 {s_Rects};
    MT::print_ctr("\nvec1 (orginal values):\n", vec1, fmt, epl_max);

    // calculation of iter_beg and num_elem skips first and last
    elements of vec1
    auto iter_beg = vec1.begin() + 1;
    auto num_elem = std::distance(iter_beg, vec1.end() - 1);
    std::println("\nnum_elem = {}", num_elem);

    // using std::copy_n (copies n elements starting from specified
    iterator)
    std::vector<Rect> vec2 {};
    std::copy_n(iter_beg, num_elem, std::back_inserter(vec2));
    MT::print_ctr("\nvec2 (after copy_n):\n", vec2, fmt, epl_max);

    // using std::ranges::copy_n (copies n elements starting from specified
    iterator)
    std::vector<Rect> vec3 {};
    std::ranges::copy_n(iter_beg, num_elem, std::back_inserter(vec3));
    MT::print_ctr("\nvec3 (after ranges::copy_n):\n", vec3, fmt, epl_max);
}
```

The STL also includes algorithms std::copy_backward() and std::ranges::copy_backward(). These functions copy elements from the source to the destination in reverse order. Here are the results for example Ch10_03:

```
----- Results for example Ch10_03 -----

----- Ch10_03_ex1() -----

arr1: 10 20 30 40 50 60 70 80 90 100

vec1: 10 20 30 40 50 60 70 80 90 100
```

CHAPTER 10   ALGORITHMS – PART 1

vec2: -10 0 10 20 30 40 50 60 70 80 90 100

vec3: -10.0 0.0 10.0 20.0 30.0 40.0 50.0 60.0 70.0 80.0 90.0 100.0

vec4: -10.0 0.0 10.0 20.0 30.0 40.0 50.0 60.0 70.0 80.0 90.0 100.0

----- Ch10_03_ex2() -----

vec1 (orginal values):
[(0, 0, 640, 480) 307200] [(0, 0, 800, 600) 480000]
[(0, 0, 1024, 768) 786432] [(0, 0, 1280, 1024) 1310720]
[(0, 0, 1600, 1200) 1920000] [(0, 0, 1920, 1080) 2073600]
[(0, 0, 3840, 2160) 8294400] [(0, 0, 7680, 4320) 33177600]

vec2 (after copy_if):
[(0, 0, 1024, 768) 786432] [(0, 0, 1280, 1024) 1310720]
[(0, 0, 1600, 1200) 1920000] [(0, 0, 1920, 1080) 2073600]

vec3 (after ranges::copy_if):
[(0, 0, 1024, 768) 786432] [(0, 0, 1280, 1024) 1310720]
[(0, 0, 1600, 1200) 1920000] [(0, 0, 1920, 1080) 2073600]

----- Ch10_03_ex3() -----

vec1 (orginal values):
[(0, 0, 640, 480) 307200] [(0, 0, 800, 600) 480000]
[(0, 0, 1024, 768) 786432] [(0, 0, 1280, 1024) 1310720]
[(0, 0, 1600, 1200) 1920000] [(0, 0, 1920, 1080) 2073600]
[(0, 0, 3840, 2160) 8294400] [(0, 0, 7680, 4320) 33177600]

num_elem = 6

vec2 (after copy_n):
[(0, 0, 800, 600) 480000] [(0, 0, 1024, 768) 786432]
[(0, 0, 1280, 1024) 1310720] [(0, 0, 1600, 1200) 1920000]
[(0, 0, 1920, 1080) 2073600] [(0, 0, 3840, 2160) 8294400]

vec3 (after ranges::copy_n):
[(0, 0, 800, 600) 480000] [(0, 0, 1024, 768) 786432]
[(0, 0, 1280, 1024) 1310720] [(0, 0, 1600, 1200) 1920000]
[(0, 0, 1920, 1080) 2073600] [(0, 0, 3840, 2160) 8294400]

CHAPTER 10   ALGORITHMS – PART 1

Move Algorithms

In C++, `std::move()` is a helper function that facilitates the transfer of an object's resources to another object without performing a copy operation. In Chapter 1, you saw an example that utilized `std::move()` to move an object of type Image (see example Ch01_04). Listing 10-4-1 shows the source code for example Ch10_04_ex1(). This function exploits `std::move()` to move an entire container of objects. It also highlights how to move individual objects within a container.

Listing 10-4-1. Example Ch10_04 – Ch10_04_ex1()

```cpp
//------------------------------------------------------------------------
// Ch10_04_ex.cpp
//------------------------------------------------------------------------

#include <algorithm>
#include <vector>
#include "Ch10_04.h"
#include "MT.h"
#include "Image.h"

void Ch10_04_ex1()
{
    const char* fmt {"{} "};
    constexpr size_t epl_max {1};

    std::vector<Image> vec1
    {
        {640, 480}, {800, 600}, {1024, 768}, {1280, 1024},
        {1600, 1200}, {1920, 1080}, {3840, 2160}, {7680, 4320},
    };

    MT::print_ctr("\nvec1 (initial values):\n", vec1, fmt, epl_max);

    // using std::move - moves entire container
    std::vector<Image> vec2 {std::move(vec1)};
    MT::print_ctr("\nvec2 (initial values):\n", vec2, fmt, epl_max);
```

```
    // using std::move - moves container's elements
    std::vector<Image> vec3 {};

    for (auto& im : vec2)
        vec3.push_back(std::move(im));

    MT::print_ctr("\nvec2 (after std::move):\n", vec2, fmt, epl_max);
    MT::print_ctr("\nvec3 (after std::move):\n", vec3, fmt, epl_max);
}
```

Function Ch10_04_ex1() commences its execution with the definition and initialization of std::vector<Image> vec1. Following the call to MT::print_ctr() is the statement std::vector<Image> vec2 {std::move(vec1)}, whose execution moves container vec1 including all of its Image elements to vec2. Following execution of this statement, vec2 contains eight objects of type Image. The state of vec1 is undefined but prepared for any requisite processing by its destructor.

In the subsequent code block, Ch10_04_ex1() utilizes a range for loop to explicitly move each Image element in vec2 to vec3. If you scan ahead to the results section, note that vec1 contains eight default-initialized Image objects following execution of the range for loop. The reason for this is that the move assignment operator Image::operator==(Image&& im) (see Listing 1-4-2) resets the source Image following a move so that it will be properly destroyed when Image::~Image() gets executed. Also, note in the results section that vec2 now contains the eight Image objects that were moved from vec1.

Listing 10-4-2 shows the source code for example Ch10_04_ex2(). This function illustrates the use of std::swap_ranges() and std::ranges::swap_ranges(). In Ch10_04_ex2(), execution of std::swap_ranges(vec1.begin(), vec1.end(), vec2.begin()) swaps (exchanges) the Image elements of vec1 and vec2. It warrants mentioning that the behavior of std::swap_ranges() is undefined if an element swap is not possible due to an invalid iterator argument. The last code block of Ch10_04_ex2() exploits std::ranges::swap_ranges(vec1, vec3) to swap the elements of vec1 and vec3.

Listing 10-4-2. Example Ch10_04 – Ch10_04_ex2()

```
void Ch10_04_ex2()
{
    const char* fmt {"{} "};
    constexpr size_t epl_max {1};
```

```cpp
    std::vector<Image> vec1 {{10, 20}, {30, 40}, {50, 60}, {70, 80}};
    std::vector<Image> vec2 {{100, 200}, {300, 400}, {500, 600},
        {700, 800}};
    std::vector<Image> vec3 {{1000, 2000}, {3000, 4000},
        {5000, 6000}, {7000, 8000}};

    // using std::swap_ranges
    std::println("\nBefore std::swap_ranges");
    MT::print_ctr("\nvec1:\n", vec1, fmt, epl_max);
    MT::print_ctr("\nvec2:\n", vec2, fmt, epl_max);
    MT::print_ctr("\nvec3:\n", vec3, fmt, epl_max);

    std::swap_ranges(vec1.begin(), vec1.end(), vec2.begin());

    std::println("\nAfter std::swap_ranges");
    MT::print_ctr("\nvec1:\n", vec1, fmt, epl_max);
    MT::print_ctr("\nvec2:\n", vec2, fmt, epl_max);
    MT::print_ctr("\nvec3:\n", vec3, fmt, epl_max);

    // using std::ranges::swap_ranges
    std::ranges::swap_ranges(vec1, vec3);
    std::println("\nAfter std::ranges::swap_ranges");
    MT::print_ctr("\nvec1:\n", vec1, fmt, epl_max);
    MT::print_ctr("\nvec2:\n", vec2, fmt, epl_max);
    MT::print_ctr("\nvec3:\n", vec3, fmt, epl_max);
}
```

The results for example Ch10_04 follow this paragraph. This output includes minor edits (the output generated by the `std::println()` statements in Image::~Image() was removed) to improve readability.

```
----- Results for example Ch10_04 -----

----- Ch10_04_ex1() -----

vec1 (initial values):
[    640    480    307200 0x0000020DB28C00A0]
[    800    600    480000 0x0000020DB290B0C0]
[   1024    768    786432 0x0000020DB2980400]
```

```
[ 1280    1024    1310720 0x0000020DB2AC2060]
[ 1600    1200    1920000 0x0000020DB2C17060]
[ 1920    1080    2073600 0x0000020DB2DF9060]
[ 3840    2160    8294400 0x0000020DB3001060]
[ 7680    4320   33177600 0x0000020DB37FC060]

vec2 (initial values):
[  640     480     307200 0x0000020DB28C00A0]
[  800     600     480000 0x0000020DB290B0C0]
[ 1024     768     786432 0x0000020DB2980400]
[ 1280    1024    1310720 0x0000020DB2AC2060]
[ 1600    1200    1920000 0x0000020DB2C17060]
[ 1920    1080    2073600 0x0000020DB2DF9060]
[ 3840    2160    8294400 0x0000020DB3001060]
[ 7680    4320   33177600 0x0000020DB37FC060]

vec2 (after std::move):
[    0       0          0 0x0000000000000000]
[    0       0          0 0x0000000000000000]
[    0       0          0 0x0000000000000000]
[    0       0          0 0x0000000000000000]
[    0       0          0 0x0000000000000000]
[    0       0          0 0x0000000000000000]
[    0       0          0 0x0000000000000000]
[    0       0          0 0x0000000000000000]

vec3 (after std::move):
[  640     480     307200 0x0000020DB28C00A0]
[  800     600     480000 0x0000020DB290B0C0]
[ 1024     768     786432 0x0000020DB2980400]
[ 1280    1024    1310720 0x0000020DB2AC2060]
[ 1600    1200    1920000 0x0000020DB2C17060]
[ 1920    1080    2073600 0x0000020DB2DF9060]
[ 3840    2160    8294400 0x0000020DB3001060]
[ 7680    4320   33177600 0x0000020DB37FC060]
```

CHAPTER 10   ALGORITHMS – PART 1

----- Ch10_04_ex2() -----

Before std::swap_ranges

vec1:
[10   20   200 0x0000020DAF9F5D70]
[30   40   1200 0x0000020DAFAE1690]
[50   60   3000 0x0000020DAFAE1B50]
[70   80   5600 0x0000020DAFAE2720]

vec2:
[100   200   20000 0x0000020DAFA83BA0]
[300   400   120000 0x0000020DAFA889E0]
[500   600   300000 0x0000020DAFB4F480]
[700   800   560000 0x0000020DB28C00A0]

vec3:
[1000   2000   2000000 0x0000020DB260E060]
[3000   4000   12000000 0x0000020DB6045060]
[5000   6000   30000000 0x0000020DB6BCE060]
[7000   8000   56000000 0x0000020DB8872060]

After std::swap_ranges

vec1:
[100   200   20000 0x0000020DAFA83BA0]
[300   400   120000 0x0000020DAFA889E0]
[500   600   300000 0x0000020DAFB4F480]
[700   800   560000 0x0000020DB28C00A0]

vec2:
[10   20   200 0x0000020DAF9F5D70]
[30   40   1200 0x0000020DAFAE1690]
[50   60   3000 0x0000020DAFAE1B50]
[70   80   5600 0x0000020DAFAE2720]

vec3:
[1000   2000   2000000 0x0000020DB260E060]
[3000   4000   12000000 0x0000020DB6045060]

```
[ 5000  6000 30000000 0x0000020DB6BCE060]
[ 7000  8000 56000000 0x0000020DB8872060]

After std::ranges::swap_ranges

vec1:
[ 1000  2000  2000000 0x0000020DB260E060]
[ 3000  4000 12000000 0x0000020DB6045060]
[ 5000  6000 30000000 0x0000020DB6BCE060]
[ 7000  8000 56000000 0x0000020DB8872060]

vec2:
[   10    20      200 0x0000020DAF9F5D70]
[   30    40     1200 0x0000020DAFAE1690]
[   50    60     3000 0x0000020DAFAE1B50]
[   70    80     5600 0x0000020DAFAE2720]

vec3:
[  100   200    20000 0x0000020DAFA83BA0]
[  300   400   120000 0x0000020DAFA889E0]
[  500   600   300000 0x0000020DAFB4F480]
[  700   800   560000 0x0000020DB28C00A0]
```

Reversal Algorithms

Reversing the order of a container's elements is a routine programming task for many applications. The STL provides several algorithms that you can use to carry out this action. Listing 10-5-1 shows the source code for Ch10_05_ex1(). This function illustrates the use of algorithms std::reverse() and std::ranges::reverse(). These algorithms perform in-place reversals. Note in the code that std::reverse() requires two iterator arguments that specify the range. The range for std::ranges::reverse() can be specified using a container name. The iterator arguments supplied to std::reverse() must be bidirectional, which means that the elements are swappable. For std::ranges::reverse(), elements of the specified container must also be swappable.

Listing 10-5-1. Example Ch10_05 - Ch10_05_ex1()

```cpp
//-------------------------------------------------------------
// Ch10_05_ex.cpp
//-------------------------------------------------------------

#include <algorithm>
#include <string>
#include <deque>
#include "Ch10_05.h"
#include "MT.h"

namespace
{
    const std::initializer_list<std::string> s_Strings {"one", "two",
    "three",
    "four", "five", "six", "seven", "eight", "nine", "ten", "eleven",
    "twelve"};
}

void Ch10_05_ex1()
{
    const char* fmt {"{:s} "};
    constexpr size_t epl_max {15};

    // using std::reverse
    std::deque<std::string> deq1 {s_Strings};
    MT::print_ctr("\ndeq1 (initial values):\n", deq1, fmt, epl_max);
    std::reverse(deq1.begin(), deq1.end());
    MT::print_ctr("\ndeq1 (after std::reverse):\n", deq1, fmt, epl_max);

    // using std::ranges::reverse
    std::deque<std::string> deq2 {s_Strings};
    MT::print_ctr("\ndeq2 (initial values):\n", deq2, fmt, epl_max);
    std::ranges::reverse(deq2);
    MT::print_ctr("\ndeq2 (after std::ranges::reverse):\n", deq2, fmt,
    epl_max);
}
```

The STL also includes reverse-copy algorithms named std::reverse_copy() and std::ranges::reverse_copy(). The use of these functions is demonstrated in Ch10_05_ex2(), whose code is shown in Listing 10-5-2. Execution of std::reverse_copy(deq1.begin(), deq1.end(), std::back_inserter(deq2)) copies elements between [deq1.begin(), deq1.end()) in reverse order and stores them in deq2. Execution of the statement std::ranges::reverse_copy(deq1, std::back_inserter(deq3)) performs the same action.

Listing 10-5-2. Example Ch10_05 – Ch10_05_ex2()

```
void Ch10_05_ex2()
{
    const char* fmt {"{:s} "};
    constexpr size_t epl_max {15};

    std::deque<std::string> deq1 {s_Strings};
    MT::print_ctr("\ndeq1 (initial values):\n", deq1, fmt, epl_max);

    // using std::reverse_copy
    std::deque<std::string> deq2 {};
    std::reverse_copy(deq1.begin(), deq1.end(), std::back_inserter(deq2));
    MT::print_ctr("\ndeq2 (after std::reverse_copy):\n", deq2, fmt,
        epl_max);

    // using std::ranges::reverse_copy
    std::deque<std::string> deq3 {};
    std::ranges::reverse_copy(deq1, std::back_inserter(deq3));
    MT::print_ctr("\ndeq3 (after std::ranges::reverse_copy):\n", deq3,
        fmt,epl_max);
}
```

Like their non-copy counterparts, algorithms std::reverse_copy() and std::ranges::reverse_copy() require ranges that support bidirectional iterators. Also, the source and destination ranges must not overlap. The STL defines other order-altering algorithms, including rotates and shifts. You'll learn about these algorithms in Chapter 13. Here are the results for example Ch10_05:

```
----- Results for example Ch10_05 -----

----- Ch10_05_ex1() -----

deq1 (initial values):
one two three four five six seven eight nine ten eleven twelve

deq1 (after std::reverse):
twelve eleven ten nine eight seven six five four three two one

deq2 (initial values):
one two three four five six seven eight nine ten eleven twelve

deq2 (after std::ranges::reverse):
twelve eleven ten nine eight seven six five four three two one

----- Ch10_05_ex2() -----

deq1 (initial values):
one two three four five six seven eight nine ten eleven twelve

deq2 (after std::reverse_copy):
twelve eleven ten nine eight seven six five four three two one

deq3 (after std::ranges::reverse_copy):
twelve eleven ten nine eight seven six five four three two one
```

Replacement Algorithms

For many applications, a container's elements are not static. Replacements are often necessary to satisfy a functional requirement. The next source code example, named Ch10_05, spotlights the use of several STL algorithm functions that replace one or more occurrences of an element within a container.

Listing 10-6-1 shows the source code for Ch10_06_01(). This example function demonstrates the use of std::replace() and std::ranges::replace(). Following the definition and initialization of std::deque<std::string> deq1, the statement std::replace(deq1.begin(), deq1.end(), "five"s, "5"s) replaces all instances of std::string("five") in deq1 with std::string("5"). Note the use of literal suffixes in the call to std::replace(). These are required since the old and new value types must match the object type of container deq1.

Listing 10-6-1. Example Ch10_06 – Ch10_06_ex1()

```
//--------------------------------------------------------------------
// Ch10_06_ex.cpp
//--------------------------------------------------------------------
#include <algorithm>
#include <deque>
#include <format>
#include <numeric>
#include <string>
#include <vector>
#include "Ch10_06.h"
#include "MT.h"
#include "MTH.h"

using namespace std::string_literals;

namespace
{
    const std::initializer_list<std::string> s_Strings {"one", "two", "three",
    "four", "five", "six", "seven", "eight", "nine", "ten", "eleven", "twelve"};
}

void Ch10_06_ex1()
{
    const char* fmt {"{:8s} "};
    constexpr size_t epl_max {6};

    // initialize deque of strings
    std::deque<std::string> deq1 {s_Strings};
    MT::print_ctr("deq1 (initial values):\n", deq1, fmt, epl_max);
```

```cpp
    // using std::replace
    std::replace(deq1.begin(), deq1.end(), "five"s, "5"s);
    MT::print_ctr("\ndeq1 (after std::replace):\n", deq1, fmt, epl_max);

    // using std::ranges::replace
    std::deque<std::string> deq2 {deq1};
    deq2.emplace_back("ten");
    deq2.emplace_front("ten");
    MT::print_ctr("\ndeq2 (initial values):\n", deq2, fmt, epl_max);

    std::ranges::replace(deq2, "ten"s, "10"s);
    MT::print_ctr("\ndeq2 (after std::ranges::replace):\n", deq2, fmt,
    epl_max);
}
```

In Ch10_06_ex1()'s second code block, execution of std::ranges::replace(deq2, "ten"s, "10"s) replaces all instances of std::string("ten") in deq2 with std::string(s, "10").

Example function Ch10_06_ex2(), shown in Listing 10-6-2-1, opens with the definition of std::vector<ll_t> vec1(n). In this expression, ll_t is an alias for long long. Also, note here that the size of vec1 is n.

Listing 10-6-2-1. Example Ch10_06 – Ch10_06_ex2()

```cpp
void Ch10_06_ex2()
{
    using ll_t = long long;
    constexpr size_t n {40};
    const char* fmt {"{:5d} "};
    constexpr size_t epl_max {10};

    // using std::iota
    std::vector<ll_t> vec1(n);
    std::iota(vec1.begin(), vec1.end(), 0);
    MT::print_ctr("vec1 (initial values):\n", vec1, fmt, epl_max);

    // using std::replace_if
    std::replace_if(vec1.begin(), vec1.end(), MTH::is_prime<ll_t>, -999);
    MT::print_ctr("\nvec1 (after std::replace_if):\n", vec1, fmt, epl_max);
```

```
    // using std::ranges::iota (C++23)
    std::vector<ll_t> vec2(n);

#ifdef __cpp_lib_ranges_iota
    std::ranges::iota(vec2, 0);
#else
    std::iota(vec2.begin(), vec2.end(), 0);
#endif
    MT::print_ctr("\nvec2 (initial values):\n", vec2, fmt, epl_max);

    // using std::ranges::replace_if
    std::ranges::replace_if(vec2, MTH::is_prime<ll_t>, -999);
    MT::print_ctr("\nvec2 (after std::ranges::replace_if):\n", vec2,
        fmt, epl_max);
    std::println("\nstd::ranges::iota() requires C++23");
}
```

Execution of the next statement, std::iota(vec1.begin(), vec1.end(), 0), fills elements [vec1.begin(), vec1.end()) with successive values starting from zero. In the current example, std::iota() carries out the following action:

```
ll_t value = 0;

for (auto iter = vec1.begin(); iter != vec1.end(); ++iter, ++value)
    *iter = value;
```

The next code block of Ch10_06_ex2() utilizes std::replace_if(vec1.begin(), vec1.end(), MTH::is_prime<ll_t>, -999) to replace each prime number in vec1 with -999. Template function MTH::is_prime(), shown in Listing 10-6-2-2, returns true if argument x is a prime number; otherwise, it returns false.

Listing 10-6-2-2. Example Ch10_06 – MTH::is_prime()

```
template <typename T> requires std::integral<T>
bool is_prime(T x)
{
    static_assert(std::is_same_v<bool, T> == false,
        "invalid use of type bool");
```

```
    if (x == 2 || x == 3)
        return true;

    if ((x % 2 == 0) || (x % 3 == 0) || (x <= 1))
        return false;

    for (T i = 5; i * i <= x; i += 6)
    {
        if ((x % i == 0) || (x % (i + 2) == 0))
            return false;
    }

    return true;
}
```

The definition of MTH::is_prime() utilizes the C++ template constraint requires std::integral<T> to preclude the use of this template function with a non-integral type. The static_assert statement is included since type bool is an integral type.

The next two code blocks in Ch10_06_ex2() demonstrate the use of std::ranges::iota() (C++23) and std::ranges::replace_if(). Execution of these functions yields the same result as their non-std::ranges counterparts.

In Listing 10-6-3, Ch10_06_ex3() employs std::replace_copy(deq1.begin(), deq1.end(), std::back_inserter(deq2), "five"s, "5"s) to copy the elements [deq1.begin(), deq1.end()) from deq1 to deq2; it also replaces each occurrence of std::string("five") with std::string("5"). The subsequent code block in Ch10_06_ex3() utilizes std::ranges::replace_copy(deq1, std::back_inserter(deq3), "five"s, "5"s) to perform the same operation.

Listing 10-6-3. Example Ch10_06 – Ch10_06_ex3()

```
void Ch10_06_ex3()
{
    const char* fmt {"{:8s} "};
    constexpr size_t epl_max {6};

    // initialize deque of strings
    std::deque<std::string> deq1 {s_Strings};
    MT::print_ctr("deq1 (initial values):\n", deq1, fmt, epl_max);
```

```cpp
    // using std::replace_copy
    std::deque<std::string> deq2 {};
    std::replace_copy(deq1.begin(), deq1.end(), std::back_inserter(deq2),
        "five"s, "5"s);
    MT::print_ctr("\ndeq2 (after std::replace_copy):\n", deq2, fmt,
    epl_max);

    // using std::ranges::replace_copy
    std::deque<std::string> deq3 {};
    std::ranges::replace_copy(deq1, std::back_inserter(deq3),
    "five"s, "5"s);
    MT::print_ctr("\ndeq3 (after std::ranges::replace_copy):\n", deq3,
    fmt,epl_max);
}
```

Listing 10-6-4 shows the final example function of Ch10_06, which is named Ch10_06_ex4(). In this function, execution of the statement std::ranges::replace_copy_if(vec1, std::back_inserter(vec2), MTH::is_prime<ll_t>, -999) copies elements [vec1.begin(), vec1.end()) from vec1 to vec2 and replaces each prime number in vec2 with -999; vec1 is not modified.

Listing 10-6-4. Example Ch10_06 - Ch10_06_ex4()

```cpp
void Ch10_06_ex4()
{
    using ll_t = long long;
    constexpr size_t n {40};
    const char* fmt {"{:5d} "};
    constexpr size_t epl_max {10};

    // initialize vector of integers
    std::vector<ll_t> vec1(n);
#ifdef __cpp_lib_ranges_iota
    std::ranges::iota(vec1, 0);
#else
    std::iota(vec1.begin(), vec1.end(), 0);
#endif
```

CHAPTER 10   ALGORITHMS – PART 1

```
    MT::print_ctr("vec1 (initial values):\n", vec1, fmt, epl_max);

    // using std::ranges::replace_copy_if
    std::vector<ll_t> vec2 {};

    std::ranges::replace_copy_if(vec1, std::back_inserter(vec2),
        MTH::is_prime<ll_t>, -999);

    MT::print_ctr("\nvec2 (after std::ranges::replace_copy_if):\n",
        vec2, fmt, epl_max);
}
```

Here are the results for example Ch10_06:

```
----- Results for example Ch10_06 -----

----- Ch10_06_ex1() -----

deq1 (initial values):
one       two       three     four      five      six
seven     eight     nine      ten       eleven    twelve

deq1 (after std::replace):
one       two       three     four      5         six
seven     eight     nine      ten       eleven    twelve

deq2 (initial values):
ten       one       two       three     four      5
six       seven     eight     nine      ten       eleven
twelve    ten

deq2 (after std::ranges::replace):
10        one       two       three     four      5
six       seven     eight     nine      10        eleven
twelve    10

----- Ch10_06_ex2() -----

vec1 (initial values):
     0     1     2     3     4     5     6     7     8     9
    10    11    12    13    14    15    16    17    18    19
434
```

```
   20    21    22    23    24    25    26    27    28    29
   30    31    32    33    34    35    36    37    38    39
vec1 (after std::replace_if):
    0     1  -999  -999     4  -999     6  -999     8     9
   10  -999    12  -999    14    15    16  -999    18  -999
   20    21    22  -999    24    25    26    27    28  -999
   30  -999    32    33    34    35    36  -999    38    39
vec2 (initial values):
    0     1     2     3     4     5     6     7     8     9
   10    11    12    13    14    15    16    17    18    19
   20    21    22    23    24    25    26    27    28    29
   30    31    32    33    34    35    36    37    38    39
vec2 (after std::ranges::replace_if):
    0     1  -999  -999     4  -999     6  -999     8     9
   10  -999    12  -999    14    15    16  -999    18  -999
   20    21    22  -999    24    25    26    27    28  -999
   30  -999    32    33    34    35    36  -999    38    39
std::ranges::iota() requires C++23

----- Ch10_06_ex3() -----

deq1 (initial values):
one     two     three   four    five    six
seven   eight   nine    ten     eleven  twelve

deq2 (after std::replace_copy):
one     two     three   four    5       six
seven   eight   nine    ten     eleven  twelve

deq3 (after std::ranges::replace_copy):
one     two     three   four    5       six
seven   eight   nine    ten     eleven  twelve
```

```
----- Ch10_06_ex4() -----
vec1 (initial values):
    0    1    2    3    4    5    6    7    8    9
   10   11   12   13   14   15   16   17   18   19
   20   21   22   23   24   25   26   27   28   29
   30   31   32   33   34   35   36   37   38   39
vec2 (after std::ranges::replace_copy_if):
    0    1 -999 -999    4 -999    6 -999    8    9
   10 -999   12 -999   14   15   16 -999   18 -999
   20   21   22 -999   24   25   26   27   28 -999
   30 -999   32   33   34   35   36 -999   38   39
```

Removal Algorithms

For many applications, it is often necessary to remove (or erase) elements from a container. In Chapters 3 and 4, you saw examples of the so-called erase-remove idiom that removed elements from a `std::vector` and `std::deque` (see examples Ch03_03 and Ch04_01). The examples of this section demonstrate additional erase-remove techniques including template usages that carry out element removals using different template types.

Listing 10-7-1 shows the source code for example `Ch10_07_ex1()`. This example demonstrates the proper use of the erase-remove idiom using `std::remove_if()`. Near the top of Listing 10-7-1 is the definition of a template function named `ch10_remove_if_and_erase()`. This template function requires argument `T& ctr` to be a sequence container that defines `ctr.erase()`.

Listing 10-7-1. Example Ch10_07 – Ch10_07_ex1()

```cpp
//------------------------------------------------------------------
// Ch10_07_ex.cpp
//------------------------------------------------------------------

#include <algorithm>
#include <deque>
#include <forward_list>
```

```cpp
#include <list>
#include <numeric>
#include <string>
#include <vector>
#include "Ch10_07.h"
#include "MT.h"
#include "MTH.h"

template <class T>
void ch10_remove_if_and_erase(const char* msg, T& ctr)
{
    const char* fmt {"{:4d} "};
    constexpr size_t epl_max {15};

    // using std::remove_if and ctr.erase (erase-remove idiom)
    std::print("{:s} - before std::remove_if", msg);
    MT::print_ctr("\n", ctr, fmt, epl_max);

    auto iter = std::remove_if(ctr.begin(), ctr.end(),
        MTH::is_prime<typename T::value_type>);

    auto num_erased = std::distance(iter, ctr.end());

    ctr.erase(iter, ctr.end());

    std::print("{:s} - after ctr.erase", msg);
    MT::print_ctr("\n", ctr, fmt, epl_max);
    std::println("num_erased: {:d}", num_erased);
}

void Ch10_07_ex1()
{
    using ll_t = long long;
    constexpr size_t n {30};

    // using ch10_remove_and_erase_if with different sequence containers
    std::vector<ll_t> vec1(n);
    std::iota(vec1.begin(), vec1.end(), 0);
    ch10_remove_if_and_erase("\nvec1", vec1);
```

```
    std::deque<ll_t> deq1(n);
    std::iota(deq1.begin(), deq1.end(), n);
    ch10_remove_if_and_erase("\ndeq1", deq1);

    std::list<ll_t> list1(n);
    std::iota(list1.begin(), list1.end(), n * 2);
    ch10_remove_if_and_erase("\nlist1", list1);
}
```

In template function ch10_remove_if_and_erase(), execution of the statement iter = std::remove_if(ctr.begin(), ctr.end(), MTH::is_prime<typename T::value_type>) "removes" all prime numbers from container ctr (see Listing 10-6-2-2 for MTH::is_prime()'s source code). Recall from the discussions in Chapters 3 and 4 that std::remove() doesn't actually remove any elements from the specified container; it merely shifts retained elements toward the container's front. Execution of std::remove_if() is almost the same except that predicate function MTH::is_prime() determines which elements to remove (true) or retain (false). Note that std::remove_if() returns an "end" iterator. This iterator can be used to calculate the number of removed elements as demonstrated by the statement num_erased = std::distance(iter, ctr.end()).

The iterator returned by remove_if() is also needed to actually delete the removed elements from ctr. Execution of the statement ctr.erase(iter, ctr.end()) carries out this action. Figure 10-2 illustrates the erase-remove idiom actions of template function ch10_remove_if_erase() in greater detail. The element movements shown in this figure are fundamentally the same as the ones you saw in Chapter 3 (see Figure 3-5). It's important to fully understand the erase-remove idiom since its use is ubiquitous in pre-C++20 code. Example function Ch10_07_ex1(), also shown in Listing 10-7-1, exercises ch10_remove_if_and_erase() using various container types.

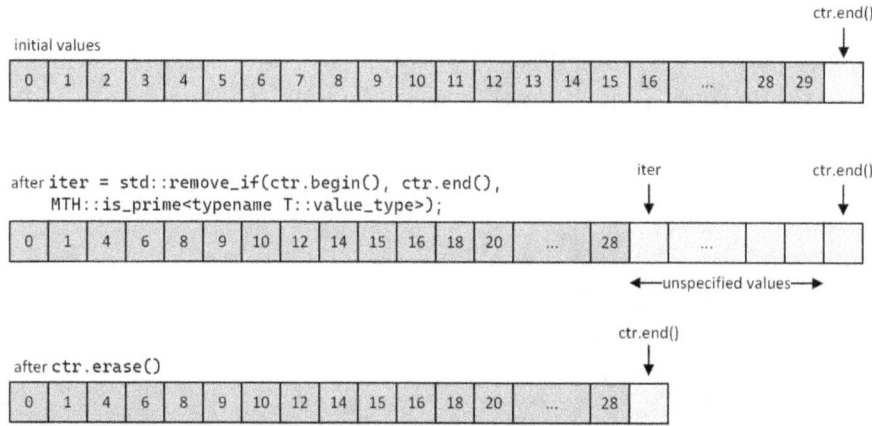

Figure 10-2. Execution of erase-remove idiom

Example function Ch10_07_ex2(), shown in Listing 10-7-2, utilizes template function ch10_erase_if() to remove elements from various container types. In ch10_erase_if(), execution of the statement num_erased = std::erase_if(ctr, MTH::is_prime<typename T::value_type>) erases all prime numbers from container ctr. No additional STL algorithm calls are necessary. The STL defines non-member overloads of std::erase_if() (and std::erase()) for all sequence containers, associative containers, and unordered associative containers. For new code, you should favor the use of either std::erase() or std::erase_if() instead of the pre-C++20 erase-remove idiom that requires explicit coding of distinct remove and erase functions.

Listing 10-7-2. Example Ch10_07 – Ch10_07_ex2()

```
template <class T> requires std::forward_iterator<typename T::iterator>
void ch10_erase_if(const char* msg, T& ctr)
{
    const char* fmt {"{:4d} "};
    constexpr size_t epl_max {15};

    // using std::erase_if (C++20)
    std::print("{:s} - before std::erase_if", msg);
    MT::print_ctr("\n", ctr, fmt, epl_max);

    auto num_erased = std::erase_if(ctr, MTH::is_prime<typename
    T::value_type>);
```

```cpp
        std::print("{:s} - after std::erase_if", msg);
        MT::print_ctr("\n", ctr, fmt, epl_max);
        std::println("num_erased: {:d}", num_erased);
    }

    void Ch10_07_ex2()
    {
    #ifdef __cpp_lib_ranges_iota
        using ll_t = long long;
        constexpr size_t n {30};

        // using ch10_erase_if with different sequence containers
        std::vector<ll_t> vec1(n);
        std::ranges::iota(vec1, 0);
        ch10_erase_if("\nvec1", vec1);

        std::deque<ll_t> deq1(n);
        std::ranges::iota(deq1, n);
        ch10_erase_if("\ndeq1", deq1);

        std::list<ll_t> list1(n);
        std::ranges::iota(list1, n * 2);
        ch10_erase_if("\nlist1", list1);

        std::forward_list<ll_t> fw_list1(n);
        std::ranges::iota(fw_list1, n * 3);
        ch10_erase_if("\nfw_list1", fw_list1);
    #else
        std::println("Ch10_07_ex2() requires __cpp_lib_ranges_iota (C++23)");
    #endif
    }
```

Here are the results for example Ch10_07:

```
----- Results for example Ch10_07 -----

----- Ch10_07_ex1() -----
vec1 - before std::remove_if
   0    1    2    3    4    5    6    7    8    9   10   11   12   13   14
  15   16   17   18   19   20   21   22   23   24   25   26   27   28   29
vec1 - after ctr.erase
   0    1    4    6    8    9   10   12   14   15   16   18   20   21   22
  24   25   26   27   28
num_erased: 10
deq1 - before std::remove_if
  30   31   32   33   34   35   36   37   38   39   40   41   42   43   44
  45   46   47   48   49   50   51   52   53   54   55   56   57   58   59
deq1 - after ctr.erase
  30   32   33   34   35   36   38   39   40   42   44   45   46   48   49
  50   51   52   54   55   56   57   58
num_erased: 7
list1 - before std::remove_if
  60   61   62   63   64   65   66   67   68   69   70   71   72   73   74
  75   76   77   78   79   80   81   82   83   84   85   86   87   88   89
list1 - after ctr.erase
  60   62   63   64   65   66   68   69   70   72   74   75   76   77   78
  80   81   82   84   85   86   87   88
num_erased: 7

----- Ch10_07_ex2() -----
vec1 - before std::erase_if
   0    1    2    3    4    5    6    7    8    9   10   11   12   13   14
  15   16   17   18   19   20   21   22   23   24   25   26   27   28   29
```

```
vec1 - after std::erase_if
    0    1    4    6    8    9   10   12   14   15   16   18   20   21   22
   24   25   26   27   28
num_erased: 10

deq1 - before std::erase_if
   30   31   32   33   34   35   36   37   38   39   40   41   42   43   44
   45   46   47   48   49   50   51   52   53   54   55   56   57   58   59

deq1 - after std::erase_if
   30   32   33   34   35   36   38   39   40   42   44   45   46   48   49
   50   51   52   54   55   56   57   58
num_erased: 7

list1 - before std::erase_if
   60   61   62   63   64   65   66   67   68   69   70   71   72   73   74
   75   76   77   78   79   80   81   82   83   84   85   86   87   88   89

list1 - after std::erase_if
   60   62   63   64   65   66   68   69   70   72   74   75   76   77   78
   80   81   82   84   85   86   87   88
num_erased: 7

fw_list1 - before std::erase_if
   90   91   92   93   94   95   96   97   98   99  100  101  102  103  104
  105  106  107  108  109  110  111  112  113  114  115  116  117  118  119

fw_list1 - after std::erase_if
   90   91   92   93   94   95   96   98   99  100  102  104  105  106  108
  110  111  112  114  115  116  117  118  119
num_erased: 6
```

Fill Algorithms

Another universal programming action in many applications is to set all elements in a container to the same value. For these use cases, you can employ std::fill(), std::ranges::fill(), std::fill_n(), or std::ranges::fill_n(). Listing 10-8-1 shows the source code for example Ch10_08_ex1(). This example spotlights the use of std::fill() and std::ranges::fill().

Listing 10-8-1. Example Ch10_08 – Ch10_08_ex1()

```cpp
//------------------------------------------------------------------------
// Ch10_08_ex.cpp
//------------------------------------------------------------------------
#include <algorithm>
#include <numeric>
#include <vector>
#include "Ch10_08.h"
#include "MT.h"
#include "Rect.h"

namespace
{
    const std::vector<Rect> s_Rectangles
    {
        {0, 0, 640, 480}, {0, 0, 800, 600}, {0, 0, 1024, 768},
        {0, 0, 1280, 1024}, {0, 0, 1600, 1200}, {0, 0, 1920, 1080},
        {0, 0, 3840, 2160}, {0, 0, 7680, 4320}
    };
}

void Ch10_08_ex1()
{
    const char* fmt {"{:4d} "};
    constexpr size_t epl_max {10};

    // using std::fill
    std::vector<int> vec1(10);
    MT::print_ctr("vec1 (initial values):\n", vec1, fmt, epl_max);
```

```
    std::fill(vec1.begin(), vec1.end(), -1);
    MT::print_ctr("\nvec1 (after std::fill):\n", vec1, fmt, epl_max);

    // using std::ranges::fill
    std::vector<int> vec2(10);
    MT::print_ctr("\nvec2 (initial values):\n", vec2, fmt, epl_max);

    std::ranges::fill(vec2, -2);
    MT::print_ctr("\nvec1 (after std::ranges::fill):\n", vec2, fmt,
    epl_max);
}
```

In Listing 10-8-1, execution of std::fill(vec1.begin(), vec1.end(), -1) sets each element in [vec1.begin(), vec1.end()) to -1. The ensuing code block utilizes std::ranges::fill(vec2, -2) to set each element in [vec2.begin(), vec2.end()) to -2.

Function Ch10_08_ex2(), shown in Listing 10-8-2, demonstrates the use of std::fill() and std::ranges::fill() with user-defined class Rect (see Listing 5-3-2-1).

Listing 10-8-2. Example Ch10_08 – Ch10_08_ex2()

```
void Ch10_08_ex2()
{
    const char* fmt {"{} "};
    constexpr size_t epl_max {2};
    const Rect fill_val {0, 0, 96, 72};

    // using std::fill
    std::vector<Rect> vec1 {s_Rectangles};
    MT::print_ctr("vec1 (initial values):\n", vec1, fmt, epl_max);
    std::fill(vec1.begin(), vec1.end(), fill_val);
    MT::print_ctr("\nvec1 (after std::fill):\n", vec1, fmt, epl_max);

    // using std::ranges::fill
    std::vector<Rect> vec2 {s_Rectangles};
    MT::print_ctr("\nvec2 (initial values):\n", vec2, fmt, epl_max);
    std::ranges::fill(vec2, fill_val);
    MT::print_ctr("\nvec2 (after std::fill):\n", vec2, fmt, epl_max);
}
```

Listing 10-8-3 shows the final fill example. In function Ch10_08_ex3(), execution of the statement std::ranges::fill_n(iter_beg, num_elem, Rect{10, 20, 30, 40}) copy-assigns Rect{10, 20, 30, 40} to each [iter, iter + num_elem) element. You can also use std::fill_n() to perform the same action.

Listing 10-8-3. Example Ch10_08 – Ch10_08_ex3()

```
void Ch10_08_ex3()
{
    const char* fmt {"{} "};
    constexpr size_t epl_max {2};

    std::vector<Rect> vec1 {s_Rectangles};
    MT::print_ctr("vec1 (initial values):\n", vec1, fmt, epl_max);

    // using std::ranges::fill_n
    auto iter_beg = vec1.begin() + 1;
    auto num_elem = std::distance(vec1.begin() + 1, vec1.end() - 1);
    std::println("\nnum_elem = {:d}", num_elem);
    std::ranges::fill_n(iter_beg, num_elem, Rect{10, 20, 30, 40});
    MT::print_ctr("\nvec1 (after std::fill_n):\n", vec1, fmt, epl_max);
}
```

Here are the results for source code example Ch10_08:

```
----- Results for example Ch10_08 -----

----- Ch10_08_ex1() -----
vec1 (initial values):
  0    0    0    0    0    0    0    0    0    0
vec1 (after std::fill):
  -1   -1   -1   -1   -1   -1   -1   -1   -1   -1
vec2 (initial values):
  0    0    0    0    0    0    0    0    0    0
vec1 (after std::ranges::fill):
  -2   -2   -2   -2   -2   -2   -2   -2   -2   -2
```

CHAPTER 10   ALGORITHMS – PART 1

----- Ch10_08_ex2() -----

vec1 (initial values):
[(0, 0, 640, 480) 307200] [(0, 0, 800, 600) 480000]
[(0, 0, 1024, 768) 786432] [(0, 0, 1280, 1024) 1310720]
[(0, 0, 1600, 1200) 1920000] [(0, 0, 1920, 1080) 2073600]
[(0, 0, 3840, 2160) 8294400] [(0, 0, 7680, 4320) 33177600]

vec1 (after std::fill):
[(0, 0, 96, 72) 6912] [(0, 0, 96, 72) 6912]
[(0, 0, 96, 72) 6912] [(0, 0, 96, 72) 6912]
[(0, 0, 96, 72) 6912] [(0, 0, 96, 72) 6912]
[(0, 0, 96, 72) 6912] [(0, 0, 96, 72) 6912]

vec2 (initial values):
[(0, 0, 640, 480) 307200] [(0, 0, 800, 600) 480000]
[(0, 0, 1024, 768) 786432] [(0, 0, 1280, 1024) 1310720]
[(0, 0, 1600, 1200) 1920000] [(0, 0, 1920, 1080) 2073600]
[(0, 0, 3840, 2160) 8294400] [(0, 0, 7680, 4320) 33177600]

vec2 (after std::fill):
[(0, 0, 96, 72) 6912] [(0, 0, 96, 72) 6912]
[(0, 0, 96, 72) 6912] [(0, 0, 96, 72) 6912]
[(0, 0, 96, 72) 6912] [(0, 0, 96, 72) 6912]
[(0, 0, 96, 72) 6912] [(0, 0, 96, 72) 6912]

----- Ch10_08_ex3() -----

vec1 (initial values):
[(0, 0, 640, 480) 307200] [(0, 0, 800, 600) 480000]
[(0, 0, 1024, 768) 786432] [(0, 0, 1280, 1024) 1310720]
[(0, 0, 1600, 1200) 1920000] [(0, 0, 1920, 1080) 2073600]
[(0, 0, 3840, 2160) 8294400] [(0, 0, 7680, 4320) 33177600]

num_elem = 6

```
vec1 (after std::fill_n):
[(0, 0, 640, 480) 307200] [(10, 20, 30, 40) 1200]
[(10, 20, 30, 40) 1200] [(10, 20, 30, 40) 1200]
[(10, 20, 30, 40) 1200] [(10, 20, 30, 40) 1200]
[(10, 20, 30, 40) 1200] [(0, 0, 7680, 4320) 33177600]
```

Summary

Here are the key learning points for this chapter:

- The C++ STL includes an extensive collection of algorithms that carry out operations using containers or ranges of elements.

- Algorithms std::count() and std::ranges::count() count the number of container/range elements that match a specified value. Algorithms std::count_if() and std::ranges::count_if() count the number of elements that return true for a specified predicate.

- Algorithms std::min_element(), std::ranges::min_element(), std::max_element(), and std::ranges::max_element() return iterators to the minimum or maximum elements in a range. Algorithms std::minmax_element() and std::ranges::minmax_element() return iterators to both the minimum and maximum elements. Algorithms std::ranges::min() and std::ranges::max() return values instead of iterators.

- Copy operations can be carried out using algorithms std::copy(), std::ranges::copy(), std::copy_if(), and std::ranges::copy_if().

- Helper function std::move() prepares an object to facilitate transfer of its resources to another object.

- Algorithms std::reverse() and std::ranges::reverse() reverse the ordering of a container's elements. Algorithms std::reverse_copy() and std::ranges::reverse_copy() generate reverse-ordered copies of a range.

- Element replacements can be performed using std::replace() and std::ranges::replace(). Predicate-controlled element replacements can be achieved using std::replace_if() or std::ranges::replace_if().

- Algorithms std::remove() and std::ranges::remove() remove all instances of an element from a container. You can also use std::remove_if() and std::ranges::remove_if() to perform predicate-controlled element removals. When necessary, use a container's erase() function to complete the erase-remove idiom. For applications developed using C++20 or later, you can use std::erase() or std::erase_if() instead of a removal function.

- Algorithms std::fill() and std::ranges::fill() set every element in a container or range to the same value. You can also use std::fill_n() and std::ranges::fill_n() to fill a sequence of n elements.

CHAPTER 11

Algorithms – Part 2

This chapter is a continuation of the previous chapter. It covers additional STL algorithms, including

- For_Each algorithms
- Transformation algorithms
- Generation algorithms
- Find algorithms
- Contains algorithms
- Search algorithms
- Accumulate and fold algorithms

Some sections in this chapter only cover the C++20/23 algorithms of namespace `std::ranges`. However, you should keep in mind that many of these algorithms also have pre-C++20 counterparts in namespace `std`. You should also keep in mind that most STL algorithms define multiple overloads. Always review all possible options and select the most appropriate overload for each use case.

For_Each Algorithms

A for_each algorithm applies a function object to each dereferenced iterator in a range. These algorithms are sometimes utilized as an alternative to an explicitly coded range for loop. Listing 11-1-1 shows the source code for example `Ch11_01_ex1()`. This example illustrates the use of `std::for_each()` and `std::ranges::for_each()`.

CHAPTER 11   ALGORITHMS – PART 2

Listing 11-1-1. Example Ch11_01 - Ch11_01_ex1()

```
//--------------------------------------------------------------------
// Ch11_01_ex.cpp
//--------------------------------------------------------------------

#include <algorithm>
#include <array>
#include <cmath>
#include <numbers>
#include <numeric>
#include "Ch11_01.h"
#include "MT.h"

void Ch11_01_ex1()
{
    using namespace std::numbers;
    const char* fmt = "{:9.2f} ";
    size_t epl_max {8};

    // initialize test array of radii
    std::array<double, 8> radii {};
    std::iota(radii.begin(), radii.end(), 1);
    MT::print_ctr("sphere radii:\n", radii, fmt, epl_max);

    // using std::for_each to print sphere areas
    auto sphere_area = [](double r)
        { std::print("{:9.2f} ", 4.0 * pi * r * r); };

    std::println("\nsphere surface areas:");
    std::for_each(radii.begin(), radii.end(), sphere_area);
    std::println("");

    // using std::ranges::for_each to print sphere volumes
    auto sphere_vol = [](double r)
        { std::print("{:9.2f} ", 4.0 * pi * r * r * r / 3.0); };
```

```
    std::println("\nsphere volumes:");
    std::ranges::for_each(radii, sphere_vol);
    std::println("");
}
```

The first code block in Ch11_01_ex1() uses std::iota() to initialize std::array<double, 8> radii. In the subsequent code block, Ch11_01_ex1() defines sphere_area(), which calculates and prints the surface area of a sphere using the supplied radius argument. In the same code block, the statement std::for_each(radii.begin(), radii.end(), sphere_area) applies sphere_area() to each dereferenced iterator in [radii.begin(), radii.end()). In the current example, execution of std::for_each() does not modify the values in array radii since radius r is passed by value to sphere_area(). The final code block of Ch11_01_ex1() utilizes std::ranges::for_each() with function object sphere_vol() to calculate sphere volumes. Note here that std::ranges::for_each() employs container name radii for the range argument.

Example Ch11_01_ex2(), shown in Listing 11-1-2, spotlights the use of std::for_each_n() and std::ranges::for_each_n(). These STL algorithms are used to calculate and print octahedron surface areas and volumes using various edge lengths. Note that both std::for_each_n() and std::ranges_for_each_n() specify the target range using a begin iterator and element count.

Listing 11-1-2. Example Ch11_01 - Ch11_01_ex2()

```
void Ch11_01_ex2()
{
    using namespace std::numbers;
    const char* fmt = "{:9.2f} ";
    size_t epl_max {8};

    // initialize test array of edge lengths
    std::array<double, 8> edge_lengths {};
    std::iota(edge_lengths.begin(), edge_lengths.end(), 1);
    MT::print_ctr("octahedron edge lengths:\n", edge_lengths, fmt,
        epl_max);
```

CHAPTER 11   ALGORITHMS – PART 2

```
    // using std::for_each_n to print octahedron areas
    auto octahedron_area = [](double el)
        { std::print("{:9.2f} ", 2.0 * sqrt3 * el * el); };

    std::println("\noctahedron surface areas:");
    std::for_each_n(edge_lengths.begin(), edge_lengths.size(),
        octahedron_area);
    std::println("");

    // using std::ranges::for_each_n to print octahedron volumes
    auto octahedron_vol = [](double el)
        { std::print("{:9.2f} ", sqrt2 * el * el * el / 3.0); };

    std::println("\noctahedron volumes:");
    std::ranges::for_each_n(edge_lengths.begin(), edge_lengths.size(),
        octahedron_vol);
    std::println("");
}
```

Listing 11-1-3 shows source code for function Ch11_01_ex3(). Note that lambda expression dodecahedron_area() specifies an argument of type double& instead of double. Also, note that dodecahedron_area() calculates x *= 15.0 * phi / std::sqrt(3.0 - phi). The use of a reference here means that following execution of std::ranges::for_each(areas, dodecahedron_area), std::array<double, 8> areas contains calculated dodecahedron areas instead of edge lengths.

Listing 11-1-3. Example Ch11_01 – Ch11_01_ex3()

```
void Ch11_01_ex3()
{
    using namespace std::numbers;
    const char* fmt = "{:9.2f} ";
    size_t epl_max {8};

    // using std::ranges::for_each to calculate dodecahedron areas
    std::array<double, 8> areas {};
    std::iota(areas.begin(), areas.end(), 1);
    MT::print_ctr("dodecahedron edge lengths:\n", areas, fmt, epl_max);
```

452

```
    auto dodecahedron_area = [](double& x)
        { x *= 15.0 * phi / std::sqrt(3.0 - phi); };

    std::ranges::for_each(areas, dodecahedron_area);
    MT::print_ctr("\ndodecahedron surface areas:\n", areas, fmt, epl_max);

    // using std::ranges::for_each to calculate dodecahedron volumes
    std::array<double, 8> volumes {};
    std::iota(volumes.begin(), volumes.end(), 1);

    auto dodecahedron_vol = [](double& x)
        { x *= 5.0 * phi * phi * phi / (6.0 - 2.0 * phi); };

    std::ranges::for_each(volumes, dodecahedron_vol);
    MT::print_ctr("\ndodecahedron volumes:\n", volumes, fmt, epl_max);
}
```

The second code block in Ch11_01_ex3() utilizes dodecahedron_vol() and std::ranges::for_each() to compute dodecahedron volumes. Like the area calculation, std::array<double, 8> volumes contains dodecahedron volumes instead of edge lengths following execution of std::ranges::for_each(). Here are the results for example Ch11_01:

```
----- Results for example Ch11_01 -----

----- Ch11_01_ex1() -----

sphere radii:
     1.00      2.00      3.00      4.00      5.00      6.00      7.00      8.00
sphere surface areas:
    12.57     50.27    113.10    201.06    314.16    452.39    615.75    804.25
sphere volumes:
     4.19     33.51    113.10    268.08    523.60    904.78   1436.76   2144.66
----- Ch11_01_ex2() -----
```

octahedron edge lengths:
```
     1.00       2.00       3.00       4.00       5.00       6.00       7.00       8.00
```
octahedron surface areas:
```
     3.46      13.86      31.18      55.43      86.60     124.71     169.74     221.70
```
octahedron volumes:
```
     0.47       3.77      12.73      30.17      58.93     101.82     161.69     241.36
```
----- Ch11_01_ex3() -----

dodecahedron edge lengths:
```
     1.00       2.00       3.00       4.00       5.00       6.00       7.00       8.00
```
dodecahedron surface areas:
```
    20.65      41.29      61.94      82.58     103.23     123.87     144.52     165.17
```
dodecahedron volumes:
```
     7.66      15.33      22.99      30.65      38.32      45.98      53.64      61.30
```

It warrants mentioning that all of the std::for_each() algorithms shown in example Ch11_01 ignore any value returned by the supplied lambda expression. For use cases where a return value is advantageous, a transformation algorithm can be applied as discussed in the next section.

Transformation Algorithms

A transformation algorithm applies a unary or binary function object to one or two input ranges. The result of each function object calculation is then saved to an output range. Listing 11-2-1 shows the source code for example function Ch11_02_ex1(). This function exemplifies the use of std::transform() and std::ranges::transform().

Listing 11-2-1. Example Ch11_02 - Ch11_02_ex1()

```cpp
//--------------------------------------------------------------------
// Ch11_02_ex.cpp
//--------------------------------------------------------------------

#include <algorithm>
#include <deque>
#include <list>
#include <numbers>
#include <numeric>
#include <vector>
#include "Ch11_02.h"
#include "AminoAcid.h"
#include "MF.h"
#include "MT.h"

void Ch11_02_ex1()
{
    using namespace std::numbers;
    const char* fmt {"{:9.2f} "};
    constexpr size_t epl_max {8};

    // create test vector of radii
    std::vector<double> radii(8);
    std::iota(radii.begin(), radii.end(), 1);
    MT::print_ctr("sphere radii:\n", radii, fmt, epl_max);

    // using std::transform
    std::vector<double> areas(radii.size());
    auto sphere_area = [](double r) { return 4.0 * pi * r * r; };
    std::transform(radii.begin(), radii.end(), areas.begin(), sphere_area);
    MT::print_ctr("\nsphere surface areas:\n", areas, fmt, epl_max);

    // using std::ranges::transform
    std::vector<double> volumes(radii.size());
    auto sphere_vol = [](double r) { return 4.0 * pi * r * r * r / 3.0; };
```

CHAPTER 11 ALGORITHMS – PART 2

```
    std::ranges::transform(radii, volumes.begin(), sphere_vol);
    MT::print_ctr("\nsphere volumes:\n", volumes, fmt, epl_max);
}
```

Example function Ch11_02_ex1() opens with the definition of std::vector<double> radii(8). The subsequent statement utilizes std::iota() to initialize the elements of radii. The definition of lambda expression sphere_area() follows. Note that this function object calculates and *returns* the surface area for a sphere of radius r. In the expression std::transform(radii.begin(), radii.end(), areas.begin(), sphere_area), the first two arguments – radii.begin() and radii.end() – specify an input range. Argument areas.begin() designates the first position of an output range. Note that the size of areas must equal or exceed the size of radii. The current use of std::transform() applies sphere_area() to each radius element in [radii.begin(), radii.end()) and saves each calculated area to the corresponding position in [areas.begin(), areas.end()).

In the ensuing code block, the expression std::ranges::transform(radii, volumes.begin(), sphere_vol) calculates sphere volumes and saves these values in std::vector<double> volumes. Like other std::ranges examples that you've already seen, container name radii specifies the input range for std::ranges::transform().

Example function Ch11_02_ex2(), shown in Listing 11-2-2, starts with the definition std::vector<char> aa1 that contains single-letter lowercase codes for several amino acids. In the subsequent code block, execution of std::ranges::transform(aa1, aa1.begin(), tr_op1) applies tr_op1() to each element in aa1. Note that the output iterator in this expression is aa1.begin(), which means that the current use of std::ranges::transform() performs an in-place lower-to-uppercase transformation of the single-letter codes in aa1.

Listing 11-2-2. Example Ch11_02 – Ch11_02_ex2()

```
void Ch11_02_ex2()
{
    const char* fmt1 {"'{:c}' "};
    const char* fmt3 {"'{:3s}' "};
    constexpr size_t epl_max {12};
```

```
    // test sequence of amino acid codes (non-standard lower case)
    // (code 'x' is intentionally invalid)
    std::vector<char> aa1 {'a', 'g', 'l', 't', 'v', 'p', 'f', 'n', 'x',
    'c', 'd'};
    MT::print_ctr("aa1 (initial values)\n", aa1, fmt1, epl_max);

    // using std::ranges::transform (inplace transformation)
    auto tr_op1 = [](char aa) { return MF::to_upper(aa); };
    std::ranges::transform(aa1, aa1.begin(), tr_op1);
    MT::print_ctr("\naa1 (after tansformation):\n", aa1, fmt1, epl_max);

    // using std::ranges::transform (non-inplace transformation)
    auto tr_op2 = [](char aa) { return AminoAcid::to_code3(aa); };
    std::deque<std::string> aa3 {};
    std::ranges::transform(aa1, std::back_inserter(aa3), tr_op2);
    MT::print_ctr("\naa3:\n", aa3, fmt3, epl_max);
}
```

The ensuing code block in Ch11_02_ex2() opens with the definition of lambda expression tr_op2(). This function object exploits AminoAcid::to_code3(aa) to convert a single letter amino acid code to a three letter std::string. Next is the definition of std::deque<std::string> aa3 {}. This is followed by a call to std::ranges::transform(aa1, std::back_inserter(aa3), tr_op2).[1] Execution of this statement converts each single letter code in [aa1.begin(), aa1.end()) to its corresponding three-letter code and saves the results in aa3. It is important to recognize here that different container types are employed for the input and output ranges.

Listing 11-2-3 shows the code for the final transformation example, which carries out a transformation operation using two input ranges. Execution of function Ch11_02_ex3() opens with the initialization of two std::vector<std::string> containers named vec1 and vec2. Next is the definition of binary operator tr_op(). This operator returns the result of an ordinary std::string concatenation using arguments s1 and s2.

---

[1] Recall that std::back_inserter() is a helper function that applies a container's push_back() member function to insert elements into the specified container.

CHAPTER 11 ALGORITHMS – PART 2

Listing 11-2-3. Example Ch11_02 - Ch11_02_ex3()

```
void Ch11_02_ex3()
{
    const char* fmt {"{:12s}  "};
    constexpr size_t epl_max {5};

    // initialize test vectors
    std::vector<std::string> vec1 {"one", "two",  "three", "four", "five"};
    std::vector<std::string> vec2 {"un",  "deux", "trois", "quatre", "cinq"};
    MT::print_ctr("vec1:  ", vec1, fmt, epl_max);
    MT::print_ctr("\nvec2:  ", vec2, fmt, epl_max);

    // using std::ranges::transform (binary operator)
    auto tr_op = [](const std::string& s1, const std::string& s2)
        { return s1 + '-' + s2; };

    std::list<std::string> list1 {};
    std::ranges::transform(vec1, vec2, std::back_inserter(list1), tr_op);
    MT::print_ctr("\nlist1: ", list1, fmt, epl_max);
}
```

Next in Listing 11-2-3 is the definition of std::list<std::string> list1 {}. The ensuing statement, std::ranges::transform(vec1, vec2, std::back_inserter(list1), tr_op), applies tr_op() using corresponding elements from [vec1.begin(), vec1.end()) and [vec2.begin(), vec2.end()). Each tr_op() result is saved in list1. STL algorithms std::transform() and std::ranges::transform() are particularly expedient in a variety of use cases. You'll see additional examples of these functions in later chapters. Here are the results for source code example Ch11_02:

```
----- Results for example Ch11_02 -----

----- Ch11_02_ex1() -----
sphere radii:
     1.00      2.00      3.00      4.00      5.00      6.00      7.00      8.00
```

```
sphere surface areas:
    12.57     50.27    113.10    201.06    314.16    452.39    615.75    804.25
sphere volumes:
     4.19     33.51    113.10    268.08    523.60    904.78   1436.76   2144.66
----- Ch11_02_ex2() -----

aa1 (initial values)
'a'   'g'   'l'   't'   'v'   'p'   'f'   'n'   'x'   'c'   'd'
aa1 (after tansformation):
'A'   'G'   'L'   'T'   'V'   'P'   'F'   'N'   'X'   'C'   'D'

aa3:
'Ala' 'Gly' 'Leu' 'Thr' 'Val' 'Pro' 'Phe' 'Asn' '???' 'Cys' 'Asp'

----- Ch11_02_ex3() -----

vec1:   one           two           three         four          five
vec2:   un            deux          trois         quatre        cinq
list1:  one-un        two-deux      three-trois   four-quatre   five-cinq
```

Generation Algorithms

A generation algorithm assigns the return value of successive user-specified function evaluations to each element of a range. These functions somewhat resemble std::iota(), but provide a greater amount of algorithmic flexibility as you'll soon see.

Listing 11-3-1 shows a simple example for std::generate(). In this listing, Ch11_03_ex1() opens with the declaration of std::vector<double> vec1(20). Next is the definition of lambda expression gen_op = [next_val = 0.0]() mutable { double x = next_val; next_val += 0.25; return x; }. Successive executions of gen_op() return 0.00, 0.25, 0.50, etc.

CHAPTER 11   ALGORITHMS – PART 2

Listing 11-3-1. Example Ch11_03 – Ch11_03_ex1()

```
//-----------------------------------------------------------------
// Ch11_03_ex.cpp
//-----------------------------------------------------------------

#include <algorithm>
#include <fstream>
#include <vector>
#include "Ch11_03.h"
#include "MF.h"
#include "MT.h"
#include "MTH.h"

void Ch11_03_ex1()
{
    const char* fmt = "{:8.2f}";
    constexpr size_t epl_max {10};

    // using std:generate
    // note: no arguments allowed for gen_op()
    std::vector<double> vec1(20);

    auto gen_op = [next_val = 0.0]() mutable
        { double x = next_val; next_val += 0.25; return x; };

    std::generate(vec1.begin(), vec1.end(), gen_op);
    MT::print_ctr("vec1:\n", vec1, fmt, epl_max);
}
```

Subsequent to the definition of gen_op() is the statement std::generate(vec1.begin(), vec1.end(), gen_op). Execution of this statement calls gen_op() for each element in [vec1.begin(), vec1.end()). The generation function supplied to std::generate() must be void of any arguments, which is why next_val is defined as a local variable in gen_op().

In example Ch11_03_ex2(), shown in Listing 11-3-2, lambda expression gen_op() includes some arbitrary logic to simulate a more sophisticated generation function. Note again that lambda expression gen_op() exploits a local variable to maintain data between successive calls.

CHAPTER 11   ALGORITHMS – PART 2

Listing 11-3-2. *Example Ch11_03 - Ch11_03_ex2()*

```
void Ch11_03_ex2()
{
    const char* fmt = "{:2c}";
    constexpr size_t epl_max {30};

    // using std::ranges::generate
    std::vector<char> vec1(26);

    auto gen_op = [next_char = 'A']() mutable
        { char c = next_char++; return (c & 0x01) ? c : MF::to_lower(c); };

    std::ranges::generate(vec1, gen_op);
    MT::print_ctr("vec1: ", vec1, fmt, epl_max);
}
```

Listing 11-3-3-1 shows the source code for example Ch11_03_ex3(). This function opens with a series of parameters that MTH::generate_sine_wave() uses to generate data points for a discrete sine wave. More on this shortly. The resultant data points generated by MTH::generate_sine_wave(), which harnesses std::ranges::generate_n(), are saved std::vector<double> vec1. The remaining code in Ch11_03_ex3() saves the data points in vec1 to a CSV file.

Listing 11-3-3-1. *Example Ch11_03 - Ch11_03_ex3()*

```
void Ch11_03_ex3()
{
    constexpr double amplitude {1.0};
    constexpr double frequency {5.0};
    constexpr double phase {0.0};
    constexpr double t_start {0.0};
    constexpr double t_end {1.0};
    constexpr double t_step {0.001};

    // create sine wave vector (uses std::generate_n)
    std::vector<double> vec1 = MTH::generate_sine_wave(amplitude, frequency,
        phase, t_start, t_end, t_step);

    std::println("vec.size(): {:d}", vec1.size());
```

```cpp
    // write sine wave vector to CSV file
    std::string fn = MF::mk_test_filename("ch11_03_ex2.csv");
    std::ofstream ofs {fn, std::ios_base::out | std::ios_base::trunc};

    if (!ofs.good())
    {
        std::println("file open failed: {:s}", fn);
        return;
    }

    double t {t_start};

    for (auto v : vec1)
    {
        std::println(ofs, "{:.6f}, {:.6f}", t, v);
        t += t_step;
    }

    ofs.close();
    std::println("results saved to file {:s}", fn);
}
```

Listing 11-3-3-2 shows the source code for MTH::generate_sine_wave() (see Common/MTH.h). Note that this template function specifies two template parameters. Parameter typename T is the floating-point data type, and class C is the return container type, which defaults to std::vector<T>.

Listing 11-3-3-2. Example Ch11_03 – MTH::generate_sine_wave()

```cpp
template <typename T, class C = std::vector<T>> requires std::floating_point<T>
auto generate_sine_wave(T amplitude, T frequency,T phase_deg,
    T t_start, T t_end, T t_step)
{
    // create target container
    auto num_points = static_cast<std::size_t>((t_end - t_start) / t_step) + 1;
    C sine_wave(num_points);
```

```
    // define lambda expression for std::ranges::generate_n
    T omega = 2 * std::numbers::pi_v<T> * frequency;
    T phase_rad = MTH::deg_to_rad(phase_deg);

    auto sw_op = [t = t_start, t_step, omega, amplitude, phase_rad]
    () mutable
    {
        auto x = amplitude * std::sin(omega * t + phase_rad);
        t += t_step;
        return x;
    };

    // using std::ranges::generate_n
    std::ranges::generate_n(std::begin(sine_wave), sine_wave.
    size(), sw_op);
    return sine_wave;
}
```

Function MTH::generate_sine_wave() calculates $x_i = Asin(2\pi ft + \phi)$ where A is the amplitude, f is the frequency, t is time, and ϕ is the phase angle. The total number of points generated for the sine wave equals static_cast<std::size_t>((t_end - t_start) / t_step) + 1. Note that this corresponds to a data point every t_step seconds between [t_start, t_stop].

In MTH::generate_sine_wave(), STL algorithm function std::ranges::generate_n() utilizes function object sw_op() to fill range [sine_wave.begin(), sine_wave.begin() + num_points) with discrete sine wave data points. Note that lambda sw_op() captures most of the previously described sine wave parameters while local variable t is the time value. Figure 11-1 shows a plot that was generated using the sine wave parameters defined near the top of Ch11_03_ex3().

Chapter 11 Algorithms – Part 2

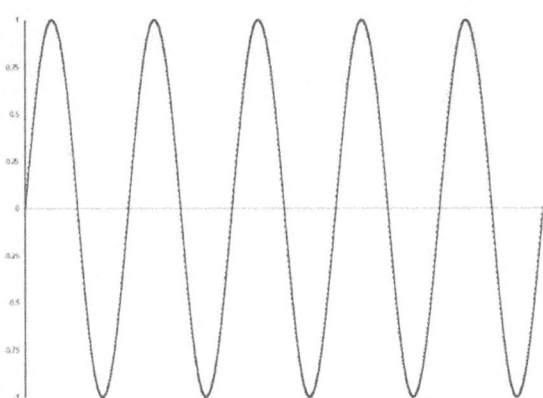

Figure 11-1. *Ch11_03_ex3() sine wave plot generated by MTH::generate_sine_wave() using std::ranges::generate_n()*

Here are the results for example Ch11_03:

```
----- Results for example Ch11_03 -----
----- Ch11_03_ex1() -----
vec1:
    0.00    0.25    0.50    0.75    1.00    1.25    1.50    1.75    2.00    2.25
    2.50    2.75    3.00    3.25    3.50    3.75    4.00    4.25    4.50    4.75
----- Ch11_03_ex2() -----
vec1: A b C d E f G h I j K l M n O p Q r S t U v W x Y z
----- Ch11_03_ex3() -----
vec.size(): 1001
results saved to file ./~~ch11_03_ex2.csv
```

Find Algorithms

Ascertaining the existence of an element in a container is a common programming task. To expedite this undertaking, the C++ STL includes several find algorithm functions that you can use. Listing 11-4-1-1 shows the header file for class `Airport`. This class is employed later in this section and in subsequent chapters.

Listing 11-4-1-1. Example Ch11_04 – Airport.h

```cpp
//-----------------------------------------------------------------------
// Airport.h
//-----------------------------------------------------------------------
#ifndef AIRPORT_H_
#define AIRPORT_H_
#include <format>
#include <optional>
#include <string>
#include <utility>
#include <vector>

class Airport
{
    friend struct std::formatter<Airport>;
public:
    class GeoCoord
    {
    public:
        enum class Units {Ignore, mi, km};

        GeoCoord() = default;

        GeoCoord(int lat_deg, int lat_min, int lat_sec, char lat_quad,
                 int lon_deg, int lon_min, int lon_sec, char lon_quad) :
            LatDeg {lat_deg}, LatMin {lat_min}, LatSec {lat_sec}, LatQuad
            {lat_quad},
            LonDeg {lon_deg}, LonMin {lon_min}, LonSec {lon_sec}, LonQuad
            {lon_quad} {}

        // validation functions for latitude and longitude
        static bool is_valid_lat(char quad) {return quad == 'N' ||
        quad == 'S';}
        static bool is_valid_lon(char quad) {return quad == 'E' ||
        quad == 'W';}
```

```cpp
        static bool is_valid_lat(double lat) {return lat >= -90.0 && lat
        <= 90.0;}
        static bool is_valid_lon(double lon) {return lon >= -180.0 && lon
        <= 180.0;}

        // misc functions (see Airport.cpp)
        static double calc_distance(const GeoCoord& gc1, const
        GeoCoord& gc2,
            Units units);
        std::pair<double, double> to_decimal() const;

        // latitude and longitude attributes
        int LatDeg {}, LatMin {}, LatSec {};
        char LatQuad {};

        int LonDeg {}, LonMin {}, LonSec {};
        char LonQuad {};
    };

    Airport() = default;
    Airport(const std::string& country_code, const std::string& iata_code,
        const std::string& name, const GeoCoord& location) :
        m_CountryCode {country_code}, m_IataCode {iata_code}, m_
        Name {name},
        m_Location {location} {};

    // accessors
    std::string CountryCode() const { return m_CountryCode; }
    void CountryCode(const std::string& country_code)
        { m_CountryCode = country_code; }

    std::string IataCode() const { return m_IataCode; }
    void IataCode(const std::string& iata_code)
        { m_IataCode = iata_code; }

    std::string Name() const { return m_Name; }
    void Name(const std::string& name) { m_Name = name; }

    GeoCoord Location() const { return m_Location; }
    void Location(const GeoCoord& location) { m_Location = location; }
```

```cpp
    // operators
    friend auto operator<=>(const Airport& ap1, const Airport& ap2)
        { return ap1.m_IataCode <=> ap2.m_IataCode; }

    friend bool operator==(const Airport& ap1, const Airport& ap2)
        { return ap1.m_IataCode == ap2.m_IataCode; }

    // misc functions
    static double calc_distance(const Airport& ap1, const Airport& ap2,
        GeoCoord::Units units)
        { return GeoCoord::calc_distance(ap1.m_Location, ap2.m_Location,
        units); }

    // static data generation functions
    static std::optional<Airport> get(const std::string& iata_code);
    static std::string get_iata_codes_string();

    static std::vector<Airport> get_vector_airports();
    static std::vector<Airport> get_vector_airports_shuffle
        (unsigned int rng_seed = 42);
    static std::vector<std::string> get_vector_iata_codes();
    static std::vector<std::string> get_vector_iata_codes_shuffle
        (unsigned int rng_seed = 57);

    static std::vector<std::string> get_vector_random_iata_codes(size_t
    num_codes,
        unsigned int rng_seed = 73);

private:
    std::string to_str() const;

    std::string m_CountryCode {};       // country code (ISO 3166-1
                                        //      alpha-2)
    std::string m_IataCode {};          // airport code (IATA, 3 letters)
    std::string m_Name {};              // airport name
    GeoCoord m_Location {};             // airport location (lat and lon)
};
```

CHAPTER 11   ALGORITHMS – PART 2

```
// class Airport formatter
template <> struct std::formatter<Airport> : std::formatter<std::string>
{
    constexpr auto parse(std::format_parse_context& pc)
        { return pc.begin(); }

    auto format(const Airport& ap, std::format_context& fc) const
        { return std::format_to(fc.out(), "{}", ap.to_str()); }
};

#endif
```

In Listing 11-4-1-1, the declaration of class Airport begins with the declaration of a subclass named GeoCoord. This class holds latitude and longitude data for an airport. Following the constructor declarations for GeoCoord is a series of is_valid_() functions that are used to validate a latitude or longitude value. Function calc_distance() computes the great-circle distance between two GeoCoord objects. More about this function shortly. The attributes section contains integer degrees, minutes, and seconds (DMS) for both latitude and longitude. Each latitude and longitude value also includes a single-letter quadrant attribute.

If you examine the declaration of class Airport, you'll notice that each instance includes a two-letter country code, a three-letter IATA[2] code that uniquely defines the airport, a name string, and a GeoCoord that specifies the airport's location. Comparison functions operator<=> and operator== carry out their actions using airport IATA codes.

Listing 11-4-1-2 shows the remaining source code for class Airport. In this listing, file Airport.cpp opens with an anonymous namespace that initializes std::vector<Airport> c_Airports. This vector contains values for 30 international airports, but only a few are shown in the listing to save space. Note that each Airport object includes all of the previously mentioned attributes.

---

[2] International Air Transport Association.

Listing 11-4-1-2. Example Ch11_04 - Airport.cpp

```cpp
//---------------------------------------------------------------------------
// Airport.cpp
//---------------------------------------------------------------------------

#include <algorithm>
#include <cmath>
#include <format>
#include <optional>
#include <random>
#include <stdexcept>
#include <string>
#include <utility>
#include <vector>
#include "Airport.h"
#include "MTH.h"

namespace
{
    const std::vector<Airport> c_Airports
    {
        // data below not suitable for navigation purposes
        Airport {"AU", "SYD", "Sydney Kingsford Smith",
            Airport::GeoCoord{33, 56, 46, 'S',  151, 10, 38, 'E'}},
        Airport {"AU", "MEL", "Melbourne",
            Airport::GeoCoord{37, 40, 24, 'S',  144, 50, 36, 'E'}},
        Airport {"BR", "BSB", "Brasilia International",
            Airport::GeoCoord{15, 52, 16, 'S',   47, 55,  7, 'W'}},

        // airports YYC - JFK excluded from listing

        Airport {"US", "LAX", "Los Angeles International",
            Airport::GeoCoord{33, 56, 33, 'N', 118, 24, 29, 'W'}},
        Airport {"US", "MCO", "Orlando International",
            Airport::GeoCoord{28, 25, 46, 'N',  81, 18, 32, 'W'}},
        Airport {"US", "ORD", "O'Hare International",
            Airport::GeoCoord{41, 58, 43, 'N',  87, 54, 17, 'W'}},
```

CHAPTER 11   ALGORITHMS – PART 2

```cpp
    };
};

double Airport::GeoCoord::calc_distance(const Airport::GeoCoord& gc1,
    const Airport::GeoCoord& gc2, Airport::GeoCoord::Units units)
{
    constexpr double earth_radius_mi = 3959.0;
    constexpr double earth_radius_km = 6371.0;

    // convert DMS to decimal
    auto [lat1, lon1] = gc1.to_decimal();
    auto [lat2, lon2] = gc2.to_decimal();
    lat1 = MTH::deg_to_rad(lat1);
    lon1 = MTH::deg_to_rad(lon1);
    lat2 = MTH::deg_to_rad(lat2);
    lon2 = MTH::deg_to_rad(lon2);

    // calculate central angle
    double t1 = std::sin(lat1) * std::sin(lat2);
    double t2 = std::cos(lat1) * std::cos(lat2);
    double t3 = std::cos(lon1 - lon2);
    double angle = std::acos(t1 + t2 * t3);

    // calculate final distance
    if (units == Airport::GeoCoord::Units::mi)
        return angle * earth_radius_mi;
    else if (units == Airport::GeoCoord::Units::km)
        return angle * earth_radius_km;
    else
        return angle;
}

std::pair<double, double> Airport::GeoCoord::to_decimal() const
{
    // make sure lat/log quads are valid
    if (!Airport::GeoCoord::is_valid_lat(LatQuad))
        throw std::runtime_error("Airport::GeoCoord::to_dec() - bad
        lat quad");
```

```cpp
    if (!Airport::GeoCoord::is_valid_lon(LonQuad))
        throw std::runtime_error("Airport::GeoCoord::to_dec() - bad
        lon quad");

    // convert DMS to decimal, both lat and lon
    auto dms_to_dec = [](int deg, int min, int sec)
        { return deg + (min * 60.0 + sec) / 3600.0; };

    double lat_dec = dms_to_dec(LatDeg, LatMin, LatSec);
    double lon_dec = dms_to_dec(LonDeg, LonMin, LonSec);

    if (LatQuad == 'S')
        lat_dec = -lat_dec;

    if (LonQuad == 'W')
        lon_dec = -lon_dec;

    return std::make_pair(lat_dec, lon_dec);
}
std::optional<Airport> Airport::get(const std::string& iata_code)
{
    // return Airport that matches iata_code
    auto pred = [iata_code](const Airport& a) { return a.IataCode() ==
    iata_code; };
    auto iter = std::ranges::find_if(c_Airports, pred);
    return (iter != c_Airports.end()) ? std::optional(*iter) :
    std::nullopt;
}

std::string Airport::get_iata_codes_string()
{
    // build string of all IATA codes
    std::string iata_codes {};

    for (const Airport& airport : c_Airports)
    {
        iata_codes += airport.IataCode();
        iata_codes += ' ';
    }
```

CHAPTER 11   ALGORITHMS – PART 2

```cpp
    return iata_codes;
}

std::vector<Airport> Airport::get_vector_airports()
{
    return c_Airports;
}

std::vector<Airport> Airport::get_vector_airports_shuffle(unsigned int rng_seed)
{
    // get shuffled vector of Airports
    std::vector<Airport> airports {c_Airports};
    std::mt19937 rng {rng_seed};
    std::shuffle(airports.begin(), airports.end(), rng);
    std::shuffle(airports.begin(), airports.end(), rng);
    return airports;
}

std::vector<std::string> Airport::get_vector_iata_codes()
{
    // get vector of all IATA codes
    std::vector<std::string> iata_codes {};
    for (const Airport& airport : c_Airports)
        iata_codes.emplace_back(airport.IataCode());
    return iata_codes;
}

std::vector<std::string> Airport::get_vector_iata_codes_shuffle
    (unsigned int rng_seed)
{
    // get shuffled vector of IATA codes
    std::vector<std::string> iata_codes {get_vector_iata_codes()};
    std::mt19937 rng {rng_seed};
    std::shuffle(iata_codes.begin(), iata_codes.end(), rng);
    std::shuffle(iata_codes.begin(), iata_codes.end(), rng);
    return iata_codes;
}
```

```cpp
std::vector<std::string> Airport::get_vector_random_iata_codes(size_t
num_codes,
    unsigned int rng_seed)
{
    // generate vector of random IATA codes
    const int dist_max = static_cast<int>(c_Airports.size() - 1);
    std::mt19937 rng {rng_seed};
    std::uniform_int_distribution<int> dist {0, dist_max};

    std::vector<std::string> iata_codes(num_codes);

    for (size_t i = 0; i < iata_codes.size(); ++i)
        iata_codes[i] = c_Airports[dist(rng)].IataCode();
    return iata_codes;
}

std::string Airport::to_str() const
{
    std::string s {};
    auto [lat, lon] = m_Location.to_decimal();

    std::format_to(std::back_inserter(s),
        "[{:2s}, {:3s}, {:s} ({:.4f}, {:.4f})]",
        m_CountryCode, m_IataCode, m_Name, lat, lon);

    return s;
}
```

Most of the remaining code in `Airport.cpp` is straightforward, but a few functions warrant some comments. Function `Airport::GeoCoord::calc_distance()` calculates the approximate distance between two GeoCoord locations. This function first calculates the central angle between the two locations using the following great-circle formula:[3]

$$\Delta\sigma = arccos(sin\phi_1\ sin\phi_2 + cos\phi_1\ cos\phi_2\ cos\Delta\lambda)$$

---

[3] This equation is valid for a perfect sphere. For oblate (flattened) sphere planet earth, the central angle formula is an approximation.

CHAPTER 11   ALGORITHMS – PART 2

In this equation, ϕ_1 and ϕ_2 are the latitudes, λ_1 and λ_2 are longitudes, and $\Delta\lambda = \lambda_1 - \lambda_2$. To calculate the actual distance, $\Delta\sigma$ is multiplied by the radius of the earth. Before continuing, please note that both the data used in c_Airports and the distance calculation performed in Airport::GeoCoord::calc_distance() are not suitable for actual navigation purposes.

Function Airport::GeoCoord::to_decimal() converts a GeoCoord latitude and longitude from DMS to decimal degrees. Note that this function returns a std::pair<double, double>. The various Airport::get_() functions format and return containers of data derived from c_Airports. You'll learn more about these functions as you study the examples that utilize class Airport.

Listing 11-4-1-3 shows the source code for example function Ch11_04_ex1(). This function uses std::ranges::find() to find airport IATA codes. Near the top of Ch11_04_ex1(), std::vector<std::string> iata_codes is initialized using Airport::get_vector_iata_codes(). Listing 11-4-1-2 shows the code for this function, which builds a std::vector<std::string> of IATA codes using the data of c_Airports.

Listing 11-4-1-3. Example Ch11_04 – Ch11_04_ex1()

```
//--------------------------------------------------------------------
// Ch11_04_ex.cpp
//--------------------------------------------------------------------

#include <algorithm>
#include <vector>
#include "Ch11_04.h"
#include "Airport.h"
#include "MT.h"

void Ch11_04_ex1()
{
    const char* fmt = "{:3s} ";
    constexpr size_t epl_max {10};

    std::vector<std::string> iata_codes {Airport::get_vector_iata_codes()};
    MT::print_ctr("\niata_codes\n", iata_codes, fmt, epl_max);
    std::println("");

    std::vector<std::string> find_codes {"AKL", "DFW", "FRA", "ORD"};
```

```cpp
    for (const std::string& find_code : find_codes)
    {
        // using std::ranges::find (uses operator==)
        std::print("IATA code: {:s} - ", find_code);
        auto iter = std::ranges::find(iata_codes, find_code);

        if (iter != iata_codes.end())
            std::println("found");
        else
            std::println("not found");
    }
}
```

The next item in Ch11_04_ex1() is the definition of std::vector<std::string> find_codes. This vector contains several IATA codes. The ensuing for loop utilizes iter = std::ranges::find(iata_codes, find_code) to search iata_codes for find_code. When searching for a match, std::ranges::find() uses operator== for the specified data type. If a match is found, iter points to the first element in iata_codes; otherwise, iter equals iata_codes.end().

Example Ch11_04_ex2(), shown in Listing 11-4-2, spotlights the use of std::ranges::find_if(). This function finds elements in a range using a unary predicate. The opening code block of Ch11_04_ex2() utilizes std::vector<Airport> airports = Airport::get_vector_airports() to initialize a vector of all Airports. Next is the definition of lambda expression find_op():

```cpp
auto find_op = [](const Airport& airport)
    { auto [lat, lon] = airport.Location().to_decimal(); return lat < 0; };
```

Predicate find_op() returns true if the airport's latitude (in decimal) is less than zero (i.e., the airport is located in the earth's southern hemisphere). Note that find_op() utilizes structured binding to parse out the latitude and longitude from the std::pair<double, double> that to_decimal() returns.

CHAPTER 11 ALGORITHMS – PART 2

Listing 11-4-2. *Example Ch11_04 - Ch11_04_ex2()*

```cpp
void Ch11_04_ex2()
{
    const char* fmt = "{} ";
    constexpr size_t epl_max {1};

    // vector of airports
    std::vector<Airport> airports = Airport::get_vector_airports();
    MT::print_ctr("\nairports\n", airports, fmt, epl_max);

    // using std::find_if (uses specfied find predicate)
    auto find_op = [](const Airport& airport)
        { auto [lat, lon] = airport.Location().to_decimal(); return
        lat < 0; };

    std::println("\nairports found:");
    auto iter = airports.begin();

    while (1)
    {
        iter = std::ranges::find_if(iter, airports.end(), find_op);

        if (iter == airports.end())
            break;

        std::println("{}", *iter);
        iter++;
    }
}
```

Following the definition of find_op() is the statement iter = airports.begin() that initializes iter to the first element in airports. Within Ch11_04_ex2()'s while loop, execution of iter = std::ranges::find_if(iter, airports.end(), find_op) returns an iterator to the next Airport in airports for which find_op() is true. It then dereferences this iterator to print the airport's data. If std::ranges::find_if() returns airports.end(), find_op() returned false for all elements in the specified range.

Listing 11-4-3 shows the source code for the next find example. In function Ch11_04_ex3(), std::vector<Airport> find_airports contains three Airports. For the current example, only the IATA codes are necessary. In Ch11_04_ex3()'s while loop, the statement iter = std::ranges::find_first_of(iter, airports. end(), find_airports.begin(), find_airports.end()) returns an iterator to the first element in [iter, airports.end()) that matches any of the elements in find_airports. For the current example, function std::ranges::find_first_of() utilizes Airport::operator==, which performs its comparisons using IATA codes.

Listing 11-4-3. Example Ch11_04 – Ch11_04_ex3()

```
void Ch11_04_ex3()
{
    std::vector<Airport> airports = Airport::get_vector_airports();

    // list of airports to find (Airport::operator== compares IATA codes)
    std::vector<Airport> find_airports
    {
        Airport {"", "CDG", "", Airport::GeoCoord {}},
        Airport {"", "ZRH", "", Airport::GeoCoord {}},
        Airport {"", "FRA", "", Airport::GeoCoord {}},
    };

    // using std::ranges::find_first_of
    std::println("\nairports found using find_first_of:");
    auto iter = airports.begin();

    while (1)
    {
        iter = std::ranges::find_first_of(iter, airports.end(),
            find_airports.begin(), find_airports.end());

        if (iter == airports.end())
            break;

        std::println("{}", *iter);
        iter++;
    }
}
```

CHAPTER 11 ALGORITHMS – PART 2

The final `std::find_` example, shown in Listing 11-4-4, demonstrates the use of `std::ranges::find_last()` (C++23). In Listing 11-4-4, function Ch11_04_ex4() utilizes `Airport::get_vector_random_iata_codes(60)` to initialize `std::vector<std::string> iata_codes` with 60 random IATA codes. The next item of note is the declaration of `std::vector<std::string> find_vals`. This vector contains several IATA codes that `std::ranges::find_last()` will search for.

Listing 11-4-4. Example Ch11_04 – Ch11_04_ex4()

```
//#define PRINT_SUBRANGE    // remove comment to enable
void Ch11_04_ex4()
{
#ifdef __cpp_lib_ranges_find_last
    const char* fmt = "{:3s} ";
    constexpr size_t epl_max {15};
    std::vector<std::string> iata_codes { Airport::get_vector_random_iata_
    codes(60) };
    MT::print_ctr("\niata_codes:\n", iata_codes, fmt, epl_max);

    // iata codes to find
    std::vector<std::string> find_vals
        {"ARN", "IAH", "MXX", "PVG", "WLG"};

    // using std::ranges::find_last
    for (const auto& find_val : find_vals)
    {
        std::print("\nfind_val: {:3s} | airport ", find_val);

        // std::ranges::find_last returns iterator subrange
        // object found         iter_sr = [iter of found obj, iata_
                                codes.end())
        // object not found     iter_sr = [iata_codes.end(), iata_
                                codes.end())
        auto iter_sr = std::ranges::find_last(iata_codes, find_val);
```

```cpp
            if (iter_sr.begin() != iata_codes.end())
            {
#ifdef PRINT_SUBRANGE
            std::println("subrange iter_sr");
            for (auto iter = iter_sr.begin(); iter != iter_sr.end();
            ++iter)
                std::print ("{:3s} ", *iter);
            std::println("");
#endif
            // calculate position
            auto find_pos = std::distance(iata_codes.begin(), iter_
            sr.begin());
            std::println("found (position = {:d})", find_pos);

            // print found airport
            std::optional<Airport> airport { Airport::get(find_val) };

            if (airport)
                std::println("{}", airport.value());
        }
        else
            std::println("not found");
    }
#else
    std::println("Ch11_04_ex4() requires __cpp_lib_ranges_find_last
    (C++23)");
#endif
}
```

In Ch11_04_ex4()'s range for loop, execution of the statement iter_sr = std::ranges::find_last(iata_codes, find_val) returns an iterator subrange. An iterator subrange is simply a range that exists within another range. If iter_sr.begin() != iata_codes.end() is true, find_last() found an IATA code match and iter_sr.begin() points to it in iata_codes. The code inside the if block utilizes find_pos = std::distance(iata_codes.begin(), iter_sr.begin()) to calculate the position of the just found IATA code in iata_codes. Execution of std::optional<Airport> airport { Airport::get(find_val) } returns an std::optional<Airport> object that's used

CHAPTER 11   ALGORITHMS – PART 2

to print the airport's data. For the current example, note that Airport::get(find_val) will always return a value. Figure 11-2 illustrates the execution of std::ranges::find_last() in greater detail.

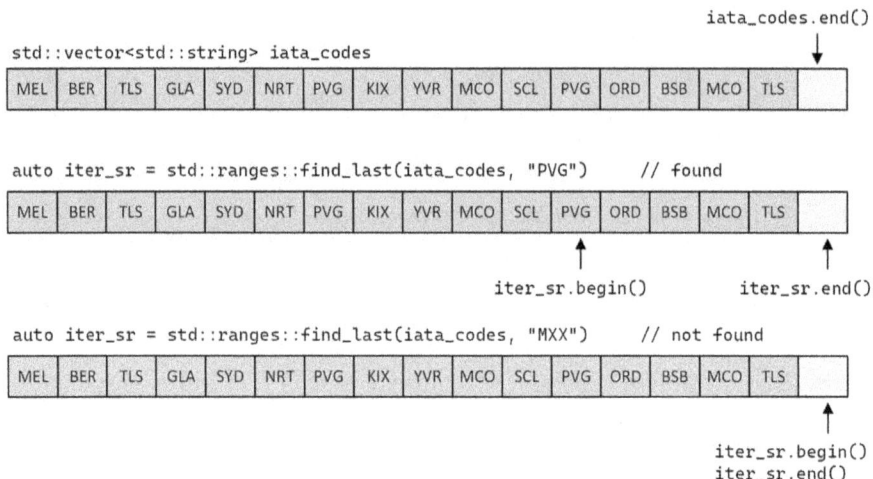

Figure 11-2. Example executions of iter_sr = std::ranges::find_last(iata_codes, find_val)

The STL includes other std::ranges::find_if_ algorithm functions, including std::ranges::find_if_not(), std::ranges::find_last_if(), std::ranges::find_last_if_not(), std::ranges::find_end(), and std::ranges::adjacent_find(). Here are the results for example Ch11_04:

```
----- Results for example Ch11_04 -----

----- Ch11_04_ex1() -----

iata_codes
SYD MEL BSB YYC YEG YVR YYZ ZRH SCL PEK
PVG BER FRA MUN CDG TLS GLA LHR DEL KIX
NRT OSL AKL WLG ARN IAH JFK LAX MCO ORD

IATA code: AKL - found
IATA code: DFW - not found
IATA code: FRA - found
IATA code: ORD - found
```

----- Ch11_04_ex2() -----

airports
[AU, SYD, Sydney Kingsford Smith (-33.9461, 151.1772)]
[AU, MEL, Melbourne (-37.6733, 144.8433)]
[BR, BSB, Brasilia International (-15.8711, -47.9186)]
[CA, YYC, Calgary International (51.1225, -114.0133)]
[CA, YEG, Edmonton International (43.6767, -79.6306)]
[CA, YVR, Vancouver International (49.1947, -123.1839)]
[CA, YYZ, Toronto Pearson International (53.3100, -113.5794)]
[CH, ZRH, Zurich (47.4314, 8.5492)]
[CL, SCL, Santiago International (-33.3928, -70.7911)]
[CN, PEK, Beijing Capital International (40.0725, 116.5975)]
[CN, PVG, Shanghai Pudong International (31.1433, 121.8053)]
[DE, BER, Berlin Brandenburg (52.3667, 13.5033)]
[DE, FRA, Frankfurt (50.0333, 8.5706)]
[DE, MUN, Munich Franz Josef Stauss (48.3539, 11.7861)]
[FR, CDG, Paris Charles de Gaulle (49.0097, 2.5478)]
[FR, TLS, Toulouse-Blagnac (43.6350, 1.3678)]
[GB, GLA, Glasgow (55.8719, -4.4331)]
[GB, LHR, Heathrow International (51.4775, -0.4614)]
[IN, DEL, Indira Gandhi International (28.5686, 77.1122)]
[JP, KIX, Kansai International (34.4306, 135.2303)]
[JP, NRT, Narita International (35.7653, 140.3856)]
[NO, OSL, Oslo Gardermoen (60.2028, 11.0839)]
[NZ, AKL, Auckland (-37.0081, 174.7917)]
[NZ, WLG, Wellington International (-41.3272, 174.8053)]
[SE, ARN, Stockholm Arlanda (59.5019, 17.9186)]
[US, IAH, George Bush International (29.9844, -95.3414)]
[US, JFK, John F Kennedy International (40.6397, -74.0789)]
[US, LAX, Los Angeles International (33.9425, -118.4081)]
[US, MCO, Orlando International (28.4294, -81.3089)]
[US, ORD, O'Hare International (41.9786, -87.9047)]

airports found:
[AU, SYD, Sydney Kingsford Smith (-33.9461, 151.1772)]
[AU, MEL, Melbourne (-37.6733, 144.8433)]

CHAPTER 11   ALGORITHMS – PART 2

[BR, BSB, Brasilia International (-15.8711, -47.9186)]
[CL, SCL, Santiago International (-33.3928, -70.7911)]
[NZ, AKL, Auckland (-37.0081, 174.7917)]
[NZ, WLG, Wellington International (-41.3272, 174.8053)]

----- Ch11_04_ex3() -----

airports found using find_first_of:
[CH, ZRH, Zurich (47.4314, 8.5492)]
[DE, FRA, Frankfurt (50.0333, 8.5706)]
[FR, CDG, Paris Charles de Gaulle (49.0097, 2.5478)]

----- Ch11_04_ex4() -----

iata_codes:
KIX PEK GLA DEL TLS YVR DEL TLS CDG PEK YYZ BSB ZRH IAH LHR
CDG WLG ARN PEK MCO FRA LHR LHR CDG ZRH JFK LAX PEK YEG AKL
LHR YYC ZRH MUN JFK YYZ LAX YVR YYC WLG ORD YYC MEL ZRH MEL
BER TLS GLA SYD NRT PVG KIX YVR MCO SCL PVG ORD BSB MCO TLS

find_val: ARN | airport found (position = 17)
[SE, ARN, Stockholm Arlanda (59.5019, 17.9186)]

find_val: IAH | airport found (position = 13)
[US, IAH, George Bush International (29.9844, -95.3414)]

find_val: MXX | airport not found

find_val: PVG | airport found (position = 55)
[CN, PVG, Shanghai Pudong International (31.1433, 121.8053)]

find_val: WLG | airport found (position = 39)
[NZ, WLG, Wellington International (-41.3272, 174.8053)]

Contains Algorithms

A contains algorithm returns a `bool` that signifies the existence of an element in a container or range. Listing 11-5-1-1 shows the source code for class `Mineral`. This class is used in example function `Ch11_05_ex1()`; it's also used in later chapters.

Listing 11-5-1-1. Example Ch11_05 – Class Mineral

```
//---------------------------------------------------------------------
// Mineral.h
//---------------------------------------------------------------------
#ifndef MINERAL_H_
#define MINERAL_H_
#include <compare>
#include <format>
#include <string>
#include <vector>

class Mineral
{
    friend struct std::formatter<Mineral>;
    static constexpr unsigned int c_RngSeedDef {119};
public:
    Mineral() = default;
    Mineral(const char* name, double hardness) : m_Name {name},
        m_Hardness {hardness} {};
    Mineral(const std::string& name, double hardness) : m_Name {name},
        m_Hardness {hardness} {};

    // accessors
    std::string Name() const { return m_Name; }
    double Hardness() const { return m_Hardness; }

    // operators
    friend auto operator<=>(const Mineral& mineral1, const Mineral&
        mineral2)
```

```cpp
    {
        auto cmp = mineral1.m_Hardness <=> mineral2.m_Hardness;
        return (cmp == 0) ? mineral1.m_Name <=> mineral2.m_Name : cmp;
    }

    friend bool operator==(const Mineral& mineral1, const Mineral&
    mineral2)
    {
        return mineral1.m_Hardness == mineral2.m_Hardness &&
               mineral1.m_Name == mineral2.m_Name;
    }

    // miscellaneous data generation functions
    static std::vector<Mineral> get_vector_all();
    static std::vector<Mineral> get_vector_all_shuffle(
        unsigned int rng_seed = c_RngSeedDef, unsigned int num_
        shuffles = 4);
    static std::vector<Mineral> get_vector_random(std::size_t vec_size,
        unsigned int rng_seed = c_RngSeedDef);
    static std::vector<Mineral> get_vector_sample(std::size_t vec_size,
        unsigned int rng_seed = c_RngSeedDef + 7);
private:
    std::string to_str() const;

    std::string m_Name {};      // mineral name
    double m_Hardness {};       // approximate hardness (Mohs scale)
};

// class Mineral formatter
template <> struct std::formatter<Mineral> : std::formatter<std::string>
{
    constexpr auto parse(std::format_parse_context& pc)
        { return pc.begin(); }

    auto format(const Mineral& mineral, std::format_context& fc) const
        { return std::format_to(fc.out(), "{}", mineral.to_str()); }
};
```

```
#endif

//--------------------------------------------------------------------------
// Mineral.cpp
//--------------------------------------------------------------------------

#include <algorithm>
#include <format>
#include <limits>
#include <random>
#include <string>
#include <vector>
#include "Mineral.h"

namespace
{
    const std::vector<Mineral> c_Minerals
    {
        Mineral {"Talc", 1.0},                  Mineral {"Dimorphite", 1.5},
        Mineral {"Todorokite", 1.5},            Mineral {"Gypsum", 2.0},
        Mineral {"Kinoite", 2.5},               Mineral {"Galena", 2.625},
        Mineral {"Chalcocite", 2.75},           Mineral {"Calcite", 3.0},
        Mineral {"Hanksite", 3.25},             Mineral {"Roselite", 3.5},
        Mineral {"Aragonite", 3.75},            Mineral {"Fluorite", 4.0},
        Mineral {"Zincite", 4.25},              Mineral
                                                {"Conichalcite", 4.5},
        Mineral {"Lindgrenite", 4.5},           Mineral {"Apatite", 5.0},
        Mineral {"Perovskite", 5.25},           Mineral {"Agrellite", 5.5},
        Mineral {"Anatase", 5.75},              Mineral
                                                {"Orthoclase", 6.0},
        Mineral {"Chloritoid", 6.5},            Mineral {"Quartz", 7.0},
        Mineral {"Bowieite", 7.0},              Mineral {"Zircon", 7.5},
        Mineral {"Topaz", 8.0},                 Mineral
                                                {"Chrysoberyl", 8.5},
        Mineral {"Tongbaite", 8.5},             Mineral {"Corundum", 9.0},
        Mineral {"Moissanite", 9.25},           Mineral {"Diamond", 10.0},
```

CHAPTER 11   ALGORITHMS – PART 2

```
    };
};
std::vector<Mineral> Mineral::get_vector_all()
{
    return c_Minerals;
}

std::vector<Mineral> Mineral::get_vector_all_shuffle(unsigned int rng_seed,
    unsigned int num_shuffles)
{
    std::mt19937_64 rng {rng_seed};
    std::vector<Mineral> minerals {c_Minerals};

    for (unsigned int i {0}; i < num_shuffles; ++i)
        std::shuffle(minerals.begin(), minerals.end(), rng);
    return minerals;
}

std::vector<Mineral> Mineral::get_vector_random(std::size_t vec_size,
    unsigned int rng_seed)
{
    const int dist_max = static_cast<int>(c_Minerals.size() - 1);
    std::mt19937 rng {rng_seed};
    std::uniform_int_distribution<int> dist {0, dist_max};

    std::vector<Mineral> minerals(vec_size);

    for (size_t i {}; i < minerals.size(); ++i)
        minerals[i] = c_Minerals[dist(rng)];
    return minerals;
}

std::vector<Mineral> Mineral::get_vector_sample(size_t vec_size,
    unsigned int rng_seed)
{
    std::vector<Mineral> minerals {};
    std::mt19937_64 rng {rng_seed};
    size_t n = std::min(c_Minerals.size(), vec_size);
```

```
    std::sample(c_Minerals.cbegin(), c_Minerals.cend(),
        std::back_inserter(minerals), n, rng);
    std::shuffle(minerals.begin(), minerals.end(), rng);
    return minerals;
}

std::string Mineral::to_str() const
{
    std::string s{};

    std::format_to(std::back_inserter(s), "[{:<13s} ", m_Name);
    std::format_to(std::back_inserter(s), "{:7.3f}]", m_Hardness);
    return s;
}
```

In Listing 11-5-1-1, note that each Mineral object includes a name attribute (m_Name) and a hardness attribute (m_Hardness). The relational operators for class Mineral, operator<=> and operator==, utilize both attributes when performing a comparison with m_Hardness having (subjectively) higher precedence.[4] Near the top of Mineral.cpp is a std::vector<Mineral> named c_Minerals. Like other user-defined classes that you have already seen, class Mineral defines a series of get_vector_() functions that return initialized std::vector< Mineral> objects for test purposes.

Listing 11-5-1-2 shows the source code for example Ch11_05_ex1(). The opening code block of this function utilizes Mineral::get_vector_all() to initialize std::vector<Mineral> minerals. Following the print statements is the definition of std::vector<Mineral> find_vals, which includes several Mineral instances. Note that each Mineral instance in find_vals includes both a name and a hardness value.

---

[4] This precedence was chosen to underscore the use of multiple attributes in operator<=> and operator==.

CHAPTER 11 ALGORITHMS – PART 2

Listing 11-5-1-2. Example Ch11_05 – Ch11_05_ex1()

```cpp
//-----------------------------------------------------------------
// Ch11_05_ex.cpp
//-----------------------------------------------------------------

#include <algorithm>
#include <vector>
#include "Ch11_05.h"
#include "MT.h"
#include "Mineral.h"

void Ch11_05_ex1()
{
#ifdef __cpp_lib_ranges_contains
    const char* fmt = "{} ";
    constexpr size_t epl_max {3};

    // create test vector
    std::vector<Mineral> minerals { Mineral::get_vector_all() };
    MT::print_ctr("\nminerals:\n", minerals, fmt, epl_max);
    std::println("");

    // using std::ranges::contains
    std::vector<Mineral> find_vals
        {{"Agrellite", 5.5}, {"Kaolinite", 2.5}, {"Zircon", 7.5}};

    for (const auto& find_val : find_vals)
    {
        std::print("find_val: {:12s} | ", find_val.Name());

        if (std::ranges::contains(minerals, find_val))
            std::println("found, hardness = {:.2f}", find_val.Hardness());
        else
            std::println("not found!");
    }
#else
    std::println("Ch11_05_ex1() requires __cpp_lib_ranges_contains (C++23)");
#endif
}
```

CHAPTER 11 ALGORITHMS – PART 2

The range for loop of Ch11_05_ex1() demonstrates the use of std::ranges::contains() (C++23). Execution of std::ranges::contains(minerals, find_val) returns true if find_val exists in minerals; otherwise, it returns false. In the current example, STL algorithm std::ranges::contains() applies Mineral::operator== to carry out its comparisons. Recall that this operator uses Mineral attributes m_Hardness and m_Name. The testing of both attributes is necessary since some minerals have the same hardness value.

Example function Ch11_05_ex2(), shown in Listing 11-5-2, spotlights the use of std::ranges::contains_subrange() (C++23). This STL algorithm searches a range for a matching subrange and returns true if the subrange exists.

Listing 11-5-2. Example Ch11_05 – Ch11_05_ex2()

```
void Ch11_05_ex2()
{
#ifdef __cpp_lib_ranges_contains
    const char* fmt = "{} ";
    constexpr size_t epl_max {3};

    // create test vector
    std::vector<Mineral> minerals { Mineral::get_vector_all() };
    MT::print_ctr("\nminerals:\n", minerals, fmt, epl_max);

    // using std::ranges::contains_subrange - example #1
    std::vector<Mineral> subrange1
        {{"Conichalcite", 4.5}, {"Lindgrenite", 4.5}, Mineral
        {"Apatite", 5.0}};
    MT::print_ctr("\nsubrange1:\n", subrange1, fmt, epl_max);

    bool bsr1 = std::ranges::contains_subrange(minerals, subrange1);
    std::println("\nsubrange1 {:s} in vector minerals",
            bsr1 ? "found" : "not found");

    // using std::ranges::contains_subrange - example #2
    std::vector<Mineral> subrange2
        {{"Kaolinite", 2.5}, {"Lindgrenite", 4.5}, Mineral
        {"Apatite", 5.0}};
    MT::print_ctr("\nsubrange2:\n", subrange2, fmt, epl_max);
```

CHAPTER 11   ALGORITHMS – PART 2

```
    bool bsr2 = std::ranges::contains_subrange(minerals, subrange2);
    std::println("\nsubrange2 {:s} in vector minerals",
        bsr2 ? "found" : "not found");
#else
    std::println("Ch11_05_ex2() requires __cpp_lib_ranges_contains (C++23)");
#endif
}
```

The use of std::ranges::contains_subrange() is clear-cut. In Listing 11-5-2, execution of std::ranges::contains_subrange(minerals, subrange1) returns true since subrange1 exists in std::vector<Mineral> minerals. However, execution of std::ranges::contains_subrange(minerals, subrange2) returns false since the specified subrange does not exist in minerals. Here are the results for example Ch11_05:

```
----- Results for example Ch11_05 -----

----- Ch11_05_ex1() -----

minerals:
[Talc           1.000] [Dimorphite    1.500] [Todorokite    1.500]
[Gypsum         2.000] [Kinoite       2.500] [Galena        2.625]
[Chalcocite     2.750] [Calcite       3.000] [Hanksite      3.250]
[Roselite       3.500] [Aragonite     3.750] [Fluorite      4.000]
[Zincite        4.250] [Conichalcite  4.500] [Lindgrenite   4.500]
[Apatite        5.000] [Perovskite    5.250] [Agrellite     5.500]
[Anatase        5.750] [Orthoclase    6.000] [Chloritoid    6.500]
[Quartz         7.000] [Bowieite      7.000] [Zircon        7.500]
[Topaz          8.000] [Chrysoberyl   8.500] [Tongbaite     8.500]
[Corundum       9.000] [Moissanite    9.250] [Diamond      10.000]

find_val: Agrellite   | found, hardness = 5.50
find_val: Kaolinite   | not found!
find_val: Zircon      | found, hardness = 7.50

----- Ch11_05_ex2() -----

minerals:
[Talc           1.000] [Dimorphite    1.500] [Todorokite    1.500]
[Gypsum         2.000] [Kinoite       2.500] [Galena        2.625]
```

```
[Chalcocite     2.750] [Calcite        3.000] [Hanksite       3.250]
[Roselite       3.500] [Aragonite      3.750] [Fluorite       4.000]
[Zincite        4.250] [Conichalcite   4.500] [Lindgrenite    4.500]
[Apatite        5.000] [Perovskite     5.250] [Agrellite      5.500]
[Anatase        5.750] [Orthoclase     6.000] [Chloritoid     6.500]
[Quartz         7.000] [Bowieite       7.000] [Zircon         7.500]
[Topaz          8.000] [Chrysoberyl    8.500] [Tongbaite      8.500]
[Corundum       9.000] [Moissanite     9.250] [Diamond       10.000]
subrange1:
[Conichalcite   4.500] [Lindgrenite    4.500] [Apatite        5.000]

subrange1 found in vector minerals

subrange2:
[Kaolinite      2.500] [Lindgrenite    4.500] [Apatite        5.000]

subrange2 not found in vector minerals
```

More Find Algorithms

To determine if a container or range starts or ends with a specific sequence of elements, you can use std::ranges::starts_with() or std::ranges::ends_with() (both C++23). Listing 11-6-1 shows the source code for example function Ch11_06_ex1(), which spotlights the use of these functions.

Listing 11-6-1. Example Ch11_06 – Ch11_06_ex1()

```
//---------------------------------------------------------------------
// Ch11_06_ex.cpp
//---------------------------------------------------------------------

#include <algorithm>
#include <vector>
#include "Ch11_06.h"
#include "AminoAcid.h"
#include "MT.h"
```

```cpp
void Ch11_06_ex1()
{
#ifdef __cpp_lib_ranges_starts_ends_with
    const char* fmt = "{:3s} ";
    std::size_t epl_max {20};
    constexpr std::size_t num_aa {80};

    // generate vector of random amino acids (code3)
    std::vector<std::string> vec1 {AminoAcid::get_vector_random_code3(num_
    aa, 100)};
    MT::print_ctr("\nvec1:\n", vec1, fmt, epl_max);

    // create test sequences of amino acids
    std::vector<std::string> seq1(vec1.begin(), vec1.begin() + 4);
    MT::print_ctr("\nseq1: ", seq1, fmt, epl_max);

    std::vector<std::string> seq2(vec1.end() - 4, vec1.end());
    MT::print_ctr("seq2: ", seq2, fmt, epl_max);

    // using std:ranges::starts_with
    bool bsw1 = std::ranges::starts_with(vec1, seq1);
    bool bsw2 = std::ranges::starts_with(vec1, seq2);
    std::println("\nvec1 starts with aminio acid sequence seq1: {:s}",
    bsw1);
    std::println("vec1 starts with aminio acid sequence seq2: {:s}", bsw2);

    // using std:ranges::ends_with
    bool bew1 = std::ranges::ends_with(vec1, seq1);
    bool bew2 = std::ranges::ends_with(vec1, seq2);
    std::println("\nvec1 ends with aminio acid sequence seq1: {:s}", bew1);
    std::println("vec1 ends with aminio acid sequence seq2: {:s}", bew2);
#else
    std::println("Ch11_06_ex1() requires __cpp_lib_ranges_starts_ends_with
    (C++23)");
#endif
}
```

CHAPTER 11   ALGORITHMS – PART 2

Near the top of Listing 11-6-1, Ch11_06_ex1() utilizes AminoAcid::get_vector_random_code3() to initialize std::vector<string> vec1. This vector contains 100 random amino acids in code3 format (see Listings 10-1-3-1 and 10-1-3-2 for class AminoAcid). Next is the instantiation of test sequences seq1 and seq2. Note that both sequences contain four code3 amino acids.

In the ensuing code block, execution of std::ranges::starts_with(vec1, seq1) returns true if vec1 starts with seq1 (i.e., the first four elements in vec1 match the four elements of seq1); otherwise, it returns false. Similarly, execution of std::ranges::starts_with(vec1, seq2) returns true if vec1 starts with seq2.

An example code block that demonstrates the use of std::ranges::ends_with() follows. This function checks the end of a range for a matching subrange. Here are the results for example Ch11_06:

```
----- Results for example Ch11_06 -----

----- Ch11_06_ex1() -----

vec1:
Leu Phe Gln His His Leu Thr Asn Ala Asp Asn Asp Phe Cys Thr Ile Asn
Trp Lys Arg
Trp Met Cys Leu Asp Lys Asn Ala Cys Glu Val Val Thr Asn Asp Arg Thr
Glu Gln Met
His Phe Tyr Met Thr Tyr Glu Gln Asp Lys Gly Asp Ala Leu Gln Met Ser
Asn Ala Lys
Lys Ile Met Gly Asn His Gly His Ala His Trp Ala Val Ser Arg Lys Trp
Gly Lys Leu

seq1: Leu Phe Gln His
seq2: Trp Gly Lys Leu

vec1 starts with aminio acid sequence seq1: true
vec1 starts with aminio acid sequence seq2: false

vec1 ends with aminio acid sequence seq1: false
vec1 ends with aminio acid sequence seq2: true
```

CHAPTER 11   ALGORITHMS – PART 2

Search Algorithms

The C++ STL also includes algorithms that search a range for a sequence of elements. Listing 11-7-1 shows the source code for example Ch11_07_ex1(). This function demonstrates the use of std::ranges::search(), which searches a range for the first occurrence of a sequence that's specified by a second range.

Listing 11-7-1. Example Ch11_07 – Ch11_07_ex1()

```
//-------------------------------------------------------------------------
// Ch11_07_ex.cpp
//-------------------------------------------------------------------------

#include <algorithm>
#include <functional>
#include <vector>
#include "Ch11_07.h"
#include "HtmlColor.h"
#include "MT.h"

std::vector<std::vector<HtmlColor>> get_sequences(size_t offset)
{
    std::vector<std::vector<HtmlColor>> sequences {};

    for (size_t i = 0; ; ++i)
    {
        // create test sequence of three HtmlColor colors
        size_t indx0 = i * offset;
        size_t indx1 = i * offset + 1;
        size_t indx2 = i * offset + 2;

        if (i == 2)
            ++indx2;     // index for non-matching sequence

        if (indx2 >= HtmlColor::num_colors())
            break;

        std::vector<HtmlColor> sequence {};
        sequence.push_back(HtmlColor::get(indx0));
```

```cpp
            sequence.push_back(HtmlColor::get(indx1));
            sequence.push_back(HtmlColor::get(indx2));

            sequences.push_back(sequence);
        }

        return sequences;
    }

    void Ch11_07_ex1()
    {
        const char* fmt = "{} ";
        constexpr size_t epl_max {2};

        // initialize vector of HtmColors
        std::vector<HtmlColor> colors = HtmlColor::get_vector();
        MT::print_ctr("\ncolors:\n", colors, fmt, epl_max);

        // generate HtmlColor color sequences
        std::vector<std::vector<HtmlColor>> sequences = get_sequences(30);

        for (const auto& sequence : sequences)
        {
            MT::print_ctr("\ntest sequence:\n", sequence, fmt, epl_max);

            // using std::ranges::search to find 'sequence' in 'colors'
            // std::ranges::search() returns iterator subrange [iter_b, iter_e)
            auto [iter_b, iter_e] = std::ranges::search(colors, sequence);

            if (iter_b != iter_e)
            {
                // sequence found, calculate position
                auto pos = std::distance(colors.begin(), iter_b);
                std::println("found sequence at position {:d}", pos);
            }
            else
                std::println("sequence not found");
        }
    }
```

Listing 11-7-1 commences with the definition of a function named get_sequences(). This function generates sequences of HtmlColor (see Listing 8-1-4-1) objects for test purposes. Note that get_sequences() returns a container of type std::vector<std::vector<HtmlColor>>.

Also shown in Listing 11-7-1 is example Ch11_07_ex1(). Near the top of this function, execution of the statement std::vector<HtmlColor> colors = HtmlColor::get_vector() creates a vector named colors that includes instances of all HtmlColors. The subsequent statement exploits the previously described get_sequences() to generate a series of std::vector<HtmlColor> test sequences.

During each iteration of Ch11_07_ex1()'s range for loop, execution of the statement [iter_b, iter_e] = std::ranges::search(colors, sequence) searches container colors for HtmlColor sequence sequence. Function std::ranges::search() returns an iterator subrange that pinpoints the first occurrence of sequence in colors (if it exists). If iter_b != iter_e is true, sequence exists in colors, and the position of sequence within colors is then calculated and printed. If the usage of subranges here looks familiar, it's because you saw the same basic technique earlier in this chapter (see Listing 11-4-4 and the accompanying explanations for std::ranges::find_last()).

Source code example Ch11_07_ex2(), shown in Listing 11-7-2, demonstrates the use of std::search().

Listing 11-7-2. Example Ch11_07 – Ch11_07_ex2()

```
void Ch11_07_ex2()
{
    const char* fmt = "{} ";
    constexpr size_t epl_max {2};

    // initialize vector of HtmColors
    std::vector<HtmlColor> colors = HtmlColor::get_vector();
    MT::print_ctr("\ncolors:\n", colors, fmt, epl_max);

    // generate HtmlColor sequences
    std::vector<std::vector<HtmlColor>> sequences = get_sequences(31);

    for (const auto& sequence : sequences)
    {
        MT::print_ctr("\ntest sequence:\n", sequence, fmt, epl_max);
```

```cpp
        // create sequence searcher
        std::boyer_moore_searcher searcher(sequence.begin(),
        sequence.end(),
            HtmlColor::hash_func_searcher);

        // using std::search to find 'sequence' in vector 'colors'
        auto iter = std::search(colors.begin(), colors.end(), searcher);

        if (iter != colors.end())
        {
            auto pos = std::distance(colors.begin(), iter);
            std::println("found sequence at position {:d}", pos);
        }
        else
            std::println("sequence not found");
    }
}
```

The code layout of Ch11_07_ex2() closely resembles that of Ch11_07_ex1(), but with a few notable differences. First, note the declaration of std::boyer_moore_searcher searcher within Ch11_07_ex2()'s range for loop. This statement specifies the sequence that the subsequent call to std::search() will look for in std::vector<HtmlColor> colors. It also specifies a custom hash function for the search algorithm. For class HtmlColor, the custom hash function utilizes the HtmlColor's name and STL's default hash function for a std::string:

```cpp
static size_t hash_func_searcher(const HtmlColor& html_color)
    { return std::hash<std::string>{} (html_color.m_Name); }
```

As mentioned in Chapter 8, defining a custom hash function that's both algorithmically efficient and statistically solid is a nontrivial undertaking. The current example applies a custom hash function merely to demonstrate the proper use of std::boyer_moore_searcher. More about this shortly.

The second item of note in Ch11_07_ex2()'s range for loop is that execution of iter = std::search(colors.begin(), colors.end(), searcher) returns a single iterator instead of a subrange. If iter != colors.end() is true, vector sequence exists in colors. STL helper function std::distance() is then exploited to calculate and print the position of vector sequence within colors.

CHAPTER 11   ALGORITHMS – PART 2

The STL also defines a std::default_searcher and a std::boyer_moore_horspool_searcher in addition to the std::boyer_moore_searcher that was used in Ch11_07_ex2(). The std::default_searcher provides functionality that corresponds to the STL's pre-C++17 implementation of std::search(). The std::boyer_moore_searcher and std::boyer_moore_horspool_searcher searchers implement search algorithms that are optimized for text strings. This is why HtmlColor::hash_function_searcher() uses std::hash<std::string>. Appendix B contains a list of references that you can consult for more information regarding these algorithms.

The final example of this section, Ch11_07_ex3(), highlights the use of std::ranges::mismatch(). This STL algorithm compares two ranges and returns iterators that identify the position of any mismatch within the two ranges. Listing 11-7-3 shows the source code for this example.

Listing 11-7-3. Example Ch11_07 – Ch11_07_ex3()

```
void Ch11_07_ex3()
{
    const char* fmt = "{:s} ";
    constexpr size_t epl_max {8};

    // initialize vector of HtmColor names
    std::vector<std::string> colors {};
    size_t num_colors {HtmlColor::num_colors()};

    for (size_t i = 0; i < num_colors; i += 25)
    {
        auto color {HtmlColor::get(i)};
        colors.emplace_back(color.Name());
    }

    for (size_t i = 0; i < 6; ++i)
    {
        // generate test vectors colors1a and colors2a
        constexpr size_t mmi {42};
        std::vector<std::string> colors1 {colors};
        std::vector<std::string> colors2 {colors};
```

```cpp
        if (i == 1)
            colors1.insert(colors1.begin() + 2, HtmlColor::get(mmi).
            Name());
        else if (i == 2)
            colors2.insert(colors2.end() - 2, HtmlColor::get(mmi).Name());
        else if (i == 3)
            colors1.erase(colors1.begin() + 3);
        else if (i == 4)
            colors1.push_back(HtmlColor::get(mmi).Name());
        else if (i == 5)
            colors2.push_back(HtmlColor::get(mmi).Name());

        // display test vectors
        std::println("\nTest #{:d}", i);
        MT::print_ctr("colors1a: ", colors1, fmt, epl_max);
        MT::print_ctr("colors2a: ", colors2, fmt, epl_max);

        // using std::ranges::mismatch
        auto [iter1, iter2] = std::ranges::mismatch(colors1, colors2);

        if (iter1 == colors1.end() && iter2 == colors2.end())
            std::println("no mistmatch found");
        else
        {
            std::println("mismatch found");

            if (iter1 != colors1.end())
                std::println("*iter1 (colors1): {}", *iter1);

            if (iter2 != colors2.end())
                std::println("*iter2 (colors2): {}", *iter2);
        }
    }
}
```

CHAPTER 11   ALGORITHMS – PART 2

The opening code block in Ch11_07_ex3() initializes std::vector<std::string> colors, which contains names of HtmlColors. The first code block in Ch11_07_ex3()'s for loop includes code that initializes two test vectors of HtmlColors named colors1 and colors2. The various if expressions ensure that colors1 and colors2 encompass a mixture of test cases when used later with std::ranges::mismatch().

Following the calls to MT::print_ctr() is the expression [iter1, iter2] = std::ranges::mismatch(colors1, colors2). The execution of this statement compares elements in the ranges specified by colors1 and colors2. If (iter1 == colors1.end() && iter2 == colorsa.end()) is true, sequences colors1 and colors2 are identical; otherwise, the sequences are different. If the sequences are different, the iterators returned by std::ranges::mismatch() point to the discrepant elements within the sequences. It's important to note that the ranges provided to std::ranges::mismatch() need not be the same size. Also, note that when a mismatch is found, one of the returned iterators may point to an end() element. This is why the else expression checks both iter1 and iter2 before they are dereferenced in the succeeding calls to std::println().

The results for example Ch11_07 follow this paragraph. This output has been edited to shorten its length (the vectors of HtmlColor names have been shortened). To see the complete output, just compile and run the code.

```
----- Results for example Ch11_07 -----

----- Ch11_07_ex1() -----

colors:
[AliceBlue           0xF0F8FF] [AntiqueWhite         0xFAEBD7]
[Aqua                0x00FFFF] [AquaMarine           0x7FFFD4]
[Azure               0xF0FFFF] [Beige                0xF5F5DC]
...

test sequence:
[AliceBlue           0xF0F8FF] [AntiqueWhite         0xFAEBD7]
[Aqua                0x00FFFF]
found sequence at position 0

test sequence:
[DarkOrchid          0x9932CC] [DarkRed              0x8B0000]
```

```
[DarkSalmon            0xE9967A]
found sequence at position 30

test sequence:
[LavenderBlush         0xFFF0F5] [LawnGreen             0x7CFC00]
[LightBlue             0xADD8E6]
sequence not found

test sequence:
[MidnightBlue          0x191970] [MintCream             0xF5FFFA]
[MistyRose             0xFFE4E1]
found sequence at position 90

test sequence:
[SeaGreen              0x2E8B57] [Seashell              0xFFF5EE]
[Sienna                0xA0522D]
found sequence at position 120

----- Ch11_07_ex2() -----
colors:
[AliceBlue             0xF0F8FF] [AntiqueWhite          0xFAEBD7]
[Aqua                  0x00FFFF] [AquaMarine            0x7FFFD4]
[Azure                 0xF0FFFF] [Beige                 0xF5F5DC]
...

test sequence:
[AliceBlue             0xF0F8FF] [AntiqueWhite          0xFAEBD7]
[Aqua                  0x00FFFF]
found sequence at position 0

test sequence:
[DarkRed               0x8B0000] [DarkSalmon            0xE9967A]
[DarkSeaGreen          0x8FBC8F]
found sequence at position 31

test sequence:
[LemonChiffon          0xFFFACD] [LightBlue             0xADD8E6]
[LightCyan             0xE0FFFF]
```

CHAPTER 11　ALGORITHMS – PART 2

sequence not found

test sequence:
[Moccasin   0xFFE4B5] [NavajoWhite   0xFFDEAD]
[Navy   0x000080]
found sequence at position 93

test sequence:
[SkyBlue   0x87CEEB] [SlateBlue   0x6A5ACD]
[SlateGray   0x708090]
found sequence at position 124

----- Ch11_07_ex3() -----

Test #0
colors1a: AliceBlue DarkGreen Gray LightYellow OrangeRed SlateBlue
colors2a: AliceBlue DarkGreen Gray LightYellow OrangeRed SlateBlue
no mistmatch found

Test #1
colors1a: AliceBlue DarkGreen Firebrick Gray LightYellow OrangeRed SlateBlue
colors2a: AliceBlue DarkGreen Gray LightYellow OrangeRed SlateBlue
mismatch found
*iter1 (colors1): Firebrick
*iter2 (colors2): Gray

Test #2
colors1a: AliceBlue DarkGreen Gray LightYellow OrangeRed SlateBlue
colors2a: AliceBlue DarkGreen Gray LightYellow Firebrick OrangeRed SlateBlue
mismatch found
*iter1 (colors1): OrangeRed
*iter2 (colors2): Firebrick

Test #3
colors1a: AliceBlue DarkGreen Gray OrangeRed SlateBlue
colors2a: AliceBlue DarkGreen Gray LightYellow OrangeRed SlateBlue
mismatch found

```
*iter1 (colors1): OrangeRed
*iter2 (colors2): LightYellow

Test #4
colors1a: AliceBlue DarkGreen Gray LightYellow OrangeRed SlateBlue
Firebrick
colors2a: AliceBlue DarkGreen Gray LightYellow OrangeRed SlateBlue
mismatch found
*iter1 (colors1): Firebrick

Test #5
colors1a: AliceBlue DarkGreen Gray LightYellow OrangeRed SlateBlue
colors2a: AliceBlue DarkGreen Gray LightYellow OrangeRed SlateBlue
Firebrick
mismatch found
*iter2 (colors2): Firebrick
```

Accumulate and Fold Algorithms

The final category of algorithms covered in this chapter includes accumulates and folds. Listing 11-8-1 shows the source code for Ch11_08_ex1(). This example function demonstrates the use of std::accumulate().

Listing 11-8-1. Example Ch11_08 – Ch11_08_ex1()

```
//-------------------------------------------------------------------------
// Ch11_08_ex.cpp
//-------------------------------------------------------------------------

#include <algorithm>
#include <functional>
#include <numeric>
#include <string>
#include <vector>
#include "Ch11_08.h"
#include "MF.h"
#include "MT.h"
```

CHAPTER 11 ALGORITHMS – PART 2

```cpp
#include "RN.h"

void Ch11_08_ex1()
{
    const char* fmt = "{:7.1f} ";
    constexpr size_t epl_max {10};

    // create vector of random values
    constexpr size_t n {20};
    constexpr int rng_min {1};
    constexpr int rng_max {1000};
    constexpr unsigned int rng_seed {5};
    std::vector vec1 {RN::get_vector<double>(n, rng_min, rng_max,
        rng_seed)};
    MT::print_ctr("\nvec1:\n", vec1, fmt, epl_max);

    // using std::accumulate
    double sum1 = std::accumulate(vec1.begin(), vec1.end(), 0.0);
    double sum2 = std::accumulate(vec1.begin(), vec1.end(),
        1'000'000'000.0);
    std::println("\nsum1: {:7.1f}  sum2: {:7.1f}", sum1, sum2);

    // using std::accumulate with binary operator
    auto acc_op = [](double x, double y) { return x - y; };
    double acc1 = std::accumulate(vec1.begin(), vec1.end(), 0.0, acc_op);
    std::println("\nacc1: {:7.1f}", acc1);
}
```

The opening code block of Ch11_08_ex1() utilizes RN::get_vector() to initialize vec1 with 20 random values of type double. In the ensuing code block, the expression sum1 = std::accumulate(vec1.begin(), vec1.end(), 0.0) sums the elements of [vec1.begin(), vec1.end()). During the execution of this expression, std::accumulate() repeatedly calculates sum1 += *iter++ where iter denotes an iterator that points to an element between [vec1.begin(), vec1.end()). The 0.0 argument is the initial value that's assigned to sum1. The next statement, sum2 = std::accumulate(vec1.begin(), vec1.end(), 1'000'000'000.0), illustrates the use of std::accumulate() with a different initial value.

The default summing behavior of std::accumulate() can be modified using a binary operator as shown in the next code block. The statement acc1 = std::accumulate(vec1.begin(), vec1.end(), 0.0, acc_op) essentially calculates acc1 = acc_op(acc1, *iter++) using all elements of the specified range. Like the non-binary operator variant, acc1 is initialized to 0.0 before the calculation commences.

Unlike most pre-C++20 algorithms, the STL doesn't define a std::ranges::accumulate(). Instead, the C++23 standard specifies a new category of fold algorithms. These algorithms are a bit more flexible than std::accumulate() as you will soon see.

A fold algorithm applies a binary operator to the elements of a range and its operation can best be explained using a short snippet of C++ code:

```cpp
std::array<double, 5> x {1.0, 2.0, 3.0, 4.0, 5.0};

auto op = [](double a, double b) { return a + b; };

double l_init {0.0};
double l_fold = op(op(op(op(op(l_init, x[0]), x[1]), x[2]), x[3]), x[4]);

double r_init {1000.0};
double r_fold = op(x[0], op(x[1], op(x[2], op(x[3], op(x[4], r_init)))));

std::println("l_fold: {:.1f}  r_fold: {:.1f}", l_fold, r_fold);
```

In this snippet, op() is a binary operator that adds two doubles. The statement l_fold = op(op(op(op(op(l_init, x[0]), x[1]), x[2]), x[3]), x[4]) is an example of a left fold. Note here that operator op() is applied left to right using successive elements of array x starting with x[0]. Also, note that each op() calculation utilizes the previous op() result and the next element in array x. Value l_init furnishes the initial value for the left fold operation. The std::accumulate() algorithm that you saw earlier performs a left fold. Returning to the snippet, the statement r_fold = op(x[0], op(x[1], op(x[2], op(x[3], op(x[4], r_init))))) is an example of a right fold. Note that a right fold applies op() to successive elements of array x in reverse order starting with the last element x[4]. Fold operations can be applied to ranges of any data type provided a suitable binary operator is defined.

Listing 11-8-2 shows the code for example Ch11_08_ex2(). This example spotlights the use of several std::ranges::fold_ algorithms.

Listing 11-8-2. Example Ch11_08 – Ch11_08_ex2()

```
void Ch11_08_ex2()
{
#ifdef __cpp_lib_ranges_fold
    const char* fmt = "{:7.1f} ";
    constexpr size_t epl_max {10};

    // create vector of random values
    std::vector<double> vec1 {10.0, 20.0, 30.0, 40.0, 50.0};
    MT::print_ctr("\nvec1:\n", vec1, fmt, epl_max);

    // using std::ranges::fold_left, std::ranges::fold_right
        (associative op)
    auto left1 = std::ranges::fold_left(vec1, 0.0, std::plus<double>());
    auto right1 = std::ranges::fold_right(vec1, 0.0, std::plus<double>());
    std::println("\nleft1: {:7.1f}   right1: {:7.1f}", left1, right1);

    // using std::ranges::fold_left, std::ranges::fold_right (non-
        associative op)
    auto left2 = std::ranges::fold_left(vec1, 0.0, std::minus<double>());
    auto right2 = std::ranges::fold_right(vec1, 0.0, std::minus<double>());
    std::println("\nleft2: {:7.1f}   right2: {:7.1f}", left2, right2);

    // using std::ranges::fold_left_first, std::ranges::fold_right_
        last (assoc)
    // left3, right3 are std::optional<double>
    auto left3 = std::ranges::fold_left_first(vec1, std::plus<double>());
    auto right3 = std::ranges::fold_right_last(vec1, std::plus<double>());
    std::println("\nleft3: {:7.1f}   right3: {:7.1f}", left3.value(),
    right3.value());

    // using std::ranges::fold_left_first, std::ranges::fold_right_last
        (non-assoc)
    // left4, right4 are std::optional<double>
    auto left4 = std::ranges::fold_left_first(vec1, std::minus<double>());
    auto right4 = std::ranges::fold_right_last(vec1, std::minus<double>());
    std::println("\nleft4: {:7.1f}   right4: {:7.1f}", left4.value(),
    right4.value());
```

```cpp
    // using std::ranges::fold_left_first, empty container
    std::vector<double> vec2 {};
    auto left5 = std::ranges::fold_left_first(vec2, std::plus<double>());

    if (left5)
        std::println("\nleft5: {:7.1f}", left5.value());
    else
        std::println("\nleft5: empty container");
#else
    std::println("Ch11_08_ex2() requires __cpp_lib_ranges_fold (C++23)");
#endif
}
```

Following the initialization of std::vector<double> vec1, execution of the statement left1 = std::ranges::fold_left(vec1, 0.0, std::plus<double>()) sums the elements of vec1. In this expression, function object std::plus<double>() calls operator+ using two doubles. As used in the current code block, std::ranges::fold_left() performs the same calculation as std::accumulate(vec1.begin(), vec1.end(), 0.0). The next statement, right1 = std::ranges::fold_right(vec1, 0.0, std::plus<double>()), performs a right fold using the elements of vec1. If you scan ahead to the results section, you'll notice that left1 and right1 are identical. The reason for this is that std::plus<double> is an associative operator. The next code block in Ch11_08_ex2() carries out left and right fold operations using vec1 and function object std::minus<double>(). Execution of these fold operations yields different values for left2 and right2 since the operations performed by std::minus<double>() are non-associative.

The next two code blocks in Ch11_08_ex2() demonstrate the use of std::ranges::fold_left_first() and std::ranges::fold_right_last(). The execution of these fold functions is slightly different. First, both functions return a value of type std::optional<T>. Recall that a std::optional<T> is an object that might contain a value. More on this shortly. The other difference is that std::ranges::fold_left_first() and std::ranges::fold_right_last() don't require an initial value; they simply use the first or last element in the specified range.

The final code block in Ch11_08_ex2() demonstrates the use of std::ranges::fold_left_first() using an empty container. This is where the std::optional<T> return value becomes useful. Note that prior to the std::println() statement that utilizes

CHAPTER 11   ALGORITHMS – PART 2

left5.value(), left5 is tested. The reason for this is that execution of left5.value() will throw a std::bad_optional_access exception if std::optional<double> left5 doesn't contain a value.

Example function Ch11_08_ex3(), shown in Listing 11-8-3, highlights left and right folds using elements of type std::string. Following the initialization of std::vector<std::string> vec1 is the definition of a binary operator named fold_op_left(). This operator carries out a concatenation action using std::string arguments s1 and s2. Note that MF::to_upper() is applied to s2_temp, which is a copy of argument s2. A copy of s2 is made since MF::to_upper() performs an in-place uppercase conversion and s2 is declared using the const qualifier. The subsequent code block in Ch11_08_ex3() defines fold_op_right(). This binary operator closely resembles fold_op_left() except that it applies MF::to_upper() to s1_temp instead of s2_temp. Both binary operators include a std::println() statement so that you can see the output of each fold concatenation step in the results section.

Listing 11-8-3. Example Ch11_08 – Ch11_08_ex3()

```
void Ch11_08_ex3()
{
#ifdef __cpp_lib_ranges_fold
    const char* fmt = "{:8s} ";
    constexpr size_t epl_max {10};

    // create test vector
    std::vector<std::string> vec1
        {"zero", "one", "two", "three", "four", "five", "six", "seven"};
    MT::print_ctr("\nvec1: ", vec1, fmt, epl_max);

    // define binary operators for left and right folds
    auto fold_op_left = [](const std::string& s1, const std::string& s2)
    {
        std::println("s1: {:35s} s2: {:35s}", s1, s2);
        auto s2_temp {s2};
        return s1 + " " + MF::to_upper(s2_temp);
    };
```

```cpp
    auto fold_op_right = [](const std::string& s1, const std::string& s2)
    {
        std::println("s1: {:35s} s2: {:35s}", s1, s2);
        auto s1_temp {s1};
        return MF::to_upper(s1_temp) + " " + s2;
    };

    // using std::ranges::fold_left_first
    std::println("\nexecuting std::ranges::fold_left_first()");
    auto left1 = std::ranges::fold_left_first(vec1, fold_op_left);
    std::println("\nleft1:  {:s}", left1.value());

    // using std::ranges::fold_left_right
    std::println("\nexecuting std::ranges::fold_right_last()");
    auto right1 = std::ranges::fold_right_last(vec1, fold_op_right);
    std::println("\nright1: {:s}", right1.value());
#else
    std::println("Ch11_08_ex3() requires __cpp_lib_ranges_fold (C++23)");
#endif
}
```

The next code block in Ch11_08_ex3() performs a left fold of vec1 using left1 = std::ranges::fold_left_first(vec1, fold_op_left). If you scan ahead to the results section, note that std::string s1 contains the accumulated result of the previous fold actions, while s2 contains the next string to concatenate. In the current example, execution of std::ranges::fold_left_first(vec1, fold_op_left) basically appends the strings of vec1 into a single string with MF::to_upper() being applied to all strings except vec[0]. The final code block of Ch11_08_ex3() performs a right fold using right1 = std::ranges::fold_right_last(vec1, fold_op_right). Execution of this expression prepends the strings of vec1 into a single string with MF::to_upper() being applied to all strings except vec[7]. Here are the results for example Ch11_08:

CHAPTER 11   ALGORITHMS – PART 2

----- Results for example Ch11_08 -----

----- Ch11_08_ex1() -----

vec1:
   222.0   56.0   871.0   832.0   207.0   364.0   919.0   980.0   489.0   90.0
   612.0   397.0   766.0   355.0   519.0   487.0   297.0   991.0   188.0   809.0

sum1: 10451.0   sum2: 1000010451.0

acc1: -10451.0

----- Ch11_08_ex2() -----

vec1:
    10.0   20.0   30.0   40.0   50.0

left1:   150.0   right1:   150.0

left2:   -150.0   right2:   30.0

left3:   150.0   right3:   150.0

left4:   -130.0   right4:   30.0

left5: empty container

----- Ch11_08_ex3() -----

vec1: zero   one   two   three   four   five   six   seven
executing std::ranges::fold_left_first()
s1: zero   s2: one
s1: zero ONE   s2: two
s1: zero ONE TWO   s2: three
s1: zero ONE TWO THREE   s2: four
s1: zero ONE TWO THREE FOUR   s2: five
s1: zero ONE TWO THREE FOUR FIVE   s2: six
s1: zero ONE TWO THREE FOUR FIVE SIX   s2: seven

left1:   zero ONE TWO THREE FOUR FIVE SIX SEVEN

510

```
executing std::ranges::fold_right_last()
s1: six                             s2: seven
s1: five                            s2: SIX seven
s1: four                            s2: FIVE SIX seven
s1: three                           s2: FOUR FIVE SIX seven
s1: two                             s2: THREE FOUR FIVE SIX seven
s1: one                             s2: TWO THREE FOUR FIVE SIX seven
s1: zero                            s2: ONE TWO THREE FOUR FIVE
SIX seven

right1: ZERO ONE TWO THREE FOUR FIVE SIX seven
```

Summary

Here are the key learning points for this chapter:

- A for_each algorithm applies a function object to each dereferenced iterator in a range. These algorithms are sometimes used as an alternative to an explicitly coded range for loop.

- A transformation algorithm applies a unary or binary function object to one or two input ranges. The result of each transformation is then saved to an output range.

- A generation algorithm assigns the return value of successive user-specified function evaluations to each element of a range.

- A find algorithm searches a range for an element that matches a specific value or satisfies the decision logic of a predicate function. The STL also defines find algorithms that determine if a range begins or ends with a sequence that's specified by a separate range.

- A contains algorithm returns a bool result that signifies the presence of a value in a range.

- A search algorithm searches a range for a sequence of elements specified by another range. The STL also predefines several searchers that can be used to accelerate the performance of searches using containers or ranges of text strings.

- A fold algorithm applies a binary operator to successive elements in a range. These algorithms are often used to carry out a "summing" action over a range.

CHAPTER 12

Algorithms – Part 3

This chapter expounds more STL algorithms, including

- Sort algorithms
- Binary search algorithms
- Partition algorithms
- Heap algorithms

Like the previous chapter, the content of this chapter mostly targets the algorithms of namespace `std::ranges`. You can also use the pre-C++20 counterparts in namespace `std`. The use of these algorithms might be a better option when maintaining an older code base, especially if switching to a C++20 or later compiler is impracticable.

Sorting Algorithms

Sorting the elements of a container is a critical task for most C++ applications. In Chapters 3 and 4, you studied several examples that exemplified basic use of STL algorithms `std::sort()` and `std::ranges::sort()`. This section briefly reviews these algorithms. It also presents other algorithms that carry out sorting operations.

Listing 12-1-1 shows the source code for example `Ch12_01_ex1()`, which illustrates the use of `std::sort()` and `std::ranges::sort()`. Near the top of `Ch12_01_ex1()`, `std::vector<Airport> airports` is initialized using `Airport::get_vector_airports_shuffle()` (see Listing 11-4-1-2). Following execution of this function, `airports` holds a collection of `Airport` objects. In the next code block, `Ch12_01_ex1()` utilizes `std::sort(airports.begin(), airports.end())` to sort the elements of `airports`.

CHAPTER 12   ALGORITHMS – PART 3

The default comparison function object for std::sort() is std::less() (or operator<), and the relational operators for class Airport utilize each airport's IATA code.[1] Following execution of std::sort(), the elements of airports are sorted by IATA code in ascending order.

Listing 12-1-1. Example Ch12_01 - Ch12_01_ex1()

```
//---------------------------------------------------------------------------
// Ch12_01_ex.cpp
//---------------------------------------------------------------------------

#include <algorithm>
#include <vector>
#include "Ch12_01.h"
#include "Airport.h"
#include "MT.h"
#include "RN.h"

void Ch12_01_ex1()
{
    const char* fmt = "{} ";
    constexpr size_t epl_max {1};

    // initialize vector of airports
    std::vector<Airport> airports = Airport::get_vector_airports_shuffle();
    MT::print_ctr("\nairports (before sort):\n", airports, fmt, epl_max);

    // using std::sort (uses Airport::operator< which uses IATA code)
    std::sort(airports.begin(), airports.end());
    MT::print_ctr("\nairports (ascending by IATA):\n", airports, fmt,
        epl_max);

    // using std::ranges::sort (custom compare, descending order using
    //   latitude)
    auto cmp_op = [](const Airport& ap1, const Airport& ap2)
    {
        auto [lat1, lon1] = ap1.Location().to_decimal();
```

---

[1] Recall that class Airport defines operator<=>, from which the compiler generates operator<.

CHAPTER 12　ALGORITHMS – PART 3

```
        auto [lat2, lon2] = ap2.Location().to_decimal();
        return lat1 > lat2;
    };

    std::ranges::sort(airports, cmp_op);
    MT::print_ctr("\nairports (descending by latitude):\n", airports, fmt,
    epl_max);
}
```

The ensuing code block opens with the definition of a lambda expression named cmp_op(). Note that this expression returns lat1 > lat2 where lat1 and lat2 are the latitudes of Airports ap1 and ap2. Execution of the subsequent std::ranges::sort(airports, cmp_op) sorts the elements of airports in descending order based on latitude. Unlike the traditional algorithms of namespace std, most algorithms in the std::ranges namespace support projections. A projection is a transformation that an algorithm applies prior to inspecting an element's value. Their use often yields simpler expressions for algorithms like std::ranges::sort(). You'll learn more about projections in Chapter 14.

Example function Ch12_01_ex2(), shown in Listing 12-1-2, highlights the use of std::ranges::stable_sort(). A stable sort preserves the range's original ordering of equivalent elements.

Listing 12-1-2. Example Ch12_01 – Ch12_01_ex2()

```
void Ch12_01_ex2()
{
    auto print_airports = [](const char* msg, const std::vector<Airport>&
    airports)
    {
        size_t nl {};
        std::println("{:s}", msg);

        for (const auto& ap : airports)
        {
            std::print("[{:2s} {:3s} {:32s}] ",
                ap.CountryCode(), ap.IataCode(), ap.Name());
```

```
            if (++nl % 2 == 0)
                std::println("");
        }

        std::println("");
    };

    // initialize vectors of airports
    std::vector<Airport> airports = Airport::get_vector_airports_shuffle();
    print_airports("airports (before stable_sort):", airports);

    // compare op for sorting
    auto cmp_op = [](const Airport& ap1, const Airport& ap2)
        { return ap1.CountryCode() < ap2.CountryCode(); };

    // using std::ranges::stable_sort - preserves equivalent orderings
    std::ranges::stable_sort(airports, cmp_op);
    print_airports("airports (after stable_sort):", airports);
}
```

In Listing 12-1-2, note that lambda expression cmp_op() compares country codes of Airports ap1 and ap2 using operator<. Execution of std::ranges::stable_sort(airports, cmp_op) carries out a stable sort using the elements of airports. Following execution of this algorithm, container airports is sorted in ascending order by country code. Note in the results section that the ordering of airports with matching country codes is the same before and after the call to std::ranges::stable_sort(). Unlike std::ranges::sort(), execution of std::ranges::stable_sort() guarantees this arrangement for equivalent elements.

For some use cases, it's only necessary to partially sort the elements of a range. Computing the median value of a data set is a common example. In Listing 12-1-3, Ch12_01_ex3() utilizes std::ranges::nth_element(vec1, iter_nth) to determine the median value of std::vector<int> vec1, which contains 60 random values. Note that iter_nth is an iterator that points to vec1's median element position at vec1.begin() + vec1.size() / 2.

Listing 12-1-3. Example Ch12_01 - Ch12_01_ex3()

```
void Ch12_01_ex3()
{
    const char* fmt = "{:5d} ";
    constexpr size_t epl_max {12};

    // initialize vector of random integers
    auto vec1 = RN::get_vector<int>(60);
    MT::print_ctr("\nvec1 (initial values):\n", vec1, fmt, epl_max);

    // using std::ranges::nth_element to find median
    auto iter_nth = vec1.begin() + vec1.size() / 2;

    std::ranges::nth_element(vec1, iter_nth);
    MT::print_ctr("\nvec1 (after nth_element):\n", vec1, fmt, epl_max);
    std::println("\nmedian value of vec1: {:d}", *iter_nth);
}
```

Following execution of std::ranges::nth_element(), iter_nth points to the *n*-th or median element in vec1. All elements in vec1 that precede iter_nth are guaranteed to be less than or equal to the iter_nth element. However, execution of std::ranges::nth_element() does not guarantee any particular ordering for the elements that occur before or after iter_nth. It only computes the same *n*-th element that would occur if the entire range were sorted.

Partial sorts are useful when it's only necessary to establish the first few elements of a completely sorted range. The final example of this section, shown in Listing 12-1-4, demonstrates the use of std::ranges::partial_sort(). Function Ch12_01_ex4() opens with the definition lambda expression named print_vec(). This function object prints the elements of std::vector<int> v. It also spotlights the use of std::ranges::is_sorted() and std::ranges::is_sorted_until(). The former returns true if the specified range is already sorted; otherwise, it returns false. Execution of iter_until = std::ranges::is_sorted_until(v) returns an iterator, and range [v.begin(), iter_until) signifies the elements of vec1 that are already sorted.

CHAPTER 12   ALGORITHMS – PART 3

Listing 12-1-4. Example Ch12_01 - Ch12_01_ex4()

```
void Ch12_01_ex4()
{
    const char* fmt = "{:5d}";
    constexpr size_t epl_max {16};

    auto print_vec = [](const std::vector<int>& v)
    {
        // using std::ranges::is_sorted
        std::println("is_sorted:       {:s}", std::ranges::is_sorted(v));

        // using std::ranges::is_sorted_until
        auto iter_until = std::ranges::is_sorted_until(v);
        std::print("is_sorted_until: ");

        if (iter_until != v.end())
            std::println("{:d}", *iter_until);
        else
            std::println("sorted");
    };

    // initialize vector of random integers
    auto vec1 = RN::get_vector<int>(16);
    MT::print_ctr("\nvec1 (initial order):\n", vec1, fmt, epl_max);
    print_vec(vec1);

    // using std::ranges::partial_sort - range, middle
    auto iter_ps = vec1.begin() + vec1.size() / 3;
    std::ranges::partial_sort(vec1, iter_ps);
    MT::print_ctr("\nvec1 (after first partial_sort):\n", vec1, fmt, epl_max);
    print_vec(vec1);

    // using std::ranges::partial_sort - first, middle, last
    std::ranges::partial_sort(iter_ps, vec1.end(), vec1.end());
    MT::print_ctr("\nvec1 (after second partial_sort):\n", vec1, fmt,
        epl_max);
    print_vec(vec1);
}
```

CHAPTER 12   ALGORITHMS – PART 3

Following the definition of print_vec(), Ch12_01_ex4() utilizes RN::get_vector<int>(16) (see Common/RN.h) to initialize vec1. In the subsequent code block, the expression iter_ps = vec1.begin() + vec1.size() / 3 computes a "middle" range position for std::ranges::partial_sort(). Execution of std::ranges::partial_sort(vec1, iter_ps) partially sorts the first vec1.size() / 3 elements of vec1. If you scan ahead to the results section, note that all of the elements in [vec1.begin(), iter_ps) are less than or equal to the element pointed to by iter_ps. Also, note the output generated by print_vec()'s use of std::ranges::is_sorted() and std::ranges::is_sorted_until().

The final code block in Ch12_01_ex4() exploits std::ranges::partial_sort(iter_ps, vec1.end(), vec1.end()) to finalize the sort of vec1. In this expression, iter_ps specifies the range's first element, while vec1.end() designates the range's "middle" and last elements. In other words, the current use of std::ranges::partial_sort() sorts all elements between [iter_ps, vec1.end()). Here are the results for example Ch12_01:

```
----- Results for example Ch12_01 -----

----- Ch12_01_ex1() -----

airports (before sort):
[US, JFK, John F Kennedy International (40.6397, -74.0789)]
[NZ, AKL, Auckland (-37.0081, 174.7917)]
[IN, DEL, Indira Gandhi International (28.5686, 77.1122)]
[DE, FRA, Frankfurt (50.0333, 8.5706)]
...
[BR, BSB, Brasilia International (-15.8711, -47.9186)]
[NZ, WLG, Wellington International (-41.3272, 174.8053)]
[CA, YYC, Calgary International (51.1225, -114.0133)]
[FR, TLS, Toulouse-Blagnac (43.6350, 1.3678)]

airports (ascending by IATA):
[NZ, AKL, Auckland (-37.0081, 174.7917)]
[SE, ARN, Stockholm Arlanda (59.5019, 17.9186)]
[DE, BER, Berlin Brandenburg (52.3667, 13.5033)]
[BR, BSB, Brasilia International (-15.8711, -47.9186)]
...
```

CHAPTER 12   ALGORITHMS – PART 3

[CA, YVR, Vancouver International (49.1947, -123.1839)]
[CA, YYC, Calgary International (51.1225, -114.0133)]
[CA, YYZ, Toronto Pearson International (53.3100, -113.5794)]
[CH, ZRH, Zurich (47.4314, 8.5492)]

airports (descending by latitude):
[NO, OSL, Oslo Gardermoen (60.2028, 11.0839)]
[SE, ARN, Stockholm Arlanda (59.5019, 17.9186)]
[GB, GLA, Glasgow (55.8719, -4.4331)]
[CA, YYZ, Toronto Pearson International (53.3100, -113.5794)]
...
[AU, SYD, Sydney Kingsford Smith (-33.9461, 151.1772)]
[NZ, AKL, Auckland (-37.0081, 174.7917)]
[AU, MEL, Melbourne (-37.6733, 144.8433)]
[NZ, WLG, Wellington International (-41.3272, 174.8053)]

----- Ch12_01_ex2() -----
airports (before stable_sort):
[US JFK John F Kennedy International   ] [NZ AKL Auckland   ]
[IN DEL Indira Gandhi International   ] [DE FRA Frankfurt   ]
[US ORD O'Hare International   ] [DE MUN Munich Franz Josef Stauss   ]
[SE ARN Stockholm Arlanda   ] [CA YVR Vancouver International   ]
[AU MEL Melbourne   ] [US LAX Los Angeles International]
[GB GLA Glasgow   ] [US IAH George Bush International]
[DE BER Berlin Brandenburg   ] [CN PVG Shanghai Pudong International]
[JP KIX Kansai International   ] [CA YEG Edmonton International   ]
[CA YYZ Toronto Pearson International   ] [US MCO Orlando International   ]

[FR CDG Paris Charles de Gaulle   ] [JP NRT Narita International   ]
[GB LHR Heathrow International   ] [AU SYD Sydney Kingsford Smith   ]
[NO OSL Oslo Gardermoen   ] [CN PEK Beijing Capital International]
[CL SCL Santiago International   ] [CH ZRH Zurich   ]
[BR BSB Brasilia International   ] [NZ WLG Wellington International   ]
[CA YYC Calgary International   ] [FR TLS Toulouse-Blagnac   ]

airports (after stable_sort):
[AU MEL Melbourne   ] [AU SYD Sydney Kingsford Smith   ]
[BR BSB Brasilia International   ] [CA YVR Vancouver International   ]
[CA YEG Edmonton International   ] [CA YYZ Toronto Pearson International]
[CA YYC Calgary International   ] [CH ZRH Zurich   ]
[CL SCL Santiago International   ] [CN PVG Shanghai Pudong International]
[CN PEK Beijing Capital International] [DE FRA Frankfurt   ]
[DE MUN Munich Franz Josef Stauss   ] [DE BER Berlin Brandenburg   ]
[FR CDG Paris Charles de Gaulle   ] [FR TLS Toulouse-Blagnac   ]
[GB GLA Glasgow   ] [GB LHR Heathrow International   ]
[IN DEL Indira Gandhi International] [JP KIX Kansai International   ]
[JP NRT Narita International   ] [NO OSL Oslo Gardermoen   ]

CHAPTER 12   ALGORITHMS – PART 3

[NZ AKL Auckland   ] [NZ WLG Wellington
                                       International   ]
[SE ARN Stockholm Arlanda   ] [US JFK John F Kennedy
                                       International   ]
[US ORD O'Hare International   ] [US LAX Los Angeles
                                       International   ]
[US IAH George Bush International   ] [US MCO Orlando
                                       International   ]

----- Ch12_01_ex3() -----

vec1 (initial values):
   375   797   951   184   732   780   599   597   157   446   156   100
    59   460   867   334   602   143   709   651   21   57   970   722
   833   939   213   1   182   993   184   618   305   612   525   8
   432   24   292   525   612   400   140   47   293   974   367   233
   457   91   786   619   200   383   515   984   593   467   47   860

vec1 (after nth_element):
    47   233   367   184   200   293   47   184   157   57   156   100
    59   21   140   334   292   143   24   8   213   1   182   305
    91   375   383   400   432   446   **457**   460   467   515   525   525
   593   597   651   709   612   602   867   599   780   732   951   797
   618   993   786   619   860   612   939   984   833   970   722   974

median value of vec1: 457

----- Ch12_01_ex4() -----

vec1 (initial order):
  375 797 951 184 732 780 599 597 157 446 156 100
59 460 867 334
is_sorted: false
is_sorted_until: 184

vec1 (after first partial_sort):
    59 100 156 157 184 951 **797** 780 732 599 597 446 375 460 867 334
is_sorted: false
is_sorted_until: 797

```
vec1 (after second partial_sort):
   59 100 156 157 184 334 375 446  460 597  599  732  780  797  867  951
is_sorted:         true
is_sorted_until: sorted
```

Binary Search Algorithms

The STL includes several binary search algorithm functions. These algorithms carry out search actions using forward iterators over *sorted* ranges. Listing 12-2-1 shows the source code for example Ch12_02_ex2(), which demonstrates the use of std::ranges::binary_search() and std::ranges::upper_bound().

Listing 12-2-1. Example Ch12_02 – Ch12_02_ex1()

```
//-------------------------------------------------------------------------
// Ch12_02_ex.cpp
//-------------------------------------------------------------------------

#include <algorithm>
#include <vector>
#include "Ch12_02.h"
#include "Airport.h"
#include "MT.h"

void print_airports(const char* msg, const std::vector<Airport>& airports)
{
    size_t nl {};
    std::println("{:s}", msg);

    for (const auto& ap : airports)
    {
        std::print("[{:2s} {:3s} {:32s}] ", ap.CountryCode(),
            ap.IataCode(),
                ap.Name());
        if (++nl % 2 == 0)
            std::println("");
    }
}
```

CHAPTER 12   ALGORITHMS – PART 3

```cpp
std::vector<Airport> Ch12_02_ex1()
{
    // using std::ranges::sort (uses Airport::operator< which uses
       IATA code)
    std::vector<Airport> airports = Airport::get_vector_airports_
    shuffle(8191);
    std::ranges::sort(airports);
    print_airports("\nairports (ascending sort by IATA code):", airports);

    // list of airports to search for (Airport::operator== compares
       IATA codes)
    std::vector<Airport> more_airports
    {
        Airport {"US", "LAX", "Los Angeles International",
            Airport::GeoCoord{33, 56, 33, 'N', 118, 24, 29, 'W'}},
        Airport {"US", "BOS", "Logan
        International",                          // new
            Airport::GeoCoord{42, 21, 47, 'N',  71,  0, 23, 'W'}},
        Airport {"US", "ORD", "O'Hare International",
            Airport::GeoCoord{41, 58, 43, 'N',  87, 54, 17, 'W'}},
        Airport {"US", "ANC", "Ted Stevens Anchorage
        Intl.",                 // new
            Airport::GeoCoord{61, 10, 27, 'N', 149, 59, 54, 'W'}},
        // repeat airports to confirm successful insertions
        Airport {"US", "BOS", "Logan Internatioal",
            Airport::GeoCoord{42, 21, 47, 'N',  71,  0, 23, 'W'}},
        Airport {"US", "ANC", "Ted Stevens Anchorage Intl.",
            Airport::GeoCoord{61, 10, 27, 'N', 149, 59, 54, 'W'}},
    };

    for (auto const& new_airport : more_airports)
    {
        // using std::ranges::binary_search
        std::println("\nsearching for airport: {:s}", new_airport.
        IataCode());
```

```cpp
        bool sea_result = std::ranges::binary_search(airports, new_
        airport);

        if (sea_result)
            std::println("airport found: {}", new_airport);
        else
        {
            // using std::ranges::upper_bound
            auto iter_insert = std::ranges::upper_bound(airports,
            new_airport);
            airports.insert(iter_insert, new_airport);
            std::println("airport not found - added to container");
        }
    }

    print_airports("\nairports (after new airport insertions):", airports);
    return airports;
}
```

Near the top of Listing 12-2-1 is the definition of a helper function named print_airports() that prints the elements of a std::vector<Airport>. Function Ch12_02_ex1() utilizes Airport::get_vector_airports_shuffle() to initialize std::vector<Airport> airports. The next statement, std::ranges::sort(airports), sorts the elements of vec1 using default comparison function object std::ranges::less(). Recall that class Airport's relation operators compare IATA codes, which means that the elements of vec1 are sorted in ascending order according to these codes. Vector std::vector<Airports> more_airports contains a list of additional Airports for example searches.

Within Ch12_02_ex1()'s range for loop, execution of std::ranges::binary_search(airports, new_airport) returns true if new_airport exists in airports; otherwise, it returns false. In the latter case, Ch12_02_ex1()'s execution continues with a call to iter_insert = std::ranges::upper_bound(airports, new_airport). Execution of this function returns an iterator to the first element in airports such that Airport::operator<(const Airport& ap1, const Airport& ap2) is false. In other words, iter_insert points to the correct insertion point in airports for new_airport. The next statement, airports.insert(iter_insert, new_airport), inserts

CHAPTER 12 ALGORITHMS – PART 3

new_airport into airports. It warrants mentioning here that the STL also includes std::ranges::lower_bound(), whose use is applicable when the source range is sorted in descending order.

Listing 12-2-2 shows the source code for example Ch12_02_ex2(). This function demonstrates the use of std::ranges::equal_range(). Prior to its range for loop, Ch12_02_ex2() re-sorts the elements of airports. Note that cmp_op utilizes each Airport's country code and operator>, which results in airports being sorted in descending order based on county code. Next is the definition of std::vector<std::string> country_codes, which includes both valid and invalid codes.

Listing 12-2-2. Example Ch12_02 – Ch12_02_ex2()

```cpp
void Ch12_02_ex2(std::vector<Airport>& airports)
{
    // sort airports in descending order by country code
    auto cmp_op = [](const Airport& ap1, const Airport& ap2)
        { return ap1.CountryCode() > ap2.CountryCode(); };

    std::ranges::sort(airports, cmp_op);
    print_airports("\nairports (descending sort by country code):",
    airports);

    // vector below contains invalid country codes for test purposes
    std::vector<std::string> country_codes {"AA", "AU", "DE", "NN",
    "US", "ZZ"};

    for (auto country_code : country_codes)
    {
        Airport ap_temp { country_code, "", "", Airport::GeoCoord{} };

        // using std::ranges::equal_range (must use same sort_op)
        auto iter_sr = std::ranges::equal_range(airports, ap_temp, cmp_op);

        std::println("\nresults for country code '{:s}' ",
                country_code);

        if (iter_sr.begin() == iter_sr.end())
            std::println("no airports found");
```

```
        else
        {
            auto f = [](const auto& ap) { std::println("{}", ap); };
            std::ranges::for_each(iter_sr, f);
        }
    }
}
```

Inside the range for loop, execution of iter_sr = std::ranges::equal_range(airports, ap_temp, cmp_op) scans airports for elements that match the country code of ap_temp. Note here that like the earlier calls to std::ranges::sort(), std::ranges::equal_range() also utilizes cmp_op(). For meaningful results, these functions must apply the same binary comparison function. If iter_sr.begin() == iter_sr.end() is true, no elements in airports matched the country code of ap_temp. Otherwise, iter_sr defines a subrange of matching country codes within airports. In this outcome, function Ch12_02_ex2() exploits std::ranges::for_each() to print the subrange's Airports. Here are the results for example Ch12_02:

```
----- Results for example Ch12_02 -----

----- Ch12_02_ex1() -----

airports (ascending sort by IATA code):
[NZ AKL Auckland                      ] [SE ARN Stockholm
                                         Arlanda                  ]
[DE BER Berlin Brandenburg            ] [BR BSB Brasilia
                                         International            ]
[FR CDG Paris Charles de Gaulle       ] [IN DEL Indira Gandhi
                                         International     ]
[DE FRA Frankfurt                     ] [GB GLA
                                         Glasgow                              ]
[US IAH George Bush International     ] [US JFK John F Kennedy
                                         International     ]
[JP KIX Kansai International          ] [US LAX Los Angeles
                                         International         ]
[GB LHR Heathrow International        ] [US MCO Orlando
                                         International            ]
```

CHAPTER 12 ALGORITHMS – PART 3

[AU MEL Melbourne   ] [DE MUN Munich Franz Josef Stauss   ]
[JP NRT Narita International   ] [US ORD O'Hare International   ]
[NO OSL Oslo Gardermoen   ] [CN PEK Beijing Capital International]
[CN PVG Shanghai Pudong International] [CL SCL Santiago International   ]
[AU SYD Sydney Kingsford Smith   ] [FR TLS Toulouse-Blagnac   ]
[NZ WLG Wellington International   ] [CA YEG Edmonton International   ]
[CA YVR Vancouver International   ] [CA YYC Calgary International   ]
[CA YYZ Toronto Pearson International] [CH ZRH Zurich   ]

searching for airport: LAX
airport found: [US, LAX, Los Angeles International (33.9425, -118.4081)]

searching for airport: BOS
airport not found - added to container

searching for airport: ORD
airport found: [US, ORD, O'Hare International (41.9786, -87.9047)]

searching for airport: ANC
airport not found - added to container

searching for airport: BOS
airport found: [US, BOS, Logan Internatioal (42.3631, -71.0064)]

searching for airport: ANC
airport found: [US, ANC, Ted Stevens Anchorage Intl. (61.1742, -149.9983)]

airports (after new airport insertions):
[NZ AKL Auckland   ] [US ANC Ted Stevens Anchorage Intl.   ]

[SE ARN Stockholm Arlanda   ] [DE BER Berlin
                                      Brandenburg   ]
[US BOS Logan International   ] [BR BSB Brasilia
                                      International   ]
[FR CDG Paris Charles de Gaulle   ] [IN DEL Indira Gandhi
                                      International   ]
[DE FRA Frankfurt   ] [GB GLA
                                      Glasgow   ]
[US IAH George Bush International   ] [US JFK John F Kennedy
                                      International   ]
[JP KIX Kansai International   ] [US LAX Los Angeles
                                      International   ]
[GB LHR Heathrow International   ] [US MCO Orlando
                                      International   ]
[AU MEL Melbourne   ] [DE MUN Munich Franz Josef
                                      Stauss   ]
[JP NRT Narita International   ] [US ORD O'Hare
                                      International   ]
[NO OSL Oslo Gardermoen   ] [CN PEK Beijing Capital
                                      International   ]
[CN PVG Shanghai Pudong International] [CL SCL Santiago
                                      International   ]
[AU SYD Sydney Kingsford Smith   ] [FR TLS Toulouse-
                                      Blagnac   ]
[NZ WLG Wellington International   ] [CA YEG Edmonton
                                      International   ]
[CA YVR Vancouver International   ] [CA YYC Calgary
                                      International   ]
[CA YYZ Toronto Pearson International] [CH ZRH
                                      Zurich   ]

----- Ch12_02_ex2() -----

airports (descending sort by country code):
[US ANC Ted Stevens Anchorage Intl.] [US BOS Logan
                                       International   ]

CHAPTER 12   ALGORITHMS – PART 3

[US IAH George Bush International   ] [US JFK John F Kennedy International   ]
[US LAX Los Angeles International   ] [US MCO Orlando International   ]
[US ORD O'Hare International   ] [SE ARN Stockholm Arlanda   ]
[NZ AKL Auckland   ] [NZ WLG Wellington International   ]
[NO OSL Oslo Gardermoen   ] [JP KIX Kansai International   ]
[JP NRT Narita International   ] [IN DEL Indira Gandhi International   ]
[GB GLA Glasgow   ] [GB LHR Heathrow International   ]
[FR CDG Paris Charles de Gaulle   ] [FR TLS Toulouse-Blagnac   ]
[DE BER Berlin Brandenburg   ] [DE FRA Frankfurt   ]
[DE MUN Munich Franz Josef Stauss   ] [CN PEK Beijing Capital International   ]
[CN PVG Shanghai Pudong International   ] [CL SCL Santiago International   ]
[CH ZRH Zurich   ] [CA YEG Edmonton International   ]
[CA YVR Vancouver International   ] [CA YYC Calgary International   ]
[CA YYZ Toronto Pearson International   ] [BR BSB Brasilia International   ]
[AU MEL Melbourne   ] [AU SYD Sydney Kingsford Smith   ]

results for country code 'AA'
no airports found

results for country code 'AU'
[AU, MEL, Melbourne (-37.6733, 144.8433)]
[AU, SYD, Sydney Kingsford Smith (-33.9461, 151.1772)]

results for country code 'DE'
[DE, BER, Berlin Brandenburg (52.3667, 13.5033)]
[DE, FRA, Frankfurt (50.0333, 8.5706)]
[DE, MUN, Munich Franz Josef Stauss (48.3539, 11.7861)]

results for country code 'NN'
no airports found

results for country code 'US'
[US, ANC, Ted Stevens Anchorage Intl. (61.1742, -149.9983)]
[US, BOS, Logan International (42.3631, -71.0064)]
[US, IAH, George Bush International (29.9844, -95.3414)]
[US, JFK, John F Kennedy International (40.6397, -74.0789)]
[US, LAX, Los Angeles International (33.9425, -118.4081)]
[US, MCO, Orlando International (28.4294, -81.3089)]
[US, ORD, O'Hare International (41.9786, -87.9047)]

results for country code 'ZZ'
no airports found

Partition Algorithms

A partition algorithm reorders the elements of a range into two groups: those that return true and those that return false for a specified unary predicate. Partitioning algorithms are handy for use cases that need to discard a large number of elements prior to more advanced processing. Listing 12-3-1 shows the source code for example Ch12_03_ex1(). This function demonstrates the use of std::ranges::partition() along with several other partition status functions.

Listing 12-3-1. Example Ch12_03 - Ch12_03_ex1()

```
//-------------------------------------------------------------------------
// Ch12_03_ex.cpp
//-------------------------------------------------------------------------

#include <algorithm>
#include <numeric>
```

CHAPTER 12   ALGORITHMS – PART 3

```cpp
#include <string>
#include <vector>
#include "Ch12_03.h"
#include "MT.h"
#include "MTH.h"

void Ch12_03_ex1()
{
    const char* fmt = "{:3d} ";
    constexpr size_t epl_max {20};
    constexpr size_t n {100};

    // initialize test vector of integers
    std::vector<int> vec1(n);
    std::iota(vec1.begin(), vec1.end(), 1);
    MT::print_ctr("\nvec1 (before partition):\n", vec1, fmt, epl_max);

    // using std::ranges::is_partitioned
    bool is_par = std::ranges::is_partitioned(vec1, MTH::is_prime<int>);
    std::println("is_partitioned (before partition): {:s}", is_par);

    // using std::ranges::partition (returns iterator subrange to
    // false group)
    std::ranges::partition(vec1, MTH::is_prime<int>);
    MT::print_ctr("\nvec1 (after partition):\n", vec1, fmt, epl_max);

    is_par = std::ranges::is_partitioned(vec1, MTH::is_prime<int>);
    std::println("is_partitioned (after partition): {:s}", is_par);

    // using std::ranges::partition_point
    auto iter_pp = std::ranges::partition_point(vec1, MTH::is_prime<int>);
    std::println("\n*iter_pp: {:d}", *iter_pp);
}
```

The code in Listing 12-3-1 is straightforward. Following initialization of std::vector<int> vec1 is the statement is_par = std::ranges::is_partitioned(vec1, MTH::is_prime<int>). The execution of this expression returns false since vec1 is currently not partitioned into two groups: prime and non-prime numbers (see Listing 10-6-2-2 for MTH::is_prime()). To partition vec1, Ch12_03_ex1()

utilizes std::ranges::partition(vec1, MTH::is_prime<int>). Execution of this statement partitions vec1 and returns an iterator subrange. More on this later. If you scan ahead to the results section, note that the elements of vec1 are organized into two groups. The front part of vec1 contains prime numbers, while the back portion contains non-primes. The prime number group is located in [vec1.begin(), iter_pp) where iter_pp = std::ranges::partition_point(vec1, MTH::is_prime<int>). Note that all STL partition functions in Ch12_03_ex1() applied predicate MTH::is_prime<int>. More importantly, note that the elements in each group are *not* sorted.

In Listing 12-3-2, example function Ch12_03_ex2() opens with the definition of lambda expression print_sr(), which prints the elements of [iter_b, iter_e). Like the previous example, Ch12_03_ex2() exploits std::ranges::partition(vec1, MTH::is_prime<int>) to partition the elements of vec1 into primes and non-primes.

Listing 12-3-2. Example Ch12_03 – Ch12_03_ex2()

```
void Ch12_03_ex2()
{
    // print_sr prints elements of [iter_b, iter_e)
    auto print_sr = [](const char* msg, auto iter_b, auto iter_e)
    {
        int add_nl {};
        std::println("\n{:s}", msg);

        for (auto iter = iter_b; iter != iter_e; ++iter)
        {
            std::print("{:3d} ", *iter);
            if (++add_nl % 20 == 0)
                std::println("");
        }
        std::println("");
    };

    // create test vector
    std::vector<int> vec1(100);
    std::iota(vec1.begin(), vec1.end(), 101);
```

```
    // using std::ranges::partition
    auto iter_sr = std::ranges::partition(vec1, MTH::is_prime<int>);

    print_sr("prime numbers", vec1.begin(), iter_sr.begin());
    print_sr("non-prime numbers", iter_sr.begin(), iter_sr.end());
}
```

The iter_sr object that's returned by std::ranges::partition() specifies a subrange of elements within vec1 for which MTH::is_prime() is false. The subsequent two calls to print_sr() utilize these iterators to print the elements in both vec1 groups. Note here that [vec1.begin(), iter_sr.begin()) identifies the prime group, while [iter_sr.begin(), iter_sr.end()) specifies the non-prime group. Also, note again in the results section that elements within the two groups are not sorted. Here are the results for example Ch12_03.

```
----- Results for example Ch12_03 -----

----- Ch12_03_ex1() -----
vec1 (before partition):
  1   2   3   4   5   6   7   8   9  10  11  12  13  14  15  16  17  18  19  20
 21  22  23  24  25  26  27  28  29  30  31  32  33  34  35  36  37  38  39  40
 41  42  43  44  45  46  47  48  49  50  51  52  53  54  55  56  57  58  59  60
 61  62  63  64  65  66  67  68  69  70  71  72  73  74  75  76  77  78  79  80
 81  82  83  84  85  86  87  88  89  90  91  92  93  94  95  96  97  98  99 100
is_partitioned (before partition): false

vec1 (after partition):
 97   2   3  89   5  83   7  79  73  71  11  67  13  61  59  53  17  47  19  43
 41  37  23  31  29  26  27  28  25  30  24  32  33  34  35  36  22  38  39  40
 21  42  20  44  45  46  18  48  49  50  51  52  16  54  55  56  57  58  15  60
 14  62  63  64  65  66  12  68  69  70  10  72   9  74  75  76  77  78   8  80
 81  82   6  84  85  86  87  88   4  90  91  92  93  94  95  96   1  98  99 100
is_partitioned (after partition): true

*iter_pp: 26
```

```
----- Ch12_03_ex2() -----

prime numbers
101 199 103 197 193 191 107 181 109 179 173 167 113 163 157 151 149
139 137 131
127

non-prime numbers
122 123 124 125 126 121 128 129 130 120 132 133 134 135 136 119 138
118 140 141
142 143 144 145 146 147 148 117 150 116 152 153 154 155 156 115 158
159 160 161
162 114 164 165 166 112 168 169 170 171 172 111 174 175 176 177 178
110 180 108
182 183 184 185 186 187 188 189 190 106 192 105 194 195 196 104 198 102 200
```

Heap Algorithms

A binary heap is a tree-based data structure where the value of each parent node is greater than or equal to its two child nodes. Heaps are advantageous in that they carry out common operations such as new element insertions and largest element retrievals with logarithmic complexity. They're also memory efficient since the nodes are typically maintained in an array, which eliminates the need for additional node pointers or other control data.

The archetypal example of real-world heap usage is a priority queue. The `std::priority_queue` container adaptor that you examined in Chapter 9 uses the same STL heap algorithms that you'll study in this section. Figure 12-1 shows an example of a binary heap in tree form. This figure also depicts the ordering of the same nodes in an array.

CHAPTER 12   ALGORITHMS – PART 3

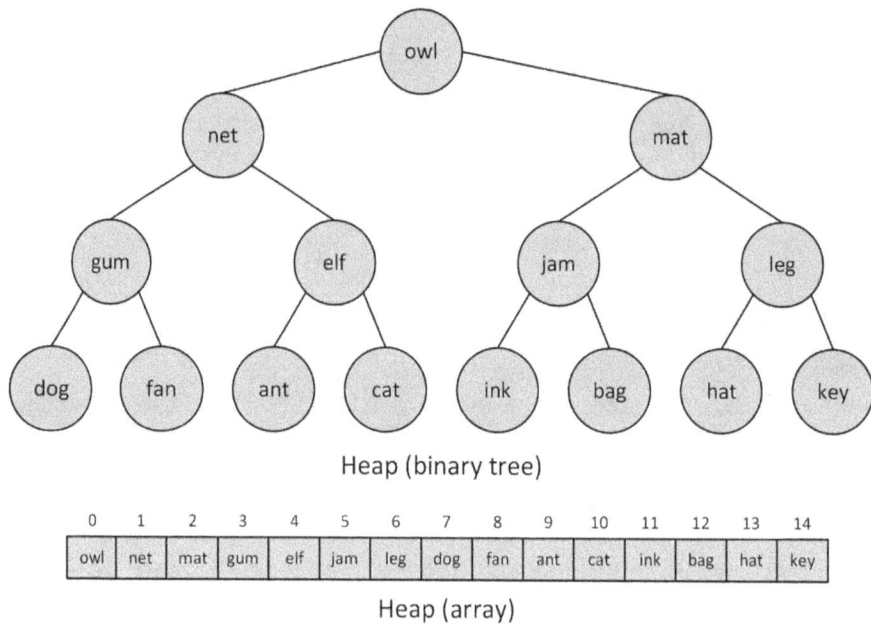

Figure 12-1. *Example heap*

In Figure 12-1, note that the topmost node is lexicographically the largest node in the tree. Also, note that each heap node is lexicographically greater than or equal to its child nodes. A heap that conforms to this parent-child node ordering scheme is called a max heap. A heap doesn't impose any ordering relationships between sibling nodes. The position of a binary heap node in an array can be easily determined using simple arithmetic. For node i, its left and right children are located at positions $2i + 1$ and $2i + 2$, respectively. The parent of node i is located at position $\lfloor (i - 1)/2 \rfloor$ for all nodes except the root node.

While pursuing the remainder of this section, it's important to keep in mind that a heap is *not* an STL container. It is a logical organization of data that satisfies the aforementioned max-heap property. The elements of a heap can be stored in any STL container that supports random access iterators.

Listing 12-4-1 shows the source code for example Ch12_04_ex1(). This example demonstrates the use of std::ranges::make_heap(). Near the top of Listing 12-4-1 is the definition of a simple function named print_heap(), which prints the elements of std::vector<std::string> heap. For now, just note that print_heap() accesses the nodes of heap2 (a copy of a heap) using std::vector member functions front(), empty(), and pop_back().

Listing 12-4-1. Example Ch12_04 – Ch12_04_ex1()

```cpp
//-------------------------------------------------------------------------
// Ch12_04_ex.cpp
//-------------------------------------------------------------------------

#include <algorithm>
#include <format>
#include <string>
#include <vector>
#include "Ch12_04.h"
#include "MT.h"

template <class CMP = std::ranges::less>
void print_heap(const std::string& msg, const
std::vector<std::string>& heap,
    CMP cmp = {})
{
    auto heap2 {heap};
    std::print("{:s}", msg);

    while (!heap2.empty())
    {
        std::print("{:3s} ", heap2.front());

        // using std::ranges::pop_heap
        std::ranges::pop_heap(heap2, cmp);
        heap2.pop_back();
    }

    std::println("");
}

void Ch12_04_ex1()
{
    const char* fmt = "{:3s} ";
    constexpr size_t epl_max {20};
```

```
// using std::ranges::make_heap with std::less (default)
// (root = largest element)
std::vector<std::string> vec1 { "ink", "elf", "leg", "fan", "cat",
    "bag", "key", "dog", "gum", "ant", "net", "jam", "mat", "hat",
    "owl" };

std::ranges::make_heap(vec1);
MT::print_ctr("\nvec1 using MT::print_ctr():\n", vec1, fmt, epl_max);
print_heap("\nvec1 using print_heap():\n", vec1);

// usng std::ranges::make_heap with std::greater
// (root = smallest element)
std::vector<std::string> vec2 { "bag", "hat", "owl", "fan", "dog",
    "ink", "key", "cat", "gum", "ant", "net", "jam", "mat", "elf",
    "leg" };

std::ranges::make_heap(vec2, std::greater {});
MT::print_ctr("\nvec2 using MT::print_ctr():\n", vec2, fmt, epl_max);
print_heap("\nvec2 using print_heap():\n", vec2, std::greater {});
}
```

The next item in Listing 12-4-1 is example Ch12_04_ex1(). Execution of this function begins with the initialization of std::vector<std::string> vec1. The elements in vec1's initializer list are arbitrarily ordered. The next statement, std::ranges::make_heap(vec1), arranges the elements of vec1 into a max heap. Like most other algorithms in namespace std::ranges, std::ranges::make_heap() defaults to std::ranges::less() for its comparison function object. However, it utilizes this function object to generate a max heap with the *largest* element positioned in the binary tree's root node as shown in Figure 12-1. The subsequent call to print_heap() prints the elements of vec1 in max-heap order. Here's a portion of the output:

```
vec1 using MT::print_ctr():
owl net mat gum elf jam leg dog fan ant cat ink bag hat key

vec1 using print_heap():
owl net mat leg key jam ink hat gum fan elf dog cat bag ant
```

CHAPTER 12   ALGORITHMS – PART 3

Note the different orderings of vec1's elements generated by the calls to MT::print_ctr() and print_heap(). The former prints the elements of vec1 as successively positioned within the container using a range for loop, while the latter prints the elements of vec1 in max-heap order.

The second half of Ch12_04_ex1() utilizes std::ranges::make_heap() to construct a heap using the elements of std::vector<std::string> vec2. Note here that std::ranges::make_heap() utilizes function object std::ranges::greater(). This organizes the elements of vec2 into a min heap, where each parent node is less than or equal to its two child nodes.

Function Ch12_04_ex2(), shown in Listing 12-4-2, demonstrates how to perform heap element insertions and removals. Like the previous example, Ch12_04_ex2() exploits std::ranges::make_heap(vec1) to create a max heap using the elements of std::vector<std::string>> vec1. In the range for loop that follows, execution of *both* vec1.push_back(val) and std::ranges::push_heap(vec1) adds a new element to the max heap in vec1. More specifically, vec1.push_back(val) appends a new element to vec1 while the ensuing call to std::ranges::push_heap(vec1) reconciles the elements of vec1 to regain the max-heap property.

Listing 12-4-2. Example Ch12_04 – Ch12_04_ex2()

```cpp
void Ch12_04_ex2()
{
    const char* fmt = "{:3s} ";
    constexpr size_t epl_max {20};

    // using std::ranges::make_heap
    std::vector<std::string> vec1 { "ink", "elf", "leg", "fan", "cat",
        "bag", "key", "dog", "gum", "ant", "net", "jam", "mat", "hat",
        "owl" };

    std::ranges::make_heap(vec1);
    print_heap("\nvec1 after make_heap():\n", vec1);

    // insert more elements
    std::vector<std::string> more_vals { "cap", "pot", "bog", "lip" };
```

```cpp
    for (const auto& val : more_vals)
    {
        // using std::ranges::push_heap
        vec1.push_back(val);
        std::ranges::push_heap(vec1);

        std::string msg = std::format(
            "\nvec1 after push_back() using '{:3s}':\n", val);
        print_heap(msg, vec1);
    }

    // remove four largest elements
    std::print("\nremoving elements: ");
    for (auto i = 0; i < 5; ++i)
    {
        auto pop_val = vec1.front();

        // using std::ranges::pop_heap
        std::ranges::pop_heap(vec1);
        vec1.pop_back();
        std::print("{:3s} ", pop_val);
    }
    print_heap("\n\nvec1 after pop_heap() operations:\n", vec1);

    // using std::ranges::is_heap
    std::println("is_heap(vec1): {:s}", std::ranges::is_heap(vec1));

    // using std::ranges::sort_heap (vec1 is no longer a heap)
    std::ranges::sort_heap(vec1);
    MT::print_ctr("\nvec1 after std::ranges::sort_heap:\n", vec1, fmt,
    epl_max);
    std::println("is_heap(vec1): {:s}", std::ranges::is_heap(vec1));
}
```

The range for loop in the next code block applies std::ranges::pop_heap(vec1) and vec1.pop_back() to remove the largest heap element from vec1. In this expression pair, function std::ranges::pop_heap(vec1) moves the largest (front) element of vec1 to its back end. It also adjusts the elements of vec1 to regain the max-heap property. Execution of vec1.pop_back() removes the last element from vec1. Recall that std::vectors are optimized for back-end element insertions and removals. When performing heap element insertions or removals, you must remember to utilize both the container's push_back()/pop_back() functions and the heap push()/pop() functions as demonstrated in example Ch12_04_ex2(). All std::ranges heap calls must also apply the same comparison function object. This is why the code in print_heap() included calls to both std::ranges::pop_heap(heap2, cmp) and heap2.pop_back().

The final code block of Ch12_04_ex2() illustrates the use of two more STL heap functions. The first one, std::ranges::is_heap(vec1), returns true if vec1 is a heap. Execution of std::ranges::sort_heap(vec1) sorts the elements of vec1. Like std::ranges::sort(), the default comparison function for std::ranges::sort_heap() is std::ranges::less(). Following execution of std::ranges::sort_heap(vec1), vec1 is no longer a heap since its elements are now sorted in ascending order. Both std::ranges::is_heap() and std::ranges::sort_heap() define overloads that accept a comparison function object to override the default use of std::ranges::less(). Here are the results for example Ch12_04:

```
----- Results for example Ch12_04 -----

----- Ch12_04_ex1() -----

vec1 using MT::print_ctr():
owl net mat gum elf jam leg dog fan ant cat ink bag hat key

vec1 using print_heap():
owl net mat leg key jam ink hat gum fan elf dog cat bag ant

vec2 using MT::print_ctr():
ant bag elf cat dog ink key fan gum hat net jam mat owl leg

vec2 using print_heap():
ant bag cat dog elf fan gum hat ink jam key leg mat net owl

----- Ch12_04_ex2() -----

vec1 after make_heap():
owl net mat leg key jam ink hat gum fan elf dog cat bag ant

vec1 after push_back() using 'cap':
owl net mat leg key jam ink hat gum fan elf dog cat cap bag ant
```

```
vec1 after push_back() using 'pot':
pot owl net mat leg key jam ink hat gum fan elf dog cat cap bag ant

vec1 after push_back() using 'bog':
pot owl net mat leg key jam ink hat gum fan elf dog cat cap bog bag ant

vec1 after push_back() using 'lip':
pot owl net mat lip leg key jam ink hat gum fan elf dog cat cap bog bag ant

removing elements: pot owl net mat lip

vec1 after pop_heap() operations:
leg key jam ink hat gum fan elf dog cat cap bog bag ant
is_heap(vec1): true

vec1 after std::ranges::sort_heap:
ant bag bog cap cat dog elf fan gum hat ink jam key leg
is_heap(vec1): false
```

The primary difference between a `std::priority_queue` and a STL heap is that the latter provides access to the underlying container. For many use cases, access to the container's elements is necessary to carry out additional processing. Access to the container's elements is also advantageous for classes whose data is dynamic instead of static (e.g., a class that processes real-time measurements or events).

Summary

Here are the key learning points for this chapter:

- The primary sorting algorithm for C++20 and later is `std::ranges::sort()`. You can also utilize `std::ranges::stable_sort()`, which preserves existing orderings of equivalent elements. Other specialized sorting algorithms include `std::ranges::nth_element()` and `std::ranges::partial_sort()`.

- Algorithm `std::ranges::binary_search()` searches a sorted container or range for element matches. Other searching algorithms include `std::ranges_lower_bound()` and `std::ranges_upper_bound()`. These functions return iterators to the first element in a sorted range that's not less than or greater than a specified value. Function `std::ranges::equal_range()` returns a subrange of elements that equal a specified value.

- Algorithm `std::ranges::partition()` arranges the elements of a container or range into two groups based on the results of a unary predicate.

- Algorithm `std::ranges::make_heap()` arranges the elements of a container or range in accordance with the max-heap (or min-heap) property. To insert a new element into a heap, call the container's `push_back()` function followed by a call to `std::ranges::push_heap()`. To remove a heap element, call `std::ranges::pop_heap()` followed by a call to the container's `pop_back()` function.

- All of the STL algorithms covered in this chapter use `std::ranges::less()` as the default comparison function object, but this can be overridden to use `std::ranges::greater()` or a user-defined comparison function.

CHAPTER 13

Algorithms – Part 4

This chapter is the final chapter that focuses primarily on STL algorithms. Topics covered in this chapter include

- Merge algorithms
- Shuffle and sample algorithms
- Rotate and shift algorithms
- Set algorithms
- Permutation algorithms

The algorithms mentioned in the preceding list tend to be used less frequently than most of the other algorithms you've studied in this book. Nevertheless, these algorithms are particularly convenient when the need arises.

Merge Algorithms

A merge algorithm merges the elements of two sorted ranges. Some container classes define member functions that merge elements of the same container type. For example, in Chapter 4 you learned how to use `std::list::merge()` (example Ch04_02). You also learned in Chapter 7 how to merge associative containers `std::set` (example Ch07_01) and `std::map` (example Ch07_02). The content of this section discusses the merge algorithms of namespace `std::ranges`.

Listing 13-1-1 shows the source code for `Ch13_01_ex1()`. This function elucidates the use of `std::ranges::merge()`. The opening code block of `Ch13_01_ex2()` harnesses `RegPolygon::get_random_polygons()` (see Listing 9-3-1-1) to initialize `std::vector<RegPolygon> polygons1` and `std::deque<RegPolygon> polygons2` with random RegPolygons. In the next code block, `Ch13_01_ex1()` exercises `std::ranges::sort()` twice to sort the elements of `polygons1` and `polygons2`.

CHAPTER 13   ALGORITHMS – PART 4

Recall that the default comparison function object for std::ranges::sort() is std::ranges::less(). Following the calls to std::ranges::sort(), the elements of polygons1 and polygons2 are sorted in ascending order by polygon area.

Listing 13-1-1. *Example Ch13_01 - Ch13_01_ex1()*

```cpp
//-------------------------------------------------------------------------
// Ch13_01_ex.cpp
//-------------------------------------------------------------------------
#include <algorithm>
#include <deque>
#include <vector>
#include "Ch13_01.h"
#include "MT.h"
#include "RegPolygon.h"

namespace
{
    // parameters for random RegPolygon generation
    constexpr unsigned int c_Seed1a {17};
    constexpr unsigned int c_Seed2a {13};
    constexpr unsigned int c_Seed1b {19};
    constexpr unsigned int c_Seed2b {23};
    constexpr size_t c_NumPolygons1 {10};
    constexpr size_t c_NumPolygons2 {6};
}

void Ch13_01_ex1()
{
    const char* fmt = "{} ";
    constexpr size_t epl_max {1};

    // create two containers of random RegPolygons
    std::vector<RegPolygon> polygons1 = RegPolygon::get_random_polygons(
        c_NumPolygons1, c_Seed1a, c_Seed2a);

    std::vector<RegPolygon> polygons_temp = RegPolygon::get_random_
    polygons(
```

```cpp
        c_NumPolygons2, c_Seed1b, c_Seed2b);

    std::deque<RegPolygon> polygons2 {};
    std::ranges::copy(polygons_temp, std::back_inserter(polygons2));

    // sort polygon containers (uses RegPolygon::operator<)
    std::ranges::sort(polygons1);
    std::println("\npolygons1 (after sort)");
    std::println("{:s}", RegPolygon::title_str());
    MT::print_ctr("", polygons1, fmt, epl_max);

    std::ranges::sort(polygons2);
    std::println("\npolygons2 (after sort)");
    std::println("{:s}", RegPolygon::title_str());
    MT::print_ctr("", polygons2, fmt, epl_max);

    // using std::ranges::merge
    std::vector<RegPolygon> polygons3 {};
    std::ranges::merge(polygons1, polygons2,
        std::back_inserter(polygons3));

    std::println("\npolygons3 (after merge)");
    std::println("{:s}", RegPolygon::title_str());
    MT::print_ctr("", polygons3, fmt, epl_max);
}
```

In its final code block, Ch13_01_ex1() applies std::ranges::merge(polygons1, polygons2, std::back_inserter(polygons3)) to merge elements from polygons1 and polygons2 into polygons3. There are a few items to note here. First, polygons1 and polygons2 are different container types. STL algorithm compatibility is usually dictated by iterator types instead of specific container classes. Second, following execution of std::ranges::merge(), the elements of polygons3 are sorted by area, while polygons1 and polygons2 are unchanged. Finally, std::ranges::merge() performs a stable merge. A stable merge preserves the ordering of equivalent elements in the output with equivalent elements from the first range preceding those from the second range.

The next source code example, shown in Listing 13-1-2, utilizes std::ranges::inplace_merge() to carry out an in-place merge operation. Like the previous example, Ch13_01_ex2() utilizes RegPolygon::get_random_polygons() to initialize polygons1 and polygons2. Next is the definition of lambda expression cmp_op(), which returns rp1.NumSides() > rp2.NumSides() for RegPolygon objects rp1 and rp2. Function Ch13_01_ex2() utilizes lambda expression cmp_op() in the ensuing two calls to std::ranges::sort(). Following execution of these sorts, the elements in both polygons1 and polygons2 are sorted in descending order based on the number of polygon sides.

Listing 13-1-2. *Example Ch13_01 - Ch13_01_ex2()*

```
void Ch13_01_ex2()
{
    const char* fmt = "{} ";
    constexpr size_t epl_max {1};

    // create two vectors of random RegPolygons
    std::vector<RegPolygon> polygons1 = RegPolygon::get_random_polygons(
        c_NumPolygons1, c_Seed1a * 2, c_Seed2a * 2);

    std::vector<RegPolygon> polygons2 =  RegPolygon::get_random_polygons(
        c_NumPolygons2, c_Seed2a * 2 , c_Seed2b * 2 );

    // comparison operator
    auto cmp_op = [](const RegPolygon& rp1, const RegPolygon& rp2)
        { return rp1.NumSides() > rp2.NumSides(); };

    // sort polygon vectors using cmp_op
    std::ranges::sort(polygons1, cmp_op);
    std::println("\npolygons1 (after sort)");
    std::println("{:s}", RegPolygon::title_str());
    MT::print_ctr("", polygons1, fmt, epl_max);

    std::ranges::sort(polygons2, cmp_op);
    std::println("\npolygons2 (after sort)");
    std::println("{:s}", RegPolygon::title_str());
    MT::print_ctr("", polygons2, fmt, epl_max);

    // move elements from polygons2 to end of polygons1
    std::ranges::move(polygons2, std::back_inserter(polygons1));
    std::println("\npolygons1 (after move)");
```

```
    std::println("{:s}", RegPolygon::title_str());
    MT::print_ctr("", polygons1, fmt, epl_max);

    // using std::ranges::inplace_merge (uses cmp_op)
    auto iter_mid = std::ranges::next(polygons1.begin(), c_NumPolygons1);
    std::ranges::inplace_merge(polygons1, iter_mid, cmp_op);

    std::println("\npolygons1 (after inplace_merge)");
    std::println("{:s}", RegPolygon::title_str());
    MT::print_ctr("", polygons1, fmt, epl_max);
}
```

To carry out an in-place merge using std::ranges::inplace_merge(), the elements of both sorted ranges must reside within the same container or range. To accomplish this, Ch13_01_ex2() employs std::ranges::move(polygons2, std::back_inserter(polygons1)) to move all RegPolygons from polygons2 into polygons1. Figure 13-1 illustrates this action in greater detail. Following execution of std::ranges::move(), polygons2 contains valid RegPolygon objects, but the actual values are unspecified per the ISO C++ standard.

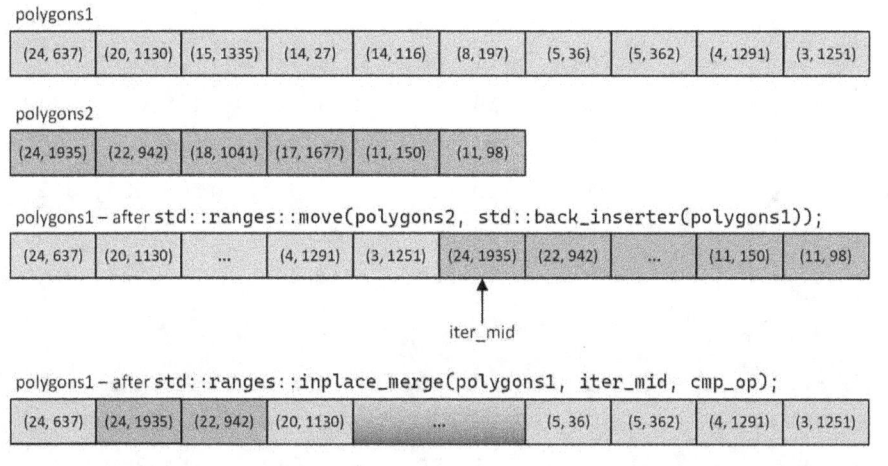

Figure 13-1. Execution of std::ranges::move() and std::ranges::inplace_merge()

CHAPTER 13 ALGORITHMS – PART 4

The final code block of Ch13_01_ex2() opens with iter_mid = std::ranges::next(polygons1.begin(), c_NumPolygons1). This statement calculates iter_mid, which points to the "middle" element between the two sorted ranges in polygons1 as shown in Figure 13-1. Execution of std::ranges::inplace_merge(polygons1, iter_mid, cmp_op) performs an in-place merge of polygons1's two sorted ranges. Note that std::ranges::inplace_merge() applies the same cmp_op() that was used earlier to sort polygons1 and polygons2. Here are the results for example Ch13_01:

```
----- Results for example Ch13_01 -----

----- Ch13_01_ex1() -----

polygons1 (after sort)
Sides      Radius1      SideLen     Radius2      Perim      VerAng        Area
================================================================================
[  26,      4.889 |      1.187,      4.925,      30.871,    166.154,     75.467]
[  14,      8.839 |      4.035,      9.066,      56.485,    154.286,    249.623]
[  25,     10.007 |      2.528,     10.087,      63.209,    165.600,    316.269]
[  11,     15.380 |      9.032,     16.029,      99.351,    147.273,    763.999]
[   4,     15.380 |     30.760,     21.750,     123.039,     90.000,    946.167]
[  27,     18.916 |      4.422,     19.044,     119.390,    166.667,   1129.175]
[   8,     19.085 |     15.811,     20.658,     126.486,    135.000,   1207.015]
[  25,     19.954 |      5.041,     20.112,     126.036,    165.600,   1257.429]
[   8,     21.556 |     17.858,     23.332,     142.861,    135.000,   1539.771]
[  17,     22.378 |      8.366,     22.766,     142.228,    158.824,   1591.399]

polygons2 (after sort)
Sides      Radius1      SideLen     Radius2      Perim      VerAng        Area
================================================================================
[  23,      5.008 |      1.377,      5.055,      31.663,    164.348,     79.281]
[  15,      5.032 |      2.139,      5.145,      32.089,    156.000,     80.739]
[   9,     11.327 |      8.245,     12.054,      74.208,    140.000,    420.271]
[  14,     14.561 |      6.647,     14.935,      93.055,    154.286,    677.476]
[   5,     16.893 |     24.547,     20.881,     122.734,    108.000,   1036.665]
[  24,     19.651 |      5.174,     19.821,     124.182,    165.000,   1220.158]
```

CHAPTER 13 ALGORITHMS – PART 4

```
polygons3 (after merge)
Sides    Radius1    SideLen    Radius2    Perim     VerAng      Area
=====================================================================
[  26,    4.889 |    1.187,     4.925,    30.871,   166.154,    75.467]
[  23,    5.008 |    1.377,     5.055,    31.663,   164.348,    79.281]
[  15,    5.032 |    2.139,     5.145,    32.089,   156.000,    80.739]
[  14,    8.839 |    4.035,     9.066,    56.485,   154.286,   249.623]
[  25,   10.007 |    2.528,    10.087,    63.209,   165.600,   316.269]
[   9,   11.327 |    8.245,    12.054,    74.208,   140.000,   420.271]
[  14,   14.561 |    6.647,    14.935,    93.055,   154.286,   677.476]
[  11,   15.380 |    9.032,    16.029,    99.351,   147.273,   763.999]
[   4,   15.380 |   30.760,    21.750,   123.039,    90.000,   946.167]
[   5,   16.893 |   24.547,    20.881,   122.734,   108.000,  1036.665]
[  27,   18.916 |    4.422,    19.044,   119.390,   166.667,  1129.175]
[   8,   19.085 |   15.811,    20.658,   126.486,   135.000,  1207.015]
[  24,   19.651 |    5.174,    19.821,   124.182,   165.000,  1220.158]
[  25,   19.954 |    5.041,    20.112,   126.036,   165.600,  1257.429]
[   8,   21.556 |   17.858,    23.332,   142.861,   135.000,  1539.771]
[  17,   22.378 |    8.366,    22.766,   142.228,   158.824,  1591.399]

----- Ch13_01_ex2() -----

polygons1 (after sort)
Sides    Radius1    SideLen    Radius2    Perim     VerAng      Area
=====================================================================
[  24,   14.204 |    3.740,    14.326,    89.759,   165.000,   637.457]
[  20,   18.894 |    5.985,    19.130,   119.702,   162.000,  1130.839]
[  15,   20.464 |    8.699,    20.921,   130.491,   156.000,  1335.167]
[  14,    2.934 |    1.339,     3.009,    18.750,   154.286,    27.504]
[  14,    6.040 |    2.757,     6.195,    38.599,   154.286,   116.564]
[   8,    7.725 |    6.400,     8.362,    51.200,   135.000,   197.771]
[   5,    3.158 |    4.589,     3.904,    22.946,   108.000,    36.234]
[   5,    9.987 |   14.512,    12.344,    72.558,   108.000,   362.312]
[   4,   17.971 |   35.942,    25.415,   143.770,    90.000,  1291.860]
[   3,   15.518 |   53.757,    31.037,   161.271,    60.000,  1251.329]
```

CHAPTER 13 ALGORITHMS – PART 4

```
polygons2 (after sort)
Sides     Radius1    SideLen    Radius2     Perim     VerAng       Area
==========================================================================
[  24,    24.747  |   6.516,    24.961,    156.386,   165.000,   1935.069]
[  22,    17.263  |   4.964,    17.441,    109.212,   163.636,    942.681]
[  18,    18.111  |   6.387,    18.390,    114.965,   160.000,   1041.061]
[  17,    22.975  |   8.589,    23.373,    146.021,   158.824,   1677.405]
[  11,     6.822  |   4.006,     7.110,     44.070,   147.273,    150.325]
[  11,     5.521  |   3.242,     5.754,     35.664,   147.273,     98.448]

polygons1 (after move)
Sides     Radius1    SideLen    Radius2     Perim     VerAng       Area
==========================================================================
[  24,    14.204  |   3.740,    14.326,     89.759,   165.000,    637.457]
[  20,    18.894  |   5.985,    19.130,    119.702,   162.000,   1130.839]
[  15,    20.464  |   8.699,    20.921,    130.491,   156.000,   1335.167]
[  14,     2.934  |   1.339,     3.009,     18.750,   154.286,     27.504]
[  14,     6.040  |   2.757,     6.195,     38.599,   154.286,    116.564]
[   8,     7.725  |   6.400,     8.362,     51.200,   135.000,    197.771]
[   5,     3.158  |   4.589,     3.904,     22.946,   108.000,     36.234]
[   5,     9.987  |  14.512,    12.344,     72.558,   108.000,    362.312]
[   4,    17.971  |  35.942,    25.415,    143.770,    90.000,   1291.860]
[   3,    15.518  |  53.757,    31.037,    161.271,    60.000,   1251.329]
[  24,    24.747  |   6.516,    24.961,    156.386,   165.000,   1935.069]
[  22,    17.263  |   4.964,    17.441,    109.212,   163.636,    942.681]
[  18,    18.111  |   6.387,    18.390,    114.965,   160.000,   1041.061]
[  17,    22.975  |   8.589,    23.373,    146.021,   158.824,   1677.405]
[  11,     6.822  |   4.006,     7.110,     44.070,   147.273,    150.325]
[  11,     5.521  |   3.242,     5.754,     35.664,   147.273,     98.448]
```

```
polygons1 (after inplace_merge)
Sides    Radius1     SideLen    Radius2     Perim      VerAng       Area
==========================================================================
[  24,    14.204 |     3.740,    14.326,    89.759,   165.000,    637.457]
[  24,    24.747 |     6.516,    24.961,   156.386,   165.000,   1935.069]
[  22,    17.263 |     4.964,    17.441,   109.212,   163.636,    942.681]
[  20,    18.894 |     5.985,    19.130,   119.702,   162.000,   1130.839]
[  18,    18.111 |     6.387,    18.390,   114.965,   160.000,   1041.061]
[  17,    22.975 |     8.589,    23.373,   146.021,   158.824,   1677.405]
[  15,    20.464 |     8.699,    20.921,   130.491,   156.000,   1335.167]
[  14,     2.934 |     1.339,     3.009,    18.750,   154.286,     27.504]
[  14,     6.040 |     2.757,     6.195,    38.599,   154.286,    116.564]
[  11,     6.822 |     4.006,     7.110,    44.070,   147.273,    150.325]
[  11,     5.521 |     3.242,     5.754,    35.664,   147.273,     98.448]
[   8,     7.725 |     6.400,     8.362,    51.200,   135.000,    197.771]
[   5,     3.158 |     4.589,     3.904,    22.946,   108.000,     36.234]
[   5,     9.987 |    14.512,    12.344,    72.558,   108.000,    362.312]
[   4,    17.971 |    35.942,    25.415,   143.770,    90.000,   1291.860]
[   3,    15.518 |    53.757,    31.037,   161.271,    60.000,   1251.329]
```

Shuffle and Sample Algorithms

A shuffle algorithm randomly rearranges the elements of a range such that each possible permutation has the same likelihood of occurrence. A sample algorithm selects N elements from a range without replacements. Both of these algorithms are handy for card game applications or data set generators.

Listing 13-2-1 shows the source code for example Ch13_02_ex1(). This example spotlights the use of std::ranges::shuffle(). Near the top of Ch13_02_ex1(), execution of the statement std::vector<std::string> vec1 = AminoAcid::get_vector_all_code3() creates a vector of all 20 standard amino acid three-letter codes (see Listings 10-1-3-1 and 10-1-3-2 for class AminoAcid). In the subsequent code block, the statement std::mt19937 rng {rng_seed} prepares a random number generator for use by std::ranges::shuffle(). Chapter 18 discusses the particulars of STL random number generators in greater detail.

CHAPTER 13   ALGORITHMS – PART 4

Listing 13-2-1. Example Ch13_02 - Ch13_02_ex1()

```cpp
//--------------------------------------------------------------------------
// Ch13_02_ex.cpp
//--------------------------------------------------------------------------

#include <algorithm>
#include <array>
#include <format>
#include <random>
#include <vector>
#include "Ch13_02.h"
#include "AminoAcid.h"
#include "MT.h"

void Ch13_02_ex1()
{
    const char* fmt = "{:3s} ";
    constexpr size_t epl_max {20};

    // create vector of random amino acid codes
    std::vector<std::string> vec1 = AminoAcid::get_vector_all_code3();
    MT::print_ctr("\nvec1 (initial values):\n", vec1, fmt, epl_max);

    // random number generator for std::ranges::shuffle
    unsigned int rng_seed {42};
    std::mt19937 rng {rng_seed};

    // using std::ranges::shuffle
    std::ranges::shuffle(vec1, rng);
    MT::print_ctr("\nvec1 (after first shuffle):\n", vec1, fmt, epl_max);

    std::ranges::shuffle(vec1, rng);
    MT::print_ctr("\nvec1 (after second shuffle):\n", vec1, fmt, epl_max);
}
```

In the code block that follows the creation of random number generator rng, Ch13_02_ex2() makes two calls to std::ranges::shuffle(vec1, rng). Each of these calls randomly reorders the elements of vec1. If you scan ahead to the results section, you'll notice that the elements of vec1 are rearranged following each call to std::ranges::shuffle().

Example function Ch13_02_ex2(), shown in Listing 13-2-2, illustrates the use of std::ranges::sample(). The execution of this algorithm randomly selects *N* elements from a range without replacements. Like the previous example, Ch13_02_ex2() initializes a std::vector<std::string> of three-letter amino acid codes. It also instantiates random number generator std::mt19937 rng {rng_seed}.

Listing 13-2-2. Example Ch13_02 - Ch13_02_ex2()

```cpp
void Ch13_02_ex2()
{
    const char* fmt = "{:3s} ";
    constexpr size_t epl_max {20};

    // create vector of random amino acid codes
    std::vector<std::string> vec1 = AminoAcid::get_vector_all_code3();
    MT::print_ctr("\nvec1 (initial values):\n", vec1, fmt, epl_max);

    // random number generator for std::ranges::sample
    unsigned int rng_seed {111};
    std::mt19937 rng {rng_seed};

    // using std::ranges::sample (sampling without replacements)
    std::array<size_t, 3> sample_sizes {5, 10, 15};

    for (size_t i = 0; i < sample_sizes.size(); ++i)
    {
        std::vector<std::string> sample(sample_sizes[i]);
        std::ranges::sample(vec1, sample.begin(), sample_sizes[i], rng);

        std::string s = std::format("\nsample #{:d}:\n", i);
        MT::print_ctr(s.c_str(), sample, fmt, epl_max);
    }
}
```

CHAPTER 13   ALGORITHMS – PART 4

The next code block in Listing 13-2-2 exhibits the use of std::ranges::sample(). The first statement inside the for loop, std::vector<std::string> sample(sample_sizes[i]), instantiates an output vector for the current iteration. This is followed by a call to std::ranges::sample(vec1, sample.begin(), sample_sizes[i], rng) that randomly selects sample_sizes[i] elements from vec1 and saves these values in sample. During execution of std::ranges::sample(), each element within [vec1.begin(), vec1.end()) has an equal chance of being selected. As mentioned earlier, std::ranges::sample() makes its selections without replacements, which means there are no duplicates in output vector sample.

The for loop in Ch13_02_ex2() also could have used the dual iterator overload of std::ranges::sample() (e.g., std::ranges::sample(vec1.begin(), vec1.end(), sample.begin(), sample_sizes[i], rng). Execution of this overload guarantees a stable sample (i.e., the relative ordering of elements in the output range matches that of the input range) if the input range supports forward iterators. It also warrants mentioning that the behavior of std::ranges::sample() is undefined if the output iterator overlaps the input range. Here are the results for example Ch13_02:

```
----- Results for example Ch13_02 -----

----- Ch13_02_ex1() -----

vec1 (initial values):
Ala Arg Asn Asp Cys Gln Glu Gly His Ile Leu Lys Met Phe Pro Ser Thr
Trp Tyr Val

vec1 (after first shuffle):
Ile Ala Met Thr Gly His Phe Val Tyr Pro Lys Trp Leu Arg Gln Cys Glu
Asn Asp Ser

vec1 (after second shuffle):
Thr Leu Tyr Lys Asp Val Gly Trp Ile Cys Gln His Arg Glu Phe Pro Ser
Met Ala Asn

----- Ch13_02_ex2() -----

vec1 (initial values):
Ala Arg Asn Asp Cys Gln Glu Gly His Ile Leu Lys Met Phe Pro Ser Thr
Trp Tyr Val
```

sample #0:
Ala Glu Met Thr Trp

sample #1:
Asp Cys Gln Glu Gly Ile Leu Phe Pro Thr

sample #2:
Ala Arg Asn Asp Cys Gln Glu Gly Ile Leu Lys Met Phe Ser Val

Rotate and Shift Algorithms

A rotate algorithm left-rotates the elements of a range. Rotate algorithms are often exploited to implement other algorithms such as sorts. A shift algorithm shifts the elements of a range toward its front or back ends. The former is a left shift, while the latter is a right shift. Figure 13-2 illustrates these operations in greater detail.

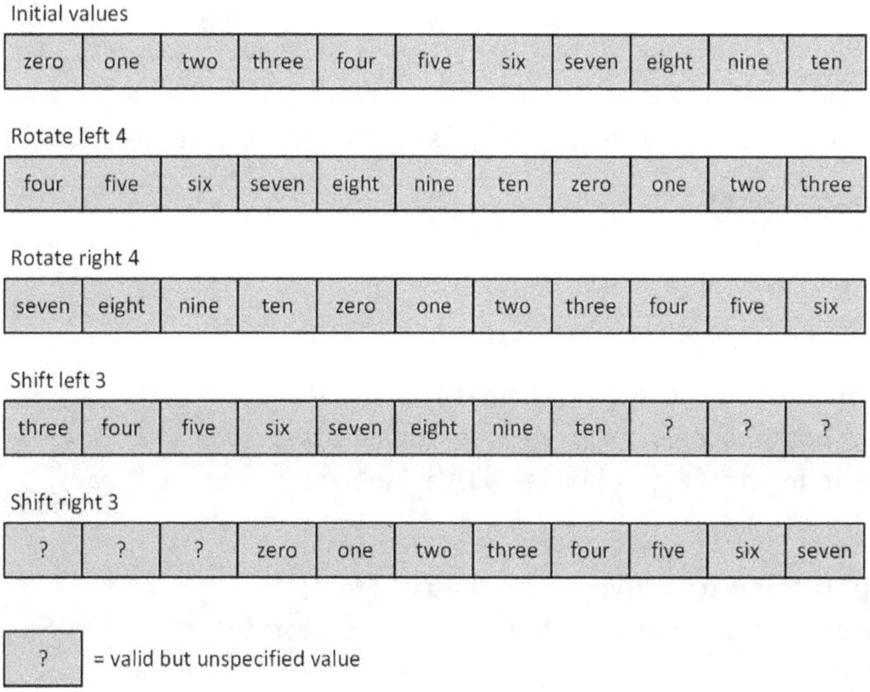

Initial values

| zero | one | two | three | four | five | six | seven | eight | nine | ten |

Rotate left 4

| four | five | six | seven | eight | nine | ten | zero | one | two | three |

Rotate right 4

| seven | eight | nine | ten | zero | one | two | three | four | five | six |

Shift left 3

| three | four | five | six | seven | eight | nine | ten | ? | ? | ? |

Shift right 3

| ? | ? | ? | zero | one | two | three | four | five | six | seven |

| ? | = valid but unspecified value

Figure 13-2. *Examples of rotate and shift operations*

CHAPTER 13   ALGORITHMS – PART 4

Listing 13-3-1 shows the source code for example Ch13_03_ex1(). This example demonstrates the use of std::ranges::rotate().

Listing 13-3-1. Example Ch13_03 – Ch13_03_ex1()

```
//-----------------------------------------------------------------------
// Ch13_03_ex.cpp
//-----------------------------------------------------------------------

#include <algorithm>
#include <deque>
#include <list>
#include <numeric>
#include <stdexcept>
#include <vector>
#include "Ch13_03.h"
#include "MT.h"

static std::initializer_list<std::string> s_StringVals {"zero", "one", "two",
    "three", "four", "five", "six", "seven", "eight", "nine", "ten"};

void Ch13_03_ex1()
{
    const char* fmt = "{:6s} ";
    constexpr size_t epl_max {12};

    // create test vector of strings
    std::vector<std::string> vec1 {s_StringVals};
    MT::print_ctr("vec1 (initial values)\n", vec1, fmt, epl_max);

    // using std::ranges::rotate (rotates left)
    std::ranges::rotate(vec1, vec1.begin() + 2);
    MT::print_ctr("\nvec1 (after std::ranges::rotate)\n", vec1, fmt,
    epl_max);

    // using std::ranges::rotate_copy (makes copy)
    std::vector<std::string> vec2 {};
```

```
    std::ranges::rotate_copy(vec1, vec1.begin() + 3,
    std::back_inserter(vec2));
    MT::print_ctr("\nvec1 (after std::ranges::rotate_copy)\n", vec1, fmt,
    epl_max);
    MT::print_ctr("\nvec2 (after std::ranges::rotate_copy)\n", vec2, fmt,
    epl_max);
}
```

Following the initialization of std::vector<std::string> vec1 is the statement std::ranges::rotate(vec1, vec1.begin() + 2). The execution of this algorithm rotates the elements of vec1 to the left (or front) by two element positions. In other words, vec1.begin() + 2 becomes the new front element of vec1. Here's a portion of the output that shows the pre- and post-rotation elements of vec1:

vec1 (initial values)
zero   one   two   three   four   five   six   seven   eight   nine   ten

vec1 (after std::ranges::rotate)
two   three   four   five   six   seven   eight   nine   ten   **zero**   one

In the next code block, execution of std::ranges::rotate_copy(vec1, vec1.begin() + 3, std::back_inserter(vec2)) stores in vec2 a copy of vec1 that's been left-rotated by three elements. Range vec1 is not modified during this execution of std::ranges::rotate_copy().

Listing 13-3-2 show the source code for example Ch13_03_ex2(). This listing opens with the definition of a template function named rotate_left(), which rotates ctr left by n element positions. A rotate element count is used here since it's often easier to express than an iterator position. Note that rotate_left() exploits middle = std::ranges::next(ctr.begin(), n) to calculate the correct "middle" iterator for std::ranges::rotate(). Execution of std::ranges:rotate() returns a pair of iterators. The first iterator points to the former front element of ctr() at its new location (shown earlier in bold text) *following* the rotate; the second iterator matches ctr.end().

CHAPTER 13   ALGORITHMS – PART 4

Listing 13-3-2. Example Ch13_03 - Ch13_03_ex2()

```
auto rotate_left(auto& ctr, size_t n)
{
    // rotate ctr left by n elements
    if (n > ctr.size())
        throw std::runtime_error("rotate_left - invalid 'n'");

    // std::ranges::rotate() returns iterators
    // { ctr.begin() + (ctr.end() - middle), ctr.end() }
    auto middle = std::ranges::next(ctr.begin(), n);
    return std::ranges::rotate(ctr, middle);
}

auto rotate_right(auto& ctr, size_t n)
{
    // rotate ctr right by n elements
    if (n > ctr.size())
        throw std::runtime_error("rotate_right - invalid 'n'");

    auto middle = std::ranges::next(ctr.begin(), ctr.size() - n);
    return std::ranges::rotate(ctr, middle);
}

void Ch13_03_ex2()
{
    const char* fmt = "{:6s} ";
    constexpr size_t epl_max {12};

    // prints elements of range returned by rotate_left() and rotate_right()
    auto print_rotate_result = [](const char* msg, auto rng)
    {
        std::print("{}", msg);
        for (auto iter = rng.begin(); iter != rng.end(); ++iter)
            std::print("{:6s} ", *iter);
        std::println("");
    };
```

```
    // using rotate_left (list)
    std::list<std::string> list1 {s_StringVals};
    MT::print_ctr("list1 (initial values):\n", list1, fmt, epl_max);

    auto result_l = rotate_left(list1, 4);
    MT::print_ctr("\nlist1 (after rotate_left, n = 4):\n", list1, fmt,
    epl_max);
    print_rotate_result("\nresult_l:\n", result_l);

    // using rotate_right (deque)
    std::deque<std::string> deq1 {s_StringVals};
    MT::print_ctr("\ndeq1 (initial values):\n", deq1, fmt, epl_max);

    auto result_r = rotate_right(deq1, 4);
    MT::print_ctr("\ndeq1 (after rotate_right, n = 4):\n", deq1, fmt,
    epl_max);
    print_rotate_result("\nresult_r:\n", result_r);
}
```

The next item in Listing 13-3-2 is template function rotate_right(), which rotates the elements of ctr to the right (or back) by n element positions. To calculate the correct iterator position for std::ranges::rotate(), rotate_right() calculates middle = std::ranges::next(ctr.begin(), ctr.size() - n). The behavior of std::ranges::rotate() is undefined if the source range is invalid or if the specified middle iterator does not reside within the source range. This is why both rotate_left() and rotate_right() throw an exception if argument n is greater than the number of container elements.

Listing 13-3-2 also shows the source code for example function Ch13_03_ex2(). This function exercises rotate_left() and rotate_right() using containers of type std::list<std::string> and std::deque<std::string>. In Ch13_03_ex2(), lambda expression print_rotate_result() prints the elements of the range that's returned from both rotate_left() and rotate_right(), which is the result returned by std::ranges::rotate().

Example function Ch13_03_ex3(), shown in Listing 13-3-3, demonstrates the use of std::ranges::shift_left() and std::ranges::shift_right() (both C++23).

CHAPTER 13　ALGORITHMS – PART 4

Listing 13-3-3. *Example Ch13_03 – Ch13_03_ex3()*

```
void Ch13_03_ex3()
{
#if __cpp_lib_shift >= 202202L
    const char* fmt = "{:6s} ";
    constexpr size_t epl_max {12};

    // transformation op for empty string
    auto tr_op = [](std::string& s) { return (s == "") ? "-----" : s; };

    // using std::ranges::shift_left (moves strings)
    std::vector<std::string> vec1 {s_StringVals};
    MT::print_ctr("vec1 (initial values):\n", vec1, fmt, epl_max);
    std::ranges::shift_left(vec1, 3);
    std::ranges::transform(vec1, vec1.begin(), tr_op);
    MT::print_ctr("\nvec1 (after shift_left, 3):\n", vec1, fmt, epl_max);

    // using std::ranges::shift_right (moves strings)
    std::vector<std::string> vec2 {s_StringVals};
    MT::print_ctr("\nvec2 (initial values):\n", vec2, fmt, epl_max);
    std::ranges::shift_right(vec2, 3);
    std::ranges::transform(vec2, vec2.begin(), tr_op);
    MT::print_ctr("\nvec2 (after shift_right, 3):\n", vec2, fmt, epl_max);
#else
    std::println("Ch13_03_ex3() requires __cpp_lib_shift >= 202202L
    (C++23)");
#endif
}
```

One notable difference between a rotate and a shift operation is that execution of the former retains all of the range's original elements, while the latter doesn't. In function Ch13_03_ex3(), execution of std::ranges::shift_left(vec1, 3) shifts the elements of vec1 to the left (front) by three positions. During its execution, std::ranges_shift_left() performs move operations to implement actual element shifts. Recall that an object move leaves the original source object in a valid but unspecified state.

Example function Ch13_03_ex3() also demonstrates the use of std::ranges::shift_right(vec2, 3). The execution of this algorithm is similar to its left-shift counterpart except that the elements of vec2 are shifted to the right (back) by three positions.

Note in Listing 13-3-1 that following each shift operation, Ch13_03_ex3() utilizes std::ranges::transform() to convert empty strings in vec1 and vec2 to "-----" for display purposes. The empty strings occur in container positions from which strings were moved to the left or right. Once again, it's important to keep in mind that while setting a moved string to empty is a sensible action, this after-effect is not guaranteed by the ISO C++ standard. Here are the results for example Ch13_03:

```
----- Results for example Ch13_03 -----

----- Ch13_03_ex1() -----
vec1 (initial values)
zero    one     two     three   four    five    six     seven   eight   nine    ten
vec1 (after std::ranges::rotate)
two     three   four    five    six     seven   eight   nine    ten     zero    one
vec1 (after std::ranges::rotate_copy)
two     three   four    five    six     seven   eight   nine    ten     zero    one
vec2 (after std::ranges::rotate_copy)
five    six     seven   eight   nine    ten     zero    one     two     three   four

----- Ch13_03_ex2() -----
list1 (initial values):
zero    one     two     three   four    five    six     seven   eight   nine    ten
list1 (after rotate_left, n = 4):
four    five    six     seven   eight   nine    ten     zero    one     two     three
result_1:
zero    one     two     three
deq1 (initial values):
zero    one     two     three   four    five    six     seven   eight   nine    ten
```

```
deq1 (after rotate_right, n = 4):
seven   eight   nine   ten     zero    one     two     three   four    five    six
result_r:
zero    one     two    three   four    five    six
```

Set Algorithms

The STL includes several algorithms that perform common set operations, including intersection, union, difference, and symmetric difference. These algorithms operate on sorted ranges. Unlike mathematical sets, the STL set algorithms support duplicate elements if they're supported by the container. Listing 13-4-1 shows the source code for example function Ch13_04_ex1(), which demonstrates the use of std::ranges::intersection(), std::ranges::union(), std::ranges::difference(), and std::ranges::symmetric_difference().

Listing 13-4-1. Example Ch13_04 - Ch13_04_ex1()

```cpp
//-------------------------------------------------------------------------
// Ch13_04_ex.cpp
//-------------------------------------------------------------------------

#include <algorithm>
#include <vector>
#include "Ch13_04.h"
#include "HtmlColor.h"
#include "MT.h"

void Ch13_04_ex1()
{
    const char* fmt = "{} ";
    constexpr size_t epl_max {2};

    // create test vectors of HtmlColors
    std::vector<size_t> indices1
        {0, 1, 1, 3, 4, 7, 7, 7, 8, 8, 9, 10, 11, 12, 12, 13, 14 };
    std::vector<HtmlColor> colors1 = HtmlColor::get_vector(indices1);
```

```cpp
    std::ranges::sort(colors1);
    MT::print_ctr("\ncolors1:\n", colors1, fmt, epl_max);

    std::vector<size_t> indices2
        {1, 1, 1, 4, 5, 6, 8, 9, 10, 10, 11, 12, 13, 16, 16} ;
    std::vector<HtmlColor> colors2 = HtmlColor::get_vector(indices2);
    std::ranges::sort(colors2);
    MT::print_ctr("\ncolors2:\n", colors2, fmt, epl_max);

    // using std::ranges::set_intersection
    std::vector<HtmlColor> colors3 {};
    std::ranges::set_intersection(colors1, colors2, std::back_
    inserter(colors3));
    MT::print_ctr("\ncolors3 (intersection):\n", colors3, fmt, epl_max);

    // using std::ranges::set_union
    std::vector<HtmlColor> colors4 {};
    std::ranges::set_union(colors1, colors2, std::back_inserter(colors4));
    MT::print_ctr("\ncolors4 (union):\n", colors4, fmt, epl_max);

    // using std::ranges::set_difference
    std::vector<HtmlColor> colors5 {};
    std::ranges::set_difference(colors1, colors2, std::back_
    inserter(colors5));
    MT::print_ctr("\ncolors5 (difference):\n", colors5, fmt, epl_max);

    // using std::ranges::symmetric_difference
    std::vector<HtmlColor> colors6 {};
    std::ranges::set_symmetric_difference(colors1, colors2,
        std::back_inserter(colors6));
    MT::print_ctr("\ncolors6 (symmetric_difference):\n", colors6, fmt,
    epl_max);
}
```

In Listing 13-4-1, the opening code block of Ch13_04_ex1() initializes two std::vector<HtmlColor> containers named colors1 and colors2 (see Listing 8-1-4-1 for class HtmlColor). Note that std::ranges::sort() is employed to sort both containers. The next code block employs std::ranges::set_intersection(colors1, colors2, std::back_inserter(colors3)) to compute the intersection of colors1 and colors2. The result of the intersection is a sorted range of elements that exist in both colors1 and colors2; these elements are saved in colors3. Note that if m and n equivalent elements exist in colors1 and colors2, respectively, the first min(m, n) from colors1 are copied in order to colors3.

In the subsequent code block, Ch13_04_ex1() utilizes std::ranges::set_union(colors1, colors2, std::back_inserter(colors4)) to compute the union of colors1 and colors2. Execution of this function saves a sorted range of elements that exist in either colors1 or colors2 to colors4. If m and n equivalent elements exist in colors1 and colors2, all elements from colors1 are copied in order to colors4, and the final max(n - m, 0) from colors2 are copied in order to colors4.

Execution of algorithm std::ranges::set_difference(colors1, colors2, std::back_inserter(colors5)) copies elements from colors1 which are *not* present in colors2 to colors5. The elements of colors5 are sorted. If m and n equivalent elements exist in colors1 and colors2, the last max(m - n, 0) elements from colors1 are copied in order to colors5.

The final set operation, std::ranges::set_symmetric_difference(colors1, colors2, std::back_inserter(colors6)), copies elements from colors1 that are nonexistent in colors2 to colors6; it also copies elements from colors2 that are nonexistent in colors1 to colors6. The elements of colors6 are sorted. If m and n equivalent elements exist in colors1 and colors2, then abs(m - n) elements are copied to colors6 as follows: the final m - n elements are copied in order from colors1 if m > n is true, and the last n - m from colors2 if m < n is true. Here are the results for example Ch13_04:

```
----- Results for example Ch13_04 -----

----- Ch13_04_ex1() -----

colors1:
[AliceBlue          0xF0F8FF]  [AntiqueWhite      0xFAEBD7]
[AntiqueWhite       0xFAEBD7]  [AquaMarine        0x7FFFD4]
[Azure              0xF0FFFF]  [Black             0x000000]
[Black              0x000000]  [Black             0x000000]
[BlanchedAlmond     0xFFEBCD]  [BlanchedAlmond    0xFFEBCD]
[Blue               0x0000FF]  [BlueViolet        0x8A2BE2]
```

CHAPTER 13 ALGORITHMS – PART 4

[Brown   0xA52A2A] [Burlywood   0xDEB887]
[Burlywood   0xDEB887] [CadetBlue   0x5F9EA0]
[Chartreuse   0x7FFF00]

colors2:
[AntiqueWhite   0xFAEBD7] [AntiqueWhite   0xFAEBD7]
[AntiqueWhite   0xFAEBD7] [Azure   0xF0FFFF]
[Beige   0xF5F5DC] [Bisque   0xFFE4C4]
[BlanchedAlmond   0xFFEBCD] [Blue   0x0000FF]
[BlueViolet   0x8A2BE2] [BlueViolet   0x8A2BE2]
[Brown   0xA52A2A] [Burlywood   0xDEB887]
[CadetBlue   0x5F9EA0] [Coral   0xFF7F50]
[Coral   0xFF7F50]

colors3 (intersection):
[AntiqueWhite   0xFAEBD7] [AntiqueWhite   0xFAEBD7]
[Azure   0xF0FFFF] [BlanchedAlmond   0xFFEBCD]
[Blue   0x0000FF] [BlueViolet   0x8A2BE2]
[Brown   0xA52A2A] [Burlywood   0xDEB887]
[CadetBlue   0x5F9EA0]

colors4 (union):
[AliceBlue   0xF0F8FF] [AntiqueWhite   0xFAEBD7]
[AntiqueWhite   0xFAEBD7] [AntiqueWhite   0xFAEBD7]
[AquaMarine   0x7FFFD4] [Azure   0xF0FFFF]
[Beige   0xF5F5DC] [Bisque   0xFFE4C4]
[Black   0x000000] [Black   0x000000]
[Black   0x000000] [BlanchedAlmond   0xFFEBCD]
[BlanchedAlmond   0xFFEBCD] [Blue   0x0000FF]
[BlueViolet   0x8A2BE2] [BlueViolet   0x8A2BE2]
[Brown   0xA52A2A] [Burlywood   0xDEB887]
[Burlywood   0xDEB887] [CadetBlue   0x5F9EA0]
[Chartreuse   0x7FFF00] [Coral   0xFF7F50]
[Coral   0xFF7F50]

colors5 (difference):
```
[AliceBlue          0xF0F8FF]  [AquaMarine         0x7FFFD4]
[Black              0x000000]  [Black              0x000000]
[Black              0x000000]  [BlanchedAlmond     0xFFEBCD]
[Burlywood          0xDEB887]  [Chartreuse         0x7FFF00]
```

colors6 (symmetric_difference):
```
[AliceBlue          0xF0F8FF]  [AntiqueWhite       0xFAEBD7]
[AquaMarine         0x7FFFD4]  [Beige              0xF5F5DC]
[Bisque             0xFFE4C4]  [Black              0x000000]
[Black              0x000000]  [Black              0x000000]
[BlanchedAlmond     0xFFEBCD]  [BlueViolet         0x8A2BE2]
[Burlywood          0xDEB887]  [Chartreuse         0x7FFF00]
[Coral              0xFF7F50]  [Coral              0xFF7F50]
```

Permutation Algorithms

A permutation is a distinct ordering of a finite set of elements. The STL defines several algorithms that you can use to generate all possible permutations using the elements of a range. Listing 13-5-1 shows the source code for example function Ch13_05_ex1(), which highlights the use of std::ranges::next_permutation(). This algorithm transforms a sequence of elements into its next permutation by assuming that the set of all possible permutations is lexicographically sorted. The initial sequence used for std::ranges::next_permutation() must be sorted in ascending order.

Listing 13-5-1. Example Ch13_05 – Ch13_05_ex1()

```
//-------------------------------------------------------------------------
// Ch13_05_ex.cpp
//-------------------------------------------------------------------------

#include <algorithm>
#include <string>
#include <vector>
#include "Ch13_05.h"
#include "HtmlColor.h"
```

CHAPTER 13　ALGORITHMS – PART 4

```cpp
#include "MT.h"

void Ch13_05_ex1()
{
    const char* fmt = "{} ";
    constexpr size_t epl_max {2};

    // create test vector of HtmlColors
    std::vector<size_t> indices1 {20, 40, 60, 80, 100};
    std::vector<HtmlColor> colors1 = HtmlColor::get_vector(indices1);

    int i {};

    while (1)
    {
        std::string s = "\niteration " + std::to_string(++i) + ":\n";
        MT::print_ctr(s.c_str(), colors1, fmt, epl_max);

        // using std::ranges::next_permutation
        // returns template<class I>
        // struct next_permutation_result { I in; bool found; };
        // in = colors1.end()
        auto np_result = std::ranges::next_permutation(colors1);

        if (!np_result.found)
            break;
    }
}
```

The opening code block of Ch13_05_ex1() utilizes HtmlColor::get_vector(indices1) to initialize std::vector<HtmlColor> colors1. Vector colors1 contains four HtmlColor objects ascendingly sorted by name. Within the while loop, example function Ch13_05_ex1() calls np_result = std::ranges::next_permutation(colors1) to generate the next permutation using the elements of colors1. The execution of this function returns a structure of type std::ranges::next_permutation_result, which includes a bool member named found. If np_result.found is true, colors1 contains the next permutation; otherwise, all possible permutations have been generated.

CHAPTER 13 ALGORITHMS – PART 4

In Listing 13-5-2, example function Ch13_05_ex2() demonstrates the use of std::ranges::is_permutation(). Execution of this function returns true if the elements of the first range can be permuted to create a sequence that matches the ordering of elements in the second range.

Listing 13-5-2. Example Ch13_05 – Ch13_05_ex2()

```
void Ch13_05_ex2()
{
    const char* fmt = "{} ";
    constexpr size_t epl_max {2};

    // create test vectors of HtmlColors
    std::vector<size_t> indices1 {100, 101, 102, 103, 104, 105, 106, 107};
    std::vector<HtmlColor> colors1 = HtmlColor::get_vector(indices1);
    MT::print_ctr("\ncolors1:\n", colors1, fmt, epl_max);

    std::vector<size_t> indices2 {101, 107, 103, 104, 102, 106, 100, 105};
    std::vector<HtmlColor> colors2 = HtmlColor::get_vector(indices2);
    MT::print_ctr("\ncolors2:\n", colors2, fmt, epl_max);

    std::vector<size_t> indices3 {101, 107, 103, 104, 102, 106, 108, 105};
    std::vector<HtmlColor> colors3 = HtmlColor::get_vector(indices3);
    MT::print_ctr("\ncolors3:\n", colors3, fmt, epl_max);

    // using std::ranges::is_permutation
    bool b12 = std::ranges::is_permutation(colors1, colors2);
    bool b13 = std::ranges::is_permutation(colors1, colors3);
    std::println("\nis_permutation (colors1, colors2): {:s}", b12);
    std::println("is_permutation (colors1, colors3): {:s}", b13);
}
```

Like most other algorithms in namespace std::ranges, you can override the default comparison function for std::ranges::next_permutation(). The STL also includes an algorithm function named std::ranges::prev_permutation(), which can be used to generate permutations in descending order. The results for example Ch13_05 follow this paragraph. Note that the output for example function Ch13_05_ex1() has been truncated to save space.

CHAPTER 13　ALGORITHMS – PART 4

----- Results for example Ch13_05 -----

----- Ch13_05_ex1() -----

iteration 1:
[Cyan   0x00FFFF] [DimGray   0x696969]
[LavenderBlush   0xFFF0F5] [Maroon   0x800000]
[OrangeRed   0xFF4500]

iteration 2:
[Cyan   0x00FFFF] [DimGray   0x696969]
[LavenderBlush   0xFFF0F5] [OrangeRed   0xFF4500]
[Maroon   0x800000]

iteration 3:
[Cyan   0x00FFFF] [DimGray   0x696969]
[Maroon   0x800000] [LavenderBlush   0xFFF0F5]
[OrangeRed   0xFF4500]

...

iteration 118:
[OrangeRed   0xFF4500] [Maroon   0x800000]
[DimGray   0x696969] [LavenderBlush   0xFFF0F5]
[Cyan   0x00FFFF]

iteration 119:
[OrangeRed   0xFF4500] [Maroon   0x800000]
[LavenderBlush   0xFFF0F5] [Cyan   0x00FFFF]
[DimGray   0x696969]

iteration 120:
[OrangeRed   0xFF4500] [Maroon   0x800000]
[LavenderBlush   0xFFF0F5] [DimGray   0x696969]
[Cyan   0x00FFFF]

CHAPTER 13   ALGORITHMS – PART 4

```
----- Ch13_05_ex2() -----
colors1:
[OrangeRed            0xFF4500]  [Orchid              0xDA70D6]
[PaleGoldenrod        0xEEE8AA]  [PaleGreen           0x98FB98]
[PaleTurquoise        0xAFEEEE]  [PaleVioletRed       0xDB7093]
[PapayaWhip           0xFFEFD5]  [PeachPuff           0xFFDAB9]

colors2:
[Orchid               0xDA70D6]  [PeachPuff           0xFFDAB9]
[PaleGreen            0x98FB98]  [PaleTurquoise       0xAFEEEE]
[PaleGoldenrod        0xEEE8AA]  [PapayaWhip          0xFFEFD5]
[OrangeRed            0xFF4500]  [PaleVioletRed       0xDB7093]

colors3:
[Orchid               0xDA70D6]  [PeachPuff           0xFFDAB9]
[PaleGreen            0x98FB98]  [PaleTurquoise       0xAFEEEE]
[PaleGoldenrod        0xEEE8AA]  [PapayaWhip          0xFFEFD5]
[Peru                 0xCD853F]  [PaleVioletRed       0xDB7093]

is_permutation (colors1, colors2): true
is_permutation (colors1, colors3): false
```

Summary

Here are the key learning points for this chapter:

- Algorithm `std::ranges::merge()` merges two sorted ranges into a single sorted range. You can also use `std::ranges::inplace_merge()` to merge two sorted subranges that exist within the same range.

- Algorithm `std::ranges::shuffle()` randomly rearranges the elements of a range where the probability of each permutation is the same. Algorithm `std::ranges::sample()` chooses *N* elements from a range without replacements.

- Algorithm `std::ranges::rotate()` left-rotates the elements of a range. Algorithm `std::ranges::rotate_copy()` also left-rotates a range but saves the result to an output range. For both of these algorithms, the number of element positions to rotate is specified by a "middle" iterator. To perform a right rotation, use `size - n` for the middle iterator where size is the number of elements in the range and n is the number of element positions to rotate.

- Algorithms `std::ranges::shift_left()` and `std::ranges::shift_right()` carry out range left and right shifts. Unlike a rotate operation, execution of a shift operation yields valid range elements with unspecified states.

- Algorithms `std::ranges::set_intersection()`, `std::ranges::union()`, `std::ranges::set_difference()`, and `std::ranges::symmetric_difference()` carry out common set operations on ranges. Unlike their mathematical counterparts, these algorithms support duplicate elements.

- Algorithms `std::ranges::next_permutation()` and `std::ranges::prev_permutation()` are permutation generator functions, whose initial permutations are an ordered (ascending or descending) range of elements.

CHAPTER 14

Ranges – Part 1

This chapter is the first of two chapters that discuss advanced programming features and techniques for C++20/23 ranges. These features and techniques extend the capabilities of ranges well beyond the predefined algorithms of namespace std::ranges. Topics examined in this chapter include

- Range views
- Range adaptors
- Range adaptor pipelines
- Projections

The discussions in this chapter assume that you have a basic understanding of STL containers and algorithms as explained thus far in this book.

Range Views and Adaptors Primer

In previous chapters, you learned how to use a variety of containers. Briefly, a container is simply an object that encompasses a collection of other objects. The elements of a container can be accessed using iterators. Pairs of iterators are often employed to define a range of elements. For example, the range [vec1.begin(), vec1.end()) includes all int elements of std::vector<int> vec1. Iterators are also used to identify a subrange of elements within a container. Subrange [vec1.begin(), vec1.begin() + 5) denotes the first five elements of vec1. Before continuing, it warrants mentioning that the C++ terms container and range are sometimes used interchangeably. For the discussions of this chapter, a container owns a collection of elements, while a range encompasses zero or more sequential members of a container or another range. Ranges are also used to access the elements of a view as explained later in this chapter.

CHAPTER 14   RANGES – PART 1

Most C++ programs exploit STL's extensive collection of algorithms to perform operations using the elements of a container or range. Previous chapters covered a wide variety of algorithms, including the explicit iterator forms formalized in C++11 and the augmented range alternatives of C++20. Recall that the algorithms of namespace `std::ranges` support variable name arguments to carry out an action using the entire container. However, the programming capabilities of `std::ranges` extends far beyond syntax simplification. Perhaps the most operative of these newer capabilities is the concept of a range view (or view).

A view is an algorithmic "window" into a range of elements. Like a range, the elements of a view can be accessed using iterators. Fundamental aspects of a view include

- A view doesn't own any elements.[1] It is a logical arrangement of elements that are typically, but not necessarily, held in a container.

- The elements of a view are generally specified using one or more filtering or transformation operations.

- Views are lazily evaluated. This means that any filtering or transformation operations aren't applied until an element is accessed.

- Views are composable. Multiple views can be chained together in a manner that resembles the piping of commands in a terminal window.

- Views are similar to other STL objects in that they can be created, destroyed, assigned, moved, etc. A view is created in constant time. In other words, the performance cost to create a view does not depend on the number of elements in the view.

- A view can be instantiated directly using the classes of namespace `std::ranges::views` or `std::views`. The latter is an alias of the former. However, it is more common and frequently more efficient to create a view using a range adaptor. A range adaptor is a utility that transforms a range into a view with explicit algorithmic behavior.

---

[1] An exception to this rule is view `std::ranges::owning_view`.

CHAPTER 14 RANGES – PART 1

One notable advantage of C++ views is that they can be created in anticipation of some future programming need. The execution cost of pre-creating one or more views is often negligible if an instantiated view is not used due to a runtime logic decision.

Figure 14-1 unifies containers, ranges, range adaptors, and views into a single diagram. Don't worry if you don't fully understand some of the entities in this figure. You'll learn more about these concepts as the chapter progresses.

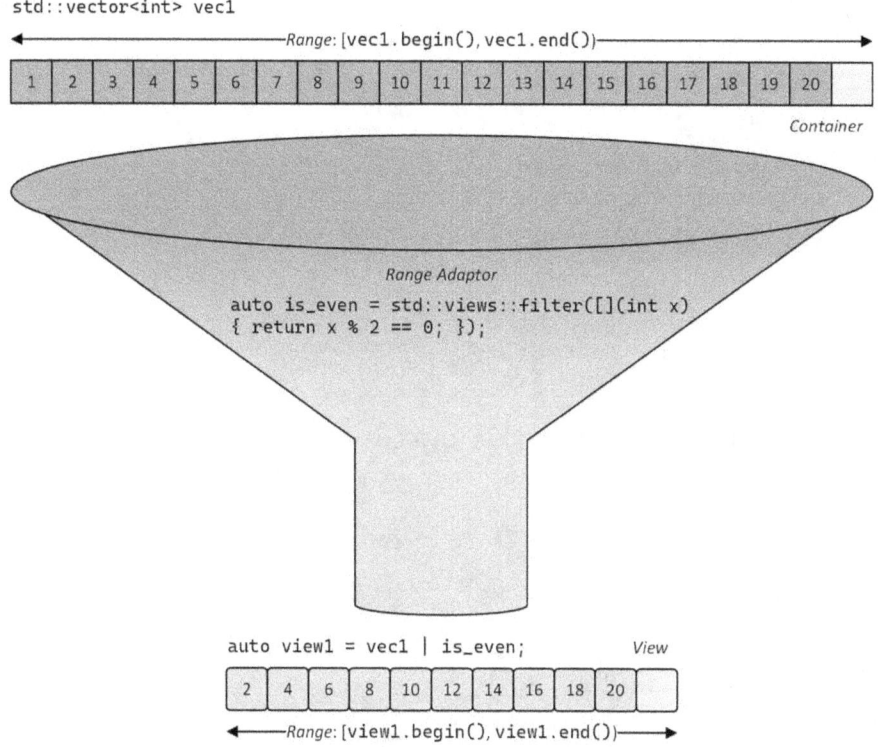

Figure 14-1. *Unified representation of a container, range, range adaptor, and view*

Range Views and Adaptors

Source code example Ch14_01 explicates elementary views. Listing 14-1-1 shows the code for example function Ch14_01_ex1(). This listing opens with the definition of get_test_vector(). Execution of this function returns a std::vector<int> of random integers. The initial code block of Ch14_01_ex1() utilizes get_test_vector() to initialize vec1. Next is the definition of lambda expression pred = [](int x) {return x > 0 && x % 10 == 0;}.

577

Listing 14-1-1. Example Ch14_01 - Ch14_01_ex1()

```cpp
//----------------------------------------------------------------------
// Ch14_01_ex.cpp
//----------------------------------------------------------------------

#include <algorithm>
#include <iostream>
#include <numeric>
#include <ranges>
#include <vector>
#include "Ch14_01.h"
#include "MT.h"
#include "MTH.h"
#include "RN.h"

auto get_test_vector()
{
    // return test vector of random integers
    return RN::get_vector<int>(60, -500, 500, 13);
}

void Ch14_01_ex1()
{
    const char* fmt = "{:6d}";
    constexpr size_t epl_max {12};

    // create test vector of random numbers
    std::vector<int> vec1 = get_test_vector();
    MT::print_ctr("\nvec1:\n", vec1, fmt, epl_max);

    auto pred = [](int x) { return x > 0 && x % 10 == 0; };

    // using std::views::filter (can also use std::ranges::views::filter)
    auto view1 = std::views::filter(vec1, pred);

    bool is_empty1 = view1.empty();
    std::println("\nview1 is empty: {:s}", is_empty1);
```

```
    // copy-construct view2 using view1
    auto view2 {view1};

    bool is_empty2 = view2.empty();
    std::println("\nview2 is empty: {:s}", is_empty2);
}
```

The second code block of Ch14_01_ex1() demonstrates how to use range adaptor std::views::filter(). The execution of view1 = std::views::filter(vec1, pred) creates a view of all elements in vec1 for which pred is true (i.e., elements that are greater than zero and evenly divisible by ten). It is important to understand that during the instantiation of view1, none of vec1's elements are accessed and pred isn't invoked. If you're unsure about this, try executing Ch14_01_ex2() using your favorite C++ debugger and set a breakpoint on the return statement inside pred.

Following creation of view1, Ch14_01_ex1() utilizes view1.empty() to check whether the view defined by view1 contains any elements. To carry out this operation, view1.empty() applies pred to the elements of vec1 starting at vec1.begin() and continues until pred returns true (non-empty view) or element vec1.end() is reached (empty view). The last code block in Ch14_01_ex1() copy-constructs view2. Note that an initializer list is used to initialize view2 just like any other C++ object.

Example function Ch14_01_ex2(), shown in Listing 14-1-2, illustrates how to enumerate the elements of a view. Like the previous example function, the initial code block of Ch14_01_ex2() initializes std::vector<int> vec1 and pred. This function also creates the same view object using view1 = std::views::filter(vec1, pred).

Listing 14-1-2. Example Ch14_01 - Ch14_01_ex2()

```
void Ch14_01_ex2()
{
    const char* fmt = "{:6d}";
    constexpr size_t epl_max {12};

    // create test vector of random numbers
    std::vector<int> vec1 = get_test_vector();
    MT::print_ctr("\nvec1:\n", vec1, fmt, epl_max);

    auto pred = [](int x) { return x > 0 && x % 10 == 0; };
```

```cpp
    // using std::views::filter
    auto view1 = std::views::filter(vec1, pred);

    // empty view?
    if (view1)
    {
        // print elements of view1
        std::println("\nprinting elements of view1 using iterators");
        for (auto iter = view1.begin(); iter != view1.end(); ++iter)
            std::print("{:d} ", *iter);
        std::println("");

        std::println("\nprinting elements of view1 using range for loop");
        for (auto val : view1)
            std::print("{:d} ", val);
        std::println("");
    }
    else
        std::println("view1 is empty");
}
```

Following instantiation of view1, Ch14_01_ex2() checks for an empty view using operator bool(), which returns !view1.empty(). If view1 is not empty, the code block inside the if statement prints the elements of view1. The first if statement code block utilizes an ordinary for loop to print the elements of [view1.begin(), view1.end()). Note that this for loop is no different than any other iterator-based for loop that accesses the elements of a range. Behind the scenes, each execution of ++iter updates iter so that it points to the next element in vec1 that returns true for pred. The second code block inside the if expression utilizes a range for loop to print the elements of view1. Once again, this expression is identical to other range for loops that you've studied.

Listing 14-1-3 shows the source code for example function Ch14_01_ex3(). This function demonstrates the use of range adaptors std::views::filter() and std::views::transform(). The opening code block of Ch14_01_ex3() utilizes std::ranges::iota(vec1, 1) to initialize the elements of std::vector<int> vec1(50). The next statement, view1 = std::views::filter(vec1, MTH::is_prime<int>), instantiates a view of all prime numbers in vec1 (see Listing 10-6-2-2 for MTH::is_prime()).

Listing 14-1-3. Example Ch14_01 - Ch14_01_ex3()

```cpp
void Ch14_01_ex3()
{
    const char* fmt = "{:7d}";
    constexpr size_t epl_max {10};

    // initialize test vector
    std::vector<int> vec1(50);
#ifdef __cpp_lib_ranges_iota          // C++23
    std::ranges::iota(vec1, 1);
#else
    std::iota(vec1.begin(), vec1.end(), 1);
#endif
    MT::print_ctr("\nvec1 (initial values):\n", vec1, fmt, epl_max);

    // using std::views::filter
    auto view1 = std::views::filter(vec1, MTH::is_prime<int>);

    // using std::views::transform
    auto view2 = std::views::transform(view1, [](int x) { return -x; });

    // print elements specfied by view1 and view2
    MT::print_ctr("\nview1 (std::views::filter):\n", view1, fmt, epl_max);
    MT::print_ctr("\nview2 (std::views::transform):\n", view2, fmt,
        epl_max);

    // print elements of vec1 (same as initial values)
    MT::print_ctr("\nvec1 (unaltered by std::views::filter, transform):\n",
        vec1, fmt, epl_max);

    // using std::ranges::to<std::vector> (C++23)
#ifdef __cpp_lib_ranges_to_container
    std::vector<int> vec2 = view2 | std::ranges::to<std::vector>();
    MT::print_ctr("\nvec2 (result of view2 | std::ranges::to<std::vec
    tor>):\n",
        vec2, fmt, epl_max);
```

#else
    std::println("std::ranges::to<std::vector>() requires C++23)");
#endif
}

Following the creation of view1 is the statement view2 = std::views::transform(view1, [](int x) { return -x; }). Execution of this range adaptor creates a view that negates all elements in view1. Once again, it's important to keep in mind that during the instantiation of view1 and view2, no elements of vec1 are accessed and neither unary predicate is invoked. The runtime cost of instantiating view1 and view2 is constant in that it's not dependent on the number of elements in vec1.

The ensuing code block in Ch14_01_ex3() utilizes MT::print_ctr() to print the elements of view1 and view2. Despite the fact that neither view1 nor view2 are containers, MT::print_ctr() successfully prints the elements of these views since it utilizes a range for loop just like you saw in example function Ch14_01_ex2(). The next statement in Ch14_01_ex3() uses MT::print_ctr() to print the elements of vec1. Note in the results section that the elements in vec1 are identical before and after the application of range adaptors std::views::filter() and std::ranges::transform().

In the final code block of Ch14_01_ex3(), execution of the statement std::vector<int> vec2 = view2 | std::ranges::to<std::vector>() (C++23) constructs vec2 using the elements of view2. Note the use of operator| in this expression. This is an example of a chained operation, the details of which are discussed in the next section. Constructing a container object using the elements of a view is sometimes necessary for subsequent processing by algorithms that perform operations using actual containers. Here are the results for example Ch14_01:

```
----- Results for example Ch14_01 -----

----- Ch14_01_ex1() -----

vec1:
    278    107   -263    360    325    393    466   -321    473    259    -47    252
    109    107    276    294    142   -112    222   -160   -465    162   -202    406
   -442    220    357    -28   -127     -3    180    -54   -244     31   -153    494
   -491    115   -142   -320    450    223   -282    440   -181     38    418    -30
   -469    125   -435    190    130   -211    374   -448   -492    288    247     26

view1 is empty: false
```

view2 is empty: false

----- Ch14_01_ex2() -----

vec1:

278	107	-263	360	325	393	466	-321	473	259	-47	252
109	107	276	294	142	-112	222	-160	-465	162	-202	406
-442	220	357	-28	-127	-3	180	-54	-244	31	-153	494
-491	115	-142	-320	450	223	-282	440	-181	38	418	-30
-469	125	-435	190	130	-211	374	-448	-492	288	247	26

printing elements of view1 using iterators
360 220 180 450 440 190 130

printing elements of view1 using range for loop
360 220 180 450 440 190 130

----- Ch14_01_ex3() -----

vec1 (initial values):

1	2	3	4	5	6	7	8	9	10
11	12	13	14	15	16	17	18	19	20
21	22	23	24	25	26	27	28	29	30
31	32	33	34	35	36	37	38	39	40
41	42	43	44	45	46	47	48	49	50

view1 (std::views::filter):

| 2 | 3 | 5 | 7 | 11 | 13 | 17 | 19 | 23 | 29 |
| 31 | 37 | 41 | 43 | 47 | | | | | |

view2 (std::views::transform):

| -2 | -3 | -5 | -7 | -11 | -13 | -17 | -19 | -23 | -29 |
| -31 | -37 | -41 | -43 | -47 | | | | | |

vec1 (unaltered by std::views::filter, transform):

1	2	3	4	5	6	7	8	9	10
11	12	13	14	15	16	17	18	19	20
21	22	23	24	25	26	27	28	29	30
31	32	33	34	35	36	37	38	39	40
41	42	43	44	45	46	47	48	49	50

```
vec2 (result of view2 | std::ranges::to<std::vector>):
    -2    -3    -5    -7   -11   -13   -17   -19   -23   -29
   -31   -37   -41   -43   -47
```

Range Adaptors and Pipelines

Source code example Ch14_02 covers additional range adaptors, including `std::views::drop()` and `std::views::reverse()`. It also explains how to define and use range adaptor pipelines (i.e., the chaining of multiple range adaptors).

Listing 14-2-1 shows the source code for example function `Ch14_02_ex1()`. Near the top of this listing is the definition of a structure named `Args`, which contains common values used by all of the example functions in Ch14_02. The opening code block of `Ch14_02_ex1()` utilizes `RN::get_vector<>()` to initialize vec1. In the subsequent code block, execution of `view2 = std::views::filter(vec1, args.IsEven)` instantiates view2. Note that the unary predicate for `std::views::filter()` is obtained from `const Args& args`, which is passed to `Ch14_02_ex1()`.

Listing 14-2-1. Example Ch14_02 - Ch14_02_ex1()

```cpp
//-------------------------------------------------------------------------
// Ch14_02_ex.cpp
//-------------------------------------------------------------------------

#include <algorithm>
#include <ranges>
#include <string>
#include "MT.h"
#include "RN.h"

// Common arguments structure
struct Args
{
    size_t NumElem {48};                // size of data vector
    unsigned int RngSeed {1003};        // random number generator seed val
    int RngMin {1};                     // random number generator min val
    int RngMax {2000};                  // random number generator max val
```

```cpp
    size_t NumDrop {5};              // number of dropped elements
    std::string Fmt {"{:6d}"};       // print format specifier
    size_t EplMax {12};              // max elements per line

    static inline auto IsEven = [](int x) { return (x % 2) == 0; };
};

void Ch14_02_ex1(const Args& args)
{
    // create vector of random values
    std::vector<int> vec1 = RN::get_vector<int>(args.NumElem, args.RngMin,
        args.RngMax, args.RngSeed);
    MT::print_ctr("\nvec1 (initial values):\n", vec1, args.Fmt,
    args.EplMax);

    // using std::views_filter (filters odd values)
    auto view2 = std::views::filter(vec1, args.IsEven);
    MT::print_ctr("\nview2:\n", view2, args.Fmt, args.EplMax);

    // using std::views_drop (deletes first NumDrop elements)
    auto view3 = std::views::drop(view2, args.NumDrop);
    MT::print_ctr("\nvec3:\n", view3, args.Fmt, args.EplMax);

    // using std::views::reverse (reverses order of elements)
    auto view4 = std::views::reverse(view3);
    MT::print_ctr("\nview4 (final result):\n", view4, args.Fmt,
    args.EplMax);

    MT::print_ctr("\nvec1 (after views::reverse):\n", vec1, args.Fmt,
    args.EplMax);
}
```

The next code block utilizes view3 = std::views::drop(view2, args. NumDrop) to create view3, which includes the elements of view2 without its first args.NumDrop elements. The final code block of Ch14_02_ex1() exploits view4 = std::views::reverse(view3) to reverse the elements of view3. Note again in the results section that vec1's elements are not modified during the execution of these range adaptors. Also, take note of each view's elements in the results section.

Source code example Ch14_02_ex2(), shown in Listing 14-2-2, computes the same view of vec1 result as Ch14_02_ex1() but uses a series of nested range adaptor calls.

Listing 14-2-2. *Example Ch14_02 – Ch14_02_ex2()*

```
void Ch14_02_ex2(const Args& args)
{
    std::vector<int> vec1 = RN::get_vector<int>(args.NumElem, args.RngMin,
        args.RngMax, args.RngSeed);
    MT::print_ctr("\nvec1 (initial values):\n", vec1, args.Fmt,
    args.EplMax);

    // Using std::views::reverse, drop, and filter (call style)
    auto view2 = std::views::reverse(std::views::drop(std::views::fi
    lter(vec1,
        args.IsEven), args.NumDrop));

    MT::print_ctr("\nview2 (final result):\n", view2, args.Fmt,
    args.EplMax);
}
```

From a functional perspective, there's nothing erroneous about the expression `view2 = std::views::reverse(std::views::drop(std::views::filter(vec1, args.IsEven), args.NumDrop))`. However, the exact calculation that gets performed may not be immediately obvious given that the innermost call to `std::views::filter()` is executed first followed by `std::views::drop()` and then `std::views::reverse()`.

In Listing 14-2-3, example function `Ch14_02_ex3()` chains together a series of range adaptor calls to create `view2`. The syntax used here resembles that of piping commands in a terminal window. Perhaps the biggest advantage of the `operator|` chaining syntax is that each range adaptor gets invoked in order as it appears in the code. It's instantly understandable exactly what's being computed.

Listing 14-2-3. *Example Ch14_02 – Ch14_02_ex3()*

```
void Ch14_02_ex3(const Args& args)
{
    std::vector<int> vec1 = RN::get_vector<int>(args.NumElem, args.RngMin,
        args.RngMax, args.RngSeed);
    MT::print_ctr("\nvec1 (initial values):\n", vec1, args.Fmt,
    args.EplMax);
```

CHAPTER 14 RANGES – PART 1

```
    // using composition of std::views::reverse, drop, filter
    auto view2 = vec1
                | std::views::filter(args.IsEven)
                | std::views::drop(args.NumDrop)
                | std::views::reverse;

    MT::print_ctr("\nview2 (final result):\n", view2, args.Fmt,
    args.EplMax);
}
```

The final example function of this section, Ch14_02_ex4(), performs the same calculation as the previous three functions but uses STL algorithms instead of range adaptors and views.

Listing 14-2-4. Example Ch14_02 – Ch14_02_ex4()

```
void Ch14_02_ex4(const Args& args)
{
    std::vector<int> vec1 = RN::get_vector<int>(args.NumElem, args.RngMin,
        args.RngMax, args.RngSeed);
    MT::print_ctr("\nvec1 (initial values):\n", vec1, args.Fmt,
    args.EplMax);

    // copy even values
    std::vector<int> temp1 {};
    std::ranges::copy_if(vec1, std::back_inserter(temp1), args.IsEven);

    // drop values
    std::vector<int> temp2(temp1.size() - args.NumDrop);
    std::ranges::copy(temp1.begin() + args.NumDrop, temp1.end(),
    temp2.begin());

    // reverse order of remaining values
    std::ranges::reverse(temp2);
    MT::print_ctr("\ntemp2: (final result)\n", temp2, args.Fmt,
    args.EplMax);
}
```

CHAPTER 14   RANGES – PART 1

The most important construct to recognize in Listing 14-2-4 is the creation of two temporary `std::vector<int>` containers that hold intermediate results. The earlier examples that utilized range adaptors were able to perform the same calculation sans these containers. The time-space performance costs of the range adaptor vs. algorithm methods will in many use cases favor the former, especially if the original source vector contains a large number of elements. Here are the results for example Ch14_02:

```
----- Results for example Ch14_02 -----

----- Ch14_02_ex1() -----
vec1 (initial values):
    1196    10   872  1399    34   504  1194  1983  1790   667  1070    57
      12   685  1805  1347  1510  1684   345  1001  1461  1106   747  1814
     365  1902   891   221   574  1091   822   685   887   955   355   900
     520    91   460   722   809   423  1020  1821   829  1234   597   859
view2:
    1196    10   872    34   504  1194  1790  1070    12  1510  1684  1106
    1814  1902   574   822   900   520   460   722  1020  1234
vec3:
    1194  1790  1070    12  1510  1684  1106  1814  1902   574   822   900
     520   460   722  1020  1234
view4 (final result):
    1234  1020   722   460   520   900   822   574  1902  1814  1106  1684
    1510    12  1070  1790  1194
vec1 (after views::reverse):
    1196    10   872  1399    34   504  1194  1983  1790   667  1070    57
      12   685  1805  1347  1510  1684   345  1001  1461  1106   747  1814
     365  1902   891   221   574  1091   822   685   887   955   355   900
     520    91   460   722   809   423  1020  1821   829  1234   597   859
```

```
----- Ch14_02_ex2() -----

vec1 (initial values):
  1196    10   872  1399    34   504  1194  1983  1790   667  1070    57
    12   685  1805  1347  1510  1684   345  1001  1461  1106   747  1814
   365  1902   891   221   574  1091   822   685   887   955   355   900
   520    91   460   722   809   423  1020  1821   829  1234   597   859
view2 (final result):
  1234  1020   722   460   520   900   822   574  1902  1814  1106  1684
  1510    12  1070  1790  1194

----- Ch14_02_ex3() -----

vec1 (initial values):
  1196    10   872  1399    34   504  1194  1983  1790   667  1070    57
    12   685  1805  1347  1510  1684   345  1001  1461  1106   747  1814
   365  1902   891   221   574  1091   822   685   887   955   355   900
   520    91   460   722   809   423  1020  1821   829  1234   597   859
view2 (final result):
  1234  1020   722   460   520   900   822   574  1902  1814  1106  1684
  1510    12  1070  1790  1194

----- Ch14_02_ex4() -----

vec1 (initial values):
  1196    10   872  1399    34   504  1194  1983  1790   667  1070    57
    12   685  1805  1347  1510  1684   345  1001  1461  1106   747  1814
   365  1902   891   221   574  1091   822   685   887   955   355   900
   520    91   460   722   809   423  1020  1821   829  1234   597   859
temp2: (final result)
  1234  1020   722   460   520   900   822   574  1902  1814  1106  1684
  1510    12  1070  1790  1194
```

CHAPTER 14 RANGES – PART 1

Range Projections

A projection is a transformation function that an algorithm applies prior to consuming an element's value. Most of the algorithms in namespace `std::ranges` support projections since they impart a substantial amount of algorithmic flexibility. Listing 14-3-1 shows the source code for example Ch14_03_ex1(). This example demonstrates how to exploit rudimentary projections.

Listing 14-3-1. Example Ch14_03 – Ch14_03_ex1()

```cpp
//------------------------------------------------------------------------
// Ch14_03_ex.cpp
//------------------------------------------------------------------------

#include <algorithm>
#include <cmath>
#include <functional>
#include <vector>
#include "Ch14_03.h"
#include "Mineral.h"
#include "MT.h"

struct Fruit
{
    std::string Name {};            // fruit name
    unsigned int Energy {};         // kJ per 100 gram serving
};

void Ch14_03_ex1()
{
    // test data
    std::vector<Fruit> fruits
    {
        {"Banana", 371},            {"Orange", 197},
        {"Apple", 281},             {"Kiwi (green)", 255},
        {"Tangerine", 223},         {"Blueberry", 240},
```

```cpp
        {"Strawberry", 136},      {"Tomato (red)", 74},
        {"Cherry (sweet)", 263},  {"Cherry (sour)", 209},
    };

    // print lambda
    auto print_fruits = [&fruits](const char* msg)
    {
        std::println("{:s}", msg);

        for (const Fruit& f : fruits)
            std::println("{:20s}  kJ: {:3d}  kcal: {:3d}", f.Name,
            f.Energy, static_cast<unsigned int>(f.Energy * 0.239f + 0.5f));
    };

    // using std::ranges::sort, by Name
    std::ranges::sort(fruits, std::ranges::greater(), &Fruit::Name);
    print_fruits("\nvector fruits (descending order by Name)");

    // using std::ranges::sort, by Energy
    std::ranges::sort(fruits, std::ranges::less(), &Fruit::Energy);
    print_fruits("\nvector fruits (ascending order by Energy)");
}
```

The code in Listing 14-3-1 opens with the declaration of a simple structure named Fruit. Note that this structure contains two members: std::string Name and unsigned int Energy. The opening code block in Ch14_03_ex1() instantiates std::vector<Fruit> fruits. Next is the definition of lambda expression print_fruits(), which prints the elements of vector fruits.

The subsequent code block utilizes std::ranges::sort(fruits, std::ranges::greater(), &Fruit::Name) to sort the elements of fruits. There are several important particulars to recognize here. First, the use of function object std::ranges::greater() means that std::ranges::sort() will sort vector fruits in descending order. Second, algorithm std::ranges::sort() will utilize attribute Fruit::Name when sorting fruits. This third argument of std::ranges::sort() is a projection. For the current example, std::ranges::sort() applies a default projection function object named std::identity(), which returns argument Fruit::Name unchanged.

CHAPTER 14 RANGES – PART 1

The next code block in Ch14_03_ex1() employs std::ranges::sort(fruits, std::ranges::less(), &Fruit::Energy) to ascendingly sort the elements of fruits using Fruit::Energy. Note that both uses of std::ranges::sort() in Ch14_03_ex1() performed practical sorts without having to define explicit comparison functions.

Listing 14-3-2 shows the next example function, which is named Ch14_03_ex2(). This function spotlights additional uses of projections using std::ranges::sort() and user-defined class Mineral (see Listing 11-5-1-1 for class Mineral). In the code block that follows the creation of std::vector<Mineral> minerals, Ch14_03_ex2() utilizes std::ranges::sort(minerals) to sort the elements of minerals. In this usage, the default comparison function object for std::ranges::sort() is std::ranges::less(), and function object std::identity() is the default projection. The relational operators for class Mineral compare attributes Mineral::Hardness first followed by Mineral::Name. This means that for the current example, std::ranges::sort()'s default comparison function is Mineral::operator<.[2]

Listing 14-3-2. *Example Ch14_03 – Ch14_03_ex2()*

```
void Ch14_03_ex2()
{
    const char* fmt = "{} ";
    constexpr size_t epl_max {3};

    // create test vector of minerals
    std::vector<Mineral> minerals = Mineral::get_vector_all_shuffle(100);

    // sort using Mineral::operator< (Hardness and Name)
    std::ranges::sort(minerals);
    MT::print_ctr("\nminerals (sorted using Mineral::operator<):\n",
        minerals, fmt, epl_max);

    // sort using std::ranges::greater and Hardness
    std::ranges::sort(minerals, std::ranges::greater(),
        &Mineral::Hardness);
```

---

[2] Class Mineral defines operator<=>, from which the compiler can generate operator< functionality.

```
    MT::print_ctr("\nminerals (sorted using std::ranges::greater and
    Hardness):\n",
        minerals, fmt, epl_max);

    // sort using std::ranges::less and Name
    std::ranges::sort(minerals, std::ranges::less(), &Mineral::Name);
    MT::print_ctr("\nminerals (sorted using std::ranges::less and
    Name):\n",
        minerals, fmt, epl_max);
}
```

The next two code blocks in Ch14_03_ex2() highlight additional exploitations of std::ranges::sort(). The first use sorts vector minerals using std::ranges::greater() and Mineral::Hardness; the second instance utilizes std::ranges::less() and Mineral::Name.

You may recall from earlier examples (e.g., Ch04_01) the use of function object std::greater(). The primary difference between this function object and std::ranges::greater() is that the use of the latter requires valid definition of all six relational operations for the type, while the former doesn't. The definition of all six relational operators is easily accomplished by defining operator<=> and operator== (see class Mineral for an example). The general rule for using predefined comparison function objects is to select std::less(), std::greater(), etc., for namespace std algorithms and std::ranges::less(), std::ranges::greater(), etc., for namespace std::ranges algorithms.

The final example function of Ch14_03, shown in Listing 14-3-3, illustrates how to define and apply custom projection functions. Near the top of Ch14_03_ex3() is the definition of std::vector<Value> values. Note that struct Value includes two members: X and Y. Next is the definition of two lambda expressions named pf1 and pf2, which are used later as projection functions. These functions carry out arbitrary calculations using members Value::X and Value::Y. The next code block defines print_values(). The execution of this lambda prints the elements of values. Note that print_values() captures its entire enclosing scope since a lambda expression cannot use a previously defined expression without capturing it.

Chapter 14 Ranges – Part 1

Listing 14-3-3. *Example Ch14_03 - Ch14_03_ex3()*

```
struct Value
{
    double X {};
    double Y {};
};
void Ch14_03_ex3()
{
    // test vector
    std::vector<Value> values
    {
        {3.0, 4.0},  {6.0, 3.0},  {12.0, 5.0},  {11.0, 10.0},
        {7.0, 8.0},  {2.0, 9.0},  {4.0, 14.0},  {6.0, 13.0}
    };

    // projection lambdas (arbitrary calculations)
    auto pf1 = [](const Value& v) { return v.X + std::log(std::fabs(v.Y)) ; };
    auto pf2 = [](const Value& v) { return v.Y + std::log10(std::fabs(v.X)); };

    // print lambda
    auto print_values = [&] (const char* msg)
    {
        std::println("{:s}", msg);
        std::print("         X          Y");
        std::print(" |        pf1        pf2");
        std::println("\n{:s}", std::string(48, '='));

        for (const Value& v : values)
        {
            auto t1 = pf1(v);
            auto t2 = pf2(v);
            std::println("[{:9.4f}, {:9.4f} | {:9.4f}, {:9.4f}]", v.X, v.Y,
            t1, t2);
        }
    };
```

```
    // sort using std::ranges::greater() and pf1
    std::ranges::sort(values, std::ranges::greater(), pf1);
    print_values("\nvalues (sorted using std::ranges::greater and pf1):");

    // sort using std::ranges::less() and pf2
    std::ranges::sort(values, std::ranges::less(), pf2);
    print_values("\nvalues (sorted using std::ranges::less and pf2):");
}
```

In the code block that follows the definition of print_values(), Ch14_03_ex3() exercises std::ranges::sort(values, std::ranges::greater(), pf1). During the execution of this algorithm, std::ranges::sort() applies pf1 to each element of vector values *before* invoking comparison function std::ranges::greater(). Thus, execution of std::ranges::sort(values, std::ranges::greater(), pf1) sorts the elements of values in descending order using the result that pf1 calculates for each Value element in values.

The final code block of Ch14_03_ex3() utilizes std::ranges::sort(values, std::ranges::less(), pf2) to ascendingly sort the elements of values using projection function pf2. Here are the results for example Ch14_03:

```
----- Results for example Ch14_03 -----

----- Ch14_03_ex1() -----

vector fruits (descending order by Name)
Tomato (red)        kJ:  74   kcal:  18
Tangerine           kJ: 223   kcal:  53
Strawberry          kJ: 136   kcal:  33
Orange              kJ: 197   kcal:  47
Kiwi (green)        kJ: 255   kcal:  61
Cherry (sweet)      kJ: 263   kcal:  63
Cherry (sour)       kJ: 209   kcal:  50
Blueberry           kJ: 240   kcal:  57
Banana              kJ: 371   kcal:  89
Apple               kJ: 281   kcal:  67
```

CHAPTER 14   RANGES – PART 1

```
vector fruits (ascending order by Energy)
Tomato (red)              kJ:  74   kcal:  18
Strawberry                kJ: 136   kcal:  33
Orange                    kJ: 197   kcal:  47
Cherry (sour)             kJ: 209   kcal:  50
Tangerine                 kJ: 223   kcal:  53
Blueberry                 kJ: 240   kcal:  57
Kiwi (green)              kJ: 255   kcal:  61
Cherry (sweet)            kJ: 263   kcal:  63
Apple                     kJ: 281   kcal:  67
Banana                    kJ: 371   kcal:  89

----- Ch14_03_ex2() -----
minerals (sorted using Mineral::operator<):
[Talc           1.000] [Dimorphite    1.500] [Todorokite    1.500]
[Gypsum         2.000] [Kinoite       2.500] [Galena        2.625]
[Chalcocite     2.750] [Calcite       3.000] [Hanksite      3.250]
[Roselite       3.500] [Aragonite     3.750] [Fluorite      4.000]
[Zincite        4.250] [Conichalcite  4.500] [Lindgrenite   4.500]
[Apatite        5.000] [Perovskite    5.250] [Agrellite     5.500]
[Anatase        5.750] [Orthoclase    6.000] [Chloritoid    6.500]
[Bowieite       7.000] [Quartz        7.000] [Zircon        7.500]
[Topaz          8.000] [Chrysoberyl   8.500] [Tongbaite     8.500]
[Corundum       9.000] [Moissanite    9.250] [Diamond      10.000]

minerals (sorted using std::ranges::greater and Hardness):
[Diamond       10.000] [Moissanite    9.250] [Corundum      9.000]
[Chrysoberyl    8.500] [Tongbaite     8.500] [Topaz         8.000]
[Zircon         7.500] [Bowieite      7.000] [Quartz        7.000]
[Chloritoid     6.500] [Orthoclase    6.000] [Anatase       5.750]
[Agrellite      5.500] [Perovskite    5.250] [Apatite       5.000]
[Conichalcite   4.500] [Lindgrenite   4.500] [Zincite       4.250]
[Fluorite       4.000] [Aragonite     3.750] [Roselite      3.500]
[Hanksite       3.250] [Calcite       3.000] [Chalcocite    2.750]
[Galena         2.625] [Kinoite       2.500] [Gypsum        2.000]
[Dimorphite     1.500] [Todorokite    1.500] [Talc          1.000]
```

minerals (sorted using std::ranges::less and Name):
```
[Agrellite      5.500] [Anatase      5.750] [Apatite       5.000]
[Aragonite      3.750] [Bowieite     7.000] [Calcite       3.000]
[Chalcocite     2.750] [Chloritoid   6.500] [Chrysoberyl   8.500]
[Conichalcite   4.500] [Corundum     9.000] [Diamond      10.000]
[Dimorphite     1.500] [Fluorite     4.000] [Galena        2.625]
[Gypsum         2.000] [Hanksite     3.250] [Kinoite       2.500]
[Lindgrenite    4.500] [Moissanite   9.250] [Orthoclase    6.000]
[Perovskite     5.250] [Quartz       7.000] [Roselite      3.500]
[Talc           1.000] [Todorokite   1.500] [Tongbaite     8.500]
[Topaz          8.000] [Zincite      4.250] [Zircon        7.500]
```

----- Ch14_03_ex3() -----

values (sorted using std::ranges::greater and pf1):
```
         X           Y |     pf1       pf2
=================================================
[   12.0000,    5.0000 |  13.6094,   6.0792]
[   11.0000,   10.0000 |  13.3026,  11.0414]
[    7.0000,    8.0000 |   9.0794,   8.8451]
[    6.0000,   13.0000 |   8.5649,  13.7782]
[    6.0000,    3.0000 |   7.0986,   3.7782]
[    4.0000,   14.0000 |   6.6391,  14.6021]
[    3.0000,    4.0000 |   4.3863,   4.4771]
[    2.0000,    9.0000 |   4.1972,   9.3010]
```

values (sorted using std::ranges::less and pf2):
```
         X           Y |     pf1       pf2
=================================================
[    6.0000,    3.0000 |   7.0986,   3.7782]
[    3.0000,    4.0000 |   4.3863,   4.4771]
[   12.0000,    5.0000 |  13.6094,   6.0792]
[    7.0000,    8.0000 |   9.0794,   8.8451]
[    2.0000,    9.0000 |   4.1972,   9.3010]
[   11.0000,   10.0000 |  13.3026,  11.0414]
[    6.0000,   13.0000 |   8.5649,  13.7782]
[    4.0000,   14.0000 |   6.6391,  14.6021]
```

CHAPTER 14 RANGES – PART 1

More Range Adaptors

The next example of this chapter spotlights a few more range adaptor usages. Listing 14-4-1 shows the source code for example Ch14_04_ex1(). This function illustrates the use of range adaptor std::views::drop_while().

Listing 14-4-1. Example Ch14_04 – Ch14_04_ex1()

```
//-------------------------------------------------------------------------
// Ch14_04_ex.cpp
//-------------------------------------------------------------------------

#include <algorithm>
#include <functional>
#include <numeric>
#include <ranges>
#include <string>
#include <vector>
#include "Ch14_04.h"
#include "HtmlColor.h"
#include "MT.h"
#include "MTH.h"

void Ch14_04_ex1()
{
    const char* fmt = "{:7d}";
    constexpr size_t epl_max {10};

    // create test vector
    std::vector<int> vec1(50);

#ifdef __cpp_lib_ranges_iota           // C++23
    std::ranges::iota(vec1, 1);
#else
    std::iota(vec1.begin(), vec1.end(), 1);
#endif
    MT::print_ctr("\nvec1 (initial values):\n", vec1, fmt, epl_max);
```

```cpp
    // drop_while predicate
    auto dw_pred = [](int x) { return x <= 25; };

    // using std::views::filter and std::views::drop_while
    auto view1 = vec1
                | std::views::filter(MTH::is_prime<int>)
                | std::views::drop_while(dw_pred);

    MT::print_ctr("\nview1 (after filter and drop_while):\n", view1, fmt,
    epl_max);
}
```

The opening code block in Ch14_04_ex1() employs std::ranges::iota(vec1, 1) to initialize std::vector<int> vec1(50). Next is the definition of predicate dw_pred = [](int x) { return x <= 25; }. In the subsequent code block, Ch14_04_ex1() instantiates view1 = vec1 | std::views::filter(MTH::is_prime<int>) | std::views::drop_while(dw_pred). This creates a view of all prime numbers less than or equal to 25.

Example function Ch14_04_ex2(), shown in Listing 14-4-2, also generates a similar view of prime numbers but uses range factory std::views::iota() to generate the initial values.

Listing 14-4-2. Example Ch14_04 – Ch14_04_ex2()

```cpp
void Ch14_04_ex2()
{
    const char* fmt = "{:7d}";
    constexpr size_t epl_max {10};

    // create view of integers [1, 51) (range factory)
    auto view0 = std::views::iota(1, 51);
    MT::print_ctr("\nview0 (result of std::views::iota):\n", view0, fmt,
    epl_max);

    // drop_while predicate
    auto dw_pred = [](int x) { return x <= 25; };

    // using std::views::filter and std::drop_while
    auto view1 = view0
```

```
                | std::views::filter(MTH::is_prime<int>)
                | std::views::drop_while(dw_pred);

    MT::print_ctr("\nview1 (after filter and drop_while):\n", view1, fmt,
    epl_max);
}
```

In Listing 14-4-2, execution of `auto view0 = std::views::iota(1, 51)` generates a view that contains values [1, 51). It is important to recognize that the view generated by range factory `std::view::iota()` *doesn't* require an underlying container. Chapter 16 discusses range factories in greater detail. Like the previous example, `Ch14_04_ex2()` utilizes `std::views::filter(MTH::is_prime<int>)` and `std::views::drop_while(dw_pred)` to generate a view of all prime numbers less than or equal to 25.

The next example in Listing 14-4-3 opens with the definition of a template function named `print_colors()`, which prints the elements of `colors`. The opening statement of the first code block in `Ch14_04_ex3()`, `std::vector<HtmlColor> colors = HtmlColor::get_vector()`, creates a test vector of `HtmlColor` objects (see Listing 8-1-4-1 for class `HtmlColor`). In the ensuing code block, execution of `std::ranges::sort(colors, std::ranges::less(), &HtmlColor::H)` sorts the elements of `colors` using accessor function `HtmlColor::H()`, which calculates hue. If you're interested in learning more about RGB to HSI color space conversion algorithms, Appendix B lists a reference that you can consult.

Listing 14-4-3. Example Ch14_04 – Ch14_04_ex3()

```
template <typename T>
void print_colors(const char* msg, T& colors)
{
    std::print("{:s}", msg);

    for (const HtmlColor& color : colors)
    {
        std::print("[{:4d} {:4d} {:4d}] ", color.R(), color.G(), color.B());
        std::println("[{:9.4f} {:9.4f} {:9.4f}] {:s}", color.H(), color.S(),
            color.I(), color.Name());
    }
}
```

```cpp
// #define PRINT_ALL

void Ch14_04_ex3()
{
    // create test vector of HtmlColors
    std::vector<HtmlColor> colors = HtmlColor::get_vector();
#ifdef PRINT_ALL
    print_colors("\ncolors (initial values):\n", colors);
#endif

    // sort colors using hue
    std::ranges::sort(colors, std::ranges::less(), &HtmlColor::H);
#ifdef PRINT_ALL
    print_colors("\ncolors (after sort by hue):\n", colors);
#endif

    // using std::views::filter to select green colors
    auto is_green = [](const HtmlColor& c)
        { return 110.0 <= c.H() && c.H() <= 160.0; };

    auto colors_g1 = colors | std::views::filter(is_green);
    print_colors("\ncolors_g1:\n", colors_g1);

    // using std::views::reverse and std::views::take (largest green hues)
    auto colors_g2 = colors_g1 | std::views::reverse | std::views::take(4);
    print_colors("\ncolors_g2 (largest green hues):\n", colors_g2);

    // using std::views::take_while
    constexpr float hue_thresh {140.0};
    auto tw_pred = [](const HtmlColor& c) { return c.H() <= hue_thresh; };
    auto colors_g3 = colors_g1 | std::views::take_while(tw_pred);

    std::string msg {};
    std::format_to(std::back_inserter(msg), "\ncolors_g3 (hue < {:.2f}):\n",
        hue_thresh);
    print_colors(msg.c_str(), colors_g3);
}
```

CHAPTER 14   RANGES – PART 1

Following the sort of vector colors, Ch14_04_ex3() uses colors_g1 = colors | std::views::filter(is_green) to create a view of "green" colors. In the ensuing code block, execution of colors_g2 = colors_g1 | std::views::reverse | std::views::take(4) yields a view that contains the four largest green colors of colors_g1. Range adaptor std::views::take() produces a view of the underlying range's first N elements. In other words, it's the opposite std::views::drop().

The final code block of Ch14_04_ex3() demonstrates the use of std::views::take_while(). The execution of colors_g3 = colors_g1 | std::views::take_while(tw_pred) creates a view of the first N elements of colors_g1 for which tw_pred is true. Note that following execution of std::views::take_while(), the resultant view might be empty; it also could contain all of the underlying range's elements. Range adaptor std::views::take_while() is the opposite of std::views::drop_while(). Here are the results for example Ch14_04:

```
----- Results for example Ch14_04 -----

----- Ch14_04_ex1() -----

vec1 (initial values):
    1    2    3    4    5    6    7    8    9   10
   11   12   13   14   15   16   17   18   19   20
   21   22   23   24   25   26   27   28   29   30
   31   32   33   34   35   36   37   38   39   40
   41   42   43   44   45   46   47   48   49   50

view1 (after filter and drop_while):
   29   31   37   41   43   47

----- Ch14_04_ex2() -----

view0 (result of std::views::iota):
    1    2    3    4    5    6    7    8    9   10
   11   12   13   14   15   16   17   18   19   20
   21   22   23   24   25   26   27   28   29   30
   31   32   33   34   35   36   37   38   39   40
   41   42   43   44   45   46   47   48   49   50

view1 (after filter and drop_while):
   29   31   37   41   43   47
```

```
----- Ch14_04_ex3() -----

colors_g1:
[ 240   255   240] [ 119.9944    0.0204    0.9608] Honeydew
[ 143   188   143] [ 119.9981    0.0949    0.6196] DarkSeaGreen
[ 144   238   144] [ 119.9991    0.1787    0.6876] LightGreen
[ 152   251   152] [ 119.9991    0.1784    0.7255] PaleGreen
[   0   100     0] [ 119.9992    1.0000    0.1307] DarkGreen
[  34   139    34] [ 119.9992    0.5073    0.2706] ForestGreen
[   0   128     0] [ 119.9993    1.0000    0.1673] Green
[  50   205    50] [ 119.9995    0.5082    0.3987] LimeGreen
[   0   255     0] [ 119.9997    1.0000    0.3333] Lime
[  46   139    87] [ 146.0907    0.4927    0.3556] SeaGreen
[  60   179   113] [ 146.3889    0.4886    0.4601] MediumSeaGreen
[   0   255   127] [ 149.8691    1.0000    0.4993] SpringGreen
[ 245   255   250] [ 149.9708    0.0200    0.9804] MintCream
[   0   250   154] [ 157.6275    1.0000    0.5281] MediumSpringGreen

colors_g2 (largest green hues):
[   0   250   154] [ 157.6275    1.0000    0.5281] MediumSpringGreen
[ 245   255   250] [ 149.9708    0.0200    0.9804] MintCream
[   0   255   127] [ 149.8691    1.0000    0.4993] SpringGreen
[  60   179   113] [ 146.3889    0.4886    0.4601] MediumSeaGreen

colors_g3 (hue < 140.00):
[ 240   255   240] [ 119.9944    0.0204    0.9608] Honeydew
[ 143   188   143] [ 119.9981    0.0949    0.6196] DarkSeaGreen
[ 144   238   144] [ 119.9991    0.1787    0.6876] LightGreen
[ 152   251   152] [ 119.9991    0.1784    0.7255] PaleGreen
[   0   100     0] [ 119.9992    1.0000    0.1307] DarkGreen
[  34   139    34] [ 119.9992    0.5073    0.2706] ForestGreen
[   0   128     0] [ 119.9993    1.0000    0.1673] Green
[  50   205    50] [ 119.9995    0.5082    0.3987] LimeGreen
[   0   255     0] [ 119.9997    1.0000    0.3333] Lime
```

CHAPTER 14   RANGES – PART 1

Range Views and Adaptors Minutiae

The final source code example of this chapter covers some of the minutiae that you need to be aware of when working with views and range adaptors. Listing 14-5-1 shows the source code for example Ch14_05_ex1(). This example spotlights a few syntactical alternatives for views.

Listing 14-5-1. Example Ch14_05 – Ch14_05_ex1()

```cpp
//-----------------------------------------------------------------
// Ch14_05_ex.cpp
//-----------------------------------------------------------------

#include <ranges>
#include <vector>
#include "Ch14_05.h"
#include "MT.h"
#include "RN.h"

auto get_test_vector(unsigned int seed)
{
    return RN::get_vector<int>(30, -200, 200, seed);
}

void Ch14_05_ex1()
{
    const char* fmt = "{:8d}";
    constexpr size_t epl_max {10};

    // create view that squares positive numbers
    auto view_ft = std::views::filter([](int x) { return x >= 0; })
                 | std::views::transform([](int x) { return x * x; });

    // create test vectors of random numbers
    std::vector<int> vec1 = get_test_vector(71);
    MT::print_ctr("\nvec1:\n", vec1, fmt, epl_max);
```

```
    std::vector<int> vec2 = get_test_vector(73);
    MT::print_ctr("\nvec2:\n", vec2, fmt, epl_max);

    // using view_ft - operator |
    auto view1a = vec1 | view_ft;
    MT::print_ctr("\nview1a:\n", view1a, fmt, epl_max);

    // using view_ft - function call syntax
    auto view2a = view_ft(vec2);
    MT::print_ctr("\nview2a:\n", view2a, fmt, epl_max);
}
```

Listing 14-5-1 begins with the definition of function get_test_vector(), which returns a std::vector<int> of random ints. Also shown in Listing 14-5-1 is example function Ch14_05_ex1(). The opening code block of this function creates a view named view_ft that exploits std::views::filter() and std::views::transform() to create a view that squares positive integers. Note that the definition of view_ft includes only range adaptors. This facilitates the use of view_ft with multiple underlying ranges. The next code block utilizes the previously defined get_test_vector() to initialize vec1 and vec2.

The final two code blocks demonstrate distinct syntaxes that you can use to apply view_ft. The first syntactical example uses view1a = vec1 | view_ft to create a view of positive integer squares. The second example employs the traditional function call syntax view2a = view_ft(vec2). Either form works, but the operator| form is usually easier to read, especially when multiple views are applied.

In Listing 14-5-2, example function Ch14_05_ex2() spotlights the use of a view that modifies elements of its underlying container. In this listing, note that the range for loop utilizes references to access each element of view1. These references ultimately correspond to elements in vec1 that were filtered by view1. Note in the results section that the positive integer elements of vec1 are squared following execution of the range for loop.

Listing 14-5-2. Example Ch14_05 – Ch14_05_ex2()

```
void Ch14_05_ex2()
{
    const char* fmt = "{:8d}";
    constexpr size_t epl_max {10};
```

CHAPTER 14   RANGES – PART 1

```
    // create test vectors of random numbers
    std::vector<int> vec1 = get_test_vector(71);
    MT::print_ctr("\nvec1 (before calculation of squares):\n", vec1, fmt,
    epl_max);

    // create view of positive numbers
    auto view1 = vec1 | std::views::filter([](int x) { return x >= 0; });

    // square positive numbers
    for (auto& val : view1)
        val *= val;

    MT::print_ctr("\nvec1 (after calculation of squares):\n", vec1, fmt,
    epl_max);
}
```

The final example of Ch14_05, shown in Listing 14-5-3, opens with the definition of function get_test_view(). Note that this function returns a view to its caller. When returning a view object, you need to ensure that any underlying containers aren't inadvertently destroyed. Note the use of preprocessor symbol STATIC_VECTOR in function get_test_view(). If this symbol is defined, vec1 is declared as static; otherwise, it's a local variable. Returning a view whose underlying container is a local variable will cause problems if the returned view object is referenced.

Listing 14-5-3. Example Ch14_05 - Ch14_05_ex3()

```
#define STATIC_VECTOR

auto get_test_view(unsigned int seed, const char* fmt, size_t epl_max)
{
    // create test vector
#ifdef STATIC_VECTOR
    static std::vector<int> vec1 {};        // ok
#else
    std::vector<int> vec1 {};               // trouble
#endif

    // create view of positive numbers
    vec1 = RN::get_vector<int>(30, -200, 200, seed);
```

```
    auto view1 = vec1 | std::views::filter([](int x) { return x >= 0; });
    MT::print_ctr("view1:\n", view1, fmt, epl_max);

    // return view to caller (trouble if vec1 not static)
    return view1;
}
void Ch14_05_ex3()
{
    const char* fmt = "{:8d}";
    constexpr size_t epl_max {10};

    auto test_view = get_test_view(77, fmt, epl_max);

    std::print("\ntest_view: ");

#ifdef STATIC_VECTOR
    MT::print_ctr("\n", test_view, fmt, epl_max);
#else
    std::println("invalid view - preprocessor symbol STATIC_VECTOR not defined");
#endif
}
```

The purpose of the example code in get_test_view() and Ch14_05_ex3() is to make sure you're aware of potential complications that can occur when passing view objects across function boundaries. Always verify that a view object doesn't reference an underlying container that might get destroyed prematurely or unexpectedly. Here are the results for example Ch14_05:

```
----- Results for example Ch14_05 -----

----- Ch14_05_ex1() -----

vec1:
    -126     104     -45    -160     133      85    -121    -133     167     106
     116    -121      89     -83     199     -51     138     -83    -107     166
     -71       6      87    -180    -159    -145      40     176    -146     116
```

CHAPTER 14   RANGES – PART 1

vec2:
```
      57     -78      15      43       5    -131      44       7      -3     -76
    -115    -166    -103     147      29      -9     109     133     -76     183
     -38      36      39      -3    -104     149     163     -71    -137     107
```

view1a:
```
   10816   17689    7225   27889   11236   13456    7921   39601   19044   27556
      36    7569    1600   30976   13456
```

view2a:
```
    3249     225    1849      25    1936      49   21609     841   11881   17689
   33489    1296    1521   22201   26569   11449
```

----- Ch14_05_ex2() -----

vec1 (before calculation of squares):
```
    -126     104     -45    -160     133      85    -121    -133     167     106
     116    -121      89     -83     199     -51     138     -83    -107     166
     -71       6      87    -180    -159    -145      40     176    -146     116
```

vec1 (after calculation of squares):
```
    -126   10816     -45    -160   17689    7225    -121    -133   27889   11236
   13456    -121    7921     -83   39601     -51   19044     -83    -107   27556
     -71      36    7569    -180    -159    -145    1600   30976    -146   13456
```

----- Ch14_05_ex3() -----
view1:
```
     168      57     102     124     115     156     102      16      77      18
     148      86     135     102      35     170      89
```

test_view:
```
     168      57     102     124     115     156     102      16      77      18
     148      86     135     102      35     170      89
```

608

Summary

Here are the key learning points for this chapter:

- A view is a window into a range of elements. The view's elements are generally owned by an underlying container. The elements of a view can be accessed using iterators.

- All views are lazily evaluated. They are also composable using `operator|`.

- A range adaptor is typically used to create a view object. View object instantiation is completed in constant time independent of the underlying range's size.

- You can use range adaptors `std::views::filter()` or `std::views::transform()` to create views that carry out filter or transformation actions.

- Range adaptors `std::views::drop()` and `std::view::drop_while()` drop elements from a view starting at the front end. The opposite range adaptors, `std::views::take()` and `std::views::take_while()`, retain elements starting from the front end.

- Range factory `std::views::iota()` is often used to create a sequence of consecutive values sans an underlying container.

- A projection is a transformation function that gets applied prior to consuming an element's value. Most algorithms in namespace `std::ranges` support projections.

CHAPTER 15

Ranges – Part 2

This chapter surveys additional range adaptors provided by C++20/23. As you saw in the previous chapter, range adaptors extend the functional capabilities of ranges far beyond the predefined algorithms of namespace `std::ranges`. Topics examined in this chapter include

- Tuple views
- Join, split, and Cartesian product views
- Slide, stride, and chunk views
- Range factories

Tuple Views

STL namespace `std::ranges` defines multiple range adaptors that build tuple-like views. This namespace also includes range adaptors that create views of elements held in multiple `std::tuples` (see Chapter 5 for a description of this class).

Source code example Ch15_01 details how to use range adaptors `std::views::keys()`, `std::views::values()`, and `std::views::elements()`. All three of these range adaptors create views of tuple elements encompassed within a container or range.

Listing 15-1-1 shows the source code for example function `Ch15_01_ex1()`. This example demonstrates the use of `std::views::keys()`. The opening code block of this function utilizes `AminoAcid::get_vector_tuple()` to initialize `std::vector<AaTuple>` aa_vec. Type `AaTuple` is an alias for `std::tuple<std::string, std::string, char, double>`, which holds the following AminoAcid attributes: Code3, Name, Code1, and MolMass (see Listings 10-1-3-1 and 10-1-3-2 for class AminoAcid).

CHAPTER 15 RANGES – PART 2

Listing 15-1-1. *Example Ch15_01 - Ch15_01_ex1()*

```cpp
//--------------------------------------------------------------------------
// Ch15_01_ex.cpp
//--------------------------------------------------------------------------

#include <algorithm>
#include <format>
#include <ranges>
#include <vector>
#include "Ch15_01.h"
#include "AminoAcid.h"

void Ch15_01_ex1()
{
    size_t add_nl {};
    constexpr size_t add_nl_max {5};

    // create vector of AminoAcid tuples
    // AaTuple = using std::tuple<std::string, std::string, char, double>;
    //                              Code3,       Name       Code1 MolMass
    std::vector<AaTuple> aa_vec = AminoAcid::get_vector_tuple();

    // using std::views::keys (first tuple element)
    auto view_keys = std::views::keys(aa_vec);

    for (const std::string& aa_code3 : view_keys)
    {
        char c = (++add_nl % add_nl_max == 0) ? '\n' : ' ';
        std::print("{:3s}{:c}", aa_code3, c);
    }
    std::println("");

    // using std::views::values (second tuple element)
    add_nl = 0;
    auto view_values = std::views::values(aa_vec);

    for (const std::string& aa_name : view_values)
    {
```

```
        char c = (++add_nl % add_nl_max == 0) ? '\n' : ' ';
        std::print("{:15s}{:c}", aa_name, c);
    }
    std::println("");
}
```

The first statement following the initialization of aa_vec, view_keys = std::views::keys(aa_vec), creates a "keys" view using the elements of aa_vec. More specifically, execution of range adaptor std::views::keys() builds a view that contains the first element (Code3) of each AaTuple in aa_vec. The range for loop in the subsequent code blocks prints the Code3 elements of view_keys. You can also use range adaptor std::views::keys() to create a view of all keys in a std::map or std::multimap.

In Ch15_01_ex1()'s next code block, execution of view_values = std::views::values(aa_vec) builds a view that contains the second element (Name) of each AaTuple in aa_vec. The ensuing range for loop prints the amino acid names specified by view_values. Range adaptor std::views::values() is also commonly employed to create a view of all values in a std::map or std::multimap.

Listing 15-1-2 shows the source code for example Ch15_01_ex2(). This example spotlights the use of std::views::elements().

Listing 15-1-2. Example Ch15_01 - Ch15_01_ex2()

```
template <typename T, size_t I>
void print_elements(const char* msg, std::vector<AaTuple>& aa_vec, const char* fmt)
{
    size_t add_nl {};
    constexpr size_t add_nl_max {5};

    std::println("{:s}", msg);

    for (const T& elem : std::views::elements<I>(aa_vec))
    {
        // format tuple element I of elem
        std::string s {};
        std::vformat_to(std::back_inserter(s), fmt, std::make_format_args(elem));
```

```cpp
        // add nl if needed, then print
        char c = (++add_nl % add_nl_max == 0) ? '\n' : ' ';
        s.push_back(c);
        std::print("{}", s);
    }
    std::println("");
}

void Ch15_01_ex2()
{
    // create vector of AminoAcid tuples
    std::vector<AaTuple> aa_vec = AminoAcid::get_vector_tuple();

    // print tuple elements in aa_vec
    print_elements<std::string, 0>("element 0 (amino acid code3)", aa_vec,
    "{:3s}");

    print_elements<std::string, 1>("element 1 (amino acid name)", aa_vec,
    "{:15s}");

    print_elements<char, 2>("element 2 (amino acid code1)", aa_vec,
    "{:3c}");

    print_elements<double, 3>("element 3 (amino acid mol mass)", aa_vec,
    "{:8.3f}");
}
```

Listing 15-1-2 commences with the definition of print_elements(). Note that this template function specifies two template parameters. Parameter T is the data type, while parameter I is the tuple element index. Recall from the discussions in Chapter 5 that the elements of a std::tuple must be accessed using compile-time constant indices.

The range for loop in print_elements() exploits range adaptor std::views::elements<I>(aa_vec) to create a view that contains the i-th element of each AaTuple in aa_vec. The remaining code inside the for loop formats the extracted element using std::vformat_to(). More specifically, function std::vformat_to() is used here instead of std::format_to() since fmt, which is passed as an argument to print_elements(), is not a compile-time constant. Execution of std::make_format_args(elem) returns an object that holds the arguments (i.e., elem) that std::vformat_to() formats. The call to std::back_inserter(s) saves the formatted result in std::string s.

Like the previous example function, Ch15_01_ex2() utilizes std::vector<AaTuple> aa_vec = AminoAcid::get_vector_tuple() to initialize a vector of AaTuples. Next is a series of calls to print_elements(). Note that each call explicitly specifies an AaTuple data type and index. Here are the results for example Ch15_01:

```
----- Results for example Ch15_01 -----

----- Ch15_01_ex1() -----
Ala Arg Asn Asp Cys
Gln Glu Gly His Ile
Leu Lys Met Phe Pro
Ser Thr Trp Tyr Val

Alanine         Arginine        Asparagine      AsparticAcid    Cysteine
Glutamine       GlutamicAcid    Glycine         Histidine       IsoLeucine
Leucine         Lysine          Methionine      Phenylalanine   Proline
Serine          Threonine       Tryptophan      Tyrosine        Valine

----- Ch15_01_ex2() -----
element 0 (amino acid code3)
Ala Arg Asn Asp Cys
Gln Glu Gly His Ile
Leu Lys Met Phe Pro
Ser Thr Trp Tyr Val

element 1 (amino acid name)
Alanine         Arginine        Asparagine      AsparticAcid    Cysteine
Glutamine       GlutamicAcid    Glycine         Histidine       IsoLeucine
Leucine         Lysine          Methionine      Phenylalanine   Proline
Serine          Threonine       Tryptophan      Tyrosine        Valine

element 2 (amino acid code1)
A   R   N   D   C
Q   E   G   H   I
L   K   M   F   P
S   T   W   Y   V
```

element 3 (amino acid mol mass)
```
  89.094   174.203   132.119   133.104   121.154
 146.146   147.131    75.067   155.156   131.175
 131.175   146.189   149.208   165.192   115.132
 105.093   119.119   204.228   181.191   117.148
```

More Tuple Views

The next source example covers additional range adaptors that create or manipulate tuple-like views. Most of these adaptors are new to C++23. Listing 15-2-1 shows the source code for example Ch15_02_ex1(). This example details how to use range adaptor std::views::enumerate().

Listing 15-2-1. Example Ch15_02 – Ch15_02_ex1()

```cpp
//------------------------------------------------------------
// Ch15_02_ex.cpp
//------------------------------------------------------------

#include <format>
#include <map>
#include <numbers>
#include <ranges>
#include <vector>
#include "Ch15_02.h"
#include "AminoAcid.h"
#include "MT.h"
#include "MF.h"
#include "RN.h"

void Ch15_02_ex1()
{
#if defined(__cpp_lib_ranges_enumerate) && defined(__cpp_lib_ranges_to_container)
    const char* fmt = "{}";
    constexpr size_t epl_max {2};
```

```cpp
    // initialize vector of amino acids
    std::vector<AminoAcid> aa_vec = AminoAcid::get_vector_all();
    MT::print_ctr("\naa_vec:\n", aa_vec, fmt, epl_max);

    // using std::views::enumerate
    auto aa_enum = aa_vec | std::views::enumerate;
    std::println("\naa_enum (size = {:d}):", aa_enum.size());

    if (!aa_enum.empty())
    {
        for (const auto& [key, value] : aa_enum)
            std::println("key: {:2d}: value: {}", key, value);
    }

    // using std::ranges::to<std::map>
    auto aa_map = aa_enum | std::ranges::to<std::map>();
    std::println("\naa_map (size = {:d}):", aa_map.size());

    if (!aa_map.empty())
    {
        for (const auto& [key, value] : aa_map)
            std::println("key: {:2d}: value: {}", key, value);
    }
#else
    std::println("Ch15_02_ex1() requires C++23");
#endif
}
```

The C++ code in example function Ch15_02_ex1() begins with the initialization of std::vector<AminoAcid> aa_vec = AminoAcid::get_vector_all(). In the subsequent code block, execution of aa_enum = aa_vec | std::views::enumerate() creates a map-like view of the elements in aa_vec. The key for each aa_enum element is an integer that corresponds to the element's position in aa_vec, while the value component is a reference to the actual data. For example, the key in view aa_enum for element aa_vec[3] is three, and the value is a reference to aa_vec[3].

In the final code block of Ch15_02_ex1(), execution of aa_map = aa_enum | std::ranges::to<std::map>() converts the view defined by aa_enum to a std::map. Note that both range for loops in Ch15_02_ex1() utilize structured binding to extract the key and value components for use with std::println().

CHAPTER 15 RANGES – PART 2

Example function Ch15_02_ex2(), shown in Listing 15-2-2, highlights the use of std::views::adjacent() and std::views::adjacent_transform(). Both of these range adaptors create views of adjacent elements in an underlying range; the latter also applies a transformation function.

Listing 15-2-2. Example Ch15_02 – Ch15_02_ex2()

```
void Ch15_02_ex2()
{
#ifdef __cpp_lib_ranges_zip
    const char* fmt = "{:3s} ";
    constexpr size_t epl_max {10};

    // initialize vector of amino acids
    std::vector<std::string> aa_vec = AminoAcid::get_vector_all_code3();
    MT::print_ctr("\naa_vec:\n", aa_vec, fmt, epl_max);

    // using std::views::adjacent
    auto adj_view1 = aa_vec | std::views::adjacent<3>;
    std::println("\nadj_view1 (size = {:d}):", adj_view1.size());

    if (adj_view1)
    {
        for (const auto [aa0, aa1, aa2] : adj_view1)
            std::println("[{:3s} {:3s} {:3s}]", aa0, aa1, aa2);
    }

    // using std::views::adjacent_transform
    auto adj_xform = [](const std::string& s1, const std::string& s2,
                        const std::string& s3, const std::string& s4)
        { return s1 + "|" + s2 + "|" + s3 + "|" + s4; };

    auto adj_view2 = aa_vec | std::views::adjacent_transform<4>(adj_xform);
    std::println("\nadj_view2 (size = {:d}):", adj_view2.size());

    if (adj_view2)
    {
        for (auto a : adj_view2)
            std::println("[{:s}]", a);
    }
```

```
#else
    std::println("Ch15_02_ex2() - std::views::adjacent_transform() requires
    C++23");
#endif
}
```

Following instantiation of aa_vec, Ch15_02_ex2() employs adj_view1 = aa_vec | std::views::adjacent<3>. The execution of this statement creates a view named aa_vec, and each element of this view incorporates three adjacent elements from aa_vec. If you scan ahead to the results section, note that the first element of adj_view1 references aa_vec[0], aa_vec[1], and aa_vec[2]; the second element of adj_view1 references aa_vec[1], aa_vec[2], and aa_vec[3]; and so on.

The ensuing code block in Ch15_02_ex2() commences with the definition of lambda expression adj_xform(), which concatenates its four std::string arguments into a single std::string. Execution of adj_view2 = aa_vec | std::views::adjacent_transform<4>(adj_xform) creates a view that applies adj_xform() to a group of four adjacent elements from aa_vec.

Listing 15-2-3 shows the source code for example function Ch15_02_ex3(). This function demonstrates the use of range adaptor std::views::zip(), which builds tuple-like views of elements using multiple ranges. Execution of Ch15_02_ex3() begins with the initialization of three vectors: std::vector<char> aa_vec_code1, std::vector<std::string> aa_vec_code3, and std::vector<double> aa_vec_mm. These vectors contain the one-letter, three-letter, and molecular mass attributes for each standard amino acid.

Listing 15-2-3. Example Ch15_02 – Ch15_02_ex3()

```
void Ch15_02_ex3()
{
#ifdef __cpp_lib_ranges_zip
    const char* fmt_code1 = "{:5c}";
    const char* fmt_code3 = "{:5s}";
    const char* fmt_mm = "{:9.3f}";
    constexpr size_t epl_max {7};

    // create text vectors of amino acid attributes
    std::vector<char> aa_vec_code1 {AminoAcid::get_vector_all_code1()};
    MT::print_ctr("\naa_vec_code1:\n", aa_vec_code1, fmt_code1, epl_max);
```

```cpp
        std::vector<std::string> aa_vec_code3 {AminoAcid::get_vector_all_
        code3()};
        MT::print_ctr("\naa_vec_code3:\n", aa_vec_code3, fmt_code3, epl_max);

        std::vector<double> aa_vec_mm {AminoAcid::get_vector_all_mol_mass()};
        MT::print_ctr("\naa_vec_mm:\n", aa_vec_mm, fmt_mm, epl_max);

        // create zip view of amino acid attributes
        auto aa_zip_view = std::views::zip(aa_vec_code1, aa_vec_code3, aa_
        vec_mm);
        std::println("\naa_zip_view:");

        // print tuples of aa_zip_view
        for (auto aa : aa_zip_view)
        {
            std::string s {};
            static const char* sep = "   ";

            std::vformat_to(std::back_inserter(s), fmt_code1,
                std::make_format_args(std::get<0>(aa)));
            s += sep;

            std::vformat_to(std::back_inserter(s), fmt_code3,
                std::make_format_args(std::get<1>(aa)));
            s += sep;

            std::vformat_to(std::back_inserter(s), fmt_mm,
                std::make_format_args(std::get<2>(aa)));

            std::println("{:s}", s);
        }
#else
        std::println("Ch15_02_ex3() - std::views::zip() requires C++23");
#endif
}
```

Execution of aa_zip_view = std::views::zip(aa_vec_code1, aa_vec_code3, aa_vec_mm) creates a view of three-element tuples. The *i*-th tuple of view aa_zip_view contains references to aa_vec_code1[i], aa_vec_code3[i], and aa_vec_mm[i], respectively. The ensuing range for loop in Ch15_02_ex3() exploits std::vformat_to() to format and print each tuple of view aa_zip_view.

The final example function of Ch15_03 illustrates how to use std::zip_transform(). Execution of this range adaptor creates tuple-like views just like std::views::zip(); it also applies a transformation function.

Listing 15-2-4. Example Ch15_02 – Ch15_02_ex4()

```
void Ch15_02_ex4()
{
#ifdef __cpp_lib_ranges_zip
    const char* fmt = "{:10.2f} ";
    constexpr size_t epl_max {6};

    constexpr size_t n {12};
    constexpr int rng_min {1};
    constexpr int rng_max {20};
    constexpr unsigned int rng_seed {511};

    // create vector of cylinder radii and heights
    std::vector radii = RN::get_vector<double>(n, rng_min, rng_max,
        rng_seed);
    MT::print_ctr("\nradii:\n", radii, fmt, epl_max);

    std::vector heights = RN::get_vector<double>(n, rng_min, rng_max, rng_
        seed / 3);
    MT::print_ctr("\nheights:\n", heights, fmt, epl_max);

    // lambda to calculate cylinder volume
    auto cyl_vol = [](double r, double h) { return std::numbers::pi * r *
        r * h; };

    // calculate volumes - vector sizes equal
    auto volumes1 = std::views::zip_transform(cyl_vol, radii, heights);
    MT::print_ctr("\nvolumes1:\n", volumes1, fmt, epl_max);
```

CHAPTER 15   RANGES – PART 2

```
    // modify test vector heights
    heights.pop_back();
    MT::print_ctr("\nheights (after pop_back):\n", heights, fmt, epl_max);

    // calculate volumes - vector sizes not equal
    auto volumes2 = std::views::zip_transform(cyl_vol, radii, heights);
    MT::print_ctr("\nvolumes2:\n", volumes2, fmt, epl_max);
#else
    std::println("Ch15_02_ex4() - std::views::zip_transform() requires
    C++23");
#endif
}
```

In Listing 15-2-4, execution of Ch15_02_ex4() opens with the instantiation of two std::vectors: radii and heights. Note that both vectors are initialized using RN::get_vector<double>(). Next is the definition of lambda expression cyl_vol, which calculates the volume of a cylinder. In the ensuing code block, execution of volumes1 = std::views::zip_transform(cyl_vol, radii, heights) creates a view of cylinder volumes using corresponding elements from vectors radii and heights.

The underlying ranges supplied to range adaptor std::views::zip_transform() need not be the same size. To demonstrate this, the next code block in Ch15_02_ex4() utilizes heights.pop_back() to modify the number of elements in heights. Execution of volumes2 = std::views::zip_transform(cyl_vol, radii, heights) creates a view that contains std::min(radii.size(), heights.size()) tuples. The results for example Ch15_02 follow this paragraph. This output has been edited to reduce its length.

```
----- Results for example Ch15_02 -----

----- Ch15_02_ex1() -----

aa_vec:
[Alanine          A|Ala|  89.094|NP][Arginine          R|Arg|174.203|B  ]
[Asparagine       N|Asn|132.119|UP][AsparticAcid      D|Asp|133.104|A  ]
[Cysteine         C|Cys|121.154|NP][Glutamine         Q|Gln|146.146|UP]
[GlutamicAcid     E|Glu|147.131|A ][Glycine           G|Gly| 75.067|NP]
[Histidine        H|His|155.156|B ][IsoLeucine        I|Ile|131.175|NP]
[Leucine          L|Leu|131.175|NP][Lysine            K|Lys|146.189|B  ]
```

```
[Methionine       M|Met|149.208|NP][Phenylalanine  F|Phe|165.192|NP]
[Proline          P|Pro|115.132|NP][Serine         S|Ser|105.093|UP]
[Threonine        T|Thr|119.119|UP][Tryptophan     W|Trp|204.228|NP]
[Tyrosine         Y|Tyr|181.191|UP][Valine         V|Val|117.148|NP]

aa_enum (size = 20):
key:  0: value: [Alanine        A|Ala| 89.094|NP]
key:  1: value: [Arginine       R|Arg|174.203|B ]
key:  2: value: [Asparagine     N|Asn|132.119|UP]
...
key: 17: value: [Tryptophan     W|Trp|204.228|NP]
key: 18: value: [Tyrosine       Y|Tyr|181.191|UP]
key: 19: value: [Valine         V|Val|117.148|NP]

aa_map (size = 20):
key:  0: value: [Alanine        A|Ala| 89.094|NP]
key:  1: value: [Arginine       R|Arg|174.203|B ]
key:  2: value: [Asparagine     N|Asn|132.119|UP]
...
key: 17: value: [Tryptophan     W|Trp|204.228|NP]
key: 18: value: [Tyrosine       Y|Tyr|181.191|UP]
key: 19: value: [Valine         V|Val|117.148|NP]

----- Ch15_02_ex2() -----

aa_vec:
Ala Arg Asn Asp Cys Gln Glu Gly His Ile
Leu Lys Met Phe Pro Ser Thr Trp Tyr Val

adj_view1 (size = 18):
[Ala Arg Asn]
[Arg Asn Asp]
[Asn Asp Cys]
[Asp Cys Gln]
[Cys Gln Glu]
[Gln Glu Gly]
[Glu Gly His]
[Gly His Ile]
```

CHAPTER 15   RANGES – PART 2

```
[His Ile Leu]
[Ile Leu Lys]
[Leu Lys Met]
[Lys Met Phe]
[Met Phe Pro]
[Phe Pro Ser]
[Pro Ser Thr]
[Ser Thr Trp]
[Thr Trp Tyr]
[Trp Tyr Val]

adj_view2 (size = 17):
[Ala|Arg|Asn|Asp]
[Arg|Asn|Asp|Cys]
[Asn|Asp|Cys|Gln]
[Asp|Cys|Gln|Glu]
[Cys|Gln|Glu|Gly]
[Gln|Glu|Gly|His]
[Glu|Gly|His|Ile]
[Gly|His|Ile|Leu]
[His|Ile|Leu|Lys]
[Ile|Leu|Lys|Met]
[Leu|Lys|Met|Phe]
[Lys|Met|Phe|Pro]
[Met|Phe|Pro|Ser]
[Phe|Pro|Ser|Thr]
[Pro|Ser|Thr|Trp]
[Ser|Thr|Trp|Tyr]
[Thr|Trp|Tyr|Val]

----- Ch15_02_ex3() -----

aa_vec_code1:
A    R    N    D    C    Q    E
G    H    I    L    K    M    F
P    S    T    W    Y    V
```

aa_vec_code3:
Ala Arg Asn Asp Cys Gln Glu
Gly His Ile Leu Lys Met Phe
Pro Ser Thr Trp Tyr Val

aa_vec_mm:
   89.094   174.203   132.119   133.104   121.154   146.146   147.131
   75.067   155.156   131.175   131.175   146.189   149.208   165.192
  115.132   105.093   119.119   204.228   181.191   117.148

aa_zip_view:
A   Ala   89.094
R   Arg   174.203
N   Asn   132.119
D   Asp   133.104
C   Cys   121.154
Q   Gln   146.146
E   Glu   147.131
G   Gly   75.067
H   His   155.156
I   Ile   131.175
L   Leu   131.175
K   Lys   146.189
M   Met   149.208
F   Phe   165.192
P   Pro   115.132
S   Ser   105.093
T   Thr   119.119
W   Trp   204.228
Y   Tyr   181.191
V   Val   117.148

----- Ch15_02_ex4() -----

radii:
        6.00   12.00   17.00   19.00   5.00   16.00
       14.00   3.00   12.00   4.00   15.00   2.00

heights:

2.00	7.00	5.00	1.00	6.00	17.00
11.00	5.00	12.00	1.00	11.00	4.00

volumes1:

226.19	3166.73	4539.60	1134.11	471.24	13672.21
6773.27	141.37	5428.67	50.27	7775.44	50.27

heights (after pop_back):

2.00	7.00	5.00	1.00	6.00	17.00
11.00	5.00	12.00	1.00	11.00	

volumes2:

226.19	3166.73	4539.60	1134.11	471.24	13672.21
6773.27	141.37	5428.67	50.27	7775.44	

Join, Split, and Cartesian Product Views

The source code example of this section expounds range adaptors that build views using std::views::join(), std::views:join_with(), std::views::split(), and std::cartesian_product().

Listing 15-3-1 contains the source code for example Ch15_03_ex1(). The execution of this example function begins with the creation of three std::vector<int> containers named vec1, vec2, and vec3. Note that RN::get_vector() is used to initialize these vectors with random values.

Listing 15-3-1. Example Ch15_03 – Ch15_03_ex1()

```
//-------------------------------------------------------------------------
// Ch15_03_ex.cpp
//-------------------------------------------------------------------------

#include <format>
#include <iterator>
#include <ranges>
#include <string>
#include <string_view>
#include <vector>
```

CHAPTER 15 RANGES – PART 2

```cpp
#include "Ch15_03.h"
#include "AminoAcid.h"
#include "MT.h"
#include "RN.h"

void Ch15_03_ex1()
{
    const char* fmt = "{:4d} ";
    constexpr size_t epl_max {15};

    constexpr size_t n {12};
    constexpr int rng_min {1};
    constexpr int rng_max {1000};
    constexpr unsigned int rng_seed {732};

    // create test vectors
    std::vector vec1 = RN::get_vector<int>(n, rng_min, rng_max, rng_seed);
    MT::print_ctr("\nvec1:\n", vec1, fmt, epl_max);

    std::vector vec2 = RN::get_vector<int>(n + 2, rng_min, rng_max, rng_seed / 3);
    MT::print_ctr("\nvec2:\n", vec2, fmt, epl_max);

    std::vector vec3 = RN::get_vector<int>(n - 1, rng_min, rng_max, rng_seed / 4);
    MT::print_ctr("\nvec3:\n", vec3, fmt, epl_max);

    std::vector<std::vector<int>> vec_of_vecs {vec1, vec2, vec3};

    // create flatten view using std::views::join
    auto view_join = vec_of_vecs | std::views::join;
    MT::print_ctr("\nview_join:\n", view_join, fmt, epl_max);
}
```

The next statement in Ch15_03_ex1(), std::vector<std::vector<int>> vec_of_vecs {vec1, vec2, vec3}, instantiates a std::vector of three std::vector<int> containers. The subsequent code block utilizes view_join = vec_of_vecs | std::views::join() to create a view that flattens vec_of_vecs. More specifically, std::views::join() makes it appear that vec1, vec2, and vec3 belong to the same range.

CHAPTER 15   RANGES – PART 2

In Listing 15-3-2, example function Ch15_03_ex2() opens with the creation of aa_vec1<std::string> using AminoAcid::get_vector_random_code3(). Execution of aa_vec1_jw = aa_vec1 | std::views::join_with("|"s) creates a view that flattens the std::string elements of aa_vec1. The "|"s argument supplied to range adaptor std::views::join_with() is a delimiter that separates the elements in aa_vec_jw. The view produced by std::views::join_width() is a flattened view of chars. This is why the std::print() statement in the subsequent range for loop utilizes a "{:c}" format specifier. You can also use the iterators of view aa_vec1_jw to construct a std::string as demonstrated in Ch15_03_ex2()'s final code block.

Listing 15-3-2. Example Ch15_03 – Ch15_03_ex2()

```
void Ch15_03_ex2()
{
#ifdef __cpp_lib_ranges_join_with
    using namespace std::string_literals;

    const char* fmt = "{:3s} ";
    constexpr size_t epl_max {20};

    // create test vector of amino acid code3 strings
    std::vector aa_vec1 = AminoAcid::get_vector_random_code3(15, 732);
    MT::print_ctr("\naa_vec1:\n", aa_vec1, fmt, epl_max);

    // using std::views::join_with
    auto aa_vec1_jw = aa_vec1 | std::views::join_with("|"s);

    // print chars using aa_vec1_jw
    std::print("\nresult #1: ");
    for (auto c : aa_vec1_jw)
        std::print("{:c}", c);
    std::println("");

    // create string using aa_vec1_jw
    std::string s(aa_vec1_jw.begin(), aa_vec1_jw.end());
    std::print("result #2: {:s}", s);
```

```
#else
    std::println("Ch15_03_ex2() std::views::join_with requires C++23");
#endif
}
```

A common string processing task of many programs is to split a string into smaller substrings based on a delimiter. Example function Ch15_03_ex3(), shown in Listing 15-3-3, demonstrates how to carry out this action using std::views::split().

Listing 15-3-3. Example Ch15_03 – Ch15_03_ex3()

```
void Ch15_03_ex3()
{
    // create vector of test strings and test delimiter
    std::vector<std::string> vec1
        { "one, two, three, four", "eins, zwei, drei, vier", "",
          "un, deux, trois, quatre" };

    std::string_view delim1 {", "};

    // using std::views::split
    for (const auto& str1 : vec1)
    {
        size_t i {};
        std::println("\ntest string:    \"{:s}\"", str1);

        for (auto sr1 : str1 | std::views::split(delim1))
        {
            // create string using sr1 (std::ranges::subrange)
            std::string s1(sr1.begin(), sr1.end());
            std::println("split string #{:d}: \"{:s}\"", i++, s1);
        }
    }
}
```

The opening code block of Ch15_03_ex3() instantiates std::vector<std::string> vec1 with test strings and std::string_view delim1 as a test delimiter. Note that delim1 contains multiple characters. Execution of for (auto sr1 : str1 | std::views::split(delim1)) splits str1 into a series of subranges at each occurrence of delim1. The ensuing statement std::string s1(sr1.begin(), sr1.end()) constructs a std::string using the iterators of subrange sr1, and this std::string is subsequently printed.

It warrants mentioning here that C++20's original std::views::split() range adaptor performed splits using forward-only ranges, which limited its usefulness for std::strings. The post-C++20 P2210R2 proposal retroactively changed this to make std::views::split() more suitable for its primary use case of splitting std::strings. Range adaptor std::views::lazy_split() now contains the functionality originally provided by std::views::split(). Appendix B contains a reference that you can consult for more information regarding this topic.

Example function Ch15_03_ex4() demonstrates the use of std::views::cartesian_product(). The execution of this range adaptor generates views of *n*-ary Cartesian product tuples (i.e., ordered groups of *n* elements) using elements from the supplied ranges.

Listing 15-3-4. Example Ch15_03 - Ch15_03_ex4()

```
void Ch15_03_ex4()
{
#ifdef __cpp_lib_ranges_cartesian_product
    using pizza_tup = std::tuple<int, const std::string&, const std::string&,
        const std::string&>;

    // create test vectors
    std::vector<int> sizes {9, 12, 15, 18};
    std::vector<std::string> crusts {"Thin", "Thick", "DeepDish"};
    std::vector<std::string> toppings {"GreenPepper", "Mushroom", "Onion",
        "Pepperoni", "Sausage"};
    std::vector<std::string> salads {"Caesar", "Garden", "Spinach"};

    // print lambda expression
    auto print_pizza = [](const pizza_tup& pizza, size_t& nl)
    {
        const auto& [size, crust, topping, salad] = pizza;
        std::print("[{:2d} {:8s} {:11s} {:11s}] ", size, crust, topping,
            salad);
```

```cpp
        if (++nl % 2 == 0)
            std::println("");
    };

    // using std::views::cartesian_product
    auto pizza_cp = std::views::cartesian_product(sizes, crusts, toppings,
    salads);

    size_t nl {0};
    for (const auto& pizza : pizza_cp)
        print_pizza(pizza, nl);
#else
    std::println("Ch15_03_ex4() - std::views::cartesian_product requires
    C++23)");
#endif
}
```

In Listing 15-3-4, execution of Ch15_03_ex4() opens with the creation of four test vectors. Vector sizes is a container of type std::vector<int>, while crusts, toppings, and salads are containers of type std::vector<std::string>. Next is the definition of a lambda expression named print_pizza(), which prints the elements of pizza_tup& pizza. Note that pizza_tup is an alias for std::tuple<int, const std::string&, const std::string&, const std::string&>.

In the subsequent code block, execution of pizza_cp = std::views::cartesian_product(sizes, crusts, toppings, salads) generates views of tuples using the elements from the supplied vectors. The range for loop that follows exploits the previously defined print_pizza() to print each pizza_tup tuple of pizza_cp. The results for example Ch15_03 follow this paragraph. The output for example Ch15_03_ex4() has been truncated to show only a few of the 180 generated pizza tuples.

----- Results for example Ch15_03 -----

----- Ch15_03_ex1() -----

vec1:
 914 606 211 775 557 832 441 634 842 581 848 655

vec2:
 291 645 100 224 250   77 397 971   73 668 218 161 991 744

CHAPTER 15   RANGES – PART 2

vec3:
  824   705   893   267   889   139   459   566   152   574   598

view_join:
  914   606   211   775   557   832   441   634   842   581   848   655   291   645   100
  224   250   77   397   971   73   668   218   161   991   744   824   705   893   267
  889   139   459   566   152   574   598

----- Ch15_03_ex2() -----

aa_vec1:
Tyr Met Cys Ser Lys Thr His Met Thr Lys Thr Phe Asn Leu Lys

result #1: Tyr|Met|Cys|Ser|Lys|Thr|His|Met|Thr|Lys|Thr|Phe|Asn|Leu|Lys
result #2: Tyr|Met|Cys|Ser|Lys|Thr|His|Met|Thr|Lys|Thr|Phe|Asn|Leu|Lys
----- Ch15_03_ex3() -----

test string: "one, two, three, four"
split string #0: "one"
split string #1: "two"
split string #2: "three"
split string #3: "four"

test string: "eins, zwei, drei, vier"
split string #0: "eins"
split string #1: "zwei"
split string #2: "drei"
split string #3: "vier"

test string: ""

test string: "un, deux, trois, quatre"
split string #0: "un"
split string #1: "deux"
split string #2: "trois"
split string #3: "quatre"

```
----- Ch15_03_ex4() -----
[ 9 Thin      GreenPepper Caesar  ] [ 9 Thin      GreenPepper Garden  ]
[ 9 Thin      GreenPepper Spinach ] [ 9 Thin      Mushroom    Caesar  ]
[ 9 Thin      Mushroom    Garden  ] [ 9 Thin      Mushroom    Spinach ]
[ 9 Thin      Onion       Caesar  ] [ 9 Thin      Onion       Garden  ]
...
[18 DeepDish  Onion       Garden  ] [18 DeepDish  Onion       Spinach ]
[18 DeepDish  Pepperoni   Caesar  ] [18 DeepDish  Pepperoni   Garden  ]
[18 DeepDish  Pepperoni   Spinach ] [18 DeepDish  Sausage     Caesar  ]
[18 DeepDish  Sausage     Garden  ] [18 DeepDish  Sausage     Spinach ]
```

Slide, Stride, and Chunk Views

The STL includes several range adaptors that create views of sliding windows, strides, or chunks of elements. In this section, you'll learn how to use std::views::slide(), std::views::stride(), std::views::chunk(), and std::views::chunk_by(). Listing 15-4-1 shows the source code for example Ch15_04_ex1(), which details the use of std::views::slide().

Listing 15-4-1. Example Ch15_04 – Ch15_04_ex1()

```
//-------------------------------------------------------------------
// Ch15_04_ex.cpp
//-------------------------------------------------------------------

#include <algorithm>
#include <ranges>
#include <vector>
#include "Ch15_04.h"
#include "MT.h"
#include "RN.h"
```

CHAPTER 15   RANGES – PART 2

```cpp
void Ch15_04_ex1()
{
#ifdef __cpp_lib_ranges_slide
    using ll_t = long long;
    const char* fmt = "{:d} ";
    constexpr size_t epl_max {10};

    // create test vector
    std::vector vec1 = RN::get_vector<ll_t>(6, 1, 50, 327);
    MT::print_ctr("\nvec1:\n", vec1, fmt, epl_max);

    // sliding window print lambda
    auto print_window = [](auto& window)
    {
        std::print("[");
        for (auto x : window)
            std::print(" {:3d}", x);
        std::print("] ");
    };

    // sliding window calculate lambda
    auto calc_window = [](auto& window)
    {
        auto sum = std::ranges::fold_left(window, 0, std::plus<ll_t>());
        auto prod = std::ranges::fold_left(window, 1,
            std::multiplies<ll_t>());
        std::println("sum: {:d} prod: {:d}", sum, prod);
    };

    for (size_t window_w = 1; window_w <= vec1.size(); ++window_w)
    {
        std::println("\nwindow width: {:d}", window_w);

        // using std::views::slide
        auto slide1 = vec1 | std::views::slide(window_w);

        for (const auto& window1 : slide1)
        {
```

634

```
            print_window(window1);
            calc_window(window1);
        }
    }
#else
    std::println("Ch15_01_ex1() - std::views::slide requires C++23)");
#endif
}
```

In Listing 15-4-1, execution of Ch15_04_ex1() commences with the instantiation of std::vector<ll_t> vec1 using RN::get_vector<ll_t> (ll_t is an alias for long long). Next is the definition of lambda expressions print_window() and calc_window(). The former prints the elements of a range, while the latter calculates a range sum and product using std::ranges::fold_left() (see example Ch11_08 for more information regarding fold algorithms).

The outermost for loop of the next code block iterates window_w (window width) between [1, vec1.size()]. Execution of the statement slide1 = vec1 | std::views ::slide(window_w) creates window_w wide views of adjacent elements from vec1. The range for loop that follows calls print_window() and calculate_window() for each view in slide1. Note in the results section that during the first iteration of the outermost for loop, std::views::slide(window_w) generates vec1.size() one-element views; during the next iteration, vec1.size() - 1 two-element views are produced; and so on.

Listing 15-4-2 contains the source code for example function Ch15_04_ex2(), which creates stride views using std::views::stride(stride_len). A stride view is a view that encompasses every *n*-th element from a range (e.g., elements ctr[stride_len * 0], ctr[stride_len * 1], etc.).

Listing 15-4-2. Example Ch15_04 – Ch15_04_ex2()

```
void Ch15_04_ex2()
{
#ifdef __cpp_lib_ranges_stride
    const char* fmt = "{:6d} ";
    constexpr size_t epl_max {10};
```

CHAPTER 15 RANGES – PART 2

```
    // create test vector
    std::vector vec1 = RN::get_vector<int>(50, 1, 50, 327);
    MT::print_ctr("\nvec1:\n", vec1, fmt, epl_max);

    // using std::views::stride
    constexpr size_t stride_len {5};

    auto stride1 = vec1 | std::views::stride(stride_len);
    MT::print_ctr("\nstride1:\n", stride1, fmt, epl_max);

    // using std::views::stride and std::views::transform
    auto stride2 = vec1
                 | std::views::stride(stride_len)
                 | std::views::transform([](int x) { return x * x; });

    MT::print_ctr("\nstride2:\n", stride2, fmt, epl_max);
#else
    std::println("Ch15_01_ex2() - std::views::stride requires C++23)");
#endif
}
```

Function Ch15_04_ex2() starts with the instantiation of std::vector vec1 = RN::get_vector<int>(50, 1, 50, 327). Execution of the expression stride1 = vec1 | std::views::stride(stride_len) creates stride_len wide views of elements from vec1 starting with vec1's first element. The subsequent code block in Ch15_04_ex2() adds std::views::transform([](int x) { return x * x; }) to perform a transformation operation using the values in each view.

The next example, shown in Listing 15-4-3, demonstrates how to use std::views::chunk(). This range adaptor produces *n*-wide views of adjacent elements from an underlying range.

Listing 15-4-3. Example Ch15_04 – Ch15_04_ex3()

```
auto print_chunk(auto& chunk)
{
    std::print("[");
```

```cpp
    for (auto x : chunk)
        std::print("{:d} ", x);
    std::print("] ");
}

void Ch15_04_ex3()
{
#ifdef __cpp_lib_ranges_chunk_by
    const char* fmt = "{:4d} ";
    constexpr size_t epl_max {12};

    // create test vector
    std::vector vec1 = RN::get_vector<int>(12, 1, 50, 327);
    MT::print_ctr("\nvec1:\n", vec1, fmt, epl_max);

    for (size_t chunk_w = 1; chunk_w <= vec1.size(); ++chunk_w)
    {
        std::println("\nchunk_w: {:d}", chunk_w);

        // using std::views::chunk
        auto chunk1 = vec1 | std::views::chunk(chunk_w);

        for (const auto& chunk : chunk1)
            print_chunk(chunk);
        std::println("");
    }
#else
    std::println("Ch15_01_ex3() - std::views::chunk requires C++23");
#endif
}
```

Listing 15-4-3 begins with the definition of template function named print_chunk(), which prints the elements of chunk. Also shown in the same listing is example function Ch15_04_ex3(). Within the outer for loop is the statement chunk1 = vec1 | std ::views::chunk(chunk_w). Execution of this expression generates chunk_w wide views of elements from vec1. Note in the results section that the last chunk of each std::views::chunk(chunk_w) generated view contains vec1 % chunk_w elements.

CHAPTER 15   RANGES – PART 2

Listing 15-4-4 shows the final example function of this section. Like the previous examples, Ch15_04_ex4() employs RN::get_vector() to create a vector of random integers. Following the instantiation of vec1, Ch15_04_ex4() harnesses std::ranges::sort() to sort the elements of vec1.

Listing 15-4-4. Example Ch15_04 – Ch15_04_ex4()

```
void Ch15_04_ex4()
{
#ifdef __cpp_lib_ranges_chunk_by
    const char* fmt = "{:4d} ";
    constexpr size_t epl_max {15};

    // create sorted test vector
    std::vector vec1 = RN::get_vector<int>(40, 1, 20, 271);
    std::ranges::sort(vec1);
    MT::print_ctr("\nvec1:\n", vec1, fmt, epl_max);

    // using std::views::chunk_by
    auto chunk_op = [](int x, int y) { return x == y; };
    auto chunk_vw = vec1 | std::views::chunk_by(chunk_op);

    size_t nl {};
    std::println("\nchunk_vw:");

    for (auto chunk : chunk_vw)
    {
        print_chunk(chunk);

        if (++nl % 4 == 0)
            std::println("");
    }
#else
    std::println("Ch15_01_ex4() - std::views::chunk_by requires C++23)");
#endif
}
```

CHAPTER 15 RANGES – PART 2

The ensuing code block in Ch15_04_ex4() opens with the definition of binary predicate chunk_op = [](int x, int y) { return x == y; }. Execution of the next statement, chunk_vw = vec1 | std::views::chunk_by(chunk_op), generates views of adjacent elements in vec1. The partitioning point between views occurs at element pairs where chunk_op() returns false. In other words, each view element generated by std::views::chunk_by(chunk_op) contains one or more instances of equivalent elements as determined by chunk_op. Here are the results for example Ch15_04:

```
----- Results for example Ch15_04 -----
----- Ch15_04_ex1() -----
vec1:
23 12 37 21 15 20

window width: 1
[  23] sum: 23 prod: 23
[  12] sum: 12 prod: 12
[  37] sum: 37 prod: 37
[  21] sum: 21 prod: 21
[  15] sum: 15 prod: 15
[  20] sum: 20 prod: 20

window width: 2
[  23  12] sum: 35 prod: 276
[  12  37] sum: 49 prod: 444
[  37  21] sum: 58 prod: 777
[  21  15] sum: 36 prod: 315
[  15  20] sum: 35 prod: 300

window width: 3
[  23  12  37] sum: 72 prod: 10212
[  12  37  21] sum: 70 prod: 9324
[  37  21  15] sum: 73 prod: 11655
[  21  15  20] sum: 56 prod: 6300
```

CHAPTER 15   RANGES – PART 2

```
window width: 4
[  23   12   37   21] sum: 93 prod: 214452
[  12   37   21   15] sum: 85 prod: 139860
[  37   21   15   20] sum: 93 prod: 233100
window width: 5
[  23   12   37   21   15] sum: 108 prod: 3216780
[  12   37   21   15   20] sum: 105 prod: 2797200
window width: 6
[  23   12   37   21   15   20] sum: 128 prod: 64335600
----- Ch15_04_ex2() -----
vec1:
    23    12    37    21    15    20    24    17    36     7
    34    17     2     2    19    28    32    32    24    46
    26     7    37    24    14     3    18     3    42    32
    13     6    35     2    16     9    11    34     9    45
    12     6    16    25    49    37    23    23    21    44
stride1:
    23    20    34    28    26     3    13     9    12    37
stride2:
   529   400  1156   784   676     9   169    81   144  1369
----- Ch15_04_ex3() -----
vec1:
  23  12  37  21  15  20  24  17  36   7  34  17
chunk_w: 1
[23 ] [12 ] [37 ] [21 ] [15 ] [20 ] [24 ] [17 ] [36 ] [7 ] [34 ] [17 ]
chunk_w: 2
[23 12 ] [37 21 ] [15 20 ] [24 17 ] [36 7 ] [34 17 ]
chunk_w: 3
[23 12 37 ] [21 15 20 ] [24 17 36 ] [7 34 17 ]
```

640

chunk_w: 4
[23 12 37 21] [15 20 24 17] [36 7 34 17]

chunk_w: 5
[23 12 37 21 15] [20 24 17 36 7] [34 17]

chunk_w: 6
[23 12 37 21 15 20] [24 17 36 7 34 17]

chunk_w: 7
[23 12 37 21 15 20 24] [17 36 7 34 17]

chunk_w: 8
[23 12 37 21 15 20 24 17] [36 7 34 17]

chunk_w: 9
[23 12 37 21 15 20 24 17 36] [7 34 17]

chunk_w: 10
[23 12 37 21 15 20 24 17 36 7] [34 17]

chunk_w: 11
[23 12 37 21 15 20 24 17 36 7 34] [17]

chunk_w: 12
[23 12 37 21 15 20 24 17 36 7 34 17]

----- Ch15_04_ex4() -----

vec1:
```
   1    1    1    2    3    3    3    4    5    5    6    6    7    7    7
   8    9   10   10   10   11   11   11   11   11   12   13   13   14   16
  16   16   16   17   18   18   18   19   20   20
```

chunk_vw:
[1 1 1] [2] [3 3 3] [4]
[5 5] [6 6] [7 7 7] [8]
[9] [10 10 10] [11 11 11 11 11] [12]
[13 13] [14] [16 16 16 16] [17]
[18 18 18] [19] [20 20]

CHAPTER 15   RANGES – PART 2

Range Factories

A range factory is a utility that creates a specialized view. Namespace `std::ranges` includes range factories that generate an incrementing sequence of values, a sequence of repeated values, and a sequence of elements generated by multiple calls to `operator>>`. In this section, you'll learn how to use the following range factories: `std::views::iota()`, `std::views::repeat()`, and `std::views::istream()`.

Listing 15-5-1 contains the source code for example `Ch15_05_ex1()`. This example demonstrates how to use `std::views::iota()` to carry out a numerical calculation. Near the top of `Ch15_05_ex1()` is the definition of a lambda expression named `calc_pi()`. The sole argument for this lambda expression is `iota_vw`, whose type corresponds to `std::ranges::iota::view`. The range for loop in `calc_pi()` calculates

$$\pi = 4\sum_{i=1}^{n} \frac{(-1)^{i+1}}{2i-1}$$

by iterating over the sequential integer values of view `iota_vw`. Before continuing, it warrants mentioning that the primary purpose of this example is to demonstrate the use of `std::view_iota()`. For the current example, employing an ordinary for loop index variable in `calc_pi()` would be simpler. Also, the equation used here to calculate π was chosen since it's easy to understand; however, it converges slowly. Appendix B contains a reference that you can consult for more information regarding formulas that calculate π.

Listing 15-5-1. Example Ch15_05 – Ch15_05_ex1()

```
//-------------------------------------------------------------------
// Ch15_05_ex.cpp
//-------------------------------------------------------------------

#include <cmath>
#include <numbers>
#include <utility>
#include <ranges>
#include <sstream>
#include <string>
#include <vector>
#include "Ch15_05.h"
```

CHAPTER 15 RANGES – PART 2

```cpp
void Ch15_05_ex1()
{
    // create vector of test bound values
    std::vector<int> n_vals { 100, 1'000, 1'000'000, 1'000'000'000 };

    // compile using /O2 or /O3 for best performance
    // iota_vw is type std::ranges::iota_view
    auto calc_pi = [](auto iota_vw)
    {
        double sum {};

        for (auto i : iota_vw)
        {
            auto num = std::pow(-1, i + 1);
            auto den = 2 * i - 1;
            sum += num / den;
        }

        return 4.0 * sum;
    };

    std::println("\nbegin test of std::views::iota, please wait");
    std::println("\npi (std::numbers::pi): {:.14f}", std::numbers::pi);

    for (auto n : n_vals)
    {
        std::println("\ncalculating pi, n: {:d}", n);

        // using std::views::iota - generates view of [1, n + 1)
        auto pi = calc_pi(std::views::iota(1, n + 1));
        auto delta = fabs(pi - std::numbers::pi);

        std::println("pi (calculated):       {:.14f}", pi);
        std::println("delta:                 {:e}", delta);
    }
}
```

CHAPTER 15   RANGES – PART 2

Later in example function Ch15_05_ex1() is the statement pi = calc_pi(std::views::iota(1, n + 1)). The execution of this expression first creates a view of sequential integer values between [1, n]. It then passes this view to calc_pi(). Following execution of calc_pi(), Ch15_05_ex1() utilizes delta = fabs(pi - std::numbers::pi) to gauge the accuracy of calc_pi().

In Listing 15-5-2, example function Ch15_05_ex2() demonstrates the use of std::views::repeat(). Execution of this range factory yields a view that contains repeated instances of the same value.

Listing 15-5-2. Example Ch15_05 – Ch15_05_ex2()

```
void Ch15_05_ex2()
{
    constexpr size_t n {10};

    // using std::views::repeat (bounded view)
    for (auto v : std::views::repeat(42.0, n))
        std::print("{:6.1f} ", v);
    std::println("");

    // using std::views::repeat (unbounded view)
    std::string s {" hello"};
    for (auto v : std::views::repeat(s) | std::views::take(n))
        std::print("{:s} ", v);
    std::println("");
}
```

The final example of this section exemplifies the use of std::views::istream(). This range factory generates a view using repetitive calls to operator>>. Near the top of Listing 15-5-3 is the container std::vector<pair_t> vec1. Note that each pair_t element includes an int and a std::string. The former is a code that the subsequent range for loop tests to select the correct template parameter for std::views::istream().

Listing 15-5-3. Example Ch15_05 - Ch15_05_ex3()

```cpp
void Ch15_05_ex3()
{
    using pair_t = std::pair<int, std::string>;

    // create test vector
    std::vector<pair_t> vec1
    {
        pair_t(0, "1 2 3 4 5 6 7 8"),
        pair_t(1, "1.0 2.0 3.0 4.0 5.0 6.0 7.0 8.0"),
        pair_t(2, "one two three four five six seven eight"),
        pair_t(0, "1 2 3 4 a 5 6 7 8"),                    // invalid
                                                            // int value
        pair_t(1, "1.0 2.0 3.0 4.0 b 5.0 6.0 7.0 8.0"),    // invalid
                                                            // FP value
    };

    for (const auto& v : vec1)
    {
        auto iss = std::istringstream(v.second);

        if (v.first == 0)
        {
            // using std::views::istream<int>
            int result0 {};
            auto iss_view = std::views::istream<int>(iss);

            for (auto val : iss_view)
                result0 += val;
            std::println("result0: {:d}", result0);

        }
        else if (v.first == 1)
        {
            // using std::views::istream<double>
            double result1 {1.0};
            auto iss_view = std::views::istream<double>(iss);
```

```
            for (auto val : iss_view)
                result1 *= val;
            std::println("result1: {:.1f}", result1);
        }
        else if (v.first == 2)
        {
            // using std::views::istream<std::string>
            std::string result2 {"|"};
            auto iss_view = std::views::istream<std::string>(iss);

            for (auto val : iss_view)
                result2 += val + "|";
            std::println("result2: {:s}", result2);
        }
    }
}
```

Within Ch15_05_ex3()'s outermost range for loop, the previously mentioned int code (v.first) determines how to process the std::string (v.second). For example, when v.first equals zero, iss_view = std::views::istream<int>(iss) creates a view that repeatedly applies operator>> to extract int values from v.second. The subsequent inner range for loop carries out a simulated calculation using values of the created view. The other two processing blocks inside the outermost range for loop perform similar actions using doubles and std::strings. Note that std::views::istream() terminates if it encounters a value that doesn't correspond to the specified data type. Here are the results for example Ch15_05:

```
----- Results for example Ch15_05 -----

----- Ch15_05_ex1() -----

begin test of std::views::iota, please wait

pi (std::numbers::pi): 3.14159265358979

calculating pi, n: 100
pi (calculated):        3.13159290355855
delta:                  9.999750e-03
```

```
calculating pi, n: 1000
pi (calculated):       3.14059265383979
delta:                 9.999997e-04

calculating pi, n: 1000000
pi (calculated):       3.14159165358977
delta:                 1.000000e-06

calculating pi, n: 1000000000
pi (calculated):       3.14159265258805
delta:                 1.001743e-09

----- Ch15_05_ex2() -----
  42.0   42.0   42.0   42.0   42.0   42.0   42.0   42.0   42.0   42.0
 hello  hello  hello  hello  hello  hello  hello  hello  hello  hello

----- Ch15_05_ex3() -----
result0: 36
result1: 40320.0
result2: |one|two|three|four|five|six|seven|eight|
result0: 10
result1: 24.0
```

Summary

Here are the key learning points for this chapter:

- Range adaptors `std::views::keys()` and `std::views::values()` create key and value views of an underlying range. These adaptors can be used to generate views of elements in a range tuples.

- Range adaptor `std::views::elements()` generates a view of the i-th element in an underlying range of tuple elements.

- Range adaptor `std::views::enumerate()` generates a key-value view of a range. The key corresponds to an element's position in an underlying range, while the value component is a reference to the actual value.

- Range adaptors of `std::views::adjacent()` and `std::views::adjacent_transform()` generate views of adjacent elements in an underlying range; the latter also applies a transformation function.

- Range adaptor `std::views::join()` creates a view that flattens multiple underlying ranges into a single view. Range adaptor `std::views::join()` performs a similar operation but adds a delimiter between elements of the resultant view.

- Range adaptor `std::views::slide()` creates sliding views of adjacent elements in underlying range. Adaptor `std::views::stride()` generates views of every *n*-th element in a range, while adaptor `std::views::chunk()` produces *n*-wide views of adjacent elements.

- Range factory `std::views::iota()` generates a view of an incrementing sequence of values. Factory `std::views::repeat()` creates a view that encompasses a sequence of repeated values. Factory `std::views::istream()` generates a view using multiple applications of `operator>>`.

CHAPTER 16

Time Library

This chapter explains prominent classes and algorithms from the time library. It also covers supplemental classes from the ratio library. Topics discussed include

- Using std::ratio
- Using std::chrono::duration
- Using clock classes
- Using std::chrono::time_point
- Date and time formatting
- Software benchmarking

Time library entities belong to namespace std::chrono. In this chapter, text references to std::chrono's classes and algorithms are mostly prefixed using chrono:: for consistency with the namespace chrono = std::chrono statements used in the source code.

Ratios

The ratio library defines a template class named std::ratio. This class represents a finite rational number using an integer (std::intmax_t) numerator and denominator. The ratio library also defines template classes that support std::ratio arithmetic and comparisons. The time library exploits std::ratio to simplify calculations using time durations (chrono::duration) and points in time (chrono::time_point). You'll learn more about these classes later in this chapter.

CHAPTER 16 TIME LIBRARY

The most important aspect to remember about a std::ratio is that the numerator and denominator are compile-time constants. Arithmetic and comparisons using std::ratios are also compile-time actions, which is advantageous in that it facilitates compile-time detection of certain errors such as division-by-zero. It also significantly reduces the risk of an arithmetic overflow error during program execution.

Listing 16-1-1 shows the source code for example Ch16_01_ex1(), which demonstrates the basic use of std::ratios. The opening statement of this function, using ra = std::ratio<12, 20>, defines an alias[1] named ra that represents the ratio 12/20. Ratios are often manipulated without creating an explicit object as shown in the current example. Class std::ratio contains two members named num and den, both of which are type static constexpr intmax_t. These members are referenced in the subsequent print statement. If you scan ahead to the results section, the output for ra shows 3 and 5 for num and den, respectively. The reason for this is that the compiler ensures that a std::ratio is always reduced to its lowest possible terms.

Listing 16-1-1. Example Ch16_01 - Ch16_01_ex1()

```
//-------------------------------------------------------------------------
// Ch16_01_ex.cpp
//-------------------------------------------------------------------------

#include <ratio>
#include "Ch16_01.h"

void Ch16_01_ex1()
{
    // using std::ratio
    using ra = std::ratio<12, 20>;          // reduced to 3 / 5
    std::println("ra::num: {:3d} ra::den: {:3d}", ra::num, ra::den);

    using rb = std::ratio<1, 15>;
    std::println("rb::num: {:3d} rb::den: {:3d}", rb::num, rb::den);

    using rc = std::ratio<42>;              // 42 / 1
    std::println("rc::num: {:3d} rc::den: {:3d}", rc::num, rc::den);
```

---

[1] In older C++ code, the keyword typedef is used instead of using (e.g., typedef std::ratio<12, 20> ra;).

```cpp
    // std::ratio arithmetic
    using rd_add = std::ratio_add<ra, rb>;
    using rd_sub = std::ratio_subtract<ra, rb>;
    using rd_mul = std::ratio_multiply<ra, rb>;
    using rd_div = std::ratio_divide<ra, rb>;

    std::println("");
    std::println("rd_add::num: {:3d} rd_add::den: {:3d}", rd_add::num,
    rd_add::den);
    std::println("rd_sub::num: {:3d} rd_sub::den: {:3d}", rd_sub::num,
    rd_sub::den);
    std::println("rd_mul::num: {:3d} rd_mul::den: {:3d}", rd_mul::num,
    rd_mul::den);
    std::println("rd_div::num: {:3d} rd_div::den: {:3d}", rd_div::num,
    rd_div::den);

    // std::ratio relational operators
    std::println("\nra == rb: {:s}", std::ratio_equal<ra, rb>::value);
    std::println("ra == rb: {:s}", std::ratio_not_equal<ra, rb>::value);
    std::println("ra <  rb: {:s}", std::ratio_less<ra, rb>::value);
    std::println("ra <= rb: {:s}", std::ratio_less_equal<ra, rb>::value);
    std::println("ra >  rb: {:s}", std::ratio_greater<ra, rb>::value);
    std::println("ra >= rb: {:s}", std::ratio_greater_equal<ra,
    rb>::value);
}
```

The next two statements in Ch16_01_ex1() define and print rb = std::ratio<1, 15>. The last std::ratio example, using rc = std::ratio<42>, creates a std::ratio<42, 1> since the default value for den is one.

The subsequent code block demonstrates the use of std::ratio arithmetic. The result of each compile-time arithmetic operation is always reduced to its lowest possible terms. The final code block of Ch16_01_ex1() spotlights std::ratio comparisons. Note that for each comparison type, member value yields true or false.

Listing 16-1-2 shows the source code for the next std::ratio example, which details how to use a few predefined SI[2] std::ratios.

---

[2] Système international d'unités (System of International Units).

CHAPTER 16 TIME LIBRARY

Listing 16-1-2. Example Ch16_01 - Ch16_01_ex2()

```
void Ch16_01_ex2()
{
    // using SI ratios
    using ra = std::milli;
    using rb = std::nano;

    std::ratio_add<ra, rb> rc_add;
    std::ratio_subtract<ra, rb> rc_sub;
    std::ratio_multiply<ra, std::micro> rc_mul;
    std::ratio_divide<ra, rb> rc_div;

    std::println("ra::num:    {:<20d} ra::den:    {:<20d}", ra::num, ra::den);
    std::println("rb::num:    {:<20d} rb::den:    {:<20d}", rb::num, rb::den);
    std::println("");
    std::println("rc_add.num: {:<20d} rc_add.den: {:<20d}", rc_add.num, rc_add.den);
    std::println("rc_sub.num: {:<20d} rc_sub.den: {:<20d}", rc_sub.num, rc_sub.den);
    std::println("rc_mul.num: {:<20d} rc_mul.den: {:<20d}", rc_mul.num, rc_mul.den);
    std::println("rc_div.num: {:<20d} rc_div.den: {:<20d}", rc_div.num, rc_div.den);

    // compile-time arithmetic overflow
//  using bad = std::ratio_multiply<rb, std::atto>;

    // more SI ratios
    using rd = std::giga;
    using re = std::tera;

    std::ratio_add<rd, std::mega> rf_add;
    std::ratio_subtract<std::peta, rd> rf_sub;
    std::ratio_multiply<std::kilo, rd> rf_mul;
    std::ratio_divide<rd, re> rf_div;
```

```
    std::println("");
    std::println("rd::num:     {:<20d} rd::den:    {:<20d}", rd::num,
    rd::den);
    std::println("re::num:     {:<20d} re::den:    {:<20d}", re::num,
    re::den);
    std::println("");
    std::println("rf_add.num: {:<20d} rf_add.den: {:<20d}", rf_add.num,
    rf_add.den);
    std::println("rf_sub.num: {:<20d} rf_sub.den: {:<20d}", rf_sub.num,
    rf_sub.den);
    std::println("rf_mul.num: {:<20d} rf_mul.den: {:<20d}", rf_mul.num,
    rf_mul.den);
    std::println("rf_div.num: {:<20d} rf_div.den: {:<20d}", rf_div.num,
    rf_div.den);
}
```

The initiating statement of Ch16_01_ex2(), using ra = std::milli, creates an alias named ra that corresponds to a std::ratio<1, 1000> (or 10^{-3}). Table 16-1 lists the predefined SI std::ratios and their corresponding units. A C++ implementation is not required to support a predefined std::ratio from Table 16-1 if the numerator or denominator is not representable using a std::intmax_t. For a C++ implementation that defines a 64-bit-wide std::intmax_t, valid SI std::ratios are between std::atto and std::exa.

Table 16-1. Standard Library Predefined SI std::ratios

Name (std::)	std::ratio<num, den>	Base 10 Ratio
quecto (C++26)	1, 1,000,000,000,000,000,000,000,000,000,000	10^{-30}
ronto (C++26)	1, 1,000,000,000,000,000,000,000,000,000	10^{-27}
yocto	1, 1,000,000,000,000,000,000,000,000	10^{-24}
zepto	1, 1,000,000,000,000,000,000,000	10^{-21}
atto	1, 1,000,000,000,000,000,000	10^{-18}

(*continued*)

Table 16-1. (*continued*)

Name (std::)	std::ratio<num, den>	Base 10 Ratio
femto	1, 1,000,000,000,000,000	10^{-15}
pico	1, 1,000,000,000,000	10^{-12}
nano	1, 1,000,000,000	10^{-9}
micro	1, 1,000,000	10^{-6}
milli	1, 1,000	10^{-3}
centi	1, 100	10^{-2}
deci	1, 10	10^{-1}
deca	10, 1	10^{1}
hecto	100, 1	10^{2}
kilo	1,000, 1	10^{3}
mega	1,000,000, 1	10^{6}
giga	1,000,000,000, 1	10^{9}
tera	1,000,000,000,000, 1	10^{12}
peta	1,000,000,000,000,000, 1	10^{15}
exa	1,000,000,000,000,000,000, 1	10^{18}
zetta	1,000,000,000,000,000,000,000 1	10^{21}
yotta	1,000,000,000,000,000,000,000,000, 1	10^{24}
ronna (C++26)	1,000,000,000,000,000,000,000,000,000, 1	10^{27}
quetta (C++26)	1,000,000,000,000,000,000,000,000,000,000, 1	10^{30}

Following the definition of alias using rb = std::nano, Ch16_01_ex2() carries out a few std::ratio arithmetic operations. Again, it's important to keep in mind that these are compile-time calculations. The compiler will flag an error if it detects an arithmetic overflow. To see this in action, remove the comment from the using bad = std::ratio_multiply<rb, std::atto> statement and compile the code.

The code in the second part of Ch16_01_ex2() is similar to its first part but uses the larger predefined std::ratios. It warrants mentioning that example function Ch16_01_ex2() employed using statements for SI std::ratios to avoid code line wraps. For production code, direct use of the predefined SI std::ratios is usually preferred. Here are the results for example Ch16_01:

```
----- Results for example Ch16_01 -----

----- Ch16_01_ex1() -----
ra::num:      3 ra::den:    5
rb::num:      1 rb::den:    15
rc::num:     42 rc::den:    1

rd_add::num:     2 rd_add::den:    3
rd_sub::num:     8 rd_sub::den:    15
rd_mul::num:     1 rd_mul::den:    25
rd_div::num:     9 rd_div::den:    1

ra == rb: false
ra == rb: true
ra <  rb: false
ra <= rb: false
ra >  rb: true
ra >= rb: true

----- Ch16_01_ex2() -----
ra::num:    1                    ra::den:    1000
rb::num:    1                    rb::den:    1000000000

rc_add.num: 1000001              rc_add.den: 1000000000
rc_sub.num: 999999               rc_sub.den: 1000000000
rc_mul.num: 1                    rc_mul.den: 1000000000
rc_div.num: 1000000              rc_div.den: 1
```

rd::num: 1000000000   rd::den: 1
re::num: 1000000000000   re::den: 1

rf_add.num: 1001000000   rf_add.den: 1
rf_sub.num: 999999000000000   rf_sub.den: 1
rf_mul.num: 1000000000000   rf_mul.den: 1
rf_div.num: 1   rf_div.den: 1000

Durations

A `chrono::duration` measures the amount of time between two points in time. Each `chrono::duration` holds a tick count and a tick period. The latter is the amount of time in seconds that transpires between two ticks. A `chrono::duration` is a rational constant and is programmatically expressed using template `std::ratio`. Namespace `std::chrono` also includes other date and time classes, and you'll learn more about these as the chapter progresses.

Listing 16-2-1 shows the source code for example `Ch16_02_ex1()`. This example demonstrates the basic use of `chrono::durations`. Near the top of this listing, the statement `namespace chrono = std::chrono` is included to reduce line length and improve readability. The first `chrono::duration` use, `chrono::duration<int, std::ratio<3600 * 24>> day {1}`, defines a duration named day as a `std::ratio<3600 * 24>` (i.e., 86400 / 1) in seconds. In other words, one tick of a day corresponds to a tick period of 86,400 seconds. The tick type for a day is `int`. Other types for a tick can be specified as you'll soon see.

Listing 16-2-1. Example Ch16_02 – Ch16_02_ex1()

```
//-------------------------------------------------------------------
// Ch16_02_ex.cpp
//-------------------------------------------------------------------

#include <chrono>
#include <typeinfo>
#include "Ch16_02.h"

namespace chrono = std::chrono;
```

CHAPTER 16 TIME LIBRARY

```cpp
//#define PRINT_DURATION_TYPEID   // remove comment to print
duration typeids

void Ch16_02_ex1()
{
    // using chrono::duration
    chrono::duration<int, std::ratio<3600 * 24>> day {1};
    chrono::duration<int, std::ratio<3600 * 24 * 7>> week {1};
    chrono::duration<int, std::ratio<3600 * 24 * 14>> fortnight {1};

    // chrono::duration arithmetic - days
    auto num_days = 2 * fortnight - 4 * day + 3 * week;
    std::println("num_days:     {}", num_days);

    // using chrono::duration_cast<>
    auto num_hours = chrono::duration_cast<chrono::hours>(num_days);
    std::println("num_hours:    {}", num_hours);

    // using chrono::duration (non-int tick type)
    chrono::duration<double, std::ratio<3600>> minutes90 {1.5};

    // more chrono::duration arithmetic
    auto num_hours_d = 20.0 * minutes90 + 0.5 * minutes90;
    auto num_minutes = chrono::duration_cast<chrono::minutes>(num_hours_d);
    std::println("\nnum_hours_d:  {}", num_hours_d);
    std::println("num_minutes:  {}", num_minutes);

#ifdef PRINT_DURATION_TYPEID
    std::println("\ntypeid(num_days):    {}", typeid(num_days).name());
    std::println("typeid(num_hours):   {}", typeid(num_hours).name());
    std::println("typeid(num_hours_d): {}", typeid(num_hours_d).name());
    std::println("typeid(num_minutes): {}", typeid(num_minutes).name());
#endif
}
```

The second `chrono::duration` used in Listing 16-2-1, `chrono::duration<int, std::ratio<3600 * 24 * 7>> week {1}`, defines week whose tick period in seconds equals `std::ratio<3600 * 24 * 7>` (or 604800 / 1). The final `chrono::duration` example of the first code block, `chrono::duration<int, std::ratio<3600 * 24 * 14>> fortnight {1}`, defines a two-week duration.

The next code block in `Ch16_02_ex1()` demonstrates simple arithmetic using the previously defined `chrono::durations`. Execution of `num_days = 2 * fortnight - 4 * day + 3 * week` calculates the number of days specified by the arithmetic expression. Why number of days? When performing arithmetic using `chrono::durations`, the compile-time calculations are carried out using the greatest common divisor for all operands in the expression. Thus, the resultant type for `num_days` is `chrono::duration<int, std::ratio<86400, 1>>`, which represents the number of seconds in one day. To see the `chrono::duration` typeids, enable preprocessor symbol `PRINT_DURATION_TYPEID`, compile, and execute the code.

Execution of the ensuing statement, `num_hours = chrono::duration_cast<chrono::hours>(num_days)`, converts `num_days` to a duration of type `chrono::duration<int, std::ratio<3600, 1>>` or hours. Table 16-2 shows the predefined duration types that you can use to specify common time durations. In this table, `intxx` denotes the minimum size in bits of a signed integer needed to represent the duration.

Table 16-2. Standard Time Duration Aliases

Name (std::chrono::)	Duration (std::chrono::duration<rep, period>)
nanoseconds	<int64, nano>
microseconds	<int55, micro>
milliseconds	<int45, milli>
seconds	<int35>
minutes	<int29, ratio<60>>
hours	<int23 ratio<3600>>
days	<int25, ratio_multiply<ratio<24>, hours::period>>
weeks	<int22, ratio_multiply<ratio<7>, days::period>>
years	<int17, ratio_multiply<ratio<146097, 400>, days::period>>
months	<int20, ratio_divide<years::period, ratio<12>>>

In Table 16-2, note that chrono::years represents 365.2425 days. Also, note that chrono::months corresponds to about 30.44 days.

The next code block in Ch16_02_ex1() defines chrono::durations minutes15 and minutes90. Note that both of these chrono::durations use tick type double. Following these definitions is another code block that demonstrates chrono::duration arithmetic and casting using chrono::duration_cast(). Like the previous example, these calculations are carried out using the greatest common divisor.

Note in the results section that the output for each chrono::duration value includes an appended unit suffix. The STL defines a template class named std::formatter<std::chrono::sys_time> that handles default formatting for time library objects. This formatter also supports a large set of explicit format specifiers for dates and times. You'll see a few examples of these later in this chapter.

CHAPTER 16 TIME LIBRARY

The code in example `Ch16_02_ex2()`, shown in Listing 16-2-2, demonstrates how to use some of the standard time duration classes of namespace `chrono::duration`. It also exemplifies the use of literal suffixes for time values. The initial line of `Ch16_02_ex2()`, using namespace `std::chrono_literals`, enables the use of `chrono`'s literal suffixes. This namespace includes suffixes for both dates and times.

Listing 16-2-2. Example Ch16_02 – Ch16_02_ex2()

```cpp
void Ch16_02_ex2()
{
    using namespace std::chrono_literals;

    // using standard durations
    chrono::days x_days {5};
    chrono::hours x_hours {18};
    chrono::minutes x_minutes {12};
    chrono::seconds x_seconds {7};

    auto a_seconds = x_days + x_hours - x_minutes + x_seconds;
    auto a_minutes = chrono::duration_cast<chrono::minutes>(a_seconds);
    auto a_hours = chrono::duration_cast<chrono::hours>(a_seconds);
    auto a_days = chrono::duration_cast<chrono::days>(a_seconds);

    auto a_err = a_seconds - a_days;

    std::println("\na_seconds:   {:8}  a_minutes: {:8}", a_seconds,
        a_minutes);
    std::println("a_hours:     {:8}  a_days:    {:8}", a_hours, a_days);
    std::println("a_err:       {:8}", a_err);

    // using time suffixes (hours, minutes, seconds)
    auto b_seconds = 17h + 47min + 18s + a_seconds;
    auto b_minutes = chrono::duration_cast<chrono::minutes>(b_seconds);
    auto b_hours = chrono::duration_cast<chrono::hours>(b_seconds);
    auto b_days = chrono::duration_cast<chrono::days>(b_seconds);

    auto b_err = b_seconds - b_days;
```

```
    std::println("\nb_seconds:    {:8}  b_minutes: {:8}", b_seconds,
    b_minutes);
    std::println("b_hours:      {:8}  b_days:    {:8}", b_hours, b_days);
    std::println("b_err:        {:8}", b_err);

    // using time suffixes (milliseconds, microseconds, nanoseconds)
    // period for duration c is std::ratio<1, 1000000000>
    auto c = 12s + 340ms + 5600us + 78901ns;

    auto c_ns  = chrono::duration_cast<chrono::nanoseconds>(c);
    auto c_us  = chrono::duration_cast<chrono::microseconds>(c);
    auto c_ms  = chrono::duration_cast<chrono::milliseconds>(c);
    auto c_sec = chrono::duration_cast<chrono::seconds>(c);

    std::println("\nc_ns: {:15} c_us:  {:15}", c_ns, c_us);
    std::println("c_ms: {:15} c_sec: {:15}", c_ms, c_sec);

    std::println("\nc_sec (decimal): {:%S}", c);    // %S specifies
                                                    decimal seconds
#ifdef PRINT_DURATION_TYPEID
    std::println("\ntypeid(b_seconds): {}", typeid(b_seconds).name());
    std::println("typeid(b_minutes): {}", typeid(b_minutes).name());
    std::println("typeid(b_hours):   {}", typeid(b_hours).name());
    std::println("typeid(c):         {}", typeid(c).name());
#endif
}
```

The opening code block of Ch16_02_ex2() initializes four duration variables using aliases from Table 16-2: chrono::days x_days, chrono::hours x_hours, chrono::minutes x_minutes, and chrono::seconds x_seconds. The next group of statements starts with an arbitrary calculation of a_seconds = x_days + x_hours - x_minutes + x_seconds. A triplet of chrono::duration_cast() usages follows that calculates a_minutes, a_hours, and a_days. The purpose of these casts is to demonstrate that just like an ordinary fundamental type cast (e.g., double to int), the use of chrono::duration_cast often results in a loss of precision. To observe this for the current example, take a look at the value of a_err = a_seconds - a_days in the results section.

CHAPTER 16   TIME LIBRARY

The next code block in Ch16_02_ex2() illustrates how to use a few literal suffixes for time values. In the statement b_seconds = 17h + 47min + 18s + a_seconds, suffixes h, min, and s denote hours, minutes, and seconds, respectively. To calculate b_seconds, the literal suffixed numbers are converted to an appropriate ratio, which means that the processor effectively computes 17 * 3600 + 47 * 60 + 18 + a_seconds. The remaining statements in this code block exercise chrono::duration_cast() just like the previous code block.

The final code block of Ch16_02_ex2() spotlights the use of additional time suffixes. In the first statement, literal suffixes ms, us, and ns correspond to milliseconds, microseconds, and nanoseconds, respectively. Calculation of c = 12s + 340ms + 5600us + 78901ns results in chrono::duration c having a period of std::ratio<1, 1000000000>. The other item to note here is the use of format specifier %S that's used to print c. This specifier formats a time duration using decimal seconds.

The concluding example function of this section highlights the use of date durations and calendar class chrono::year_month_day. Listing 16-2-3 shows the source code for Ch16_02_ex3(). Near the top of this function is the definition of a lambda expression named print_rel_ops(), which prints a complete set of comparison results for ymd1 and ymd2.

Listing 16-2-3. Example Ch16_02 – Ch16_02_ex3()

```
void Ch16_02_ex3()
{
    using namespace std::chrono_literals;

    // print rel ops results
    auto print_rel_ops = [](const auto& ymd1, const auto& ymd2)
    {
        std::print("\nymd1 == ymd2: {:5s}   ", ymd1 == ymd2);
        std::println("ymd1 != ymd2: {:5s}", ymd1 != ymd2);
        std::print("ymd1 <  ymd2: {:5s}   ", ymd1 <  ymd2);
        std::println("ymd1 <= ymd2: {:5s}", ymd1 <= ymd2);
        std::print("ymd1 >  ymd2: {:5s}   ", ymd1 >  ymd2);
        std::println("ymd1 >= ymd2: {:5s}", ymd1 >= ymd2);
    };
```

```
    // using chrono date suffixes
    chrono::year_month_day ymd1 {2025y/6/21d};
    chrono::year_month_day ymd2 {2027y/6/21d};
    std::println("ymd1 | ymd2 (initial values):   {} | {}", ymd1, ymd2);
    print_rel_ops(ymd1, ymd2);

    // using chrono date suffixes - more formats
    auto ymd3 {9/20d/2026y};
    auto ymd4 {19d/3/2028y};
    std::println("\nymd3 | ymd4 (initial values):   {} | {}", ymd3, ymd4);

    // ymd calendar arithmetic - months and years
    ymd1 += chrono::months(6);
    ymd2 -= chrono::months(18);
    std::println("\nymd1 | ymd2 (after arithmetic): {} | {}", ymd1, ymd2);
    print_rel_ops(ymd1, ymd2);

    auto ymd5 = ymd3 + chrono::years(4);
    auto ymd6 = ymd4 - chrono::years(1);
    std::println("\nymd5 | ymd6 (initial values):   {} | {}", ymd5, ymd6);

    // ymd calendar arithmetic - days
    auto ymd7 = chrono::sys_days(ymd5) + chrono::days(7);
    auto ymd8 = chrono::sys_days(ymd6) - chrono::days(28);
    std::println("\nymd7 | ymd8 (initial values):   {} | {}", ymd7, ymd8);
}
```

Next is the definition of chrono::year_month_day ymd1 {2025y/6/21d}. In this expression, note the use of the literal suffixes y (year) and d (day) (there is no month literal suffix). The definition of ymd2 follows. After initialization of ymd1 and ymd2, Ch16_02_ex3() prints their values and invokes print_rel_ops() to demonstrate chrono::year_month_day comparisons. You can also use the keyword auto and month-day-year or day-month-year orderings[3] to instantiate a chrono::year_month_day object as shown in the subsequent code block with ymd3 and ymd4.

---

[3] The time library defines multiple overloads for operator/ that convert common Gregorian calendar date orderings to a suitable std::chrono calendar object.

CHAPTER 16   TIME LIBRARY

The subsequent code block in Ch16_02_ex3() demonstrates how to perform calendar arithmetic using chrono::year_month_day objects. For example, execution of ymd1 += chrono::months(6) adds six months to ymd1, while ymd2 -= chrono::months(18) subtracts 18 months from ymd2. You can also carry out calendar arithmetic using years as illustrated in the statements ymd5 = ymd3 + chrono::years(4) and ymd6 = ymd4 - chrono::years(1).

Class chrono::year_month_day doesn't support calendar arithmetic using days. To carry out these types of calculations, a chrono::year_month_day object must be converted to a chrono::time_point object using operator chrono::sys_days() as shown in the final code block of Ch16_02_ex3(). The next section discusses chrono::time_points in greater detail. Here are the results for example Ch16_02:

```
----- Results for example Ch16_02 -----
----- Ch16_02_ex1() -----
num_days:      45d
num_hours:     1080h

num_hours_d:   30.75h
num_minutes:   1845min

----- Ch16_02_ex2() -----

a_seconds:    496087s    a_minutes: 8268min
a_hours:      137h       a_days:    5d
a_err:        64087s

b_seconds:    560125s    b_minutes: 9335min
b_hours:      155h       b_days:    6d
b_err:        41725s

c_ns: 12345678901ns    c_us:   12345678us
c_ms: 12345ms          c_sec:  12s

c_sec (decimal): 12.345678901
```

```
----- Ch16_02_ex3() -----
ymd1 | ymd2 (initial values):    2025-06-21 | 2027-06-21

ymd1 == ymd2: false     ymd1 != ymd2: true
ymd1 <  ymd2: true      ymd1 <= ymd2: true
ymd1 >  ymd2: false     ymd1 >= ymd2: false

ymd3 | ymd4 (initial values):    2026-09-20 | 2028-03-19

ymd1 | ymd2 (after arithmetic): 2025-12-21 | 2025-12-21

ymd1 == ymd2: true      ymd1 != ymd2: false
ymd1 <  ymd2: false     ymd1 <= ymd2: true
ymd1 >  ymd2: false     ymd1 >= ymd2: true

ymd5 | ymd6 (initial values):    2030-09-20 | 2027-03-19

ymd7 | ymd8 (initial values):    2030-09-27 | 2027-02-19
```

Clocks and Timepoints

To perform time measurements and time-oriented arithmetic, the time library provides two interdependent classes: clocks and chrono::time points. A clock bundles an epoch (time reference point) and a tick period. The epoch for commonly used clocks such as chrono::system_clock and chrono::utc_clock is 1970-01-01 00:00:00 UTC (Coordinated Universal Time). A clock's tick period in seconds is represented using a std::ratio. As implied by its name, a chrono::time_point instance represents a point in time. It's implemented as a positive or negative time interval (std::duration) from a clock's epoch.

The time library defines several different clock classes that target specific use cases as outlined in Table 16-3. In this table, the column labeled Monotonic signifies whether the chrono::time_point object returned by a clock's now() function increases monotonically (i.e., the value returned by now() is *always* greater than or equal to the value returned by any earlier call).

Table 16-3. Time Library Clock Classes

Name (std::chrono)	Description	Epoch	Leap Seconds/ Monotonic
system_clock	Represents wall clock time from the system's real-time clock; subject to adjustments due to DST, Network Time Protocol synchronizations, user changes, etc.	1970-01-01 00:00:00 UTC	No/Optional
utc_clock	Mostly similar to system clock except for leap seconds	1970-01-01 00:00:00 UTC	Yes/Optional
steady_clock	Monotonic clock independent of wall clock time; used to measure time intervals	Unspecified	No/Yes
high_resolution_clock	Clock with the shortest tick period; may be a distinct clock or an alias for system_clock or steady_clock	Unspecified	No/Optional
tai_clock	International Atomic Time (TAI)	1958-01-01 00:00:00 (1957-12-31 23:59:50 UTC)	No/Optional
gps_clock	Global Positioning System	1980-01-06 00:00:00 UTC	No/Optional
file_clock	Alias for std::filesystem::file_time_type; used for file times	Unspecified	No/Optional

The source code examples in this chapter consider clock classes chrono::system_clock, chrono::utc_clock, and std::steady_clock. Most of explanations also apply to specialized clocks chrono::tai_clock and chrono::gps_clock. You'll learn more about clock chrono::file_clock and file system times in Chapter 17.

Listing 16-3-1 shows the source code for example function Ch16_03_ex1(). This example prints attribute information for commonly used clocks. Near the top of Listing 16-3-1 is the definition of a lambda expression named print_clock_info(). In this lambda, template parameter CLK represents a chrono clock class. All clock classes define a static constexpr bool value named is_steady, whose value is true if calls to the clock's now() function return monotonically increasing values; otherwise, is_steady is false. Clock attribute CLK::period is a std::ratio that defines the clock's tick period in seconds.

Listing 16-3-1. Example Ch16_03 – Ch16_03_ex1()

```
//-------------------------------------------------------------------
// Ch16_03_ex.cpp
//-------------------------------------------------------------------

#include <chrono>
#include <thread>
#include <typeinfo>
#include <vector>
#include "Ch16_03.h"

namespace chrono = std::chrono;
using namespace std::chrono_literals;

void Ch16_03_ex1()
{
    // clock information lambda
    auto print_clock_info = []<class CLK>(const char* msg, const CLK& clk)
    {
        std::println("\n{:s} ", msg);
        std::println("type name: {:s}", typeid(clk).name());
        std::println("is_steady: {:s}", clk.is_steady);
        std::println("period:    {:s}", typeid(typename CLK::period).name());
    };
```

```cpp
    // print clock information for various clocks
    chrono::system_clock clk1 {};
    print_clock_info("clk1 (chrono::system_clock)", clk1);

    chrono::utc_clock clk2 {};
    print_clock_info("clk2 (chrono::utc_clock)", clk2);

    chrono::steady_clock clk3 {};
    print_clock_info("clk3 (chrono::steady_clock)", clk3);

    chrono::high_resolution_clock clk4 {};
    print_clock_info("clk4 (chrono::high_resolution_clock)", clk4);
}
```

The ensuing code blocks in Ch16_03_ex1() utilize print_clock_info() to print information for clocks chrono::system_clock, chrono::utc_clock, chrono::steady_clock, and chrono::high_resolution_clock. Table 16-4 summarizes the information displayed by print_clock_info() for two different test computers.

Table 16-4. *Clock Class Attribute Information*

Clock (std::chrono::)	Attribute	Windows 11 (msvc)	Ubuntu 23.10 (GCC)
system_clock	is_steady	false	false
	period	std::ratio<1,10000000>	std::ratio<1,1000000000>
utc_clock	is_steady	false	false
	period	std::ratio<1,10000000>	std::ratio<1,1000000000>
steady_clock	is_steady	true	true
	period	std::ratio<1,1000000000>	std::ratio<1,1000000000>
high_resolution_clock	is_steady	true	false
	period	std::ratio<1,1000000000>	std::ratio<1,1000000000>

CHAPTER 16　TIME LIBRARY

Example Ch16_03_ex2(), shown in Listing 16-3-2, opens with the definition of chrono::time_point<chrono::system_clock> tp1_sys {}. Note that a chrono::timepoint object requires a clock class as a template parameter. The specified clock's epoch is utilized when performing certain chrono::time_point operations. The next statement instantiates tp1_utc as a chrono::utc_clock.

Listing 16-3-2. Example Ch16_03 – Ch16_03_ex2()

```
void Ch16_03_ex2()
{
    // using chrono::time_point
    chrono::time_point<chrono::system_clock> tp1_sys {};
    chrono::time_point<chrono::utc_clock> tp1_utc {};

    // print epochs
    // %F = yyyy-mm-dd, %X = locale's time format, %Z = time zone
    std::println("\ntp1_sys epoch: {0:%F} {0:%X} {0:%Z}", tp1_sys);
    std::println("\ntp1_utc epoch: {0:%F} {0:%X} {0:%Z}", tp1_utc);

    // using chrono::system_clock
    auto tp2_sys = chrono::system_clock::now();
    auto tp2_sys_tse = tp2_sys.time_since_epoch();
    std::println("\ntp2_sys: {0:%F} {0:%X} {0:%Z}", tp2_sys);
    std::println("tp2_sys.time_since_epoch(): {}", tp2_sys_tse);

    // using chrono::utc_clock
    auto tp2_utc = chrono::utc_clock::now();
    auto tp2_utc_tse = tp2_utc.time_since_epoch();
    std::println("\ntp2_utc: {0:%F} {0:%X} {0:%Z}", tp2_utc);
    std::println("tp2_utc.time_since_epoch(): {}", tp2_utc_tse);

    // calculate sys/utc time difference (number of leap seconds
    since epoch)
    auto tp2_delta = tp2_utc_tse - tp2_sys_tse;
    std::println("\ntp2_delta: {:%S}", tp2_delta);

    // using zoned time (current zone)
    chrono::zoned_time tp2_sys_zt(chrono::current_zone(), tp2_sys);
    std::println("\ntp2_sys: {0:%F} {0:%X} {0:%Z}", tp2_sys_zt);
```

```
    // using chrono::steady_clock
    auto tp3_start = chrono::steady_clock::now();
    std::this_thread::sleep_for(500ms);
    auto tp3_stop = chrono::steady_clock::now();
    auto tp3_diff = tp3_stop - tp3_start;
    auto tp3_diff_ms = chrono::duration_cast<chrono::milliseconds>
    (tp3_diff);

    std::println("\ntp3_diff:    {}", tp3_diff);
    std::println("tp3_diff_ms: {}", tp3_diff_ms);
}
```

The time default value for a chrono::timepoint is its clock's epoch. The next two std::println() statements print the epoch values for tp1_sys and tp1_utc. The important items to note here are the format specifiers used to print each epoch's date (%F for yyyy-mm-dd), time (%X for locale time), and time zone (%Z). The time library defines an extensive set of distinct format specifiers for date and times. You'll see other examples of these format specifiers later.

In the subsequent code block, Ch16_03_ex2() utilizes tp2_sys = chrono::system_clock::now() to obtain the current system time in UTC. The following statement, tp2_sys_tse = tp2_sys.time_since_epoch(), acquires a std::duration object that represents the amount of time between tp2_sys and its clock's epoch. The subsequent code block performs these same actions using chrono::utc_clock. Calculation of tp2_delta = tp2_utc_tse - tp2_sys_tse effectively determines the time difference between clocks of type chrono::system_clock and chrono:utc_clock. Note in the results section that the value of tp2_delta is marginally greater than 27 seconds. Recall that a chrono::utc_clock includes leap seconds, and, as I write this, there have been 27 leap seconds since the 1970-01-01 00:00:00 epoch.

To convert a time obtained using chrono::system_clock::now() from UTC to local time, Ch16_03_ex2() exploits class chrono::zoned_time as demonstrated in the next code block.

The final code block of Ch16_03_ex2() highlights the use of chrono::steady_clock::now(). Recall that instances of chrono::steady_clock() are useful for measuring time intervals. Note that sandwiched between the two calls to chrono::steady_clock::now() is a call to std::this_thread::sleep_for(500ms), which blocks execution of the current thread for a minimum of 500 milliseconds.

Execution of tp3_diff = tp3_stop - tp3_start computes the actual delay time, and tp3_diff_ms = chrono::duration_cast<chrono::milliseconds>(tp3_diff) casts this value to milliseconds.

The next chrono example function, shown in Listing 16-3-3, details how to carry out chrono::time_point additive arithmetic.

Listing 16-3-3. Example Ch16_03 – Ch16_03_ex3()

```
void Ch16_03_ex3()
{
    // %H = hours, %M = minutes, %S = decimal seconds
    auto print_tp = [](const char* msg, const auto& tp)
        { std::println("{0:<30s} {1:%F} {1:%H:%M:%S}", msg, tp); };

    // create time_point using specific date
    chrono::time_point<chrono::system_clock> tp = chrono::sys_days
    {2026y/7/4d};
    std::println("");
    print_tp("tp (initial value):", tp);

    // chrono::time_point arithmetic (date)
    tp += chrono::years(4) + chrono::months(5) + chrono::days(7);
    print_tp("tp (after date adjustments):", tp);

    // chrono::time_point arithmetic (time)
    tp += 12h + 30min + 45s + 123ms + 456us;
    print_tp("tp (after time adjustments):", tp);
}
```

In Listing 16-3-3, Ch16_03_ex3() utilizes chrono::time_point<chrono::system_clock> tp = chrono::sys_days {2026y/7/4d} to initialize tp to a specific date. Note that chrono literal suffixes are employed for the years and days in this expression. Following its initialization, tp equals 2026-07-04 00:00:00.

The ensuing two code blocks demonstrate chrono::time_point additive arithmetic. The first additive expression exploits chrono::duration aliases from Table 16-2 for dates, while the second one applies literal suffixes for time quantities. When performing arithmetic using chrono::timepoints, always keep in mind that this arithmetic is carried out using the chrono::durations from Table 16-2. Leap seconds are accounted

CHAPTER 16　TIME LIBRARY

for if a chrono::time_point's clock is a chrono::utc_clock. Class chrono::time_point also supports subtractive arithmetic using operator- and operator-=. You can also use operator++ and operator-- to adjust the year of a chrono::time_point.

Listing 16-3-4 shows the source code for example Ch16_03_ex4(). This function illustrates how to use chrono::time_point relational operators.

Listing 16-3-4. Example Ch16_03 - Ch16_03_ex4()

```
void Ch16_03_ex4()
{
    // initialize chrono::time_points (%T = %H:%M:%S)
    auto tp1 = chrono::system_clock::now();
    std::this_thread::sleep_for(300ms);
    auto tp2 = chrono::system_clock::now();
    std::this_thread::sleep_for(200ms);
    auto tp3 = chrono::system_clock::now();

    std::println("tp1: {0:%F} {0:%T}", tp1);
    std::println("tp2: {0:%F} {0:%T}", tp2);
    std::println("tp3: {0:%F} {0:%T}", tp3);

    // perform chrono::time_point compares
    auto cmp_tp = [](const auto& tp1, const auto& tp2)
    {
        std::print("\ntp1 == tp2: {:5s}", tp1 == tp2);
        std::println("  tp1 != tp2: {:5s}", tp1 != tp2);
        std::print("tp1 <  tp2: {:5s}", tp1 <  tp2);
        std::println("  tp1 <= tp2: {:5s}", tp1 <= tp2);
        std::print("tp1 >  tp2: {:5s}", tp1 >  tp2);
        std::println("  tp1 >= tp2: {:5s}", tp1 >= tp2);
    };

    cmp_tp(tp1, tp2);
    cmp_tp(tp3, tp1);
}
```

The opening code block of Ch16_03_ex4() initializes chrono::time_points tp1, tp2, and tp3 using chrono::system_clock::now(). The two calls to std::this_thread::sleep_for() are included to ensure value differences between tp1, tp2, and tp3 since now() might return the same value. The std::print() statements in lambda cmp_op() include all six standard relational operators. As you can see, performing comparisons using chrono::time_points is basically the same as fundamental types.

The final example function of this section, Ch16_03_ex5(), spotlights the use of chrono::time_point mathematical operations. The code in Listing 16-3-5 commences with the initialization of tp_now = chrono::system_clock::now(). Execution of the next statement, tp_cast = chrono::time_point_cast<chrono::milliseconds>(tp_now), casts the value of tp_now to milliseconds (i.e., a new std::duration) and saves the result to tp_cast.

Listing 16-3-5. Example Ch16_03 – Ch16_03_ex5()

```
void Ch16_03_ex5()
{
    auto tp_now = chrono::system_clock::now();
    std::println("tp_now:   {0:%F} {0:%T}", tp_now);

    // using chrono::time_point_cast
    auto tp_cast = chrono::time_point_cast<chrono::milliseconds>(tp_now);
    std::println("\ntp_cast:  {0:%F} {0:%T}", tp_cast);

    // using chrono::ceil, chrono::floor, chrono::round
    auto tp_ceil  = chrono::ceil<chrono::microseconds>(tp_now);
    auto tp_floor = chrono::floor<chrono::microseconds>(tp_now);
    auto tp_round = chrono::round<chrono::microseconds>(tp_now);

    std::println("\ntp_ceil:  {0:%F} {0:%T}", tp_ceil);
    std::println("tp_floor: {0:%F} {0:%T}", tp_floor);
    std::println("tp_round: {0:%F} {0:%T}", tp_round);
}
```

The final code block of Ch16_03_ex5() illustrates the use of chrono::ceil(), chrono::floor(), and chrono::round(). These three functions carry out mathematical rounding operations (up, down, and nearest) using chrono::time_points. The results for example Ch16_03 follow this paragraph. These results will vary depending on the compiler and target system.

----- Results for example Ch16_03 -----

----- Ch16_03_ex1() -----

clk1 (chrono::system_clock)
type name: struct std::chrono::system_clock
is_steady: false
period: struct std::ratio<1,10000000>

clk2 (chrono::utc_clock)
type name: class std::chrono::utc_clock
is_steady: false
period: struct std::ratio<1,10000000>

clk3 (chrono::steady_clock)
type name: struct std::chrono::steady_clock
is_steady: true
period: struct std::ratio<1,1000000000>

clk4 (chrono::high_resolution_clock)
type name: struct std::chrono::steady_clock
is_steady: true
period: struct std::ratio<1,1000000000>

----- Ch16_03_ex2() -----

tp1_sys epoch: 1970-01-01 00:00:00 UTC

tp1_utc epoch: 1970-01-01 00:00:00 UTC

tp2_sys: 2024-06-01 20:28:47 UTC
tp2_sys.time_since_epoch(): 17172737276003474[1/10000000]s

tp2_utc: 2024-06-01 20:28:47 UTC
tp2_utc.time_since_epoch(): 17172737546003588[1/10000000]s

tp2_delta: 27.0000114

tp2_sys: 2024-06-01 15:28:47 CDT

tp3_diff: 511917400ns
tp3_diff_ms: 511ms

```
----- Ch16_03_ex3() -----
```

tp (initial value):   2026-07-04 00:00:00.0000000
tp (after date adjustments):   2030-12-10 03:42:18.0000000
tp (after time adjustments):   2030-12-10 16:13:03.1234560

```
----- Ch16_03_ex4() -----
tp1: 2024-06-01 20:28:48.1515212
tp2: 2024-06-01 20:28:48.4642883
tp3: 2024-06-01 20:28:48.6673747

tp1 == tp2: false   tp1 != tp2: true
tp1 <  tp2: true    tp1 <= tp2: true
tp1 >  tp2: false   tp1 >= tp2: false

tp1 == tp2: false   tp1 != tp2: true
tp1 <  tp2: false   tp1 <= tp2: false
tp1 >  tp2: true    tp1 >= tp2: true

----- Ch16_03_ex5() -----
tp_now:   2024-06-01 20:28:48.6675935

tp_cast:  2024-06-01 20:28:48.667

tp_ceil:  2024-06-01 20:28:48.667594
tp_floor: 2024-06-01 20:28:48.667593
tp_round: 2024-06-01 20:28:48.667594
```

More Clocks and Timepoints

In Listing 16-4-1, example function Ch16_01_ex4() demonstrates the use of additional chrono format specifiers.

CHAPTER 16　TIME LIBRARY

Listing 16-4-1. Example Ch16_04 - Ch16_04_ex1()

```
//--------------------------------------------------------------------------
// Ch16_04_ex.cpp
//--------------------------------------------------------------------------
#include <chrono>
#include <string>
#include <typeinfo>
#include <vector>
#include "Ch16_04.h"

namespace chrono = std::chrono;
using namespace std::chrono_literals;

void Ch16_04_ex1()
{
    // display current UTC time
    auto now_sys = chrono::system_clock::now();
    std::println("now_sys:     {0:%F} {0:%X} {0:%Z}", now_sys);

    // using zoned time (current zone)
    chrono::zoned_time now_sys_zt(chrono::current_zone(), now_sys);

    // %r = %H:%M (locale's 12 hour time), %c = locale's date and time
    std::println("\nother formatting examples using now_sys_zt");
    std::println("now_sys_zt:  {0:%F} {0:%X} {0:%Z}", now_sys_zt);
    std::println("12 hour time: {0:%F} {0:%r}", now_sys_zt);
    std::println("explicit YMD: {0:%Y}-{0:%m}-{0:%d}", now_sys_zt);
    std::println("explicit MDY: {0:%m}/{0:%d}/{0:%y}", now_sys_zt);
    std::println("locale:      {0:%c}", now_sys_zt);

    // using zoned time (explicit zones)
    std::vector<std::string> zones
        { "America/New_York", "Europe/Berlin", "Asia/Kolkata",
          "Asia/Shanghai","Asia/Tokyo", "America/Vancouver" };

    std::println("\ndate and time using explicit zones");

    for (auto zone : zones)
```

```
    {
        chrono::zoned_time now_sys_zt {zone, now_sys};
        std::println("{0:25s} {1:%F} {1:%X} {1:%Z}", zone, now_sys_zt);
    }
}
```

The opening code block of this function employs now_sys = chrono::system_clock::now() and chrono::zoned_time now_sys_zt(chrono::current_zone(), now_sys) to obtain the current system and zoned times. The subsequent code block prints now_sys_zt using a variety of chrono format specifiers. The new specifiers to note here are %r (locale's HH:MM 12-hour time) and %c (locale's date and time). Appendix B contains a reference that you can consult for additional information regarding chrono format specifiers, including the large number of specifiers not exercised in this book.

The final code block of Ch16_04_ex1() demonstrates how to format a time for a specific global time zone. In this code block, std::vector<std::string> zones contain area/location strings for several global time zones from the IANA time zone database (see Appendix B for a reference). In the subsequent range for loop, execution of chrono::zoned_time now_sys_zt {zone, now_sys} converts time now_sys from UTC to zone's local time. The std::println() statement that follows prints this value.

Listing 16-4-2 shows the source code for example Ch16_02_ex4(). The opening code block of this example demonstrates how to calculate the number of leap seconds inserted on or before a particular date. Execution of sys_days1 = chrono::sys_days(2000y/1/1d) instantiates a chrono::time_point for 2000-01-01. The next two statements, sys_seconds1 = chrono::sys_seconds(sys_days1) and sys_tse1 = sys_seconds1.time_since_epoch(), calculate the number of seconds since sys_day1's epoch.

Listing 16-4-2. Example Ch16_04 – Ch16_04_ex2()

```
//#define PRINT_TYPE_INFO     // remove comment to print type info

void Ch16_04_ex2()
{
    // calculate number of leap seconds since 2000-01-01
    auto sys_days1 = chrono::sys_days(2000y/1/1d);
    auto sys_seconds1 = chrono::sys_seconds(sys_days1);
    auto sys_tse1 = sys_seconds1.time_since_epoch();
```

```cpp
    auto utc_seconds1 = chrono::clock_cast<chrono::utc_clock>
    (sys_seconds1);
    auto utc_tse1 = utc_seconds1.time_since_epoch();
    auto num_leap_seconds1 = utc_tse1 - sys_tse1;

    std::println("sys_days1:         {0:%F} {0:%X} {0:%Z}", sys_days1);
    std::println("sys_tse1:          {}", sys_tse1);
    std::println("utc_tse1:          {}", utc_tse1);
    std::println("num_leap_seconds1: {}", num_leap_seconds1);

    // calculate number of leap seconds since now()
    auto tp_now = chrono::system_clock::now();
    auto tp_now_utc = chrono::clock_cast<chrono::utc_clock>(tp_now);
    auto tp_tse_delta = tp_now_utc.time_since_epoch() - tp_now.time_since_epoch();
    auto num_leap_seconds2 = chrono::duration_cast<chrono::seconds>
    (tp_tse_delta);

    std::println("\ntp_now:          {0:%F} {0:%X} {0:%Z}", tp_now);
    std::println("num_leap_seconds2: {}", num_leap_seconds2);

    // confirm chrono class types
#ifdef PRINT_TYPE_INFO
    std::println("\nsys_day1:    {:s}", typeid(sys_days1).name());
    std::println("sys_seconds1: {:s}", typeid(sys_seconds1).name());
    std::println("sys_tse1:     {:s}", typeid(sys_tse1).name());
    std::println("utc_seconds1: {:s}", typeid(utc_seconds1).name());
#endif

    static_assert(typeid(sys_days1)
        == typeid(chrono::time_point<chrono::system_clock, chrono::days>));
    static_assert(typeid(sys_seconds1)
        == typeid(chrono::time_point<chrono::system_clock,
        chrono::seconds>));
    static_assert(typeid(sys_tse1) == typeid(chrono::seconds));
    static_assert(typeid(utc_seconds1)
        == typeid(chrono::time_point<chrono::utc_clock, chrono::seconds>));
}
```

Execution of utc_seconds1 = chrono::clock_cast<chrono::utc_clock>(sys_seconds1) converts sys_seconds1 time from a chrono::system_clock to a chrono::utc_clock. The ensuing statement, utc_tse1 = utc_seconds1.time_since_epoch(), obtains the number of seconds since sys_day1's epoch using a chrono::utc_clock. Calculation of num_leap_seconds1 = utc_tse1 - sys_tse1 yields the number of leap seconds since sys_days1.

The next code block illustrates how to determine the number of leap seconds since tp_now = chrono::system_clock::now(). To achieve this, Ch16_04_ex2() calculates tp_now_utc, which is tp_now's time based on a chrono::utc_clock. It then computes tp_tse_delta = tp_now_utc.time_since_epoch() - tp_now.time_since_epoch() and converts this value to seconds using num_leap_seconds2 = chrono::duration_cast<chrono::seconds>(tp_tse_delta).

The time library contains a large number of classes, and it's easy to get confused about a particular object's exact type. The final code block of Ch16_04_ex2() highlights the use of typeid() and static_assert() to view or confirm class types. Application of these language features is often helpful during initial development or when tracking down an obscure bug involving chrono objects. Here are the results for example Ch16_04:

```
----- Results for example Ch16_04 -----

----- Ch16_04_ex1() -----
now_sys:        2024-06-01 20:28:48 UTC

other formatting examples using now_sys_zt
now_sys_zt:     2024-06-01 15:28:48 CDT
12 hour time:   2024-06-01 03:28:48 PM
explicit YMD:   2024-06-01
explicit MDY:   06/01/24
locale:         06/01/24 15:28:48

date and time using explicit zones
America/New_York         2024-06-01 16:28:48 EDT
Europe/Berlin            2024-06-01 22:28:48 GMT+2
Asia/Kolkata             2024-06-02 01:58:48 GMT+5:30
Asia/Shanghai            2024-06-02 04:28:48 GMT+8
Asia/Tokyo               2024-06-02 05:28:48 GMT+9
```

CHAPTER 16   TIME LIBRARY

```
America/Vancouver         2024-06-01 13:28:48 PDT

----- Ch16_04_ex2() -----
sys_days1:          2000-01-01 00:00:00 UTC
sys_tse1:           946684800s
utc_tse1:           946684822s
num_leap_seconds1:  22s

tp_now:             2024-06-01 20:28:48 UTC
num_leap_seconds2:  27s
```

Software Benchmarking

The final example of this chapter describes how to use chrono components to perform elementary software benchmarking. When developing an algorithm that makes heavy use of floating-point arithmetic, one critical decision involves the use of single- vs. double-precision values. Conventional wisdom suggests that a double-precision floating-point algorithm should take roughly twice as long to execute compared to a single-precision variant. One could accept this assertion as always being true, but it's always more prudent to base an important performance-precision trade-off decision using actual timing measurements.

Listing 16-5-1-1 shows the source code for example Ch16_05_ex1(). This example contains demonstration code that exercises a benchmarking timing class named BmTimer. Execution of Ch16_05_ex1() opens with the initialization of std::vector<float> vec0 and std::vector<double> vec1. Both of these vectors contain random values. The ensuing code block defines two lambda expressions, tr_f32() and tr_f64(), that perform identical calculations using single- and double-precision arithmetic, respectively.

Listing 16-5-1-1. Example Ch16_05 – Ch16_05_ex1()

```
//------------------------------------------------------------
// Ch16_05_ex.cpp
//------------------------------------------------------------

#include <algorithm>
#include <cmath>
```

CHAPTER 16   TIME LIBRARY

```cpp
#include <iostream>
#include <vector>
#include "Ch16_05.h"
#include "BmTimer.h"
#include "RN.h"

void Ch16_05_ex1()
{
    constexpr int rng_min {1};
    constexpr int rng_max {2000};
    constexpr size_t vec_size {10'000'000};

    // create test vectors
    auto vec0 = RN::get_vector<float>(vec_size, rng_min, rng_max);
    auto vec1 = RN::get_vector<double>(vec_size, rng_min, rng_max);

    // create test transformation lambdas (std::cbrt(x) is cube root of x)
    auto tr_f32 = [](float x) { return x + std::cbrt(x); };
    auto tr_f64 = [](double x) { return x + std::cbrt(x); };

    // create BmTimer using steady clock
    constexpr size_t num_iter {40};
    constexpr size_t num_alg {2};
    BmTimerSteadyClk bm_timer(num_iter, num_alg);

    std::print("example Ch16_05_ex1 is running, please wait ");

    // execute test algorithms
    for (size_t i {0}; i < num_iter; ++i)
    {
        bm_timer.start(i, 0);
        std::ranges::transform(vec0, vec0.begin(), tr_f32);
        bm_timer.stop(i, 0);

        if (i % 4 == 0)
            std::cout << '.' << std::flush;
    }
```

```
    for (size_t i {0}; i < num_iter; ++i)
    {
        bm_timer.start(i, 1);
        std::ranges::transform(vec1, vec1.begin(), tr_f64);
        bm_timer.stop(i, 1);

        if (i % 4 == 0)
            std::cout << '.' << std::flush;
    }

    // save results to CSV file
    std::println("");
    std::string fn {"Ch16_05_ex1_results.csv"};
    bm_timer.save_to_csv(fn, "{:..2f}", BmTimerSteadyClk::EtUnit::MilliSec);
    std::println("Benchmark times save to file {:s}", fn);
}
```

The next code block in Ch16_05_ex1() instantiates BmTimerSteadyClk bm_timer(num_iter, num_alg). Class BmTimerSteadyClock is an alias for BmTimer<std::chrono::steady_clock> that exploits elements of the time library to perform benchmark timing measurements. The two constructor arguments for bm_timer, num_iter and num_alg, correspond to the number of test iterations and the number of test algorithms, respectively.

Each for loop in Ch16_05_ex1() performs num_iter executions of a test algorithm using a previously defined vector and lambda. In the first for loop, execution of bm_timer.start(i, 0) records the start time for the *i*-th iteration of std::ranges::transform(vec0, vec0.begin(), tr_f32). Similarly, execution of bm_timer.stop(i, 0) records the stop time. The second for loop performs the same actions using tr_f64(). Following the execution of both for loops, Ch16_05_ex1() utilizes bm_timer.save_to_csv(fn, "{:..2f}", BmTimerSteadyClk::EtUnit::MilliSec) to save bm_timer's time measurements to CSV file.

Listing 16-5-1-2 shows the source code for template class BmTimer. Note that this class specifies a template parameter named CLK. This parameter represents the chrono clock class that BmTimer uses to record time values. Next in Listing 16-5-1-2 is the definition of chrono::time_point alias TP and an enum class named EtUnit. This enum defines time units for member function BmTimer::save_to_csv().

Listing 16-5-1-2. *Example Ch16_05 – Class BmTimer*

```cpp
//-------------------------------------------------------------------
// BmTimer.h
//-------------------------------------------------------------------
#ifndef BM_TIMER_H_
#define BM_TIMER_H_
#include <chrono>
#include <format>
#include <fstream>
#include <stdexcept>
#include <string>
#include <vector>
#include "Common.h"

template <class CLK>
class BmTimer
{
    // time point alias
    using TP = std::chrono::time_point<CLK, typename CLK::duration>;
public:
    enum class EtUnit
        { NanoSec, MicroSec, MilliSec, Sec, Default = Sec };

    BmTimer() = delete;

    BmTimer(size_t num_iter, size_t num_alg) : m_NumIter {num_iter},
        m_NumAlg {num_alg}
    {
        static_assert(CLK::is_steady);

        m_StartTimes.resize(num_iter * num_alg);
        m_StopTimes.resize(num_iter * num_alg);
    }

    void save_to_csv(const std::string& fn, const char* fmt,
                     EtUnit et_unit = EtUnit::Default)
```

```cpp
{
    namespace chrono = std::chrono;

    std::ofstream ofs(fn);

    if (!ofs.good())
        throw std::runtime_error("BmTimer::save_to_csv - file open
        error");

    for (size_t i = 0; i < m_NumIter; ++i)
    {
        for (size_t j = 0; j < m_NumAlg; ++j)
        {
            auto t_start =  m_StartTimes[i * m_NumAlg + j];
            auto t_stop = m_StopTimes[i * m_NumAlg + j];
            auto t_temp1 = t_stop - t_start;
            auto t_temp2 =
                chrono::duration_cast<std::chrono::duration<double>>
                (t_temp1);

            double t_elapsed = static_cast<double>(t_temp2.count());
            // seconds

            switch (et_unit)
            {
                case EtUnit::NanoSec:
                    t_elapsed *= 1.0e9;
                    break;

                case EtUnit::MicroSec:
                    t_elapsed *= 1.0e6;
                    break;

                case EtUnit::MilliSec:
                    t_elapsed *= 1.0e3;
                    break;

                default:
                    break;
```

```cpp
            }

            // write formatted time to output file
            const char* sep = (j + 1 < m_NumAlg) ? ", " : "\n";
            std::string s {std::vformat(fmt, std::make_format_args
                (t_elapsed))};
            std::print(ofs, "{:s}", s);
            std::print(ofs, "{:s}", sep);
        }
    }

    ofs.close();
}

void start(size_t iter_id, size_t alg_id)
    { m_StartTimes[iter_id * m_NumAlg + alg_id] = CLK::now(); }

void stop(size_t iter_id, size_t alg_id)
    { m_StopTimes[iter_id * m_NumAlg + alg_id] = CLK::now(); }
private:
    size_t m_NumIter {};
    size_t m_NumAlg {};
    std::vector<TP> m_StartTimes {};
    std::vector<TP> m_StopTimes {};
};

// convenience aliases
using BmTimerSteadyClk = BmTimer<std::chrono::steady_clock>;
using BmTimerHighResClk = BmTimer<std::chrono::high_resolution_clock>;

#endif
```

The first statement of class BmTimer's constructor, static_assert(CLK::is_steady), ensures that BmTimer's specified clock class is a steady clock.[4] The subsequent two statements resize vectors m_StartTimes and m_StopTimes using the provided arguments.

---

[4] Using a non-steady clock may yield invalid results.

Next in Listing 16-5-1-2 is the definition of member function save_to_csv(). Execution of this function performs elapsed time calculations using the values in m_StartTimes and m_StopTimes. It also writes these values to the designated CSV file using the time units specified by argument et_unit.

Class BmTimer member functions start() and stop() record times to either m_StartTimes or m_StopTimes using CLK::now(). In these functions, vectors m_StartTimes and m_StopTimes are interpreted as 2D arrays. Calculation of iter_id * m_NumAlg + alg_id ensures that a timing measurement is stored at the correct "row" and "column."

The final two statements of Listing 16-5-1-2 define two BmTimer convenience aliases named BmTimerSteadyClk and BmTimerHighResClk. Recall that chrono::steady_clock is always monotonic, while the monotonicity of chrono::high_resolution_clock is optional.

Table 16-5 summarizes the timing measurements obtained by running Ch16_05's code on two test computers.[5] Note that the single-precision algorithm is faster than its double-precision counterpart, but the ratio is closer than one might expect.

Table 16-5. *Benchmark Performance Results for Example Ch16_05 – Mean (Standard Deviation) in Milliseconds*

Platform	Single-Precision	Double-Precision	Ratio (Double/Single)
Test Computer #1	260.7 (3.4)	359.7 (2.1)	1.38
Test Computer #2	91.6 (0.2)	103.5 (0.4)	1.13

Ch16_05's primary purpose is to provide another interesting and practical example of time library features. Its secondary aim is to serve as a reminder that it's often imprudent to make critical design decisions regarding the performance of an algorithm based on conjecture or mistaken assumptions. Always carry out measurements using techniques that are appropriate for the specific use case.

---

[5] See Appendix A for specification information regarding the test computers.

Summary

Here are the key learning points for this chapter:

- An instance of class `std::ratio` represents a finite rational number using an integer (`std::intmax_t`) numerator and denominator, which are compile-time constants. Time library classes such as `chrono::duration` and `chrono::time_point` utilize `std::ratio`s to carry out compile-time error checks and simplify time calculations.

- An instance of `chrono::duration` measures the amount of time between two points in time. Each `chrono::duration` holds a tick count and a tick period in seconds. A `chrono::duration` is a rational constant and is programmatically expressed using a `std::ratio`.

- A time library clock bundles an epoch and a tick period. A clock's tick period in seconds is represented using a `std::ratio`. Table 16-3 summarizes important aspects of each time library clock.

- A `chrono::time_point` represents a point in time. It's implemented as a positive or negative time interval (`std::duration`) from a clock's epoch.

- STL template class `std::formatter<std::chrono::sys_time>` defines default formatting rules for time library objects. When using `std::println()` or `std::format()`, you can also use one of the many explicit specifiers to format a date or time.

CHAPTER 17

File Systems

This chapter explains important file system classes and functions. It also describes useful programming techniques that you can exploit to perform universal file system operations. Topics discussed include

- Class `std::filesystem::path`
- Class `std::filesystem::recursive_directory_iterator`
- Class `std::filesystem::directory_entry`
- Directory creation and removal functions
- Directory and file copy functions
- File type functions

STL's file system classes and functions are defined in namespace `std::filesystem`. References to this namespace in the text and source code are prefixed using `fs::`. Prefix `chrono::` is also employed for time library classes from namespace `std::chrono`. The discussions in this chapter assume that you have a basic understanding of Windows, Linux, or macOS directories, files, and pathnames.

File System Path Classes

One of namespace `std::filesystem`'s most useful classes is `fs::path`. An instance of class `fs::path` encompasses a character string pathname that denotes a file system path. This representation involves only lexical and syntactical aspects. Principal details to understand about class `fs:path` include

- Elements of a path include a root name, root directory, and a sequence of filenames partitioned using separator characters. The root name and root directory components of a `fs::path` are optional.

- Class fs::path supports a variety of pathname representations, including absolute, relative, and canonical.

- A fs::path object does not necessarily correspond to the existence of an actual directory or file on a storage device.

- The pathname encompassed by a fs::path object is not guaranteed to be valid for a particular operating system or any of its supported file systems.

- The maximum length of a fs::path's pathname is established by the operating system. The operating system also determines valid pathname characters.

Example function Ch17_01_ex1(), shown in Listing 17-1-1, introduces class fs::path. In its opening code block, Ch17_01_ex1() utilizes fs::path path1 = fs::current_path() to obtain the current working directory. Execution of fs::current_path() returns an absolute pathname in native OS format (e.g., X:\CppSTL\SourceCode\Chapter17 or /home/homer/CppSTL/Code/Chapter17). The subsequent std::println() statement utilizes path1.string() to print path1's pathname.[1] The next statement in Listing 17-1-1, path1.append("test1.txt"), appends either \test1.txt or /test1.txt to path1. Note that the appended text includes an OS-specific separator character.

Listing 17-1-1. Example Ch17_01 – Ch17_01_ex1()

```
//-----------------------------------------------------------------------
// Ch17_01_ex.cpp
//-----------------------------------------------------------------------

#include <filesystem>
#include <fstream>
#include "Ch17_01.h"
#include "MF.h"

namespace fs = std::filesystem;

void Ch17_01_ex1()
```

---

[1] C++26 defines a new specialization, std::formatter<std::filesystem::path>, that facilitates direct formatting of fs::path objects using std::println(), std::format(), etc.

CHAPTER 17 FILE SYSTEMS

```cpp
{
    // using fs::current_path
    fs::path path1 = fs::current_path();
    std::println("\npath1: {:s}", path1.string());
    path1.append("test1.txt");
    std::println("path1: {:s}", path1.string());

    // using fs::temp_directory_path
    fs::path path2 = fs::temp_directory_path();
    std::println("\npath2: {:s}", path2.string());
    path2 /= "test2.txt";
    std::println("path2: {:s}", path2.string());

    // using fs::current_path - bad path
    fs::path path3 = fs::current_path();
    std::println("\npath3: {:s}", path3.string());
    path3 /= "Bad//Filename.txt";
    std::println("path3: {:s}", path3.string());

    std::ofstream ofs(path3);
    std::println("\nofs.good(): {:s} (expecting false)", ofs.good());
}
```

The next code block in Listing 17-1-1 exploits `fs::path path2 = fs::temp_directory_path()` to obtain the current temporary directory. The directory path returned by `fs::temp_directory_path()` is guaranteed to exist. In the same code block, execution of `path2 /= "test2.txt"` appends an OS-specific directory separator to path2 (if necessary) followed by the text `test2.txt`.

The final code block of `Ch17_01_ex1()` utilizes `fs::path path3 = fs::current_path()` and `path3 /= "Bad//Filename.txt"` to form an invalid pathname for demonstration purposes. Recall that the pathname represented by a `fs::path` object need not be valid. However, using path3 to create a file will fail as shown during the instantiation of `std::ofstream ofs(path3)`.

In Listing 17-1-2, example function `Ch17_01_ex2()` exercises `fs::path path1 = fs::current_path() / "test1.txt"` to create an absolute pathname for file test1.txt in the current working directory. The subsequent code block demonstrates the use of various `fs::path` decomposition functions that extract distinct components of a `fs::path`.

CHAPTER 17 FILE SYSTEMS

Listing 17-1-2. Example Ch17_01 - Ch17_01_ex2()

```
void Ch17_01_ex2()
{
    // create test path
    fs::path path1 = fs::current_path() / "test1.txt";
    std::println("path1:                 {:s}", path1.string());

    // using fs::path decomposition functions
    fs::path path1_root_name = path1.root_name();
    fs::path path1_root_dir = path1.root_directory();
    fs::path path1_root_path = path1.root_path();
    fs::path path1_relative_path = path1.relative_path();
    fs::path path1_parent_path = path1.parent_path();
    fs::path path1_filename = path1.filename();
    fs::path path1_stem = path1.stem();
    fs::path path1_extension = path1.extension();

    std::println("path1_root_name:       {:s}", path1_root_name.string());
    std::println("path1_root_dir:        {:s}", path1_root_dir.string());
    std::println("path1_root_path:       {:s}", path1_root_path.string());
    std::println("path1_relative_path:   {:s}", path1_relative_path.string());
    std::println("path1_parent_path:     {:s}", path1_parent_path.string());
    std::println("path1_filename:        {:s}", path1_filename.string());
    std::println("path1_stem:            {:s}", path1_stem.string());
    std::println("path1_extension:       {:s}", path1_extension.string());
}
```

All of the fs::path member functions used in Ch17_01_ex2() return objects of type fs::path. Tables 17-1 and 17-2 summarize the results obtained using test computers running Windows and Linux. Note in these tables that the decomposition functions properly handle the presence or absence of a drive letter (i.e., root name) specifier.

Table 17-1. *File System Decomposition Function Usage Results – Windows*

Path Component	Result
absolute path	X:\CppSTL\SourceCode\Chapter17\test1.txt
root_name	X:
root_dir	\
root_path	X:\
relative_path	CppSTL\SourceCode\Chapter17\test1.txt
parent_path	X:\CppSTL\SourceCode\Chapter17
filename	test1.txt
stem	test1
extension	.txt

Table 17-2. *File System Decomposition Function Usage Results – Linux*

Path Component	Result
absolute path	/home/homer/SambaWin/CppSTL/SourceCode/Chapter17/test1.txt
root_name	
root_dir	/
root_path	/
relative_path	home/homer/SambaWin/CppSTL/SourceCode/Chapter17/test1.txt
parent_path	/home/homer/SambaWin/CppSTL/SourceCode/Chapter17
filename	test1.txt
stem	test1
extension	.txt

CHAPTER 17 FILE SYSTEMS

The next example elucidates the use of common fs directory creation, existence, and removal functions. In Listing 17-1-3, execution of Ch17_01_ex3() begins with the initialization of fs::path sub_dir1 = fs::current_path() / "sub1". The ensuing code block utilizes rc = fs::exists(sub_dir1) to ascertain the existence of sub_dir1.

Listing 17-1-3. Example Ch17_01 – Ch17_01_ex3()

```
void Ch17_01_ex3()
{
    // initialize test subdirectory path
    fs::path sub_dir1 = fs::current_path() / "sub1";

    // using fs::exists
    bool rc = fs::exists(sub_dir1);
    std::println("\nfs::exists({:s})\nrc = {:s}", sub_dir1.string(), rc);

    if (!rc)
    {
        // using fs::create_directory
        rc = fs::create_directory(sub_dir1);
        std::println("\nfs::create_directory({:s})\nrc = {:s}",
            sub_dir1.string(), rc);

        if (!rc)
            return;
    }

    // write a test file to sub_dir1
    fs::path fn1 = sub_dir1 / "TestA.txt";
    rc = MF::create_test_file(fn1);
    std::println("\nwrite_test_file({:s})\nrc = {:s}", fn1.string(), rc);

    // using fs::exists
    rc = fs::exists(fn1);
    std::println("\nfs::exists({:s})\nrc = {:s}", fn1.string(), rc);

    // using fs::remove to delete test file
    rc = fs::remove(fn1);
    std::println("\nfs::remove({:s})\nrc = {:s}", fn1.string(), rc);
```

CHAPTER 17 FILE SYSTEMS

```
    // using fs::remove to delete test subdirectory (must be empty)
    rc = fs::remove(sub_dir1);
    std::println("\nfs::remove({:s})\nrc = {:s}", sub_dir1.string(), rc);
}
```

If sub_dir1 does not exist, Ch17_01_ex3() exercises rc = fs::create_directory(sub_dir1) to create it. File system function fs::create_directory(sub_dir1) returns true if it created the specified directory; otherwise, it returns false. A value of false is also returned if the specified directory already exists. This scenario is considered later in greater detail.

The next code block in Ch17_01_ex3() utilizes fs::path fn1 = sub_dir1 / "TestA.txt" and MF::create_test_file(fn1) (see Listing 17-2-2-2) to create test file fn1. Another example usage of fs:exists() follows. The penultimate code block of Ch17_01_ex3() exercises rc = fs::remove(fn1) to remove test file fn1. The execution of this function returns true if the specified file was deleted. The final code block of Ch17_01_ex3() exploits rc = fs::remove(sub_dir1) to delete sub_dir1. When using fs::remove() to delete a directory, the directory *must* be empty. Otherwise, a fs::filesystem_error exception may be thrown. File system exceptions are covered later in this chapter.

Listing 17-1-4 shows the source code for example Ch17_01_ex4(), which illustrates how to create and delete multiple levels of directories. The opening code block Ch17_01_ex4() utilizes fs::temp_directory_path() and several fs::path append operations to initialize fs::path sub_tree_top and fs::path sub_tree_bot. In the subsequent code block, execution of fs::create_directories(sub_tree_bot) creates directory sub_tree_bot including any required intermediate directories. For the current example, this creates the directory subtree d1/d2/d3/d4 in fs::temp_directory_path().

Listing 17-1-4. Example Ch17_01 - Ch17_01_ex4()

```
void Ch17_01_ex4()
{
    // create fs::paths
    fs::path base_dir = fs::temp_directory_path();
    fs::path sub_tree_top = base_dir / "d1";
    fs::path sub_tree_bot = sub_tree_top / "d2/d3/d4";
```

```cpp
    // path sub_tree_bot exists?
    bool rc = fs::exists(sub_tree_bot);
    std::println("\nfs::exists({:s})\nrc = {:s}", sub_tree_bot.
    string(), rc);

    if (!rc)
    {
        // using fs::create_directories to create sub_tree_bot
        rc = fs::create_directories(sub_tree_bot);
        std::println("\nfs::create_directories({:s})\nrc = {:s}",
            sub_tree_bot.string(), rc);

        if (!rc)
            return;
    }

    // write test file to sub_tree_top
    fs::path fn1 = sub_tree_top / "TestA.txt";
    rc = MF::create_test_file(fn1);
    std::println("\nfn1.generic_string(): {:s}", fn1.generic_string());
    std::println("fn1.string():          {:s}", fn1.string());
    std::println("rc:                    {:s}", rc);

    // write test file to sub_tree_bot
    fs::path fn2 = sub_tree_bot / "TestB.txt";
    rc = MF::create_test_file(fn2);
    std::println("\nfn2.generic_string(): {:s}", fn2.generic_string());
    std::println("fn2.string():          {:s}", fn2.string());
    std::println("rc:                    {:s}", rc);

    // using fs::remove_all to delete sub_tree_top
    auto num_deletes = fs::remove_all(sub_tree_top);
    std::println("\nfs::remove_all({:s})\nnum_deletes = {:d}",
        sub_tree_top.generic_string(), num_deletes);
}
```

CHAPTER 17   FILE SYSTEMS

The next code block in Ch17_01_ex4() utilizes MF::create_test_file(fn1) to create file fs::path fn1, whose value equals sub_tree_top / "TestA.txt". The ensuing std::println() statement exercises fn1.generic_string() to print the value of fn1. Execution of this function returns a std::string of fn1's encompassed pathname in fs generic format. This is different than fn1.string(), which returns a std::string in native OS format. Native pathnames are sometimes required when calling OS-specific API functions.

Execution of Ch17_01_ex4() continues with the creation of test file fs::path fn2 = sub_tree_bot / "TestB.txt" using MF::create_test_file(fn2). The final code block of Ch17_01_ex4() exploits num_deletes = fs::remove_all(sub_tree_top) to completely remove directory sub_tree_top including all files and lower-level subdirectories. Following execution of fs::remove_all(), num_deletes contains the total number of deleted directories and files. The results for example Ch17_01 follow this paragraph. For function Ch17_01_ex4(), note the difference between the generic and native pathname formats on a Windows system.

```
----- Results for example Ch17_01 -----

----- Ch17_01_ex1() -----

path1: X:\CppSTL\SourceCode\Chapter17
path1: X:\CppSTL\SourceCode\Chapter17\test1.txt

path2: C:\Users\dan\AppData\Local\Temp\
path2: C:\Users\dan\AppData\Local\Temp\test2.txt

path3: X:\CppSTL\SourceCode\Chapter17
path3: X:\CppSTL\SourceCode\Chapter17\Bad//Filename.txt

ofs.good(): false (expecting false)

----- Ch17_01_ex2() -----
path1:                 X:\CppSTL\SourceCode\Chapter17\test1.txt
path1_root_name:       X:
path1_root_dir:        \
path1_root_path:       X:\
path1_relative_path:   CppSTL\SourceCode\Chapter17\test1.txt
path1_parent_path:     X:\CppSTL\SourceCode\Chapter17
```

CHAPTER 17   FILE SYSTEMS

```
path1_filename:      test1.txt
path1_stem:          test1
path1_extension:     .txt

----- Ch17_01_ex3() -----

fs::exists(X:\CppSTL\SourceCode\Chapter17\sub1)
rc = false

fs::create_directory(X:\CppSTL\SourceCode\Chapter17\sub1)
rc = true

write_test_file(X:\CppSTL\SourceCode\Chapter17\sub1\TestA.txt)
rc = true

fs::exists(X:\CppSTL\SourceCode\Chapter17\sub1\TestA.txt)
rc = true

fs::remove(X:\CppSTL\SourceCode\Chapter17\sub1\TestA.txt)
rc = true

fs::remove(X:\CppSTL\SourceCode\Chapter17\sub1)
rc = true

----- Ch17_01_ex4() -----

fs::exists(C:\Users\dan\AppData\Local\Temp\d1\d2/d3/d4)
rc = false

fs::create_directories(C:\Users\dan\AppData\Local\Temp\d1\d2/d3/d4)
rc = true

fn1.generic_string(): C:/Users/dan/AppData/Local/Temp/d1/TestA.txt
fn1.string():         C:\Users\dan\AppData\Local\Temp\d1\TestA.txt
rc:                   true

fn2.generic_string(): C:/Users/dan/AppData/Local/Temp/d1/d2/d3/d4/TestB.txt
fn2.string():         C:\Users\dan\AppData\Local\Temp\d1\d2\d3\d4\TestB.txt
rc:                   true

fs::remove_all(C:/Users/dan/AppData/Local/Temp/d1)
num_deletes = 6
```

File System Directory Iterator Classes

For many applications, searching a directory for files is a common programming requirement. To handle this need, the file system library provides a set of classes that can be used to iterate the elements of a directory, its files, and any subdirectories. Listing 17-2-1 shows the source code for example Ch17_02_ex1(). This example describes how to use classes fs::recursive_directory_iterator and fs::directory_entry. It also covers a few ancillary functions related to these classes.

Listing 17-2-1. Example Ch17_01 – Ch17_02_ex1()

```
void Ch17_02_ex1()
{
    // NOTE - change code_path to book's source code directory on
    your system
#if defined(_WIN32) || defined(_WIN64)
    fs::path code_path = "x:\\CppSTL\\SourceCode";
#else
    fs::path code_path = "/home/homer/SambaWin/CppSTL/SourceCode";
#endif
    std::println("code_path: {:s}", code_path.string());

    // using fs::is_directory
    bool is_dir = fs::is_directory(code_path);
    std::println("fs::is_directory({:s}): {:s}", code_path.string(),
    is_dir);

    if (!is_dir)
        return;

    // initialize recursive_directory_iterator
    fs::directory_options options = fs::directory_options::skip_
    permission_denied;
    fs::recursive_directory_iterator rdi =
        fs::recursive_directory_iterator(code_path, options);

    // search for .cpp and .h files
    size_t num_files {0};
```

```
    size_t num_files_h {0};
    size_t num_files_cpp {0};

    for (const fs::directory_entry& dir_entry : rdi)
    {
        // using is_regular_file
        if (fs::is_regular_file(dir_entry))
        {
            // extract extension
            fs::path file = dir_entry.path();
            const std::string& file_ext = file.extension().string();

            // update file counts
            ++num_files;

            if (file_ext == ".cpp")
                ++num_files_cpp;
            else if (file_ext == ".h")
                ++num_files_h;
        }
    }

    std::println("\nnum_files:     {:d}", num_files);
    std::println("num_files_cpp: {:d}", num_files_cpp);
    std::println("num_files_h:   {:d}", num_files_h);
}
```

The opening code block of Ch17_02_ex1() initializes fs:path code_path to the root source code directory for this book. Before executing this example, you *must* change the value of code_path to the correct directory for your system.[2] In the next code block, file system function fs::is_directory(code_path) is exercised to confirm that code_path is a directory.

The first statement in the subsequent code block, fs::directory_options options = fs::directory_options::skip_permission_denied, sets traversal options for fs::recursive_directory_iterator. Option fs::directory_options::skip_permission_denied instructs fs::recursive_directory_iterator to skip any

---

[2] See Appendix A for more information regarding this book's source code.

directory that would generate a permission denied error. You can also specify fs::follow_directory_symlink, which enables traversals of any symbolic links. Execution of rdi = fs::recursive_directory_iterator(code_path, options) initializes a fs::recursive_directory_iterator that will be used to iterate over the fs::directory_entry elements of code_path and its subdirectories. Before continuing, it warrants mentioning that the current example uses explicit class names to accelerate understanding of classes that might be new to you. For production code, the use of keyword auto is probably a better option.

Each iteration of for (const fs::directory_entry& dir_entry : rdi) updates dir_entry so that it references the next element of [rdi.begin(), rdi.end()). The first range for loop statement, if (fs::is_regular_file(dir_entry)), tests dir_entry to see if it references a normal file. Table 17-3 lists other supported file type checks that can be performed using fs::directory_entry or fs::path objects. You'll study other examples of these functions throughout this chapter.

Table 17-3. Supported File Type Checks for fs::directory_entry and fs::path Objects

Name	fs::directory_entry	fs::path
is_block_file	Y	Y
is_character_file	Y	Y
is_directory	Y	Y
is_empty	N	Y
is_fifo	Y	Y
is_other	Y	Y
is_regular_file	Y	Y
is_socket	Y	Y
is_symlink	Y	Y
status_known	N	Y

If `fs::is_regular_file(dir_entry)` is true, `Ch17_02_ex1()` utilizes `fs::path file = dir_entry.path()` and `const std::string& file_ext = p.extension().string()` to obtain a reference to file's extension. The subsequent code block updates counters `num_files`, `num_files_cpp`, and `num_files_h`.

Many applications use temporary files to maintain intermediate results or other data. Over time, the number of old temporary files may become large enough to adversely affect overall system performance. Performing a periodic temporary file cleanup will help mitigate this condition. Listing 17-2-2-1 shows the source code for example `Ch17_02_ex2()`. This example demonstrates how to traverse the temporary file directory and identify old files based on a threshold value in days.

Listing 17-2-2-1. Example Ch17_01 – Ch17_02_ex2()

```
void Ch17_02_ex2()
{
    // set old file threshold in days
    constexpr chrono::days num_days {15};

    // base path for old file search
    fs::path base_path = fs::temp_directory_path();

    // get current time
    auto now = chrono::file_clock::now();

    // create old test files (ensures that some files are found)
    constexpr size_t num_levels {4};
    constexpr size_t num_files {3};
    fs::path test_path = base_path / "Ch17_02_ex3";

    std::println("test_path: {:s}", test_path.string());

    MF::create_test_files(test_path, "Ch17_02_ex3", num_levels, num_files,
        now, -num_days, false);

    // set recursive directory iterator options
    auto options = fs::directory_options::skip_permission_denied;
    auto rdi = fs::recursive_directory_iterator(base_path, options);
```

```
        size_t num_directories {};
        size_t num_old_files {};
        constexpr size_t num_old_files_print_max {25};

        // search base_path for old files
        for (auto const& dir_entry : rdi)
        {
            // using is_directory
            if (fs::is_directory(dir_entry))
                ++num_directories;

            // using is_regular_file
            if (fs::is_regular_file(dir_entry))
            {
                auto lwt = dir_entry.last_write_time();

                // found old file?
                if (now - lwt >= num_days)
                {
                    if (++num_old_files <= num_old_files_print_max)
                    {
                        auto s = MF::to_string(lwt);
                        std::println("old {:2d}: {:s} {:s}", num_old_files, s,
                            dir_entry.path().string());
                    }
                }
            }
        }

        // print counts and remove test_path
        std::println("\nnum_directories: {:d}", num_directories);
        std::println("num_old_files:   {:d}", num_old_files);
        fs::remove_all(test_path);
}
```

The opening code block in Ch17_02_ex2() initializes chrono::days num_days {15} as an old file threshold. Object fs::path base_path, which is the top-level traversal path, is then initialized using fs::temp_directory_path(). The next code block utilizes `auto now = chrono::file_clock::now()` to obtain the current time. Example Ch17_02_ex2() utilizes `chrono::file_clock` since this is the same clock that's used by other fs classes.

To ensure that the traversal code finds some files, Ch17_02_ex2() exploits `MF::create_test_files()` to create a small subtree of test directories and files under base_path. Listing 17-2-2-2 shows the source code for this function, which is discussed later. Following the call to `MF::create_test_files()`, Ch17_02_ex2() utilizes `auto options = fs::directory_options::skip_permission_denied` and `auto rdi = fs::recursive_directory_iterator(base_path, options)` to initialize a recursive directory iterator just like the previous example, except for the use of keyword `auto`.

The recursive directory iterator traversal code in Ch17_02_ex2() follows the same pattern as the previous example. The first code block within the range for loop exercises `fs::is_directory(dir_entry)` to count the number of directories in base_path. If `fs::is_regular_file(dir_entry)` is true, execution of `lwt = dir_entry.last_write_time()` acquires dir_entry's last data modification time. If (now - lwt >= num_days) is true, dir_entry is at least num_days old. Execution of `MF::to_string(lwt)` (see Common/MF.cpp) converts lwt to a `std::string` for display purposes. Note that the display code in the range for loop prints a maximum of num_old_files_print_max files. A call to `fs::remove(dir_entry.path())` can be inserted here to delete old file dir_entry.

Listing 17-2-2-2 shows the source code for `MF::create_test_files()`. As previously mentioned, this function creates a small subtree of directories and files under directory base_dir. Argument num_levels specifies the number of directory levels while num_files denotes the number of test files to create in each subdirectory. Arguments tp_base and tp_adj_days are used to set the last data modification time for each created test file as you'll soon see.

Listing 17-2-2-2. Example Ch17_02 – MF::create_test_files()

```
void MF::create_test_files(const fs::path& base_dir, const std::string&
base_name, size_t num_levels, size_t num_files,
    const chrono::time_point<chrono::file_clock>& tp_base, chrono::days
    tp_adj_days, bool verbose)
{
    // create base_dir
    if (fs::exists(base_dir))
    {
```

```cpp
        if (!fs::is_directory(base_dir))
            throw std::runtime_error("fs::is_directory() failed");
    }
    else
    {
        if (!fs::create_directory(base_dir))
            throw std::runtime_error("fs::create_directory() failed");
    }

    fs::path sub_dir = base_dir;

    // create subdirs and files
    for (size_t i = 0; i < num_levels; ++i)
    {
        sub_dir /= std::format("D{:02d}", i);

        if (!fs::exists(sub_dir))
        {
            if (!fs::create_directory(sub_dir))
                throw std::runtime_error("fs::create_directory() failed");
        }

        for (size_t j = 0; j < num_files; ++j)
        {
            fs::path fn = sub_dir /
                std::format("{:s}-{:02d}-{:02d}.txt", base_name, i, j);

            if (!MF::create_test_file(fn.string()))
                throw std::runtime_error("MF::create_test_file() failed");

            if (verbose)
                std::println("created {:s}", fn.string());

            // set last write_time
            if (tp_adj_days != chrono::days{0})
                fs::last_write_time(fn, tp_base + tp_adj_days);
        }
    }
}
```

CHAPTER 17 FILE SYSTEMS

```cpp
bool MF::create_test_file(const std::string& name, bool empty)
{
    // create test file
    std::ofstream ofs(name, std::ios_base::out | std::ios_base::trunc);

    if (!ofs.good())
        return false;

    if (!empty)
    {
        // write sample data to test file
        auto tp_now = chrono::system_clock::now();
        chrono::zoned_time tp_now_zt {chrono::current_zone(), tp_now};

        std::println(ofs, "test file:  {:s}", name);
        std::println(ofs, "created on: {0:%F} {0:%T} {0:%Z}", tp_now);
        std::println(ofs, "created on: {0:%F} {0:%T} {0:%Z}", tp_now_zt);
    }

    ofs.close();
    return !ofs.fail();
}

bool MF::create_test_file(const fs::path& name, bool empty)
{
    return MF::create_test_file(name.string(), empty);
}
```

The opening code block of MF::create_test_files() exercises fs::exists(base_dir), fs::is_directory(base_dir), and fs::create_directory(base_dir) to ensure that base_dir exists. The first code block in MF::create_test_files()'s outer for loop creates subdirectory sub_dir /= std::format("D{:02d}", i). The inner for loop creates test files named fs::path fn = sub_dir / std::format("{:s}-{:02d}-{:02d}.txt", base_name, i, j). For function Ch17_02_ex2(), the directory-file structure created by these for loops looks like the following:

```
Ch17_02_ex3\D00\Ch17_02_ex3-00-00.txt
Ch17_02_ex3\D00\Ch17_02_ex3-00-01.txt
Ch17_02_ex3\D00\Ch17_02_ex3-00-02.txt
Ch17_02_ex3\D00\D01\Ch17_02_ex3-01-00.txt
Ch17_02_ex3\D00\D01\Ch17_02_ex3-01-01.txt
Ch17_02_ex3\D00\D01\Ch17_02_ex3-01-02.txt
Ch17_02_ex3\D00\D01\D02\Ch17_02_ex3-02-00.txt
Ch17_02_ex3\D00\D01\D02\Ch17_02_ex3-02-01.txt
Ch17_02_ex3\D00\D01\D02\Ch17_02_ex3-02-02.txt
Ch17_02_ex3\D00\D01\D02\D03\Ch17_02_ex3-03-00.txt
Ch17_02_ex3\D00\D01\D02\D03\Ch17_02_ex3-03-01.txt
Ch17_02_ex3\D00\D01\D02\D03\Ch17_02_ex3-03-02.txt
```

The other item to note near the bottom of Listing 17-2-2-2 is the utilization of fs::last_write_time(fn, tp_base + tp_adj_days). Execution of this overload changes the last data modification time for file fn to tp_base + tp_adj_days. Recall that example function Ch17_02_ex2() called MF::create_test_files() using values now (chrono::file_clock::now()) and -num_days (chrono::days num_days {15}). This means that the new last data modification time for file fn is 15 days earlier than now.[3] The results for example Ch17_02 follow this paragraph. These results will vary depending on the target system.

```
----- Results for example Ch17_02 -----

----- Ch17_02_ex1() -----
code_path: x:\CppSTL\SourceCode
fs::is_directory(x:\CppSTL\SourceCode): true

num_files:      10219
num_files_cpp:  318
num_files_h:    175
```

---

[3] When using fs::last_write_time() to set a file time, the actual time may vary depending on the time granularity of the underlying file system.

```
----- Ch17_02_ex2() -----
test_path: C:\Users\dan\AppData\Local\Temp\Ch17_02_ex3
old  1: [2024-05-24 13:49:27]
C:\Users\dan\AppData\Local\Temp\Ch17_02_ex3\D00\Ch17_02_ex3-00-00.txt
old  2: [2024-05-24 13:49:27]
C:\Users\dan\AppData\Local\Temp\Ch17_02_ex3\D00\Ch17_02_ex3-00-01.txt
old  3: [2024-05-24 13:49:27]
C:\Users\dan\AppData\Local\Temp\Ch17_02_ex3\D00\Ch17_02_ex3-00-02.txt
old  4: [2024-05-24 13:49:27]
C:\Users\dan\AppData\Local\Temp\Ch17_02_ex3\D00\D01\Ch17_02_ex3-01-00.txt
old  5: [2024-05-24 13:49:27]
C:\Users\dan\AppData\Local\Temp\Ch17_02_ex3\D00\D01\Ch17_02_ex3-01-01.txt
old  6: [2024-05-24 13:49:27]
C:\Users\dan\AppData\Local\Temp\Ch17_02_ex3\D00\D01\Ch17_02_ex3-01-02.txt
old  7: [2024-05-24 13:49:27]
C:\Users\dan\AppData\Local\Temp\Ch17_02_ex3\D00\D01\D02\Ch17_02_
ex3-02-00.txt
old  8: [2024-05-24 13:49:27]
C:\Users\dan\AppData\Local\Temp\Ch17_02_ex3\D00\D01\D02\Ch17_02_
ex3-02-01.txt
old  9: [2024-05-24 13:49:27]
C:\Users\dan\AppData\Local\Temp\Ch17_02_ex3\D00\D01\D02\Ch17_02_
ex3-02-02.txt
old 10: [2024-05-24 13:49:27]
C:\Users\dan\AppData\Local\Temp\Ch17_02_ex3\D00\D01\D02\D03\Ch17_02_
ex3-03-00.txt
old 11: [2024-05-24 13:49:27]
C:\Users\dan\AppData\Local\Temp\Ch17_02_ex3\D00\D01\D02\D03\Ch17_02_
ex3-03-01.txt
old 12: [2024-05-24 13:49:27]
C:\Users\dan\AppData\Local\Temp\Ch17_02_ex3\D00\D01\D02\D03\Ch17_02_
ex3-03-02.txt

num_directories: 25
num_old_files:   12
```

File System Helper Functions

Namespace `std::filesystem` includes numerous helper functions that carry out useful operations using `fs::paths`. This section covers some of these functions. It also discusses exception class `fs::filesystem_error`.

Listing 17-3-1 shows the source code for `Ch17_03_ex1()`, which highlights the use of functions that generate various forms of a `fs::path` object.

Listing 17-3-1. Example Ch17_03 – Ch17_03_ex1()

```cpp
//------------------------------------------------------------------
// Ch17_03_ex.cpp
//------------------------------------------------------------------

#include <filesystem>
#include "Ch17_03.h"
#include "MF.h"

namespace fs = std::filesystem;

void Ch17_03_ex1()
{
    auto print_path_info = []
        (const char* msg, const fs::path& p)
    {
        // print paths
        std::println("\n{:s}", msg);
        std::println("raw string:     {:s}", p.string());
        std::println("generic string: {:s}", p.generic_string());

        // compose path forms
        fs::path absolute = fs::absolute(p);
        fs::path canonical = fs::canonical(p);
        fs::path relative = fs::relative(p);
        std::println("absolute:      {:s}", absolute.string());
        std::println("canonical:     {:s}", canonical.string());
        std::println("relative:      {:s}", relative.string());
    };
```

CHAPTER 17   FILE SYSTEMS

```
    // print_path_info example #1
    fs::path path1 = "../../test1.txt";
    MF::create_test_file(path1);
    print_path_info("path1 information:", path1);
    fs::remove(path1);

    // print_path_info example #2
    fs::path path2_base = fs::current_path() / "D0";
    fs::path path2 = path2_base / "D1/D2";
    fs::create_directories(path2);

    path2 /= "test2.txt";
    MF::create_test_file(path2);
    print_path_info("path2 information:", path2);
    fs::remove_all(path2_base);
}
```

Function Ch17_03_ex1() commences with the definition of lambda expression print_path_info(), which prints path information related to argument const fs::path& p. The first two std::println() statements in this lambda utilize p.string() and p.generic_string() to print the pathname encompassed in p. Recall that the former returns a std::string pathname in native OS format, while the latter returns a pathname in fs (i.e., std::filesystem) generic format.

The next three statements generate various fs::path formats. For example, fs::path absolute = fs::absolute(p) composes an unambiguous path to the file system object represented by p. Per the ISO C++23 specification, implementations are "strongly encouraged" to avoid file system queries and nonexistent file errors (i.e., fs::exists(p) is false) in fs::absolute(), but this is not guaranteed.

Next is fs::path canonical = fs::canonical(p), which composes an absolute path in fs generic format that lacks symbolic link, dot, or dot-dot elements. Execution of fs::canonical(p) throws an exception if the file specified by p does not exist.

The final path composition example, fs::path relative = fs::relative(p), composes a fs::path relative (non-absolute) to fs::current_path(). In this usage example, execution of fs::relative(p) throws an exception if an OS API error prevents successful composition of the relative path. More about this shortly.

The remaining code in Ch17_03_ex1() exercises print_path_info(). The first example uses fs::path path1 = "../../test1.txt" as a test path, while the second example uses fs::current_path() / "D0/D1/D2/test2.txt". Here's an example of the output that print_path_info() produced on a Windows system:

```
path1 information:
raw string:      ../../test1.txt
generic string:  ../../test1.txt
absolute:        X:\CppSTL\test1.txt
canonical:       \\carbon2\SambaShare\CppSTL\test1.txt
relative:        ..\..\test1.txt

path2 information:
raw string:      X:\CppSTL\SourceCode\Chapter17\D0\D1/D2\test2.txt
generic string:  X:/CppSTL/SourceCode/Chapter17/D0/D1/D2/test2.txt
absolute:        X:\CppSTL\SourceCode\Chapter17\D0\D1\D2\test2.txt
canonical:       \\carbon2\SambaShare\CppSTL\SourceCode\Chapter17\D0\D1\D2\
                 test2.txt
relative:        D0\D1\D2\test2.txt
```

For Linux, the output looks like this:

```
path1 information:
raw string:      ../../test1.txt
generic string:  ../../test1.txt
absolute:        /home/homer/SambaWin/CppSTL/SourceCode/Chapter17/../../
                 test1.txt
canonical:       /home/homer/SambaWin/CppSTL/test1.txt
relative:        ../../test1.txt

path2 information:
raw string:      /home/homer/SambaWin/CppSTL/SourceCode/Chapter17/D0/D1/D2/
                 test2.txt
generic string:  /home/homer/SambaWin/CppSTL/SourceCode/Chapter17/D0/D1/D2/
                 test2.txt
absolute:        /home/homer/SambaWin/CppSTL/SourceCode/Chapter17/D0/D1/D2/
                 test2.txt
```

```
canonical:      /home/homer/SambaWin/CppSTL/SourceCode/Chapter17/D0/D1/D2/
                test2.txt
relative:       D0/D1/D2/test2.txt
```

The std::filesystem examples presented thus far in this chapter have exercised function overloads that throw a fs::filesystem_error exception if an underlying OS API error occurs. Most fs functions also define a noexcept overload that returns error information via a std::error_code. Listing 17-3-2 shows the source code for example Ch17_03_ex2(), which demonstrates both error reporting methods in greater detail.

Listing 17-3-2. Example Ch17_03 – Ch17_03_ex2()

```
void create_dir(const char* msg, const fs::path& dir)
{
    std::println("\n{:s} - dir: {:s}", msg, dir.string());

    // using fs::create_directory (noexcept) and std::error_code
    std::error_code ec {};

    if (fs::create_directory(dir, ec))
        std::println("#1 - created directory {:s}", dir.string());
    else
    {
        if (!ec)
            std::println("#1 - directory {:s} already exists",
                dir.string());
        else
        {
            std::println("ec.value:   {:d}", ec.value());
            std::println("ec.message: {:s}", ec.message());
        }
    }

    // using fs::create_directory and fs::filesystem_error
    try
    {
        if (fs::create_directory(dir))
            std::println("#2 - created directory {:s}", dir.string());
```

```cpp
        else
            std::println("#2 - directory {:s} already exists",
                dir.string());
    }

    catch (const fs::filesystem_error& ex)
    {
        // std::exception information
        std::println("\ncaught fs::filesystem_error exception");
        std::println("what():           {:s}", ex.what());

        // fs::filesystem_error information
        std::println("path1():          {:s}", ex.path1().string());
        std::println("path2():          {:s}", ex.path2().string());
        std::println("code().value():   {:d}", ex.code().value());
        std::println("code().message(): {:s}", ex.code().message());
    }
}

void Ch17_03_ex2()
{
    // using create_dir with valid path
    fs::path dir1 = fs::temp_directory_path() / "good_dir_name";
    create_dir("test case #1", dir1);
    create_dir("test case #2", dir1);
    fs::remove(dir1);

    // using create_dir with invalid path
    fs::path dir2 = fs::temp_directory_path() / "bad//_dir_name";
    create_dir("test case #3", dir2);
}
```

Listing 17-3-2 opens with the definition of a function named create_dir(). Execution of this function exercises two different overloads of fs::create_directory().

Near the top of create_dir(), fs::create_directory(dir, ec) is utilized to create directory dir. This function returns true if dir is *newly* created; otherwise, false is returned. Note that a return value of false includes the case of an existing directory with the same name as dir. Should an OS API error occur during the execution of

CHAPTER 17 FILE SYSTEMS

fs::create_directory(dir, ec), an OS-specific error code is returned via argument std::error_code ec. If fs::create_directory(dir, ec) returns false, create_dir() tests ec to ascertain if dir already exists or if an OS API error occurred. If it's the latter, create_dir() prints ec.value() and ec.message(), which contain an OS-specific error code and message.

The second part of create_dir() utilizes fs::create_directory(dir) and a try-catch construct to create directory dir. Like its std::error_code overload counterpart, execution of fs::create_directory(dir) returns true if dir is newly created; otherwise, it returns false (dir already exists). Should an OS API occur that prevents successful creation of dir, fs::create_directory() throws a fs::filesystem_error exception.

In create_dir()'s catch block, ex.path1() returns a fs::path that corresponds to dir, while ex.code().value() and ex.code().message() contains OS-specific error information. More generally, when a fs function throws fs::filesystem_error exception& ex, ex.path1() corresponds to the first fs::path argument of the function that threw the exception, while ex.path2() corresponds to the second fs::path argument (if any). Execution of ex.code() returns a const std::error_code& reference that contains OS-specific information regarding the exception.

The C++ code in function Ch17_03_ex2() exercises create_dir() using both valid and invalid directory names.

Example Ch17_03_ex3(), shown in Listing 17-3-3, spotlights the use of additional file type checking functions from Table 17-3. Near the top of Listing 17-3-3 is the definition of lambda expression print_types(), which prints type information related to argument const fs::path& p if it exists. Note that this function utilizes std::error_code overloads to preclude the throwing of std::filesystem_error exceptions. The reason for this is that calling a fs::is_ function using a Windows-specific path (e.g., C:\Windows\notepad.exe) on a Linux system will generate a fs::filesystem_error exception.

Listing 17-3-3. Example Ch17_03 – Ch17_03_ex3()

```
void Ch17_03_ex3()
{
    auto print_types = [](const fs::path& p)
    {
        std::println("\npath: {:s}", p.string());

        // code below uses fs std::error_code overloads, which are noexcept
```

```cpp
        std::string s {"| "};
        std::error_code ec {};

        if (fs::exists(p, ec))
        {
            if (fs::is_block_file(p, ec))
                s += "is_block_file | ";
            if (fs::is_character_file(p, ec))
                s += "is_character_file | ";
            if (fs::is_directory(p, ec))
                s += "is_directory | ";
            if (fs::is_fifo(p, ec))
                s += "is_fifo | ";
            if (fs::is_other(p, ec))
                s += "is_other | ";
            if (fs::is_regular_file(p, ec))
                s += "is_regular_file | ";
            if (fs::is_socket(p, ec))
                s += "is_socket | ";
            if (fs::is_symlink(p, ec))
                s += "is_symlink | ";
            if (fs::is_empty(p, ec))
                s += "is_empty |";
        }
        else
            s += "does not exist |";

        if (s == "")
            s += "unknown or implementation specific |";

        std::println("{:s}", s);
};

// using create_directory
fs::path test_path1 = fs::temp_directory_path() / "Ch17_03_ex2";
fs::create_directory(test_path1);
fs::path test_path2 = test_path1 / "EmptyDir";
fs::create_directory(test_path2);
```

CHAPTER 17 FILE SYSTEMS

```cpp
    // create test files
    fs::path test_file1 = test_path1 / "test1-data-file.txt";
    MF::create_test_file(test_file1);
    fs::path test_file2 = test_path1 / "test2-empty-file.txt";
    MF::create_test_file(test_file2, true);

    // print types
    print_types(test_path1);
    print_types(test_path2);
    print_types(test_file1);
    print_types(test_file2);

    // test paths for Windows
    print_types("C:\\");
    print_types("C:\\Windows\\notepad.exe");
    print_types("\\\\carbon2\\projects");

    // test paths for Linux and similar operating systems
    print_types("/etc");
    print_types("/etc/fstab");
    print_types("/dev/sda");
    print_types("/dev/tty0");

    fs::remove_all(test_path1);
}
```

Following the definition of print_types(), Ch17_03_ex3() utilizes fs::create_directory() and MF::create_test_file() to create several test directories and files. The ensuing code block exploits print_types() to display type information about these files. The final two code blocks of Ch17_03_ex3() exercise print_types() using Windows- and Linux-specific fs::paths. Here are the results for example Ch17_03:

```
----- Results for example Ch17_03 -----

----- Ch17_03_ex1() -----

path1 information:
raw string:     ../../test1.txt
generic string: ../../test1.txt
```

716

```
absolute:      X:\CppSTL\test1.txt
canonical:     \\carbon2\SambaShare\CppSTL\test1.txt
relative:      ..\..\test1.txt

path2 information:
raw string:    X:\CppSTL\SourceCode\Chapter17\D0\D1/D2\test2.txt
generic string: X:/CppSTL/SourceCode/Chapter17/D0/D1/D2/test2.txt
absolute:      X:\CppSTL\SourceCode\Chapter17\D0\D1\D2\test2.txt
canonical:     \\carbon2\SambaShare\CppSTL\SourceCode\Chapter17\D0\D1\D2\
test2.txt
relative:      D0\D1\D2\test2.txt

----- Ch17_03_ex2() -----

test case #1 - dir: C:\Users\dan\AppData\Local\Temp\good_dir_name
#1 - created directory C:\Users\dan\AppData\Local\Temp\good_dir_name
#2 - directory C:\Users\dan\AppData\Local\Temp\good_dir_name already exists

test case #2 - dir: C:\Users\dan\AppData\Local\Temp\good_dir_name
#1 - directory C:\Users\dan\AppData\Local\Temp\good_dir_name already exists
#2 - directory C:\Users\dan\AppData\Local\Temp\good_dir_name already exists

test case #3 - dir: C:\Users\dan\AppData\Local\Temp\bad//_dir_name
ec.value:    3
ec.message: The system cannot find the path specified.

caught fs::filesystem_error exception
what():          create_directory: The system cannot find the path
specified.:
                 "C:\Users\dan\AppData\Local\Temp\bad//_dir_name"
path1():         C:\Users\dan\AppData\Local\Temp\bad//_dir_name
path2():
code().value():  3
code().message(): The system cannot find the path specified.

----- Ch17_03_ex3() -----

path: C:\Users\dan\AppData\Local\Temp\Ch17_03_ex2
| is_directory |
```

path: C:\Users\dan\AppData\Local\Temp\Ch17_03_ex2\EmptyDir
| is_directory | is_empty |

path: C:\Users\dan\AppData\Local\Temp\Ch17_03_ex2\test1-data-file.txt
| is_regular_file |

path: C:\Users\dan\AppData\Local\Temp\Ch17_03_ex2\test2-empty-file.txt
| is_regular_file | is_empty |

path: C:\
| is_directory |

path: C:\Windows\notepad.exe
| is_regular_file |

path: \\carbon2\projects
| is_directory |

path: /etc
| does not exist |

path: /etc/fstab
| does not exist |

path: /dev/sda
| does not exist |

path: /dev/tty0
| does not exist |

File System Copy Functions

The final example of this chapter explains how to use copy functions `fs::copy_file()` and `fs::copy()`. In Listing 17-4-1, execution of `Ch17_04_ex1()` begins with creation of a test directory named `fs::temp_directory_path() / "Ch17_04_ex1"`. In the next code block, `Ch17_04_ex1()` utilizes `fs::path test_file1 = test_path / "TestFile1.txt"` and `MF::create_test_file(test_file1)` to create a source test file. The subsequent statement, `fs::path test_file2 = test_path / "TestFile2.txt"`, establishes a test destination file.

Listing 17-4-1. Example Ch17_04 - Ch17_04_ex1()

```cpp
//---------------------------------------------------------------------
// Ch17_04_ex.cpp
//---------------------------------------------------------------------

#include <filesystem>
#include "Ch17_04.h"
#include "MF.h"

namespace fs = std::filesystem;

void Ch17_04_ex1()
{
    // create test directory
    std::error_code ec {};
    fs::path test_path = fs::temp_directory_path() / "Ch17_04_ex1";

    if (fs::exists(test_path))
        remove_all(test_path);        // for debug/test

    if (!fs::create_directory(test_path, ec))
    {
        std::println("ec: {:s}", ec.message());
        return;
    }

    // create test files
    fs::path test_file1 = test_path / "TestFile1.txt";   // source file
    MF::create_test_file(test_file1);
    fs::path test_file2 = test_path / "TestFile2.txt";   // destination file

    for (int i = 0; i < 3; ++i)
    {
        // set copy_options (default is fs:copy_options::none)
        fs::copy_options copy_opt {};

        if (i == 2)
            copy_opt = fs::copy_options::overwrite_existing;

        std::println("\nusing fs::copy_file() - test #{:d}", i);
```

```
            std::println("source file:     {:s}", test_file1.string());
            std::println("destination file: {:s}", test_file2.string());

            // using copy_file (fails when i == 1 is true)
            bool status = fs::copy_file(test_file1, test_file2, copy_opt, ec);
            std::println("status:          {:s}", status);
            std::println("ec.message():    {:s}", ec.message());
        }

        fs::remove_all(test_path);
}
```

Within Ch17_04_ex1()'s for loop, the statement fs::copy_options copy_opt {} default initializes copy_opt to fs::copy_options::none for later use. Class fs::copy_options is an enum of bitmask constants that specify copy behavior preferences for fs::copy_file() and fs::copy(). Table 17-4 lists the available options.

Table 17-4. Bitmask Constants for Class copy_options

Group (Copy Type)	Bitmask Constant (fs::copy_options::)	Description
Existing target files fs::copy_file()	none	Error if file exists
	skip_existing	Skip overwrite of existing file
	overwrite_existing	Overwrite existing file
	update_existing	Overwrite existing file if older than replacement file
Subdirectories fs::copy()	none	Do not copy subdirectories
	recursive	Recursively copy subdirectories and their files

(continued)

Table 17-4. *(continued)*

Group (Copy Type)	Bitmask Constant (fs::copy_options::)	Description
Symbolic links fs::copy()	none	Follow symbolic links
	copy_symlinks	Copy symbolic link as symbolic links
	skip_symlinks	Ignore symbolic links
Form of copying fs::copy()	none	Copy content
	directories_only	Copy only directories; skip non-directory files
	create_symlinks	Create symbolic links instead of copies of files; source path must be an absolute path unless the destination path is in the current directory
	create_hard_links	Make hard links instead of copies of files

The for loop in Ch17_04_ex1() executes three times. During its first iteration, execution of fs::copy_file(test_file1, test_file2, copy_opt, ec) copies test_file1 to test_file2. During the second iteration, execution of fs:copy_file() fails since test_file2 already exists. To modify this default behavior, Ch17_04_ex1() sets copy_opt = fs::copy_options::overwrite_existing prior to calling fs::copy_file() during the for loop's third iteration.

Listing 17-4-2 shows the source code for example Ch17_04_ex2(). This example exploits fs::copy() to recursively copy the files of a directory to a new directory.

Listing 17-4-2. *Example Ch17_04 - Ch17_04_ex2()*

```cpp
void Ch17_04_ex2()
{
    std::error_code ec {};

    // create path names
    fs::path source_dir = fs::temp_directory_path() / "Ch17_04_ex2_S";
    fs::path dest_dir = fs::temp_directory_path() / "Ch17_04_ex2_D";

    fs::remove_all(source_dir, ec);     // remove old dirs
    fs::remove_all(dest_dir, ec);       // (for debug/test)

    // create test files in source_dir (remove_all delete
    if (!fs::create_directory(source_dir))
        throw std::runtime_error("create_directory() failed");

    MF::create_test_files(source_dir, "Ch17_04_ex2", 4, 3);

    // copy source_dir to dest_dir (fs::copy() is void)
    fs::copy_options copy_opt = fs::copy_options::recursive;
    fs::copy(source_dir, dest_dir, copy_opt, ec);

    if (ec)
    {
        std::println("error: {:s}", ec.message());
        return;
    }

    // display files in source_dir and des_dir
    for (int i = 0; i < 2; ++i)
    {
        fs::path display_path = (i == 0) ? source_dir : dest_dir;
        std::println("\ndisplay_path: {:s}", display_path.string());

        for (auto const& de : fs::recursive_directory_
        iterator(display_path))
        {
            if (fs::is_directory(de) || fs::is_regular_file(de))
```

```
            std::println("{:s}", de.path().string());
        }
    }

    fs::remove_all(source_dir);
    fs::remove_all(dest_dir);
}
```

Function Ch17_04_ex2() utilizes MF::create_test_files(source_dir, "Ch17_04_ex2", 4, 3) to create a directory tree under source_dir (see Listing 17-2-2-2 for MF::create_test_files()). In the next code block, execution of fs::copy(source_dir, dest_dir, copy_opt, ec) recursively copies all subdirectories and files in source_dir to des_dir. Note here that copy_opt is set to fs::copy_options::recursive, which enables the recursive copy. Following execution of fs::copy(), std::error_code ec is checked to determine if any errors occurred.

The final code block of Ch17_04_ex2() contains a for loop that exploits fs::recursive_directory_iterator() to print the files in both source_dir and dest_dir. Here are the results for example Ch17_04:

```
----- Results for example Ch17_04 -----

----- Ch17_04_ex1() -----

using fs::copy_file() - test #0
source file:       C:\Users\dan\AppData\Local\Temp\Ch17_04_ex1\TestFile1.txt
destination file:  C:\Users\dan\AppData\Local\Temp\Ch17_04_ex1\TestFile2.txt
status:            true
ec.message():      The operation completed successfully.

using fs::copy_file() - test #1
source file:       C:\Users\dan\AppData\Local\Temp\Ch17_04_ex1\TestFile1.txt
destination file:  C:\Users\dan\AppData\Local\Temp\Ch17_04_ex1\TestFile2.txt
status:            false
ec.message():      The file exists.

using fs::copy_file() - test #2
source file:       C:\Users\dan\AppData\Local\Temp\Ch17_04_ex1\TestFile1.txt
```

CHAPTER 17 FILE SYSTEMS

```
destination file: C:\Users\dan\AppData\Local\Temp\Ch17_04_ex1\TestFile2.txt
status:          true
ec.message():    The operation completed successfully.

----- Ch17_04_ex2() -----

display_path: C:\Users\dan\AppData\Local\Temp\Ch17_04_ex2_S
C:\Users\dan\AppData\Local\Temp\Ch17_04_ex2_S\D00
C:\Users\dan\AppData\Local\Temp\Ch17_04_ex2_S\D00\Ch17_04_ex2-00-00.txt
C:\Users\dan\AppData\Local\Temp\Ch17_04_ex2_S\D00\Ch17_04_ex2-00-01.txt
C:\Users\dan\AppData\Local\Temp\Ch17_04_ex2_S\D00\Ch17_04_ex2-00-02.txt
C:\Users\dan\AppData\Local\Temp\Ch17_04_ex2_S\D00\D01
C:\Users\dan\AppData\Local\Temp\Ch17_04_ex2_S\D00\D01\Ch17_04_ex2-01-00.txt
C:\Users\dan\AppData\Local\Temp\Ch17_04_ex2_S\D00\D01\Ch17_04_ex2-01-01.txt
C:\Users\dan\AppData\Local\Temp\Ch17_04_ex2_S\D00\D01\Ch17_04_ex2-01-02.txt
C:\Users\dan\AppData\Local\Temp\Ch17_04_ex2_S\D00\D01\D02
C:\Users\dan\AppData\Local\Temp\Ch17_04_ex2_S\D00\D01\D02\Ch17_04_
ex2-02-00.txt
C:\Users\dan\AppData\Local\Temp\Ch17_04_ex2_S\D00\D01\D02\Ch17_04_
ex2-02-01.txt
C:\Users\dan\AppData\Local\Temp\Ch17_04_ex2_S\D00\D01\D02\Ch17_04_
ex2-02-02.txt
C:\Users\dan\AppData\Local\Temp\Ch17_04_ex2_S\D00\D01\D02\D03
C:\Users\dan\AppData\Local\Temp\Ch17_04_ex2_S\D00\D01\D02\D03\Ch17_04_
ex2-03-00.txt
C:\Users\dan\AppData\Local\Temp\Ch17_04_ex2_S\D00\D01\D02\D03\Ch17_04_
ex2-03-01.txt
C:\Users\dan\AppData\Local\Temp\Ch17_04_ex2_S\D00\D01\D02\D03\Ch17_04_
ex2-03-02.txt

display_path: C:\Users\dan\AppData\Local\Temp\Ch17_04_ex2_D
C:\Users\dan\AppData\Local\Temp\Ch17_04_ex2_D\D00
C:\Users\dan\AppData\Local\Temp\Ch17_04_ex2_D\D00\Ch17_04_ex2-00-00.txt
C:\Users\dan\AppData\Local\Temp\Ch17_04_ex2_D\D00\Ch17_04_ex2-00-01.txt
C:\Users\dan\AppData\Local\Temp\Ch17_04_ex2_D\D00\Ch17_04_ex2-00-02.txt
C:\Users\dan\AppData\Local\Temp\Ch17_04_ex2_D\D00\D01
C:\Users\dan\AppData\Local\Temp\Ch17_04_ex2_D\D00\D01\Ch17_04_ex2-01-00.txt
```

C:\Users\dan\AppData\Local\Temp\Ch17_04_ex2_D\D00\D01\Ch17_04_ex2-01-01.txt
C:\Users\dan\AppData\Local\Temp\Ch17_04_ex2_D\D00\D01\Ch17_04_ex2-01-02.txt
C:\Users\dan\AppData\Local\Temp\Ch17_04_ex2_D\D00\D01\D02
C:\Users\dan\AppData\Local\Temp\Ch17_04_ex2_D\D00\D01\D02\Ch17_04_ex2-02-00.txt
C:\Users\dan\AppData\Local\Temp\Ch17_04_ex2_D\D00\D01\D02\Ch17_04_ex2-02-01.txt
C:\Users\dan\AppData\Local\Temp\Ch17_04_ex2_D\D00\D01\D02\Ch17_04_ex2-02-02.txt
C:\Users\dan\AppData\Local\Temp\Ch17_04_ex2_D\D00\D01\D02\D03
C:\Users\dan\AppData\Local\Temp\Ch17_04_ex2_D\D00\D01\D02\D03\Ch17_04_ex2-03-00.txt
C:\Users\dan\AppData\Local\Temp\Ch17_04_ex2_D\D00\D01\D02\D03\Ch17_04_ex2-03-01.txt
C:\Users\dan\AppData\Local\Temp\Ch17_04_ex2_D\D00\D01\D02\D03\Ch17_04_ex2-03-02.txt

Summary

Here are the key learning points for this chapter:

- An instance of class fs::path encompasses a character string pathname that denotes a file system path.
- Class fs::path supports a variety of pathname representations, including absolute, relative, and canonical.
- A fs::path object does not necessarily correspond to the existence of an actual file on a storage device.
- Functions fs::current_path() and fs::temp_directory_path() return fs::path objects that contain the current working and temporary directories.
- Classes fs::recursive_directory_iterator and fs::directory_entry are used to iterate the elements of a directory, its files, and any subdirectories.

- File system functions `fs::create_directory()` and `fs::remove()` create and remove a single directory. File system functions `fs::create_directories()` and `fs::remove_all()` create and remove a directory and all of its files and subdirectories.

- File system functions `fs::copy_file()` and `fs::copy()` copy files and directories. Copy operation behavior preferences are specified using the bitmask values of `enum class fs:copy_options`.

- Most `fs` functions define two overloads. The first type includes functions that require an explicit `std::error_code` argument for error results. These functions are declared `noexcept`. The non-`std::error_code` overloads throw `fs::filesystem_error` exceptions to report critical errors, including API errors from the underlying OS.

CHAPTER 18

Numerical Processing – Part 1

The STL includes a variety of classes and algorithms that expedite numerical processing. These constructs are also convenient in applications that are less numerical. This chapter is the first of two that describe mainstream classes and algorithms from the C++ numerics library. Topics covered include

- Mathematical constants
- Complex numbers
- Random number generators
- Random number distributions

Some of the discussions in this chapter tacitly assume previous exposure to certain mathematical disciplines. If you need a refresher, Appendix B contains a few references that you can consult.

Mathematical Constants

The C++ programming language did not include library definitions of frequently used mathematical constants until C++20. Prior to this, it was not uncommon for a large program to incorporate multiple definitions of universal constants such as π and e using `const` or `constexpr`. In legacy C++ code, mathematical constants were often formed using preprocessor directive `#define`.

CHAPTER 18 NUMERICAL PROCESSING – PART 1

The C++ numerics library includes several pre-initialized constant variable templates as shown in Table 18-1. These templates are encompassed in namespace std::numbers (<numbers>). For example, the mathematical constant π can be realized in code using std::numbers::pi_v<T> where T corresponds to float, double, or long double. Table 18-1 also shows the corresponding inline constexpr double aliases.

Table 18-1. Mathematical Constants of Namespace std::numbers

Template Form	Alias (inline constexpr double)	Constant
e_v<T>	e	Mathematical constant e (2.71828…)
log2e_v<T>	log2e	$\log_2 e$
log10e_v<T>	log10e	$\log_{10} e$
pi_v<T>	pi	Mathematical constant π (3.14159…)
inv_pi_v<T>	inv_pi	$1/\pi$
inv_sqrtpi_v<T>	inv_sqrtpi	$1/\sqrt{\pi}$
ln2_v<T>	ln2	$\ln 2$
ln10_v<T>	ln10	$\ln 10$
sqrt2_v<T>	sqrt2	$\sqrt{2}$
sqrt3_v<T>	sqrt3	$\sqrt{3}$
inv_sqrt3_v<T>	inv_sqrt3	$\dfrac{1}{\sqrt{3}}$
egamma_v<T>	egamma	Euler-Mascheroni constant γ (0.57721…)
phi_v<T>	phi	Golden ratio constant $\varphi = \dfrac{(1+\sqrt{5})}{2}$ (1.61803…)

CHAPTER 18 NUMERICAL PROCESSING – PART 1

Some of the mathematical constants shown in Table 18-1 were used in earlier chapters. The examples of this section spotlight a few more examples.

In Listing 18-1-1, example function Ch18_01_ex1() calculates Fibonacci numbers using the golden ratio constant φ and the following equation:

$$F_n = \frac{\varphi^n - (-\varphi)^{-n}}{2\varphi - 1}$$

Listing 18-1-1. Example Ch18_01 – Ch18_01_ex1()

```cpp
//-------------------------------------------------------------------------
// Ch18_01_ex.cpp
//-------------------------------------------------------------------------

#include <cmath>
#include <concepts>
#include <numbers>
#include <numeric>
#include <vector>
#include "Ch18_01.h"
#include "MT.h"

void Ch18_01_ex1()
{
    // calculate Fibonacci numbers using golden ratio
    bool add_nl {false};
    std::println("\nFibonacci numbers using golden ratio");

    for (int n = 0; n < 20; ++n)
    {
        auto t1 = std::pow(std::numbers::phi, n);
        auto t2 = std::pow(-std::numbers::phi, -n);
        auto fib = (t1 - t2) / (2.0 * std::numbers::phi - 1.0);
```

```
        const char* s = (add_nl) ? "\n" : "    ";
        std::print("{:4d}   {:10.4f} {:s}", n, fib, s);
        add_nl = !add_nl;
    }
}
```

In function Ch18_01_ex1(), std::numbers::phi is an alias for std::numbers::phi_v<double>. There are no library-defined aliases for float or long double mathematical constants. To carry out calculations using these types, the template form of the constant must be used (e.g., std::numbers::phi_v<float> or std::numbers::phi_v<long double>. You can also define your own aliases (e.g., using phi_f32 = std::numbers::phi_v<float>).

Example function Ch18_01_ex2(), shown in Listing 18-1-2, exemplifies the use of template constant std::numbers::pi_v<> in a lambda expression. Note that lambda expression calc_area() specifies an explicit floating-point template parameter, and this parameter is utilized to calculate circle areas using std::numbers::pi_v<T>.

Listing 18-1-2. Example Ch18_01 - Ch18_01_ex2()

```
void Ch18_01_ex2()
{
    const char* fmt = "{:12.6f} ";
    constexpr size_t epl_max {5};
    constexpr size_t n {10};

    std::vector<float> radii_f(n);
    std::vector<double> radii_d(n);
    std::iota(radii_f.begin(), radii_f.end(), 1.0f);
    std::iota(radii_d.begin(), radii_d.end(), 1.0);

    // using std::numbers::pi_v<T>
    auto calc_area = []<typename T>(T r) requires std::floating_point<T>
        { return r * r * std::numbers::pi_v<T>; };

    // calculate circle areas (float)
    std::vector<float> areas_f {};
    for (auto r : radii_f)
```

```
        areas_f.push_back(calc_area(static_cast<float>(r)));
    MT::print_ctr("\nareas_f:\n", areas_f, fmt, epl_max);

    // calculate circle areas (double)
    std::vector<double> areas_d {};
    for (auto r : radii_d)
        areas_d.push_back(calc_area(static_cast<double>(r)));
    MT::print_ctr("\nareas_d:\n", areas_d, fmt, epl_max);
}
```

You may have noticed that Table 18-1 includes a few "unusual" mathematical constants. For example, why is $\log_{10}e$ (std::numbers::log10e<T>) defined? The reason is that this value can be exploited to calculate logarithms for any number base[1] using the following equation:

$$\log_b x = \log_e x (\log_{10} e / \log_{10} b)$$

Example function Ch18_01_ex3(), shown in Listing 18-1-3, utilizes this equation to calculate base 3 and base 5 logarithms. The opening statement of Ch18_01_ex3(), using namespace std::numbers, imports members of std::numbers into the current scope. Next is the definition of lambda expression log_b_x. Note here that log10e_v<T> is used directly without a namespace prefix.

Listing 18-1-3. Example Ch18_01 - Ch18_01_ex3()

```
void Ch18_01_ex3()
{
    using namespace std::numbers;

    const char* fmt = "{:8.4f}";
    constexpr size_t epl_max {10};
    constexpr size_t n_f {81};
    constexpr size_t n_d {125};

    std::vector<float> vec0_f(n_f);
    std::vector<double> vec0_d(n_d);
```

---

[1] The standard library defines std::log(), std::log10(), and std::log2() for computing natural, common, and base 2 logarithms.

```cpp
    std::iota(vec0_f.begin(), vec0_f.end(), 1.0f);
    std::iota(vec0_d.begin(), vec0_d.end(), 1.0);

    // calculate log base b of x
    auto log_b_x = []<typename T>(T b, T x) requires std::floating_point<T>
        { return std::log(x) * log10e_v<T> / std::log10(b); };

    // calculate log3 values (float)
    std::println("\nlog3 values of [{:d}, {:d}]: ", 1, n_f);
    std::vector<float> vec_f {};
    for (auto x : vec0_f)
        vec_f.push_back(log_b_x(3.0f, static_cast<float>(x)));
    MT::print_ctr("", vec_f, fmt, epl_max);

    // calculate log5 values (double)
    std::println("\nlog5 values of [{:d}, {:d}]: ", 1, n_d);
    std::vector<double> vec_d {};
    for (auto x : vec0_d)
        vec_d.push_back(log_b_x(5.0, static_cast<double>(x)));
    MT::print_ctr("", vec_d, fmt, epl_max);
}
```

In the subsequent code block, Ch18_01_ex3() exercises log_b_x(3.0f, static_cast<float>(x)) to calculate $\log_3 x$ for each value in vec0_f. The final code block of Ch18_01_ex3() calculates $\log_5 x$ for each value in vec0_d. Here are the results for example Ch18_01:

```
----- Results for example Ch18_01 -----

----- Ch18_01_ex1() -----

Fibonacci numbers using golden ratio
    0      0.0000      1      1.0000
    2      1.0000      3      2.0000
    4      3.0000      5      5.0000
    6      8.0000      7     13.0000
    8     21.0000      9     34.0000
   10     55.0000     11     89.0000
```

```
    12     144.0000         13      233.0000
    14     377.0000         15      610.0000
    16     987.0000         17     1597.0000
    18    2584.0000         19     4181.0000
```

----- Ch18_01_ex2() -----

areas_f:
```
     3.141593       12.566371      28.274334       50.265484      78.539818
   113.097336      153.938049     201.061935      254.469009     314.159271
```

areas_d:
```
     3.141593       12.566371      28.274334       50.265482      78.539816
   113.097336      153.938040     201.061930      254.469005     314.159265
```

----- Ch18_01_ex3() -----

log3 values of [1, 81]:
```
   0.0000   0.6309   1.0000   1.2619   1.4650   1.6309   1.7712   1.8928   2.0000   2.0959
   2.1827   2.2619   2.3347   2.4022   2.4650   2.5237   2.5789   2.6309   2.6801   2.7268
   2.7712   2.8136   2.8540   2.8928   2.9299   2.9656   3.0000   3.0331   3.0650   3.0959
   3.1257   3.1546   3.1827   3.2098   3.2362   3.2619   3.2868   3.3111   3.3347   3.3578
   3.3802   3.4022   3.4236   3.4445   3.4650   3.4850   3.5046   3.5237   3.5425   3.5609
   3.5789   3.5966   3.6139   3.6309   3.6476   3.6640   3.6801   3.6960   3.7115   3.7268
   3.7419   3.7567   3.7712   3.7856   3.7997   3.8136   3.8273   3.8408   3.8540   3.8671
   3.8801   3.8928   3.9053   3.9177   3.9299   3.9420   3.9539   3.9656   3.9772   3.9887
   4.0000
```

log5 values of [1, 125]:
```
   0.0000   0.4307   0.6826   0.8614   1.0000   1.1133   1.2091   1.2920   1.3652   1.4307
   1.4899   1.5440   1.5937   1.6397   1.6826   1.7227   1.7604   1.7959   1.8295   1.8614
   1.8917   1.9206   1.9482   1.9746   2.0000   2.0244   2.0478   2.0704   2.0922   2.1133
   2.1337   2.1534   2.1725   2.1911   2.2091   2.2266   2.2436   2.2602   2.2763   2.2920
   2.3074   2.3223   2.3370   2.3512   2.3652   2.3789   2.3922   2.4053   2.4181   2.4307
   2.4430   2.4550   2.4669   2.4785   2.4899   2.5011   2.5121   2.5229   2.5335   2.5440
   2.5542   2.5643   2.5743   2.5841   2.5937   2.6032   2.6125   2.6217   2.6308   2.6397
   2.6486   2.6572   2.6658   2.6743   2.6826   2.6908   2.6990   2.7070   2.7149   2.7227
   2.7304   2.7380   2.7456   2.7530   2.7604   2.7676   2.7748   2.7819   2.7889   2.7959
```

2.8028   2.8095   2.8163   2.8229   2.8295   2.8360   2.8424   2.8488   2.8551   2.8614
2.8675   2.8737   2.8797   2.8857   2.8917   2.8976   2.9034   2.9092   2.9149   2.9206
2.9262   2.9318   2.9373   2.9428   2.9482   2.9536   2.9589   2.9642   2.9694   2.9746
2.9798   2.9849   2.9900   2.9950   3.0000

Complex Numbers

A number of the form $z = a + bi$ where both a and b are real numbers is called a complex number. Note that complex number z includes two components: a real part a and an imaginary part b. Symbol i denotes $\sqrt{-1}$ and $i^2 = -1$. Complex numbers are frequently applied to solve a wide variety of mathematical problems that can't be solved using only real numbers. They are used extensively in scientific and engineering applications.

The source code examples of this section demonstrate basic arithmetic and other operations using complex numbers and class std::complex. Feel free to either skim or skip this section if complex numbers are not relevant to your programming endeavors.

Listing 18-2-1 shows the source code for example Ch18_02_ex1(). This example demonstrates how to define objects of type std::complex. It also covers common arithmetic operations using std::complex values. The initial statement of Ch18_02_ex1(), using namespace std::complex_literals, enables the use of complex literal suffixes for imaginary numbers. More about this shortly.

Listing 18-2-1. Example Ch18_02 - Ch18_02_ex1()

```cpp
//------------------------------------------------------------------
// Ch18_02_ex.cpp
//------------------------------------------------------------------

#include <complex>
#include <concepts>
#include <format>
#include "Ch18_02.h"
#include "MTH.h"

void Ch18_02_ex1()
{
    using namespace std::complex_literals;
```

```cpp
// complex variables
std::complex<double> z0 {};                    // 0 + 0i
std::complex<double> z1 {3.0, 4.0};
std::complex<double> z2 {7.0, -3.0};

std::println("\nz0: ({:.3f}, {:.3f})", z0.real(), z0.imag());
std::println("z1: ({:.3f}, {:.3f})", z1.real(), z1.imag());
std::println("z2: ({:.3f}, {:.3f})", z2.real(), z2.imag());

// complex arithmetic
std::complex<double> z3 = z1 + z2;
std::complex<double> z4 = z1 - z2;
std::complex<double> z5 = z1 * z2;
std::complex<double> z6 = z1 / z2;

std::println("\nz3: ({:.3f}, {:.3f})", z3.real(), z3.imag());
std::println("z4: ({:.3f}, {:.3f})", z4.real(), z4.imag());
std::println("z5: ({:.3f}, {:.3f})", z5.real(), z5.imag());
std::println("z6: ({:.3f}, {:.3f})", z6.real(), z6.imag());

// more complex arithmetic (using complex literals)
z1 += 1.0 + 2.0i;
z2 -= 2.0;
z3 *= 4.0i;
std::complex<double> z7 = z1 + 1.5 + 3.0i;

std::println("\nz1: ({:.3f}, {:.3f})", z1.real(), z1.imag());
std::println("z2: ({:.3f}, {:.3f})", z2.real(), z2.imag());
std::println("z3: ({:.3f}, {:.3f})", z3.real(), z3.imag());
std::println("z7: ({:.3f}, {:.3f})", z7.real(), z7.imag());

// relational ops
std::complex<double> z8 {4.0, 6.0};
std::complex<double> z9 {5.0, 12.0};
std::println("\nz8: ({:.3f}, {:.3f})", z8.real(), z8.imag());
std::println("z9: ({:.3f}, {:.3f})", z9.real(), z9.imag());
std::println("z8 == z9: {:s}", z8 == z9);
std::println("z8 != z9: {:s}", z8 != z9);
```

CHAPTER 18 NUMERICAL PROCESSING – PART 1

```
    std::println("z9 == (4.0 + 6.0i): {:s}", z9 == 4.0 + 6.0i);
    std::println("z9 != (4.0 + 6.0i): {:s}", z9 != 4.0 + 6.0i);
}
```

The opening code block of Ch18_02_ex1() defines three values of type std::complex<double>. The first value, std::complex<double> z0 {}, corresponds to a complex variable whose real and imaginary components are doubles and equal to 0.0 (i.e., z0 = 0.0 + 0.0i). Template class std::complex also supports value types of float and long double. The next two statements, std::complex<double> z1 {3.0, 4.0} and std::complex<double> z2 {7.0, -3.0}, set z1 = 3.0 + 4.0i and z2 = 7.0 - 3.0i, respectively. The ensuing group of std::println() statements prints z0, z1, and z2. Note in these statements that std::complex member functions real() and imag() obtain the real and imaginary components of a std::complex value.

The next code block illustrates how to carry out elementary arithmetic operations using std::complex values. Thanks to operator overloading, performing complex arithmetic using std::complex values mostly resembles ordinary arithmetic using fundamental types. Table 18-2 details the math behind the four elementary arithmetic operations.

Table 18-2. *Elementary Arithmetic Operations Using Complex Numbers*

Operation	Calculation
Addition	$z_1 + z_2 = (a_1 + a_2) + (b_1 + b_2)i$
Subtraction	$z_1 - z_2 = (a_1 - a_2) + (b_1 - b_2)i$
Multiplication	$z_1 z_2 = (a_1 a_2 - b_1 b_2) + (a_1 b_2 + b_1 a_2)i$
Division	$\dfrac{z_1}{z_2} = \dfrac{a_1 a_2 + b_1 b_2}{a_2^2 + b_2^2} + \dfrac{b_1 a_2 - a_1 b_2}{a_2^2 + b_2^2} i$

The third code block in Ch18_02_ex1() performs arithmetic calculations using std::complex objects and complex literals. The first statement of this block, z1 += 1.0 + 2.0i, adds complex literal 1.0 + 2.0i to z1. During execution of this expression, 1.0 is added to z1.real(), and 2.0 is added to z1.imag(). Note the use of complex literal suffix i, which signifies that 2.0 is a std::complex imaginary value. Without this suffix, 3.0 would be added to z1.real(). The next statement, z2 -= 2.0 subtracts

CHAPTER 18   NUMERICAL PROCESSING – PART 1

2.0 from z2.real(). Execution of z3 *= 4.0i calculates z3 *= 0 + 4.0i. Finally, std::complex<double> z7 = z1 + 1.5 + 3.0i sums z1 and 1.5 + 2.0i and saves the result to z7. Once again, the use of the i suffix is required to denote the imaginary component.

The final code block of Ch18_02_ex1() demonstrates how to compare two std::complex values using operator== and operator!=. Unlike ordinary numbers, two complex numbers can't be compared using operator< or operator>. However, the magnitudes of complex numbers are comparable, and you'll learn how to calculate this shortly.

Example Ch18_02_ex2(), shown in Listing 18-2-2, exemplifies the use of several common functions using std::complex values. In this example, execution of auto z1_abs = std::abs(z1) calculates the magnitude (std::hypot(std::real(z1), std::imag(z1))) of z1. In this expression, the value type of z1_abs corresponds to the value type of z1 (i.e., it's a double). The next statement, auto z1_arg = std::arg(z1) calculates z1's phase angle (std::atan2(std::imag(z1), std::real(z1))). Like z1_abs, the value type of z1_arg is a double. Execution of auto z1_conj = std::conj(z1) computes the complex conjugate of z1, which means that it flips the sign of z1's imaginary component.

Listing 18-2-2. Example Ch18_02 – Ch18_02_ex2()

```
void Ch18_02_ex2()
{
    // using common complex functions
    std::complex<double> z1 {3.0, 4.0};
    auto z1_abs = std::abs(z1);
    auto z1_arg = std::arg(z1);
    auto z1_conj = std::conj(z1);

    std::println("\nz1:      ({:.3f}, {:.3f})", z1.real(), z1.imag());
    std::println("z1_abs:  {:.4f}", z1_abs);
    std::println("z1_arg:  {:.4f} radians", z1_arg);
    std::println("z1_arg:  {:.4f} degrees)", MTH::rad_to_deg(z1_arg));
    std::println("z1_conj: ({:.4f}, {:.4f})", z1_conj.real(), z1_conj.
    imag());
}
```

CHAPTER 18 NUMERICAL PROCESSING – PART 1

Class `std::complex` supports a variety of common complex mathematical functions, including trigonometric (`std::cos()`, `std::sin()`, `std::tan()`, etc.), logarithmic (`std::exp()`, `std::log()`, `std::log10()`), and hyperbolic (`std::cosh()`, `std::sinh()`, etc.). The mathematical operations carried out by these functions are different than their real counterparts. One frequently used algorithm that's based on complex arithmetic and `std::exp()` is the discrete Fourier transform (DFT).

The standard DFT decomposes a sampled time-domain signal into its component frequencies. Mathematically, the DFT is defined as follows:

$$X_k = \sum_{n=0}^{N-1} x_n \cdot e^{-i\left(\frac{2\pi kn}{N}\right)} \quad k = 0,1,\ldots N-1.$$

In this equation, x is the input (real[2] or complex) time-domain signal, X is the output (complex) spectrum of frequencies, and N represents the number of values in both x and X. To recover a time-domain signal from its DFT spectrum, the following inverse equation is used:

$$x_n = \frac{1}{N}\sum_{k=0}^{N-1} X_k \cdot e^{i\left(\frac{2\pi kn}{N}\right)} \quad n = 0,1,\ldots N-1.$$

The DFT is widely used in signal processing applications and numerous tomes have been written about its underlying mathematics. Appendix B contains a valuable reference that you can consult for more information. For the next source code example, the most important property to recognize about the DFT equations is that they sum products of two complex numbers. Also, note that the DFT equation and its inverse differ only by a minus sign in the exponential term and pre-factor $\frac{1}{N}$.

Listing 18-2-3-1 shows the source code for template function `MTH::dft()`, which calculates a DFT or inverse DFT using the previously defined equations. The opening code block of `MTH::dft()` instantiates `std::vector<std::complex<T>> result(N)` to hold the calculated result. The next statement, `const T sign = (inv) ? 1 : -1`, sets `sign` to ensure correction calculation of a normal or inverse DFT.

---

[2] Real number a is equal to a+0i in the complex plane.

CHAPTER 18 NUMERICAL PROCESSING – PART 1

Listing 18-2-3-1. Example Ch18_02 - MTH::dft()

```
template <typename T> requires std::floating_point<T>
std::vector<std::complex<T>> dft(const std::vector<std::complex<T>>& x,
bool inv)
{
    // create result vector
    const size_t N = x.size();
    std::vector<std::complex<T>> result(N);

    // set sign for normal or inverse
    const T sign = (inv) ? 1 : -1;

    for (size_t k = 0; k < N; ++k)
    {
        std::complex<T> sum {};

        for (size_t n = 0; n < N; ++n)
        {
            T t1 = 2 * std::numbers::pi_v<T> * n * static_cast<T>(k) / N;
            std::complex<T> t2(0, sign * t1);

            // using std::exp(std::complex)
            sum += x[n] * std::exp(t2);
        }

        // apply pre-factor
        if (inv)
            sum /= static_cast<T>(N);

        result[k] = sum;
    }

    return result;
}
```

The two nested for loops in MTH::dft() carry out the actual DFT calculation. The first two statements inside the inner for loop, T t1 = 2 * std::numbers::pi_v<T> * n * static_cast<T>(k) / N and std::complex<T> t2(0, sign * t1) compute the exponent for std::exp(). Note that the real component of T t2 is zero. The next

739

statement, sum += x[n] * std::exp(t2), adds the product of complex values x[n] and std::exp(t2) to sum. Following execution of the inner for loop, MTH::dft() applies the pre-factor (if necessary) and saves sum to result[k].

Listing 18-2-3-2 shows the source code for example Ch18_02_ex3(). This listing opens with the definition of template function print_complex_vec(), which prints the elements of argument std::vector<std::complex<T>>& x.

Listing 18-2-3-2. Example Ch18_02 – Ch18_02_ex3()

```
template <typename T> requires std::floating_point<T>
void print_complex_vec(const char* msg, const
std::vector<std::complex<T>>& x,
    T eps = 0)
{
    std::print("{:s}", msg);
    for (const std::complex<T>& z : x)
    {
        T re = z.real();
        T im = z.imag();

        // flush to zero (for display purposes only)
        if (eps > 0)
        {
            if (fabs(re) < eps)
                re = 0;
            if (fabs(im) < eps)
                im = 0;
        }

        std::println("({:11.6f}, {:11.6f})", re, im);
    }
}

void Ch18_02_ex3()
{
    constexpr double eps = 1.0e-9;
    using namespace std::complex_literals;
```

```
    // initialize test input signal
    std::vector<std::complex<double>> x
    {
        {1.0}, {3.0 - 1.0i}, {5.0i}, {-1.0 + 2.0i},
        {-8.0 - 3.0i}, {7.0 - 4.0i}, {5.0 + 11.0i}, {-6.0 - 2.0i}
    };

    print_complex_vec("\noriginal signal x:\n", x);

    // calculate discrete Fourier transform
    std::vector<std::complex<double>> X = MTH::dft(x, false);
    print_complex_vec("\nDFT signal X:\n", X);

    // calculate inverse discrete Fourier transform
    std::vector<std::complex<double>> X_inv = MTH::dft(X, true);
    print_complex_vec("\ninverse DFT signal X_inv:\n", X_inv, eps);
}
```

Execution of Ch18_02_ex3() begins with the initialization of test input signal std::vector<std::complex<double>> x. The values used to initialize x are arbitrary. In the next code block, Ch18_02_ex3() exercises std::vector<std::complex<double>> X = MTH::dft(x, false) to calculate the DFT of x. The final code block in Ch18_02_ex3() utilizes std::vector<std::complex<double>> X_inv = MTH::dft(X, true) to demonstrate the calculation of an inverse DFT. Note in the results section that the values in vectors x and X_inv are equal.

The primary purpose of example Ch18_02 was to demonstrate additional usages of std::complex values and std::complex mathematical functions. Most math libraries and signal processing applications calculate DFTs using fast Fourier transforms (FFT). The advantage of this algorithm is its improved time complexity, which equals $O(n \log n)$ compared to $O(n^2)$ for the DFT. Here are the results for example Ch18_02:

```
----- Ch18_02_ex1() -----

z0: (0.000, 0.000)
z1: (3.000, 4.000)
z2: (7.000, -3.000)
```

CHAPTER 18   NUMERICAL PROCESSING – PART 1

```
z3: (10.000, 1.000)
z4: (-4.000, 7.000)
z5: (33.000, 19.000)
z6: (0.155, 0.638)

z1: (4.000, 6.000)
z2: (5.000, -3.000)
z3: (-4.000, 40.000)
z7: (5.500, 9.000)

z8: (4.000, 6.000)
z9: (5.000, 12.000)
z8 == z9: false
z8 != z9: true
z9 == (4.0 + 6.0i): false
z9 != (4.0 + 6.0i): true

----- Ch18_02_ex2() -----

z1:       (3.000, 4.000)
z1_abs:   5.0000
z1_arg:   0.9273 radians
z1_arg:   53.1301 degrees)
z1_conj: (3.0000, -4.0000)

----- Ch18_02_ex3() -----

original signal x:
(    1.000000,     0.000000)
(    3.000000,    -1.000000)
(    0.000000,     5.000000)
(   -1.000000,     2.000000)
(   -8.000000,    -3.000000)
(    7.000000,    -4.000000)
(    5.000000,    11.000000)
(   -6.000000,    -2.000000)
```

DFT signal X:
(1.000000, 8.000000)
(1.585786, 6.585786)
(-17.000000, -36.000000)
(26.313708, -2.000000)
(-5.000000, 18.000000)
(4.414214, 9.414214)
(-7.000000, -2.000000)
(3.686292, -2.000000)

inverse DFT signal X_inv:
(1.000000, 0.000000)
(3.000000, -1.000000)
(0.000000, 5.000000)
(-1.000000, 2.000000)
(-8.000000, -3.000000)
(7.000000, -4.000000)
(5.000000, 11.000000)
(-6.000000, -2.000000)

Random Number Generation

Random number generation is a requisite task for many applications. For example, game programs often need to simulate the rolling of dice, dealing of playing cards, or unpredictability in natural phenomena. Computerized production of synthetic data sets for software test and debugging is another common use for random number generation. To address these and other use cases, the STL defines several classes that facilitate random number generation for a wide variety of ordinary and specialized usages. Here's a brief description of these classes:

- **Uniform random bit generator** – Concept[3] for a function object that generates an unsigned integer value from a range of values. Ideally, each value within the range has an equal probability of being generated.

- **Random number engine** – Specific type of uniform random bit generator that encompasses a source of entropy (i.e., degree of randomness).

- **Random number engine adaptor** – Adjusts the output of an underlying random number engine to alter its generation characteristics.

- **Random number generator** – Incorporates a random number engine and an optional random number engine adaptor.

- **Random number distribution** – Adjusts the output of a random number generator to conform to a probability density function.

You'll learn more about these class types as the chapter progresses.

STL's random number engines and engine adaptors impart a significant amount of algorithmic flexibility for individuals who possess the requisite statistical expertise. For the rest of us, the STL predefines several random number generators using parameters that implement established algorithms. These generators, shown in Table 18-3, are suitable for many use cases with cryptography being a notable exception.

---

[3] Recall that a concept facilitates compile-time validation of a template's arguments.

Table 18-3. Random Number Generators

Generator	Engine	Adaptor
minstd_rand0	linear_congruential_engine	
minstd_rand	linear_congruential_engine	
mt19937	mersenne_twister_engine	
mt19937_64	mersenne_twister_engine	
ranlux24_base	subtract_with_carry_engine	
ranlux48_base	subtract_with_carry_engine	
ranlux24	Same as ranlux24_base	discard_block_engine
ranlux48	Same as ranlux48_base	discard_block_engine
knuth_b	Same as minstd_rand0	shuffle_order_engine
default_random_engine	Implementation defined	

All of the classes shown in Table 18-3 belong to namespace std. A discussion of the algorithmic differences between the various random number generators is beyond the scope of this book and my expertise, but basically involves a trade-off between computational overhead and improved statistical randomness. Appendix B contains some references that you can consult for more information.

CHAPTER 18 NUMERICAL PROCESSING – PART 1

Each STL random number generator class is designed to be used with a random number distribution. A random number distribution transforms the output generated by a random number engine to produce random values that conform to a probability density function. Table 18-4 lists STL's random number distribution classes. Like the engine classes, all of the classes shown in this table are defined in namespace std.

Table 18-4. Random Number Distribution Classes

Distribution Category	Class Name	Data Type
Uniform	uniform_int_distribution	Integer
	uniform_real_distribution	Floating-point
Bernoulli	bernoulli_distribution	bool
	binomial_distribution	Integer
	negative_binomial_distribution	Integer
	geometric_distribution	Integer
Poisson	poisson_distribution	Integer
	exponential_distribution	Floating-point
	gamma_distribution	Floating-point
	weibull_distribution	Floating-point
	extreme_value_distribution	Floating-point
Normal	normal_distribution	Floating-point
	lognormal_distribution	Floating-point
	chi_squared_distribution	Floating-point
	cauchy_distribution	Floating-point
	fisher_f_distribution	Floating-point
	student_t_distribution	Floating-point
Sampling	discrete_distribution	Integer
	piecewise_constant_distribution	Floating-point
	piecewise_linear_distribution	Floating-point

CHAPTER 18 NUMERICAL PROCESSING – PART 1

As mentioned earlier, the classes shown in Table 18-4 principally model different probability density functions. Some of these distribution names are likely familiar if you have ever taken a course in probability and statistics. The ISO C++ specification document defines the exact probability density function that each distribution class realizes. However, the algorithm employed to produce a specified distribution is implementation defined.

Using Generators and Distributions

Listing 18-3-1 shows the source code for example Ch18_03_ex1(). This example demonstrates the basic use of random number generator and random number distribution classes.

Listing 18-3-1. Example Ch18_03 – Ch18_03_ex1()

```
//-----------------------------------------------------------------------
// Ch18_03_ex.cpp
//-----------------------------------------------------------------------

#include <algorithm>
#include <format>
#include <fstream>
#include <random>
#include <vector>
#include "Ch18_03.h"

void Ch18_03_ex1()
{
    constexpr size_t n {60};
    constexpr int rng_min {1};
    constexpr int rng_max {100};
    constexpr unsigned int rng_seed {42};

    // create random number generator (std::minstd_rand) & distribution
    std::minstd_rand rng1(rng_seed);
    std::uniform_int_distribution<int> dist1(rng_min, rng_max);
```

```
    // generate random numbers (integers)
    std::println("\nrandom values using generator std::minstd_rand");
    size_t add_nl = 0;
    for (size_t i = 0; i < n; ++i)
    {
        int rng_val = dist1(rng1);
        std::print("{:4d} ", rng_val);

        if (++add_nl % 15 == 0)
            std::println("");
    }

    // create random number generator (std::mt19937) & distribution
    std::println("\nrandom values using generator std::mt19937");
    std::mt19937 rng2(rng_seed);
    std::uniform_real_distribution<float> dist2(rng_min, rng_max);

    // generate random numbers (integers)
    add_nl = 0;
    for (size_t i = 0; i < n; ++i)
    {
        float rng_val = dist2(rng2);
        std::print("{:7.2f} ", rng_val);

        if (++add_nl % 10 == 0)
            std::println("");
    }
}
```

In the opening code block of Ch18_03_ex1(), the statement std::minstd_rand rng1(rng_seed) instantiates an instance of random number generator std::minstd_rand. Argument rng_seed is the seed value for generator. A seed value sets the internal state of a random number generator. How this value is actually used varies depending on the generator. What's important to understand is that a specific seed value always yields the same sequence of "random" values. In other words, it's deterministic. This is one of the reasons why STL's random number generators and their underling algorithms are often called pseudo-random. Later in this section, you'll learn how to create a non-deterministic random number generator.

CHAPTER 18   NUMERICAL PROCESSING – PART 1

The next line in Ch18_03_ex1(), std::uniform_int_distribution<int> dist1(rng_min, rng_max), instantiates a random number distribution. Class std::uniform_int_distribution generates random integers that are uniformly distributed between [rng_min, rng_max]. In other words, each integer value in [rng_min, rng_max] has an equal probability of being generated. The subsequent code block in Ch18_03_ex1() utilizes rng1 and dist1 to generate random integers. Inside the first for loop, execution of rng_val = dist1(rng1) returns a uniformly distributed random integer between [rng_min, rng_max].

Function Ch18_03_ex1() also demonstrates how to instantiate objects of type std::mt19937 and std::uniform_real_distribution<float>. Class std::uniform_real_distribution<float> differs from its integer counterpart in that random values are generated uniformly over open interval [rng_min, rng_max). The current example also highlights the use of Mersenne Twister generator class std::mt19937. The second for loop utilizes float rng_val = dist2(rng2) to generate a floating-point random value between [rng_min, rng_max). It warrants mentioning here that the random number generators listed in Table 18-3 can be used with any of the random number distributions shown in Table 18-4, which provides a tremendous amount of algorithmic flexibility. It also simplifies experimentation.

Source code example Ch18_03_ex2(), shown in Listing 18-3-2, spotlights the use of distribution class std::normal_distribution.

Listing 18-3-2. Example Ch18_03 – Ch18_03_ex2()

```
void Ch18_03_ex2()
{
    constexpr size_t num_iter {2};

    for (size_t iter = 0; iter < num_iter; ++iter)
    {
        constexpr size_t n {32};
        constexpr double rng_mean {5.0};
        constexpr double rng_sd {2.0};
        constexpr unsigned int rng_seed {42};

        // create random number generator and distribution
        std::mt19937 rng(rng_seed);
        std::normal_distribution<double> dist(rng_mean, rng_sd);
```

749

CHAPTER 18 NUMERICAL PROCESSING – PART 1

```
        size_t add_nl {0};
        std::println("\niteration #{:d}", iter);

        for (size_t i = 0; i < n; ++i)
        {
            double rng_val = dist(rng);
            std::print("{:8.4f} ", rng_val);

            if (++add_nl % 8 == 0)
                std::println("");
        }
    }
}
```

Class `std::normal_distribution` generates floating-point random numbers using the probability density function:

$$p(x|\mu,\sigma) = \frac{1}{\sigma\sqrt{2\pi}} \cdot exp\left(-\frac{(x-\mu)^2}{2\sigma^2}\right)$$

where μ and σ correspond to the distribution's mean and standard deviation, respectively. Figure 18-1 depicts a few prototypical normal distribution bell-shaped curves using $\mu = 0.0$ and different values for σ.

CHAPTER 18 NUMERICAL PROCESSING – PART 1

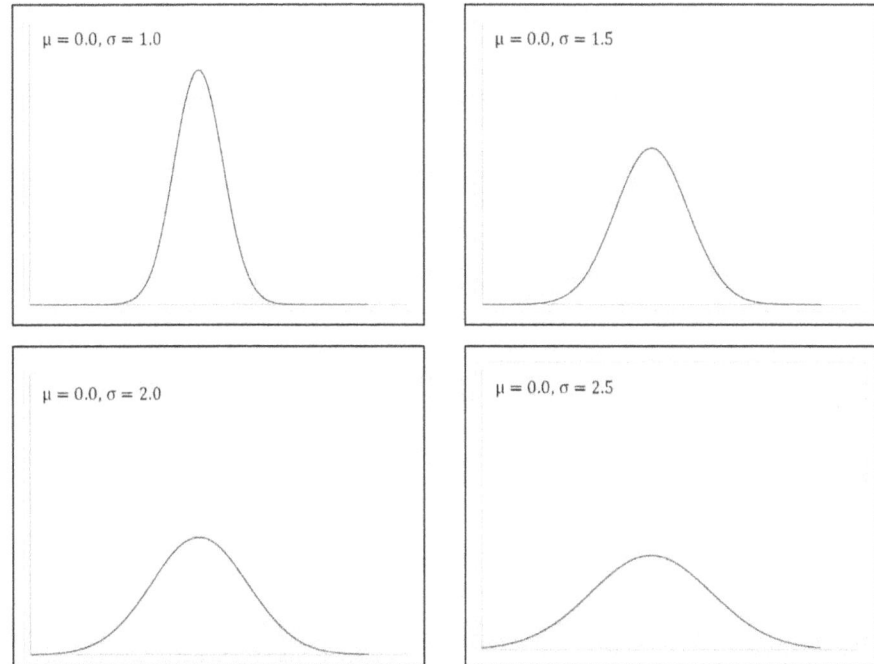

Figure 18-1. Examples of normal distributions

The code in Ch18_03_ex2() incorporates two for loops. The inner for loop uses std::mt19937 rng(rng_seed) and std::normal_distribution<double> dist(rng_mean, rng_sd) to generate random values. The outer for loop is included to demonstrate that the use of the same seed value yields the same sequence of random numbers.

Listing 18-3-3 shows the source code for example Ch18_03_ex3(). This listing opens with the definition of template function save_histogram(). Execution of this function creates a num_bucket sized histogram for the values in std::vector<T>& vec1. The bucket counts are written to the file specified by std::string& fn.

Listing 18-3-3. Example Ch18_03 – Ch18_03_ex3()

```
template <typename T> bool save_histogram(const std::string& fn,
const std::vector<T>& vec1, int num_buckets = 100)
{
    std::ofstream ofs(fn, std::ios::out | std::ios::trunc);

    if (!ofs.good())
        throw std::runtime_error("save_histogram - file open error");
```

751

```cpp
        auto histo_min = std::ranges::min(vec1);
        auto histo_max = std::ranges::max(vec1);
        auto bucket_size = (histo_max - histo_min) / num_buckets;

        // create histogram vector (extra bucket holds counts for histo_max)
        std::vector<int> histo(num_buckets + 1);

        // build and save histogram
        for (auto v : vec1)
        {
            int bucket_index = static_cast<int>((v - histo_min) / bucket_size);
            ++histo.at(bucket_index);
        }

        for (auto bucket_count : histo)
            std::println(ofs, "{:d}", bucket_count);

        ofs.close();
        return ofs.good();
}

void Ch18_03_ex3()
{
    constexpr size_t num_iter {4};
    constexpr size_t num_vals {25'000};
    constexpr double rng_mean {10.0};
    constexpr double rng_sd {2.0};
    const std::string fn_base = "Ch18_03_ex3-histogram";

    // instantiate non-deterministic random integer generator
    std::random_device rng_dev {};

    for (size_t i = 0; i < num_iter; ++i)
    {
        // create vectors for random numbers
        std::vector<double> vec1(num_vals);

        // create non-deterministic random number generator, distribution
        std::mt19937 rng(rng_dev());
        std::normal_distribution<double> dist(rng_mean, rng_sd);
```

```
        // fill vec1 with random values
        for (size_t j = 0; j < num_vals; ++j)
            vec1[j] = dist(rng);

        // save histogram
        std::string fn_histo = std::format("{:s}-{:02d}.csv", fn_base, i);
        save_histogram(fn_histo, vec1);
        std::println("Saved histogram to file {:s}", fn_histo);
    }
}
```

In the opening code block of Ch18_03_ex3(), execution of std::random_device rng_dev {} instantiates a random number generator that produces non-deterministic random numbers of type unsigned int. The entropy source for this non-determinism is typically a hardware device. An implementation will substitute an implementation-defined alternative if a non-deterministic hardware device is unavailable. In this case, multiple instances of std::random_device might generate the same sequence of values.

To spotlight the non-determinism of std::random_device, function Ch18_03_ex3() utilizes a for loop that generates num_iter histograms of random number sequences using std::mt19937 rng(rng_dev()) and std::normal_distribution<double> dist(rng_mean, rng_sd). Execution of rng_dev() generates a non-deterministic seed value for random number generator rng. Figure 18-2 shows the histograms generated by Ch18_03_ex3(). Note that all of the histograms in this figure have the general form of a bell-shaped curve but are clearly distinct. If you replace rng_dev() with a constant value, all four histograms will be identical.

CHAPTER 18 NUMERICAL PROCESSING – PART 1

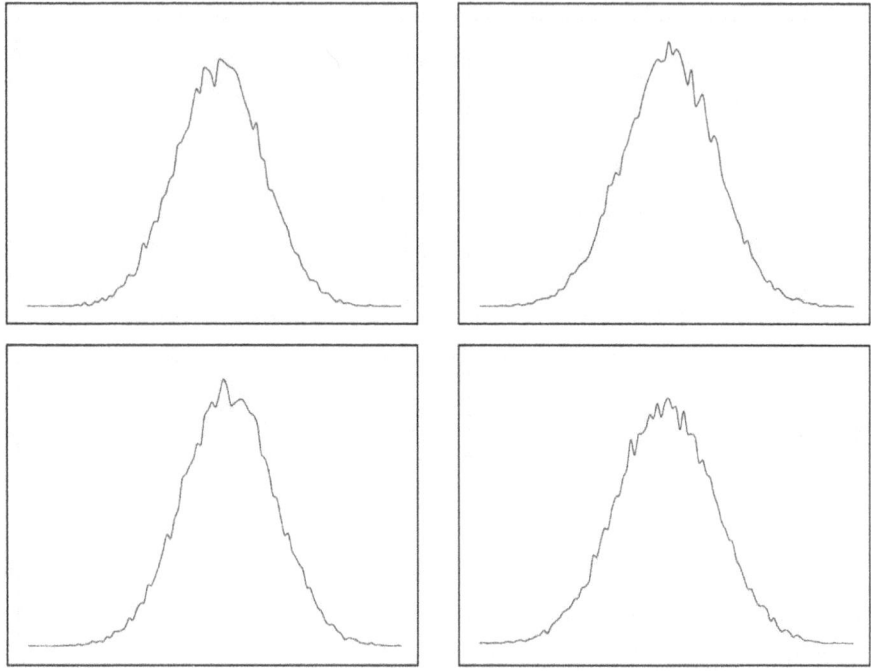

Figure 18-2. *Histograms of normal distributions using non-deterministic seed values*

The results for example Ch18_03 follow this paragraph. These results will vary depending on the C++ implementation.

```
----- Results for example Ch18_03 -----

----- Ch18_03_ex1() -----

random values using generator std::minstd_rand
    1   52   90    9   46   91    1   99   96   86   77    8   18   70   65
   84   35   31   37   98   92    2   12   79   65   11   39   87   61   35
   48   68   13   29   41   82   67   35   64   63   75    4   52   27   51
   68   83   63   73    6   44   51   71   20   71   61   70    1   79   30
```

```
random values using generator std::mt19937
    38.08   79.86   95.12   19.16   73.47   78.19   60.27   60.09   16.45   45.14
    16.44   10.90    6.75   46.47   86.75   34.04   60.51   15.14   71.10   65.44
     3.04    6.58   97.02   72.48   83.41   93.92   22.02    1.08   19.00   99.23
    19.16   62.13   31.12   61.55   52.95    1.70   43.76    3.28   29.83   52.95
    61.57   40.59   14.81    5.62   29.92   97.40   37.27   24.04   46.15    9.97
    78.73   62.22   20.77   38.86   51.91   98.34   59.65   47.21    5.60   86.13
----- Ch18_03_ex2() -----
iteration #0
   6.0309  3.8995  7.7369  5.9477  4.7517  3.1663  4.0144  0.9781
   3.1416  5.7852  4.6810  5.1597  4.1444  5.0444  4.7650  3.9364
   3.4640  5.4442  4.9307  5.2849  4.7905  7.2687  8.8255  3.9498
   7.2388  0.9466  2.7978  6.5584  5.7462  7.2605  2.6825  4.2271

iteration #1
   6.0309  3.8995  7.7369  5.9477  4.7517  3.1663  4.0144  0.9781
   3.1416  5.7852  4.6810  5.1597  4.1444  5.0444  4.7650  3.9364
   3.4640  5.4442  4.9307  5.2849  4.7905  7.2687  8.8255  3.9498
   7.2388  0.9466  2.7978  6.5584  5.7462  7.2605  2.6825  4.2271
----- Ch18_03_ex3() -----
Saved histogram to file Ch18_03_ex3-histogram-00.csv
Saved histogram to file Ch18_03_ex3-histogram-01.csv
Saved histogram to file Ch18_03_ex3-histogram-02.csv
Saved histogram to file Ch18_03_ex3-histogram-03.csv
```

Dice Games

Dice games are another common use case for random numbers. Class DiceSet, shown in Listing 18-4-1-1, is a simple class that simulates the rolling of num_dice dies with each having num_sides (faces). The opening section of Listing 18-4-1-1 contains the definition of class DiceSet. Note that the private section DiceSet contains two parts. The first part includes attributes related to the simulated dice, while the second defines the requisite members for random number generation.

CHAPTER 18　NUMERICAL PROCESSING – PART 1

Listing 18-4-1-1. Example Ch18_04 – Class DiceSet

```
//---------------------------------------------------------------
// DiceSet.h
//---------------------------------------------------------------
#ifndef DICE_SET_H_
#define DICE_SET_H_
#include <random>
#include <string>
#include <vector>

class DiceSet
{
public:
    DiceSet() = delete;
    DiceSet(unsigned int num_dice, unsigned int num_sides, unsigned int
    rng_seed);

    unsigned int NumDice() const { return m_NumDice; }
    unsigned int NumSides() const { return m_NumSides; }

    std::vector<unsigned int> roll(unsigned int offset = 1);
    std::vector<std::string> roll_names();

    void set_side_names(unsigned int die_num,
        const std::vector<std::string>& side_names);

private:
    bool check_args(unsigned int num_dice, unsigned int num_sides);

    // dice attributes
    unsigned int m_NumDice {};
    unsigned int m_NumSides {};
    unsigned int m_RngSeed {};
    std::vector<std::string> m_SideNames {};

    // random number generation attributes
    std::random_device m_RngDevice {};
```

```cpp
    std::mt19937 m_RngEngine {};
    std::uniform_int_distribution<unsigned int> m_RngDist {};
};

#endif


//---------------------------------------------------------------------
// DiceSet.cpp
//---------------------------------------------------------------------

#include <random>
#include <stdexcept>
#include <string>
#include <vector>
#include "DiceSet.h"

DiceSet::DiceSet(unsigned int num_dice, unsigned int num_sides,
    unsigned int rng_seed)
{
    // save DiceSet parameters
    if (!check_args(num_dice, num_sides))
        throw std::runtime_error("DiceSet ctor - invalid argument value");

    m_NumDice = num_dice;
    m_NumSides = num_sides;
    m_RngSeed = rng_seed;

    // initialize default side names (or face labels)
    m_SideNames.resize(m_NumDice * m_NumSides);
    for (size_t i = 0; i < m_NumDice; ++i)
    {
        for (size_t j = 0; j < m_NumSides; ++j)
            m_SideNames[i * m_NumSides + j] = std::to_string(j + 1);
    }

    // initialize RNG engine
    if (m_RngSeed == 0)
        m_RngEngine.seed(m_RngDevice());
```

```cpp
        else
            m_RngEngine.seed(m_RngSeed);

        // initialize distribution
        std::uniform_int_distribution<unsigned int> temp_dist
        (0, num_sides - 1);
        m_RngDist.param(temp_dist.param());
    }

    void DiceSet::set_side_names(unsigned int dice_num,
        const std::vector<std::string>& side_names)
    {
        if ((dice_num >= m_NumDice || side_names.size() != m_NumSides))
        {
            const char* msg = "DiceSet::set_side_names - invalid argument";
            throw std::runtime_error(msg);
        }

        for (unsigned int j = 0; j < m_NumSides; ++j)
            m_SideNames[dice_num * m_NumSides + j] = side_names[j];
    }

    std::vector<unsigned int> DiceSet::roll(unsigned int offset)
    {
        // perform simulated roll, return integer values
        std::vector<unsigned int> roll_values(m_NumDice);

        for (size_t i = 0; i < roll_values.size(); ++i)
            roll_values[i] = m_RngDist(m_RngEngine) + offset;

        return roll_values;
    }

    std::vector<std::string> DiceSet::roll_names()
    {
        // perform simulated roll, return side names
        std::vector<unsigned int> roll_values {roll(0)};
        std::vector<std::string> roll_names(roll_values.size());
```

```cpp
    for (size_t i = 0; i < roll_names.size(); ++i)
        roll_names[i] = m_SideNames[i * m_NumSides + roll_values[i]];

    return roll_names;
}

bool DiceSet::check_args(unsigned int num_dice, unsigned int num_sides)
{
    // validate num_dice (arbitrary value for maximum number of dice)
    if (num_dice > 20)
        return false;

    // validate num_sides (most common die sizes are valid, can change)
    bool rc = (num_sides == 6  || num_sides == 4  || num_sides == 8 ||
               num_sides == 10 || num_sides == 12 || num_sides == 20);
    return rc;
}
```

The second part of Listing 18-4-1-1 shows the definitions for class DiceSet. Execution of DiceSet's constructor begins with the validation of arguments num_dice and num_sides. Following argument validation, each die side is assigned a default name. If m_RngSeed == 0 is true, the constructor's penultimate code block initializes m_RngEngine using a non-deterministic seed value returned by m_RngDevice(). Otherwise, deterministic seed m_RngSeed is used, which is useful for testing purposes. In the constructor's final code block, the statement std::uniform_int_distribution<unsigned int> temp_dist(0, num_sides - 1) instantiates a uniform integer distribution for DiceSet rolls. Execution of the next statement, m_RngDist.param(temp_dist.param()), copies temp_dist's internal parameters and assigns them to class attribute m_RngDist. All STL random number distribution classes define a member function named param() that can be used to get or set a distribution object's parameters. The object type returned by the get variant of param() varies depending on the distribution class.

The two other member functions of note in Listing 18-4-1-1 are std::vector<unsigned int> DiceSet::roll(unsigned int offset) and std::vector<std::string> DiceSet::roll_names(). The former returns a std::vector<unsigned int> of values that represent a simulated roll of m_NumDice. The value of each unsigned integer element in the returned vector is [0 + offset, m_NumSides + offset). Execution of std::vector<std::string> DiceSet::roll_names() is similar but returns a vector of side names (or face labels)

CHAPTER 18 NUMERICAL PROCESSING – PART 1

Listing 18-4-1-2 shows the source code for example Ch18_04_ex1(). This example demonstrates the use of class DiceSet using two dice. In the outer for loop, execution of roll_values = dice.roll() simulates a roll of both dice in object dice. Note that dice's constructor used a seed value of zero, which means different results for each execution of Ch18_04_ex1() (recall that DiceSet's constructor non-deterministically initializes its random number when the specified seed equals zero).

Listing 18-4-1-2. Example Ch18_04 – Ch18_04_ex1()

```
//-----------------------------------------------------------------------
// Ch18_04_ex.cpp
//-----------------------------------------------------------------------

#include "Ch18_04.h"
#include "AminoAcid.h"
#include "DiceSet.h"

void Ch18_04_ex1()
{
    constexpr size_t num_rolls {30};
    constexpr unsigned int num_dice {2};
    constexpr unsigned int num_sides {6};
    constexpr unsigned int seed {0};

    // allocate dice set (uses default values for side names)
    DiceSet dice(num_dice, num_sides, seed);

    // perform simulated rolls
    std::println("\nusing class DiceSet ");
    std::println("(num_dice = {:d}, num_sides = {:d})\n", num_dice,
        num_sides);

    for (unsigned int i = 0; i < num_rolls; ++i)
    {
        std::print("roll {:2d}: ", i);

        // roll dice
        std::vector<unsigned int> roll_values = dice.roll();
```

CHAPTER 18   NUMERICAL PROCESSING – PART 1

```
        // sum values of all dice
        unsigned int total {};
        for (unsigned int j = 0; j < num_dice; ++j)
        {
            total += roll_values[j];
            std::print("{:1d} ", roll_values[j]);
        }
        std::print(" ({:2d})", total);

        if ((i + 1) % 2 == 0)
            std::println("");
        else
            std::print("  |  ");
    }
}
```

The second `DiceSet` example, shown in Listing 18-4-2, instantiates a `DiceSet` that includes 15 dice, and each die contains 20 sides. You may recall from earlier examples that there are 20 standard amino acids. Given this and the fact that an icosahedron is sometimes used as a physical die, it's easy to imagine dozens of thrilling peptide or protein assembly games that could be created for both PCs and mobile devices.

Listing 18-4-2. Example Ch18_04 – Ch18_04_ex2()

```
void Ch18_04_ex2()
{
    constexpr size_t num_rolls {20};
    constexpr unsigned int num_dice {15};
    constexpr unsigned int num_sides {20};
    constexpr unsigned int seed {0};

    // allocate dice set and initialize side names
    DiceSet dice_aa(num_dice, num_sides, seed);

    std::vector<std::string> aa_code3 = AminoAcid::get_vector_all_code3();
    for (unsigned int i = 0; i < num_dice; ++i)
        dice_aa.set_side_names(i, aa_code3);
```

CHAPTER 18   NUMERICAL PROCESSING – PART 1

```
    // perform simulated rolls
    std::println("\nusing class DiceSet ");
    std::println("(num_dice = {:d}, num_sides = {:d})\n", num_dice,
        num_sides);

    for (unsigned int i = 0; i < num_rolls; ++i)
    {
        std::vector<std::string> roll_values = dice_aa.roll_names();

        std::print("roll {:2d}:   ", i);
        for (unsigned int j = 0; j < num_dice; ++j)
            std::print("{:4s} ", roll_values[j]);
        std::println("");
    }
}
```

Following instantiation of dice_aa, Ch18_04_ex2() employs AminoAcid::get_vector_all_code3() to obtain a std::vector<std::string> that contains all code3 amino acids. The ensuing for loop utilizes dice_aa.set_side_names(i, aa_code3) to assign code3 symbols to the sides of each die in dice_aa. Each iteration of the outer for loop executes std::vector<std::string> roll_values = dice_aa.roll_names(). The inner for loop then prints the code3 result for each die in dice_aa. Expansion of the code in Ch18_04_ex2() to simulate assembly of genuine peptides or proteins is left as an exercise for the reader. Here are the results for example Ch18_04:

```
----- Results for example Ch18_04 -----

----- Ch18_04_ex1() -----

using class DiceSet
(num_dice = 2, num_sides = 6)

roll  0: 5 1  ( 6) |  roll  1: 3 5  ( 8)
roll  2: 3 5  ( 8) |  roll  3: 3 1  ( 4)
roll  4: 2 1  ( 3) |  roll  5: 6 5  (11)
roll  6: 1 2  ( 3) |  roll  7: 1 1  ( 2)
roll  8: 5 1  ( 6) |  roll  9: 4 3  ( 7)
roll 10: 2 2  ( 4) |  roll 11: 3 5  ( 8)
```

```
roll 12: 2 5  ( 7) | roll 13: 2 6  ( 8)
roll 14: 6 3  ( 9) | roll 15: 5 6  (11)
roll 16: 5 2  ( 7) | roll 17: 6 2  ( 8)
roll 18: 6 3  ( 9) | roll 19: 2 1  ( 3)
roll 20: 1 5  ( 6) | roll 21: 4 4  ( 8)
roll 22: 4 3  ( 7) | roll 23: 5 4  ( 9)
roll 24: 3 1  ( 4) | roll 25: 5 1  ( 6)
roll 26: 6 4  (10) | roll 27: 3 4  ( 7)
roll 28: 1 2  ( 3) | roll 29: 5 1  ( 6)

----- Ch18_04_ex2() -----

using class DiceSet
(num_dice = 15, num_sides = 20)

roll  0: Met Ala Gln Gln Lys Val Gln Tyr Asp Ile Thr Phe Leu Ser Trp
roll  1: Ala Met Ser Asn Cys Met Ala Asp Trp His Gln Thr Gly Ile Trp
roll  2: His Phe Lys Asp His Ser Leu Val Leu Tyr Arg Trp Trp Val Gly
roll  3: Gln Lys Lys Tyr Glu Phe Gly Leu Thr Arg Gly Cys Tyr Gln Ser
roll  4: Cys Ala Thr Leu Trp Asn Val Arg Met Ala Pro Gly Pro His Pro
roll  5: Ile Glu Phe His Leu Tyr Met Glu Glu Val Gln Trp Lys Tyr Pro
roll  6: Cys Phe Ala Ala Ser Lys Trp Glu Ser Val Arg Gln Gly Gly Ser
roll  7: Asn Asn Cys Ala His His Cys Tyr Phe Trp Pro Met Ile Cys Arg
roll  8: Pro Tyr Tyr Gln Glu Lys Asp Leu Cys Trp Arg His Asp Phe Glu
roll  9: Val Asp Leu Trp Arg Gln Gly Gly Cys Phe Arg Cys Arg Ile Asn
roll 10: Trp Gly Gly Asn Phe Tyr Met His Ser Arg Glu Tyr Tyr Phe His
roll 11: Phe Glu Lys Lys Gln Asp Asn Ser Val His Gly Gln Ala Tyr Ala
roll 12: Val Gln Lys Arg Arg Gln Leu Asp Met Val Tyr Glu Trp Tyr Phe
roll 13: Ala Pro Gly Gln Ile Ser Glu His Phe Glu Ile Pro Ala Lys Trp
roll 14: Asn Cys Asp Tyr Trp Met Trp Val Val Thr Trp Glu Trp Tyr Met
roll 15: Met Arg His Arg Asn Gly Gly His Gln Leu Gly Leu Leu Lys Ala
roll 16: Arg Trp His Trp Ser Ser Asn Asn Gly Asn Leu His Glu Glu Asp
roll 17: Arg Cys Tyr Trp His Trp Arg Phe Phe Leu Met Ser Phe Gly Val
roll 18: Gln Asn His His Pro Leu Lys Asn Asn Pro Leu Ile Thr Leu Asn
roll 19: His Glu Ser Ile Gln Trp Gln Met Cys Gly Ala Met Arg Glu Trp
```

CHAPTER 18 NUMERICAL PROCESSING – PART 1

Vector of Random Numbers

In earlier chapters, some of the source examples exploited function RN::get_vector() (Common/RN.h) to obtain a vector of random numbers (see Ch10_02, Ch11_08, Ch12_01, and others). Listing 18-5-1-1 shows the source code for this function.

Listing 18-5-1-1. Example Ch18_05 – RN::get_vector()

```
template <typename T> std::vector<T> get_vector(size_t n,
    int rng_min = s_RngMinDef, int rng_max = s_RngMaxDef,
    unsigned int rng_seed = s_RngSeedDef)
{
    // create random number generator and distribution
    std::mt19937 rng {};
    std::uniform_int_distribution<int> rng_dist(rng_min, rng_max);

    // seed generator
    if (rng_seed == 0)
    {
        std::random_device rd {};
        rng.seed(rd());
    }
    else
        rng.seed(rng_seed);

    // generate vector with random numbers
    std::vector<T> vec(n);
    for (auto& x : vec)
        x = static_cast<T>(rng_dist(rng));
    return vec;
}
```

The reason why the source code for RN::get_vector() wasn't shown until now is that it utilizes several STL random number generation classes first expounded in this chapter. Execution of RN::get_vector() opens with the instantiation of std::mt19937 rng_engine {} and std::uniform_int_distribution<int> rng_dist(rng_min, rng_max).

CHAPTER 18   NUMERICAL PROCESSING – PART 1

If argument seed equals zero, RN::get_vector() exploits std::random_device rd {} and rng_engine.seed(rd()) to non-deterministically seed rng_engine; otherwise, rng_engine.seed(rng_seed) is used.

Listing 18-5-1-2 shows the source code for example function Ch18_05_ex1(), which exercises RN::get_vector(). Note in this function that the first two usages of RN::get_vector() use a nonzero value, which means that vec1 and vec2 are equal. The second pair of RN::get_vector() usages employs a seed value of zero. This instructs RN::get_vector() to seed its underlying random number generator using std::random_device() as previously explained.

Listing 18-5-1-2. Example Ch18_05 – Ch18_05_ex1()

```
//-------------------------------------------------------------------
// Ch18_05_ex.cpp
//-------------------------------------------------------------------

#include <vector>
#include "Ch18_05.h"
#include "MT.h"
#include "RN.h"

void Ch18_05_ex1()
{
    const char* fmt1 = "{:7.1f}";
    const char* fmt2 = "{:7d}";
    constexpr size_t epl_max1 {10};
    constexpr size_t epl_max2 {10};

    constexpr size_t n {50};
    constexpr int rng_min {1};
    constexpr int rng_max {500};
    constexpr unsigned int rng_seed {99};

    // using RN::get_vector (constant seed)
    std::vector vec1 = RN::get_vector<double>(n, rng_min, rng_max,
        rng_seed);
    MT::print_ctr("\nvec1:\n", vec1, fmt1, epl_max1);
```

```
    std::vector vec2 = RN::get_vector<double>(n, rng_min, rng_max,
    rng_seed);
    MT::print_ctr("\nvec2:\n", vec2, fmt1, epl_max1);
    std::println("\nvec1 == vec2: {:s} (expect true)", vec1 == vec2);

    // using RN::get_vector (hardware seed)
    std::vector vec3 = RN::get_vector<int>(n, rng_min, rng_max, 0);
    MT::print_ctr("\nvec3:\n", vec3, fmt2, epl_max2);

    std::vector vec4 = RN::get_vector<int>(n, rng_min, rng_max, 0);
    MT::print_ctr("\nvec4:\n", vec4, fmt2, epl_max2);
    std::println("\nvec3 == vec3: {:s} (expect false)", vec3 == vec4);
}
```

The results for example Ch18_05 follow this paragraph. These results will vary for each execution.

```
----- Results for example Ch18_05 -----

----- Ch18_05_ex1() -----
vec1:
   337.0  362.0  245.0  416.0  413.0  368.0   16.0  351.0  405.0   97.0
   283.0  489.0  149.0  289.0   24.0  257.0  496.0  426.0    4.0  191.0
   385.0  137.0  374.0  321.0  189.0  247.0  248.0  169.0  465.0  309.0
   198.0  181.0  487.0  166.0  263.0  314.0   47.0  347.0  407.0  164.0
   106.0  205.0  278.0  368.0  147.0  355.0  409.0  142.0  415.0  462.0

vec2:
   337.0  362.0  245.0  416.0  413.0  368.0   16.0  351.0  405.0   97.0
   283.0  489.0  149.0  289.0   24.0  257.0  496.0  426.0    4.0  191.0
   385.0  137.0  374.0  321.0  189.0  247.0  248.0  169.0  465.0  309.0
   198.0  181.0  487.0  166.0  263.0  314.0   47.0  347.0  407.0  164.0
   106.0  205.0  278.0  368.0  147.0  355.0  409.0  142.0  415.0  462.0
```

CHAPTER 18   NUMERICAL PROCESSING – PART 1

```
vec1 == vec2: true (expect true)
vec3:
       164    102    440    360    455     20    308    389    186     89
       360    332    293    362    188    371    221    137    500    467
       304     37    139    183    128    101    489     26    397     81
       249    372    218    340    161     37    145    273    454    132
       328    164    120    307    242    289    213    304    420     95
vec4:
        37    297    461    499    417    289     80    109    227    203
        34    286    468    343    125    490    302    446    426    114
       427    380    133    390     73    354     72    199    152    494
         6     51    486    241    345    180    243    335    315    215
       115    447    328     20      6    238    190    325     56    263
vec3 == vec3: false (expect false)
```

Summary

Here are the key learning points for this chapter:

- The C++ numerics library includes constant variable templates for common mathematical constants as shown in Table 18-1. These variable templates are encompassed in namespace `std::numbers`.

- Class `std::complex` supports arithmetic using complex numbers.

- A random number engine is a uniform random bit generator that encompasses a source of entropy.

- A random number engine adaptor adjusts the output of an underlying random number engine to modify its generation characteristics.

- A random number generator incorporates a random number engine and an optional random number engine adaptor. The STL predefines several random number generators, shown in Table 18-3, that implement common algorithms.

- A random number distribution adjusts the output of a random number generator to conform to a probability density function. Table 18-4 lists STL's random number distribution classes.

- Random number generators are deterministic in that a given seed value always generates the same sequence of values. Class `std::random_device` can be used to generate non-deterministic random numbers using a hardware source of entropy if supported by the implementation.

CHAPTER 19

Numerical Processing – Part 2

This chapter covers additional numerical processing classes and algorithms. Topics covered include

- Using std::valarray
- Using std::slice
- Inner products
- Reductions

Like the previous chapter, some of the discussions in this chapter assume previous exposure to certain mathematical disciplines. You may either skim or skip any sections that are irrelevant to your programming interests.

Class std::valarray

Template class std::valarray is a one-dimensional array-like construct that's specifically designed for numerical operations. Unlike similar containers such as std::array and std::vector, class std::valarray excludes certain forms of aliasing, which facilitates more aggressive optimizations by the compiler. Higher-dimensional arrays can be modeled using classes std::valarray and std::slice. You'll learn more about this later.

CHAPTER 19   NUMERICAL PROCESSING – PART 2

Arithmetic Functions

Listing 19-1-1 shows the source code for example Ch19_01_ex1(). This example demonstrates a few elementary operations using instances of class std::valarray.

Listing 19-1-1. Example Ch19_01 – Ch19_01_ex1()

```cpp
//------------------------------------------------------------
// Ch19_01_ex.cpp
//------------------------------------------------------------

#include <algorithm>
#include <numeric>
#include <valarray>
#include "Ch19_01.h"
#include "MT.h"
#include "RN.h"

void Ch19_01_ex1()
{
    const char* fmt1 = "{:7d}";
    const char* fmt2 = "{:7.1f}";
    constexpr size_t epl_max {10};

    constexpr size_t n {25};
    constexpr int rng_min {1};
    constexpr int rng_max {500};
    constexpr unsigned int rng_seed {19011};

    // using std::valarray<int>
    std::valarray va1 = RN::get_valarray<int>(n, rng_min, rng_max,
        rng_seed);
    MT::print_ctr("\nva1:\n", va1, fmt1, epl_max);

    std::println("\nva1 - sum: {:d}, min: {:d}, max: {:d}",
        va1.sum(), va1.min(), va1.max());

    // using std::valarray<> operator+=
    va1 += 5;
    MT::print_ctr("\nva1 (after operator+=):\n", va1, fmt1, epl_max);
```

```
    // using std::valarray<double>
    std::valarray va2 = RN::get_valarray<double>(n, rng_min, rng_max,
    rng_seed + 1);
    MT::print_ctr("\nva2:\n", va2, fmt2, epl_max);

    std::println("\nva2 - sum: {:..1f}, min: {:..1f}, max: {:..1f}",
        va2.sum(), va2.min(), va2.max());

    // using std::valarray<> operator-=
    va2 -= 0.5;
    MT::print_ctr("\nva2 (after operator-=):\n", va2, fmt2, epl_max);

    // using operator[]
    for (size_t i = 0; i < n; ++i)
        va2[i] = static_cast<double>(va1[i] % 3);
    MT::print_ctr("\nva2 (after operator[] calculations):\n",
        va2, fmt2, epl_max);
}
```

In Ch19_01_ex1()'s opening code block, execution of std::valarray va1 = RN::get_valarray<int>(n, rng_min, rng_max, rng_seed) initializes va1 with n random integers between [rng_min, rng_max]. Function RN::get_valarray() is the std::valarray counterpart of RN::get_vector() (see Listing 18-5-1-1 and Common/RN.h). Execution of va1.sum() computes the sum of all elements in va1, while va1.min() and v1.max() calculate minimum and maximum values. In the next code block, execution of va1 += 5 adds five to each element in va1.

The next std::valarray example in Listing 19-1-1 uses std::valarray va2 = RN::get_valarray<double>(n, rng_min, rng_max, rng_seed) to initialize va2 with random values. Like the previous example, execution of va2.sum() sums the elements of va2, while va2.min() and va2.max() determine va2's minimum and maximum values. The statement va2 -= 0.5 subtracts 0.5 from each element in va2. Other common arithmetic operators can also be used to adjust the elements in a std::valarray.

The final code block in Ch19_01_ex1() illustrates how to use operator[] to access individual elements in a std::valarray. Like std::array and std::vector, std::valarray's operator[] does not check for invalid indices; execution behavior is undefined if one is used. Class std::valarray also doesn't define bounds checking member function at().

CHAPTER 19   NUMERICAL PROCESSING – PART 2

Example function Ch19_01_ex2(), shown in Listing 19-1-2, highlights a few more operations using instances of class std::valarray. Execution of Ch19_01_ex2() begins with the initialization of test std::valarrays va1, va2, and va3. Note that the first two contain elements of type int, while the latter holds long longs.

Listing 19-1-2. Example Ch19_01 – Ch19_01_ex2()

```
void Ch19_01_ex2()
{
    const char* fmt = "{:7d}";
    constexpr size_t epl_max {10};

    // create test valarray<> objects
    std::valarray<int> va1 {10, 20, 30, 40, 50};
    std::valarray<int> va2 {100, 200, 300, 400, 500, 600, 700, 800};
    std::valarray<long long> va3 {1000, 2000, 3000, 4000, 5000, 6000,
    7000, 8000};
    MT::print_ctr("\nva1:\n", va1, fmt, epl_max);
    MT::print_ctr("\nva2:\n", va2, fmt, epl_max);
    MT::print_ctr("\nva3:\n", va3, fmt, epl_max);

    // using valarray<>::operator=
    va2 = va1;
    MT::print_ctr("\nva2 (after operator=):\n", va1, fmt, epl_max);
//  va3 = va1;      // illegal - different element types

    // using valarray<>::apply
    auto apply_op = [](int x) { return x * x - 1; };

    std::valarray<int> va4 = va1.apply(apply_op);
    MT::print_ctr("\nva4:\n", va4, fmt, epl_max);
}
```

Following the calls to print_ctr(), execution of va2 = va1 assigns va1 to va2. Class std::valarray's assignment operator only supports assignments using objects that hold the same element type. The statement va3 = va1 is commented out since it's invalid; object va3 holds long longs, while va1 contains ints. The final code block of Ch19_01_ex2() demonstrates the use of std::valarray::apply(). Execution of std::valarray<int> va4 = va1.apply(apply_op) returns a new std::valarray whose values correspond to va4[i] = apply_op(va1[i]).

In Listing 19-1-3, example function Ch19_01_ex3() utilizes std::iota(std::begin(va1), std::end(va1), fp_t {1}) to initialize std::valarray<double> va1(n). Unlike most other STL containers, class std::valarray does not define iterator member functions begin() and end(). Global functions std::begin() and std::end() must be used to acquire iterators for an instance of std::valarray.

Listing 19-1-3. Example Ch19_01 - Ch19_01_ex3()

```
void Ch19_01_ex3()
{
    const char* fmt = "{:12.4f}";
    constexpr size_t epl_max {5};

    // create test valarray<>
    // must use std::begin() and std::end() for std::valarray iterators
    constexpr size_t n {20};

    std::valarray<double> va1(n);
    std::iota(std::begin(va1), std::end(va1), 1.0);
    MT::print_ctr("\nva1:\n", va1, fmt, epl_max);

    // using std::valarray<> math overloads
    std::valarray<double> va2 = std::sqrt(va1);
    MT::print_ctr("\nva2 (after sqrt):\n", va2, fmt, epl_max);

    va2 = std::pow(va2, 3.0);
    MT::print_ctr("\nva2 (after pow):\n", va2, fmt, epl_max);

    va2 = std::log10(va1);
    MT::print_ctr("\nva2 (after log10):\n", va2, fmt, epl_max);
}
```

The remaining code in Ch19_01_ex3() demonstrates the use of std::valarray non-member functions std::sqrt(), std::pow(), and std::log10(). Each of these functions applies a mathematical operation to each element in the specified std::valarray. The STL also defines std::valarray overloads for common trigonometric and hyperbolic operations.

CHAPTER 19 NUMERICAL PROCESSING – PART 2

In Listing 19-1-4, example function Ch19_01_ex4() illustrates the use of operator<, operator==, and operator>. These operators return objects of type std::valarray<bool>. For example, execution of std::valarray<bool> va_lt = va1 < va2 returns a std::valarray<bool> whose *i*-th element equals va1[i] < va2[i]. When performing comparisons using std::valarrays, both arrays must hold the same number of elements.

Listing 19-1-4. Example Ch19_01 – Ch19_01_ex4()

```
void Ch19_01_ex4()
{
    const char* fmt = "{:7.1f}";
    constexpr size_t epl_max {11};
    constexpr size_t n {10};

    // create test valarray<> objects
    std::valarray<float> va1(n);
    std::iota(std::begin(va1), std::end(va1), 1.0f);

    std::valarray<float> va2(va1);
    va2[0] += 1.0f;
    va2[n / 4] -= 2.0f;
    va2[n / 2] *= 3.0f;
    va2[n - 1] /= 4.0f;

    MT::print_ctr("\nva1:\n", va1, fmt, epl_max);
    MT::print_ctr("\nva2:\n", va2, fmt, epl_max);

    // using operator< (returns std::valarray<bool>)
    std::valarray<bool> va_lt = va1 < va2;
    MT::print_ctr("\nva_lt:\n", va_lt, "{:>7s}", epl_max);

    // using operator== (returns std::valarray<bool>)
    std::valarray<bool> va_eq = va1 == va2;
    MT::print_ctr("\nva_cmp:\n", va_eq, "{:>7s}", epl_max);

    // using operator> (returns std::valarray<bool>)
    std::valarray<bool> va_gt = va1 > va2;
    MT::print_ctr("\nva_gt:\n", va_gt, "{:>7s}", epl_max);
}
```

Here are the results for example Ch19_01:

```
----- Results for example Ch19_01 -----

----- Ch19_01_ex1() -----

va1:
    16    454    341    466    394    276    327    115    203    373
   450    260    219    491     18    487    187     84    166     64
    22    131    222    210    129

va1 - sum: 6105, min: 16, max: 491

va1 (after operator+=):
    21    459    346    471    399    281    332    120    208    378
   455    265    224    496     23    492    192     89    171     69
    27    136    227    215    134

va2:
  70.0   238.0  206.0   77.0  330.0  210.0  473.0  453.0  210.0  135.0
  82.0   222.0  211.0  217.0   86.0   72.0  330.0  425.0  241.0  408.0
 124.0    60.0  461.0  335.0  259.0

va2 - sum: 5935.0, min: 60.0, max: 473.0

va2 (after operator-=):
  69.5   237.5  205.5   76.5  329.5  209.5  472.5  452.5  209.5  134.5
  81.5   221.5  210.5  216.5   85.5   71.5  329.5  424.5  240.5  407.5
 123.5    59.5  460.5  334.5  258.5

va2 (after operator[] calculations):
   0.0    0.0    1.0    0.0    0.0    2.0    2.0    0.0    1.0    0.0
   2.0    1.0    2.0    1.0    2.0    0.0    0.0    2.0    0.0    0.0
   0.0    1.0    2.0    2.0    2.0
```

CHAPTER 19   NUMERICAL PROCESSING – PART 2

----- Ch19_01_ex2() -----

va1:
    10   20   30   40   50

va2:
   100   200   300   400   500   600   700   800

va3:
  1000   2000   3000   4000   5000   6000   7000   8000

va2 (after operator=):
    10   20   30   40   50

va4:
    99   399   899   1599   2499

----- Ch19_01_ex3() -----

va1:
    1.0000   2.0000   3.0000   4.0000   5.0000
    6.0000   7.0000   8.0000   9.0000   10.0000
   11.0000   12.0000   13.0000   14.0000   15.0000
   16.0000   17.0000   18.0000   19.0000   20.0000

va2 (after sqrt):
    1.0000   1.4142   1.7321   2.0000   2.2361
    2.4495   2.6458   2.8284   3.0000   3.1623
    3.3166   3.4641   3.6056   3.7417   3.8730
    4.0000   4.1231   4.2426   4.3589   4.4721

va2 (after pow):
    1.0000   2.8284   5.1962   8.0000   11.1803
   14.6969   18.5203   22.6274   27.0000   31.6228
   36.4829   41.5692   46.8722   52.3832   58.0948
   64.0000   70.0928   76.3675   82.8191   89.4427

va2 (after log10):
    0.0000   0.3010   0.4771   0.6021   0.6990
    0.7782   0.8451   0.9031   0.9542   1.0000
    1.0414   1.0792   1.1139   1.1461   1.1761
    1.2041   1.2304   1.2553   1.2788   1.3010

```
----- Ch19_01_ex4() -----
va1:
    1.0    2.0    3.0    4.0    5.0    6.0    7.0    8.0    9.0   10.0

va2:
    2.0    2.0    1.0    4.0    5.0   18.0    7.0    8.0    9.0    2.5

va_lt:
   true  false  false  false  false   true  false  false  false  false

va_cmp:
  false   true  false   true   true  false   true   true   true  false

va_gt:
  false  false   true  false  false  false  false  false  false   true
```

Statistical Calculations

Many applications need to calculate common statistical properties using the elements in an array. The first source example of this section illustrates how to compute the mean and standard deviation using the elements in a `std::valarray`. The second example explains a somewhat more intricate least-squares computation. Here are the equations that example Ch19_02 uses to calculate the sample mean and standard deviation of a `std::valarray`:

$$\bar{x} = \frac{1}{n}\sum_i x_i$$

$$s = \sqrt{\frac{1}{n-1}\sum_i (x_i - \bar{x})^2}$$

Listing 19-2-1 shows the source code for example `Ch19_02_ex1()`. Like the previous example, the opening code block in `Ch19_02_ex1()` utilizes `std::valarray va = RN::get_valarray<double>(n, rng_min, rng_max, rng_seed)` to instantiate a `std::valarray` of random values. Execution of the expression `double va_mean = va.sum() / va.size()` calculates the mean.

CHAPTER 19 NUMERICAL PROCESSING – PART 2

Listing 19-2-1. Example Ch19_02 - Ch19_02_ex1()

```cpp
//-------------------------------------------------------------
// Ch19_02_ex.cpp
//-------------------------------------------------------------

#include <algorithm>
#include <cmath>
#include <concepts>
#include <expected>
#include <valarray>
#include <utility>
#include "Ch19_02.h"
#include "MT.h"
#include "RN.h"

void Ch19_02_ex1()
{
    const char* fmt = "{:7.1f}";
    constexpr size_t epl_max {10};

    constexpr size_t n {50};
    constexpr int rng_min {1};
    constexpr int rng_max {50};
    constexpr unsigned int rng_seed {19014};

    // create test valarray<>
    std::valarray va = RN::get_valarray<double>(n, rng_min, rng_max,
        rng_seed);
    MT::print_ctr("\nva:\n", va, fmt, epl_max);

    // calculate mean
    double va_mean = va.sum() / va.size();

    // calculate standard deviation using std::ranges::fold_left
    auto sd_fold_op = [&va_mean](double sum, double x) -> double
        { return sum + (x - va_mean) * (x - va_mean); };

    double va_sd_sum = std::ranges::fold_left(va, 0.0, sd_fold_op);
    double va_sd = std::sqrt(va_sd_sum / (va.size() - 1));
```

```
        std::println("\nva_mean: {:.4f}", va_mean);
        std::println("va_sd    {:.4f}", va_sd);
}
```

In Chapter 11, you learned how to use algorithm `std::ranges::fold_left()` to sum the elements of a container (see example Ch11_08). In the current example, this same algorithm can be exploited to compute the standard deviation's sum-of-squares component. In Listing 19-2-1, lambda expression

```
auto sd_fold_op = [&va_mean](double sum, double x) -> double
    { return sum + (x - va_mean) * (x - va_mean); };
```

is invoked during execution of `va_sd_sum = std::ranges::fold_left(va, 0.0, sd_fold_op)` to calculate the sum of squares. More specifically, `std:ranges::fold_left()` applies `sd_fold_op()` to each element in va and sums the calculated squares. The subsequent statement, `va_sd = std::sqrt(va_sd_sum / (va.size() - 1))`, computes the final standard deviation.

Another widely used statistical technique is linear regression, which models a linear relationship between two sets of data. The least-squares method of linear regression finds a best-fit $y = mx + b$ line. In this equation, x is the independent variable, y is the dependent (or measured) variable, and b is the line's y-axis intercept point. The regression line's slope and intercept point can be calculated using series of computations that minimize the sum of the squared deviations between the line and the sample data points. Least-squares lines are often exploited to predict an unknown y value using a known x value. The following equations are used to calculate the slope and intercept point of a least-squares line:

$$m = \frac{n \sum_i x_i y_i - \sum_i x_i \sum_i y_i}{n \sum_i x_i^2 - \left(\sum_i x_i\right)^2}$$

$$b = \frac{\sum_i x_i^2 \sum_i y_i - \sum_i x_i \sum_i x_i y_i}{n \sum_i x_i^2 - \left(\sum_i x_i\right)^2}$$

CHAPTER 19   NUMERICAL PROCESSING – PART 2

At first glance, these equations seem a bit complicated. However, note that the denominators are the same in both equations. Also, note that the least-squares equations contain only four distinct sum variables:

$$sum_x = \sum_i x_i$$

$$sum_y = \sum_i y_i$$

$$sum_{xy} = \sum_i x_i y_i$$

$$sum_{xx} = \sum_i x_i^2$$

Following calculation of the sum variables, the least-squares line slope and intercept point are easily derived using simple arithmetic.

Listing 19-2-2 shows the source code for example Ch19_02_ex2(). This example spotlights a least-squares calculation using the elements of two std::valarrays.

Listing 19-2-2. Example Ch19_02 - Ch19_02_ex2()

```
#if __cpp_lib_expected >= 202211L
template <typename T> requires std::floating_point<T>
std::expected<std::pair<T, T>, bool> least_squares(const
std::valarray<T>& va_x,
    const std::valarray<T>& va_y, T epsilon)
{
    if (va_x.size() != va_y.size())
        return std::unexpected(false);

    // calculate sum_x and sum_y
    T sum_x = va_x.sum();
    T sum_y = va_y.sum();

    // calculate sum_xx
    auto sum_xx_op = [](T sum, T x) -> T { return sum + x * x; };
    T sum_xx = std::ranges::fold_left(va_x, T {1}, sum_xx_op);
```

```cpp
        // calculate sum_xy
        auto iter_y = std::begin(va_y);
        auto sum_xy_op = [&iter_y](T sum, T x) -> T
            { return sum + x * *iter_y++; };

        T sum_xy = std::ranges::fold_left(va_x, T {1}, sum_xy_op);

        // calculate slope and intercept
        auto n = va_x.size();
        T den = n * sum_xx - sum_x * sum_x;

        if (std::fabs(den) < epsilon)
            return std::unexpected(false);

        T slope = (n * sum_xy - sum_x * sum_y) / den;
        T intercept = (sum_xx * sum_y - sum_x * sum_xy) / den;
        return std::make_pair(slope, intercept);
}
#endif

void Ch19_02_ex2()
{
#if __cpp_lib_expected >= 202211L
    using fp_t = float;

    const char* fmt = "{:7.1f}";
    constexpr size_t epl_max {10};
    constexpr size_t n {50};
    constexpr int rng_min {1};
    constexpr int rng_max {1000};
    constexpr unsigned int rng_seed {19014};

    // create test valarray va_x
    std::valarray<fp_t> va_x =
        RN::get_valarray<fp_t>(n, rng_min, rng_max, rng_seed);
```

```
    MT::print_ctr("\nva_x:\n", va_x, fmt, epl_max);

    // create test valarray va_y
    std::valarray<fp_t> va_y(va_x.size());
    std::ranges::transform(va_x, std::begin(va_y), [](fp_t x)
    {
        fp_t adjust = static_cast<fp_t>(RN::get_value<int>() % 25) /
        fp_t {100};
        return x + x * adjust;
    });

    MT::print_ctr("\nva_y:\n", va_y, fmt, epl_max);

    // using least_squares
    auto result = least_squares(va_x, va_y, fp_t {1.0e-9});

    if (result.has_value())
    {
        auto [slope, intercept] = result.value();
        std::println("\nslope: {:.4f}, intercept: {:.4f}", slope,
        intercept);
    }
    else
        std::println("\nleast_squares() failed");
#else
    std::println("Example Ch19_02_ex2() requires std::expected (C++23)");
#endif
}
```

Listing 19-2-2 begins with the definition of a template function named least_squares(). Note that this function requires three arguments: const std::valarray& va_x, const std::val_array& va_y, and epsilon. This last argument is used to preclude potential arithmetic underflows. Also, note that least_squares() returns a std::expected<std::pair<T, T>, bool>. Recall that a std::expected value combines an expected object and an unexpected (or error) object into a single entity (see example Ch05_06).

CHAPTER 19 NUMERICAL PROCESSING – PART 2

Following size validation of va_x and va_y, least_squares() utilizes sum_x = va_x. sum() and sum_y = va_y.sum() to sum the elements of va_x and va_y. The next code block employs auto sum_xx_op = [](T sum, T x) -> T { return sum + x * x; } and T sum_xx = std::ranges::fold_left(va_x, T {1}, sum_xx_op) to calculate va_x's sums of squares.

To calculate sum_xy, Ch19_02_ex2() utilizes the following:

```
auto iter_y = std::begin(va_y);
auto sum_xy_op = [&iter_y](T sum, T x) -> T
    { return sum + x * *iter_y++; };

T sum_xy = std::ranges::fold_left(va_x, T {1}, sum_xy_op);
```

Algorithm std::ranges::fold_left() normally applies the specified function object to the elements of a single range. However, calculation of sum_xy involves elements from both va_x and va_y. To handle this, lambda expression sum_xy_op captures an iterator to va_y and updates this iterator during each invocation.

Following calculation of sum_xy, the common slope and offset denominator are calculated using auto n = va_x.size() and T den = n * sum_xx - sum_x * sum_x. If (std::fabs(den) < epsilon) is true, the denominator is too close to zero for the result to be valid. In this case Ch19_02_ex2() returns std::unexpected(false). Otherwise, the final slope and intercept are calculated, and Ch19_02_ex2() returns std::make_pair(slope, intercept).

Also shown in Listing 19-2-2 is example function Ch19_02_ex2(). Execution of this function commences with the instantiation of two test std::valarrays: va_x and va_y. Note that algorithm std::ranges::transform() is employed to generate values for va_y using the values of va_x and a linear transformation operator. This was done to facilitate a quick accuracy check of least_squares()'s results (the slope should be close to 1.0). Following generation of the test arrays, Ch19_02_ex2() exercises result = least_squares(va_x, va_y, fp_t {1.0e-9}) to perform a least-squares calculation. If result.has_value() is true, structured binding is employed to obtain the slope and intercept values from result.value(). Otherwise, an error message is printed.

The results for example Ch19_02 follow this paragraph. These results will vary for each execution since RN::get_value() utilizes std::random_device rd {} to generate non-deterministic random numbers.

CHAPTER 19 NUMERICAL PROCESSING – PART 2

```
----- Results for example Ch19_02 -----

----- Ch19_02_ex1() -----

va:
     5.0    18.0    24.0     2.0    18.0    37.0    13.0    33.0     3.0    13.0
    35.0    27.0    40.0    44.0    46.0    33.0    31.0     9.0    31.0    43.0
    48.0    28.0    29.0    41.0    43.0    16.0    13.0    31.0    30.0    37.0
    14.0    17.0    48.0    29.0    10.0    31.0    50.0    43.0    39.0    14.0
    36.0    27.0    19.0    14.0     2.0    15.0    29.0    19.0    36.0     3.0
va_mean: 26.3200
va_sd    13.6702

----- Ch19_02_ex2() -----

va_x:
    97.0   345.0   479.0    25.0   343.0   729.0   259.0   644.0    44.0   257.0
   687.0   536.0   798.0   864.0   919.0   656.0   616.0   165.0   608.0   852.0
   957.0   559.0   574.0   813.0   842.0   304.0   241.0   620.0   590.0   738.0
   270.0   323.0   954.0   576.0   196.0   602.0   983.0   856.0   779.0   273.0
   718.0   528.0   366.0   262.0    32.0   300.0   565.0   369.0   713.0    51.0
va_y:
   112.5   362.2   536.5    25.2   404.7   736.3   274.5   669.8    53.2   272.4
   714.5   578.9   933.7  1045.4  1084.4   675.7   640.6   178.2   747.8  1005.4
  1043.1   682.0   637.1   845.5   993.6   343.5   257.9   694.4   672.6   848.7
   318.6   381.1  1106.6   656.6   213.6   686.3  1169.8  1001.5   779.0   330.3
   782.6   607.2   402.6   293.4    32.3   324.0   689.3   446.5   755.8    63.2
slope: 1.1355, intercept: -5.4492
```

Class std::slice

An instance of std::slice resembles a BLAS[1] slice. A std::slice doesn't hold or own any elements. It simply groups three std::size_t values – a start index, a size (length), and a stride – that collectively specify elements from a std::valarray. Figure 19-1 shows a few std::slice examples. Slices are frequently used to simplify the coding of matrix-vector operations and linear algebra functions.

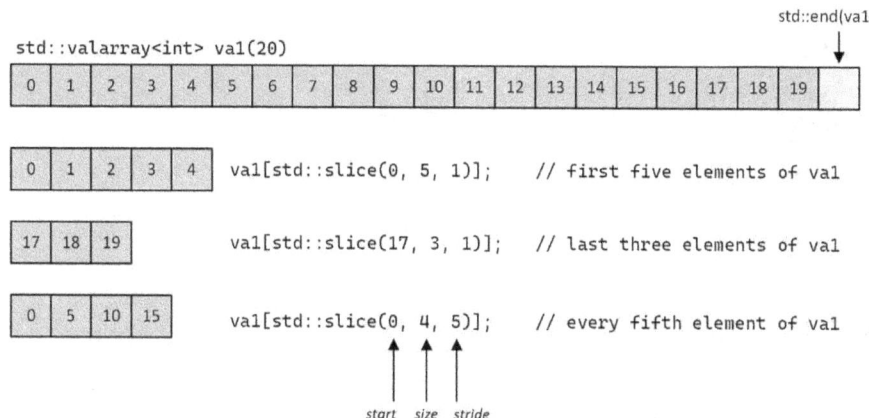

Figure 19-1. Examples of std::slice objects

Basic Operations

Listing 19-3-1 shows the source code for example Ch19_03_ex1(). This example demonstrates elementary use of class std::slice. It also illustrates how to use std::valarray::operator[] to retrieve elements from a std::valarray. The opening code block of Ch19_03_ex1() defines a lambda expression named print_va(), which prints the elements of std::valarray<int>& va. Note that print_va() exploits a range for loop to print va's elements just like an ordinary container.

---

[1] Basic Linear Algebra Subprograms, a specification that describes low-level functions for linear algebra and matrix-vector operations.

CHAPTER 19   NUMERICAL PROCESSING – PART 2

Listing 19-3-1. Example Ch19_03 - Ch19_03_ex1()

```cpp
//-----------------------------------------------------------------------
// Ch19_03_ex.cpp
//-----------------------------------------------------------------------

#include <algorithm>
#include <format>
#include <numeric>
#include <stdexcept>
#include <valarray>
#include "Ch19_03.h"
#include "Matrix.h"

void Ch19_03_ex1()
{
    auto print_va = [](const char* msg, const std::valarray<int>& va)
    {
        std::print("{:s}", msg);
        for (int x : va)
            std::print("{:3d}", x);
        std::println("");
    };

    // create test valarray<>
    std::valarray<int> va1(20);
    std::iota(std::begin(va1), std::end(va1), 0);
    print_va("va1: ", va1);

    // using std::slice - first four elements of va1
    size_t size = 4;
    std::slice sl1(0, size, 1);
    std::slice_array<int> sa1 = va1[sl1];
    std::valarray<int> va2 = sa1;
    print_va("va2: ", va2);
```

```cpp
    // using std::slice - last n elements of va1
    size = 7;
    std::valarray<int> va3 = va1[std::slice(va1.size() - size, size, 1)];
    print_va("va3: ", va3);

    // using std::slice - even elements of va1
    size = va1.size() / 2 + va1.size() % 2;
    std::valarray<int> va4 = va1[std::slice(0, size, 2)];
    print_va("va4: ", va4);

    // using std::slice - odd elements va1
    size = va1.size() / 2;
    std::valarray<int> va5 = va1[std::slice(1, size, 2)];
    print_va("va5: ", va5);

    // using std::slice - every fifth element of va1
    size = va1.size() / 5;
    std::valarray<int> va6 = va1[std::slice(0, size, 5)];
    print_va("va6: ", va6);
}
```

In the ensuing code block, Ch19_03_ex1() initializes the elements of std::valarray<int> va1(20) using std::iota(std::begin(va1), std::end(va1), 0). The second line of the subsequent code block instantiates std::slice sl1(0, size, 1). This std::slice can be used to retrieve the first size (four) elements from a std::valarray. Execution of std::slice_array<int> sa1 = va1[sl1] copy-constructs sa1. Class std::slice_array<> is a helper class that operator[ ] uses to maintain reference semantics to the subset of elements in std::valarray va1 specified by std::slice sl1. Function Ch19_03_ex1() then uses std::valarray<int> va2 = sa1 to copy the first size elements from va1 into va2.

For most std::valarray::operator[] usages, the explicit use of std::slice_array<> is unnecessary as exemplified in the subsequent code block. Here, function Ch19_03_ex1() utilizes size = 7 and std::valarray<int> va3 = va1[std::slice(va1.size() - size, size, 1)] to initialize va3 using the last seven elements of va1. The final three code blocks of Ch19_03_ex1() highlight additional std::slice usages. Note that for each example, size is recalculated to ensure that no element positions within the specified std::slice equal or exceed va1.size().

CHAPTER 19   NUMERICAL PROCESSING – PART 2

Example function `Ch19_03_ex2()`, shown in Listing 19-3-2, details how to perform common matrix operations using `std::valarrays` and `std::slices`. This example utilizes a template class named `Matrix`, whose source code is located in Common/ Matrix.h. The C++ code for class `Matrix` is lengthy. To save some space, I'll show relevant snippets from Matrix.h instead of a complete listing.

Listing 19-3-2. Example Ch19_03 – Ch19_03_ex2()

```
void Ch19_03_ex2()
{
    // create test matrix
    Matrix<double> m1(4, 4);
    m1.iota(1);
    std::println("\nm1:\n{:9.1f}", m1);

    // print rows and columns of matrix m1
    for (size_t i = 0; i < m1.NumRows(); ++i)
    {
        Matrix<double> m1_row(1, m1.NumCols(), m1.row(i));
        std::println("\nm1 row {:d}:\n{:9.1f}", i, m1_row);
    }

    for (size_t i = 0; i < m1.NumCols(); ++i)
    {
        Matrix<double> m1_col(m1.NumRows(), 1, m1.col(i));
        std::println("\nm1 col {:d}:\n{:9.1f}", i, m1_col);
    }

    // create test matricies
    Matrix<double> m2(4, 7);
    m2.iota(10);
    std::println("\nm2:\n{:9.1f}", m2);

    Matrix<double> m3(7, 4);
    m3.iota(20);
    std::println("\nm3:\n{:9.1f}", m3);

    // matrix multiplication
    Matrix<double> m4 = m2 * m3;
    std::println("\nm4:\n{:9.1f}", m4);
```

```cpp
    // matrix multiplication (::mul uses for loops and indicies)
    Matrix<double> m5 = Matrix<double>::mul(m2, m3);
    std::println("\nm4 == m5: {:s} (expect true)", m4 == m5);

    // matrix addition
    Matrix<double> m6 = m4 + m1;
    std::println("\nm6:\n{:9.1f}", m6);

    // matrix trace
    std::println("\nm1.trace(): {:.1f}", m1.trace());
}
```

Execution of Ch19_03_ex2() commences with the definition of test matrix Matrix<double> m1(4, 4). The two constructor arguments specify the number of rows and columns in m1. Internally, class Matrix maintains the following private attributes:

```cpp
size_t m_NumRows {};
size_t m_NumCols {};
std::valarray<T> m_Data {};
```

The next statement in Listing 19-3-2, m1.iota(1), initializes the elements of m1. Member function Matrix::iota() executes std::iota(std::begin(m_Data), std::end(m_Data), val). Class Matrix defines its own std::formatter (see Chapter 2), and this facilitates the use of std::println("\nm1:\n{:9.1f}", m1) to print the elements of m1.

The for loop that follows prints the elements of each row in m1. Execution of m1.row(i) obtains a std::valarray whose elements correspond to row i of Matrix m1. Here's the code from class Matrix that performs this operation:

```cpp
std::valarray<T> row(size_t row) const { return m_Data[row_slice(row)]; }

std::slice row_slice(size_t row) const
{
    if (row >= m_NumRows)
        throw std::runtime_error("Matrix::row_slice - invalid row index");

    return std::slice(row * m_NumCols, m_NumCols, 1);
}
```

CHAPTER 19   NUMERICAL PROCESSING – PART 2

Note that member function `Matrix::row_slice()` returns an object of type `std::slice`, which represents the specified matrix row. The statement `Matrix<double> m1_row(1, m1.NumCols(), m1.row(i))` constructs a 1 × m1.NumCols() Matrix using the elements of m1.row(). The ensuing `std::println("\nm1 row {:d}:\n{:9.1f}", i, m1_row)` statement prints the elements of m1_row.

The next code block in `Ch19_03_ex2()` prints the columns of m1 using a similar for loop and member function `m1.col(i)`:

```
std::valarray<T> col(size_t col) const { return m_Data[col_slice(col)]; }

std::slice col_slice(size_t col) const
{
    if (col >= m_NumCols)
        throw std::runtime_error("Matrix::col_slice - invalid col index");

    return std::slice(col, m_NumRows, m_NumCols);
}
```

A brief digression. The product of two matrices, **C** = **AB** where **A** is an $m \times p$ (rows × columns) matrix, **B** is a $p \times n$ matrix, and **C** is an $m \times n$ matrix, can be calculated using the following equation:

$$c_{ij} = \sum_{k=0}^{p-1} a_{ik} b_{kj} \quad i = 0, \ldots, m-1; \quad j = 0, \ldots, n-1$$

Note that this equation uses zero-based subscripts since this simplifies translating the equation into C++ source code; most mathematical texts use one-based subscripts.

Returning to the source code in Listing 19-3-2, following initialization of `Matrix<double> m2(4, 7)` and `Matrix<double> m3(7, 4)`, `Ch19_03_ex2()` utilizes `Matrix<double> m4 = m2 * m3` to calculate a matrix product. The following code in class Matrix performs this calculation:

```
friend Matrix operator*(const Matrix& m1, const Matrix& m2)
{
    if (m1.m_NumCols != m2.m_NumRows)
        throw std::runtime_error("Matrix::operator* - invalid size");

    Matrix m3(m1.m_NumRows, m2.m_NumCols);
```

```
    for (size_t i = 0; i < m1.m_NumRows; ++i)
    {
        std::valarray<T> m1_row = m1.m_Data[m1.row_slice(i)];

        for (size_t j = 0; j < m2.m_NumCols; ++j)
        {
            std::valarray<T> m2_col = m2.m_Data[m2.col_slice(j)];

            // m3(i, j) = inner product of m1 row i, and m2 col j
            T dp = (m1_row * m2_col).sum();
            m3.m_Data[i * m3.m_NumCols + j] = dp;
        }
    }

    return m3;
}
```

To calculate the product of two matrices, a series of dot (inner) products must be computed using the rows of multiplicand m1 and the columns of multiplier m2. To accomplish this, operator* exploits m1.row_slice(i) and m2.col_slice(j) to extract row i from m1 and column j from m2. Execution of T dp = (m1_row * m2.m_Data[col_sl]).sum() computes the required dot product.

The next code block in Ch19_03_ex2() utilizes Matrix<double> m5 = Matrix<double>::mul(m2, m3) to calculate m5 = m2 * m3. Function mul() (source code not shown) performs matrix multiplication using classic for loops and explicit indices. This variant is included for comparison purposes.

Class Matrix also defines operator+ as follows:

```
friend Matrix operator+(const Matrix& m1, const Matrix& m2)
{
    if (!same_size(m1, m2))
        throw std::runtime_error("Matrix::operator+ - size error");

    Matrix m3 = m1;
    m3.m_Data += m2.m_Data;
    return m3;
}
```

CHAPTER 19   NUMERICAL PROCESSING – PART 2

To perform matrix addition, operator+ simply adds the two std::valarrays. Calculation of a matrix trace (sum of its diagonal elements) is also straightforward:

```
T trace() const
{
    if (m_NumRows != m_NumCols)
        throw std::runtime_error("Matrix::trace - non-square matrix");

    auto tr_slice = std::slice(0, m_NumRows, m_NumRows + 1);
    return m_Data[tr_slice].sum();
}
```

The statement std::slice(0, m_NumRows, m_NumRows + 1) defines a slice that represents the Matrix's diagonal elements. Execution of m_Data[tr_slice].sum() calculates the trace.

The results for example Ch19_03 follow this paragraph. These results include some minor edits to improve readability.

```
----- Results for example Ch19_03 -----

----- Ch19_03_ex1() -----
va1:    0  1  2  3  4  5  6  7  8  9 10 11 12 13 14 15 16 17 18 19
va2:    0  1  2  3
va3:   13 14 15 16 17 18 19
va4:    0  2  4  6  8 10 12 14 16 18
va5:    1  3  5  7  9 11 13 15 17 19
va6:    0  5 10 15

----- Ch19_03_ex2() -----

m1:
        1.0         2.0         3.0         4.0
        5.0         6.0         7.0         8.0
        9.0        10.0        11.0        12.0
       13.0        14.0        15.0        16.0

m1 row 0:
        1.0         2.0         3.0         4.0
```

```
m1 row 1:
    5.0         6.0         7.0         8.0

m1 row 2:
    9.0        10.0        11.0        12.0

m1 row 3:
   13.0        14.0        15.0        16.0

m1 col 0:    m1 col 1:   m1 col 2:   m1 col 3:
    1.0         2.0         3.0         4.0
    5.0         6.0         7.0         8.0
    9.0        10.0        11.0        12.0
   13.0        14.0        15.0        16.0

m2:
   10.0        11.0        12.0        13.0        14.0        15.0        16.0
   17.0        18.0        19.0        20.0        21.0        22.0        23.0
   24.0        25.0        26.0        27.0        28.0        29.0        30.0
   31.0        32.0        33.0        34.0        35.0        36.0        37.0

m3:
   20.0        21.0        22.0        23.0
   24.0        25.0        26.0        27.0
   28.0        29.0        30.0        31.0
   32.0        33.0        34.0        35.0
   36.0        37.0        38.0        39.0
   40.0        41.0        42.0        43.0
   44.0        45.0        46.0        47.0

m4:
 3024.0      3115.0      3206.0      3297.0
 4592.0      4732.0      4872.0      5012.0
 6160.0      6349.0      6538.0      6727.0
 7728.0      7966.0      8204.0      8442.0

m4 == m5: true (expect true)
```

CHAPTER 19 NUMERICAL PROCESSING – PART 2

m6:
```
    3025.0    3117.0    3209.0    3301.0
    4597.0    4738.0    4879.0    5020.0
    6169.0    6359.0    6549.0    6739.0
    7741.0    7980.0    8219.0    8458.0
```

m1.trace(): 34.0

Covariance Matrix

Covariance is a statistical measure that quantifies the extent that two random variables vary together. When analyzing multiple random variables, it is often necessary to calculate a matrix of all possible covariances. Once calculated, a covariance matrix can be utilized to perform a wide variety of advanced statistical analyses (e.g., principal component analysis).

The calculation of a covariance matrix begins with a sample data matrix as shown in Figure 19-2. In this figure, each row of matrix X represents one random variable (or feature), while each column is a multivariate observation.

$$\begin{array}{c} \leftarrow\text{Observations}\rightarrow \\ \begin{array}{c} x_0 \\ x_1 \\ x_2 \\ x_3 \end{array} \begin{bmatrix} 10.75 & 6.39 & 6.60 & \cdots & 21.37 & 1.86 & 13.17 \\ 8.30 & 7.46 & 8.32 & \cdots & 24.99 & 16.70 & 4.12 \\ 21.73 & 22.89 & 14.32 & \cdots & 9.65 & 0.40 & 6.40 \\ 15.65 & 22.62 & 2.34 & \cdots & 15.02 & 16.10 & 12.18 \end{bmatrix} \end{array}$$

Data matrix X (4 × N)

$$\begin{bmatrix} 49.33 & 14.69 & 4.28 & 7.37 \\ 14.69 & 64.62 & -4.54 & 9.24 \\ 4.28 & -4.54 & 46.54 & 7.27 \\ 7.37 & 9.24 & 7.27 & 34.70 \end{bmatrix}$$

Covariance matrix C (4 × 4)

Figure 19-2. *Covariance matrix*

Element c_{ij} of covariance matrix C is calculated using the following equation:

$$c_{ij} = \frac{\sum_{k=0}^{n_{obv}-1}(x_{ik}-\bar{x}_i)(x_{jk}-\bar{x}_j)}{n_{obv}-1}$$

CHAPTER 19 NUMERICAL PROCESSING – PART 2

where $i = 0, 1, \cdots, n_{var} - 1$ and $j = 0, 1, \cdots, n_{var} - 1$. In this equation, symbols n_{obv} and n_{var} signify the number of observations and variables, respectively. A covariance matrix is always a square ($n_{var} \times n_{var}$) symmetric ($c_{ij} = c_{ji}$) matrix as shown in Figure 19-2. Each c_{ij} element represents the covariance between random variables x_i and x_j, while each main diagonal element c_{ii} is the variance for variable x_i.

Listing 19-4-1-1 shows the source code example function Ch19_04_ex1(). The purpose of this example is to demonstrate the calculation of a covariance matrix using classes std::valarray and std::slice.

Listing 19-4-1-1. Example Ch19_04 - Ch19_04_ex1()

```cpp
//-------------------------------------------------------------------------
// Ch19_04_ex.cpp
//-------------------------------------------------------------------------

#include <iostream>
#include <valarray>
#include "Ch19_04.h"
#include "BmTimer.h"
#include "CovData.h"

void Ch19_04_ex1()
{
    using fp_t = double;
    constexpr size_t num_vars {8};
    constexpr size_t num_obvs {100};
    constexpr fp_t rng_min {0.0};
    constexpr fp_t rng_max {25.0};
    constexpr unsigned int rng_seed {1111};

    // create CovData object
    CovData<fp_t> cov_data(num_vars, num_obvs);
    cov_data.generate_data(rng_min, rng_max, rng_seed);

    // calculate covariance matrix
    cov_data.covariance();
    cov_data.save_results("Ch19_04_ex1-results.txt", "{:9.4f}");
}
```

CHAPTER 19 NUMERICAL PROCESSING – PART 2

Near the top of Listing 19-4-1-1, the statement CovData<fp_t> cov_data(num_vars, num_obvs) creates an instance of CovData. Template class CovData (see Common/CovData.h) is a helper class that bundles several data structures related to the calculation of a covariance matrix. It also includes code that writes results to a text file. Each CovData object encompasses the following private attributes:

```
Matrix<T> m_Data {};              // data matrix (num_vars x num_obvs)
Matrix<T> m_CovMat {};            // covariance matrix (num_vars x num_vars)
std::valarray<T> m_VarMeans {};   // var means (num_vars)
std::valarray<T> m_VarStdDevs{};  // var standard deviations (num_vars)
```

The next statement in Listing 19-4-1-1, cov_data.generate_data(rng_min, rng_max, rng_seed), fills CovData::m_Data with random values using a distribution of type std::uniform_real_distribution. Execution of cov_data.covariance() calculates a covariance matrix for CovData::m_Data and saves this result to CovData::m_CovMat. Here's the code for member function CovData::covariance():

```
void covariance()
{
    m_VarMeans = m_Data.row_means();
    m_CovMat = m_Data.covariance(m_VarMeans);

    // main diagonal of covariance matrix contains variable variances
    auto variances = m_CovMat.main_diag();
    m_VarStdDevs = std::sqrt(variances);
}
```

Member function CovData::covariance() utilizes Matrix<T>::row_means() (see Common/Matrix.h) to calculate the required variable means. Calculation of the actual covariance matrix is carried out in Matrix<T>::covariance(), whose code is shown in Listing 19-4-1-2. More about this function shortly. Following calculation of the covariance matrix, CovData::covariance() computes the corresponding variable standard deviations using m_VarStdDevs = std::sqrt(variances).

Listing 19-4-1-2. Example Ch19_04 – Matrix<T>::covariance()

```
Matrix covariance(const std::valarray<T>& var_means) const
{
    const size_t num_vars = m_NumRows;
    const size_t num_obvs = m_NumCols;

    if (var_means.size() != num_vars)
        throw std::runtime_error("Matrix::covariance - invalid size");

    Matrix cvm(num_vars, num_vars);      // covariance matrix

    for (size_t i = 0; i < num_vars; i++)
    {
        std::slice row_i = std::slice(i * num_obvs, num_obvs, 1);
        std::valarray<T> t1 = m_Data[row_i] - var_means[i];

        for (size_t j = 0; j < num_vars; j++)
        {
           if (i <= j)
           {
                // calculate cvm(i, j)
                std::slice row_j = std::slice(j * num_obvs, num_obvs, 1);
                std::valarray<T> t2 = m_Data[row_j] - var_means[j];
                T t3 = (t1 * t2).sum();

                cvm.m_Data[i * num_vars + j] = t3 / (num_obvs - 1);
           }
           else
                cvm.m_Data[i * num_vars + j] = cvm.m_Data[j *
                num_vars + i];
        }
    }

    return cvm;
}
```

CHAPTER 19 NUMERICAL PROCESSING – PART 2

If you take a closer look at the previously defined covariance matrix equation, note that the numerator essentially calculates $(x_{i*} - \bar{x}_i)(x_{j*} - \bar{x}_j)$ where x_{i*} and x_{j*} denote the i-th and j-th rows of matrix X. Extracting rows from a matrix is easily accomplished using std::slices as you have already seen (see example Ch19_03_ex2()). In Listing 19-4-1-2, the first two statements of Matrix<T>::covariance()'s outer for loop, std::slice row_i = std::slice(i * num_obvs, num_obvs, 1) and std::valarray<T> t1 = m_Data[row_i] - var_means[i], extract the i-th row from m_Data and subtract $\bar{x}_i$ from each row element. The inner for loop first checks i <= j. If true, a similar set of statements extracts the j-th row from m_Data and subtracts $\bar{x}_j$. Execution of the statement T t3 = (t1 * t2).sum() completes calculation of the numerator expression, while cvm.m_Data[i * num_vars + j] = t3 / (num_obvs - 1) calculates and saves c_{ij}. If i <= j is false, $c_{ij} = c_{ji}$ is executed (recall that a covariance matrix is always symmetrical).

It warrants mentioning that for a large matrix, extracting and saving a row to a std::valarray is likely to be slower than accessing the row's elements using explicit integer indices. Class Matrix also includes a member function named covariance_indx(const std::valarray<T>& var_means) that computes a covariance matrix using integer indices. You can study this example and compare it to covariance() at your convenience. Example function Ch19_04_ex2() (source code not shown) includes code that benchmarks the performance of both covariance calculating functions. You are encouraged to execute this code on your computer. Here are the results for example Ch19_04_ex1(), which were copied from the output results file and edited to save space:

```
----- Data Matrix (transposed) -----
  0:    10.7505  16.2671  12.3094  15.1944   2.5068  19.8886   5.0283  23.7072
  1:     6.3864   7.9719  14.9163   2.2310  19.7471  14.0313  18.9222  10.3168
  2:     6.6014   1.1641  18.9931   3.9612  20.9191   5.0176  19.6103  19.1253
  ...
 97:    15.0232  15.6809   1.5589  10.5805   3.6461   3.6828  17.0885  11.6744
 98:    16.0958  13.7763   9.5595  10.3423   4.3967   4.3943  22.4331  23.6863
 99:    12.1817   8.3819  12.5211  21.3646   9.0977  14.0633   1.2102   1.7706

----- Variable Means -----
        13.4349  11.8191  13.8101  12.2710  12.3101  12.0714  11.7752  11.9075
```

```
----- Covariance Matrix -----
   0:    51.1491    9.0192   -8.0377   -2.7088   -4.7136    3.3254   -2.3661   -2.9640
   1:     9.0192   46.8772    5.6651   -4.7371   -1.1666    5.7336    0.7252    4.6614
   2:    -8.0377    5.6651   45.9784    0.2774   -0.5157   13.9864    5.7252    2.6287
   3:    -2.7088   -4.7371    0.2774   50.7602    9.7805   -1.8174   -5.5411   -4.8787
   4:    -4.7136   -1.1666   -0.5157    9.7805   55.8655   -8.2996   -3.0797    7.6506
   5:     3.3254    5.7336   13.9864   -1.8174   -8.2996   55.5117    0.8668   -4.4321
   6:    -2.3661    0.7252    5.7252   -5.5411   -3.0797    0.8668   53.7989    7.0524
   7:    -2.9640    4.6614    2.6287   -4.8787    7.6506   -4.4321    7.0524   57.6110
----- Variable Standard Deviations -----
          7.1519    6.8467    6.7807    7.1246    7.4743    7.4506    7.3348    7.5902
```

Inner Products and Reductions

The STL defines several useful functions that perform practical numerical operations. You have already seen a few of these, including std::iota (examples Ch10_06, Ch10_07, etc.) and std::accumulate (examples Ch03_01 and Ch11_08). The source code examples of this section covers a few more numerical operations, including std::inner_product(), std::reduce(), and std::transform_reduce().

Listing 19-5-1 shows the source code for example function Ch19_05_ex1(), which illustrates the basic use of std::inner_product(). Execution of Ch19_05_ex1() opens with the creation of two std::valarray<double> objects named va1 and va2. The next statement, double ip_va1_va2 = std::inner_product(std::begin(va1), std::end(va1), std::begin(va2), 0.0), computes sum += (*iter1++) * (*iter2++) where iter1 and iter2 are iterators that reference elements in va1 and va2, respectively. The initial value for sum is 0.0.

CHAPTER 19 NUMERICAL PROCESSING – PART 2

Listing 19-5-1. Example Ch19_05 - Ch19_05_ex1()

```cpp
//---------------------------------------------------------------
// Ch19_05_ex.cpp
//---------------------------------------------------------------

#include <algorithm>
#include <cmath>
#include <numeric>
#include <string>
#include <valarray>
#include <vector>
#include "Ch19_05.h"
#include "MT.h"
#include "RN.h"

void Ch19_05_ex1()
{
    const char* fmt = "{:7.1f}";
    constexpr size_t epl_max {10};

    constexpr size_t n {10};
    constexpr int rng_min {1};
    constexpr int rng_max {50};
    constexpr unsigned int rng_seed {3400};

    // create test valarrays
    auto va1 = RN::get_valarray<double>(n, rng_min, rng_max, rng_seed);
    MT::print_ctr("\nva1:\n", va1, fmt, epl_max);

    auto va2 = RN::get_valarray<double>(n, rng_min, rng_max, rng_seed + 1);
    MT::print_ctr("\nva2:\n", va2, fmt, epl_max);

    // using std::inner_product
    double ip_va1_va2 = std::inner_product(std::begin(va1), std::end(va1),
        std::begin(va2), 0.0);

    std::println("\nip_va1_va2: {:7.1f}", ip_va1_va2);
}
```

CHAPTER 19 NUMERICAL PROCESSING – PART 2

Function std::inner_product() can be used with other containers provided they support input or forward iterators. Custom binary function objects can also be supplied to replace the defaults of addition and multiplication as demonstrated in example function Ch19_05_ex2(), which is shown in Listing 19-5-2.

Listing 19-5-2. Example Ch19_05 – Ch19_05_ex2()

```
void Ch19_05_ex2()
{
    // create test vectors
    std::vector<std::string> vec1 {"A", "B", "C", "D", "E"};
    std::vector<std::string> vec2 {"a", "b", "c", "d", "e"};

    // binary operators for std::inner_product
    auto ip_op1 = [](const std::string& s1, const std::string& s2)
        { return s1 + " + " + s2; };

    auto ip_op2 = [](const std::string& s1, const std::string& s2)
        { return s1 + " * " + s2; };

    // operation performed below by std::inner_product:
    //
    //   acc = "#"; iter1 = vec1.begin(); iter2 = vec2.begin()
    //   while (iter1 != vec1.end())
    //   {
    //       acc = ip_op1(acc, ip_op2(*iter1, *iter2))
    //       ++iter1; ++iter2
    //   {

    std::string ip_vec1_vec2 = std::inner_product(vec1.begin(), vec1.end(),
        vec2.begin(), std::string("#"), ip_op1, ip_op2);

    std::println("\nip_vec1_vec2: {:s}", ip_vec1_vec2);
}
```

Function Ch19_05_ex2() opens with the definition of two std::vector<std::string> objects named vec1 and vec2. Next is the definition of two lambda expressions:

CHAPTER 19 NUMERICAL PROCESSING – PART 2

```
auto ip_op1 = [](const std::string& s1, const std::string& s2)
    { return s1 + " + " + s2; };

auto ip_op2 = [](const std::string& s1, const std::string& s2)
    { return s1 + " * " + s2; };
```

Note that both ip_op1 and ip_op2 perform simple string concatenations. Execution of

```
std::string ip_vec1_vec2 = std::inner_product(vec1.begin(), vec1.end(),
    vec2.begin(), std::string("#"), ip_op1, ip_op2);
```

calculates acc = ip_op1(acc, ip_op2(*iter1, *iter2)) for iter1 = [vec1.begin(), vec1.end()) and iter2 = [vec2.begin(), vec2.end()). In the current example, std::inner_product() utilizes ip_op1() and ip_op2() instead of addition and multiplication. The initial value for acc is std::string("#").

Example function Ch19_05_ex3(), shown in Listing 19-5-3, typifies the use of std::reduce(). The first use of this function, double reduce1 = std::reduce(vec1.begin(), vec1.end()), sums the elements of [vec1.begin(), vec1.end()). The difference between std::reduce() and std::accumulate() is that the former does not guarantee a specific execution order. This means that non-deterministic results are possible for non-associative and non-communicative operations, such as floating-point addition.

Listing 19-5-3. Example Ch19_05 – Ch19_05_ex3()

```
void Ch19_05_ex3()
{
    const char* fmt = "{:7.1f}";
    constexpr size_t epl_max {10};

    constexpr size_t n {20};
    constexpr int rng_min {1};
    constexpr int rng_max {50};
    constexpr unsigned int rng_seed {3400};

    auto vec1 = RN::get_vector<double>(n, rng_min, rng_max, rng_seed);
    MT::print_ctr("\nvec1:\n", vec1, fmt, epl_max);
```

```
    // using std::reduce (initial value = 0)
    double reduce1 = std::reduce(vec1.begin(), vec1.end());
    std::println("\nreduce1: {:7.1f}", reduce1);

    // using std::reduce (initial value = 1000.0)
    double reduce2 = std::reduce(vec1.begin(), vec1.end(), 1000.0);
    std::println("\nreduce2: {:7.1f}", reduce2);

    // using std::reduce (initial value = 1000.0, custom binary_op)
    std::println("");
    auto reduce_op = [](double sum, double x)
    {
        std::println("{:8.4f} {:8.4f} {:8.4f}", sum, x, sqrt(x));
        return sum + std::sqrt(x);
    };

    double reduce3 = std::reduce(vec1.begin(), vec1.end(), 0.0, reduce_op);
    std::println("\nreduce3: {:8.4f}", reduce3);
}
```

The next code block in Ch19_05_ex3() utilizes double reduce2 = std::reduce(vec1.begin(), vec1.end(), 1000.0). Note here that an initial value is supplied (the default is T{}). The final code block in Ch19_05_ex3() starts with the definition of a custom binary reduction operator:

```
auto reduce_op = [](double sum, double x)
{
    std::println("{:8.4f} {:8.4f} {:8.4f}", sum, x, sqrt(x));
    return sum + std::sqrt(x);
};
```

Execution of reduce3 = std::reduce(vec1.begin(), vec1.end(), 0.0, reduce_op) applies reduce_op() to the elements of [vec1.begin(), vec1.end()).

The final example function of this section, Ch19_05_ex4(), illustrates the use of std::transform_reduce(). The operation performed by this STL function resembles std::reduce() but also carries out a transformation operation. In Listing 19-5-4, execution of Ch19_05_ex4() commences with the initialization of two std::vector<int> containers named vec1 and vec2. In the ensuing code block, the statement int tr1

= std::transform_reduce(vec1.begin(), vec1.end(), vec2.begin(), 0) sums products of corresponding elements from vec1 and vec2 (i.e., sum = vec1[0] * vec2[0] + vec1[1] * vec2[1] +...). In this usage example, std::transform_reduce() uses std::plus() and std::multiplies() as default reduce and transform operators.

Listing 19-5-4. Example Ch19_05 - Ch19_05_ex4()

```
#define ENABLE_PRINT

void Ch19_05_ex4()
{
    const char* fmt = "{:5d}";
    constexpr size_t epl_max {10};
    constexpr size_t n {8};

    // create test vectors
    std::vector<int> vec1(n);
    std::ranges::iota(vec1, 1);
    MT::print_ctr("\nvec1:\n", vec1, fmt, epl_max);

    std::vector<int> vec2(n);
    std::ranges::iota(vec2, 10);
    MT::print_ctr("\nvec2:\n", vec2, fmt, epl_max);

    // using std::transform_reduce
    // uses default std::plus (reduce_op) and std::multiplies
    (transform_op)
    int tr1 = std::transform_reduce(vec1.begin(), vec1.end(), vec2.begin(), 0);
    std::println("\ntr1: {:d}\n", tr1);

    // using std::transform_reduce
    // calculates reduce_op2(transform_op2(vec1[i])) for all i
    auto reduce_op2 = [](int sum, int x)
    {
#ifdef ENABLE_PRINT
        std::println("reduce_op2: [sum: {:5d}, x: {:5d}]", sum, x);
#endif
```

```cpp
        return sum + x;
    };

    auto transform_op2 = [](int x)
        { return x * x; };

    int tr2 = std::transform_reduce(vec1.begin(), vec1.end(), 0,
        reduce_op2, transform_op2);
    std::println("\ntr2: {:d}\n", tr2);

    // using std::transform_reduce
    // calculates reduce_op3(transform_op3(vec1[i], vec2[i])) for all i
    auto reduce_op3 = [](int sum, int z)
    {
#ifdef ENABLE_PRINT
        std::println("reduce_op3:    [sum: {:5d}, z: {:5d}]", sum, z);
#endif
        return sum + z;
    };

    auto transform_op3 = [](int x, int y)
    {
#ifdef ENABLE_PRINT
        std::println("transform_op3: [x:   {:5d}, y: {:5d}]", x, y);
#endif
        return 2 * x + 2 * y;
    };

    int tr3 = std::transform_reduce(vec1.begin(), vec1.end(), vec2.begin(), 0,
        reduce_op3, transform_op3);
    std::println("\ntr3: {:d}\n", tr3);
}
```

The subsequent code block in Ch19_05_ex4() exercises std::transform_reduce() using a single container. In this usage example, execution of tr2 = std::transform_reduce(vec1.begin(), vec1.end(), 0, reduce_op2, transform_op2) calculates reduce_op2(transform_op2(vec1[i]) for all elements in vec1.

CHAPTER 19   NUMERICAL PROCESSING – PART 2

The third and final std::transform_reduce() example starts with the definition of custom operators reduce_op3() and transform_op3(). Execution of int tr3 = std::transform_reduce(vec1.begin(), vec1.end(), vec2.begin(), 0, reduce_op3, transform_op3) calculates reduce_op3(transform_op3(vec1[i], vec2[i])) for all elements in vec1 and vec2. Here are the results for example Ch19_05:

```
----- Results for example Ch19_05 -----

----- Ch19_05_ex1() -----

va1:
    24.0    31.0    36.0    18.0    11.0    21.0    36.0    22.0    40.0    9.0

va2:
     7.0    47.0     2.0    39.0     7.0    44.0    29.0    47.0    17.0    8.0

ip_va1_va2:   6230.0

----- Ch19_05_ex2() -----

ip_vec1_vec2: # + A * a + B * b + C * c + D * d + E * e

----- Ch19_05_ex3() -----

vec1:
    24.0    31.0    36.0    18.0    11.0    21.0    36.0    22.0    40.0    9.0
    35.0    13.0    15.0     8.0    39.0    13.0    48.0    50.0     2.0   26.0

reduce1:    497.0

reduce2:   1497.0

  0.0000   24.0000    4.8990
  4.8990   31.0000    5.5678
 10.4667   36.0000    6.0000
 16.4667   18.0000    4.2426
 20.7094   11.0000    3.3166
 24.0260   21.0000    4.5826
 28.6086   36.0000    6.0000
 34.6086   22.0000    4.6904
 39.2990   40.0000    6.3246
```

```
    45.6236     9.0000    3.0000
    48.6236    35.0000    5.9161
    54.5396    13.0000    3.6056
    58.1452    15.0000    3.8730
    62.0182     8.0000    2.8284
    64.8466    39.0000    6.2450
    71.0916    13.0000    3.6056
    74.6971    48.0000    6.9282
    81.6254    50.0000    7.0711
    88.6964     2.0000    1.4142
    90.1106    26.0000    5.0990

reduce3:   95.2097

----- Ch19_05_ex4() -----

vec1:
    1    2    3    4    5    6    7    8
vec2:
   10   11   12   13   14   15   16   17
tr1: 528

reduce_op2: [sum:      0, x:      1]
reduce_op2: [sum:      1, x:      4]
reduce_op2: [sum:      5, x:      9]
reduce_op2: [sum:     14, x:     16]
reduce_op2: [sum:     30, x:     25]
reduce_op2: [sum:     55, x:     36]
reduce_op2: [sum:     91, x:     49]
reduce_op2: [sum:    140, x:     64]

tr2: 204

transform_op3: [x:      1, y:     10]
reduce_op3:    [sum:     0, z:     22]
transform_op3: [x:      2, y:     11]
reduce_op3:    [sum:    22, z:     26]
```

```
transform_op3:  [x:        3, y:    12]
reduce_op3:     [sum:     48, z:    30]
transform_op3:  [x:        4, y:    13]
reduce_op3:     [sum:     78, z:    34]
transform_op3:  [x:        5, y:    14]
reduce_op3:     [sum:    112, z:    38]
transform_op3:  [x:        6, y:    15]
reduce_op3:     [sum:    150, z:    42]
transform_op3:  [x:        7, y:    16]
reduce_op3:     [sum:    192, z:    46]
transform_op3:  [x:        8, y:    17]
reduce_op3:     [sum:    238, z:    50]

tr3: 288
```

Summary

Here are the key learning points for this chapter:

- Class `std::valarray` is a one-dimensional array construct that's specifically designed for numerical operations. The implementation of this class avoids certain forms of aliasing, which facilitates more aggressive optimizations by the compiler.

- Class `std::valarray` supports common binary arithmetic operations such as addition, subtraction, multiplication, and division. The operations are applied to corresponding elements from the two `std::valarray` operands.

- The STL defines `std::valarray` overloads for common arithmetic functions, including exponential, logarithmic, trigonometric, and hyperbolic.

- Class `std::valarrary` does not define iterator member functions `begin()` and `end()`. However, global iterator functions `std::begin()` and `std::end()` can be used.

- Class std::slice resembles a BLAS slice. A std::slice doesn't hold or own any elements. It simply bundles a start index, a size (length), and a stride that collectively designate elements in a std::valarray as shown in Figure 19-1.

- Instances of std::slice can be used with operator[] to extract groups of elements from a std::valarray. This capability also facilitates the modeling of higher-dimensional arrays using std::valarray.

- Calculations that use std::slices to copy large numbers of elements from one std::valarray to another may be less efficient than performing the same calculation using explicit integer indices.

- Function std::inner_product() calculates inner products using the elements of two ranges. This function supports arguments that replace an inner product's normal operations of addition and multiplication.

- Functions std::reduce() reduces the elements of a range to a single value using std::plus or another supplied function object. Function std::reduce() does not guarantee a specific execution order, which means non-deterministic results are possible for non-associative and non-communicative operations such as floating-point addition.

- Function std::transform_reduce() closely resembles std::reduce() but also performs a transformation operation.

CHAPTER 20

Concurrency – Part 1

This chapter explains essential classes and algorithms related to concurrency and the C++ concurrency support library. Topics covered include

- Execution policies
- Mutexes
- Thread classes
- Atomic classes and operations
- Multithreaded algorithms

The C++ concurrency support library provides classes and algorithms that facilitate the creation and management of multithreaded programs for a wide variety of use cases. The discussions and source code examples of this chapter emphasize elements of the library that are typically used to create worker threads that execute background algorithms.

Concurrency Primer

Before examining the basics of C++ concurrency, a few words regarding concurrency and parallelism are warranted. Concurrency is the coordinated execution of an algorithm's (or program's) executable components. Coordinated execution encompasses a variety of computational factors, including the partitioning of a task into smaller subtasks, interleaving of task operations via time slicing and context switching, or alterations to flow control that don't affect the final result. Parallelism is the simultaneous execution of an algorithm's executable components. For many modern hardware and software platforms, parallelism exploits the notion of a thread.

CHAPTER 20 CONCURRENCY – PART 1

A thread is an independent sequence of instructions that can be executed on a processor. On a single processor system, parallelism is often simulated using time sharing and context switching. In a time-sharing system, each thread is allowed to execute for a fixed period of time. The length of this period is classically based on a priority scheme. An operating system's context switcher preserves the execution state (i.e., processor registers, status flags, etc.) of a thread so that it can be resumed later following the execution of another thread. A multiprocessor computer system can achieve true parallelism since it's capable of executing multiple threads simultaneously, which significantly improves performance.

Another type of (data-level) parallelism that's an integral part of modern processor architectures is single instruction multiple data (SIMD). A SIMD instruction executes a single operation using multiple data values. For example, suppose a program needs to compute `c[i] = a[i] + b[i]` using all N elements in arrays a, b, and c. A non-SIMD implementation of this operation requires the processor to perform N distinct additions. However, a SIMD capable processor can perform the same calculation using multiple array elements. In other words, it can execute `c[i:i+m] = a[i:i+m] + b[i:i+m]` where m corresponds to the number of simultaneous elements. The optimization process that a C++ compiler employs to transform a scalar expression into SIMD code is called vectorization.

Designing and coding algorithms that properly exploit concurrency and parallelism can be challenging, even for experienced software developers. When designing such algorithms, two issues merit meticulous attention: data races and deadlocks. A data race occurs when multiple executing threads attempt to modify the same data value using a non-atomic operation (i.e., an operation that can be interrupted before its completion). A deadlock transpires when two computing entities are unable to continue since each entity is waiting for a resource that is controlled by the other.

As mentioned earlier, the C++ concurrency support library provides classes and algorithms that facilitate creation and runtime management of threads. It also includes components that can be used to prevent data races and deadlocks including atomic operations, mutexes, condition variables, and semaphores. The remaining sections of this chapter and the next explore these topics in greater detail.

Execution Policies

Most of the algorithms defined in namespace `std` support overloads that accept an execution policy argument. An execution policy object specifies the types of parallelism that an algorithm is permitted to employ during its execution. Table 20-1 summarizes the four standard execution policies, which belong to namespace `std::execution`. A C++ compliant implementation is authorized to define additional execution policies beyond those shown in Table 20-1 to support specialized parallel architectures (e.g., GPU).

Table 20-1. Standard Execution Policies

Policy Type (std::execution)	Policy Object (std::execution)	Description
sequenced_policy	seq	Sequenced execution only. An algorithm may not be parallelized
unsequenced_policy	unseq	Execution of an algorithm may be parallelized using vectorization on a single thread
parallel_policy	par	Execution of an algorithm may be parallelized using multiple threads
parallel_unsequenced_policy	par_unseq	Execution of an algorithm may be parallelized using multiple threads and vectorization

It's important to keep in mind that the specification of an explicit execution policy is merely a suggestion. A C++ implementation will complete an algorithm sequentially if the host system lacks the requisite hardware resources to properly execute multiple threads or implement vectorization. It is also important to understand that the use of an execution policy does not preclude data races or deadlocks. It is the programmer's responsibility to either avoid or properly handle these scenarios.

Listing 20-1-1 shows the source code for function `Ch20_01_ex1()`. This example demonstrates how to specify execution policies using STL algorithm `std::transform()`. Near the top of Listing 20-1-1 is the statement `namespace ex = std::execution`. As mentioned earlier, execution policy objects belong to namespace `std::execution`, and alias `ex` is used in this chapter to improve readability and save a few keystrokes.

CHAPTER 20 CONCURRENCY – PART 1

Listing 20-1-1. Example Ch20_01 - Ch20_01_ex1()

```cpp
//-------------------------------------------------------------------
// Ch20_01_ex.cpp
//-------------------------------------------------------------------

#include <algorithm>
#include <array>
#include <execution>
#include <iostream>
#include "Ch20_01.h"
#include "BmTimer.h"
#include "MT.h"
#include "RN.h"

namespace ex = std::execution;

void Ch20_01_ex1()
{
    const char* fmt = "{:9.1f} ";
    constexpr size_t epl_max {8};
    constexpr int rng_min {-200};
    constexpr int rng_max {200};
    constexpr size_t vec_size {50};

    // create test vectors
    std::vector<double> vec0 = RN::get_vector<double>(vec_size, rng_min,
        rng_max);
    MT::print_ctr("\nvec0 (initial values):\n", vec0, fmt, epl_max);
    std::vector<double> vec1(vec0.size());
    std::vector<double> vec2(vec0.size());
    std::vector<double> vec3(vec0.size());
    std::vector<double> vec4(vec0.size());

    // transformation lambda
    auto tr_op = [](auto x) { return 3 * x * x + 2 * x + 1; };

    // using transform - sequenced
    std::transform(ex::seq, vec0.begin(), vec0.end(), vec1.begin(), tr_op);
```

CHAPTER 20   CONCURRENCY – PART 1

```
    // using transform - unsequenced
    std::transform(ex::unseq, vec0.begin(), vec0.end(),
    vec2.begin(), tr_op);

    // using transform - parallel sequenced
    std::transform(ex::par, vec0.begin(), vec0.end(), vec3.begin(), tr_op);

    // using transform - parallel unsequenced
    std::transform(ex::par_unseq, vec0.begin(), vec0.end(),
    vec4.begin(), tr_op);

    // verify results
    std::print("\nresult vector compare check: ");
    if (vec1 == vec2 && vec1 == vec3 && vec1 == vec4)
        std::println("OK");
    else
        std::println("Failed!");
}
```

The opening code block of example function Ch20_01_ex1() initializes std::vector<double> vec0 using get_vector<double>(vec_size, rng_min, rng_max). Next is the instantiation of std::vector<double> objects vec1 to vec4. These vectors store the results that std::transform() calculates. The ensuing statement, auto tr_op = [](auto x) { return 3 * x * x + 2 * x + 1; }, defines an arbitrary function object for std::transform().

The next four executable statements in Ch20_01_ex1() invoke STL algorithm std::transform() using the execution policy objects from the middle column of Table 20-1. Note that the execution policy is specified as the first argument. This argument ordering pattern is typical of STL algorithms that support execution policies. It warrants mentioning at this point that execution policies can only be used with algorithms in namespace std. The algorithm variants of namespace std::ranges (e.g., std::ranges::transform()) do not support execution policies.

Listing 20-1-2 shows the source code for example Ch20_01_ex2(). This example spotlights the use of std::for_each(). Execution of this algorithm applies a unary function object to an iterator that dereferences each element of a specified range.

CHAPTER 20 CONCURRENCY – PART 1

Listing 20-1-2. Example Ch20_01 - Ch20_01_ex2()

```
void Ch20_01_ex2()
{
    // create test vector
    constexpr size_t n {1'000'000};
    std::vector<int> vec0(n);
    std::iota(vec0.begin(), vec0.end(), 0);
    std::vector<int> vec1 {};

    // function object for for_each
    auto fe_op = [&vec1](int x)
            { vec1.push_back(3 * x * x + 2 * x + 1); };

    // OK
    std::for_each(ex::seq, vec0.begin(), vec0.end(), fe_op);
    std::println("after std::for_each(ex::seq)\n");

    // trouble - data race condition - calls std::terminate()
//    std::for_each(ex::par, vec0.begin(), vec0.end(), fe_op);
//    std::println("after std::for_each(ex::par)\n");
}
```

In Listing 20-1-2, note that the first use of std::for_each() specifies an execution policy of ex::seq. This means that during execution of std::for_each(), an iterator is employed to sequentially dereference each element of [vec0.begin(), vec0.end()). Function object fe_op() is then applied to the value obtained via this dereferencing action. Function object fe_op() utilizes vec1.push_back() to store results in a separate vector since std::for_each() ignores function object return values (the value pointed to by std::for_each()'s iterator can be updated if the function object specifies a reference argument).

The next use of std::for_each() is commented out since the specification of execution policy ex:::par here introduces a data race condition. Recall that execution policy ex::par signifies that a C++ implementation can utilize multiple threads to execute an algorithm. The data race condition occurs since fe_op()'s use of vec1.push_back() does not support synchronized access to vec1 from multiple threads. To address this condition, a mutex could be used. You'll learn more about mutexes later in this chapter.

CHAPTER 20 CONCURRENCY – PART 1

The primary advantage of C++'s execution policies is that they permit a program to exploit the hardware capabilities of modern processor architectures sans the coding fuss that's sometimes associated with concurrency and parallelization. Deciding when and which execution policy to use is a design decision that should be driven using realistic benchmark timing measurements. The next source code example, shown in Listing 20-1-3, contains code that measures the performance of std::transform() using different execution policies.

Listing 20-1-3. Example Ch20_01 - Ch20_01_ex3()

```cpp
void Ch20_01_ex3()
{
    constexpr int rng_min {1};
    constexpr int rng_max {2000};
    constexpr size_t vec_size = {10'000'000};

    // create test vectors
    auto vec0 = RN::get_vector<float>(vec_size, rng_min, rng_max);
    auto vec1(vec0);
    auto vec2(vec0);
    auto vec3(vec0);
    auto vec4(vec0);

    // create BmTimer using steady clock
    constexpr size_t num_iter {25};
    constexpr size_t num_alg {5};
    BmTimerSteadyClk bm_timer(num_iter, num_alg);

    // transform lambda
    auto transform_policy = [&bm_timer]<typename T>(std::vector<T>& vec,
        size_t alg_id, bool use_default, auto policy)
    {
        auto tr_op = [](T x) { return x + std::cbrt(x); };

        if (use_default)
        {
            for (size_t i = 0; i < num_iter; ++i)
            {
```

```cpp
                    bm_timer.start(i, alg_id);
                    std::transform(vec.begin(), vec.end(), vec.begin(), tr_op);
                    bm_timer.stop(i, alg_id);

                    if (i % 4 == 0)
                        std::cout << '.' << std::flush;
                }
            }
            else
            {
                for (size_t i = 0; i < num_iter; ++i)
                {
                    bm_timer.start(i, alg_id);
                    std::transform(policy, vec.begin(), vec.end(),
                        vec.begin(), tr_op);
                    bm_timer.stop(i, alg_id);

                    if (i % 4 == 0)
                        std::cout << '.' << std::flush;
                }
            }
    };

    // benchmark std::transform() using execution policies
    std::print("example Ch20_01_ex3 is running, please wait ");

    transform_policy(vec0, 0, true,  ex::seq);
    transform_policy(vec1, 1, false, ex::seq);
    transform_policy(vec2, 2, false, ex::unseq);
    transform_policy(vec3, 3, false, ex::par);
    transform_policy(vec4, 4, false, ex::par_unseq);

    // save results to CSV file
    std::println("");
    std::string fn = "Ch20_01_ex3_results.csv";
    bm_timer.save_to_csv(fn, "{:.2f}", BmTimerSteadyClk::EtUnit::MilliSec);
    std::println("Benchmark times save to file {:s}", fn);
}
```

CHAPTER 20　CONCURRENCY – PART 1

The first thing to note in Listing 20-1-3 is the number of elements in each test vector. The execution of an algorithm that consumes multiple threads to carry out its operations involves a certain amount of computational overhead. This means that it rarely makes sense to specify an execution policy of ex::par or ex::par_unseq using containers that hold a small number of elements.[1]

Example function Ch20_01_ex3() utilizes class bm_timer (see Listing 16-5-1-2) to measure the performance of std::transform() using an arbitrary function object and different execution policies. The core code for this example resides in lambda function transform_policy(). Note that this lambda contains code that also calls the overload of std::transform() that lacks an execution policy.

Table 20-2 summarizes the results obtained by executing Ch20_01_ex3() on two different test computers.[2] These results clearly show that the parallel execution policies std::par and std::par_unseq offer superior performance to their nonparallel counterparts.

Table 20-2. Mean Execution Times (Milliseconds) Using std::transform() (10,000,000 Elements) with Different Execution Policies

Execution Policy	Test Computer #1	Test Computer #2
None	266	105
ex::seq	265	106
ex::unseq	266	107
ex::par	21	14
ex::par_unseq	21	14

Source code example Ch20_01_ex4() (source code not shown) essentially replicates Ch20_01_ex3() except that it benchmarks STL algorithm std::sort() using different execution policies. Table 20-3 shows the results for this source code example. Once again, the use of a parallel execution policy yields a significant improvement in performance.

---

[1] The precise meaning of small varies depending on the algorithm and data type, which is why execution policy section should always be based on real-world benchmark timing measurements.
[2] See Appendix A for detailed information regarding each test computer.

CHAPTER 20　CONCURRENCY – PART 1

Table 20-3. *Mean Execution Times (Milliseconds) Using* `std::sort` *(5,000,000 Elements) with Different Execution Policies*

Execution Policy	Test Computer #1	Test Computer #2
None	306	264
ex::seq	306	262
ex::unseq	306	261
ex::par	54	37
ex::par_unseq	54	36

To compile and execute a program that exploits execution policies, some C++ implementations require a third-party thread building block library to be installed on the host system. Also, the default code generation option for most C++ compilers may not fully utilize the SIMD capabilities of the target processor. Appendix A contains more information regarding these topics. Here are the results for example Ch20_01:

```
----- Results for example Ch20_01 -----

----- Ch20_01_ex1() -----

vec0 (initial values):
     -50.0     119.0     181.0    -127.0      93.0     112.0      40.0      39.0
    -138.0     -22.0    -138.0    -160.0    -177.0     -16.0     147.0     -67.0
      41.0    -143.0      83.0      61.0    -192.0    -178.0     188.0      89.0
     133.0     176.0    -115.0    -200.0    -128.0     197.0    -127.0      47.0
     -78.0      45.0      10.0    -198.0     -27.0    -191.0     -84.0      10.0
      45.0     -40.0    -145.0    -182.0     -83.0     190.0     -54.0    -107.0
     -18.0    -164.0

result vector compare check: OK

----- Ch20_01_ex2() -----
after std::for_each(ex::seq)
```

```
----- Ch20_01_ex3() -----
example Ch20_01_ex3 is running, please wait ..................................
Benchmark times save to file Ch20_01_ex3_results.csv

----- Ch20_01_ex4() -----
example Ch20_01_ex4 is running, please wait ..................................
Benchmark times save to file Ch20_01_ex4_results.csv
```

Mutexes

A mutex is a synchronization mechanism that allows only one thread to access a critical section. A critical section contains code that typically manipulates a shared resource (e.g., data structure, hardware device, etc.). Mutexes are used extensively to prevent race conditions and ensure that only a single thread can access a shared resource at a given instance.

Source code example Ch20_02_ex1(), shown in Listing 20-2-1, demonstrates the basic use of class std::mutex. Following instantiation of test vectors vec0 to vec3, Ch20_02_ex1() utilizes std::for_each(ex::seq, vec0.begin(), vec0.end(), fe_op1) to apply fe_op1() to each element in [vec0.begin(), vec0.end()). Note that fe_op1() employs vec1.push_back(), which saves calculated results in vec1.

Listing 20-2-1. Example Ch20_02 – Ch20_02_ex1()

```
//-------------------------------------------------------------------------
// Ch20_02_ex.cpp
//-------------------------------------------------------------------------

#include <algorithm>
#include <execution>
#include <mutex>
#include <vector>
#include "Ch20_02.h"

namespace ex = std::execution;
```

```cpp
void Ch20_02_ex1()
{
    // create test vectors
    constexpr size_t n {10'000'000};
    std::vector<long long> vec0(n);
    std::iota(vec0.begin(), vec0.end(), 0);
    std::vector<long long> vec1 {};
    std::vector<long long> vec2 {};
    std::vector<long long> vec3 {};

    // using std::for_each with ex::seq
    auto fe_op1 = [&vec1](long long x) { vec1.push_back(x + x); };

    std::for_each(ex::seq, vec0.begin(), vec0.end(), fe_op1);
    auto sum1 = std::accumulate(vec1.begin(), vec1.end(), 0LL);
    std::println("after std::for_each(ex::seq) - sum1: {:d}", sum1);

    // using std::for_each with ex::par and std::mutex
    std::mutex mtx2 {};

    auto fe_op2 = [&vec2, &mtx2](long long x)
    {
        mtx2.lock();
        vec2.push_back(x + x);
        mtx2.unlock();
    };

    std::for_each(ex::par, vec0.begin(), vec0.end(), fe_op2);
    auto sum2 = std::accumulate(vec2.begin(), vec2.end(), 0LL);
    std::println("after std::for_each(ex::par) - sum2: {:d}", sum2);

    // using std::for_each with ex::par, std::lock_guard, and std::mutex
    std::mutex mtx3 {};

    auto fe_op3 = [&vec3, &mtx3](long long x)
    {
        std::lock_guard<std::mutex> lg3(mtx3);
        vec3.push_back(x + x);
    };
```

```
    std::for_each(ex::par, vec0.begin(), vec0.end(), fe_op3);
    auto sum3 = std::accumulate(vec3.begin(), vec3.end(), 0LL);
    std::println("after std::for_each(ex::par) - sum3: {:d}", sum3);

    // verify sums
    std::println("\nsum1 == sum2: {:s} (expect true)", sum1 == sum2);
    std::println("sum2 == sum3: {:s} (expect true)", sum2 == sum3);

    // print location of first vec1/vec2 element mismatch (if any)
    auto mm_pair = std::mismatch(vec1.begin(), vec1.end(), vec2.begin());
    auto mm_pos = std::distance(vec1.begin(), mm_pair.first);

    if (mm_pos == n)
        std::println("\nvec1 and vec2 are identical");
    else
    {
        std::println("\nvec1 and vec2 are different");
        std::println("  vec1[{:d}]: {:d}", mm_pos, vec1[mm_pos]);
        std::println("  vec2[{:d}]: {:d}", mm_pos, vec2[mm_pos]);
    }
}
```

The subsequent code block in Ch20_02_ex1() opens with the definition of std::mutex mtx2. Next is the definition of function object fe_op2(). The first executable statement of this function object, mtx2.lock(), locks std::mutex mtx2. The locking of mtx2 prevents any other thread from accessing vec2 until the lock is removed. If another thread utilizes fe_op2() while mtx2 is locked, execution of that thread is blocked (i.e., suspended) until the lock is removed. Following execution of vec2.push_back(x + x), fe_op2() employs mtx2.unlock() to unlock mtx2. This allows another thread to safely add another element to vec2. To summarize, fe_op2()'s use of mutex mtx2 avoids a data race during execution of std::for_each(ex::par, vec0.begin(), vec0.end(), fe_op2), which calls fe_op2() from multiple threads.

The explicit locking and unlocking of a mutex somewhat resembles memory allocation using operators new and delete. A locked mutex must always be unlocked by the same thread that locked it. Failure to do this will likely cause problems that can be difficult to trace. Program behavior is undefined if a thread attempts to lock a mutex it already owns. If a C++ implementation is able to detect this state, it may throw a std::system_error exception; otherwise, a deadlock may transpire.

CHAPTER 20   CONCURRENCY – PART 1

To avoid some of the undesirable side effects of failing to unlock a `std::mutex`, the STL provides a helper class named `std::lock_guard` that can automatically unlock a mutex. In Ch20_02_ex1(), function object fe_op3() utilizes `std::lock_guard<std::mutex> lg3(mtx3)` to lock mtx3. Following completion of fe_op3(), mtx3 is automatically unlocked during execution of lg3's destructor. For most use cases, the combined use of `std::lock_guard` and `std::mutex` should be favored instead of explicit mutex unlocks.

If you scan ahead to the results section, you'll notice that the values of sum1, sum2, and sum3 are identical as expected. However, vectors vec1 and vec2 are different (vec1 and vec3 are also likely different). This may be surprising, but expected since the use of execution policy ex::par (or ex::par_unseq) does not guarantee a specific order of execution. In other words, the threads spawned during execution of `std::for_each(ex::par, vec0.begin(), vec0.end(), fe_op2)` add new elements to vec2 non-deterministically. Here are the results for example Ch20_02:

```
----- Results for example Ch20_02 -----

----- Ch20_02_ex1() -----
after std::for_each(ex::seq) - sum1: 99999990000000
after std::for_each(ex::par) - sum2: 99999990000000
after std::for_each(ex::par) - sum3: 99999990000000

sum1 == sum2: true (expect true)
sum2 == sum3: true (expect true)

vec1 and vec2 are different
  vec1[3273]: 6546
  vec2[3273]: 39064
```

The C++ concurrency support library also defines several other mutex classes, including `std::timed_mutex`, which implements timeouts when attempting a lock operation. You'll see other examples of `std::mutex` use later in this book.

Threads

The C++ concurrency support library provides two basic thread classes: std::thread and std::jthread. Class std::thread has been part of the library since C++11, and class std::jthread was first included with C++20. Either class can be used to create thread objects, but the newer std::jthread class incorporates a few capabilities that make it superior for new code.

Listing 20-3-1 shows the source code for example Ch20_03_ex1(). Near the top of this listing is the definition of a function named get_test_vector() that returns a std::vector<int> of random numbers for test purposes.

Listing 20-3-1. Example Ch20_03 – Ch20_03_ex1()

```cpp
//-------------------------------------------------------------------------
// Ch20_03_ex.cpp
//-------------------------------------------------------------------------

#include <chrono>
#include <format>
#include <mutex>
#include <sstream>
#include <thread>
#include <vector>
#include "Ch20_03.h"
#include "MTH.h"
#include "RN.h"
#include "THR.h"

std::vector<int> get_test_vector(unsigned int rng_seed = 1000)
{
    constexpr size_t n {50'000'000};
    constexpr int rng_min {1};
    constexpr int rng_max {100'000'000};

    std::vector<int> vec1 = RN::get_vector<int>(n, rng_min, rng_max,
        rng_seed);
    return vec1;
}
```

CHAPTER 20   CONCURRENCY – PART 1

```cpp
void count_primes_a(const char* name, const std::vector<int>& vec,
    size_t ib, size_t ie, size_t& num_primes)
{
    std::string id = THR::get_this_thread_id();
    std::println("\nENTER count_primes_a() | name: {:s}, id: {:s}",
    name, id);

    num_primes = 0;
    for (size_t i = ib; i < ie; ++i)
    {
        if (MTH::is_prime(vec[i]))
            num_primes++;
    }

    std::println("\nEXIT  count_primes_a() | name: {:s}, id: {:s}, num_primes {:d}",
        name, id, num_primes);
}

void Ch20_03_ex1()
{
    // number of concurrent threads may be different than number of
    // physical processor threads
    auto num_concurrent_threads = std::thread::hardware_concurrency();
    std::println("number of supported concurrent threads: {}",
        num_concurrent_threads);

    // create test vector
    std::vector<int> vec1 = get_test_vector();
    size_t num_primes1 {};
    size_t num_primes2 {};

    // count primes using multiple threads
    std::println("\nlaunching thread1 and thread2");

    std::thread thread1(count_primes_a, "thread1", std::cref(vec1),
        0, vec1.size() / 2, std::ref(num_primes1));

    std::thread thread2(count_primes_a, "thread2", std::cref(vec1),
```

```
    vec1.size() / 2, vec1.size(), std::ref(num_primes2));

// count primes from current thread (for comparison purposes)
// executes in parallel with other threads
size_t num_primes3 {};
count_primes_a("Ch20_03_ex1", vec1, 0, vec1.size(), num_primes3);

// wait for threads to complete
thread1.join();
thread2.join();
std::println("\nthread1 and thread2 joined");

// check prime number counts
bool count_check = num_primes1 + num_primes2 == num_primes3;
std::println("\ncount_check: {:s} (expect true)", count_check);
}
```

The next function in Listing 20-3-1, count_primes_a(), counts the number of prime numbers in std::vector<int>& vec between [ib, ie). The opening line of this function, std::string id = THR::get_this_thread_id(), obtains a std::string id for the currently executing thread. The source code for this function, located in Common/THR.h, is as follows:

```
std::string get_this_thread_id()
{
    auto thread_id {std::this_thread::get_id()};

#if __cpp_lib_formatters >= 202302L
    return std::format("{}", thread_id);
#else
    std::ostringstream oss {};
    oss << thread_id;
    return oss.str();
#endif
}
```

Execution of function std::this_thread::get_id() returns a std::thread::id object for the currently executing thread. Function THR::get_this_thread_id() then builds a std::string for thread_id using std::format(), if supported by the compiler, or operator<<.

The remaining code in count_primes_a() utilizes a single for loop and MTH::is_prime() (see Listing 10-6-2-2) to count the number of prime numbers between [ib, ie).

In Listing 20-3-1, the initial statement of Ch20_03_ex1(), auto num_concurrent_threads = std::thread::hardware_concurrency(), obtains the number of available hardware thread contexts. Note that the value is only a hint and may not equal the actual number of concurrent threads supported by the system's physical processors. Function std::thread::hardware_concurrency() will return zero if the number of hardware thread contexts cannot be determined. When implementing a multithreaded algorithm, the value returned by hardware_concurrency() can be exploited as a guide to determine the actual number of std::thread or std::jthread objects to use.

The next code block in Ch20_03_ex1() utilizes the previously described get_test_vector() to obtain a std::vector<int> of random integers. In Ch20_03_ex1(), execution of the statement

```
std::thread thread1(count_primes_a, "thread1", std::cref(vec1),
    0, vec1.size() / 2, std::ref(num_primes1));
```

creates a std::thread object named thread1. The first argument of thread1's constructor, count_primes_a, designates a start function for the new thread. The remaining constructor arguments are passed by value to count_primes_a(). Note that the data types for these arguments match the ones that are defined for count_primes_a(). More about this shortly.

The next statement in Ch20_03_ex1():

```
std::thread thread2(count_primes_a, "thread2", std::cref(vec1),
    vec1.size() / 2, vec1.size(), std::ref(num_primes2));
```

launches a second thread that also utilizes count_primes_a() as its start function. Note that this second thread launch uses different index values. To summarize, thread1 exploits count_primes_a() to count prime numbers in vec1 between [0, vec1.size() / 2), while thread2 utilizes the same thread function to count prime numbers between [vec1.size() / 2, vec1.size()).

When using std::thread (or std::jthread) to launch a new thread, all arguments are passed by value to the designated start function; arguments can also be moved. Passing arguments by value involves making copies, but making copies of containers that hold large number of elements consumes additional resources unnecessarily. This is why the constructors for thread1 and thread2 use std::cref(vec1), which passes a constant reference to count_primes_a(). Unlike a normal function call, passing a reference to a thread's start function requires the use of std::cref() or std::ref(). Pointers can also be passed to a thread.

Execution of a thread's start function can begin any time following its instantiation. When launching more than one thread as illustrated in the current example, there's no guarantee which thread will begin executing first. This is something that needs to be considered when launching multiple threads that process data using a pipeline approach.

Following the launching of threads thread1 and thread2, Ch20_03_ex1() invokes count_primes_a("Ch20_03_ex1", vec1, 0, vec1.size(), num_primes3), which executes in parallel with thread1 and thread2. The next code block utilizes thread2.join(), which waits for thread2 to complete. Similarly, execution of thread1.join() blocks further execution of Ch20_03_ex1() until thread1 finishes. A std::thread object should always be joined prior to the execution of its destructor. Failure to do this is considered an error and may result in a thrown exception. Another option is to use std::thread::detach(), which allows a thread to continue executing independently. When using std::thread::detach(), it is extremely important to ensure that any objects accessed in the thread via a reference or pointer aren't prematurely destroyed.

If you scan ahead to the results section, note the distinct thread ids for the three executions of count_primes_a(). Also, note the order of count_primes_a() executions, which may vary depending on the target system.

In Listing 20-3-2, example function Ch20_03_ex2() demonstrates how to use std::jthread. The most important difference between a std::thread and std::jthread object is that the latter calls request_stop() (discussed later in this section) followed by join() in its destructor. This guarantees that the specified thread function finishes before the thread object is destroyed. Note in Listing 20-3-2 that Ch20_03_ex2() doesn't explicitly call join().

Listing 20-3-2. Example Ch20_03 – Ch20_03_ex2()

```
void Ch20_03_ex2()
{
    size_t num_primes1 {};
    size_t num_primes2 {};
    std::vector<int> vec1 = get_test_vector();
```

```
    std::println("launching thread1 and thread2");

    std::jthread thread1(count_primes_a, "thread1", std::cref(vec1),
        0, vec1.size() / 2, std::ref(num_primes1));

    std::jthread thread2(count_primes_a, "thread2", std::cref(vec1),
        vec1.size() / 2, vec1.size(), std::ref(num_primes2));

    // thread1.join() and thread2.join() called in destructors
}
```

Listing 20-3-3 opens with the definition of function count_primes_b(). The primary difference between this function and the count_primes_a() function is that the former periodically checks to see if a stop request has been issued for the thread. Note that the first argument of count_primes_b() is a std::stop_token. If stop_tkn.stop_requested() is true, count_primes_b() prints a simple stop message and immediately returns. Unlike class std::jthread, class std::thread does not support the use of std::stop_tokens and stop requests.

Listing 20-3-3. Example Ch20_03 - Ch20_03_ex3()

```
void count_primes_b(std::stop_token stop_tkn, const char* name,
    const std::vector<int>& vec, size_t ib, size_t ie, size_t& num_primes)
{
    std::string id = THR::get_this_thread_id();
    std::println("ENTER count_primes_b() | name: {:s}, id: {:s}, ",
        name, id);

    num_primes = 0;

    for (size_t i = ib; i < ie; ++i)
    {
        if (i % 1000)
        {
            // check for stop request
            if (stop_tkn.stop_requested())
            {
                std::println("\ncount_primes_b() - stop request received");
```

```cpp
            std::println("EXIT  count_primes_b() | name: {:s}, "
                id: {:s}, "
                    "num_primes: {:d}", name, id, num_primes);
            return;
        }
    }

    if (MTH::is_prime(vec[i]))
        num_primes += 1;
    }

    std::println("\ncount_primes_b() - normal termination");
    std::println("EXIT  count_primes_b() | name: {:s}, id: {:s}, "
        "num_primes: {:d}", name, id, num_primes);
}

void Ch20_03_ex3()
{
    // launch test thread
    std::println("launching thread1");

    std::vector<int> vec1 = get_test_vector();
    size_t num_primes1 {};
    std::jthread thread1(count_primes_b, "thread1", vec1, 0, vec1.size(),
        std::ref(num_primes1));

    // wait a bit, then send stop request to thread1
    THR::sleep_for_random_ms(1500, 2000);
    thread1.request_stop();

    // explict join() used to ensure value of num_primes1 is final
    thread1.join();
    std::println("\nnum_primes1: {:d}", num_primes1);

    // running count_primes_b() to completion
    std::println("launching thread2");
    size_t num_primes2 {};
    std::jthread thread2(count_primes_b, "thread2", vec1, 0, vec1.size(),
        std::ref(num_primes2));
```

```
        // explict join() used since jthread destructor calls request_stop()
        thread2.join();
        std::println("\nnum_primes2: {:d}", num_primes2);
}
```

Also shown in Listing 20-3-3 is example function Ch20_03_ex3(). The purpose of this example is to demonstrate how to issue a thread stop request. Following initialization of std::jthread thread1, Ch20_03_ex3() calls THR::sleep_for_random(1500, 2000), which suspends execution of the current thread for a random time period between [1500, 2000) milliseconds (see Common/THR.h for the source code). After the sleep period, Ch20_03_ex3() utilizes thread1.request_stop(). Execution of this statement sends a stop request to thread1. The next statement, thread1.join(), blocks execution of the current thread until count_primes_b() returns. This is done to ensure that the value of num_primes1 is final.

The second part of Ch20_03_ex3() launches std::jthread thread2. An explicit call to thread2.join() is used here since thread2's destructor calls request_stop(). Without the join(), thread2 would receive an unintentional stop request and terminate prematurely. To see this in action, comment out the statement thread2.join() and execute the code. Here are the results for example Ch20_03_ex3():

```
----- Results for example Ch20_03 -----

----- Ch20_03_ex1() -----
number of supported concurrent threads: 16

launching thread1 and thread2

ENTER count_primes_a() | name: Ch20_03_ex1, id: 13432

ENTER count_primes_a() | name: thread1, id: 2428

ENTER count_primes_a() | name: thread2, id: 9280

EXIT  count_primes_a() | name: thread2, id: 9280, num_primes 1439615

EXIT  count_primes_a() | name: thread1, id: 2428, num_primes 1439675

EXIT  count_primes_a() | name: Ch20_03_ex1, id: 13432, num_primes 2879290

thread1 and thread2 joined

count_check: true (expect true)
```

----- Ch20_03_ex2() -----
launching thread1 and thread2

ENTER count_primes_a() | name: thread1, id: 13620

ENTER count_primes_a() | name: thread2, id: 10080

EXIT count_primes_a() | name: thread2, id: 10080, num_primes 1439615

EXIT count_primes_a() | name: thread1, id: 13620, num_primes 1439675

----- Ch20_03_ex3() -----
launching thread1
ENTER count_primes_b() | name: thread1, id: 4124,

count_primes_b() - stop request received
EXIT count_primes_b() | name: thread1, id: 4124, num_primes: 496308

num_primes1: 496308
launching thread2
ENTER count_primes_b() | name: thread2, id: 13264,

count_primes_b() - normal termination
EXIT count_primes_b() | name: thread2, id: 13264, num_primes: 2879290

num_primes2: 2879290

Atomic Operations

An atomic operation is an operation on an atomic object whose execution is allowed to finish without being interrupted. Atomic operations facilitate lockless concurrent programming actions, which enables a program to avoid data race conditions without having to explicitly use a mutex or other synchronization object. The principal template for an atomic object is std::atomic<T>. Type T is often a fundamental type, such as a bool, char, int, long, double, etc.[3] Type T can also be a user-defined type provided it satisfies certain conditions.[4]

---

[3] The STL defines type aliases for integral atomic types (e.g., atomic_int for std::atomic<int>). This text uses the explicit template form.

[4] The type must be trivially copyable, copy/move assignable, and copy/move constructable.

CHAPTER 20   CONCURRENCY – PART 1

Listing 20-4-1 shows the source code for example function Ch20_04_ex1(). This listing opens with the definition of struct Values. Note that this structure includes two fundamental types and two atomic types. Next is the definition of thread1_func(), which contains a simple for loop that repeatedly adds one to each element in Values& v.

Listing 20-4-1. Example Ch20_04 – Ch20_04_ex1()

```cpp
//-------------------------------------------------------------------
// Ch20_04_ex.cpp
//-------------------------------------------------------------------

#include <array>
#include <atomic>
#include <format>
#include <random>
#include <string>
#include <thread>
#include <vector>
#include "Ch20_04.h"
#include "THR.h"

struct Values
{
    int Ival {};
    double Dval {};

    std::atomic<int> IvalAtomic {};
    std::atomic<double> DvalAtomic {};
};

void thread1_func(Values& v, int n)
{
    for (int i = 0; i < n; ++i)
    {
        // non-atomic adds
        v.Ival += 1;
        v.Dval += 1.0;
```

834

```cpp
        // atomic adds
        v.IvalAtomic += 1;
        v.DvalAtomic += 1.0;
    }
}

void Ch20_04_ex1()
{
    Values v {};

    // print lock_free status
    std::println("v.IvalAtomic.is_lock_free(): {:s}", v.IvalAtomic.is_lock_free());
    std::println("v.DvalAtomic.is_lock_free(): {:s}", v.DvalAtomic.is_lock_free());

    std::println("\nstd::atomic<int>::is_always_lock_free:    {:s}",
        std::atomic<int>::is_always_lock_free);

    std::println("std::atomic<double>::is_always_lock_free: {:s}",
        std::atomic<double>::is_always_lock_free);

    constexpr int n {100000};
    constexpr int n_threads {5};

    auto run_threads = [&v, n]()
    {
        {
            // elements of thread_pool default initialized, not
            actual threads
            std::array<std::jthread, n_threads> thread_pool {};

            // std::jthread::operator= performs move
            for (size_t i = 0; i < thread_pool.size(); ++i)
                thread_pool[i] = std::jthread(thread1_func,
                    std::ref(v), n);
        }

        // all threads joined here
    };
```

CHAPTER 20   CONCURRENCY – PART 1

```
    // run threads, print results
    run_threads();
    std::println("\nv.Ival:        {:7d}   v.Dval:        {:9.1f}", v.Ival,
                                                                  v.Dval);
    std::println("v.IvalAtomic: {:7d}   v.DvalAtomic: {:9.1f}",
            int(v.IvalAtomic), double(v.DvalAtomic));
    std::println("\nexpected result for all values: {:d}", n * n_threads);
}
```

The first code block in Ch20_04_ex1() utilizes v.IvalAtomic.is_lock_free() and v.DvalAtomic.is_lock_free() to ascertain the lock-free status of v.IvalAtomic and v.DvalAtomic. A return value of true signifies that the specified atomic object can be locked without using a mutex or other locking mechanism. Lock-free access is generally faster compared to the alternatives. The next two std::println() statements utilize std::atomic<int>::is_always_lock_free and std::atomic<double>::is_always_lock_free to print the lock-free status of specific atomic classes.

The middle portion of Ch20_04_ex1() contains code that launches n_thread threads. Near the top of run_threads(), the statement std::array<std::jthread, n_threads> thread_pool {} instantiates a container that can hold n_thread objects of type std::jthread. Following execution of this statement, the members of thread_pool are default initialized but not actual threads. The ensuing for loop creates the actual threads. Execution of the statement thread_pool[i] = std::jthread(thread1_func, std::ref(v), n) first creates a new std::jthread object and then moves this object to thread_pool[i]. Note that the thread creation code in run_threads resides in a distinct scope, which means it doesn't return until all threads in thread_pool have been joined.

The final code block of Ch20_04_ex1() contains several std::println() statements that print the values of Values v following execution of run_threads(). Note in the results section that atomic values v.IvalAtomic and v.DvalAtomic are correct, while non-atomic elements v.Ival and V.Dval are invalid. Also, note that the final std::println() statement employs operator int() and operator double() to obtain the current values of v.IvalAtomic and v.DvalAtomic, respectively.

You may be wondering why discrepancies exist between the atomic and non-atomic values when the same arithmetic operations are performed. The reason for this is as follows. Execution of a simple expression such as x += 1 requires the processor to perform three distinct operations: read the current value of x from memory, add one to this value, and write the result back to memory. If x is a non-atomic value, one thread might be performing the addition, while another thread is saving a new value to x. To address this, modern processor architectures such as Arm and X86 incorporate instructions that perform the three steps involved in executing x += 1 without any intervening operations. Doing this takes a bit longer to complete compared to a non-atomic value, which is why atomic variables should be used only when the possibility of a data race exists. On systems with processors that don't support atomic memory operations, a mutex or other synchronization mechanism must be used.

Listing 20-4-2 shows the source code for the next std::atomic<T> example. This listing opens with the definition of a function named thread2_func(). Following an initial delay using std::this_thread::sleep_for(), thread_func2() utilizes x +=1 to update std::atomic<int>& x. The next statement, x.notify_one(), sends a notification that unblocks at least one thread that's currently waiting for the value of x to change.

Listing 20-4-2. Example Ch20_04 – Ch20_04_ex2()

```
void thread2_func(std::atomic<int>& x, size_t delay_ms)
{
    std::println("\nENTER thread2_func() | x: {:d}, delay_ms = {:d}",
    int(x), delay_ms);
    std::this_thread::sleep_for(std::chrono::milliseconds(delay_ms));

    // change value and send notification
    x += 1;
    x.notify_one();

    std::this_thread::sleep_for(std::chrono::milliseconds(delay_ms));
    std::println("EXIT thread2_func()  | x: {:d}, delay_ms = {:d}", int(x),
    delay_ms);
}
void Ch20_04_ex2()
{
    constexpr size_t delay_ms {1000};

    // launch test thread
    constexpr int test_val1 {100};
    std::atomic<int> at_int1 {test_val1};
```

```
    std::jthread thread2(thread2_func, std::ref(at_int1), delay_ms);

    // wait for change notification
    at_int1.wait(test_val1);
    std::println("at_int1.wait() complete | at_int1: {:d}", int(at_int1));
}
```

In Ch20_04_ex2(), the statement at_int1.wait(test_val1) blocks execution of Ch20_04_ex2() while at_int1 equals test_val1. Execution of Ch20_04_ex2() resumes following thread2_func()'s use of x.notify_one(). It's important to note that if x.notify_one() (or x.notify_all()) is never called, Ch20_04_ex2() will continue to wait *ad infinitum*.

The final std::atomic<T> example spotlights the unlocking of multiple threads using atomic<T>::notify_all(). In Listing 20-4-3, thread_func3() employs x.wait(false) to block further execution while std::atomic<bool>& x is false.

Listing 20-4-3. Example Ch20_04 - Ch20_04_ex3()

```
void thread3_func(std::string name, std::atomic<bool>& x)
{
    std::print("ENTER thread3_func() | name: {:s}, x: {:s}\n", name,
    bool(x));

    x.wait(false);
    std::print("recevied notification | name: {:s}\n", name);

    // sleep_for_random_ms() used to simulate work following wait()
    THR::sleep_for_random_ms(500, 1000);
    std::print("EXIT thread3_func() | name: {:s}, x: {:s}\n", name,
    bool(x));
}

void Ch20_04_ex3()
{
    // launch test threads using thread3_func
    std::atomic<bool> at_bool1 {};
    std::array<std::jthread, 10> thread_pool {};

    for (size_t i = 0; i < thread_pool.size(); ++i)
```

```cpp
    {
        std::string name = std::format("thread{:02d}", i);
        thread_pool[i] = std::jthread(thread3_func, name, std::ref
        (at_bool1));
    }

    // allow time for all threads to begin wait
    std::this_thread::sleep_for(std::chrono::milliseconds(2000));

    // change value and notify all waiting threads
    at_bool1 = true;
    at_bool1.notify_all();
    std::println("Ch20_04_ex3() - after at_bool1.notify_all()");

    // all threaded joined here
}
```

Example function Ch20_04_ex3() commences its execution by launching ten threads using thread3_proc(). Note that std::atomic<bool> at_bool1 is passed by reference to each thread. Following a short delay using std::this_thread::sleep_for(std::chrono::milliseconds(2000)), which allows time for all launched threads to begin executing, Ch20_04_ex3() changes the value of at_bool1 to true. It then exercises at_bool1.notify_all() to notify all ten waiting threads. Note in the results section that the order of thread resumption is different than the launch order, which is not surprising since notify_all() does not stipulate any resumption guarantees for waiting threads. Here are the results for example Ch20_04:

```
----- Results for example Ch20_04 -----

----- Ch20_04_ex1() -----
v.IvalAtomic.is_lock_free(): true
v.DvalAtomic.is_lock_free(): true

std::atomic<int>::is_always_lock_free:     true
std::atomic<double>::is_always_lock_free: true

v.Ival:         277576  v.Dval:         273984.0
v.IvalAtomic:   500000  v.DvalAtomic:   500000.0

expected result for all values: 500000
```

CHAPTER 20   CONCURRENCY – PART 1

```
----- Ch20_04_ex2() -----
ENTER thread2_func() | x: 100, delay_ms = 1000
at_int1.wait() complete | at_int1: 101
EXIT thread2_func()  | x: 101, delay_ms = 1000
----- Ch20_04_ex3() -----
ENTER thread3_func() | name: thread00, x: false
ENTER thread3_func() | name: thread05, x: false
ENTER thread3_func() | name: thread02, x: false
ENTER thread3_func() | name: thread03, x: false
ENTER thread3_func() | name: thread04, x: false
ENTER thread3_func() | name: thread06, x: false
ENTER thread3_func() | name: thread07, x: false
ENTER thread3_func() | name: thread09, x: false
ENTER thread3_func() | name: thread01, x: false
ENTER thread3_func() | name: thread08, x: false
recevied notification | name: thread08
Ch20_04_ex3() - after at_bool1.notify_all()
recevied notification | name: thread01
recevied notification | name: thread00
recevied notification | name: thread07
recevied notification | name: thread06
recevied notification | name: thread04
recevied notification | name: thread03
recevied notification | name: thread05
recevied notification | name: thread09
recevied notification | name: thread02
EXIT thread3_func() | name: thread00, x: true
EXIT thread3_func() | name: thread08, x: true
EXIT thread3_func() | name: thread02, x: true
EXIT thread3_func() | name: thread01, x: true
EXIT thread3_func() | name: thread05, x: true
EXIT thread3_func() | name: thread06, x: true
EXIT thread3_func() | name: thread03, x: true
```

```
EXIT thread3_func() | name: thread09, x: true
EXIT thread3_func() | name: thread04, x: true
EXIT thread3_func() | name: thread07, x: true
```

The examples of this section performed simple addition and assignment using `std::atomic<T>` variables. Instances of `std::atomic<T>` also support a few other basic operations, including `operator-=`, `operator++`, `operator--`, `operator&=`, `operator|=`, and `operator^=`. Floating-point atomic types can use `operator=+` and `operator-=`, while the other operators are only valid for integral types. Appendix B lists a few references that you can consult for additional information regarding these and other `std::atomic<T>` operators and member functions.

Multithreaded Algorithms

Multiple threads are frequently used to accelerate the performance of a computationally intense algorithm. One such algorithm from the domain of signal processing is called convolution. A 1D discrete convolution can be calculated using the following equation:

$$y[i] = \sum_{k=-M}^{M} x[i-k]g[k] \quad i=0,1,\ldots N-1$$

In this equation, x is the input signal, y is the output signal, and g is the response signal or convolution kernel. Summation index variable $M = \lfloor N_g/2 \rfloor$ where N_g is the size of the convolution kernel. The source code examples in this book assume that N_g is an odd integer greater than or equal to three. Figure 20-1 illustrates the calculation of $y[i]$ using input signal point $x[i]$ and five-element convolution kernel g. Note in this figure that convolution kernel g is reflected, while the convolution equation reflects input signal x; either form is correct since convolution is algebraically commutative.

CHAPTER 20   CONCURRENCY – PART 1

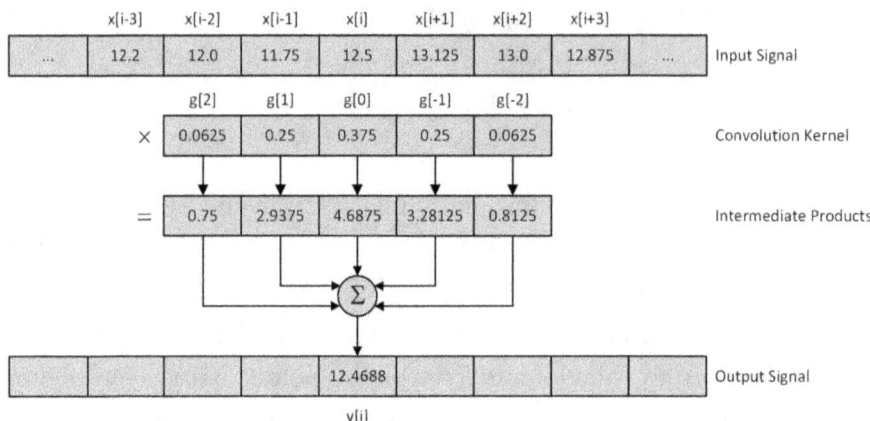

Figure 20-1. *Calculation of 1D discrete convolution signal point y[i]*

The smoothing of a sampled digital signal to reduce noise is a common signal processing use case for a convolution. The top plot in Figure 20-2 illustrates a raw data signal that contains a noticeable amount of noise. The bottom plot in the same figure shows the signal following the application of a smoothing operator using a convolution kernel that approximates a low-pass (or Gaussian) filter. The calculation of a discrete 1D convolution is computationally intense, especially for large signal arrays. Using multiple threads to carry out this calculation often results in a significant increase in performance as you'll soon see.

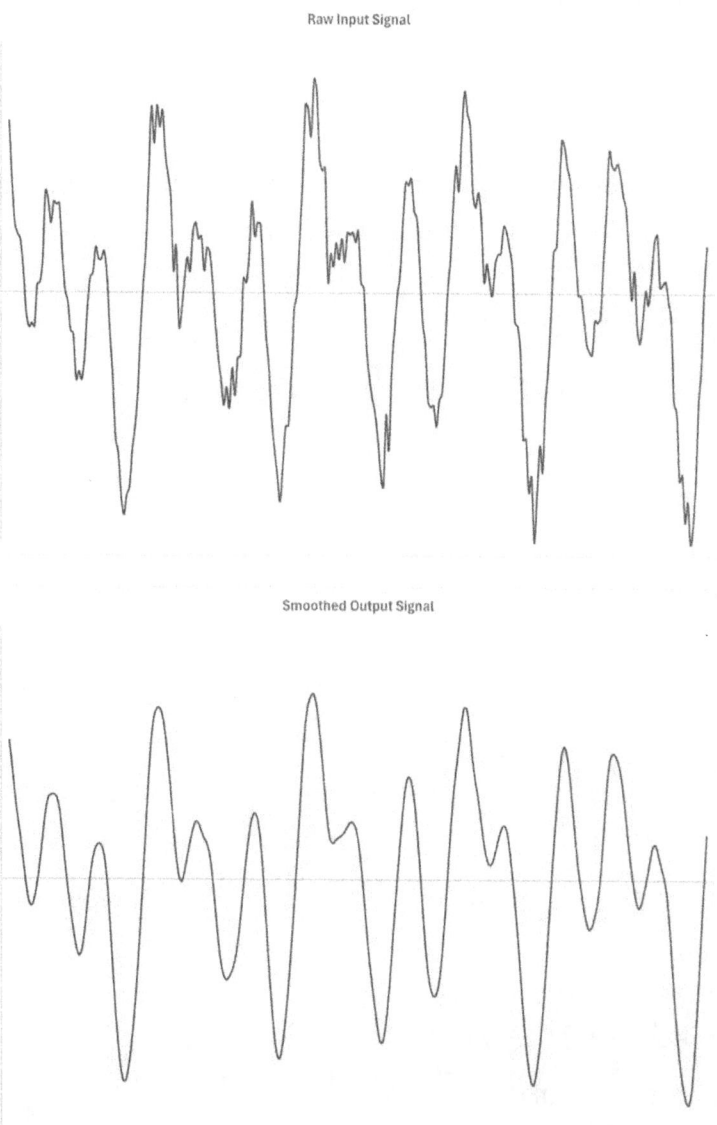

Figure 20-2. *Raw input data signal (top) and its smooth counterpart (bottom)*

The source code example of this section, named Ch20_05, illustrates how to code a multithreaded convolution algorithm. The concurrency classes and algorithms demonstrated in this example can also be used to code other types of multithreaded algorithms. Example Ch20_05 utilizes a data structure named ConvData that holds the input and output signal arrays. It also defines a few member functions that you'll soon see. A large portion of the code in ConvData relates to the generation of a synthetic test

CHAPTER 20   CONCURRENCY – PART 1

signal and the writing of results to an output file. To save some space, the listings in this section only show the code from ConvData that's directly related to concurrency and the convolution algorithm. The complete source code for ConvData is located in Common/ConvData.h.

Listing 20-5-1-1 shows the source code for a common initialization function named init_conv_data(). Execution of this function begins with the instantiation of ConvData<fp_t> cd(num_rs). Variable num_rs represents the number of raw signals that are used to generate a test input signal.

Listing 20-5-1-1. Example Ch20_05 – init_conv_data()

```cpp
//-----------------------------------------------------------------------
// Ch20_05_ex.cpp
//-----------------------------------------------------------------------

#include <iostream>
#include <valarray>
#include "Ch20_05.h"
#include "BmTimer.h"
#include "ConvData.h"

using fp_t = float;

ConvData<fp_t> init_conv_data(fp_t end_time, std::valarray<fp_t>& kernel)
{
    constexpr size_t num_rs {3};
    ConvData<fp_t> cd(num_rs);

    // generate test signal
    cd.StartTime = fp_t {0.0};
    cd.EndTime = end_time;
    cd.StepTime = fp_t {1.0 / 256.0};

    cd.Amplitudes  = std::valarray {fp_t{1.0}, fp_t{0.8},  fp_t{1.20}};
    cd.Frequencies = std::valarray {fp_t{5.0}, fp_t{9.0},  fp_t{14.0}};
    cd.PhaseAngles = std::valarray {fp_t{0.0}, fp_t{60.0}, fp_t{90.0}};

    cd.generate_signal_x(true);
    std::println("SignalX.size(): {:d}", cd.SignalX.size());
```

```
    // generate convolution kernel
    kernel = std::valarray<fp_t>
        { 1.0 / 64.0, 6.0 / 64.0, 15.0 / 64.0,
          20.0 / 64.0,
          15.0 / 64.0, 6.0 / 64.0, 1.0 / 64.0 };

    return cd;
}
```

Structure ConvData incorporates the following data attributes:

```
// signal arrays
std::valarray<T> SignalX {};                // input signal array
std::valarray<T> SignalY {};                // output signal array

// raw signal data (used to initialize SignalX)
size_t NumRs {};                            // number of raw signals
T StartTime {};                             // raw signal start time
T EndTime {};                               // raw signal end time
T StepTime {};                              // raw signal time step size

std::valarray<T> Amplitudes {};             // raw signal ampltudes
std::valarray<T> Frequencies {};            // raw signal frequecies
std::valarray<T> PhaseAngles {};            // raw signal phase angles
std::vector<std::valarray<T>> RawSignals {}; // raw signals used to
                                            //   build SignalX
```

In init_conv_data(), execution of cd.generate_signal_x(true) generates input signal cd.SignalX. This signal is built by summing three discrete sinusoidal waveforms using different amplitudes, frequencies, and phase angles. Argument value true signifies that random additive noise should be included in the generated signal. The statements just before the call to cd.generate_signal_x() define the parameters for the waveforms. The cd.SignalX generated by cd.generate_signal_x() closely resembles the top plot of Figure 20-2. The final code block of init_conv_data() instantiates a seven-element discrete convolution kernel that approximates a low-pass filter.

Listing 20-5-1-2 shows the source code for example function Ch20_05_ex1(). The opening code block of this function employs init_conv_data() to initialize ConvData<fp_t> cd and std::valarray<fp_t> kernel. The next three code blocks

CHAPTER 20   CONCURRENCY – PART 1

utilize `ConvData<fp_t>::convolve()` to perform convolutions using one, three, and seven threads. The result of each convolution is saved to a CSV file to verify that the same `cd.SignalY` result is obtained for each execution.

Listing 20-5-1-2. *Example Ch20_05 – Ch20_05_ex1()*

```
void Ch20_05_ex1()
{
    // initialize convolution data struct
    std::valarray<fp_t> kernel {};
    ConvData<fp_t> cd = init_conv_data(1.0, kernel);

    // perform convolution using 1 thread
    ConvData<fp_t>::convolve(cd, kernel, 1);
    cd.save_data("ch20_05_ex1_cd_data-a.csv");

    // perform convolution using 3 threads
    ConvData<fp_t>::convolve(cd, kernel, 3);
    cd.save_data("ch20_05_ex1_cd_data-b.csv");

    // perform convolution using 7 threads
    ConvData<fp_t>::convolve(cd, kernel, 7);
    cd.save_data("ch20_05_ex1_cd_data-c.csv");
}
```

Listing 20-5-1-3 shows the convolution calculating code from `ConvData`. The opening statements of `Convolve<T>::convolve()` validate critical convolution size parameters. If `num_threads == 1`, `convolve()` directly executes `ConvData::convole_thread()` since it's not necessary to explicitly launch any additional threads.

Listing 20-5-1-3. *Example Ch20_05 – Convolution Calculating Code*

```
    static void convolve(
        ConvData<T>& cd, const std::valarray<T>& kernel,
        size_t num_threads = 1)
    {
        size_t ss = cd.SignalX.size();
        size_t ks = kernel.size();
        size_t ks2 = ks / 2;
```

CHAPTER 20 CONCURRENCY – PART 1

```cpp
    if (ks < 3 || (ks & 1) == 0 || ss < ks)
        throw std::runtime_error("convolve_par - invalid kernel size");

    if (num_threads == 0)
        throw std::runtime_error("convolve_par - invalid num_threads");

    if (num_threads == 1)
    {
        // perform convolution on current thread
        convolve_thread(cd, kernel, ks2, ss - ks2);
        return;
    }

    // calc npts_per_thread, npts_adj (residual points added to
    first thread)
    size_t npts = ss - 2 * ks2;
    size_t npts_per_thread = npts / num_threads;
    size_t npts_adj = npts - npts_per_thread * num_threads;

    // launch convolution threads
    size_t ib = ks2;
    size_t ie = ib + npts_per_thread + npts_adj;
    std::vector<std::jthread> thread_pool(num_threads);

    for (size_t i = 0; i < num_threads; ++i)
    {
        thread_pool[i] = std::jthread(convolve_thread, std::ref(cd),
            std::cref(kernel), ib, ie);

        ib = ie;
        ie += npts_per_thread;
    }
}

static void convolve_thread(
    ConvData<T>& cd, const std::valarray<T>& kernel, size_t ib,
    size_t ie)
{
    try
```

```
    {
        size_t ks = kernel.size();
        size_t ks2 = ks / 2;

        // create reverse copy of kernel
        std::valarray<T> kernel_rev(ks);
        std::ranges::reverse_copy(kernel, std::begin(kernel_rev));

        // perform convolution using SignalX [ib, ie)
        for (size_t i = ib; i < ie; ++i)
        {
            T y_val {};

            for (size_t k = 0; k < ks; ++k)
                y_val += cd.SignalX[i - ks2 + k] * kernel_rev[k];
            cd.SignalY[i] = y_val;
        }
    }
    catch (const std::exception& ex)
    {
        std::println("Exception occured in convolve_thread");
        std::println("{:s}", ex.what());
    }
}
```

The ensuing code block calculates the number of signal points that each thread will process. Note that the number of points for the first thread is adjusted to include any residual points if npts is not an integral multiple of num_threads. The final code block of ConvData::convolve() contains a for loop that launches num_threads threads that execute ConvData::convole_thread(). Note that each executing thread performs calculations using the points from ConvData::SignalX specified by interval [ib, ie).

Function ConvData::convolve_thread(), also shown in Listing 20-5-1-3, implements the previously defined 1D discrete convolution equation over the specified interval. Note that prior to the calculating for loops, ConvData::convolve_thread() creates a reverse copy of kernel. Doing this simplifies the indexing in the for loops.

CHAPTER 20 CONCURRENCY – PART 1

One topic that hasn't been previously discussed is what happens if an executing thread throws an exception. If an executing thread throws an exception that is not caught, `std::terminate()` is called. How to handle thrown exceptions is frequently an application-specific concern. Function `ConvData::convolve_thread()` simply prints an error message, but a more robust solution should be employed for production code.

Listing 20-5-2 shows the source code for example `Ch20_05_ex2()`. This function exploits class `BmTimer` (see Listing 16-5-1-2) to measure convolution performance based on the number of threads.

Listing 20-5-2. Example Ch20_05 – Ch20_05_ex2()

```
void Ch20_05_ex2()
{
    std::println("example Ch20_05_ex2() is running, please wait ");

    // initialize convolution data struct
    std::valarray<fp_t> kernel {};
    ConvData<fp_t> cd = init_conv_data(250'000.0, kernel);

    // initailize BmTimer using steady clock
    constexpr size_t num_iter {40};
    constexpr size_t num_threads_max {8};
    BmTimerSteadyClk bm_timer(num_iter, num_threads_max);

    // run test convolutions
    for (size_t i = 0; i < num_iter; ++i)
    {
        for (size_t j = 0; j < num_threads_max; ++j)
        {
            bm_timer.start(i, j);
            ConvData<fp_t>::convolve(cd, kernel, j + 1);
            bm_timer.stop(i, j);
        }

        std::cout << '.' << std::flush;
    }
```

849

```
// save measurements to CSV file
std::println("");
std::string fn {"Ch20_05_ex2-results.csv"};
bm_timer.save_to_csv(fn, "{:..2f}", BmTimerSteadyClk::EtUnit::MilliSec);
std::println("Benchmark times save to file {:s}", fn);
}
```

Figure 20-3 summarizes the data from two executions of Ch20_05_ex2() using two different test computers. The processor for test computer #1 contains 8 cores/16 threads, while test computer #3's processor supports 4 cores/4 threads. For test computer #1, performance dramatically improves as the number of threads increases to four, after which the rate of improvement slows. For test computer #3, a similar trend is observed for one to four threads. However, performance starts to degrade after that since the processor only supports four concurrent threads. The principal takeaway point from this example is that, once again, algorithmic design decisions should be driven using real-world benchmark timing measurements on representative hardware platforms and not baseless conjecture.

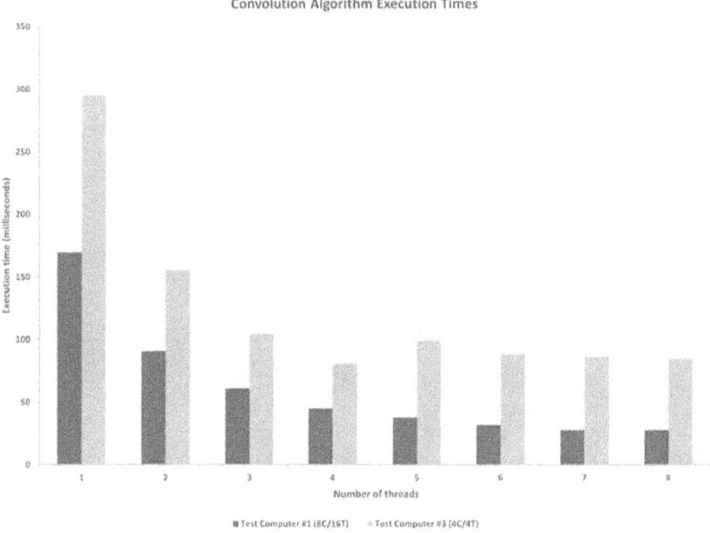

Figure 20-3. *Convolution algorithm execution times using multiple threads*

Summary

Here are the key learning points for this chapter:

- Most of the algorithms defined in namespace `std` support execution policies. An execution policy specifies the types of parallelism that an algorithm is permitted to use during its execution.

- When using an execution policy, the programmer is responsible for addressing any potential data race conditions or deadlock scenarios.

- A `std::mutex` restricts access to a critical section of code that typically manipulates a shared resource. Mutexes are used extensively to prevent race conditions and ensure that only a single thread can access a shared resource at a given instance.

- A thread is an independent sequence of instructions that can be executed on a processor. The concurrency support library includes thread classes `std::thread` and `std::jthread`. The latter class supports automatic joining and stop requests.

- An atomic operation is an operation on an atomic object whose execution is allowed to finish without being interrupted. Atomic operations facilitate lockless concurrent programming actions sans mutexes or other synchronization objects. The primary template for an atomic object is `std::atomic<T>`.

- The performance of a computationally intensive algorithm can be significantly improved by partitioning the workload across multiple threads. The number of algorithmic threads to use in production code should be established using representative benchmark timing measurements.

CHAPTER 21

Concurrency – Part 2

This chapter is a continuation of the previous chapter. It covers additional classes and algorithms related to C++ concurrency, including

- Semaphores
- Latches
- Condition variables
- Futures

Like the previous chapter, the discussions and source code examples of this chapter spotlight elements of the C++ concurrency support library that are frequently utilized to create worker threads that execute background algorithms.

Semaphores

A semaphore is a synchronization primitive that's used to coordinate concurrent access to a shared resource. The primary difference between a C++ semaphore and a mutex is that the latter can only be unlocked by the same thread that locked the mutex. Semaphores can be locked and unlocked by different threads.

The concurrency support library provides two different types of semaphores: std::binary_semaphore and std::counting_semaphore. A std::binary_semaphore is a semaphore that supports only two states. A std::counting_semaphore encompasses an internal counter that's decremented during an acquire operation and incremented by a release. A thread gets blocked if it attempts to acquire a std::counting_semaphore when its internal counter equals zero.

Listing 21-1-1 shows the source code for example Ch21_01_ex1(). This example details how to use std::binary_semaphores as thread start-stop signals. Near the top of Listing 21-1-1 is the definition of struct BinSemVec<T>. Note that this structure includes

CHAPTER 21 CONCURRENCY – PART 2

two std::binary_semaphores named Sem1 and Sem2. Also, note that both of these semaphores are default initialized, which means that they are in an acquired state. An instance of BinSemVec<T> also holds a std::vector<T> named Vec, which is constructor-initialized using std::ranges::iota(Vec, 0).

Listing 21-1-1. Example Ch21_01 - Ch21_01_ex1()

```
//--------------------------------------------------------------------
// Ch21_01_ex.cpp
//--------------------------------------------------------------------

#include <chrono>
#include <format>
#include <numeric>
#include <semaphore>
#include <string>
#include <thread>
#include <vector>
#include "Ch21_01.h"
#include "MT.h"
#include "MTH.h"
#include "THR.h"

template <typename T> struct BinSemVec
{
    BinSemVec() = delete;

    explicit BinSemVec(size_t vec_size)
    {
        Vec.resize(vec_size);
#ifdef __cpp_lib_ranges_iota         // C++23
        std::ranges::iota(Vec, 0);
#else
        std::iota(Vec1.begin(), Vec1.end(), 0);
#endif
    }
```

CHAPTER 21   CONCURRENCY – PART 2

```cpp
    static void thread_proc(BinSemVec<T>& bin_sem_vec)
    {
        std::print("\nwaiting to acquire Sem1\n");
        bin_sem_vec.Sem1.acquire();

        // sleep period added to simulate long processing time
        THR::sleep_for_random_ms(1000, 1500);
        std::ranges::transform(bin_sem_vec.Vec, bin_sem_vec.Vec.begin(),
            [](T x) { return x * x; });

        std::print("\nreleasing Sem2\n");
        bin_sem_vec.Sem2.release();
    }

    std::vector<T> Vec {};                  // test vector
    std::binary_semaphore Sem1 {0};         // thread start start
    std::binary_semaphore Sem2 {0};         // thread end signal
};

void Ch21_01_ex1()
{
    const char* fmt = "{:5d} ";
    constexpr size_t epl_max {12};

    // instantiate BinSemVec
    BinSemVec<int> bin_sem_vec1(24);
    MT::print_ctr("\nbin_sem_vec1.Vec (initial values):\n",
        bin_sem_vec1.Vec, fmt, epl_max);

    // start thread_proc
    std::println("\nlaunching thread_proc");
    std::jthread thread1(BinSemVec<int>::thread_proc, std::ref
    (bin_sem_vec1));
    THR::sleep_for_random_ms(1000, 1500);
    bin_sem_vec1.Sem1.release();

    // wait for Sem2
    std::println("\nwaiting to acquire Sem2");
    bin_sem_vec1.Sem2.acquire();
```

```
    MT::print_ctr("\nbin_sem_vec1.Vec (after processing):\n",
        bin_sem_vec1.Vec, fmt, epl_max);
}
```

The main component of BinSemVec<T> is its definition of static member function thread_proc(BinSemVec<T>& bin_sem_vec). Following an initial std::print(), thread_proc() invokes bin_sem_vec.Sem1.acquire() to acquire Sem1. Subsequent to the acquisition of Sem1, a simulated algorithm is carried out using THR::sleep_for_random(1000, 1500) (see Listing 20-3-3) and std::ranges::transform(). The final statement of thread_proc(), bin_sem_vec.Sem2.release(), releases Sem2. This notifies the thread that launched thread_proc() that its execution is complete.

Also shown in Listing 21-1-1 is example function Ch21_01_ex1(), whose execution commences with the instantiation of BinSemVec<int> bin_sem_vec1(24). In the next code block, Ch21_01_ex1() utilizes std::jthread thread1(BinSemVec<int>::thread_proc, std::ref(bin_sem_vec1)) to launch a new thread. Following a random delay, bin_sem_vec1.Sem1.release() releases Sem1. Execution of this expression unblocks thread_proc(). Function Ch21_01_ex1() then exercises bin_sem_vec1.Sem2.acquire(), which blocks further execution of Ch21_01_ex1() until thread_proc() releases Sem2.

The next example function illustrates how to use a std::counting_semaphore. The archetypal use case for a counting semaphore is to regulate the use of a limited resource. For example, suppose a server launches a new thread each time it receives a request from client. To prevent the system from becoming overloaded, the server can limit the maximum number of concurrently executing threads using a std::counting_semaphore.

In Listing 21-1-2, count_primes_thread() counts the number of prime numbers between [begin, end). Toward the end of this function, execution of cs.release() releases std::counting_semaphore<>& cs. This enables Ch21_01_ex2() to launch another thread.

Listing 21-1-2. Example Ch21_01 – Ch21_01_ex2()

```
void count_primes_thread(std::string name, int begin, int end, int& count,
    std::counting_semaphore<>& cs)
{
    std::print("{:s} - ENTER count_primes_thread()\n", name);
    std::print("{:s} - counting primes between [{:d}, {:d})\n", name,
    begin, end);
```

```cpp
    // count primes
    count = 0;
    for (int i = begin; i < end; ++i)
    {
        if (MTH::is_prime(i))
            count++;
    }

    // release semaphore (sleep added to force timeout errors)
    THR::sleep_for_random_ms(50, 60);
    cs.release();
    std::print("{:s} - EXIT count_primes_thread()\n", name);
}

void Ch21_01_ex2()
{
    // size counts and data vectors
    constexpr size_t num_total_threads {12};            // total
                                                        threads to run
    constexpr size_t num_active_threads_max {3};        // max
                                                        active threads

    std::vector<std::jthread> threads(num_total_threads);   // thread pool
    std::vector<std::string> names(num_total_threads);      // thread names
    std::vector<int> counts(num_total_threads);             // prime
                                                            num counts

    // counting semaphore to restrict number of active threads
    std::counting_semaphore<> cs(num_active_threads_max);

    // vars for count ranges
    constexpr int step {25000};
    int begin {};
    int end {step};
    size_t i {};
```

```
    while (i < threads.size())
    {
        if (!cs.try_acquire_for(std::chrono::milliseconds(5)))
            std::println("cs.try_acquire_for() time out occurred");
        else
        {
            // launch thread to count primes between [begin, end)
            names[i] = std::format("Thread{:02d}", i);

            threads[i] = std::jthread(count_primes_thread, names[i],
            begin, end,
                std::ref(counts[i]), std::ref(cs));

            begin = end;
            end += step;
            ++i;
        }
    }

    // wait for all threads to finish
    for (auto& thread : threads)
        thread.join();

    // print results
    begin = 0;
    end = step;
    std::println("");

    for (size_t i = 0; i < threads.size(); ++i)
    {
        std::println("{:10s}: [{:8d}, {:8d}) = {:5d}   ",
            names[i], begin, end, counts[i]);
        begin = end;
        end += step;
    }
}
```

Function Ch21_01_ex2() opens with the definition of num_total_threads and num_active_threads_max. The former specifies the total number of threads to launch, while the latter denotes the maximum number of active threads. Following the definition of various thread pool and data vectors, Ch21_01_ex2() utilizes std::counting_semaphore<> cs(num_active_threads_max) to instantiate a counting semaphore. Constructor argument num_active_threads_max represents the maximum number of active acquires supported by cs.

Inside Ch21_01_ex2()'s while loop, execution of cs.try_acquire_for(std::chrono::milliseconds(5)) attempts to acquire counting semaphore cs. If the attempt fails to occur within the specified duration, num_active_threads_max are currently executing. If execution of cs.try_acquire_for(std::chrono::milliseconds(5)) successfully acquires cs, Ch21_01_ex2() launches another thread using std::jthread(count_primes_thread, names[i], begin, end, std::ref(counts[i]), std::ref(cs)).

The penultimate code block in Ch21_01_ex2() contains a range for loop that executes a series of join()s to ensure completion of all launch threads. The final code block prints the prime number counts in std::vector<int> counts. The results for example Ch21_01 follow this paragraph. Note the number of timeouts that occurred during execution of cs.try_aquire_for(), which may be different for other systems.

```
----- Results for example Ch21_01 -----

----- Ch21_01_ex1() -----

bin_sem_vec1.Vec (initial values):
    0    1    2    3    4    5    6    7    8    9   10   11
   12   13   14   15   16   17   18   19   20   21   22   23

launching thread_proc

waiting to acquire Sem1

waiting to acquire Sem2

releasing Sem2

bin_sem_vec1.Vec (after processing):
    0    1    4    9   16   25   36   49   64   81  100  121
  144  169  196  225  256  289  324  361  400  441  484  529
```

CHAPTER 21   CONCURRENCY – PART 2

```
----- Ch21_01_ex2() -----
Thread00 - ENTER count_primes_thread()
Thread00 - counting primes between [0, 25000)
Thread01 - ENTER count_primes_thread()
Thread01 - counting primes between [25000, 50000)
Thread02 - ENTER count_primes_thread()
Thread02 - counting primes between [50000, 75000)
cs.try_acquire_for() time out occurred
cs.try_acquire_for() time out occurred
cs.try_acquire_for() time out occurred
Thread02 - EXIT count_primes_thread()
Thread01 - EXIT count_primes_thread()
Thread00 - EXIT count_primes_thread()
Thread03 - ENTER count_primes_thread()
Thread03 - counting primes between [75000, 100000)
Thread05 - ENTER count_primes_thread()
Thread05 - counting primes between [125000, 150000)
Thread04 - ENTER count_primes_thread()
Thread04 - counting primes between [100000, 125000)
cs.try_acquire_for() time out occurred
cs.try_acquire_for() time out occurred
cs.try_acquire_for() time out occurred
Thread04 - EXIT count_primes_thread()
Thread05 - EXIT count_primes_thread()
Thread03 - EXIT count_primes_thread()
Thread06 - ENTER count_primes_thread()
Thread06 - counting primes between [150000, 175000)
Thread07 - ENTER count_primes_thread()
Thread07 - counting primes between [175000, 200000)
Thread08 - ENTER count_primes_thread()
Thread08 - counting primes between [200000, 225000)
cs.try_acquire_for() time out occurred
cs.try_acquire_for() time out occurred
cs.try_acquire_for() time out occurred
Thread07 - EXIT count_primes_thread()
```

```
Thread06 - EXIT count_primes_thread()
Thread10 - ENTER count_primes_thread()
Thread10 - counting primes between [250000, 275000)
Thread09 - ENTER count_primes_thread()
Thread09 - counting primes between [225000, 250000)
cs.try_acquire_for() time out occurred
Thread08 - EXIT count_primes_thread()
Thread11 - ENTER count_primes_thread()
Thread11 - counting primes between [275000, 300000)
Thread10 - EXIT count_primes_thread()
Thread09 - EXIT count_primes_thread()
Thread11 - EXIT count_primes_thread()
Thread00 : [      0,  25000) = 2762
Thread01 : [  25000,  50000) = 2371
Thread02 : [  50000,  75000) = 2260
Thread03 : [  75000, 100000) = 2199
Thread04 : [ 100000, 125000) = 2142
Thread05 : [ 125000, 150000) = 2114
Thread06 : [ 150000, 175000) = 2068
Thread07 : [ 175000, 200000) = 2068
Thread08 : [ 200000, 225000) = 2036
Thread09 : [ 225000, 250000) = 2024
Thread10 : [ 250000, 275000) = 1994
Thread11 : [ 275000, 300000) = 1959
```

Latches

Starting with C++20, the concurrency support library includes two new thread coordination classes: std::latch and std::barrier. A std::latch can be used to block a group of threads until an expected number of threads arrive at the latch. Once this happens, all blocked threads are unblocked. A std::latch is a single-use thread coordination mechanism in that its internal counter is set during construction and cannot be increased or reset thereafter. A std::barrier is similar to a std::latch, but its internal counter can be reset. This facilitates object reuse.

CHAPTER 21   CONCURRENCY – PART 2

Listing 21-2-1 shows the source code for example Ch21_02, which demonstrates the use of a std::latch. Near the top of Listing 21-2-1 is the definition of struct CountPrimesThread. This structure incorporates all of the computing elements necessary to count prime numbers using multiple background threads and two std::latches.

Listing 21-2-1. Example Ch21_02 – Ch21_02_ex1()

```
//-------------------------------------------------------------------------
// Ch21_02_ex.cpp
//-------------------------------------------------------------------------

#include <array>
#include <chrono>
#include <latch>
#include <string>
#include <thread>
#include "Ch21_02.h"
#include "MTH.h"
#include "THR.h"

struct CountPrimesThread
{
    CountPrimesThread() = delete;

    explicit CountPrimesThread(const char* name, int begin, int end) :
        Name(name), Begin(begin), End(end) {};

    static void thread_proc(CountPrimesThread& cpt, std::latch& start_latch,
        std::latch& finish_latch)
    {
        std::print("{:s} - ENTER thread_proc()\n", cpt.Name);
        std::print("{:s} - waiting for start_latch\n", cpt.Name);

        // wait for latch
        start_latch.arrive_and_wait();

        //
```

```cpp
        cpt.Count = 0;
        std::print("{:s} - counting primes between [{:d}, {:d})\n",
            cpt.Name, cpt.Begin, cpt.End);

        for (int i = cpt.Begin; i < cpt.End; ++i)
        {
            if (MTH::is_prime(i))
                ++cpt.Count;
        }

        // update finish latch
        finish_latch.count_down();
        std::print("{:s} - EXIT thread_proc()\n", cpt.Name);
    }

    std::string Name {};                    // thread name
    int Begin {}, End {}, Count {};         // count data
    std::jthread Thread {};                 // thread object
};

void Ch21_02_ex1()
{
    std::println("Ch21_02_ex1() - this example may take a while to
    complete");

    // CountPrimeThread instances
    std::array<CountPrimesThread, 4> cpts
    {
        CountPrimesThread {"CPT0",             0,    50'000'001},
        CountPrimesThread {"CPT1",    50'000'000,    75'000'001},
        CountPrimesThread {"CPT2",    75'000'000,   175'000'001},
        CountPrimesThread {"CPT3",   175'000'000,   250'000'001}
    };

    // thread start and finish latches
    std::latch start_latch(cpts.size() + 1);
    std::latch finish_latch(cpts.size());

    // launch threads
```

```
    for (size_t i = 0; i < cpts.size(); ++i)
    {
        cpts[i].Thread = std::jthread(CountPrimesThread::thread_proc,
            std::ref(cpts[i]), std::ref(start_latch), std::ref
            (finish_latch));
    }

    // commence execution of threads
    THR::sleep_for_random_ms(50, 75);
    start_latch.count_down();

    // wait for finish latch to signal all threads complete
    std::println("Ch21_02_ex1() - waiting for finish_latch");
    finish_latch.wait();
    std::println("Ch21_02_ex1() - all threads finished\n");

    for (size_t i = 0; i < cpts.size(); ++i)
    {
        std::println("Name: {:6s}  Begin: {:10d}  End: {:10d}
        Count: {:10d}",
            cpts[i].Name, cpts[i].Begin, cpts[i].End, cpts[i].Count);
    }
}
```

The principal element of struct CountPrimeThread is static member function thread_proc(CountPrimesThread& cpt, std::latch& start_latch, std::latch& finish_latch). In this function, execution of start_latch.arrive_and_wait() atomically decrements an internal counter in start_latch by one and blocks further execution of thread_proc() until start_latch's counter equals zero. Following the for loop that counts prime numbers between [cpt.Begin, cpt.End), thread_proc() utilizes finish_latch.count_down() to decrement finish_latch's internal counter by one without blocking.

The opening code block of Ch21_02_ex1() contains the statement std::array<CountPrimesThread, 4> cpts that instantiates four instances of CountPrimeThread. Note that each thread utilizes different values for its counting range. The subsequent code block includes definitions for latch objects std::latch start_latch(cpts.size() + 1) and std::latch finish_latch(cpts.size()). In these expressions, the constructor argument specifies the initial value for the std::latch's internal counter. The reason for the extra count on start_latch will be explained shortly.

The next code block in Ch21_02_ex1() utilizes a for loop to launch cpts.size() threads. Note that references to both start_latch and finish_latch are passed to CountPrimeThread::thread_proc(). Following a short delay using THR::sleep_for_random_ms(50, 75), Ch21_02_ex1() utilizes start_latch.count_down() to unblock all launched threads. Recall that CountPrimeThread::thread_proc() called start_latch.arrive_and_wait() to block execution until start_latch's internal counter reached zero. In the current example, this happens when Ch21_02_ex3() exercises start_latch.count_down(). The reason for start_latch's extra count should now be apparent.

The final code block in Ch21_02_ex1() employs finish_latch.wait() to block further execution until finish_latch's internal counter reaches zero. This transpires following the execution of finish_latch.count_down() in CountPrimesThread::thread_proc() by all cpts active threads. Here are the results for example Ch21_02:

```
----- Results for example Ch21_02 -----

----- Ch21_02_ex1() -----
Ch21_02_ex1() - this example may take a while to complete
CPT2 - ENTER thread_proc()
CPT2 - waiting for start_latch
CPT3 - ENTER thread_proc()
CPT3 - waiting for start_latch
CPT1 - ENTER thread_proc()
CPT1 - waiting for start_latch
CPT0 - ENTER thread_proc()
CPT0 - waiting for start_latch
Ch21_02_ex1() - waiting for finish_latch
CPT1 - counting primes between [50000000, 75000001)
CPT2 - counting primes between [75000000, 175000001)
CPT3 - counting primes between [175000000, 250000001)
CPT0 - counting primes between [0, 50000001)
CPT1 - EXIT thread_proc()
CPT0 - EXIT thread_proc()
```

```
CPT3 - EXIT thread_proc()
CPT2 - EXIT thread_proc()
Ch21_02_ex1() - all threads finished

Name: CPT0      Begin:           0  End:   50000001  Count:      3001134
Name: CPT1      Begin:    50000000  End:   75000001  Count:      1393170
Name: CPT2      Begin:    75000000  End:  175000001  Count:      5372468
Name: CPT3      Begin:   175000000  End:  250000001  Count:      3912546
```

Condition Variables

A condition variable is a synchronization primitive that blocks execution of a thread until notified by another thread that a predetermined condition has been met or a timeout occurs. An instance of std::condition_variable requires a std::mutex to carry out its actions. Condition variables are typically exploited to signify the occurrence of an event. One such use case is the producer-consumer model where one thread generates data, while a second thread processes it as elucidated in source code example Ch21_03.

Listing 21-3-1-1 shows declaration for struct ConditionVarDemo. The first group of items in this structure – Mutex, ConditionVar, DataReady, and NoMoreData – are used in example Ch21_03 to generate and detect an event. The next three items, Airports, Distances, and Units, represent the generated and processed data. Member RngSeed is used as a random number generator seed value.

Listing 21-3-1-1. Example Ch21_03 – ConditionVarDemo

```
//------------------------------------------------------------------------
// Ch21_03_ex.cpp
//------------------------------------------------------------------------

#include <algorithm>
#include <chrono>
#include <condition_variable>
#include <mutex>
#include <string>
#include <vector>
#include <thread>
```

```cpp
#include "Ch21_03.h"
#include "Airport.h"
#include "THR.h"

struct ConditionVarDemo
{
    // event signaling
    std::mutex Mutex {};
    std::condition_variable ConditionVar {};
    bool NoMoreData {};
    bool DataReady {};

    // generated data
    std::vector<Airport> Airports {};
    std::vector<double> Distances {};
    Airport::GeoCoord::Units Units {};

    // miscellaneous data
    unsigned int RngSeed {};
};
```

The data generation function generate_data(), shown in Listing 21-3-1-2, utilizes a simple for loop to generate several sets of data. Within this for loop, the first code block exercises airports = get_random_airports(n, cvd.RngSeed + n) to obtain a std::vector<Airports> of n random Airports. The next statement, auto distances = calc_distance_matrix(airports, cvd.Units), constructs the n × n distance matrix of all Airports in container airports. The source code for both get_random_airports() and calc_distance_matrix() is not shown in a listing but located in Ch21_03_misc.cpp.

Listing 21-3-1-2. Example Ch21_03 – generate_data()

```cpp
static void generate_data(ConditionVarDemo& cvd)
{
    std::print("\nENTER generate_data\n");

    for (unsigned int n = 3; n < 8; ++n)
    {
        // generate data
```

```
        auto airports = get_random_airports(n, cvd.RngSeed + n);
        auto distances = calc_distance_matrix(airports, cvd.Units);

        // move data into cvd
        {
            std::lock_guard<std::mutex> lock(cvd.Mutex);
            cvd.Airports = std::move(airports);
            cvd.Distances = std::move(distances);
            cvd.DataReady = true;
        }

        // send data ready notification
        // (sleep added to simulate random processing delays)
        cvd.ConditionVar.notify_one();
        THR::sleep_for_random_ms(250, 500);
    }

    // signal end of data
    {
        std::lock_guard<std::mutex> lock(cvd.Mutex);
        cvd.NoMoreData = true;
    }

    cvd.ConditionVar.notify_one();
    THR::sleep_for_random_ms(25, 50);
    std::print("\nEXIT   generate_data\n");
}
```

The next code block in generate_data(), which is distinctly scoped, utilizes std::lock_guard<std::mutex> lock(cvd.Mutex) to lock the event signaling mutex in ConditionVarDemo cvd. This allows safe execution of the subsequent two statements, cvd.Airports = std::move(airports) and cvd.Distances = std::move(distances). Following the data move, cvd.DataReady is set to true for reasons that will be explained later. The final code block of generate_data()'s for loop exercises cvd.ConditionVar.notify_one(), which notifies the thread executing process_data() that new data has been generated.

The final code block in generate_data() locks mutex cvd.Mutex and sets cvd.NoMoreData to true. Function process_data() utilizes this flag to terminate its for loop. Execution of cvd.ConditionVar.notify_one() notifies process_data() of this change.

Listing 21-3-1-3 shows the source code for process_data(). Within this function's while loop is a scoped block whose first statement, std::unique_lock<std::mutex> lk(cvd.Mutex), obtains control of mutex cvd.Mutex.

Listing 21-3-1-3. Example Ch21_03 - process_data()

```
static void process_data(ConditionVarDemo& cvd)
{
    std::print("\nENTER process_data\n");

    // miscellanous data items
    bool done {};
    std::vector<Airport> airports {};
    std::vector<double> distances {};
    std::string units {"Uknown"};

    if (cvd.Units == Airport::GeoCoord::Units::mi)
        units = "Miles";
    else if (cvd.Units == Airport::GeoCoord::Units::km)
        units = "Kilometers";

    while (!done)
    {
        {
            // wait for event
            std::unique_lock<std::mutex> lk(cvd.Mutex);

            cvd.ConditionVar.wait(lk,
                [&cvd] { return cvd.NoMoreData || cvd.DataReady; });

            if (cvd.NoMoreData)
                done = true;
            else
            {
                cvd.DataReady = false;
                airports = std::move(cvd.Airports);
```

```
                distances = std::move(cvd.Distances);
            }
        }

        // above lock released, generate_data() can now lock again
        if (!done)
        {
            std::string title = std::format(
                "---- Distance Matrix ({:d} airports in {:s}) -----",
                airports.size(),
                units);

            print_distance_matrix(title, airports, distances);
        }
    }

    std::print("\nEXIT  process_data\n");
}
```

During execution of cvd.ConditionVar.wait(lk, [&cvd] { return cvd.NoMoreData || cvd.DataReady}), process_data() is blocked until either cvd.NoMoreData or cvd.DataReady is true. If cvd.NoMoreData is true, process_data()'s while loop terminates. If cvd.DataReady is true, execution of airports = std::move(cvd.Airports) and distances = std::move(cvd.Distances) moves the previously generated data from cvd to local containers for later printing by print_distance_matrix(). Note that this function is called outside of the scoped block, which means that cvd.Mutex is no longer locked. This allows generate_data() to resume generating data, while print_distance_matrix() (see Ch21_03_misc.cpp) prints the airport distance matrix.

The reason for using bools NoMoreData and DataReady is that std::mutex cvd.Mutex might spuriously wake up (i.e., unlock) during execution of cvd.ConditionVar.wait(). The use of predicate cvd.NoMoreData || cvd.DataReady ensures that a genuine event has occurred and not a spurious wakeup. The possibility of a spurious wakeup, while unlikely, varies depending on the target system. For the current example, if another thread were to change the state of cvd.ConditionVar, a spurious wakeup is theoretically possible following completion of generate_data()'s inner for loop scope (i.e., just before cvd.ConditionVar.notify_one()) and process_data()'s use of std::unique_lock<std::mutex> lk(cvd.Mutex).

CHAPTER 21 CONCURRENCY – PART 2

Listing 21-3-1-4 shows the source code for example function Ch21_03_ex1().
Execution of this function launches std::jthreads thread1 and thread2, which execute
generate_data() and process_data(), respectively.

Listing 21-3-1-4. Example Ch21_03 - Ch21_03_ex1()

```
void Ch21_03_ex1()
{
    ConditionVarDemo cvd {};
    cvd.RngSeed = 73;
    cvd.Units = Airport::GeoCoord::Units::mi;

    // launch process_data and generate_data threads
    // (sleep allows time for process_data thread to begin)
    std::jthread thread1(process_data, std::ref(cvd));
    std::this_thread::sleep_for(std::chrono::milliseconds(25));
    std::jthread thread2(generate_data, std::ref(cvd));

    // threads joined here
}
```

Here are the results for example Ch21_03:

```
----- Results for example Ch21_03 -----

----- Ch21_03_ex1() -----

ENTER process_data

ENTER generate_data

---- Distance Matrix (3 airports in Miles) -----
        CDG        LHR        WLG
CDG     0.00       216.20     11787.11
LHR     216.20     0.00       11701.23
WLG     11787.11   11701.23   0.00
```

871

CHAPTER 21   CONCURRENCY – PART 2

```
---- Distance Matrix (4 airports in Miles) -----
         YYC       MEL       KIX       ZRH
YYC      0.00      8628.59   5191.03   4825.08
MEL      8628.59   0.00      5020.28   10146.40
KIX      5191.03   5020.28   0.00      5889.41
ZRH      4825.08   10146.40  5889.41   0.00

---- Distance Matrix (5 airports in Miles) -----
         YVR       IAH       SYD       YYZ       ZRH
YVR      0.00      1969.50   7768.23   502.72    5164.39
IAH      1969.50   0.00      8597.70   1854.57   5310.57
SYD      7768.23   8597.70   0.00      8260.13   10296.00
YYZ      502.72    1854.57   8260.13   0.00      4694.37
ZRH      5164.39   5310.57   10296.00  4694.37   0.00

---- Distance Matrix (6 airports in Miles) -----
         LAX       IAH       GLA       YYC       ORD       TLS
LAX      0.00      1376.47   5123.76   1207.45   1741.27   5873.40
IAH      1376.47   0.00      4563.66   1748.00   926.30    5129.72
GLA      5123.76   4563.66   0.00      4024.02   3665.78   883.54
YYC      1207.45   1748.00   4024.02   0.00      1382.08   4834.85
ORD      1741.27   926.30    3665.78   1382.08   0.00      4288.94
TLS      5873.40   5129.72   883.54    4834.85   4288.94   0.00

---- Distance Matrix (7 airports in Miles) -----
         PVG       DEL       MCO       CDG       BER       ORD       JFK
PVG      0.00      2666.21   8049.10   5758.48   5236.96   7043.04   7374.60
DEL      2666.21   0.00      8248.58   4080.23   3585.95   7470.10   7311.38
MCO      8049.10   8248.58   0.00      4498.05   4879.07   1006.73   937.85
CDG      5758.48   4080.23   4498.05   0.00      532.01    4141.22   3637.71
BER      5236.96   3585.95   4879.07   532.01    0.00      4415.49   3982.33
ORD      7043.04   7470.10   1006.73   4141.22   4415.49   0.00      722.74
JFK      7374.60   7311.38   937.85    3637.71   3982.33   722.74    0.00

EXIT   process_data

EXIT   generate_data
```

CHAPTER 21 CONCURRENCY – PART 2

Futures

The futures section of the C++ concurrency support library provides components that a thread can use to asynchronously retrieve a value or exception produced by another (or the same) thread. More specifically, an instance of `std::promise<T>` stores an object of type T for later retrieval by an instance of `std::future<T>`. Function template `std::async()` asynchronously launches a thread function and returns a `std::future<T>`, which eventually incorporates the thread function's returned result. These three components, plus a few others not discussed in this book, facilitate the execution of threads using a somewhat higher level of abstraction compared to the explicit use of `std::thread` and `std::jthread`.

Example function `Ch21_04_ex1()`, shown in Listing 21-4-1, elucidates the basic use of classes `std::promise<T>` and `std::future<T>`. Near the top of this listing is the definition of alias `using result_t = std::pair<double, double>`. The next code block defines function object `calc_sphere_area_vol()`, which calculates the surface area and volume of a sphere. Note that `calc_sphere_area_vol()` returns an object of type `result_t`.

Listing 21-4-1. Example Ch21_04 – Ch21_04_ex1()

```
//------------------------------------------------------------------------
// Ch21_04_ex.cpp
//------------------------------------------------------------------------

#include <future>
#include <numbers>
#include <thread>
#include <utility>
#include "Ch21_04.h"
#include "MTH.h"
#include "THR.h"

void Ch21_04_ex1()
{
    // define result type
    using result_t = std::pair<double, double>;
```

```cpp
    // lambda to calculate sphere surface area & volume
    auto calc_sphere_area_vol = [](double r)
    {
        double area = 4 * std::numbers::pi * r * r;
        double volume = area * r / 3;
        return result_t {area, volume};
    };

    // calculate sphere surface areas and volumes
    std::vector<double> radii { 1.0, 2.0, 3.0, 4.0, 5.0 };

    for (double radius : radii)
    {
        // using std::promise
        std::promise<result_t> promise1 {};
        promise1.set_value(calc_sphere_area_vol(radius));

        // using std::future
        std::future<result_t> future1 { promise1.get_future() };
        result_t result1 = future1.get();

        // print result
        std::println("radius: {:6.2f}  surface area: {:6.2f}  volume: {:6.2f}",
            radius, result1.first, result1.second);
    }
}
```

The first statement inside Ch21_04_ex1()'s for loop, std::promise<result_t> promise1 {}, default initializes a std::promise<T> object that holds a result_t. Execution of promise1.set_value(calc_sphere_area_vol(radius)) *atomically* sets promise1's result_t value using the return value from calc_sphere_area_vol(). The next code block opens with std::future<result_t> future1 { promise1.get_future() }. Execution of this statement obtains the std::future<result_t> object that's associated with promise1. This is followed by result_t result1 = future1.get(), which obtains the actual result_t value from future1.

Example function Ch21_04_ex1() exercises instances of std::promise<T> and std::future<T> on the same thread. The more common use case for these classes is the storing and retrieval of a value using different threads. Listing 21-4-2 shows the source code for example function Ch21_04_ex2(). This function sets a std::promise<T> value on one thread that is retrieved using a std::future<T> on a second thread.

Listing 21-4-2. Example Ch21_04 – Ch21_04_ex2()

```
void Ch21_04_ex2()
{
    // define result type
    using result_t = std::pair<double, double>;

    // lambda to calculate sphere surface area & volume
    auto calc_sphere_area_vol = [](double r, std::promise<result_t>& prom)
    {
        double area = 4 * std::numbers::pi * r * r;
        double volume = area * r / 3;

        prom.set_value(result_t {area, volume});
    };

    // calculate sphere surface areas and volumes
    std::vector<double> radii { 1.0, 2.0, 3.0, 4.0, 5.0 };

    for (double radius : radii)
    {
        // create std::promise and std::future objects
        std::promise<result_t> promise1 {};
        std::future<result_t> future1 { promise1.get_future() };

        // launch thread to perform calculation
        std::jthread thread1(calc_sphere_area_vol, radius,
            std::ref(promise1));

        // get future result, current thread blocked until result is ready
        result_t result1 = future1.get();
```

```
        // print result
        std::println("radius: {:6.2f}  surface area: {:6.2f}
        volume: {:6.2f}",
            radius, result1.first, result1.second);

        // thread1 joined here
    }
}
```

In Listing 21-4-2, note that the definition of function object calc_sphere_area_vol() includes an argument of type std::promise<result_t>& prom. Also, note that the last line of calc_sphere_area_vol() utilizes prom.set_value(result_t {area, volume}) to set prom's value.

Like the previous example, function Ch21_04_ex2() creates std::promise<result_t> promise1 {} and std::future<result_t> future1 { promise1.get_future() } inside its range for loop. The next statement, std::jthread thread1(calc_sphere_area_vol, radius, std::ref(promise1)), launches a thread using start function calc_sphere_area_vol(). Note that a reference to promise1 is passed to calc_sphere_area_vol(). Execution of result_t result1 = future1.get() blocks execution of the current thread until future1's result is ready. This transpires following execution of prom.set_value(result_t {area, volume}) in calc_sphere_area_vol(). What's important to recognize here is that the result from calc_sphere_area_vol() is retrieved and printed prior to the joining of thread1, which occurs automatically following execution of the std::println() statement.

In Listing 21-4-3, example function Ch21_04_ex3() demonstrates the retrieval of a std::future<T> value from a thread launched using template function std::async(). Near the top of Ch21_04_ex3() is the definition of struct result_t { std::string ThreadId {}; ll_t Sum {}; }. Function object sum_primes(ll_t n) sums prime numbers between 2 and n; it then returns a result_t that contains the calculated sum along with executing thread's id number.

Listing 21-4-3. Example Ch21_04 - Ch21_04_ex3()

```
void Ch21_04_ex3()
{
    // define types
    using ll_t = long long;
    struct result_t { std::string ThreadId {}; ll_t Sum {}; };
```

```cpp
// sum_primes lambda
auto sum_primes = [](ll_t n, const char* policy)
{
    std::print("ENTER sum_primes() - policy: {:s}\n", policy);

    ll_t sum {0};

    for (ll_t i = 2; i <= n; ++i)
        { if (MTH::is_prime(i)) sum += i; }

    std::print("EXIT  sum_primes() - policy: {:s}\n", policy);
    return result_t { THR::get_this_thread_id(), sum };
};

// print current thread_id
constexpr ll_t n {10'000'000};
std::println("Ch21_04_ex2() - n: {:d}, thread_id: {:s}\n", n,
    THR::get_this_thread_id());

// launch async threads using different launch policies
const char* ps0 = "default";
const char* ps1 = "async";
const char* ps2 = "deferred";
const char* ps3 = "async | deferred";

auto async_result0 = std::async(sum_primes, n, ps0);
auto async_result1 = std::async(std::launch::async, sum_primes,
n, ps1);
auto async_result2 = std::async(std::launch::deferred, sum_primes,
n, ps2);
auto async_result3 = std::async(std::launch::async | std::launch::
deferred,
    sum_primes, n, ps3);

// print results
auto print_result = [](std::future<result_t>& result, const char*
policy)
{
```

```
        // print result, get() blocks until result is ready
        result_t r = result.get();

        std::println("result - Sum: {:12d}  ThreadId: {:6s}  policy: {:s}",
            r.Sum, r.ThreadId, policy);
    };

    print_result(async_result0, ps0);
    print_result(async_result1, ps1);
    print_result(async_result2, ps2);
    print_result(async_result3, ps3);
}
```

Function Ch21_04_ex3() utilizes std::async() to asynchronously execute sum_primes(), whose execution occurs on the current thread or a newly launched thread. More about this shortly. Function std::async() returns a std::future<result_t> that eventually holds the result returned by sum_primes().

Template function std::async() defines an overload that includes a launch policy parameter. Launch policy std::launch::async instructs std::async() to begin asynchronous execution of the specified function object as soon as possible. Policy std::launch::deferred postpones execution of the specified function object until get() is called for the std::future<T> object that std:async() returns. When using this launch policy, failure to call get() (or std::future<T>::wait()) means that the function object will never execute. Policy selection is implementation-defined when std::launch::async | std::launch::deferred is specified. This policy is also the default for the overload of std::async() that lacks an explicit launch policy parameter.

The results for example Ch21_04 follow this paragraph. Note that for function Ch21_04_ex3(), all std::async() launches of sum_primes() were executed on different threads except for launch policy std::launch::deferred. These results may vary depending on the target system.

```
----- Results for example Ch21_04 -----

----- Ch21_04_ex1() -----
radius:   1.00  surface area:  12.57  volume:    4.19
radius:   2.00  surface area:  50.27  volume:   33.51
radius:   3.00  surface area: 113.10  volume:  113.10
radius:   4.00  surface area: 201.06  volume:  268.08
radius:   5.00  surface area: 314.16  volume:  523.60

----- Ch21_04_ex2() -----
radius:   1.00  surface area:  12.57  volume:    4.19
radius:   2.00  surface area:  50.27  volume:   33.51
radius:   3.00  surface area: 113.10  volume:  113.10
radius:   4.00  surface area: 201.06  volume:  268.08
radius:   5.00  surface area: 314.16  volume:  523.60

----- Ch21_04_ex3() -----
Ch21_04_ex2() - n: 10000000, thread_id: 10556

ENTER sum_primes() - policy: default
ENTER sum_primes() - policy: async
ENTER sum_primes() - policy: async | deferred
EXIT  sum_primes() - policy: async
EXIT  sum_primes() - policy: async | deferred
EXIT  sum_primes() - policy: default
result - Sum: 3203324994356  ThreadId: 11176   policy: default
result - Sum: 3203324994356  ThreadId: 8660    policy: async
ENTER sum_primes() - policy: deferred
EXIT  sum_primes() - policy: deferred
result - Sum: 3203324994356  ThreadId: 10556   policy: deferred
result - Sum: 3203324994356  ThreadId: 924     policy: async | deferred
```

Class std::future<T> can also be used to return a container object by value from a thread function. Source code example Ch21_05 illustrates this design pattern using thread functions that calculate discrete cosine transforms (DCT). DCTs are the foundation of many lossy compression algorithms for audio and video, including the original JPEG and MPEG algorithms. A DCT and its inverse can be calculated using the following textbook equations:

CHAPTER 21   CONCURRENCY – PART 2

$$X_k = \frac{1}{N}\sum_{n=0}^{N-1} x_n \cos\left(\frac{\pi k}{N}\left(n+\frac{1}{2}\right)\right) \quad k=0,1,2,\ldots N-1$$

$$x_k = X_0 + 2\sum_{n=1}^{N-1} X_n \cos\left(\frac{\pi n}{N}\left(k+\frac{1}{2}\right)\right) \quad k=0,1,2,\ldots N-1$$

Listing 21-5-1-1 shows the source code for template functions dct() and dct_inv(). Note that both functions require an argument of type std::vector<T>& and return a result of std::vector<T>. The code used in these functions is a direct implementation of the DCT equations.

Listing 21-5-1-1. Example Ch21_05 - DCT Functions

```
//-------------------------------------------------------------------
// Ch21_05_ex.cpp
//-------------------------------------------------------------------

#include <algorithm>
#include <chrono>
#include <cmath>
#include <future>
#include <numbers>
#include <stdexcept>
#include <vector>
#include "Ch21_05.h"
#include "RN.h"

template <typename T> requires std::floating_point<T>
std::vector<T> dct(const std::vector<T>& x)
{
    const size_t N = x.size();
    std::vector<T> X(N);

    // calculate DCT
    for (size_t k = 0; k < N; ++k)
    {
        T sum {};
```

```
        for (size_t n = 0; n < N; ++n)
        {
            T t1 = std::numbers::pi_v<T> * k / N;
            sum += x[n] * std::cos(t1 * (n + 0.5));
        }

        X[k] = T(1.0) / N * sum;
    }

    return X;
}
template <typename T> requires std::floating_point<T>
std::vector<T> dct_inv(const std::vector<T>& X)
{
    const size_t N = X.size();
    std::vector<T> x(N);

    // calculate inverse DCT
    for (size_t k = 0; k < N; ++k)
    {
        T sum {};

        for (size_t n = 1; n < N; ++n)
        {
            T t1 = std::numbers::pi_v<T> * n / N;
            sum += X[n] * std::cos(t1 * (k + 0.5));
        }

        x[k] = X[0] + T(2) * sum;
    }

    return x;
}
```

Template function compare_vectors(), shown in Listing 21-5-1-2, compares two std::vector<T> objects for equivalence. This function is used later to validate DCT results.

CHAPTER 21 CONCURRENCY – PART 2

Listing 21-5-1-2. *Example Ch21_05 - compare_vectors()*

```
template <typename T> requires std::floating_point<T>
void compare_vectors(const std::vector<T>& vec1, const
std::vector<T>& vec2,
    T epsilon = 1.0e-7)
{
    auto eq_pred = [epsilon](T a, T b) { return std::fabs(a - b)
    <= epsilon; };
    bool ok = std::ranges::equal(vec1, vec2, eq_pred);

    std::print("\ncompare_vectors(): ");
    std::println("{:s}", ok ? "ok" : "failed!");
}
```

Example function Ch21_05_ex1(), shown in Listing 21-5-1-3, demonstrates the use of dct() and dct_inv() using a small std::vector<fp_t> of random numbers. Note that both DCT functions return by value objects of type std::vector<fp_t>. Also, note that compare_vectors() is employed to validate the equivalence of x0 and x1.

Listing 21-5-1-3. *Example Ch21_05 - Ch21_05_ex1()*

```
// #define PRINT_DCT_VALUES

void Ch21_05_ex1()
{
    using fp_t = double;

    // create test vector
    constexpr int rng_min {0};
    constexpr int rng_max {1000};
    constexpr unsigned int rng_seed {879};
    constexpr size_t npts {20};

    std::vector<fp_t> x0 = RN::get_vector<fp_t>(npts, rng_min, rng_max,
    rng_seed);

    // perform DCT and inverse DCT, compare results
    auto X0 = dct<fp_t>(x0);
```

```
        auto x1 = dct_inv<fp_t>(X0);
        compare_vectors(x0, x1);

#ifdef PRINT_DCT_VALUES
        for (size_t i = 0; i < npts; ++i)
            std::println("{:3d}: {:12.6f}, {:12.6f}, {:12.6f}", i, x0[i],
            X0[i], x1[i]);
#endif
}
```

Source code example, shown in Listing 21-5-2, employs `std::async()` and `std::future<T>` to carry out asynchronous DCT calculations. The opening function of this listing, `wait_for_future()`, contains a simple while loop that waits for `std::future<std::vector<T>>&` future to obtain a result. Note the use of `auto status = future.wait_for(wait_time)`. Execution of this function returns a status code that signals the availability of a result or a timeout. The timeout capabilities of `wait_for_future()` can be used to perform other processing while waiting for the future's result. Timeouts are also useful for monitoring purposes to ensure that an executing thread completes its execution within an expected time period.

Listing 21-5-2. Example Ch21_05 – Ch21_05_ex2()

```
template <typename T> requires std::floating_point<T>
std::chrono::milliseconds wait_for_future(std::future<std::vector<T>
>& future,
    std::chrono::milliseconds wait_time)
{
    std::chrono::milliseconds total_wait {};

    while (1)
    {
        auto status = future.wait_for(wait_time);

        if (status == std::future_status::ready)
            return total_wait;

        if (status != std::future_status::timeout)
            throw std::runtime_error("wait_for_future() - unexpected
            status");
```

```cpp
        // other processing can be added here
        total_wait += wait_time;
        std::println("waiting for result ({})", total_wait);
    }
}

void Ch21_05_ex2()
{
    using fp_t = double;
    constexpr auto wait_time {std::chrono::milliseconds(500) };

    // create test vector
    constexpr int rng_min {0};
    constexpr int rng_max {1000};
    constexpr unsigned int rng_seed {879};
    constexpr size_t npts {25'000};
    std::vector<fp_t> x0 = RN::get_vector<fp_t>(npts, rng_min, rng_max,
    rng_seed);

    // perform DCT
    auto future_dct = std::async(std::launch::async, dct<fp_t>, x0);

    auto total_wait_time1 = wait_for_future(future_dct, wait_time);
    std::println("dct() complete - total_wait_time1 = {}",
    total_wait_time1);

    // perform inverse DCT
    auto X0 = future_dct.get();
    auto future_dct_inv = std::async(std::launch::async,
    dct_inv<fp_t>, X0);

    auto total_wait_time2 = wait_for_future(future_dct_inv, wait_time);
    std::println("dct_inv() complete - total_wait_ms = {}",
    total_wait_time2);

    // confirm results
    auto x1 = future_dct_inv.get();
    compare_vectors(x0, x1);
}
```

Execution of Ch21_05_ex2() opens with the instantiation of std::vector<fp_t> x0. The next code block utilizes auto future_dct = std::async(lp, dct<fp_t>, x0) to asynchronously calculate a DCT using launch policy std::launch::async. Function Ch21_05_ex2() then exploits wait_for_future(future_dct, wait_time) to wait for a result.

The subsequent code block in Ch21_05_ex2() commences with auto X0 = future_dct.get(). During execution of this statement, the std::vector<fp_t> result held in future is *moved* to X0. The inverse DCT for X0 is then calculated using future_dct_inv = std::async(std::launch::async, dct_inv<fp_t>, X0). Following the call to wait_for_future(future_dct_inv, wait_time), the final code block in Ch21_05_ex2() utilizes auto x1 = future_dct_inv.get() and compare_vectors(x0, x1) to confirm that x0 is equivalent to x1. Here are the results for example Ch21_05:

```
----- Results for example Ch21_05 -----
----- Ch21_05_ex1() -----
compare_vectors(): ok
----- Ch21_05_ex2() -----
waiting for result (500ms)
waiting for result (1000ms)
waiting for result (1500ms)
waiting for result (2000ms)
waiting for result (2500ms)
waiting for result (3000ms)
dct() complete - total_wait_time1 = 3000ms
waiting for result (500ms)
waiting for result (1000ms)
waiting for result (1500ms)
waiting for result (2000ms)
waiting for result (2500ms)
waiting for result (3000ms)
waiting for result (3500ms)
waiting for result (4000ms)
dct_inv() complete - total_wait_ms = 4000ms

compare_vectors(): ok
```

CHAPTER 21   CONCURRENCY – PART 2

Summary

Here are the key learning points for this chapter:

- Semaphores facilitate coordinated concurrent access to a shared resource. Unlike a mutex, a semaphore can be locked and unlocked by different threads.

- The concurrency support library defines two semaphore classes: `std::binary_semaphore` and `std::counting_semaphore`. The former only supports two states; the latter maintains an internal counter that's decremented during an acquire operation and incremented during a release. A thread is blocked if it attempts to acquire a `std::counting_semaphore` when its internal counter equals zero.

- A `std::latch` blocks execution of one or more threads until an expected number of threads arrive at the latch. Following this, all waiting threads are unblocked. A `std::latch` is a single-use thread mechanism; its internal counter is set during construction and cannot be increased later.

- A condition variable is a synchronization primitive that blocks execution of a thread until a predetermined condition has been met or a timeout occurs. A `std::condition_variable` requires a `std::mutex` to carry out its actions. Condition variables are typically exploited to signal application-related events.

- An instance of `std::promise<T>` stores an object of type T for later retrieval by a `std::future<T>`. These classes simplify asynchronously retrieval of a value produced on one thread by another thread.

- Function template `std::async()` asynchronously launches a thread function and returns a `std::future<T>`, which eventually incorporates the thread function's returned result.

APPENDIX A

Source Code and Development Tools

This appendix explains how to download, build, and execute this book's source code examples. It also contains important information regarding the software development tools used to create the source code.

Source Code Download

Perform the following steps to download and install the source code for *Practical C++ STL Programming*:

1. Using your favorite browser, navigate to the following GitHub website: https://github.com/Apress/Practical-CPP-STL-Programming.

2. Click the **Code** button and select **Download ZIP**. Save[1] the .zip file in your Documents[2] folder.

3. Open a File Manager (or Finder) and navigate to your Documents folder.

4. Rename the downloaded .zip file to CppSTL.zip.

5. Right-click CppSTL.zip and select **Extract All...** (Windows), or **Extract** (Linux), or **Open With ➤ Archive Utility.app** (macOS).

---

[1] You may need to copy the .zip file from the Downloads folder.
[2] You can select a different folder. If you do this, some subsequent instructions will need to be adapted.

© Daniel Kusswurm 2024
D. Kusswurm, *Practical C++ STL Programming*, https://doi.org/10.1007/979-8-8688-0774-9

APPENDIX A   SOURCE CODE AND DEVELOPMENT TOOLS

6. Open subfolder CppSTL and rename Practical-CPP-STL-Programming (or similarly named subfolder) to Code.

7. Figure A-1 shows the correct contents for subfolder Code. This subfolder may also contain additional files or subfolders besides those shown in the figure.

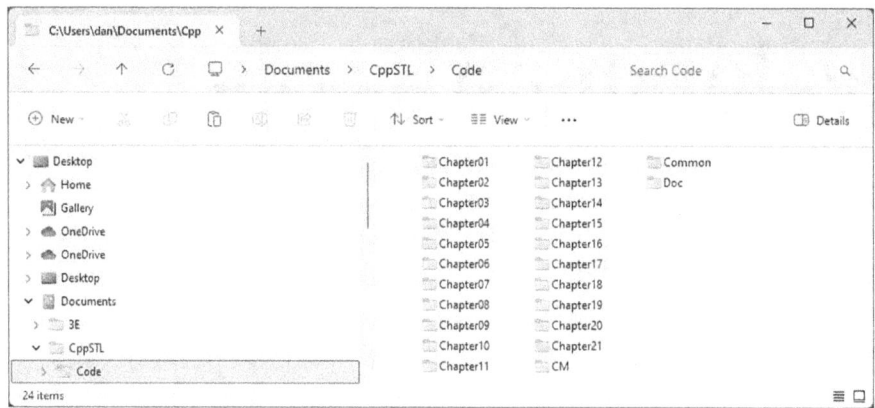

Figure A-1. *Source code folder tree*

Some of the source code examples and build scripts use relative pathnames. You may need to change these if you use a folder structure that differs from the default one created in this section.

Source Code Development Tools

The source code for *Practical C++ STL Programming* was developed using Windows 11 and Visual Studio 2022 (MSVC 19.40). The source code examples were also compiled and tested on computers running Ubuntu 24.04 LTS (GCC[3] 13.2 and Clang 18.1) and macOS 14.5 (GCC 13.3). Other required tools for Ubuntu[4] and macOS include CMake (3.27 or later) and Intel's Threading Building Blocks library. If any source code or build script changes are necessary to support future tool releases, they can be downloaded from the book's GitHub site.

---

[3] GNU Compiler Collection.

[4] The same development tools must be used with other Linux distributions.

APPENDIX A   SOURCE CODE AND DEVELOPMENT TOOLS

The remainder of this section is partitioned into three subsections. The first subsection covers Windows and Visual Studio. The second subsection details Linux and GCC, while the third subsection discusses macOS and GCC.

Windows and Visual Studio

The source code examples in this book were created using Visual Studio Professional 2022, but you can use any 2022 edition, including the free Community edition. For more information regarding Visual Studio installation and use, visit https://visualstudio.microsoft.com/.

Perform the following steps to build and execute a chapter's source code examples:

1. If necessary, use the Visual Studio Installer and install Visual Studio's C++ CMake tools for Windows.

2. From the Windows **Start** menu, open **Visual Studio 2022** and select **Developer Command Prompt for VS 2022**.

3. Enter cd C:\Users\<UserName>\Documents\CppSTL\Code to change the current directory (replace <UserName> with your Windows username).

4. Change the current directory to a specific chapter subdirectory. For example, to compile and execute the code for Chapter 1, use cd Chapter01.

5. Use mk.bat to compile and link the chapter's source code examples.

6. Use r.bat to execute the chapter's source code examples.

To use the Visual Studio IDE, double-click the chapter's solution (.sln) file.

Linux and GCC

To compile and execute the source code on a computer running Ubuntu 23.10 or later, you'll need to install the build-essential meta package for GCC (13.2 or later), CMake (3.27 or later), and the Intel Threading Building Blocks library on your computer. Open a terminal window and enter the following commands:

APPENDIX A   SOURCE CODE AND DEVELOPMENT TOOLS

```
sudo apt update
sudo apt upgrade
sudo apt install build-essential
sudo apt install cmake
sudo apt install libtbb-dev
```

Please consult the appropriate documentation to install the required development tools on a computer running an older version of Ubuntu or another Linux distribution. To use Clang instead of GCC with Ubuntu or another Linux distribution, please consult the appropriate resources listed in the last section of this appendix.

Build Script File Permissions

Perform the following steps to set the correct file permissions for the build scripts:

1. Open a terminal window.

2. Enter the following commands:

   ```
   cd ~/Documents/CppSTL
   find . -name '*.sh' -type f | xargs chmod a+x
   ```

The steps shown in this section only need to be performed once.

Compile and Execute

Perform the following steps to build and execute a chapter's source code examples:

1. Open a terminal window.

2. Enter cd ~/Documents/CppSTL.

3. Change the current directory to a specific chapter subdirectory. For example, to compile and execute the code for Chapter 1, use cd Code/Chapter01.

4. Use sh mk.sh to compile and link the chapter's source code examples.

5. Use sh r.sh to run the chapter's source code examples.

macOS and GCC

To compile and execute the source code on macOS 14 (Sonoma) or later, you'll need to install GCC (13.2 or later), CMake (3.27 or later), and the Intel Threading Building Blocks library on your computer. To do this, perform the steps detailed in this section. These steps assume that the macOS Terminal app is configured to use shell zsh, which is the default[5] for macOS 10.15 and later.

1. If necessary, install package manager Homebrew on your computer. To do this, open https://brew.sh/ in a browser. Follow the instructions on this web page to download a macOS .pkg installer file (look for "Download it from Homebrew's latest GitHub release"). Save the .pkg file in the Downloads folder.

2. Open the Downloads folder in Finder and double-click the Homebrew-<version>.pkg file to install Homebrew. Follow the installer's instructions, *except* those on the final screen regarding modifications to file .zprofile.

3. Open a terminal window and enter the command cd ~.

4. Enter the command nano .zprofile. This opens a simple text editor in the terminal window. Add the following lines to the end of this (possibly empty) file:

   ```
   export PATH="/opt/homebrew/bin:${PATH}"
   eval "$(/opt/homebrew/bin/brew shellenv)"
   ```

5. Press control-X, y, and Enter to save the modified .zprofile file and exit the editor. Then close the terminal window.

---

[5] If the Terminal app's default shell is bash or another shell, visit https://support.apple.com/en-us/102360 for instructions on how to make zsh the new default.

APPENDIX A   SOURCE CODE AND DEVELOPMENT TOOLS

6. To install GCC 13, CMake, and the Intel Threading Building Blocks library, open a new terminal window and enter the following commands:

   ```
   brew install gcc@13
   brew install cmake
   brew install tbb
   ```

7. Enter the command `cd ~`. Then enter the command `nano .zprofile` and add the following lines to the end of the file:

   ```
   export CC="$(brew --prefix gcc@13)/bin/gcc-13"
   export CXX="$(brew --prefix gcc@13)/bin/g++-13"
   ```

8. Press `control-X`, `y`, and `Enter` to save the modified `.zprofile` file and exit the editor. Then close the terminal window.

9. Open a new terminal window and enter the following command:

   ```
   $CXX -version
   ```

You should see a printed message that shows GCC's version number.

Perform the steps shown earlier in sections "Build Script File Permissions" and "Compile and Execute" to build and execute a chapter's source code examples. When compiling the source code examples for some chapters, GCC may print several "note" messages. These can be ignored.

Apple's Xcode IDE also supports C++. Unfortunately, the version of Clang that's supplied with Xcode 15 is outdated. The next release of Xcode is expected to provide better support for C++20/23. Visit https://developer.apple.com/xcode/cpp/ for more information. You can also use Microsoft's Visual Studio Code. For more information, see https://code.visualstudio.com/docs/cpp/config-clang-mac.

Test Computers

Table A-1 shows the specifications for the test computers that were used to perform benchmark timing measurements in some of the source code examples.

Table A-1. *Test Computer Specifications*

	Test Computer #1	**Test Computer #2**	**Test Computer #3**
Processor	Intel i7-11700K	Intel i5-11600K	Arm Cortex A-76 (Raspberry Pi 5)
Cores/Threads	8/16	6/12	4/4
OS	Windows 11	Ubuntu 23.10	Ubuntu 23.10
Compiler	MSVC 19.40 (VS 2022)	GCC 13.2	GCC 13.2

All benchmark timing measurements were made using executables that were compiled for maximum optimization (/O2 or -O3). Default settings were used for other compiler options, including SIMD code generation. Mainstream C++ compilers such as MSVC, GCC, and Clang support a plethora of code generation options that affect performance. The sole purpose of the benchmark timing measurements published in this book is to provide additional insights regarding C++ STL performance. The techniques and compiler options used to perform these measurements may not be suitable for other benchmarking purposes.

Additional Information

Additional information regarding the software tools mentioned in this appendix can be obtained from the following websites:

Clang, https://clang.llvm.org/

CMake, https://cmake.org/

GNU GCC, www.gnu.org/software/gcc/

Intel Threading Building Blocks, www.intel.com/content/www/us/en/developer/tools/oneapi/onetbb-download.html

Microsoft Visual Studio, https://visualstudio.microsoft.com/

Ubuntu, https://ubuntu.com/

APPENDIX B

References and Resources

Appendix B lists the references that were consulted during the writing of this book. It also contains additional resources that you might find useful or interesting.

Principal C++ Resources

This section lists the principal resources that were consulted during the writing of this book:

Working Draft, Standard for Programming Language C++, N4950, 2023-05-10, www.open-std.org/jtc1/sc22/wg21/docs/standards

C++ Reference, https://en.cppreference.com/w/

Standard C++, https://isocpp.org/

Ivor Horton, *Using the C++ Standard Template Libraries*, Apress, ISBN 978-1-4842-0005-6, 2015

Nicolai M. Josuttis, *The C++ Standard Library – A Tutorial and Reference, Second Edition*, Addison Wesley, ISBN 978-0-321-62321-8, 2012

Bjarne Stroustrup, *The C++ Programming Language, Fourth Edition*, Addison Wesley, ISBN 978-0-321-56384-2, 2013

Bjarne Stroustrup, *A Tour of C++, Third Edition*, Addison Wesley, ISBN 978-0-13-681648-5, 2023

David Vandevoorde, Nicolai Josuttis, Douglas Gregor, *C++ Templates – The Complete Guide, Second Edition*, Addison Wesley, ISBN 978-0-321-71412-1, 2018

Anthony Williams, *C++ Concurrency in Action*, Manning, ISBN 978-1933988771, 2012

APPENDIX B   REFERENCES AND RESOURCES

Additional C++ Resources

The readers of this book may find the following C++ resources useful:

C++ FAQ, https://isocpp.org/faq

C++ Standard Library Reference (STL), https://learn.microsoft.com/en-us/cpp/standard-library/cpp-standard-library-reference?view=msvc-170

ISO/IEC 14882:2020, www.iso.org/standard/79358.html

ISO/IEC PRF 14882, www.iso.org/standard/83626.html

Modernes C++, www.modernescpp.com/

Chrono Format Specifiers (std::formatter<std::chrono::sys_time>), https://en.cppreference.com/w/cpp/chrono/system_clock/formatter#Format_specification

Superior String Splitting, www.open-std.org/jtc1/sc22/wg21/docs/papers/2021/p2210r2.html

Ivor Horton and Peter Van Weert, *Beginning C++23*, Apress, ISBN 978-1484293423, 2023

Algorithm References

The following resources were consulted to develop some of the source code example algorithms. This section also includes references to ancillary algorithm resources:

Bruce Alberts, et al. *Essential Cell Biology*, Fifth Edition, W.W. Norton & Company, Inc. 2019

Rafael C. Gonzalez and Richard E. Woods, *Digital Image Processing, Fourth Edition*, Pearson, ISBN 978-0-133-35672-4, 2018

Bryan Manly, *Multivariate Statistical Methods: A Primer, Second Edition*, Chapman & Hall, ISBN 04126030004, 1994

Robert Sedgewick, *Algorithms in C++*, Addison-Wesley, ISBN, 0-201-51059-0, 1992

APPENDIX B REFERENCES AND RESOURCES

Julius O. Smith III, *Mathematics of the Discrete Fourier Transform (DFT)*, Second Edition, W3K Publishing, ISBN 978-0-9745607-4-8, 2007

Eric Weisstein, *Convolution*, MathWorld, http://mathworld.wolfram.com/Convolution.html

Eric Weisstein, *Covariance*, MathWorld, https://mathworld.wolfram.com/Covariance.html

Eric W. Weisstein, *Least Squares Fitting*, MathWorld, http://mathworld.wolfram.com/LeastSquaresFitting.html

Eric W. Weisstein, *Matrix Multiplication*, MathWorld, http://mathworld.wolfram.com/MatrixMultiplication.html

Eric Weisstein, *Pi Formulas*, MathWorld, https://mathworld.wolfram.com/PiFormulas.html

Eric Weisstein, *Prime Number*, MathWorld, https://mathworld.wolfram.com/PrimeNumber.html

IANA, *Time Zone Database*, www.iana.org/time-zones

Wikipedia, *Binary Heap*, https://en.wikipedia.org/wiki/Binary_heap

Wikipedia, *Boyer-Moore String-Search Algorithm*, https://en.wikipedia.org/wiki/Boyer%E2%80%93Moore_string-search_algorithm

Wikipedia, *Discrete Cosine Transform*, https://en.wikipedia.org/wiki/Discrete_cosine_transform

Wikipedia, *Great Circle Distance*, https://en.wikipedia.org/wiki/Great-circle_distance

Wikipedia, *Heap (Data Structure)*, https://en.wikipedia.org/wiki/Heap_(data_structure)

Wikipedia, *IATA Airport Code*, https://en.wikipedia.org/wiki/IATA_airport_code

APPENDIX B REFERENCES AND RESOURCES

Wikipedia, *List of Random Number Generators*, https://en.wikipedia.org/wiki/List_of_random_number_generators

Wikipedia, *Mohs Scale*, https://en.wikipedia.org/wiki/Mohs_scale

Wikipedia, *Tower of Hanoi*, https://en.wikipedia.org/wiki/Tower_of_Hanoi

Index

A

AaTuple, 611, 613–615
Accumulate and fold algorithms, 503–509
add_values() function, 7, 10
Airport::GeoCoord::calc_distance(), 473, 474
Airport::GeoCoord::to_decimal() function, 474
Airport::get_() functions, 474
Airport::get_vector_iata_codes(), 474
Algorithm resources, 896–897
AminoAcid class, 396, 397, 400, 553, 611
AminoAcid::get_vector_all_code3(), 553, 762
AminoAcid::get_vector_random_code3(), 493, 628
AminoAcid::get_vector_tuple(), 611, 615
AminoAcid::to_code3(aa), 457
Apple's Xcode IDE, 892
Arithmetic functions, 770–777
Iterators arr1.begin() and arr1.end(), 131
Associative container, 302
    objects collection, 259
    primary advantage, 259
    std::map (*see* std::map)
    std::multimap, 292
    std::multiset (*see* std::multiset)
    std::set (*see* std::set)
Atomic operation, 833, 851
    Ch20_04_ex1(), 836
    Ch20_04_ex3(), 839
    modern processor architectures, 837

operators and member functions, 841
principal template, 833
source code, 834
auto future_dct = std::async(lp, dct<fp_t>, x0), 885
auto now = chrono::file_clock::now(), 704
auto status = future.wait_for(wait_time), 883
auto X0 = future_dct.get(), 885

B

Bidirectional iterators, 158, 161, 263, 427
Binary heap, 535, 536
Binary reduction operator, 803
Binary search algorithms, 523–527
bin_sem_vec1.Sem1.release(), 856
BinSemVec<int>& bin_sem_vec1(24), 856
BinSemVec<T&>, 854, 856
bin_sem_vec.Sem2.release(), 856
BmTimer, 682
    BmTimer<std::chrono::steady_clock>, 682
    BmTimer::save_to_csv(), 682
    BmTimerSteadyClk and BmTimerHighResClk, 686
    BmTimerSteadyClk bm_timer(num_iter, num_alg), 682
    BmTimerSteadyClk::EtUnit::MilliSec), 682
    BmTimerSteadyClock, 682
    m_StartTimes and m_StopTimes, 686

INDEX

BmTimer (*cont.*)
   start() and stop(), 686
   static_assert(CLK::is_steady), 685

C

C++ concurrency, 853
C++ concurrency support library, 811, 812, 824, 825, 873
C++ FAQ, 896
C++20 formatting library <format>, 80
C++23 functions, 2, 93, 123, 162, 163, 355, 358, 387, 389, 710
C++ input/output library, 103
C++ numerics library, 727, 728, 767
C++ resources, 895, 896
C++'s execution policies, 817
C++ Standard Library Reference (STL), 412, 447, 464, 896
C++ templates
   add_values() function, 7
   algorithms, 1
   argument values, 7
   calc_mean() function, 8
   #include "Common.h" statement, 2
   #include <string> statement, 7
   integer variables, 7
   parameterized data type, 1, 61
   Point2D class, 8, 10
   source code examples, 2, 11
   std::println(), 7
C++ views, 577
calc_area(), 730
calc_distance() function, 468
calc_pi(), 642, 644
calc_sphere_area_vol(), 876
cbegin() function, 16
cend() function, 16

Ch20_03_ex3(), 830, 832
Ch20_04_ex2(), 838
Ch20_05_ex1(), 845
Ch20_05_ex2(), 850
chrono format specifiers, 675, 677
chrono::ceil(), 673
chrono::days num_days {15}, 703
chrono::file_clock, 704
chrono::floor(), 673
Chrono Format Specifiers, 896
chrono::round(), 673
chrono::time_point, 649
chrono::utc_clock, 672
chrono::year_month_day ymd1
   {2025y/6/21d}, 663
chrono::zoned_time now_sys_
   zt(chrono::current_zone(),
   now_sys), 677
chrono::zoned_time now_sys_zt
   {zone, now_sys}, 677
chunk_op(), 639
chunk_op = [](int x, int y)
   { return x == y; }, 639
chunk_w wide views, 637
Clang, 12, 890, 893
Class BmTimerSteadyClock, 682
Class chrono::year_month_day, 662, 664
Class fs::path, 689
   elements, 689
   fn1.generic_string(), 697
   fs::create_directories(sub_tree_
      bot), 695
   fs::create_directory(sub_dir1), 695
   fs::current_path(), 690
   fs::filesystem_error, 695
   fs::path fn1, 697
   fs::path fn1 = sub_dir1 / "TestA.txt", 695
   fs::path path1 = fs::current_path(), 690

fs::path path1 = fs::current_
    path()/"test1.txt", 691
fs::path path2 = fs::temp_directory_
    path(), 691
fs::path path3 = fs::current_path(), 691
fs::temp_directory_path(), 691, 695
maximum length, 690
path component, 693
pathname representations, 690
path1.string(), 690
std::ofstream ofs(path3), 691
std::println(), std::format(), 690

Class Image
    assignments, 30
    function definitions, 26
    Image's copy constructor, 30
    Image() = default, 26
    move constructor, 30
    m_PixelBuff.resize(m_Height *
        m_Width), 26
    new and delete, 29
    parameterized constructor, 26
    pixel_t, 25
    private attributes, 26
    public declarations, 26
    relational operators, 30
    reset(), 30
    std::move(), 32
    std::println(), 30, 32
    std::unique_ptr<>, 29
    std::vector, 29
    private member function to_str(), 30

Class Rect, 193, 444

Class std::array
    advantages, 106
    arithmetic calculation, 110
    expression auto iter_a = areas.
        begin(), 111
    begin() and end() functions, 109
    description, 106
    for loop's initializer statement, 108
    int elements, 107
    iterators, 109
    MT::print_ctr(), 112
    operator[] vs. at(), 108
    operator++, 109
    operator=, 116
    operator==, 114
    parameterized template
        objects, 116
    primary purpose, 115
    radii.size(), 110
    required items, 107
    reverse iterator, 109
    RN::fill_ctr(), 111
    std::accumulate(), 112
    std::print(), 109
    std::ranges::sort(), 114
    std::sort(), 113, 114
    x_vals, 108

Class std::bitset<>, 74

Class std::forward_list
    definition, 158
    fw_list1, 159
    insert_range_after(), 164
    logical structure, 159
    iterator operator++
        executions, 160
    resource perspective, 158
    size() function, 160
    std::distance(), 160
    std::erase_if(), 164
    std::forward_list<std::string>), 161
    std::forward_list::prepend_range(), 162
    std::forward_list::sort(), 161
    unary lambda expression, 162

INDEX

Class std::list
    advantage, 158
    auto iter_mid = list1.begin(), 150
    cbegin(), 153
    common operations, 149
    definition, 148
    emplace_back() and emplace_front(), 154
    iterators, 150, 153
    list1.reverse(), 156
    list1.size(), 152
    logical structure, 148
    mid-container insertions and removals, 148
    push_front() and push_back(), 149
    random access operations, 148
    splicing, 152
    std::advanced(), 152
    std::line::remove_if(), 151
    std::list::insert(), 151
    std::list::merge(), 155
    std::list::remove(), 151
    std::list::sort(), 154
    std::remove(), 151

Class std::pair
    bundling, 174
    constructs pair2, 175
    std::get<0> and std::get<1>, 177
    std::make_pair(), 175
    std::pair<int, double> pair1 {}, 174
    std::pair<int, float>, 177
    std::pair<std::int, double>, 175
    std::pair<std::string, double>, 175
    std::println(), 174
    std::println() statements, 177
    std::print_vec(), 177
    std::ranges::sort(), 178
    std::vector vec1, 177
    template class, 174

Class std::deque
    definition, 137
    elements storage, 137
    emplace_front() and emplace_back(), 141
    int type objects, 138
    LIFO/FIFO, 137
    line_t = Line<double> statement, 142
    logical structure, 138
    manipulations, 140
    operator[] and at() functions, 139
    relational operators, 144
    std::deque::append_range(), 142
    std::deque::insert(), 142
    std::deque::insert_range(), 142
    std::deque::push_back(), 139
    std::deque::push_front(), 139
    std::ranges::sort(), 144
    std::remove() and std::deque::erase(), 144
    std::sort(), 144
    vs. std::vector, 137, 148

Class std::ratio
    arithmetic and comparisons, 649
    Ch16_01_ex1(), 651
    Ch16_01_ex2(), 653
    chrono::duration<int, std::ratio<3600 * 24>> day {1}, 656
    chrono::duration<int, std::ratio<3600, >>, 1, 658
    chrono::duration<int, std::ratio<86400, >>, 1, 658
    compile-time actions, 650
    num and den, 650
    std::ratio<1, 1000000000>, 662
    using ra = std::ratio<12, >, 20, 650

INDEX

Standard Library Predefined SI
    std::ratios, 653, 654
using bad = std::ratio_multiply<>, 655
using rb = std::nano, 655
Class std::string, 173
Class std::tuple
    bundling, 174
    print_tuple(), 184-186
    std::array, 188
    std::get<I>(), 184
    std::get<I>(std::tuple), 180
    std::make_tuple(), 182
    std::println(), 180, 186
    std::tie(), 187
    std::tuple_cat(), 188
    std::tuple_element<>, 182
    std::tuple<int, 180
    std::tuple<std::string, int, double>, 183
    std::tuple_size<>, 182
    template class, 180
Class std::vector
    copy constructor, 123
    definition, 116
    disadvantage, 116
    end-of-container insertions, 121
    erase-remove idiom, 130
    insert() function, 122
    lambda expression, 119
    member functions, 119
    multiple elements insertions, 121
    objects insertion, 134
    Point2D, 124
    prints of vectors, 119
    relational comparisons, 124
    size attribute encapsulation, 116
    size attributes, 121
    std::copy(), 122
    std::erase(), 126
    std::find(), 124
    std::ranges, 124
    std::vector::emplace_back(), 124
    std::vector<int> vec1, 117
    std::vector<int> vec2(vec1.size()), 117
    use case multiplicity, 128
    vec2{vec1.size()}, 117
Class std::vector forward and reverse iterators, 15
Clock classes, 665-666
    chrono::steady_clock, 668
    chrono::system_clock, 665, 667, 668, 670
    chrono::system_clock::now(), 670
    and chrono::time points, 665
    chrono::time_point<chrono::system_clock> tp1_sys {}, 669
    chrono::utc_clock, 665, 667-670, 679
    CLK::period, 667
    clock's now() function, 667
    file_clock, 666
    gps_clock, 666
    high_resolution_clock, 666, 668
    now() function, 665
    print_clock_info(), 667, 668
    std::steady_clock, 667
    steady_clock, 666, 668
    system_clock, 666, 668
    tai_clock, 666
    tp2_sys = chrono::system_clock::now(), 670
    utc_clock, 666, 668
CMake, 888, 891-893
cmp_op(), 515, 516
cmp_protein(), 412
compare_vectors(), 881, 882
Compiler-supplied default constructors, 32

INDEX

Complex number, 734
  auto z1_abs = std::abs(z1), 737
  and class std::complex, 734
  DFT, 738
  elementary arithmetic
      operations, 736
  inverse DFT, 738
  MTH::dft(), 738–740
  namespace std::complex_literals, 734
  operator< or operator>, 737
  print_complex_vec(), 740
  real() and imag(), 736
  std::complex, 736, 738
  std::vector<std::complex
      <double>> x, 741
  trigonometric, logarithmic and
      hyperbolic, 738
  z1_conj = std::conj(z1), 737
Concurrency
  basics, 811
  classes and algorithms, 812
  computational factors, 811
  data race condition, 816
  designing and coding algorithms, 812
  execution policies, 813, 819, 820
  function object, 816
  parallel architectures, 813
  parallelism, 812, 813
  processor system, 812
  SIMD capabilities, 820
  STL algorithms, 815
  std::for_each(), 816
  std::transform(), 819
  vectors, 815
Concurrency support library, 853, 861,
    873, 886
ConditionVar, 866, 868
ConditionVarDemo cvd, 868

Condition variable
  calc_distance_matrix(), 867
  cvd.ConditionVar.notify_one(), 868
  generate_data(), 867, 868
  get_random_airports(), 867
  struct ConditionVarDemo, 866
Condition variables, 866
const, 727
const iterators, 16
constexpr, 727
const fs::path& p, 710
Constructor's Image&& im argument, 30
const std::string& file_ext = p.extension().
    string(), 702
Container, 575, 577
Container adaptors
  flat, 387, 388
  std::stack (see std::stack)
  std::priority_queue, 535
  std::priority_queue (see
      std::priority_queue)
  std::queue (see std::queue)
  STL, 355, 356
Containers and iterators
  operator++ prefix, 15
  rbegin() and rend(), 16
  std::begin() and std::end()
      functions, 16
  std::vector, 14
  std::vector<long long> y_vals, 15
  std::vector::operator[], 14
  std::vector<std::string>, 16
  typeid(y_vals.begin()).name())
      prefix, 15, 16
Contains algorithm, 483–490, 511
ConvData::SignalX, 848
Convolution, 841, 846
Convolution algorithm execution, 850

Copy algorithms, 414–418
Copy assignment (Image&
    Image::operator=(const
    Image& im)), 30
Copy functions, 718
Copy operations, 447
copy_pred(), 416, 417
Counting algorithms
    AminoAcid.cpp, 400
    AminoAcid::get_vector_all(), 405
    AminoAcid.h, 397
    amino acids, 396, 397
    class AminoAcid, 397, 400
    pre-C++20 counterpart functions, 406
    pred_mm(), 406
    std::count(), 393–395
    std::count_if(), 395, 396
    std::ranges::count(), 395
count_primes_a(), 828
count_primes_b(), 830
count_primes_thread(), 856
CountPrimeThread, 864
CountPrimeThread::thread_proc(), 865
covariance_indx(const std::valarray<T>&
    var_means), 798
Covariance matrix, 794–799
CovData, 796
CovData::covariance(), 796
crbegin() function, 16
create_dir(), 713, 714
crend() function, 16
cs.try_aquire_for(), 859
ctr.bucket_count(), 303
ctr.erase(), 436
Custom data types, 23
Custom hash function, 497
cvd.Airports = std::move(airports), 868
cvd.ConditionVar.notify_one(), 868

cvd.ConditionVar.wait(), 870
cvd.DataReady, 868, 870
cvd.Distances = std::move(distances), 868
cvd.Mutex, 868–870

D

DataReady, 866
dct(), 880
dct_inv(), 880
dice_aa.set_side_names(i, aa_code3), 762
DiceSet, 755, 759–761
Discrete Fourier transform (DFT), 738,
    739, 741
dodecahedron_area(), 452
dodecahedron_vol(), 453
Double-precision floating-point
    algorithm, 680

E

Emplace member functions, 142
enum class ErrorCode, 223
Erase-remove idiom, 438, 439
Exceptions
    advantage, 61
    C++ program, 61
    definition, 58
    std::domain_error, 58, 60
    std::stod(), 60
    try and catch blocks, 58
ex.code().message(), 714
ex.code().value(), 714

F

Fibonacci numbers, 729
File input streams, 68

INDEX

File streams std::ofstream and
    std::ifstream, 97–101
Fill algorithms, 443–445
Find algorithms, 464–480, 511
find_op(), 475, 476
finish_latch.count_down(), 865
First-in-first-out (FIFO), 137, 370
Flat container adaptors, 387–389
Floating-point addition, 802, 809
Format specifier (fmt), 112
fn1.string(), 697
Fold algorithm, 512
For_each algorithm, 449–454, 511
for loop, 266, 475, 479, 525–527, 540
format() function, 91
Format specifier fields, 81, 82
Format specifiers, 66, 80, 81, 103
Formatted output using std::format()
    + sign, 86
    alignment character, 84
    argument, 85
    bool formatting, 84
    definition, 80
    floating-point specifiers, 85
    format specifier field, 81
    hexadecimal notation, 85
    integer value, 87
    nested replacement field, 82
    nested replacement specifier, 86
    protection feature, 87
    source code example, 82
    static_cast<> conversions, 85
    std::back_inserter(), 91
    std::formatter<Line<>>, 91
    std::string, 81
    std::vformat(), 88
    to_str(), 91
    user-defined class, 90

Formatted output using std::print() and
    std::println(), 93, 96, 103
Formatted output using std::printf()
    C-style null-terminated format
        string, 65
    conversion specifier %d, 66
    fundamental types, 67
    length field, 66
    modern alternatives, 67
    modifier field, 66
    specification characters, 66
Formatted output using streams
    C++ I/O stream libraries, 70
    floating-point values, 74, 76
    global I/O streams, 69, 70
    I/O streams class hierarchy, 68, 69
    manipulators, 72–74
    MF::mk_test_filename(), 77
    namespace std::numbers (C++20)
        statement, 75
    ofs.close(), 78
    ofs.good(), 78
    operator<<, 72
    std::basic_ios<> functions, 78
    std::basic_string<>, 68
    std::cerr vs. std::clog, 70
    std::cout, 72
    std::cout << std::dec, 74
    std::cout << value, 72
    std::ios_base, 70
    std::scientific manipulators, 76
    std::setfill('_'), 76
    STL alias, 68
Formatting library, 103
fs::copy(), 718, 720, 721, 723
fs::copy_file(), 718, 720, 721
fs::copy_file(test_file1, test_file2,
    copy_opt, ec), 721

fs::copy_options::recursive, 723
fs::copy(source_dir, dest_dir,
    copy_opt, ec), 723
fs::create_directories(sub_tree_bot), 695
fs::create_directory(), 713, 716
fs::create_directory(dir), 714
fs::create_directory(dir, ec), 713, 714
fs::current_path(), 710
fs::current_path() / "D0/D1/D2/
    test2.txt", 711
fs::directory_entry, 699, 701
fs:exists(), 695
fs::filesystem_error, 709, 712
fs::filesystem_error exception& ex,
    ex.path1(), 714
fs::is_directory(code_path), 700
fs::is_directory(dir_entry), 704
fs::is_regular_file(dir_entry), 701, 702, 704
fs::last_write_time(), 707
fs::last_write_time(fn, tp_base +
    tp_adj_days), 707
fs::path, 689–692, 695, 709, 710, 714
fs::path base_path, 703
fs::path canonical = fs::canonical(p), 710
fs::path code_path, 700
fs::path relative = fs::relative(p), 710
fs::path sub_dir1 = fs::current_path() /
    "sub1", 694
fs::recursive_directory_iterator(),
    699–701, 723
fs::temp_directory_path(), 695, 703

G

generate_data(), 867, 868, 870
Generation algorithm, 459–464, 511
gen_op(), 460

GeoCoord, 468
get() function, 878
get_sequences() function, 496
get_test_nut() function, 216
get_test_vector(), 577, 825
get_vector_() functions, 487
Global functions, 773
Global I/O stream, 69
GNU GCC, 893

H

Hash function, 302, 303, 352, 353
Hash table, 302
Hash value, 302
Heap algorithms, 535–542
Helper functions, 709
Heterogeneous objects, 173
Homebrew-<version>.pkg file, 891

I, J, K

~Image(), 29
Image<uint8_t> functions, 38
Inner products, 799–808
insert_range_after() function, 164
Intel Threading Building Blocks library,
    889, 891
Inverse DFT, 738, 741
iota_vw, 642
ISO/IEC 14882:2020, 896
ISO/IEC PRF 14882, 896
is_valid_() functions, 468
Iterator functions, 153
Iterators, 109, 575
    categories, 165, 166, 168
    compiler error, 168

Iterators (*cont.*)
    iter, 166
    operator++, 165
    pointer-like operations, 165, 172
    print_concepts(), 170
    sentinel value, 168
    std::distance(), 171
    taxonomy of concepts, 166, 167
iter_sr object, 534

L

Lambda expressions, 779, 785, 801
    [=] and [&] capture, 48
    keyword auto, 46
    calc1, 46
    capture list, 41
    capval, 46
    defining, 42
    definition, 41
    elements, 42
    explicit template
        parameter list, 42
    func_transform(), 213
    local_var, 47
    operator<, 41
    replace_if_pred, 132
    std::vectors, 46
    STL algorithms, 62
    sum_if(), 46
Last-in-first-out (LIFO), 137
Latches
    cpts.size() threads, 865
    finish_latch.count_down(), 865
    start_latch, 864
    start_latch.arrive_and_wait(), 865
    std::array<CountPrimesThread, 4>
        cpts, 864

std::barrier, 861
std::latch, 861, 862
Least-squares lines, 779, 780
Linear algebra functions, 785
Linear regression, 779
Linear transformation operator, 783
Load factor, 353

M

macOS Terminal app, 891
Manipulators, 103
Mathematical constants
    const or constexpr, 727
    Fibonacci numbers, 729
    log_b_x(3.0f, static_cast<float>(x)), 732
    namespace std::numbers, 728
    π, 728
    std::numbers, 731
    std::numbers::log10e<T>, 731
    std::numbers::log10e<T>), 731
    std::numbers::phi, 730
    std::numbers::phi_v<double>, 730
    std::numbers::pi_v<>, 730
    std::numbers::pi_v<T>, 730
Matrix operations, 788–791
Matrix-vector operations, 785
Max heap, 536
Maximum load factor, 353
Mean Execution Times, 819
Merge algorithms, 545
    iter_mid, 550
    RegPolygon::get_random_
        polygons(), 547
    results, 550–553
    std::ranges, 545
    std::ranges::inplace_merge(), 547, 549, 550, 572

INDEX

std::ranges::merge(), 545–547, 572
std::ranges::move(), 549
std::ranges::sort(), 545, 548
MF::create_test_files(), 704, 706, 707, 716
MF::to_upper(), 508, 509
Microsoft Visual Studio, 893
Mineral object, 487
Mineral class, 483
Mineral::get_vector_all(), 487
Minimum and maximum
    algorithms, 408–413
Modern alternatives, 67
Modernes C++, 896
Move algorithms, 420–422
Move assignment (Image&
    Image::operator=(Image&& im))
    operator, 30
m_PixelBuffer's data pointer, 32
m_PixelBuff {im.m_PixelBuff}
    initializer, 30
m_RngDevice(), 759
m_RngDist, 759
m_RngDist.param(temp_dist.param()), 759
m_RngEngine, 759
m_RngSeed, 759
MTH::dft(), 738–740
MTH::dft(x, false), 741
MTH::generate_sine_wave(),
    461–464
MTH::is_prime(), 431, 432
MT::print_ctr() function, 112, 500
Multithreaded algorithms
    ConvData, 843
    convolution, 841
    convolution equation, 841
    discrete 1D convolution, 842
    performance, 841
    smoothing operator, 842

Multithreaded convolution algorithm, 843
Mutex, 821, 853, 866, 886
    execution policy, 824
    locking and unlocking, 823
    side effects, 824

N

nano .zprofile, 891, 892
Nested replacement fields, 82
NoMoreData, 866
Non-associative operations, 802
Non-communicative operations, 802
Non-member functions, 773
num_active_threads_max, 859
num_dice, 755, 759
Numerical processing
    inner products, 799–808
    reductions, 799–808
    std::slice, 785–799
    std::valarray, 769–784
num_old_files_print_max files, 704
num_sides, 759

O

op() operator, 505
operator+, 10, 791, 792
operator!=, 30
operator==, 30, 56
Monadic member function or_else(), 213
Count_primes_a()., 829

P, Q

param(), 759
parse() function, 91
Partition algorithms, 531–534

INDEX

path1.string(), 690
Permutation, 568
Permutation algorithms
    HtmlColor::get_vector(indices1), 569
    np_result = std::ranges::next_
        permutation(colors1), 569
    results, 571, 572
    std::ranges::is_permutation(), 570
    std::ranges::next_permutation(), 568, 570, 573
    std::ranges::prev_permutation(), 570, 573
p.generic_string(), 710
Point2D class, 8, 10
Class Point2D, 124
PointCoord2D template constraint, 8, 10
pop_back() function, 543
Practical C++ STL Programming, 887, 888
Prime number group, 533
Principal C++ resources, 895
print_airports(), 525
print_chunk(), 637
print_concepts() function, 170
print_ctr(), 772
print_elements(), 614, 615
print_heap(), 536
print_path_info(), 710, 711
print_rel_ops(), 662, 663
print_sr(), 533, 534
print_types(), 714, 716
print_vec(), 519
process_data(), 870
process_message() function, 221
Projections, 590, 609
    members, 591
    Mineral::Hardness, 592
    particulars, 591
    print_values(), 593
    results, 595, 597
    std::ranges, 593
    std::ranges namespace, 590
    std::ranges::sort(), 592, 593, 595
    std::vector<Value> values, 593
p.string(), 710
push_back()/pop_back() functions, 457, 541, 543

R

Random number generation, 743
    dice games, 755-762
    game programs, 743
    generators, 744, 745
    probability density functions, 747
    random number distribution, 744, 746
    random number engine, 744
    random number engine adaptor, 744
    random number generator, 744
    STL's random number distribution classes, 746
    uniform random bit generator, 744
    using generators and distributions, 747-754
    vector of random numbers, 764-766
Random variables, 794
Range adaptor pipelines, 584
Range adaptors, 576, 577, 609
    calculation, 587
    colors, 602
    HtmlColor::H(), 600
    prime numbers, 599
    print_colors(), 600
    results, 588, 589, 602, 603
    RN::get_vector<>(), 584
    std::vector<int> containers, 588
    calculation, 587

colors, 602
HtmlColor::H(), 600
prime numbers, 599
print_colors(), 600
results, 588, 589, 602, 603
RN::get_vector<>(), 584
std::vector<int> containers, 588
std::views::adjacent(), 648
std::views::adjacent_transform(), 648
std::views::drop_while(), 598
std::views::elements(), 611, 647
std::views::elements<I>(aa_vec), 614
std::views::enumerate(), 616, 647
std::views::filter(), 584, 586
std::views::iota(), 599, 600
std::views::join(), 648
std::views::join_with(), 628
std::views::keys(), 611, 613, 647
std::views::lazy_split(), 630
std::views::slide(), 648
std::views::split(), 630
std::views::take_while(), 602
std::views::values(), 611, 613, 647
std::views::zip(), 619
std::views::zip_transform(), 622
tuple-like views, 611, 616, 621
view2, 586
view4 = std::views::
    reverse(view3), 585
Range factories, 642, 644, 648
Ranges, 575, 577
Ratio library
    Ch16_01_ex1(), 651
    Ch16_01_ex2(), 653, 655
    std::ratio, 649
Ratio library
    definition, 649
    num and den, 650

Raw/native C++ pointer
    definition, 233
    std::println(), 235
    test_ptr1(), 234
    test_ptr2(), 234
    test_ptr3(), 234, 235
rbegin() and rend() functions, 109
Reductions, 799–808
Removal algorithms, 436–439
remove_if(), 438
Replacement algorithms, 428–433
Reversal algorithms, 425, 427
Reverse iterators, 109
RN::fill_ctr() function, 111
rng_dev(), 753
rng_engine.seed(rd()), 765
rng_engine.seed(rng_seed), 765
RN::get_valarray(), 771
RN::get_vector(), 504, 626, 638, 764, 765
RN::get_vector() (Common/RN.h), 764
RN::get_vector<double>(), 622
RN::get_vector<ll_t> (ll_t, 635
rng_seed, 748, 866
Rotate algorithm, 557
    rotate_left(), 559, 561
    rotate_right(), 561
    std::ranges::rotate(),
        558, 559, 561, 573
    std::ranges::rotate_copy(), 573

S

Sample algorithm, 553
    for loop, 556
    results, 556
    std::ranges::sample(), 555, 556, 572
save_histogram(), 751
Search algorithms, 494–500, 512

INDEX

Semaphores, 853
    BinSemVec<T>, 856
    and mutex, 853
    num_active_threads_max, 859
    num_total_threads, 859
    std::binary_semaphore, 853
    std::counting_semaphore, 853, 856
    std::counting_semaphore<>& cs, 856
    std::counting_semaphore<> cs
        (num_active_threads_max), 859
    std::vector<int> counts, 859
    struct BinSemVec<T>, 853
    types, 853
Sequence container
    class std::forward_list (*see* Class
        std::forward_list)
    definition, 105
    objects collection, 134
    std::array (*see* Class std::array)
    std::deque, 137–148
    std::list, 148–158
    std::vector (*see* Class std::vector)
Set algorithms, 564, 573
    containers, 565
    results, 566–568
    std::ranges::difference(), 564
    std::ranges::intersection(), 564
    std::ranges::set_difference(colors1,
        colors2, std::back_
        inserter(colors5)), 566
    std::ranges::set_symmetric_
        difference(colors1, colors2,
        std::back_inserter(colors6)), 566
    std::ranges::set_union(colors1, colors2,
        std::back_inserter(colors4)), 566
    std::ranges::sort(), 565
    std::ranges::symmetric_difference(), 564
    std::ranges::union(), 564

Shift algorithm, 557, 561–563, 573
Shuffle algorithm, 553
    std::ranges::shuffle(), 553, 555, 572
SIMD code generation, 893
Smart pointer
    definition, 235
    std::shared_ptr, 248–252
    std::weak_ptr, 254–257
Software benchmarking, 680
    BmTimer, 680, *see also* BmTimer
    bm_timer.start(i, 0), 682
    BmTimer<std::chrono::steady_
        clock>, 682
    class BmTimerSteadyClock, 682
    performance results, 686
    timing measurements, 682
    tr_f32() and tr_f64(), 680
Software tools, 893
Sorting algorithms, 513–519
Source code
    for Practical C++ STL
        Programming, 887–888
Source code development tools
    Linux and GCC
        build-essential meta package, 889
        build script file permissions, 890
        commands, 889
        compile and execute, 890
    macOS and GCC, 891–893
    for Practical C++ STL
        Programming, 888
    Ubuntu and macOS, 888
    Windows and Visual Studio, 889
sphere_area(), 451, 456
splice_after() operation, 161
Standard Library Predefined SI
    std::ratios, 653, 654
start_latch.arrive_and_wait(), 864

INDEX

start_latch.count_down(), 865
std::accumulate() algorithm, 503, 505, 799
std::advance() function, 150
std::any class
    const char*, 220
    non-template container, 219
    process_message(), 221
    std::println() statement, 219
    val1.emplace<Rect>(0, 0, 3, 4)
        statement, 220
std::array, 769
std::array<std::string> function, 131
std::async(), 876, 878, 883, 886
std:async(), 878
std::back_inserter() function, 91, 457
std::barrier, 861
std::binary_semaphores, 853, 854, 886
std::boyer_moore_horspool_searcher, 498
std::boyer_moore_search, 498
std::cartesian_product(), 626
std::chrono::duration class template
    a_seconds = x_days + x_hours-x_
        minutes + x_seconds, 661
    b_seconds = 17h + 47min + 18s +
        a_seconds, 662
    Ch16_02_ex1(), 658
    Ch16_02_ex2(), 660
    Ch16_02_ex2(), duration variables, 661
    chrono::days x_days, 661
    chrono::duration, 656
    chrono::duration_cast(), 659, 661, 662
    chrono::duration<int, std::ratio
        <3600 * 24 * 7>> week {1}, 658
    chrono::durations minutes15 and
        minutes90, 659
    chrono::minutes x_minutes, 661
    chrono::seconds x_seconds, 661
    chrono::year_month_day, 662, 664
    chrono::year_month_day ymd1
        {2025y/6/21d}, 663
    namespace chrono = std::chrono, 656
    namespace std::chrono_literals, 660
    num_days, 658
    num_hours = chrono::duration_cast
        <chrono::hours>
        (num_days), 658
    std::formatter<std::chrono::
        sys_time>, 659
std::chrono::duration class template
    Ch16_02–Ch16_02_ex1(), 656, 658
    standard time duration aliases, 659
std::chrono::time_point class template
    chrono::ceil(), chrono::floor(), and
        chrono::round(), 673
    chrono::sys_days(), 664
    chrono::system_clock::now(), 673
    chrono::time_point<chrono::system_
        clock> tp = chrono::sys_days
        {2026y/7/4d}, 671
    chrono::time_point<chrono::system_
        clock> tp1_sys {}, 669
    chrono::time_point relational
        operators, 672
    chrono::utc_clock, 672
    EtUnit, 682
    now() function, 665
    tp_now = chrono::system_
        clock::now(), 673
std::chrono::time_point class template
    additive arithmetic, 671
    time default value, 670
std::complex, 734, 738
std::complex<double>, 736
std::condition_variable, 866, 886
std::copy(), 122
std::copy_backward(), 418

INDEX

std::copy_if(), 416
std::copy_n(), 417
std::count(), 447
std::count_if(), 447
std::counting_semaphore, 853, 856, 886
std::counting_semaphore<>& cs, 856
std::default_searcher, 498
std::deque, 357, 358, 387, 388
std::deque::append_range() function, 142
std::distance() function, 160, 171
std::domain_error, 60
std::emplace(), 281
std::erase() function, 126, 131, 439
std::erase_if() function, 126, 164, 439
std::error_code, 712, 714
std::exp(), 738, 739
std::expected class
    calc_result(), 227, 229
    compiler support, 223
    ErrorCode's string, 223
    file_op() function, 226, 227
    monadic operations, 231
    print_vec(), 229
    return fn statement, 227
    std::println() statement, 227
    std::strings, 227
    template class, 223
std::filesystem, 689, 709, 710, 712
std::filesystem_error, 714
std::fill(), 444, 448
std::fill_n(), 448
std::find() algorithm, 124
std::floating_point, 8
std::for_each() algorithms, 454
std::for_each_n(), 451
std::format(), 10
std::formatter<Line<>>, 91
std::formatter<std::chrono::sys_time>, 659

std::formatter<std::filesystem::path>, 690
std::forward_list<std::string>) function, 161
std::forward_list::prepend_range()
    function, 162
std::forward_list::sort() function, 161
std::future<result_t>, 874, 878
std::future<result_t> future1 { promise1.
    get_future() }, 874, 876
std::future<std::vector<T>>& future, 883
std::future<T>, 875
std::future<T>., 873, 876, 878, 879, 883, 886
std::future<T>::wait(), 878
std::generate(), 459
std::get_if<>(), 193
std::get<I>(tuple), 186
std::inner_product(), 799–808
std::input_iterator iterator argument, 171
std::integral, 8
std::iota(), 431, 451, 799
std::iota(std::begin(va1), 773
std::jthread thread1(BinSemVec
    <int>::thread_proc, 856
std::latch, 861, 862, 865, 886
std::latch finish_latch(cpts.size(), 864
std::latch start_latch(cpts.size() + 1), 864
std::launch::async, 878, 885
std::launch::async |
    std::launch::deferred, 878
std::launch::deferred, 878
std::list::merge() function, 155
std::list::remove() function, 151
std::list::sort() function, 154
std::lock_guard<std::mutex> lock(cvd.
    Mutex), 868
std::make_format_args(elem), 614
std::make_tuple(), 182
std::make_unique_for_overwrite()
    function, 245, 246, 248

std::map, 300
    associative container, 276
    cmap_lt_t or cmap_gt_t map, 284, 286, 287
    map1.clear(), 278
    MT::print_map(), 276
    operator[], 278
    results, source code example, 287
    class RGB, 282
    std::map::emplace(), 281
    std::map::find(), 281
    std::map<int, std::string> map1, 276
    vs. std::set, 276
    std::string_view, 278
    try_emplace(), 281
std::max_element(), 413
std::min_element(), 413
std::minstd_rand, 748
std::minstd_rand rng1(rng_seed), 748
std::mt19937, 749
std::mt19937 rng_engine {}, 764
std::mt19937 rng(rng_dev()), 753
std::mt19937 rng(rng_seed), 751
std::multimap, 300
    find(), 294
    mmap1.contains() (C++20), 294
    mulmap_t mmap1, 292
    std::equal_range(), 297
    std::maps, 292
    std::mmap1.find(find_key), 296
    std::multimap::equal_range(), 294, 299
    std::multimap::find(), 299
    std::multimap::try_emplace(), 294
    std::println() statement, 292
    std::string_view objects, 292, 296
std::multiset, 300
    associative container, 271
    mset1.count(count_val), 273
    mset1.insert_range(vals1) (C++23), 273
    std::greater<std::string>>, 273
    std::multiset::emplace(), 274
    std::multiset<int> mset1, 271
    std::multiset<std::string, 273
    vs. std::set, 271
    while loop, 274
std::mutex, 866, 886
std::mutex cvd.Mutex, 870
std::normal_distribution, 749, 750
std::normal_distribution<double> dist(rng_mean, rng_sd), 751, 753
std::numbers, 728, 731
std::numbers (<numbers>), 728
std::numbers::phi, 730
std::numbers::phi_v<double>, 730
std::numbers::pi_v<>, 730
std::numbers::pi_v<T>, 728, 730
std::optional object
    binary, 201
    func_and_then(), 213
    get_test_nut(), 214, 216
    has_value()=, 207
    monadic operation, 211
    class Nut, 201, 205
    Nut.cpp, 205
    object's destructor, 201
    operator<=> and operator==, 205
    opt.value(), 213
    or_else(), 213
    protein_per_ounce(), 214
    relational operator usage, 207, 209
    std::bad_optional_access, 207
    std::optional::bool(), 207
    std::optional::operator=, 207
    monadic member function transform(), 213
std::optional<T> objects, 209

INDEX

std::partial_ordering, 52
std::path file = dir_entry.path(), 702
std::print(), 2
std::printf() sibling functions, 67
std::println(), 2, 10, 690, 697, 710
std::println() statement, 251
std::priority_queue, 388
    member function calc_values(), 381
    container adaptor, 376
    emplace(), 385
    get_random_polygons(), 382
    MT::print_priority_queue(), 382
    pop(), 385
    pq_t, 384
    push() and emplace(), 384
    push() and pop(), 375
    push_range() (C++23), 385
    class RegPolygon, 376, 377, 381
    RegPolygons.cpp, 382
    std::greater<>, 375
    std::greater<RegPolygon>, 384
    std::less<>, 375
    std::println(), 384
    std::priority_queue<RegPolygon>, 382
    vs. std::queue, 375
    std::vector, 376
    top() or pop(), 384
std::priority_queue container adaptor, 535
std::priority_queue *vs.* STL heap, 542
std::promise<result_t>, 874, 876
std::promise<result_t>& prom, 876
std::promise<T>, 873–875, 886
std::queue, 388
    back() and front(), 371
    container adaptor, 370
    FIFO functionality, 370
    push() and emplace(), 371
    push_range() (C++23), 372

    result, 374
    std::deque<int>, 371
    std::println(), 372
    std::queue<int>, 372
    std::queue<std::string>, 372
    std::queue::pop(), 370
    std::queue::push(), 370, 371
std::random_device(), 753, 765
std::random_device rd {}, 765
std::random_device rng_dev {}, 753
std::ranges, 449, 611, 642
std::ranges::binary_search(), 523, 543
std::ranges::contains(), 489
std::ranges::contains_subrange(), 489, 490
std::ranges::copy_backward(), 418
std::ranges::copy_n(), 417
std::ranges::count(), 447
std::ranges::count_if(), 447
std::ranges::ends_with(), 491, 493
std::ranges::equal_range(), 543
std::ranges::fill(), 444, 448
std::ranges::fill_n(), 448
std::ranges::find(), 474
std::ranges::find_if(), 475
std::ranges::find_if_ algorithm
    functions, 480
std::ranges::find_last(), 478
std::ranges::fold_ algorithms, 505
std::ranges::fold_left_first(), 507
std::ranges::fold_right_last(), 507
std::ranges::for_each(), 451, 453
std::ranges_for_each_n(), 451
std::ranges::generate_n(), 464
std::ranges::greater(), 543
std::ranges::iota(Vec, 0), 854
std::ranges::iota::view, 642
std::ranges::is_heap(vec1), 541
std::ranges::is_sorted(), 517

INDEX

std::ranges::is_sorted_until(), 517
std::ranges::less(), 525, 543
std::ranges_lower_bound(), 543
std::ranges::make_heap(), 536, 539, 543
std::ranges::max(), 412
std::ranges::max_element(), 413
std::ranges::min(), 412
std::ranges::min_element(), 413
std::ranges::minmax(), 412
std::ranges::minmax_element(), 410, 411
std::ranges::min_max_result, 410
std::ranges::mismatch(), 498, 500
std::ranges namespace, 576
std::ranges::nth_element(), 517, 542
std::ranges::partial_sort(), 517, 519, 542
std::ranges::partition(), 531, 543
std::ranges::pop_heap(), 540, 543
std::ranges::push_heap(), 539, 543
std::ranges::remove(), 448
std::ranges::remove_if(), 448
std::ranges::replace(), 428, 448
std::ranges::replace() algorithm, 132, 134
std::ranges_replace_if() algorithm, 132
std::ranges::reverse(), 425, 447
std::ranges::reverse_copy(), 427, 447
std::ranges::search() function, 494, 496
std::ranges::shuffle(), 553–555
std::ranges::sort() function, 114, 144, 178, 513, 542, 638
std::ranges::stable_sort(), 515, 542
std::ranges::starts_with(), 491
std::ranges::swap_ranges(), 421
std::ranges::transform(), 454, 856
std::ranges::upper_bound(), 523
std::reduce(), 799–808
std::ref(bin_sem_vec1), 856
std::remove() function, 130, 448
std::remove_if(), 436, 438, 448

std::replace() algorithm, 132, 429, 448
std::reverse(), 425, 447
std::reverse_copy(), 427, 447
std::search(), 496, 497
std::set, 300
    bidirectional iterators, 263
    emplacements, 261
    for loop, 263, 266
    MT::print_ctr() statement, 260
    red-black tree, 259
    relational operators, 263
    sequence containers, 259
    set::merge(), 266
    std::greater<>, 262
    std::println() statement, 260
    std::set::clear(), 267
    std::set::contains() (C++20), 265
    std::set::insert(), 261
    std::set<int> set1, 259
    std::set<T>, 263
std::slice
    copy-constructs, 787
    covariance matrix, 794–799
    dot (inner) products, 791
    for loop, 789, 790
    lambda expression, 785
    matrix operations, 788–791
    matrix row, 790
    matrix-vector operations and linear algebra functions, 785
    m_Data[tr_slice].sum(), 792
    function mul(), 791
    std::valarray<int> val(20), 787
    std::valarray::operator[], 787
    test matrix, 789
    usages, 787
    zero-based subscripts, 790

INDEX

std::shared_ptr
    buy_copies(), 250
    ControlBlock object, 248
    logical relationships, 248
    m_NumCopies, 251
    sharing object's ownership, 248
    std::println() statements, 250
    std::shared_ptr<Book>, 251, 252
std::sort() function, 41, 144, 513
std::stack, 388
    Ch09_01_ex1(), 358
    class TowerOfHanoi, 362, 363, 367
    Hanoi algorithm peg and disc arrangements, 362
    Hanoi disc moves, 367
    LIFO, 357
    move_disc(), 367
    peg_t, 362
    pop() operations, 357
    print_pegs(), 367
    print_words(), 360
    push() operations, 357, 367
    std::deque, 357
    std::deque<std::string>, 360
    std::vector or std::list, 358
    TOH algorithm, 362
    TOH disc move algorithm code, 367
    TOH_VERBOSE_TEST, 368
    top() and pop(), 358, 360
    top_and_pop() member function, 360
    TowerOfHanoi::run(), 362, 368
    uint_t, 363
    words1.emplace("four"), 360
    words1.push("score"), 360
    words2.push_range() (C++ 23), 361
std::string, 508, 619, 628, 630, 644, 697, 704, 710
std::string& fn, 751
std::string, char, double>, 611
std::string::contains() class, 21, 22
std::string::find(), 21
std::string::operator+, 17
std::string::operator+= class, 17
std::string::replace(), 21
std::string_view class, 21
std::swap_ranges(), 421
std::terminate(), 849
std::tie(), 187
std::transform(), 454
std::transform_reduce(), 799–808
std::tuple_cat(), 188
std::tuple_element<>, 182
std::tuple<std::string, 611
std::tuples, 611
std::tuple_size<>, 182
std::uniform_int_distribution, 749
std::uniform_int_distribution<int> dist1(rng_min, rng_max), 749
std::uniform_int_distribution<int> rng_dist(rng_min, rng_max), 764
std::uniform_int_distribution <unsigned int> temp_dist (0, num_sides-1), 759
std::uniform_real_distribution<float>, 749
std::unique_lock<std::mutex> lk(cvd.Mutex), 869, 870
std::unique_ptr, 249std::slice, 769, 795, 798
std::unordered_map, 353
    get_airports(), 334, 336
    hash_func, 339
    insert_range(), 340
    merge(), 338
    pred, 339
    public interface, 333
    std::string, 333
    vs. std::unordered_set, 333

uno_map_hf_t, 333, 340
uno_map_t, 333, 342
std::unordered_multimap, 353
   equal_range(), 349
   get_airport(), 346
   get_airports(), 348
   print_buckets(), 346, 348
   std::string_view, 345
   std::unordered_set, 348
std::unordered_multiset, 353
   colors.emplace(HtmlColor::
      get(i)), 331
   colors.find(test_color), 331
   colors.insert(HtmlColor::get(i)), 331
   colors.merge(more_colors), 331
   extract()/insert() operation, 331
   HtmlColor, 327
   HtmlColor::hash_func_bucket_
      count, 329
   print_buckets(), 327
   std::unordered_set, 331
   uno_mset_t, 329
std::unordered_set, 311, 353
   colors, 321
   class HtmlColor, 304, 312, 319
   HtmlColor::hash_func(), 320
   HtmlColor::hash_func_bucket_
      count, 320
   max_load_factor(), 321
   print_buckets(), 306, 308, 310
   print_stats(), 308
   set2.insert(std::move(node_
      handle)), 310
   std::string, 304, 310
   std::unordered_set::extract(), 310
   strings.bucket_size(i), 308
   unordered associative container, 303
   uno_set_hc_t, 320

uno_set_str_t, 311
uno_set_str_t set1, 306
std::valarray, 795, 798
   arithmetic functions, 770-777
   assignment operator, 772
   code block, 771
   non-member functions, 773
   operator[], 771
   operators, 774
   random values, 771
   statistical calculations, 777
      code block, 777
      lambda expression, 779
      least_squares(), 782
      least-squares lines, 779, 780
      linear regression, 779
      mean and standard deviation, 777
      RN::get_value(), 783
      std::ranges::fold_left(), 783
      std::ranges::transform(), 783
      subsequent statement, 779
      validation, 783
   std::begin() and std::end(), 773
   trigonometric and hyperbolic
      operations, 773
std::valarray::apply(), 773
std::valarray<double> val(n), 773
std::valarray's operator[], 771
std::variant class
   class Rect, 193
   C++ template class, 190
   elementary operations, 190
   i = v.index(), 198
   operator<=> and operator==, 193
   relational operators, 196, 198
   std::bad_variant_access exception, 192
   std::get_if<>(), 193
   std::get<>(), 192

INDEX

std::variant class (*cont.*)
   std::variant::emplace<>(), 196
   std::variant<double, int> var1 {}, 192
   vs. unions, 190
   valueless_by_exception(), 198
std::vector, 363, 387, 388, 769
std::vector::at() function, 119
std::vector::back() function, 119
std::vector::begin(), 15
std::vector::capacity() function, 121
std::vector class, 14
std::vector::clear() function, 119
std::vector::emplace_back()
   function, 124
std::vector::end(), 15
std::vector::front() function, 119
std::vector<Airport> find_airports, 477
std::vector<Airports>, 867
std::vector<double> vectors, 130
std::vector<fp_t>, 882
std::vector<fp_t> x0, 885
std::vector<int>, 626, 627, 631
std::vector<int> vec1 function, 117
std::vector<Rect1> vec1, 416
std::vector<std::string>, 762
std::vector<std::string> colors, 500
std::vector<std::string> containers,
   457, 458
std::vector<std::string> DiceSet::
   roll_names(), 759
std::vector<std::string> find_codes, 475
std::vector<std::string> objects, 801
std::vector<std::string> roll_values =
   dice_aa.roll_names(), 762
std::vector<T>, 854, 880, 881
std::vector<T>&, 880
std::vector<T>& vec1, 751
std::vector<unsigned int>, 759

std::vector<unsigned int> DiceSet::roll
   (unsigned int offset), 759
std::vector::operator[], 14
std::vector::operator== vectors, 30
std::vector::pop_back(), 121
std::vector::push_back() function, 119
std::vector::reserve() function, 121
std::vector::resize(), 248
std::vector::size() function, 121
std::vformat_to(), 614, 621
std::views::adjacent(), 618, 648
std::views::cartesian_product(), 630
std::views::chunk(), 633, 636, 648
std::views::chunk_by(chunk_op), 639
std::views::chunk(chunk_w), 637
std::views::elements(), 611, 613, 647
std::views::enumerate(), 616, 647
std::views::iota(), 642, 648
std::views::iota() range factory, 599,
   600, 609
std::views::istream(), 642, 644, 646, 648
std::views::join(), 626, 627, 648
std::views::join_width(), 628
std::views::join_with(), 626, 628
std::views::keys(), 611, 613, 647
std::views::repeat(), 642, 644, 648
std::views::slide(), 633, 648
std::views::slide(window_w), 635
std::views::split(), 626, 629, 630
std::views::stride(), 633, 648
std::weak_ptr
   book1_wp_locked, 255
   constructors, 257
   description, 254
   expression, 257
   operator->/operator*(), 255
   s1_sp and s2_sp, 256
   structure S2, 257

std::println(), 254
structures, 255
std::zip_transform(), 621
STL algorithm library, 391
STL algorithms, 41
- C++, 392
- C++11, 391
- C++20, 392
- global algorithms, 393
- member functions, 392
- std::sort(), 392

STL algorithm std::accumulate(), 112
STL algorithm std::sort(), 113
STL container adaptors, 356
STL container class std::map, 173
STL container object, 29
STL sequence container classes, 105, 106, 134
Stride views, 635
Strings
- alias classes, 17
- __cpp_lib_string_contains, 22
- std::basic_string, 17
- std::string
  - :operator+, 17
- std::string::ends_with(), 21
- std::string::find(), 21
- std::string::replace(), 21
- std::string::starts_with(), 21
- string member functions, 21

struct BinSemVec<T>, 853
struct ConditionVarDemo, 866
struct CountPrimesThread, 862
struct result_t { std::string ThreadId {}; ll_t Sum {}; }, 876
sub_tree_bot, 695
Summation index variable, 841
sum_primes(), 878
sum_primes(llt_n), 876
Superior String Splitting, 896

T

template <typename T> T add_values(T a, T b, T c), 7
Test computers, 892, 893
Test matrix, 789
thread_proc(), 856
thread_proc(BinSemVec<T>& bin_sem_vec), 856
Thread's start function, 829
Three-way comparison operator <=>
- comparing integer types, 52
- definition, 48
- floating-point types, 52
- #include <compare> statement, 48
- lengths comparison, 56
- class Line, 55
- operator==, 56
- ordering class, 51
- relational operators, 52
- std::println() statement, 49
- std::weak_ordering, 52

Time library
- clock (see Clock classes)
- durations (see std::chrono::duration class template)
- ratio (see Ratio library)
- software benchmarking, 680–687

Time Zone Database (IANA), 897
TOH algorithm, 362
TowerOfHanoi algorithm, 367
TowerOfHanoi::run(), 362
Transformation algorithms, 454–458, 511

INDEX

Tuple-like views
    AaTuple, 613–615
    aa_zip_view, 621
    pizza_tup tuple, 631
    std::min(radii.size(), heights.size())
        tuples, 622
    std::views::zip(), 619
Tuple-like views, 611

U

Ubuntu, 890, 893
Unordered associative container
    hash function, 301–303
    maximum load factor, 303
    objects/elements, collection, 301
    std::unordered_map (*see*
        std::unordered_map)
    std::unordered_multimap (*see*
        std::unordered_multimap)
    std::unordered_multiset (*see*
        std::unordered_multiset)
    std::unordered_set (*see*
        std::unordered_set)
User-defined class
    class Image, 24 (*see* class Image)
    compiler-supplied default, 61
User-defined template classes
    class definition, 38
    design pattern, 38
    Image class templates
        implemented, 34
    Image<> *vs.* Image, 38
    Image<uint8_t>, 38
    requires clause, 38
    std::basic_string<class CharT>, 34

Utility classes
    std::optional (*see* std::optional object)
    std::variant, 190–198
Utility class std::any, 219–222

V

vec1.pop_back(), 541
vec4.size() function, 119
Views, 576, 577, 609
    for loop, 580, 605
    get_test_vector(), 577, 605
    get_test_view(), 606, 607
    MT::print_ctr(), 582
    results, 582, 583, 607, 608
    statement, 582
    std::views::filter(), 579, 580
    std::views::transform(), 580
    syntactical alternatives, 604
    vec2/view2, 582
    view1 = std::views::filter(vec1, pred), 579
    view1.empty(), 579
    view2, 579, 582
    view_ft, 605
Visual Studio (MSVC), 12

W, X, Y

wait_for_future(), 883
wait_for_future(future_dct_inv,
    wait_time), 885
while loop, 476, 477

Z

z1.real(), 736
zprofile file, 891, 892

GPSR Compliance

The European Union's (EU) General Product Safety Regulation (GPSR) is a set of rules that requires consumer products to be safe and our obligations to ensure this.

If you have any concerns about our products, you can contact us on

ProductSafety@springernature.com

In case Publisher is established outside the EU, the EU authorized representative is:

Springer Nature Customer Service Center GmbH
Europaplatz 3
69115 Heidelberg, Germany

www.ingramcontent.com/pod-product-compliance
Lightning Source LLC
LaVergne TN
LVHW080308260326
834688LV00038B/1008